2015 NHL DRAFT BLACK BOOK
PROSPECT SCOUTING REPORTS & DRAFT RANKINGS

by HockeyProspect.com

© 2015 by The Hockey Press

ALL RIGHTS RESERVED.

The Hockey Press
ISBN-13: 978-0991677566
ISBN-10: 0991677560

TABLE OF CONTENTS — 3

2015 NHL DRAFT RANKINGS **11**
2015 NHL DRAFT PROSPECTS **17**

★ Abols, Rodrigo	18
★ Addison, Jeremiah	18
★ Adams, Jack	18
★ Afonasyevsky, Semyon	18
★ Ahl, Filip	19
★ Aho, Sebastian	19
★ Aho, Sebastian	19
★ Alain, Alexandre	20
★ Alsing, Olle	20
★ Andersson, Rasmus	21
★ Appleby, Ken	22
★ Appleton, Mason	22
★ Artemov, Artem	22
★ Askew, Cam	22
★ Bachman, Karch	23
★ Baer, Alec	23
★ Baille, Tyson	24
★ Baird, Mike	24
★ Balcers, Rudolfs	24
★ Barre-Boulet, Alex	25
★ Barwell, Jesse	25
★ Barzal, Matt	25
★ Bast, Gabe	26
★ Bear, Ethan	26
★ Beaudin, Jean-Christophe	27
★ Beauvillier, Anthony	28
★ Bednard, Ryan	28
★ Bell, Jason	28
★ Bengtsson, Lukas	29
★ Benglund, Filip	29
★ Bernhardt, Daniel	30
★ Bethune, Jared	30
★ Betz, Nick	30
★ Betzold, Greg	31
★ Birdsall, Chris	31
★ Bittner, Paul	31
★ Björkqvist, Kasper	32
★ Black, Alex	32
★ Blackwood, Mackenzie	33
★ Blaisdell, Doug	33
★ Boeser, Brock	34
★ Boka, Nick	34
★ Bondra, Radovan	35
★ Borgen, Will	35
★ Bouramman, Gustav	35
★ Boikov, Sergei	36
★ Booth, Callum	36
★ Bourque, Simon	37
★ Bowman, Zack	38
★ Bracco, Jeremy	38
★ Bradley, Matt	39
★ Brisebois, Guillaume	39
★ Bruce, Riley	40
★ Burns Andrew	40
★ Bushnell, Noah	40
★ Capobianco, Kyle	41
★ Carbonara, Adrian	41
★ Carlo, Brandon	41
★ Carlsson, Gabriel	42
★ Carlsson, Lucas	43
★ Carpenter, Robert	43
★ Carrier, Alexandre	43
★ Cecconi, Joseph	44
★ Cernak, Erik	45
★ Chabot, Thomas	45
★ Chebykin, Nikolai	46
★ Chlapik, Filip	46
★ Cirelli, Anthony	47
★ Clapham, Austin	47
★ Connor, Kyle	48
★ Conrad, Colton	49
★ Corneil, Johnny	49
★ Corriveau, Taggart	49
★ Cotton, David	50
★ Coyle, Josh	50
★ Craievich, Adam	50
★ Crawford, Marcus	51
★ Crawley, Brandon	51
★ Crouse, Lawson	51
★ Cukste, Karlis	52
★ Dahlstrom, John	53
★ Demler, Brendan	53
★ Davidsson, Jonathan	53
★ Davies, Mike	54
★ Davis, Kevin	54
★ DeBrusk, Jake	55
★ Dello, Tory	55
★ Dergachyov, Alexander	55
★ Dermott, Travis	56
★ Deschene, Luc	56
★ Didur, Bo	57
★ Diffley, Brien	57
★ Dostie, Alex	58
★ Dove-McFalls, Samuel	58
★ Dufek, Jan	59
★ Dunda, Liam	59
★ Dunn, Vince	59
★ Dzierkals, Martins	60
★ Edmonds, Ty	61
★ Eichel, Jack	61
★ Eriksson Ek, Joel	62
★ Estephan, Giorgio	63
★ Falkovsky, Stepan	63
★ Fanjoy, Ben	64

★ Fazio, Justin	64
★ Fellows, Patrick	65
★ Fiala, Evan	65
★ Finlay, Liam	65
★ Fischer, Christian	66
★ Flanagan, McKay	66
★ Fitzgerald, Casey	66
★ Foley, Erik	67
★ Fontaine, Gabriel	67
★ Forsbacka-Karlsson, Jakob	68
★ Forsberg, Fredrik	68
★ Fortin, Alexandre	69
★ Fournier, Jordan Ty	69
★ Fox, Trent	69
★ Franzen, Gustaf	70
★ Freytag, Matthew	70
★ Fronk, Jiri	70
★ Gabrielle, Grant	71
★ Gabrielle, Jesse	71
★ Gagne, Gabriel	72
★ Galipeau, Olivier	72
★ Gardiner, Reid	73
★ Garland, Conor	73
★ Gatenby, Joe	74
★ Gates, Brent	74
★ Gaudette, Adam	75
★ Gavrikov, Vladislav	75
★ Gibson, Stephen	75
★ Gawdin, Glenn	76
★ Gennaro, Matteo	76
★ Gilbert, Dennis	77
★ Godla, Denis	77
★ Greenway, Jordan	78
★ Greer, A.J.	78
★ Gropp, Ryan	78
★ Grzelewski, Zach	79
★ Guhle, Brendan	79
★ Guryanov, Denis	80
★ Hall, Austin	81
★ Halladay, Logan	81
★ Hanifin, Noah	82
★ Hansson, Petter	82
★ Harding, Sam	83
★ Harkins, Jansen	83
★ Haudum, Lukas	84
★ Henderson, Jacob	84
★ Henley, David	84
★ Henley, Troy	85
★ Herbst, Liam	85
★ Hill, Adin	86
★ Hintz, Roope	86
★ Hobbs, Connor	87
★ Hodgson, Hayden	88
★ Holmes, Michael	88
★ Huether, Kenny	89
★ Hughes, Cameron	89
★ Hunt, Dryden	89
★ Huska, Adam	90
★ Imama, Bokondji	90
★ Impose, Auguste	91
★ Ingram, Connor	91
★ Jaremko, Jacob	92
★ Jaros, Christian	92
★ Järvinen, Ville	92
★ Jasek, Lukas	92
★ Jaycox, Luke	93
★ Johnston, Brendan	93
★ Jones, Caleb	93
★ Joseph, Mathieu	94
★ Jutting, Tyler	94
★ Juulsen, Noah	94
★ Kalapudas, Antti	95
★ Kaprizov, Kirill	95
★ Karnaukhov, Pavel	96
★ Kase, David	96
★ Kielly, Kameron	97
★ Kiviranta, Joel	97
★ Knott, Graham	97
★ Kodola, Vladislav	98
★ Kohn, Mason	98
★ Kolesar, Keegan	99
★ Konecny, Travis	99
★ Korostelev, Nikita	100
★ Korshkov, Yegor	101
★ Kotala, Jakub	101
★ Kovacs, Robin	101
★ Kreis, Matthew	102
★ Kuhlman, Karson	102
★ Kupsky, Jake	103
★ Kylington, Oliver	103
★ Laberge, Samuel	104
★ Lackey, Michael	104
★ Laishram, Adam	105
★ Lajeunesse, Troy	105
★ Lalonde, Bradley	105
★ Larkin, Ryan	106
★ Larsson, Jacob	106
★ Lauzon, Jeremy	107
★ Lazarev, Leo	107
★ Lemcke, Justin	108
★ Leschenko, Vyacheslav	108
★ Leskinen, Otto	109
★ Léveillé, Loïk	109
★ Lindberg, Brandon	109
★ Lindgren, Jesper	110
★ Lindholm, Max	110

★ Lizotte, Cameron	110	★ Norman, Ryan	133
★ Llewellyn, Darby	111	★ Novak, Thomas	133
★ Looke, Jens	111	★ O'Brien, Brogan	134
★ Luchuk, Aaron	112	★ Ohlsson, Sebastian	134
★ Luff, Matt	112	★ Okulov, Konstantin	134
★ MacArthur, Tyler	112	★ Olund, Linus	135
★ MacAdams, Eric	113	★ Oldham, Kris	135
★ Mackie, Gage	113	★ Olson, Jacob	135
★ Malgin, Denis	113	★ Olson, Tate	136
★ Malmquist, Dylan	114	★ Opilka, Luke	136
★ Malone, Seamus	115	★ Orban, Ryan	137
★ Mangiapane Andrew	115	★ Osipov, Dmitry	137
★ Marcoux, Antoine	116	★ Paigin, Ziyat	137
★ Marino, John	116	★ Paliani, Devon	138
★ Marner, Mitchell	116	★ Palmu, Petrus	138
★ Marody, Cooper	117	★ Papirny, Jordan	138
★ Marsh, Adam	117	★ Parikka, Jarkko	139
★ Martenet, Chris	118	★ Parsells, Adam	139
★ Massie, Jake	119	★ Pavlychev, Nikita	139
★ McBride, Nick	119	★ Pawlenchuk, Grayson	140
★ McCool, Hayden	119	★ Pearson, Chase	140
★ McCormick, Sam	120	★ Pelton-Byce, Ty	141
★ McDavid, Connor	120	★ Peters, Collin	141
★ McDermott, John	121	★ Pfeifer, Tristen	142
★ McDonald, Dylan	121	★ Phelps, Chase	142
★ McEwan, James	121	★ Philp, Luke	142
★ McFadden, Garrett	122	★ Piipponen Topi	143
★ McKenzie, Brett	122	★ Pilipenko, Kirill	143
★ McNeely, Jack	122	★ Pilon, Ryan	144
★ McNiven, Michael	123	★ Podluboshnov, Pavel	144
★ Meier, Timo	123	★ Poehling, Jack	145
★ Meloche, Nicolas	124	★ Provorov, Ivan	145
★ Mercer, Cullen	125	★ Radke, Roy	146
★ Merkley, Nick	125	★ Rantanen, Mikko	146
★ Meyer, Jarret	126	★ Ratelle, Joey	146
★ Michaud, Lucas	126	★ Reddekopp, Chaz	147
★ Mikkola, Niko	126	★ Richard, Anthony	147
★ Miller, David	127	★ Roslovic, Jack	148
★ Montembeault, Samuel	127	★ Roy, Jeremy	148
★ Moberg, Sebastian	127	★ Roy, Nicolas	149
★ Moore, Ryan	128	★ Ruuskanen, Waltteri	150
★ Morris, Cale	128	★ Rykov, Yegor	150
★ Morrison, Brad	128	★ Saarela, Aleksi	151
★ Murray, Liam	129	★ Saarijarvi, Vili	151
★ Murray, Troy	129	★ Saban, Jesse	152
★ Musil, Adam	129	★ Saccoman, Colin	152
★ Mustonen, Aleksi	130	★ Sadek, Jack	152
★ Myers, Philippe	130	★ Salituro, Dante	152
★ Nättinen, Julius	131	★ Samsonov, Ilya	153
★ Nielsen Andrew	131	★ Sandberg, Johannes	154
★ Niemelä, Joonas	132	★ Sandstrom, Felix	154
★ Niku, Sami	132	★ Schemitsch, Thomas	154
★ Noel, Nathan	132	★ Schneider, Nick	155

★ Schweri, Kay	155	
★ Seney, Brett	156	
★ Senyshyn, Zachary	156	
★ Sharov, Alexander	157	
★ Shaw, Austin	157	
★ Sherwood, Kole	157	
★ Sideroff, Deven	158	
★ Siegenthaler, Jonas	158	
★ Simion, Dario	159	
★ Shea, Ryan	160	
★ Simon, Dominik	160	
★ Smallman, Spencer	160	
★ Smejkal, Jiri	161	
★ Smith, Evan	161	
★ Smolin, Mikhail	161	
★ Somers, Will	162	
★ Sorensen, George	162	
★ Soustal, Tomas	162	
★ Soy, Tyler	163	
★ Spacek, Michael	164	
★ Spaxman, Ethan	164	
★ Speers, Blake	164	
★ Spencer, Matthew	165	
★ Sprong, Daniel	166	
★ Stadel, Riley	167	
★ Stenlund, Kevin	168	
★ Stephens, Devante	168	
★ Stephens, Mitchell	169	
★ Stevens, Luke	169	
★ Stewart, Chase	170	
★ Stezka, Ales	170	
★ Strand, Austin	170	
★ Strome, Dylan	171	
★ Suter, Pius	172	
★ Svechnikov, Evgeny	173	
★ Sweezey, Bill	174	
★ Szypula, Ethan	174	
★ Tammela, Jonne	174	
★ Tavernier, Sami	174	
★ Terry, Troy	175	
★ Texeira, Keoni	175	
★ Tiffels, Frederik	175	
★ Thurkauf, Calvin	176	
★ Timashov, Dmytro	176	
★ Tkachev, Vladimir	176	
★ Tomek, Matej	177	
★ Trenin, Yakov	177	
★ Trinkberger, David	178	
★ Tuulola, Joni	178	
★ Vainio, Veeti	179	
★ Vande Sompel, Mitchell	179	
★ Vehviläinen, Veini	179	
★ Vejdemo, Lukas	180	
★ Vela, Marcus	180	
★ Vladar, Daniel	181	
★ Vladimirov, Artem	181	
★ Vorobyov, Mikhail	181	
★ Wagner, Austin	182	
★ Wahlin, Jake	182	
★ Walters, Connor	183	
★ Warren, Brendan	183	
★ Webster, Bailey	183	
★ Weinger, Evan	184	
★ Werenski, Zach	184	
★ White, Colin	185	
★ White, Colton	186	
★ Wilkie, Chris	186	
★ Wotherspoon, Parker	186	
★ Yan, Dennis	187	
★ Yetman, Bryce	187	
★ Younan, Alexander	187	
★ Zacha, Pavel	188	
★ Zboril, Jakub	189	
★ Zborosky, Zak	190	
★ Zborovskiy, Sergei	190	
★ Zeppieri, David	191	
★ Zhukenov, Dmitri	191	
★ Zipp, Michael	191	
★ Zuhlsdorf, Ryan	192	
2016 NHL DRAFT TOP 30	**193**	
2016 NHL DRAFT PROSPECTS	**197**	
★ Abramov, Vitaly	198	
★ Amundrud, Nik	198	
★ Andersson, Alexander	198	
★ Anderson, Joey	198	
★ Anderson, Josh	199	
★ Ang, Johnathan	199	
★ Allard, Frederic	199	
★ Allison, Wade	199	
★ Asplund, Rasmus	200	
★ Badini, Jack	200	
★ Bain, Maxim	200	
★ Bajkov, Patrik	200	
★ Balmas, Mitchell	201	
★ Barron, Travis	201	
★ Bastian, Nathan	201	
★ Bean, Jake	201	
★ Beaudin, Jeremie	202	
★ Bellows, Kieffer	202	
★ Benson, Tyler	202	
★ Bilodeau, Gabriel	203	
★ Bitten, Will	203	
★ Bourque, Trenton	203	
★ Bratt, Jesper	203	
★ Brown, Logan	204	
★ Brushett, Ryan	204	

TABLE OF CONTENTS — 7

★ Budik, Vojtech 204
★ Bunnaman, Connor 205
★ Caamano, Nicholas 205
★ Campbell, Chase 205
★ Campoli, Michael 205
★ Candella, Cole 205
★ Carroll, Noah 206
★ Cederholm, Jacob 206
★ Chychrun, Jakob 206
★ Clague, Kale 207
★ Cormier, Evan 207
★ Crone, Hank 207
★ Crossley, Brett 207
★ Dahlen, Jonathan 208
★ Daschke, Derek 208
★ Day, Sean 208
★ DeBrincat, Alex 209
★ DeNoble, Logan 209
★ Dineen, Cam 210
★ Dmytriw, Jared 210
★ Dubois, Pierre-Luc 210
★ Durflinger, Jake 210
★ Eliot, Mitch 211
★ Fabbro, Dante 211
★ Fallstrom, William 211
★ Farmer, Ty 211
★ Felhaber, Tye 212
★ Felixson, Oliver 212
★ Fitzpatrick, Evan 212
★ Forsmark, Filip 213
★ Fortier, Maxime 213
★ Fox, Adam 213
★ Frederic, Trent 213
★ Gauthier, Julien 214
★ Getson, Keith 214
★ Gettinger, Tim 214
★ Girard, Samuel 215
★ Gleason, Benjamin 215
★ Green, Luke 215
★ Greenway, James 216
★ Gregoire, Thomas 216
★ Grundstrom, Carl 216
★ Gustavsson, Filip 216
★ Hajek, Libor 217
★ Hanson, Bo 217
★ Hart, Carter 217
★ Harvey, Samuel 217
★ Hawerchuk, Ben 218
★ Hellickson, Matthew 218
★ Hotchkiss, Matthew 218
★ Howdeshell, Keeghan 218
★ Hylland, Tyler 219
★ Jones, Max 219
★ Jost, Tyson 219
★ Juolevi, Olli 219
★ Kalyayev, Maxim 220
★ Katerinakis, Alexander 220
★ Keller, Clayton 220
★ Kilgour, Jack 221
★ Kirwan, Luke 221
★ Kluuskeri, Jan 221
★ Knierim, Willie 221
★ Krassey, Evan 221
★ Krys, Chad 222
★ Kryski, Jake 222
★ Kunin, Luke 223
★ Kuokkanen, Janne 223
★ Kyrou, Jordan 223
★ Laberge, Pascal 223
★ Laine, Patrik 224
★ Lajoie, Max 224
★ Latorella, Michael 224
★ Lauzon, Felix 224
★ Leonard, John 225
★ Lindgren, Ryan 225
★ Lindstrom, Linus 225
★ Luce, Griffin 225
★ Lundh, Gusten 226
★ Maher, Jordan 226
★ Mäkinen, Otto 226
★ Maksimovich, Kyle 226
★ Malenstyn, Beck 227
★ Mascherin, Adam 227
★ Matthews, Auston 227
★ Mattson, Mitchell 228
★ McAvoy, Charlie 228
★ McGing, Hugh 228
★ McInnis, Luke 228
★ McLeod, Michael 228
★ McPhee, Graham 229
★ Mete, Victor 229
★ Middleton, Keaton 229
★ Mityakin, Evgeny 230
★ Moverare, Jacob 230
★ Nauss, Morgan 230
★ Neveu, Jacob 231
★ Niemeläinen, Markus 231
★ Nother, Tyler 231
★ Nylander, Alexander 232
★ Paquette, Christopher 232
★ Parsons, Tyler 232
★ Pastujov, Nick 232
★ Peeke, Andrew 233
★ Pezzetta, Michael 233
★ Picard, Miguel 233
★ Pickard, Reilly 233

- ★ Poirier, Zach — 234
- ★ Pu, Cliff — 234
- ★ Puljujärvi, Jesse — 234
- ★ Raaymakers, Joseph — 235
- ★ Raddysh, Taylor — 235
- ★ Reunanen, Tarmo — 235
- ★ Reynolds, Keenan — 236
- ★ Rossini, Sam — 236
- ★ Rubtsov, German — 236
- ★ Ruotsalainen, Arttu — 236
- ★ Rymsha, Drake — 236
- ★ Saigeon, Brandon — 237
- ★ Salinitri, Anthony — 237
- ★ Sanchez, James — 237
- ★ Sarthou, Evan — 237
- ★ Sartoris, Matt — 238
- ★ Schaefer, Jonathon — 238
- ★ Sergachyov, Mikhail — 238
- ★ Sevigny, Mathieu — 239
- ★ Smith, Givani — 239
- ★ Sokolov, Dmitri — 239
- ★ Somppi, Otto — 240
- ★ Sproviero, Franco — 240
- ★ Stanley, Logan — 240
- ★ Steel, Sam — 241
- ★ Sukhachyov, Vladislav — 241
- ★ Suthers, Keenan — 241
- ★ Sylvestre, Gabriel — 241
- ★ Tessier, Julien — 242
- ★ Thierus, Lucas — 242
- ★ Timleck, Adam — 242
- ★ Timms, Matthew — 243
- ★ Tkachuk, Matthew — 243
- ★ Tufte, Riley — 243
- ★ Tuulola, Eetu — 243
- ★ Verbeek, Hayden — 244
- ★ Wait, Garrett — 244
- ★ Walker, Zach — 244
- ★ Weissbach, Linus — 244
- ★ Wells, Dylan — 244
- ★ Woll, Joseph — 245
- ★ Yakovenko, Alexander — 245
- ★ Zelenak, Vojtech — 245

2017 NHL DRAFT PROSPECTS 247

- ★ Aucoin, Yan — 248
- ★ Baribeau, Dereck — 248
- ★ Boudrias, Shawn — 248
- ★ Bowers, Shane — 248
- ★ Bulitka, Shane — 249
- ★ Burt, Robbie — 249
- ★ Cardinal, Tommy — 249
- ★ Chainey, Jocktan — 250
- ★ Chmelevski, Sasha — 250
- ★ Comtois, Maxime — 250
- ★ Côté, Louis-Filip — 251
- ★ Crête-Belzile, Antoine — 251
- ★ Davis, Hayden — 251
- ★ DiPietro, Michael — 252
- ★ D'Orio, Alex — 252
- ★ Durandeau, Arnaud — 252
- ★ Eder, Tobias — 253
- ★ Gadjovich, Jonah — 253
- ★ Gallant, Zach — 253
- ★ Gilmour, Brady — 253
- ★ Hawel, Liam — 254
- ★ Hischier, Nico — 254
- ★ Hoyt, Peyton — 254
- ★ Hughes, Aidan — 255
- ★ Jones, Ben — 255
- ★ Keating, Austen — 255
- ★ Krief, Alexander — 256
- ★ Lacombe, Charlie — 256
- ★ Lefebvre, Simon — 256
- ★ Martineau, Vincent — 257
- ★ McGregor, Ryan — 257
- ★ Meireles, Greg — 257
- ★ Morand, Antoine — 258
- ★ O'Grady, Reagan — 258
- ★ Paquette, Jacob — 258
- ★ Pataki, Brady — 258
- ★ Pettersson, Elias — 259
- ★ Phillips, Markus — 259
- ★ Popugayev, Nikita A. — 260
- ★ Poulin, Anthony — 260
- ★ Proner, Robert — 260
- ★ Ratcliffe, Isaac — 260
- ★ Roberts, Elijah — 261
- ★ Stevens, Liam — 261
- ★ Strome, Matthew — 261
- ★ Suzuki, Nicholas — 262
- ★ Teasdale, Joel — 262
- ★ Thomas, Robert — 262
- ★ Tippett, Owen — 263
- ★ Vilardi, Gabriel — 263
- ★ Voyer, Alex-Olivier — 263
- ★ Webb, Reilly — 264
- ★ Willms, Jason — 264

SCOUTS GAME REPORTS 265

CREDITS 485

2015 NHL DRAFT RANKINGS

RANK	PLAYER	TEAM	LEAGUE	POS	HEIGHT	WEIGHT	GOALS	ASSISTS
1	MCDAVID, CONNOR	ERIE	OHL	C	6' 0.75"	195	44	76
2	EICHEL, JACK	BOSTON UNIVERSITY	H-EAST	C	6' 2.0"	196	26	45
3	MARNER, MITCHELL	LONDON	OHL	C	5' 11.0"	160	44	82
4	HANIFIN, NOAH	BOSTON COLLEGE	H-EAST	D	6' 2.75"	203	5	18
5	CONNOR, KYLE	YOUNGSTOWN	USHL	LW	6' 1.0"	177	34	46
6	STROME, DYLAN	ERIE	OHL	C	6' 3.0"	185	45	84
7	ZACHA, PAVEL	SARNIA	OHL	C	6' 3.0"	210	16	18
8	CROUSE, LAWSON	KINGSTON	OHL	LW	6' 4.0"	215	29	22
9	PROVOROV, IVAN	BRANDON	WHL	D	6' 0.5"	201	15	46
10	RANTANEN, MIKKO	TPS	FINLAND	RW	6' 3.5"	211	9	19
11	WERENSKI, ZACHARY	U OF MICHIGAN	BIG10	D	6' 2.0"	206	9	16
12	BARZAL, MATHEW	SEATTLE	WHL	C	5' 11.25"	175	12	45
13	MEIER, TIMO	HALIFAX	QMJHL	RW	6' 1.0"	209	44	46
14	MERKLEY, NICHOLAS	KELOWNA	WHL	RW	5' 10.5"	191	20	70
15	ERIKSSON EK, JOEL	FARJESTAD	SWEDEN	C	6' 1.75"	180	4	2
16	GURIANOV, DENIS	TOGLIATTI 2	RUSSIA-JR.	RW	6' 2.5"	183	15	10
17	SVECHNIKOV, EVGENY	CAPE BRETON	QMJHL	LW	6' 1.75"	199	32	46
18	BOESER, BROCK	WATERLOO	USHL	RW	6' 0.5"	191	35	33
19	KONECNY, TRAVIS	OTTAWA	OHL	C	5' 9.75"	175	29	39
20	CHABOT, THOMAS	SAINT JOHN	QMJHL	D	6' 1.5"	180	12	29
21	SAMSONOV, ILYA	MAGNITOGORSK 2	RUSSIA-JR.	G	6' 3.0"	200	2.66	0.918
22	JUULSEN, NOAH	EVERETT	WHL	D	6' 1.5"	174	9	43
23	WHITE, COLIN	USA U-18	USHL	C	6' 0.0"	183	4	13
24	ROSLOVIC, JACK	USA U-18	USHL	C	6' 0.5"	182	11	27
25	ZBORIL, JAKUB	SAINT JOHN	QMJHL	D	6' 0.75"	184	13	20
26	ROY, JEREMY	SHERBROOKE	QMJHL	D	6' 0.0"	188	5	38
27	CARLO, BRANDON	TRI-CITY	WHL	D	6' 5.0"	196	4	21
28	DeBRUSK, JAKE	SWIFT CURRENT	WHL	LW	5' 11.75"	174	42	39
29	KYLINGTON, OLIVER	FARJESTAD	SWEDEN	D	6' 0.0"	180	2	3
30	BITTNER, PAUL	PORTLAND	WHL	LW	6' 4.0"	204	34	37
31	LARSSON, JACOB	FROLUNDA JR.	SWEDEN-JR.	D	6' 2.0"	191	8	11
32	MELOCHE, NICOLAS	BAIE-COMEAU	QMJHL	D	6' 2.5"	204	10	24
33	CARLSSON, GABRIEL	LINKOPING JR.	SWEDEN-JR.	D	6' 4.0"	183	0	7
34	HARKINS, JANSEN	PRINCE GEORGE	WHL	C	6' 1.25"	182	20	59
35	KOVACS, ROBIN	AIK	SWEDEN-2	RW	6' 0.0"	172	17	11
36	TRENIN, YAKOV	GATINEAU	QMJHL	C	6' 1.75"	194	18	49
37	SPRONG, DANIEL	CHARLOTTETOWN	QMJHL	RW	6' 0.0"	180	39	49
38	SIEGENTHALER, JONAS	ZURICH	SWISS	D	6' 2.5"	220	0	3
39	BLACKWOOD, MACKENZIE	BARRIE	OHL	G	6' 4.0"	215	3.09	0.906
40	BEAUVILLIER, ANTHONY	SHAWINIGAN	QMJHL	LW	5' 10.25"	173	42	52
41	FOLEY, ERIK	CEDAR RAPIDS	USHL	LW	5' 11.5"	185	27	27
42	NATTINEN, JULIUS	JYP 2	FINLAND-2	C	6' 1.75"	191	11	18
43	CHLAPIK, FILIP	CHARLOTTETOWN	QMJHL	C	6' 1.0"	196	33	42
44	HINTZ, ROOPE	ILVES	FINLAND	LW	6' 2.5"	185	5	12
45	GAGNE, GABRIEL	VICTORIAVILLE	QMJHL	RW	6' 4.75"	186	35	24
46	DUNN, VINCE	NIAGARA	OHL	D	5' 11.75"	187	18	38
47	DERMOTT, TRAVIS	ERIE	OHL	D	5' 11.25"	197	8	37
48	BRISEBOIS, GUILLAUME	ACADIE-BATHURST	QMJHL	D	6' 1.75"	175	4	24
49	FISCHER, CHRISTIAN	USA U-18	USHL	RW	6' 1.0"	212	15	15
50	CARRIER, ALEXANDRE	GATINEAU	QMJHL	D	5' 11.0"	174	12	43
51	STEPHENS, MITCHELL	SAGINAW	OHL	C	5' 11.25"	188	22	26
52	VLADAR, DANIEL	KLADNO	CZREP-2	G	6' 5.25"	185	2.78	0.926
53	KOROSTELEV, NIKITA	SARNIA	OHL	RW	6' 1.25"	195	24	29
54	BRACCO, JEREMY	USA U-18	USHL	RW	5' 9.25"	173	14	18
55	WAGNER, AUSTIN	REGINA	WHL	LW	6' 1.0"	178	20	19
56	KNOTT, GRAHAM	NIAGARA	OHL	LW	6' 3.25"	190	25	18
57	SENYSHYN, ZACHARY	SAULT STE. MARIE	OHL	RW	6' 1.0"	192	26	19
58	NOVAK, THOMAS	WATERLOO	USHL	C	6' 0.5"	179	14	34
59	BEAUDIN, JEAN-CHRISTOPHE	ROUYN-NORANDA	QMJHL	C	6' 1.0"	181	14	39
60	ANDERSSON, RASMUS	BARRIE	OHL	D	6' 0.0"	212	12	52

2015 NHL DRAFT RANKINGS — 13

RANK	PLAYER	TEAM	LEAGUE	POS	HEIGHT	WEIGHT	GOALS	ASSISTS
61	FORSBACKA KARLSSON, JACOB	OMAHA	USHL	C	6' 0.75"	190	15	38
62	GROPP, RYAN	SEATTLE	WHL	LW	6' 2.0"	187	30	28
63	JOSEPH, MATHIEU	SAINT JOHN	QMJHL	RW	6' 0.75"	166	21	21
64	GUHLE, BRENDAN	PRINCE ALBERT	WHL	D	6' 1.75"	184	5	27
65	STENLUND, KEVIN	HV 71 JR.	SWEDEN-JR.	C	6' 3.0"	205	14	22
66	BOOTH, CALLUM	QUEBEC	QMJHL	G	6' 2.75"	199	2.49	0.904
67	ROY, NICOLAS	CHICOUTIMI	QMJHL	C	6' 4.0"	195	16	34
68	LAUZON, JEREMY	ROUYN-NORANDA	QMJHL	D	6' 1.75"	193	15	21
69	MORRISON, BRAD	PRINCE GEORGE	WHL	C	5' 11.5"	154	23	27
70	GREER, A.J	BOSTON UNIVERSITY	H-EAST	LW	6' 2.5"	204	3	4
71	YAN, DENNIS	SHAWINIGAN	QMJHL	LW	6' 1.25"	184	33	31
72	GREENWAY, JORDAN	USA U-18	USHL	LW	6' 4.75"	222	5	15
73	CAPOBIANCO, KYLE	SUDBURY	OHL	D	6' 1.0"	178	10	30
74	COTTON, DAVID	CUSHING ACADEMY	HIGH-MA	C	6' 2.5"	200	27	42
75	MARINO, JOHN	SOUTH SHORE	USPHL PRE.	D	6' 0.5"	171	4	24
76	KOLESAR, KEEGAN	SEATTLE	WHL	RW	6' 1.25"	217	19	19
77	CIRELLI, ANTHONY	OSHAWA	OHL	C	5' 11.5"	160	13	23
78	NOEL, NATHAN	SAINT JOHN	QMJHL	C	5' 10.75"	172	24	38
79	MARTENET, CHRIS	LONDON	OHL	D	6' 7.0"	198	7	9
80	CERNAK, ERIK	KOSICE	SLOVAKIA	D	6' 3.0"	203	5	8
81	SPENCER, MATTHEW	PETERBOROUGH	OHL	D	6' 1.5"	203	6	24
82	MUSIL, ADAM	RED DEER	WHL	C	6' 2.75"	202	15	24
83	NIELSEN, ANDREW	LETHBRIDGE	WHL	D	6' 3.0"	207	7	17
84	GABRIELLE, JESSE	REGINA	WHL	LW	5' 10.75"	205	23	21
85	PILON, RYAN	BRANDON	WHL	D	6' 2.0"	206	11	41
86	MANGIAPANE, ANDREW	BARRIE	OHL	LW	5' 10.0"	170	43	61
87	BORGEN, WILLIAM	MOORHEAD	HIGH-MN	D	6' 1.75"	189	3	16
88	VANDE SOMPEL, MITCHELL	OSHAWA	OHL	D	5' 10.0"	182	12	51
89	DOVE-MCFALLS, SAMUEL	SAINT JOHN	QMJHL	LW	6' 2.0"	207	14	20
90	SPEERS, BLAKE	SAULT STE. MARIE	OHL	C	5' 11.0"	181	24	43
91	DERGACHYOV, ALEXANDER	SKA ST. PETERSBURG 2	RUSSIA-JR.	C	6' 4.0"	200	10	29
92	AHL, FILIP	HV 71 JR.	SWEDEN-JR.	LW	6' 3.25"	211	20	22
93	MALGIN, DENIS	ZURICH	SWISS	C	5' 8.0"	163	2	6
94	PFEIFER, TRISTEN	EVERETT	WHL	D	6' 4.0"	180	2	7
95	BOURQUE, SIMON	RIMOUSKI	QMJHL	D	6' 0.25"	184	10	28
96	BEAR, ETHAN	SEATTLE	WHL	D	5' 11.0"	200	13	25
97	REDDEKOPP, CHAZ	VICTORIA	WHL	D	6' 3.25"	219	5	16
98	GAWDIN, GLENN	SWIFT CURRENT	WHL	C	6' 0.5"	191	15	39
99	LOOKE, JENS	BRYNAS	SWEDEN	RW	6' 0.5"	180	2	4
100	GARLAND, CONOR	MONCTON	QMJHL	RW	5' 8.0"	163	35	94
101	RICHARD, ANTHONY	VAL-D'OR	QMJHL	C	5' 9.5"	163	43	48
102	MONTEMBEAULT, SAMUEL	BLAINVILLE-BOISBRIAND	QMJHL	G	6' 2.5"	173	2.59	0.891
103	GAVRIKOV, VLADISLAV	YAROSLAVL	RUSSIA	D	6' 2.5"	205	1	6
104	GILBERT, DENNIS	CHICAGO	USHL	D	6' 2.25"	201	4	23
105	TIMASHOV, DMYTRO	QUEBEC	QMJHL	LW	5' 9.25"	192	19	71
106	SOY, TYLER	VICTORIA	WHL	C	5' 11.5"	172	28	35
107	TOMEK, MATEJ	TOPEKA	NAHL	G	6' 2.5"	180	1.83	0.928
108	MASSIE, JAKE	KIMBALL UNION	HIGH-NH	D	6' 0.5"	172	5	15
109	WOTHERSPOON, PARKER	TRI-CITY	WHL	D	6' 0.25"	171	9	33
110	TIFFELS, FREDERIK	WESTERN MICH	NCAA	LW	6' 1.0"	201	11	10
111	SCHEMITSCH, THOMAS	OWEN SOUND	OHL	D	6' 3.0"	205	14	35
112	STEZKA, ALES	LIBEREC JR.	CZREP-JR.	G	6' 3.25"	178	2.77	0.907
113	CECCONI, JOSEPH	MUSKEGON	USHL	D	6' 2.25"	209	3	14
114	MARODY, COOPER	SIOUX FALLS	USHL	C	6' 0.25"	173	20	29
115	KARNAUKHOV, PAVEL	CALGARY	WHL	LW	6' 2.5"	194	20	22
116	GABRIELE, GRANT	USA U-18	USHL	D	6' 0.75"	167	1	4
117	OLUND, LINUS	BRYNAS JR.	SWEDEN-JR.	C	5' 11.25"	178	15	11
118	VEHVILAINEN, VEINI	JYP 2	FINLAND-2	G	6' 0.5"	180	3.09	0.918
119	MCNIVEN, MICHAEL	OWEN SOUND	OHL	G	6' 0.75"	221	2.79	0.914
120	SUTER, PIUS	GUELPH	OHL	C	5' 11.0"	165	43	29

RANK	PLAYER	TEAM	LEAGUE	POS	HEIGHT	WEIGHT	GOALS	ASSISTS
121	FIALA, EVAN	SPOKANE	WHL	RD	6' 4.0"	193	0	12
122	SANDSTROM, FELIX	BRYNAS JR.	SWEDEN-JR.	G	6' 2.0"	191	2.63	0.907
123	MARSH, ADAM	SAINT JOHN	QMJHL	LW	6' 0.0"	160	24	20
124	YOUNAN, ALEXANDER	HV 71 JR.	SWEDEN-JR.	D	6' 0.75"	189	3	17
125	RADKE, ROY	BARRIE	OHL	RW	6' 2.5"	203	9	9
126	TAMMELA, JONNE	KALPA	FINLAND	RW	5' 10.0"	180	4	0
127	AHO, SEBASTIAN	KARPAT	FINLAND	RW	5' 11.25"	172	4	7
128	TUULOLA, JONI	HPK	FINLAND	D	6' 2.5"	180	5	5
129	BONDRA, RADOVAN	KOSICE	SLOVAKIA	RW	6' 5.25"	220	2	2
130	JAROS, CHRISTIAN	LULEA JR.	SWEDEN-JR.	D	6' 3.0"	201	4	8
131	GATES, BRENT	GREEN BAY	USHL	C	6' 1.75"	196	10	17
132	VELA, MARCUS	LANGLEY	BCHL	C	6' 0.5"	204	20	26
133	BEDNARD, RYAN	JOHNSTOWN	NAHL	G	6' 3.75"	179	2.66	0.913
134	LEVEILLE, LOIK	CAPE BRETON	QMJHL	D	5' 11.5"	223	13	41
135	HUNT, DRYDEN	MEDICINE HAT	WHL	LW	6' 0.0"	199	19	17
136	ESTEPHAN, GIORGIO	LETHBRIDGE	WHL	C	6' 0.0"	188	23	28
137	STEWART, CHASE	SAGINAW	OHL	RD	6' 2.0"	212	0	5
138	WILKIE, CHRISTOPHER	TRI-CITY	USHL	RW	5' 11.5"	199	35	20
139	NIKU, SAMI	JYP 2	FINLAND-2	D	6' 0.5"	176	3	22
140	SPACEK, MICHAEL	PARDUBICE	CZREP	RW	5' 11.0"	187	5	17
141	LABERGE, SAMUEL	RIMOUSKI	QMJHL	LW	6' 1.5"	206	15	11
142	WARREN, BRENDAN	USA U-18	USHL	LW	6' 0.25"	191	7	6
143	WEBSTER, BAILEY	SAINT JOHN	QMJHL	D	6' 3.0"	210	1	5
144	RYKOV, YEGOR	SKA ST. PETERSBURG 2	RUSSIA-JR.	D	6' 1.25"	216	5	16
145	KIELLY, KAMERON	CHARLOTTETOWN	QMJHL	RW	6' 0.0"	180	16	33
146	LINDGREN, JESPER	MODO JR.	SWEDEN-JR.	D	6' 0.0"	161	6	27
147	LEMCKE, JUSTIN	BELLEVILLE	OHL	D	6' 2.25"	200	9	14
148	VOROBYOV, MIKHAIL	UFA 2	RUSSIA-JR.	C	6' 2.0"	194	8	12
149	BRADLEY, MATTHEW	MEDICINE HAT	WHL	C	5' 11.25"	187	17	23
150	KASE, DAVID	CHOMUTOV	CZREP-2	RW	5' 11.0"	169	7	7
151	JASEK, LUKAS	TRINEC	CZREP	RW	5' 11.25"	165	0	2
152	DESROCHER, STEPHEN	OSHAWA	OHL	D	6' 3.75"	198	10	13
153	PEARSON, CHASE	YOUNGSTOWN	USHL	C	6' 2.0"	189	12	14
154	HILL, ADIN	PORTLAND	WHL	G	6' 3.5"	198	2.81	0.921
155	SAARELA, ALEKSI	ASSAT	FINLAND	C	5' 10.5"	198	6	6
156	WEINGER, EVAN	PORTLAND	WHL	RW	5' 11.25"	184	7	19
157	SIDEROFF, DEVEN	KAMLOOPS	WHL	RW	5' 11.0"	171	17	25
158	FALKOVSKY, STEPAN	YUNOST MINSK 2	RUSSIA-JR.	D	6' 6.0"	203	4	7
159	FREYTAG, MATTHEW	TRI-CITY	USHL	LW	6' 0.75"	195	15	15
160	SHAROV, ALEXANDER	TOGLIATTI	RUSSIA	LW	6' 2.0"	191	3	3
161	KAPRIZOV, KIRILL	NOVOKUZNETSK	RUSSIA	LW	5' 9.0"	185	4	4
162	BOURAMMAN, GUSTAV	SAULT STE. MARIE	OHL	D	5' 11.25"	184	5	39
163	GAUDETTE, ADAM	CEDAR RAPIDS	USHL	C	6' 0.75"	170	13	17
164	PETERS, COLLIN	SIOUX FALLS	USHL	C	5' 11.5"	166	6	5
165	APPLETON, MASON	TRI-CITY	USHL	RC	6' 2.0"	194	12	28
166	LARKIN, RYAN	CEDAR RAPIDS	USHL	G	6' 0.5"	192	2.43	0.919
167	CARLSSON, LUCAS	BRYNAS JR.	SWEDEN-JR.	D	6' 0.0"	180	6	12
168	TERRY, TROY	USA U-18	USHL	C/RW	5' 10.5"	160	6	8
169	SADEK, JACK	LAKEVILLE NORTH	HIGH-MN	D	6' 1.5"	185	4	9
170	MICHAUD, LUCAS	PORTLAND JR. PIRATES	USPHL PRE.	C	5' 10.5"	205	22	23
171	STEVENS, LUKE	NOBLE & GREENOUGH	HIGH-MA	LW	6' 3.75"	192	11	28
172	BOKA, NICHOLAS	USA U-18	USHL	D	6' 0.25"	197	5	6
173	VEJDEMO, LUKAS	DJURGARDEN JR.	SWEDEN-JR.	C	6' 2.0"	194	23	25
174	ALAIN, ALEXANDRE	GATINEAU	QMJHL	C	6' 0.25"	173	9	18
175	KOHN, MASON	KITCHENER	OHL	LC	5' 10.5"	188	7	8
176	FITZGERALD, CAVAN	HALIFAX	QMJHL	D	6' 0.0"	196	4	27
177	SIMON, DOMINIK	HC PLEZEN	CZE	LW	5' 11.0"	176	18	12
178	PERESSINI, LUCAS	KINGSTON	OHL	G	6' 2.25"	198	2.32	0.922
179	VAINIO, VEETI	BLUES JR.	FINLAND-JR.	D	6' 1.75"	169	13	31
180	WHITE, COLTON	SAULT STE. MARIE	OHL	D	6' 0.0"	182	6	16

2015 NHL DRAFT RANKINGS — 15

RANK	PLAYER	TEAM	LEAGUE	POS	HEIGHT	WEIGHT	GOALS	ASSISTS
181	HANSSON, PETTER	LINKOPING JR.	SWEDEN-JR.	D	6' 1.0"	187	15	19
182	PARSELLS, ADAM	WAUSAU WEST	HIGH-WI	D	6' 5.5"	192	5	12
183	ASKEW, CAMERON	MONCTON	QMJHL	C	6' 2.25"	203	17	28
184	PAWLENCHUK, GRAYSON	RED DEER	WHL	LW	5' 11.5"	183	9	17
185	ALSING, OLLE	ALMTUNA	SWEDEN-2	D	5' 11.0"	161	2	9
186	DUNDA, LIAM	OWEN SOUND	OHL	LW	6' 4.25"	212	2	7
187	KUPSKY, JAKE	LONE STAR	NAHL	G	6' 5.0"	209	2.16	0.911
188	MCBRIDE, NICK	PRINCE ALBERT	WHL	G	6' 3.5"	179	3.41	0.895
189	STEPHENS, DEVANTE	KELOWNA	WHL	D	6' 1.25"	171	4	7
190	SHEA, RYAN	BOSTON COLLEGE H.S.	HIGH-MA	D	6' 0.5"	175	6	29
191	AHO, SEBASTIAN	SKELLEFTEA	SWEDEN	D	5' 9.25"	165	1	8
192	PAVLYCHEV, NIKITA	DES MOINES	USHL	C	6' 7.0"	200	6	10
193	LALONDE, BRADLEY	CAPE BRETON	QMJHL	D	6' 0.0"	196	7	22
194	MERCER, CULLEN	PLYMOUTH	OHL	RC	5' 11.75"	189	7	8
195	DZIERKALS, MARTINS	HK RIGA	MHL	RW	5' 11.0"	170	15	23
196	LINDBERG, BRANDON	SARNIA	OHL	C	6' 0.5"	205	13	14
197	FORTIN, ALEXANDRE	ROUYN-NORANDA	QMJHL	C	6' 0.0"	173	11	29
198	LIZOTTE, CAMERON	PETERBOROUGH	OHL	D	6' 1.25"	193	2	7
199	BRUCE, RILEY	NORTH BAY	OHL	D	6' 6.0"	205	0	3
200	HUSKA, ADAM	GREEN BAY	USHL	G	6' 3.25"	189	3.66	0.901
201	INGRAM, CONNOR	KAMLOOPS	WHL	G	6' 0.5"	212	2.96	0.904
202	GENNARO, MATTEO	PRINCE ALBERT	WHL	C	6' 2.25"	187	16	15
203	SAARIJARVI, VILI	GREEN BAY	USHL	D	5'9"	161	6	17
204	BETZ, NICK	ERIE	OHL	RW	6' 4.0"	220	22	32
205	SHERWOOD, KOLE	OHIO BLUE JACKETS U18	T1EHL	RW	6' 0.0"	185	22	26
206	OPILKA, LUKE	USA U-18	USHL	G	6' 1.0"	192	2.77	0.883
207	MCNEELY, JACK	LAKEVILLE NORTH	HIGH-MN	D	6' 2.5"	178	1	20
208	ADDISON, JEREMIAH	OTTAWA	OHL	LW	5' 11.75"	182	19	28
209	PELTON-BYCE, TY	MADISON MEMORIAL	HIGH-WI	LC	6' 1.0"	176	36	46
210	JONES, CALEB	USA U-18	USHL	D	5' 11.75"	194	6	18
211	CRAWLEY, BRANDON	LONDON	OHL	D	6' 0.5"	198	3	13

2015 NHL DRAFT PROSPECTS

Abols, Rodrigo
LC – HK Riga (MHL) – 6'3" 179
HockeyProspect.com Ranking: NR

In his second year of eligibility for the draft Abols had good numbers in the MHL, saw some KHL action in the new year and managed to grab a spot in the Latvian roster for the World Championships in Prague.

He still needs to fill out his frame, but he has nice size and decent speed to go along with it. However, Rodrigo doesn't take advantage of his size, as he doesn't make very good use of it in puck battles and is not a physical player. His hands are average and his performance in our live viewings at the U20 Div.I World Championships in Asiago was disappointing. Even though has some scoring ability around the net, he doesn't look apt for the smaller rinks and the North American game. Right now it's hard to envision a role for him in North American pro hockey, as he doesn't have the skills to play there on a top six, and doesn't bring the elements required to be effective in a bottom six role.

Addison, Jeremiah
RW - Ottawa 67's (OHL) 6'00" 186
HockeyProspect.com Ranking: 208

Even dating back to his Minor Midget days, Addison never really showed us much offensively. He was primarily a two-way forward who was hard to play against. While he projects to be that type of player at the next level, he showed some impressive offensive ability never seen before by him. He improved his shot from last season. He also displayed good hands and made some decent passes to create chances as well. Jeremiah finishes his checks effectively and is a tough player who quickly picks up his man on the backcheck. He played in all game situations for the 67's and is a very capable penalty killer. Addison won't be a high pick but could be a pick later on as a forward who would make a solid penalty killer, but who also may be a late bloomer in regards to talent and puck skills.

Adams, Jack
RW – Malden Catholic (HIGH – MA) – 6'5" 190
HockeyProspect.com Ranking: NR

He's a big winger that really made great progress from his sophomore to junior season at perennial Massachusetts high school powerhouse Malden Catholic. Until this year, his stride was a little awkward as he learned to play with his size. His lower body strength and work put in with skating coach Paul Vincent showed as he became adept at leveraging opponents with good edge work and size. He's a smart player who sees the ice well and can finish. His strong play earned him several offers from Hockey East and ECAC schools before ultimately committing to Princeton.

Afonasyevsky, Semyon
LW – Belye Medvedi (MHL) – 6'2" 196
HockeyProspect.com Ranking: NR

Afonasyevsky is a Russian winger with solid size coming off a strong junior season. A late '96 born, he relies on his solid wrist shot to score a good chunk of his goals, but he is not afraid of driving the net when he sees an opening for that. He is certainly more of a scorer than a playmaker, but he is defensively responsible and sees time on the penalty kill. Semyon lacks however a dynamic element both in terms of skills and skating, and the question is if he can develop the skills to buy himself chances at the next level.

Ahl, Filip
LW – HV 71 (SWE) – 6'3.5" 211
HockeyProspect.com Ranking: 92

When watching a junior game where Ahl is playing, eyes usually fall on him. He brings to the ice a terrific, massive frame, and he is able to carry the puck and make some skilled moves in the offensive zone; his NHL potential is immediately obvious. When he is coming down the offensive zone with his powerful stride and the puck on his stick he is hard to contain for his peers. An intelligent player with the puck, he knows how to suck a defender in and then thread a pass to a linemate that is skating into open ice, or he can protect it to complete a short feed and create some room for a linemate close by; passing is an underrated part of his game. Ahl also knows where to go without the puck in the offensive zone and when on his game he makes life difficult for defenders, whether trying to find the inside lane, sneaking back door, or simply using his body mass to shield the puck. He can use his reach to complete plays in uncomfortable situations while engaged with opponents. Usually tries to take the puck to the net once down deep, showing his impressive strength, but he can also use a good low wrister off the rush and has a good eye for finding holes on goalies.

For a guy of his size he can show good mobility, as once he gets going he moves well in all directions. However his footwork is often troublesome and when he is not on top shape, a lack of agility becomes very evident and a reason for concern. He needs to keep his feet going, and he often doesn't, particularly when he gets tired, something that has been happening too often too soon this season, raising some question marks on his conditioning. Filip can be caught flat-footed in the neutral zone and his overall defensive game needs a lot of improvement, on some shifts he looks lost in his zone. Ahl can be very physical, but like other parts of his game, that isn't a consistent trait. Coming off a very disappointing showing at the U18 World Championships, there is still a lot to like about Ahl and his potential, but also good reasons for concern.

Quotable: "I've seen him play some great stretches of hockey but he seems to struggle more after the mid point of the game. - Mark Edwards

Aho, Sebastian
LW – Kärpät (Fin Elite) – 5'11" 172
HockeyProspect.com Ranking: 127

He's an offensive-minded winger with quick feet and good vision. Aho likes to use his speed to challenge defenders and his passing in the offensive-zone is great, but he doesn't have any spectacular strengths. He has represented Finland internationally many times already from the world junior hockey championship, U18 world championship and U18 Ivan Hlinka tournament this season alone. This season he played majority of the season in Finland men's league playing 27 games with Kärpät. He's not the biggest kid, but he will go to traffic and doesn't shy away from the corners. His two-way game is decent and he's really versatile kid but there aren't any strength that suggest to us that he's a special prospect. He's not a pure scorer, we have doubt at how well he will be able to translate his game to the NHL.

Aho, Sebastian
LD – Skelleftea (SWE) – 5'10" 170
HockeyProspect.com Ranking: 191

The other Sebastian Aho of this draft, this one is a defenseman from Sweden who was passed over in last year draft. He's an undersized defenseman who moves the puck quickly out of his zone and makes smart decisions with it. This year he played with Skelleftea of the Swedish elite league and also took part of the world junior hockey championship in Canada where he recorded 4 points in 7 games helping Sweden finishing in 4th place. He has good feet and moves very well around the ice and that also makes him a threat on the power play. His lack of size definitely hurts him, we would had been drafted last season if it was not for that. It also hurt him in the defensive zone when he battles for the puck against bigger forwards. He brings a dynamic presence on the blue line and can stickhandle with ease while moving around the ice exploring his options. The WJC showed both his good part (in the preliminary rounds) and his bad part (medal rounds).

Alain, Alexandre
RC/RW – Gatineau Olympiques (QMJHL) – 6'0" 168
HockeyProspect.com Ranking: 174

Alain was selected in the first round of the 2013 QMJHL draft by Gatineau, even after missing a good chunk of the season due to a non-cancerous tumor on his spinal cord. For his 16 year old season, it was decided that he would go back to Midget AAA for one more year with Séminaire St-Francois and he didn't have the best of seasons, still feeling the effect of his illness.

This season, Alain made the Olympiques' roster out of training camp and had a strong start to his season, scoring 7 goals and 14 points in the first 2 months. However, Alain finished the season with no goals in his last 42 regular season games, being moved around in the lineup often to form different line combinations, moving from center to the wing as well.

The Quebec native is a versatile forward who can either play on the wing or at center and is a smart player at both ends of the rink. He makes good use of his speed and smarts as an effective penalty killer, unafraid of blocking shots. Like last year, it's offensively that he showed he has trouble in being a consistent producer. There's nothing wrong with his work ethic and with luck he should have scored more than he did this year. He keeps his play simple and he's usually first on the puck, seeing the ice very well. He's capable of playing on a checking line and playing versus the opposing team's top line. He's not an overly physical player, but knows how to win puck battles and he's smart on the forecheck. Alain struggled to produce after a hot start and that cost him in our rankings during the course of the year. He could still get drafted due to his smarts and hockey sense.

Alsing, Olle
LD – Almtuna (SWE 2) – 5'11" 161
HockeyProspect.com Ranking: 185

Alsing is a slight defenseman with quick feet that effectively starts up plays from the back end, often before the opponents have the time to shut down his best option or put pressure on him. He has decent puck skills, his head up and he immediately recognizes the best passing lane available. When no good one is available straight away, he has the notable capability of waiting an extra split second for a lane to open up. He takes some risks, but overall his passing game is excellent and certainly his main strength. He doesn't mind joining the play in the offensive zone, but doesn't possess great acceleration to make up for it when he gets caught.

After playing almost the entire season against men, Olle doesn't look intimidated by bigger opponents, but inevitably his size somewhat limits his defensive efficiency. How he would fare against the most talented forwards in the top Swedish league is a question mark, and he certainly will have to bulk up to increase his chances to succeed at the next level.

Andersson, Rasmus
RD - Barrie Colts (OHL) 6'00" 210
HockeyProspect.com Ranking: 60

Andersson is one of the better puck-moving defensemen to come out of the OHL this year. He usually makes the accurate first pass up ice hitting his man in stride, but does have a tendency to sometimes not see when a lane has been taken away from him. Andersson keeps his head up when skating up ice with the puck, which allows him to read the ice effectively and anticipate how the play will develop. If no outlets are available, Andersson has no problem taking what the defense gives him and skating the puck up ice. He's a good puck handler and is good at eluding traffic in space. His stride isn't the smoothest looking, but he gets around the ice pretty well. He could use more explosiveness in his first few steps.

Andersson is very good at quarterbacking powerplay. He distributes the puck quickly, doesn't force anything that isn't available and regularly gets shots through traffic. Andersson has a powerful slap shot, but he doesn't force it if there is no clear shooting lane. He's good at holding the line and for the most part, he's smart with his pinches and has no problem jumping into the play. He usually picks his spots well, as he regularly helps keep the play alive and doesn't get caught often.

Without the puck, Andersson's game progressed as the year went on. He's good at keeping opponents to the outside, as he uses his stick to steer opposing forwards wide before sealing them off and finishing them along the wall. He doesn't take himself out of position for the big hit quite as often and has some edge to his game. He doesn't shy away from physical play and he was a regular on Barrie's penalty killing units. He's good at taking lanes away with his stick and doesn't hesitate to block shots. At times he's not as aggressive as he should be while battling in front of his net or along walls, though he did pick up his physical play as the season went on.

Quotable: "Smart player, an early 2nd rounder for me." - NHL Scout

Quotable: "Good offensive player and I like his offensive tools but his play in his own zone was spotty at times. His fitness level is an area for concern. He struggled late in games in too many of my viewings. When you see him off ice, his body needs work. Had him just outside the first round early in the season but the more I saw him, the more he slid for me." - Mark Edwards

Quotable: "If I'm choosing between him and a guy like Dermott, I'm going Dermott. He was a good interview at the combine though." - NHL Scout

Quotable: "Really impressive interview (Combine) he answered tough questions about his off ice (fitness, high weight and body fat as examples) and met them head on. He was honest and understood the concerns." - NHL Scout

Quotable: "May have been our best interview in Buffalo (Combine)." - NHL Scout

Quotable: "Andersson is an excellent passer and regularly gets his shots through...is the kind of player you want quarterbacking a powerplay" - HP Scout Todd Cordell

Appleby, Ken
G - Oshawa Generals (OHL) 6'04" 205
HockeyProspect.com Ranking: NR

While the re-entry goaltender Appleby benefits from having one of the top teams in the CHL in front of him, he showed on multiple occasions the potential that could make him a solid pick up in the 2015 NHL Entry Draft. Appleby has excellent size and uses it very well to take away angles. He has made some great saves at point blank this year. He is technically sound going post to post and covering up all the holes between him and the post then pushes off to the top to the crease well. If there is a weakness in his game it would be how much his five hole opens up and this has been exploited by some good players.

Quotable: "Appleby played a big part in the Generals successful season and run to becoming OHL champs. He competes hard and has the size NHL teams love. His rebound control was hit and miss in my viewings." - Mark Edwards

Appleton, Mason
RC – Tri City Storm (USHL) 6'2" 190
HockeyProspect.com Ranking: 165

Mason is a 96' birth who plays a very simple but smart effective game. He progressed as the season moved along and caught our eye as a potential re-entry player. He does a lot of little things well and plays hard every game. His biggest strength is probably that he doesn't have any glaring weaknesses. Mason could be a free agent invite or might even be a late round selection.

Quotable: "I've watched this kid for a few years now and he just keeps getting better. He plays a smart game and competes." - HP scout, Justin Schreiber

Artemov, Artem
RW - Saginaw Spirit (OHL) 6'00" 198
HockeyProspect.com Ranking: NR

Artemov's skating is average despite possessing quick feet. He has a good frame and can protect the puck effectively in the offensive zone. He has average size but struggles in battles down low. His strongest asset is his hands which are very quick and when he's on his game he can create offense for himself and his linemates. He can sometimes get caught trying to do too much. Artem still has a fair amount of room for improvement and is not a player we would rank or a player we expect to see drafted at the 2015 NHL Entry Draft.

Askew, Cam
Right Wing/RC - Moncton Wildcats (QMJHL) – 6'2" 204
HockeyProspect.com Ranking: 183

Askew was drafted by Drummondville, 11th overall during the 2013 QMJHL Draft but after a tough first season in the league, he was traded to Moncton in the off-season.

After starting the season slowly, Askew had his best moment in December after Moncton traded Vladimir Tkachev to Quebec, thus granting Askew an opportunity to play a top-6 role on the team. Playing often on a line with Barbashev and Garland surely helped him produce more and he became a more confident player offensively. Consistency remains an issue with him and he didn't stay on that line for the remainder of the year. The South Boston native is positionally strong, usually finding himself in the right position in the offensive zone. Askew has a good, quick shot and can create numerous scoring chances with his skilled play. He has an NHL wrist shot and can score from anywhere in the offensive zone. He has a good stride for a bigger forward, but still needs more explosiveness in them.

We would like to see him be more active on the ice instead of waiting to get the puck back while not moving his feet. However, he has gotten better this season in this aspect; maybe playing a bigger role on the team is one of the reasons why. Askew has good hockey sense and skates himself into good position to be an offensive threat. He sees the ice very well and is a bit underrated with his playmaking abilities. Askew has good size and can be dominant physically, but not often enough for us. He still lacks consistency in that area. He has showed that if he plays with skilled players in an offensive role he's a capable point producer. Last year and early on this year, his play in a bottom-6 role showed that he struggled playing on a grinding / energy line. He's a bit one-dimensional in that he does a fine job without the puck, but won't be known as a defensive specialist. He won't hurt you in the defensive zone either.

With Askew, you like the size and his shot but he always seems to leave you wanting more and that will probably cost him at the draft, looking more like his value is that of a late pick at this point in our view.

Bachman, Karch
LC - Culver Military Academy (US Prep – Ind.) 5'11 179
HockeyProspect.com Ranking: NR

Bachman is average size as still a tad under the 6-foot mark. His best asset is his skating as he shows good speed and can get going pretty quick with the first three strides. Another great aspect to his game is his shot release. He possesses a very quick shot release that catches goalies off guard. His stick skills are pretty good as shows good handle around the net and can finish. In viewings have seen Bachman be one of the better players on the ice and then at other times at Culver just going throwing the motions. He will need to grow mentally by bringing a consistent compete level each and every night. He is expected to attend Miami (NCHC) for the 2016-17 season.

Baer, Alec
LW – Vancouver Giants (WHL) – 5'11" 168
HockeyProspect.com Ranking: NR

Alec Baer is a light-footed forward from St. Louis Park, Minnesota. Baer is a talented puckhandler who weaves and winds his way through traffic, often choosing to take the long route to tough areas of the ice. He transitions the play to offense quickly. He's agile and crafty with the puck, he changes directions naturally and without sacrificing a lot of speed. On more than one occasion, we saw him get wiped out with a huge open-ice hit, only to return to the game and score one of his patented goals. That 'head-down' approach, however, not only left Baer vulnerable physically, but led to some untimely turnovers this season.

It would still be difficult to downplay his offensive skill. When he's focused and swivel-headed, Baer is a real offensive threat, as his puckhandling, passing and above all his shooting are all exceptionally good assets. He is a threat from just about anywhere in the offensive zone, as his passes and shots are all very accurate and have a long range. Both quick-footed and crafty with the puck on his stick, he is also capable of 'deking and streaking'—making unconventional and unpredictable routes to the net that aren't always effective but can be breathtaking when they are. He can pick his shots, but too often shoots high and wide, causing turnovers.

During the miserable first-half the Giants had, bad habits somehow crept deeply into Baer's game, who made multiple turnovers per game, some of which were costly. A lack of versatility is troubling.

He was trusted a few times on the penalty kill and performed poorly; his assignments on the power play were similarly disastrous. Baer witnessed a slight rebound in his game after the mid-season coaching change to Claude Noel. He even some ice-time on the top line and on the power play. Consistency remains an issue. Immature both physically and mentally.

Baille, Tyson
LW – Kelowna Rockets (WHL) – 5'11" 195
HockeyProspect.com Ranking: NR

The Kelowna Rockets forward Tyson Baillie is a Prairie-bred fast skating two-way winger with good hands and instincts. A late 1995-born player who went undrafted in 2014—his first year of eligibility—he's now played in four full seasons in the WHL and will have to register as an overager next year. Baillie is a fairly fluid skater with a good first-step but lacks an elite level stride when accelerating straight ahead. He possesses a nice blend of vision and natural skill, allowing him to thread passes or unleash his shot at will.

After going undrafted last June, Baillie really improved on his defensive game and transitional ability this year. Fairly durable, he relies on his endurance, skating and shooting as he is undersized, underpowered and predominantly a finesse player. A slippery guy in the offensive end who sneaks into areas that are just a step away from where the puck is going Baillie possesses very good hockey IQ, vision and awareness. He uses quick initial step and a quick release to pounce on loose pucks and put them in the net. While he's not a pure sniper or goal scorer, his wristshot, slapshot, backhand and one-timer are all released with power and accuracy.

At this point, he's already one of the best 'undersized' forwards at his age group in terms of puck separation techniques along the boards and is often the catalyst for the breakout. He transitions the puck quickly up the boards with his superior first steps. Doing a lot of penalty killing duty this year, Baillie plays in all situations and good in the faceoff circle.

Baird, Mike
LW - North Bay Battalion (OHL) 6'02" 168
HockeyProspect.com Ranking: NR

Baird is about as straight forward and simple as it comes for a player. He's a big, physical hitting machine that likes to drop the gloves. He plays a tough fourth line role and gets in the face of opposing players. He doesn't show much talent wise, but will go hard into the corners and compete for pucks. His skating is well below average and needs to get better before he will be able to make more of an impact. He has decent power in his shot, which helped him net five goals this season. There was more room for a player like him in the old NHL and he isn't a player we would draft at the 2015 NHL Entry Draft.

Balcers, Rudolfs
LW – Stavanger (NOR) – 5'11" 165
HockeyProspect.com Ranking: NR

Balcers is a Latvian winger who, oddly enough, has been developing in Norway for years. He played most of this season in the senior league and represented his country in both the U18 and U20 IIHF World Championships. In both competitions he was able to display his talent, and against his peers in Switzerland he was still dangerous offensively while facing the top nations in the World. Rudolfs is an impressive skater, possesses deceptive speed and he is able to hit another gear apparently without further effort. His skills and skating allow him to get into good shooting positions and his wrist shot is legit. However, too often he doesn't look determined enough to take his chances as soon as they come up. He looks weak physically and not overly competitive, getting softer as the game gets tougher, even if in April he did show some improvement in that area. He is a prospect that will need a long development path, but given his talent level he might be worth the wait.

Barre-Boulet, Alex
LC – Drummondville Voltigeurs (QMJHL) – 5'9" 156
HockeyProspect.com Ranking: NR

Drummondville drafted Barre-Boulet in the 6th round of the 2013 QMJHL draft out of the Midget Espoir league. After playing a year in Midget AAA last season with Lévis, Barre-Boulet made his QMJHL debut this year.

The Montmagny native had a decent first season in the QMJHL, becoming an important player in the future of the Voltigeurs. After starting the year on their bottom-6, he quickly became a big part of their top-6 during the season, centering one of their top-2 lines. He is still not overly large and needs to gain a lot of strength before thinking about playing professional hockey. He struggled in battles along the wall and in front of the net, one reason why playing on the point on the power play was a smart move by the Drummondville coaching staff. He's a smart player with the puck, showing good creativity and vision. He's a good puck-rusher and likes to have it on his stick, but does a real good job moving it quickly to his wingers. He's an above-average skater but he always keeps his feet moving, which makes him tough to defend against. If he was bigger, Barre-Boulet is a player who would be drafted for sure.

Barwell, Jesse
LC - Saginaw Spirit (OHL) 5'11" 189
HockeyProspect.com Ranking: NR

After showing excellent skill and talent at the Minor Midget level, Barwell has struggled to get things going at the OHL level. Thing started to improve for him later on in the season and he started to develop and create more offense towards the end of the year. He is an excellent skater who absorbs contact fairly well. He plays with a fair amount of energy and competes for pucks in all three zones. Despite showing good signs of improvement, We don't expect Barwell to be selected at the 2015 NHL Entry Draft. However, if he continues to adjust his game and improve like he has in the past few months he could give himself a shot at an invite or re-entry pick.

Barzal, Matt
LC – Seattle Thunderbirds (WHL) – 5'11" 175
HockeyProspect.com Ranking: 12

Former 1st overall pick in the WHL Bantam Draft Matthew Barzal of the Seattle Thunderbirds is an elite level playmaker with above-average skating ability. While his 'compete level' has not always been at top gear, the staple of Matt Barzal's game is undoubtedly elite level passing ability. He has a unique knack for sneaking into areas just between defensive zone coverage and is able to stop-up with the puck and wait for an opening. When the opening presents itself, he's able to thread the needle and deliver a perfect pass for an easy tap-in goal. His shooting game isn't bad either, but he doesn't score a lot of goals because he's best utilized on the perimeter as he sees the game so well and is able to make incredible things happen from the half-wall. As a centre, we would like to see Barzal play a bit more of a 200-foot game and to improve in the faceoff circle. He became more physical as the year went on, which was definitely an encouraging development.

His talent definitely shows when he has the puck on his stick in the offensive zone. He's one of the most talented natural playmaker available in this year's draft. Barzal had a good performance at the

U18 in April, where he was relied on to play a ton of minutes. At times he plays the game all on his own and passes up moving the puck when he has available options. He needs to decrease the number of turnovers he creates, most come just by holding onto the puck too long and trying to do too much.

Quotable: " Plays to the beat of his own drummer at times." - NHL Scout

Quotable: " You can't deny the talent but our coach will snap if he brings some of that unnessacary turnover crap with him to the NHL." - NHL Scout

Quotable: " This isn't a kid I get to see play live as much as the Ontario kids. That said, the U18 this year was the best I have persoanlly seen him play and was light years better than what I thought of him at last years U18. He still needs a lot of work on his play without the puck but I really like pure talent." - Mark Edwards

Quotable: " If a Marner or Konecny loses a puck, they hound it trying to get it back. He (Barzall) waits for someone to get it back for him." - NHL Scout

Bast, Gabe
RD – Penticton Vees (BCHL) – 5'10" 185
HockeyProspect.com Ranking: NR

Gabe Bast is a diminutive puck possession defenseman who played this season on a powerhouse Penticton Vees club, in what was considered something of a 'down-year' for the BCHL in terms of draft-eligibles. Bast is an above-average skater with high-end skills from the blueline who benefited greatly from being on a strong club, as exhibited by his 40 points in 49 regular season games. He was named to Canada West's roster for the World Junior A Challenge and struggled at that tournament—definitely a concern for us, as we were monitoring how he would play in a different environment. He's a fast skater, a talented puckhandler, a great shooter and a smart passer.

Even though he's small by pro standards, Bast manages to pokecheck well and isn't afraid to play a fairly robust physical game. He navigates the point with ease thanks to fancy footwork and advanced lateral agilitiy. He's a key playmaking defender for the Vees and their number one quarterback (despite the fact that highly touted 2016-eligible defenseman Dante Fabbro also plays on the Vees back-end) and has been a big part of their success this season when it comes to special teams. Aside from his failure to meet expectations at the World Junior A tournament, Bast remains undersized. He expects to spend several years at the University of North Dakota beginning in 2016. His major junior rights belong to the Victoria Royals.

Bear, Ethan
RD – Seattle Thunderbirds (WHL) – 5'11" 200
HockeyProspect.com Ranking: 96

Bear is a mid-sized two-way defenseman who has been quarterbacking the second power play unit of the Seattle Thunderbirds since he was just sixteen-years-old. A bit slow in terms of first steps and a bit clumsy in transition, he's just an alright skater at this point. If he can improve his footwork, there could be a future for Ethan Bear in the NHL, as he is blessed with good puck sense, great passing ability and a cannon of a shot from the point.

Bear is a stocky kid that finds ways to effectively utilize his less-than-ideal physical stature. He finds ways to win a lot of races and is learning to generate better acceleration speed. He doesn't necessarily use perfect skating technique to do it, but he wins the vast majority of the puck races he's involved in through hard work. He can lead the rush if he needs to as well, but he's not quite naturally skilled, fast or mobile enough to lead the rush on a regular basis without making mistakes. Thus, he prefers to use outlet passes, which he is very good at delivering to his teammates—sometimes sending the puck tape-to-tape from his own goalline to the opposition's blueline. His ability to make smart chips and bank-plays off of the boards was something we noted several times.

You can also see Bear playing on Seattle's top penalty killing unit, where he is more likely to show off his defensive assets. Preferring to keep things simple in his own end, Bear is generally very well positioned and is a renowned shot blocker. He's not the world's most punishing bodychecker, but he works really hard below his own goal line and is very good at using his upper-body strength to rub opposition guys off of the puck. Graced with a fairly bulky upper-body, he likes to force opponents to the outside to press them into the corner to wear them out. Overall, Bear provides a strong presence at both ends of the ice and will only get better as he gets bigger and improves his footwork.

Beaudin, Jean-Christophe
RW/RC – Rouyn-Noranda Huskies (QMJHL) – 6'1" 180
HockeyProspect.com Ranking: 59

Beaudin is a player we scouted in his QMJHL draft year, but unfortunately he hurt both of his shoulders and missed a good chunk of that season. He was finally drafted in the 4th round by Rouyn-Noranda in the 2013 QMJHL Draft. Beaudin played an extra season of Midget with Antoine-Girouard last year, where he was one of the better scorers in the league.

In his rookie season this year with the Huskies, he was able to establish himself as a top-6 forward and was a strong performer at both ends of the ice. Beaudin is a smart player who takes pride in playing a strong defensive game before thinking about any offense. He's a very good skater who uses his speed well defensively by coming back quickly to help out in the defensive zone.
He has very nice burst of speed and uses it well to gain speed in the neutral zone so that he is able to attack the offensive zone with a lot of speed down the wing. He has a good quick shot, but doesn't use it enough and prefers setting up plays. Beaudin sees the ice very well and makes players around him better.

He played the point on the power play in some of our viewings during the season, mostly on the 2nd unit where he was able to show off his playmaking skills. He still needs to add mass to his frame, he's going to be tougher to play against once he's physically stronger as he will have a nice mix of strength and speed. There's not much to dislike in Beaudin's game, he shouldn't wait too long on day 2 of the draft.

Quotable: "Very underrated, strong defensive game and has great speed. Look for offensive game to take another step next season." - HP scout Jérôme Bérubé

Quotable: "I really like this kid. He has some skill but doesn't look to have high-end offensive upside for the NHL level. He's a very smart player. He looks like a player coaches will love. He seemed to execute on the ice with amazing attention to detail...great stick position, angling, defensive positioning etc...I would draft this kid and I'm not going to totally rule out him posting some surprising numbers moving forward." - Mark Edwards

Beauvillier, Anthony
LW – Shawinigan Cataractes (QMJHL) – 5'10" 181
HockeyProspect.com Ranking: 40

The Cataractes drafted Beauvillier 2nd overall in the 2013 QMJHL draft after he scored 39 goals in 40 games with College Antoine-Girouard in the Quebec Midget AAA league. After and up-and-down season last year, Beauvillier became the offensive leader of the Cataractes this season and one of the best offensive players in the league.

The Sorel native played for Team Canada in August at the Hlinka tournament but suffered an injury there. He was back healthy for the start of the regular season and what a season he had. He finished in the league's top-10 in scoring, playing in all situations for the Cataractes. Beauvillier is a shoot-first center, averaging over five shots per game this season. On the power play, he's very dangerous when he's able to use his accurate shot from the faceoff circle, where he likes to position himself. He has a great scoring touch around the net and he's dangerous to score from anywhere in the offensive zone.

He's not afraid to get his nose dirty in front of the net and plays with a lot of heart. He's a good skater with a nice burst of speed and is able to change direction quickly which allows him to create space for himself on the ice. He also loves to carry the puck in the offensive zone. He's fast and agile on his skates, which makes him tough to defend against on the rush. This year he got better by learning to use his linemates better and formed a nice duo with import winger Dennis Yan. Beauvillier's size could be an issue at the pro level, but he plays bigger than his listed size and adds a lot of energy.

At times, like with Team Canada at the Ivan Hlinka camp and before his injury, he showed good versatility and an ability to play in more of an energy role on the team, performing very well in that aspect. We had some good debates on Beauvillier's rankings all year long.

Quotable: "Scored a lot more this year than I anticipated, love his speed and energy that he brings to the table." - HP scout Jérôme Bérubé

Quotable: "He's a shooter." NHL Scout

Bednard, Ryan
G - Johnstown (NAHL) 6'3.75" 179
HockeyProspect.com Ranking: 133

Bednard is a big goalie who takes up a lot of space in the net. He will need to continue to put on weight as he's a little wiry at 179 lbs. His footwork and quickness in net leave something to be desired at this point, but there is a lot of potential there. He is fundamentally sound but just lacks the athleticism and footwork to take him to an elite level. He will need to continue to develop, whether it's back with Johnstown in the North American Hockey League or perhaps a USHL team next year before heading to Bowling Green State in 2016.

Bell, Jason
LD – Saint John Sea Dogs (QMJHL) – 6'2" 190
HockeyProspect.com Ranking: 217

Bell was acquired by Saint John in January from Cape-Breton in exchange for Sea Dogs' captain Olivier Leblanc (Columbus 7th rounder in 2014). The Screaming Eagles originally drafted Bell 12th overall in the 2013 QMJHL draft.

Bell, who is originally from Montreal, is a solid defenseman who gets a lot of ice time on the power play. He does a good job joining his team on the rush; he's an offensive defenseman with a great shot from the point. Bell's shot is heavy and he has a good, quick release to go with it. The former member of the Laval-Montreal Rousseau-Royal that won the Quebec Midget AAA playoff championship in 2013 is always involved offensively. In the offensive zone, Bell takes risks and jumps in the play often. He often acts as a 4th forward on the ice for his team. Playing for Team Quebec at the U-17 Hockey Challenge, he was also used as a forward at times during the tournament by head coach Donald Audette. When Bell has the opportunity offensively, he doesn't waste any time, jumping low in the offensive zone or in the rush but often carrying the puck himself. Bell makes good passes and also shows good hands and vision. He has good puck skills and is a good stickhandler with soft hands. He does need to do a better job defending one-on-one and use his stick better in those situations. We would love to see a better understanding of the game from him in his own zone as he's still raw in there. His decision-making also needs some improvement. He needs to be smarter and not be a liability defensively. There is some potential with Bell but also a lot of questions marks.

Bengtsson, Lukas
RD – Frolunda (SWE) – 5'11" 172
HockeyProspect.com Ranking: NR

Bengtsson is a righty puck moving defenseman in the last year of draft eligibility. He has below average size for a defenseman, especially if compared with NHL standards. What makes him an interesting prospect is how quick he is at distributing the puck, an attribute that helps him to still play an effective puck possession game when the intensity of the play raises. Lukas is a cerebral player but he can rush the puck when he sees the room for it. He has a very good first step and moves particularly well laterally, his mobility helps him when carrying the puck but also defensively. In his own zone his size puts him at a disadvantage, and even if he competes he struggles in physical confrontations. He will definitely need to get stronger and is better paired with a physical defenseman that can clear the slot, as long as he can still play a possession game. Bengtsson has very good reach for his size and can be a regular feature on the powerplay, as he possesses a legit shot on top of his puck moving abilities.

After another successful season with Mora in the second tier Swedish league, this Spring he joined Frolunda for the playoffs and he was able to gain more icetime as the games went by, a promising sign for his first full SHL season next year.

Benglund, Filip
RD – Skelleftea (SWE) – 6'2" 198
HockeyProspect.com Ranking: NR

Berglund is a strapping right shooting defenseman who can move well with the puck. He uses his size better with the puck than to play a physical game. At the junior level he has the ability to shake off attackers, shielding the puck, and then make a crisp, flat pass when breaking out. He has very good puck control, the puck looks safe on his stick while he quickly spots his passing options and he has terrific passing skills, regularly hitting his targets with precision and promptness. He has good hands and can softly place pucks in the right spots. Filip tries to play a reliable and defensively sound game. Sometimes he gets caught with both hands on his stick though, which makes defending against skilled forwards more difficult. The main knock on Berglund right now is he lacks straight-ahead acceleration and he struggles to get first on loose pucks as a result.

Bernhardt, Daniel
RW – Djurgardens (SWE Jr.) – 6'3" 191
HockeyProspect.com Ranking: NR

In his second year of eligibility Bernhardt's offensive production exploded playing alongside Lukas Vejdemo, as the pair led Djurgardens to winning the SuperElit title. Daniel's most remarkable trait is his acceleration with the puck, he has the capability of increasing his speed while stickhandling through the neutral zone or coming off the corners. He shows very good agility with the puck for a big man and he is a really skilled puckhandler. That's something that however doesn't always benefit his game, as Bernhardt likes to get a little too fancy with the puck. His talent shines through some creative plays and beautiful passes, but he needs to stay more focused when attempting much easier plays, he can miss common passes with the same ease he completes ingenious ones. He should pay more attention at avoiding turnovers, sometimes they come from trying difficult plays on the offensive blueline, sometimes they just look like careless plays. As of now, Bernhardt has flaws in his game and doesn't bring a physical game despite his frame, but he possesses the tools to potentially become a relevant player.

Bethune, Jared
LW – Prince George Cougars (WHL) – 6'00" 174
HockeyProspect.com Ranking: NR

Jared is a big powerful and forward who played his midget years in the Minnesota high school system and is now plying his trade with the Prince George Cougars in the WHL.

A big-bodied forward with good adaptability, Bethune is still a bit slow-footed and spastic in terms of his upper-body motions while skating at full stride. He nonetheless has good net drive and competitiveness and comes at the opposition with a ton of size and the ability to make plays happen off of his stick. His shot isn't bad either.

One of the best aspects of Bethune's game is the sheer power with which he does everything. He hits hard, shoots hard and passes hard. A bit of a 'hot head' at times, we love his competitiveness but feel he would benefit greatly from keeping his frustrations in check and not losing concentration during the games' important moments. If he can focus his attention on consistency of effort and better net drive, better times are ahead for Jared Bethune.

Betz, Nick
RW - Erie Otters (OHL) 6'04" 220
HockeyProspect.com Ranking: 204

After spending the past three seasons in the OHL, generally playing a depth role on the bottom two lines for the Otters providing a big, physical presence, Betz really turned the corner this season.
He caught our eye early on in exhibition match-up's standing out both physically and with a much improved shot. His veteran presence was also felt playing in the top six with primarily younger skilled forwards, allowing him to play a power forward mentoring role, rather than an energy line checker. Betz' skating is decent for his size, but the most improved asset is his powerful, dangerous shot. Often when he didn't beat the goaltender, the goalie would still struggle to control the shot, resulting in rebounds for his linemates. Betz is tough to knock off the puck down low and impossible to move out front, making things even more difficult for goaltenders than it already is facing the talent level of the Otters.

Betz showed this season that he isn't just a big tough guy and can contribute a bit skill wise as well. While he doesn't project to be a first or second line forward at the NHL level he certainly has shown this season that he could become a reliable contributor in the bottom six.

Quotable: "Stood out as the best player on the ice in a pre-season game I saw (McDavid didn't dress) and I liked him in some other early season viewings. I didn't think he played nearly as well later on in the season." - Mark Edwards

Betzold, Greg
LW - Peterborough Petes (OHL) 6'03" 202
HockeyProspect.com Ranking: NR

Playing in his third OHL season Betzold became much more consistent offensively. He has a powerful shot and his accuracy has improved as well. If not for a suspension earlier on in the season Betzold may have pushed for 40 goals this year. Dangerous on the cycle game and in the corners, he has good size and is tough to play against along the wall and will use his long reach to break up passes and poke free loose pucks. Betzold was relied upon heavily for the Petes and seemed to score goals at key times for his team. He has power forward size but could stand to add more of a mean streak. His skating will also need improvements.

Quotable: "We have ranked him previously talking about his offensive potential. This year he showed some of it, but questionable off ice decisions may keep NHL teams from using a draft pick on him. He might get another free agent invite if he's not drafted. He's attended the St. Louis Blues camp the past two seasons." - Mark Edwards

Birdsall, Chris
G - Youngstown (USHL) 5'11" 181
HockeyProspect.com Ranking: NR

It's incredible that Birdsall's first eligible draft year comes after his third full season in the USHL. Birdsall entered the league as a sixteen year old in 2012 with the Cedar Rapids RoughRiders, where he played last season as well. He had struggled with Cedar Rapids in the 2012-13 and 2013-14 seasons leading Birdsall to be traded to Youngstown prior to this season. With Youngstown, Birdsall had a very solid third year in the league and entered the NHL Draft discussion as the season went on.

He is a smaller goalie as far as typically NHL goalie prospects go, but he plays a fairly athletic game and challenges shooters. Birdsall tends to sometimes be too aggressive leading to him getting beat. He also tends to rely on his athleticism too much and doesn't get set as early as we'd like to see, making him float back and have to work harder in net than he should have to. Birdsall will attend Boston College in the fall.

Quotable: "He's one of those players who just doesn't have enough to make our list. His lack of size hurts him." - Mark Edwards

Bittner, Paul
LW – Portland Winterhawks (WHL) – 6'04" 204
HockeyProspect.com Ranking: 30

At least physically speaking, Bittner is already one of the most physically mature players available in the 2015 NHL Entry Draft. He possesses good upside, but we question whether or not he will ever be the type of player who drives the play or whether he will remain something of a support player, as despite having some good puck skills and intangibles, his game lacks explosiveness.

Already equipped with an NHL-sized frame that just requires some filling out, Bittner is tall and reasonably heavy already. His legs are long and strong and his strides are decently powerful. He is able to generate slightly above-average top-speed acceleration. In spite of less than ideal footwork and quickness, his solid positioning, backwards manoeuvrings and long wingspan make him a threatening presence without the puck and he causes many turnovers. His backcheck lacks speed and effort at times. Even when moving at his slowest pace, this is a player who maintains good self-awareness and knows how to fully utilize his big body. Taking it, for instance, to the areas of the ice that smaller players can't easily get to—i.e., at the top of the crease or in the corners with a big bull coming his way. While he had strings of inconsistency this, he combines size and a good level of skill. Bittner has a knack for finding his way into good scoring areas. While he was able to acquire plenty of scoring opportunities in these areas, we felt that he simply didn't capitalize enough on these chances despite the numbers.

Quotable: "I don't think he can score in the NHL." - NHL Scout

Quotable: "He lacks consistency in multiple areas of is game including his physical play. He does use his long reach effectively and is solid in protecting the puck. Skating is fine and continues to improve, it's better now then it was in September. One thing I haven't liked in my viewings is his lack of ability to see all his options in the offensive zone. I'd like to see him bury chances more consistently too." - Mark Edwards

Björkqvist, Kasper
LW – Blues (Fin Jr.) 6'1" 187
HockeyProspect.com Ranking: NR

Kasper is a forward with great speed and attitude. Kasper likes to play tough and he's always giving his best effort. He has scoring opportunities but misses them too often. Kasper has a good wrister with a quick release and likes to use his shot. He's not a great puck handler but he's always one of the fastest skaters on ice. He's an average sized player but he's great battling around corners and he's decent two play player.

Black, Alex
LD - Sarnia Sting (OHL) 6'01" 190
HockeyProspect.com Ranking: NR

Black entered his rookie season with the Sting this season and primarily played on the third pairing. He is a physical shutdown defender who has good strength, but still has some development ahead of him. He finishes his checks hard and can be tough to play against but can also get beat and had more than his share of "rookie" moments in the defensive zone. He is a decent skater but his turns and pivots are not very good and this cost him in several one on one match-up's on the rush. While he can be tough on the wall, he needs to check his man in the slot because he can sometimes make it too easy for the opposition to stand there. Will chase the play out of position at times. Puck playing ability needs improvement and needs to make the safe simple play in order to be more successful with the puck. We don't expect Alex to be selected at the 2015 NHL Entry Draft.

Blackwood, Mackenzie
G - Barrie Colts (OHL) 6'04" 215
HockeyProspect.com Ranking: 39

Mackenzie Blackwood is one of the top goaltenders available for the 2015 NHL Entry Draft. He's very calm in the crease and doesn't tend to get rattled if he allows a soft goal. Blackwood is very good at squaring up to his shooters and he takes away a lot of the net in the butterfly because of his size. He's quite quick for a goaltender his size and his lateral movement is good too, as he has no issue stretching out to make a sprawling save on a backdoor play. For the most part his rebound control is good, though he does cough out some rebounds on high shots around his shoulders.

He has a quick glove and while making some impressive saves, we felt consistency catching the puck was an issue at times. Blackwood's rebound control is more than adequate, he is capable of making flurries of stops if necessary, he battles hard and doesn't give up on plays. Blackwood is also a capable puck handler. He regularly comes out to play the puck in order to disrupt the forecheck and help shift play up ice.

While Mackenzie has the total package of size skill positioning and awareness, his biggest concern is consistency. He had some rough nights where nothing seemed to be going right for him. In most of our viewings he was excellent, but he did have a few forgettable performances and he will need to play to his ability on a game by game basis to reach his potential.

Quotable: "I'm not a huge fan, I think he's one of the more overrated players in the draft." NHL Scout

Quotable: "He's our top ranked goalie in this years draft." - NHL Scout

Quotable: "He can't seem to catch a puck. Every time I saw him he flat our missed pucks with his trapper." - NHL Scout

Quotable: "He's the number two on our goalie list." - NHL Scout

Quotable: "Mackenzie has such a great combination of size, athleticism and talent. If he can just become more consistent, watch out." - HP Scout Ryan Yessie

Blaisdell, Doug
LD - Kitchener Rangers (OHL) 6'03" 206
HockeyProspect.com Ranking: NR

Blaisdell projects as a shutdown defenseman at the next level but he has a fair amount of work ahead of him to accomplish that feat. He has the natural size on the back end to play a solid defensive role, along with the mentality required for a stay at home shutdown defender. He's not an overly physical defender but doesn't back down either. His skating is average, he gets around decent in all directions but it isn't really a strength. He isn't a great player with the puck but will consistently make the smart, simple first pass.

On the offensive line he's made some smart low risk pinches to keep the plays alive in the offensive zone. He has good shooting/passing decisions and won't fire at the net unless he's confident he has shooting lane in front of him. He does have a tendency to be caught napping positionally in the defensive zone from time to time. He can also get beat one on one occasionally as well. Blaisdell is a low risk, low reward defenseman that has value later on in the draft.

Boeser, Brock
RW – Waterloo (USHL) 6'0.5" 191
HockeyProspect.com Ranking: 18

Boeser put together an incredible season in his draft year. He plays a well-rounded game and can really do it all. After de-committing from Wisconsin early in the year, Boeser flipped to North Dakota where he will head next season. He is an extremely talented offensive player that can play a physical game and works hard in his own zone.

Offensively, there's not many flaws to Boeser's game. He has a very heavy shot and a quick release. He can pick his corners well, and is able to beat goalies in a variety of ways – he possesses every shot type in his arsenal and knows how to use them. Outside of scoring goals, he had a very productive year setting up his linemates. Boeser sees the ice really well, sees the passing lanes and has the ability to find his teammates with crisp tape to tape passes. With the puck on his stick, he's almost impossible to knock off the puck. He has an incredible ability to protect the puck from poke checks and is super strong on his skates so even the strongest defensemen in the league struggle to separate him from the puck. He's not the fastest guy but skates with such a strong base.

For how good he is offensively, Boeser puts in the same amount of work on the backcheck. He is always skating hard back and plays a good game in his own zone. He's not afraid to throw the body around and play physical. He really is a very well-rounded player. Boeser was one of the most impressive players in the USHL this year in our viewings and has made a push to be selected early in the draft.

Quotable:" Looks like an pure goal scorer who possesses and NHL caliber shot. I like the way he will score in different ways. He will take the puck to net and score in tight as much as he will fire his great shot. His compete level stood out to me. Strong kid who just needs to keep improving his skating." - Mark Edwards

Quotable:" One of my favorite players to watch in the USHL. His combination of speed, skill, and strength makes him one of the most exciting players coming out of the league." - HP Scout Justin Schreiber

Boka, Nick
RD – USNTDP (USHL) 6'0.25" 197
HockeyProspect.com Ranking: 172

He is a decent sized D-man and his mobility isn't bad as moves well in all directions although he will still need to improve his foot speed and quickness for the next level. There are times he is exposed because he does not open up with pivots fast enough to keep up with speedy forwards. He makes the breakout passes, although too often will make some questionable plays with the puck and gets caught out of position in his own zone. He does possess a good, strong shot from the point. He has limited offensive instincts. Overall he's lacking some skill and has more of a vanilla game when projecting him for the higher level.

Quotable:" I like his toughness but question his smarts. He didn't show me much in the skill department in my viewings. Not really a guy for my list." - Mark Edwards

Bondra, Radovan
RW – Kosice (SVK) – 6'5" 220
HockeyProspect.com Ranking: 129

Bondra is a player who caught our eye at the 2014 U18 hockey championship and we had high hope for him coming into the 2014-2015 season. In our viewings of him this season from the U-18 to the WJC he was not able to make as good of an impact. He's a smart player who can be a valuable player on the PK thanks to a solid understanding of the game defensively. He anticipates the play well and makes good use of his long stick. He's not an overly physical player but makes good use of his size along the board and in front of the net. His offensive game yet to be developed to be a threat vs good competition as he struggled be an impact player offensively in international tournament. He has a long reach and can be useful in puck protection situations and also his big frame also helps in that department. In possession of the puck we would like to see him take quicker decisions, seems a step behind often. He's still a project and still very raw. This season back in Slovakia he split the season between the men's league and the U-18 national team.

Quotable: "Frustrating player. As an example, he was one of the best players on the ice in an early game at the U18 in Switzerland. He was a no-show in the rest of my viewings. Kid is huge though." - Mark Edwards

Borgen, Will
RD – Moorhead (MN-HS) 6'1.75" 189LBS
HockeyProspect.com Ranking: 87

Borgen is a big bodied defenseman with a solid build and is still growing. Borgan reads the play in his own end very well and makes decisive plays with the puck. He doesn't possess a lot of dynamic offensive ability apart from having a big shot from the point and has pretty good passing ability out of his own end. Borgen plays a physical style. He likes to punish players but doesn't take a lot of penalties. Does a good job clearing the front of the net for his goaltender. While his skating style is a bit unorthodox he is agile on his skates and uses his reach and positioning to his advantage against more shifty forwards. Has good gap control. Always seems to give an honest effort and doesn't shy away from blocking shots. Borgen finished his 14/15 season playing for Omaha of the USHL where he played 18 games for the Lancers and handled himself well, gaining more confidence with every game. He will likely return to Omaha next season, then off the St. Cloud St. in 16/17.

Quotable: "Good skater, good size, used his stick well. He's raw and made mental gaffes but I liked his gap and his aggressiveness on his man. Didn't show me NHL offensive upside." - Mark Edwards

Bouramman, Gustav
RD - Sault Ste. Marie Greyhounds (OHL) 6'00" 185
HockeyProspect.com Ranking: 162

Bouramman came over from Luela in Sweden to the Greyhounds and instantly added offensive depth on the back end. Bouramman skates well and is a capable puck rusher. He can take the puck end to end pretty regularly but will sometimes take dangerous skating lanes, which has led to turnovers. He's an offensively minded defenseman who moves the puck reasonably well in the offensive zone and he gets shots through from the point.

Defensively he has decent reaction time but isn't always in the most ideal position. He lacks physicality and will use his stick to make the play. Gustav projects as an offensive defenseman and he put up good numbers on the regular season champion Greyhounds but he's not blessed with great size.

Quotable: "I'm not sure he is dynamic enough to make up for what he lacks in size." NHL Scout

Quotable: "The only Greyhounds player we have on our list is this guy." (pointed at Speers on the lineup sheet) - NHL Scout

Boikov, Sergei
LD – Drummondville Voltigeurs (QMJHL) – 6'2" 195
HockeyProspect.com Ranking: NR

Boikov finished his second season with the Voltigeurs this season, after he went undrafted in last year's NHL Draft. This year he established himself as part of Drummondville's top 4 D, by playing against opposing top lines and being tough to play against in his own zone.

Boikov is very useful on the penalty killing unit, and he's very courageous on the ice as he's willing to take hits to move the puck out of his zone. He has also become, since last year, an excellent shot-blocker. Boikov also has become a feared open-ice hitter around the league, with good anticipation to deliver good open-ice hits. With the puck, like last year, his decision-making is a bit slow, and that's put him in trouble when facing pressure on the forecheck. He can be victim to turning the puck over because of his slow reaction time, putting himself in a bad position to get hit because of this slow process. With the puck on his stick he keeps things simple; he will get it deep, on net or make simple short passes on the transition game. Overall his puck skills are average; he is at his best when he keeps things simple. Boikov won't ever be known for his offensive skills but he's a solid stay-at-home defenseman at the QMJHL level. Boikov's hockey sense still needs work, as he needs to make better reads in his zone. He often tends to follow the puck and forget his position or man in front of the net. We feel Boikov could go undrafted again this season, he made some progress in his overall game this year but his hockey sense will hurt him on draft day.

Quotable: "Boikov has become one of the best hitters in the QMJHL in his second season with the Voltigeurs." - HP scout Jérôme Bérubé

Booth, Callum
G – Quebec Remparts (QMJHL) – 6'3" 196
HockeyProspect.com Ranking: 66

Booth was drafted by the Remparts in the 3rd round of the 2013 QMJHL draft, a late pick due to his NCAA intentions at the time. We had him ranked 10th overall in our draft guide that year after playing a year with Salisbury Prep School in Connecticut. Playing in his 2nd season with the Remparts, playing in a high-pressure situation will only help Booth in the future. Started the year by winning gold the U-18 Ivan Hlinka tournament in August, but played the role of backup during the tournament.

In the first half of the season with the Remparts, we felt his game was a bit up-and-down, featuring some good games and some bad ones. He had some struggles in December when there were a lot of rumors with him being on the move for the QMJHL trade deadline. Finally Booth was never traded, and Quebec still acquired Zachary Fucale from Halifax. Fucale had some struggles of his own in the 2nd half and Booth did very well when given the opportunity. He even won the starting job to start the playoffs against Cape-Breton.

Similar to his rookie season, it was another year of up-and-down this year for the Montreal goaltender. He has great size and excellent positioning; rarely will you see Booth out of position or deep in his crease. He covers a lot of room in his crease, even when he's on his knees. Since his rookie year, the biggest improvement in his game has been his lateral movements, where he used to rely more on his size to make saves. He also has a good glove side.

His consistency from game to game is still a weakness; he has a ton of potential but we're still waiting for him to take charge and become a dominant goaltender in the QMJHL. He showed flashes of it in the 2nd half of the season for a bit; we should see it more next season as this will be his team from now on. Booth's consistency might keep him out of the first two rounds at the NHL draft, other goalies have had the chance to prove themselves more at this point than he has.

Quotable: "Big and calm netminder, up and down this year but has all the tools to be an NHL goaltender. Next season will be key one for him with Fucale gone." - HP scout Jérôme Bérubé

Bourque, Simon
LD – Rimouski Oceanic (QMJHL) – 6'0" 189
HockeyProspect.com Ranking: 95

Bourque was drafted by the Oceanic in the 2nd round of the 2013 QMJHL draft and made a good impact with the team last year, as he played big minutes in the 2nd half of the season. Again this year, Bourque played a big role with the team, playing in a top-4 role, being used in all situations and wearing an A on his jersey.

Bourque is a player who plays with a lot of heart and works extremely hard on the ice. He has a very good compete level even if he lacks ideal size for a defenseman. He's a capable puck mover; he's able to play on the power play and makes smart decisions with the puck. On the power play he played more the role of the playmaker, he likes to set up his teammates on the man-advantage instead of being the shooter from the point. He's more of a complimentary player on the man-advantage at this point in his development. He has a good, accurate shot from the point, but his velocity could see an improvement. Defensively he's reliable, with above-average mobility and an ability to keep up with the best forwards in the league. He's capable of playing physical in his own zone but relies more on his smarts and a good active stick to counter those top forwards. He's consistent from game to game, rarely having a bad one, and always bounces back after a bad shift or game. It wouldn't surprise us to see him wear the C as soon as next season with the Oceanic, as the management and coaching staff are really high on him. Bourque doesn't have any great qualities and lacks the ideal size for a defensive NHL defenseman and that could cost him a chance to go in the first three rounds of the NHL draft, a mid-round pick for us.

Quotable: "Bourque is a player who does everything well on the ice but lacks a high end qualities, I love his compete level and has reminded me since his midget days of former Habs defenseman Josh Gorges." - HP scout Jérôme Bérubé

Bowman, Zack
G - Plymouth Whalers (OHL) 6'00" 170
HockeyProspect.com Ranking: NR

Bowman went into this season with a certain expectation despite receiving time behind veteran Alex Nedeljkovic, however he struggled in many of our viewings this season. Bowman does a good job of not overextending himself under pressure, which allows him to change directions quickly and to stick with the play. He's a low risk goaltender with the puck and will take a lot of whistles instead of some who are very active with the puck. He cut down angles well. Sometimes goaltenders develop a little later on.

Bowman showed good promise as a Minor Midget goaltender in his OHL draft year and flashes in his rookie season, so while we don't expect him to get selected this year, he could be a goaltender to watch moving forward.

Bracco, Jeremy
LW – USNTDP (USHL) 5'9.25" 173
HockeyProspect.com Ranking: 54

Bracco is a player that might scare off some scouts because of his size. He can wheel and handle the puck all at the same time. He shows exceptional edge work in the offensive zone, as he likes to open up to his inside edges and circle around the zone to create scoring threats. He has tamed this habit a little bit this season and has developed a more north-south game. As he gains muscle he will be more effective with his good balance and low center-of-gravity. He has elusive moves and is a skilled player. His vision is very, very good too, as he can find the seams and has great awareness of his teammates. He has very good stick skills in tight and is always a scoring threat when the puck is on his stick.

You cannot deny Bracco's offensive instincts, silky hands and vision, as he has kept performing since the youth playing days. While his defensive game will need work as well as big improvement in his physical strength, there is potential here. Despit his lack of size, some teams might not want to pass on his skills for too long on draft day.

Quotable: "He will be an interesting one to watch on draft day. I could see him slide as late as the 4th or as early as an early 2nd." - NHL Scout

Quotable: "Remember scouting Bracco at USA Hockey Select 155 Camp in Rochester a few summers back. He picked up the puck wheeled it in the offensive zone circling around, opening up on his inside edges until he scored or feathered a pass to a teammate for the goal. Immediately I was captivated, as not many players have that skating, stick handling, and play making ability. Even though his size is a concern, he gets it done at each level." - HP Scout Russ Bitely

Quotable: "I liked him entering this season but he lost me a bit along the path to the draft. Too much perimeter play and he couldn't win his own pucks. He can score when given the opportunity and often looks fantastic doing it. I just question how his game translates to the next level given his weaknesses. For me his weaknesses started to add up and it dropped him down my list a bit." - Mark Edwards

Bradley, Matt
RC – Medicine Hat Tigers (WHL) – 5'11" 187
HockeyProspect.com Ranking: 149

Bradley, a two-way centreman is an energetic, fleet-footed and strong-willed forward who saw his draft stock steadily rise over the course of this season. Bradley excels most in terms of footspeed, faceoff skill and hockey IQ and saw his ice-time increase concurrently with his rise in draft stock. Over the course of the last season he transitioned from a depth role to a top-six role. His promotion came as a result of his consistent play, as he finds a way to create a good amount of offense, a lot of energy down the middle and a ton of turnovers in all three zones on a game-to-game basis. His decision-making is also consistently good, making him a dependable presence on the ice most of the time. We also really like his work in the faceoff circle.

Bradley's is solid on the forecheck, as he can turn into most passing lanes with surprising ease and unpredictability. His high hockey IQ allows him to consistently anticipate where the passes are going. His hockey sense additionally allows him to make good passes and properly anticipate where his teammates are going, which makes him very good on the cycle and at keeping the offense alive. His shot is yet another threat, as exhibited by his 17 goals in his rookie season.

All in all, Bradley is a dependable player in terms of faceoffs, offensive awareness and attention to defensive details. That dependability earned Bradley considerable time on the penalty kill this year, which allowed him to additionally show off some of his defensive skills. Even though he struggled to keep those minutes as the year wore on, he showed improvements in his shot blocking and clearing abilities. He's already trustworthy enough in the faceoff circle to be used in careful own-zone situations, so improvements in his defensive game and penalty killing capabilities will surely help him in developing in the future.

Brisebois, Guillaume
LD – Acadie-Bathurst Titan (QMJHL) – 6'2" 173
HockeyProspect.com Ranking: 48

Brisebois was the 5th overall pick by Acadie-Bathurst in the 2013 QMJHL Draft. He played his midget hockey with the Antoine-Girouard Gaulois, who had many good players that year with the likes of Jeremy Roy, Anthony Beauvillier and Jean-Christophe Beaudin. Brisebois has represented his province and country the past two seasons in international events, including the U-17 in Cape-Breton last season and the U-18 Ivan Hlinka tournament this past August. He was also part of Team QMJHL during the Subway Super Series against Russia in November.

The Mont St-Hilaire native was named the Acadie-Bathurst Titan's team captain in October. Brisebois gets offensively involved, but also stays defensively responsible; he sets up the Titan power play by carrying the puck and setting up in zone. He moves the puck quickly and efficiently. His quick decision-making and skills allow him to be involved offensively, and he keeps his team on offense, as he does not turn the puck over. He does a good job using his size to protect the puck and to win battles. When the forwards are rushing the puck, he does a good job joining the rush, creating another offensive threat and confusion for his opponents' backcheck. He could use a little more strength and size, as he is sometimes outmatched physically in the defensive end. However, other times he shows the work ethic and ability to beat opponents and separate them from the puck. By playing on the worst team in the league, Brisebois didn't get as much help as other prospects had this year, finding himself exposed at times. He's a capable point producer from the back end, but with an offensively challenged team, it was hard to produce as many points as others. We do love his poise with the puck and his skating abilities, as he has a good burst and good lateral agility.

Brisebois is a safe bet, good all-around defenseman with some untapped potential. He has a chance to play in a top-4 role in the NHL due to his smarts and mobility, but safe bet would be as a bottom pairing.

Quotable: "I have him in the 3rd." - NHL Scout

Quotable: "He's a smart player who executes well. He knows how to play smart effective hockey. Good skater, first pass takes good angles, I like him." - Mark Edwards

Bruce, Riley
RD - North Bay Battalion (OHL) 6'06" 207
HockeyProspect.com Ranking: 199

Bruce is a hulking defender with good physical tools, but he is still very raw. Very light for his size at 207 lbs, Bruce needs to physically mature into his body. Skating needs work as he was exposed laterally too often. He uses his stick and reach effectively on opposition rushes. He plays a simple game and displays good gap control and instincts. Bruce has been able to benefit from playing on a team that plays the type of game that is most beneficial towards his development as a prospect. He isn't a defenseman with big upside but he projects to be a safe third pairing defenseman who understands his role clearly, has great size and has a willingness to use it.

Quotable: "He's too raw, just too far off for me to use a pick on him." NHL Scout

Burns Andrew
LD - Windsor Spitfires (OHL) 6'00" 184
HockeyProspect.com Ranking: NR

After some very promising play late last season including the playoffs, Burns looked poised for a breakout season and while he wasn't a bad defender for Windsor, he didn't quite live up to those expectations this season. Burns shows good offensive tools in his puck rush, smooth skating ability and puck moving ability, but played a minimal role for the Spitfires this season primarily in a third pairing capacity. Burns has a decent shot from the point. Defensively he still has room for improvement as he can chase the play a little bit and get caught out of position at times. Burns will have the opportunity to move up Windsor's depth chart and get a chance as a re-entry player, but isn't likely to be selected at the 2015 NHL Entry Draft.

Bushnell, Noah
RW - Sarnia Sting (OHL) 6'02" 211
HockeyProspect.com Ranking: NR

Bushnell is a big physical power winger who showed a lot of potential after a decent rookie season with the Sting but didn't improve enough from last season to this season. His skating is an area that needed improvement that didn't materialize. He scored 10 goals and posted 120 penalty minutes and has a powerful shot that can beat some of the better goaltenders at the junior level. He plays a very tough game, loves to finish his hits and isn't hesitant to drop the gloves whenever necessary. He projects as a tough, mean, physical winger who will hit, fight and battle for pucks.

Possessing his good shot will only make him more valuable, but right now he does not project to be selected at the 2015 NHL Entry Draft. However, if his skating ever improves enough that he can get some speed behind him and get to plays quicker, he could be an intriguing re-entry guy later on in his junior career.

Capobianco, Kyle
LD - Sudbury Wolves (OHL) 6'01" 170
HockeyProspect.com Ranking: 73

Kyle Capobianco is a smooth skating puck-moving defenseman that had a good year on a bad Sudbury team. Capobianco makes a good first pass and is capable of carrying the puck up ice if no outlets are made available to him. He possesses good hands, can elude checkers in space and is poised while carrying the puck. Capobianco anticipates the play well without the puck and has the skating ability to close gaps and intercept passes. He is a capable quarterback on the powerplay and has a good shot he'll utilize if no better options are available. At times he can try and do too much, though that may be a result of not having much help around him.

Defensively, his good stick, patience and skating ability make him tough to get around. He's not as physical as he could be and doesn't always finish his checks when he has the opportunity. Capobianco has shown a willingness to block shots and is a capable penalty killer.

Quotable: "I have time for him." NHL Scout

Quotable: "I've liked him going back to his OHL Draft year where he was my favorite D-man from his OHL Cup winning Oakville Rangers team. He's a smart player with offensive talent but the drawback on him for me has always been that he can be prone to playing a bit scared. Too often he goes just fast enough to lose races retrieving dump-ins. I hope his lack of minutes at the U18 doesn't hurt his draft stock, he deserved to play more in my opinion." - Mark Edwards

Carbonara, Adrian
RW - Barrie Colts (OHL) 6'02" 190
HockeyProspect.com Ranking: NR

Adrian Carbonara struggled for icetime early in the year, but seemed to dress more often as the season went on. He plays the proto-typical 4th line game, as he chips pucks in, finishes his checks and can be disruptive on the forecheck. He hits with a purpose and he's smart about it, he rarely lays dirty hits or takes stupid penalties. He doesn't back down physically to anyone and has no problem sticking up for teammates. His puck skills are better than most 4th liners and at times throughout the year he took a couple shifts on one of the top two lines to spark the team. He generates good straight-line speed, which allows him to get on the forecheck quickly and close gaps. He's not a liability defensively and leaves it all on the ice every shift. While he doesn't hold much NHL potential at this point, he is one of those guys you love to have on your team and hate to play against.

Carlo, Brandon
RD – Tri-City Americans (WHL) – 6'05" 196
HockeyProspect.com Ranking: 27

Carlo is a big and strong defensive defenseman who played with the Tri-City Americans in the WHL this year. Carlo also made an appearance at the World Juniors this year, suiting up for the American national team. Carlo brings a great combination of size, speed, strength and talent. There are some gaps in his game. Namely, he needs to work on his balance, consistency and competitiveness, but when he's playing on cue, in consideration of his physical dimensions and long-term upside, he's one of the better defenseman available in this year's crop. We think the offensive game of Brandon Carlo is limited, but his size, mobility, decision making and ability to move puck are attractive. Everytime an NHL team can add a mobile 6'5" defensemen they will do it, Carlo is exactly that. He has fluid feet with good top speed and acceleration that are tough to find in big size defenseman. He's best at handling the puck when he's keeping things simple—making smart, short and simple passes or playing the dump and chase game in the neutral zone—but we see some potential in his puck carrying abilities. In his zone he typically plays a steady game on the back end using his big body to limit opposition chances and to clear his crease. For the most part, Carlo rarely does anything really flashy on the ice but he's very efficient at what he can brings to the table, he looks for us as safe bet to reach the NHL.

Quotable: " I've been a little bit all over the map on him. I was beating him up last year but he's grown on me." – NHL Scout

Quotable: " He's an elite skater for a guy that big." – NHL Scout

Quotable: " Less is more with him. As soon as he tries to do too much he goes south in a hurry." – NHL Scout

Quotable: " I want more out of a 1st round pick." – NHL Scout

Quotable: " He's a guaranteed NHL player." – NHL Scout

Quotable: " He has zero offense so forget about that part of his game. He's a huge kid who can skate and defend." – NHL Scout

Quotable: " I liked the kid a lot when I interviewed him. He's not physical though and I don't see the offensive NHL upside that some seem to see. I just see a huge kid who skates well. He's a shutdown defensive prospect for me. Where do you rank that in this draft?" – Mark Edwards

Carlsson, Gabriel
LD – Linkoping (SWE) – 6'4" 183
HockeyProspect.com Ranking: 33

Gabriel is a defensive defenseman with tremendous reach who can move properly despite his size. He has been getting better along the season, and in February has found a spot on his SHL team. His game is still inconsistent though, especially during puck possession. He will probably never be someone who demands the puck on his stick or likes to carry it up ice, but in his good days he looks quite comfortable with the puck on his stick and able to complete steady plays after managing it away from his opponent. On his bad moments, he struggles with the puck and against the forecheck, relying on his solid decision making to limit the damage. As of now he needs well set up zone exits to be consistently effective against the forecheck.

He is usually out of his comfort zone on the offensive blueline, where his mistakes become more frequent, but he is a player able to surprise you with the odd, impressive play that makes you wonder about his real ceiling. In Switzerland at the U18 there was a play in the offensive zone where he was forced to extemporize and he managed to keep possession with a quick twirl, to promptly backcheck with nice speed when his teammate lost the puck. Even if his skating is a strength (especially his backwards agility for such a tall guy), it looks less good when he gets closer to the boards and needs improvement when he needs to make snap stops. In general though, his skating allows him to have good gaps, something that paired with his reach gives the forwards he is facing lots of troubles. With his stature he cannot be the most reactive guy on rebounds, but overall he seems on the verge of becoming a very serviceable defenseman, someone whose name won't last long on the draft board.

Carlsson, Lucas
LD – Brynas (SWE) – 6'0" 185
HockeyProspect.com Ranking: 167

Lucas is an all around type of defensemen, a strong competitor who likes to move around the ice trying to impact the game in all areas. Sometimes that brings him out of position, however, and he can be caught chasing the play. He loves to join the play inside the offensive zone and for that matter he picks his spots quite well. He is a pretty good stickhandler that can find lanes to carry the puck beyond the offensive blueline and doesn't look out of place when he gets closer to the net. His most regular offensive contribution still comes from his shots from the blueline though, as he likes to use his solid slap shot at any given chance, even when he is given room and he would be better served waiting and taking advantage of it. His decision making is definitely one of the areas he will need to improve on. Carlsson doesn't mind engaging in battles and can bring a physical element to his game. He is pretty strong on his skates and fairly mobile, but not the fastest skater, he will probably need to become a bit quicker for his game to be effective at the next level. He is active in front of his net, competes hard on the penalty kill and goes down whenever needed, but in those situations shows a tendency to try to block shots too close to his net instead of keeping his feet moving and closing in on the shooter.

Carpenter, Robert
LW – Sioux City (USHL) 5'11" 174
HockeyProspect.com Ranking: NR

After getting passed over in the 2014 draft, Carpenter made a strong case for himself to be reconsidered this June. Moving at a over a point-per-game clip this season, the Boston University commit turned some heads in his first full season in the USHL. He plays a strong two-way game, and while he doesn't necessarily have any elite skills that jump off the ice at you, he does everything pretty well. Carpenter finished the year in the three-way tie for the league lead in goals with Wilkie and Boeser. He has a good shot that was amplified by his linemates' ability to find him in open space as well as above average playmaking skills. He plays hard and competes every shift. He's not an explosive skater but did well enough with a quick first step to beat defenders at the junior level. He will need to continue to improve his stride at Boston to be a difference maker in college. Overall, Carpenter is a very solid two-way player that made the most of his first full year in the USHL. While his numbers might have been inflated by the quality of his linemates, his goal-scoring ability and compete level will garner him some attention his second eligible draft year.

Carrier, Alexandre
RD – Gatineau Olympiques (QMJHL) – 5'11" 168
HockeyProspect.com Ranking: 50

Carrier was in his 3rd season with the Olympiques after being selected 4th overall in the 2012 QMJHL draft. The former Antoine-Girouard midget player was the Olympiques captain this season and was the 3rd leading scoring defenseman finishing with 55 points.
Carrier strongest trait is his hockey sense; he sees the ice very well and makes good accurate passes out of his zone. He's a quarterback on the power play, has good vision and always seems to make the smart play when distributing the puck from the point. He's not afraid to get involved deep in the offensive zone and takes some calculated chances. In the offensive zone he could use his shot more,

as he tends to look too feed the puck to his teammates. At even strength he will jump into the play and act as a 4th forward trying to create odd man rushes for his team. Carrier is not an over flashy defenseman offensively, but one that will make the smart plays that help his team.

Defensively, Carrier can be used in a shutdown role, much like he has been used for the majority of the last two years with the Olympiques. He has very good mobility and can keep up with speedy forwards, has good body positioning and good active stick. Carrier doesn't have the ideal size of an NHL defensemen but we love his compete level and he doesn't back down from any physical confrontation. His lack of size can hurt him at times down low or in front of the net battling bigger forwards. He has a good gap, doesn't give opposing forwards a lot of time or space react when they enter the offensive zone.

Carrier has played numerous times in international event from the U-17, U-18 Hlinka tournament & U18 world championship. We really like a lot about Carrier's game, but feel his size will cost him a few ranking spots at the NHL draft, his lack of strength to be more clear. We think Carrier has some pretty big upside for a team that will be a bit patient. He needs time to gain weight, get stronger and than adjust to playing in a bigger frame. We see him as a player that in time could easily develop into a top for D-man in the NHL.

Quotable: "To be honest, it took me a few games to see the full package that Carrier brings to the table. Jérôme Bérubé was always singing his praises to me last year, but it took me some time to jump on board the 'Carrier bandwagon'. Maybe I wrote him off a bit too early because of his size. Regardless, I am a big fan now. He's a heart and soul player and a really smart one too. He is a fluid skater who plays a two-way game. He has a ton of poise and I'd describe his play as very under control. I think he's worth the time it will take him to get bigger and stronger. I expect it will be time well invested." - Mark Edwards

Cecconi, Joseph
RD – Muskegon (USHL) 6'2.25", 209
HockeyProspect.com Ranking: 113

One of the key components to Muskegon's deep playoff run to the Clark Cup Final has a lot to do with the consistent play of Joseph Cecconi at both ends of the ice all season. A fluid skater with great agility, who is able to use his body and feet well along the boards and does a good job pinning opposing players and buying time until support arrives. Uses his size to his advantage whenever possible, doesn't try to distribute punishing body checks but has enough physically when it's needed to get the job done.

Maybe the most impressive aspect of Cecconi's game is he seems to show excellent poise with and without the puck. He makes strategic plays with the puck and doesn't try to force anything that may pose a risk. He doesn't panic when under pressure, always seems to have an outlet or a plan for the puck. Cecconi see's the ice well and makes a very good first pass out of the zone; has the skill and skating ability to bring the puck up the ice when it's warranted. He moves the puck quickly from the point in the offensive zone and doesn't take unnecessary risks at the blue line. He does a good job using his quick release to get it toward the net or getting the puck down low to his forwards. Cecconi likes to pick his spots on the power play and creep down the blind side. If his offensive game continues to make strides, Cecconi could turn out to be a solid prospect down the road. Cecconi joins a very deep and talented blue line at the University of Michigan in 15/16.

Quotable: "NHL size and he's pretty good in his own end. Good showing in the play-offs won't hurt him any. No real offense to speak of though." - NHL Scout

Cernak, Erik
RD – Kosice (SVK) – 6'4" 203
HockeyProspect.com Ranking: 80

He's what you want physically at 6'3" with a big frame. Mobility is ok and he can play with a bit of an attitude at times. He won't wow you with puck skills but he can move the puck when he's on his game.

We saw the good and the bad with Cernak. When he was on, he would have you thinking he could crack the first round. Our problem was that he was off more than he was one. Big is great, but if he can't play the size is useless. One thing we like is that he will use his size to his advantage. Some big guys don't play big and that can be frustrating unless they play like the Pietrangelo's of the world. He does ok with moving the puck, we don't suspect he will become a guy skating the puck and gaining far bluelines all on his own. He's not a player with any uncanny vision or playmaking ability in the offensive zone. He handles the oncoming rush ok, his feet could be better, pivots are inconsistent.

Inconsistent play with the puck, showing us questionable hockey sense is what dictates his ranking with us. He has positives in his game for sure but lacks consistency in the hockey IQ department.

Quotable: "Right handed shot will help him. I loved this kid the first time I saw him in Sochi (U18) two years ago. Thought he played really poorly in Finland (U18) last April. This year I thought he better but still had those brain cramps that make me cool off on him. I like his size and the fact that he will use it. He's got a good hard shot too...both slap and wrister." - Mark Edwards

Chabot, Thomas
LD – Saint John Sea Dogs (QMJHL) – 6'2" 179
HockeyProspect.com Ranking: 20

Chabot slipped in the 2nd round of the QMJHL Draft and was selected 22nd overall by Saint-John in 2013. We had him rated as a first-round prospect (ranked 14th in our QMJHL draft guide) that year due to his upside offensively and his skating abilities. Chabot never played in international events for his province or country until the recent U18 World Championship in April, where he did very well for Canada. After a decent first season in the league, Chabot was much better this season and was without a doubt one of the most improved players in the league.

His play in his own end is where we saw the biggest improvement from last year; he was scratched for one game early in the season for poor commitment in the defensive end and ever since, he has become an impact player for the Sea Dogs at both ends of the ice. Another area where we saw improvement is on his explosiveness, as he was a good skater before this year but looks to have added an extra gear to his skating strides over the past year. It became one of the items in his skillset that has positioned him to become one of the best skating defensemen in this draft class. He has success retrieving the puck and making plays in pressure situations. He doesn't mind the physical play and is successful in winning battles on the boards, but still lacks consistency with his physical game from game to game. Becoming stronger would definitely help in that area.

Chabot has an excellent stride, making him dangerous offensively. He can rush the puck out of his zone with ease. He makes good decisions on his team's pressure breakouts and works hard to get the puck out of his defensive zone. Chabot likes to jump up in on his team's offensive rushes, but works hard to get back defensively if caught. He sees a lot of time on the power play and started playing more regularly on the penalty kill unit. He directs play when he is on the ice, directing the backcheck as play comes towards him. Chabot protects the puck well on his backhand, using his body to carry the puck where he wants. He has an above average shot from the point, there was some improvement made from last year but it could still get better to help him to be more of a threat to score from the point.

Chabot should be playing in a top 4 role at the NHL level and playing a key role on a teams power play. Puck moving defensemen with good feet are in high demand in the NHL.

Quotable:" Chabot was one the most improved players in the QMJHL this season, still work to be done in his own zone but his offensive potential and skating are top notch" - HP scout Jérôme Bérubé

Quotable:" I saw Roy and Chabot on back to back nights this season. That was when I first thought Chabot had a chance to be a real climber on our draft board. He played with amazing confidence and created a lot of offense for his team. He had a few brain cramps in Switzerland but the kid has pretty big upside." - Mark Edwards

Chebykin, Nikolai
RW – MVD (MHL) – 6'0" 183
HockeyProspect.com Ranking: NR

Listed by CSS at 6'0", Chebykin looks actually much taller than that. Around 6'3", he is a big left shooting right winger that may generate interest because of his growing size and a good showing in December at the World Junior A Challenge in *Saskatchewan*. The Russian has pretty nice hands and good stickhandling, which along with his frame help him keep possession and maneuver inside the offensive zone. However, for someone that is mainly effective in that third of the rink, he is currently lacking from a purely offensive standpoint, as showed by his mediocre numbers. As of now he rarely succeeds when he challenges the defenseman one on one or tries to pull off flashy plays, he needs to better choose when to make those attempts and has to add quickness to his game. Nikolai doesn't consistently play a physical game, even if he can throw the odd strong check along the boards. A draft selection right now would be heavily based on projection and potential, and his performance at the U18 in Switzerland didn't help his case.

Chlapik, Filip
LC – Charlottetown Islanders (QMJHL) – 6'1" 190
HockeyProspect.com Ranking: 43

Chlapik was acquired by the Islanders during the 2014 CHL Import draft after being selected 11th overall in the draft. Before joining the Islanders, we first saw Chlapik at the 2014 U-17 Hockey Challenge in Cape Breton, where he was one of the better Czech players. He also played at the 2014 U-18 World Championship as an under-ager and at the recent Ivan Hlinka tournament last August before making the move to the CHL.

In our viewings at international competitions, we saw Chlapik as a well-rounded player at both ends of the ice with some offensive upside. He was a bit of a surprise offensively for us at the rate he produced with the Islanders this year, averaging over a point a game and finishing 3rd in rookie scoring with 75 points. Chlapik is a smart player in his zone; we loved his attention to detail in his zone and how he supported his defense well by coming deep in his zone. The Czech forward possesses a good, heavy, accurate shot. During the season he was more consistent than his teammate and fellow draft-eligible prospect Daniel Sprong. With the puck, he's a smart player and sees the ice very well. He's a very good playmaker who's able to analyze things quickly on the ice and move the puck to his teammates rapidly for offensive chances.

Chlapik's biggest flaw is his skating; he lacks explosiveness and doesn't win enough puck races on a consistent basis due to his lack of speed. He's not able to create separation between himself and defenders because of this. In possession of the puck, he does a good job using his size to protect it along the boards, using his body to shield opponents away. Chlapik skating will be a big factor in dictating where he winds up playing pro hockey.

Quotable: "Kid has bad boots." - NHL Scout

Cirelli, Anthony
LC - Oshawa Generals (OHL) 6'00" 165
HockeyProspect.com Ranking: 77

Cirelli is a high energy two-way forward for the Oshawa Generals. In his rookie season, Anthony was given a big role for the 2015 OHL Champion Generals and was up to the challenge. He has ok size and excellent skating ability. He has a very high compete level and is intense on the forecheck. He is also an excellent backchecker and forces a ton of turnovers on any given night. In addition to his effective defensive game he has shown some good flashes with the puck and is capable of creating offense for his linemates by making smart puck decisions. He isn't a big goal scorer yet but when in alone he has the moves to beat the goaltender.

Cirelli will need to bulk up more because while he isn't afraid to get into physical battles and finish his checks, he lacks the strength to match up with some of the bigger older players. We love the skating and this kid really competes. He did a great job making an impact as a rookie on a team that was ranked 1st in the OHL all season long. He's easily worth a mid round pick and Anthony will get a chance to show his stuff on the big stage at the Memorial Cup.

Clapham, Austin
RD - Sudbury Wolves (OHL) 6'01" 195
HockeyProspect.com Ranking: NR

Clapham is a big right shooting defenseman playing in his first full season with the Sudbury Wolves. Austin played a physical shutdown role for the Wolves on the blueline switching between second and third pairing depending on the night. He also got some experience on his team's second penalty killing unit. Austin is a physical defender who is very tough on the wall. He has good size and likes to finish his hits whenever possible. He has decent backwards skating and overall was fairly reliable in 2 on 1 and 1 on 1 defensive assignments. He made a few errors in the defensive zone and playing on the worst team in the OHL this season, he spent a lot of time in his own end.

All in all, Clapham is a pretty simple defenseman who would benefit from further improving his mobility and improving positional consistency. He has a chance to go late in the draft due to his size and projects as a low-end physical shutdown defenseman.

Connor, Kyle
LC - Youngstown (USHL) 6'1" 177
HockeyProspect.com Ranking: 5

The thing we like most about Connor is that he has a very high hockey IQ. He combines his hockey smarts with skill and creativity and it translates into making him one of the more dangerous offensive players available in this draft.

Connor is a fantastic skater. He can explode through checks and excels using his edges. He reaches his top speed in a hurry and attacks the opposing blueline carrying a lot of speed. Once in the zone, he utilizes his great short area quickness and high-end skills. He is great at buying himself time and space. He's great keeping his feet moving and reading and reacting to changing situations. Connor's a player you want to have control the puck. His hands are soft. He's both a creative playmaker and goal scorer. His shot is good and he often flashes a very quick release. If he doesn't have the puck, he supports it well. He reads openings and jumps into areas making him available to get the puck.

He's good without the puck too and plays pretty hard defensively. He supports the puck well and makes sure he's an option on the breakout. His smarts translate to the defensive zone as well and he understands defensive positional hockey. He uses his speed to be an effective forechecker and also applies great back-pressure.

He isn't known for his physical game but he goes to dirty areas and doesn't shy away from contact. He's not afraid and will take a hit to make a play.

There's not much not to like about Connor. Sometimes he might over-handle a puck or try to do too much but it's not something that troubled us. The skills, smarts and speed he possesses are what get you excited about his potential going forward. He has the ability to translate into a top line player in the NHL. Like many players his age he, needs to fill out his frame and gain more strength.

Quotable: "He was really good in his interview. He came across multiple times as a team first player." - NHL Scout

Quotable: "After seeing him play great hockey at the U18 in Finland last April, I saw Kyle again in Lake Placid last summer prior to him beginning his draft season in Youngstown. It was an impressive performance and foreshadowed what we would see from him this season. One play that sticks out in my mind was when he used a burst of speed to split two defenders right through the middle of their own zone. Kyle uses his assets well to maximize his performance. Some of his games late in the year were especially impressive. I hear some scouts saying they are concerned about his body. I saw him at the combine and I think he will be fine. He's no Zacha or Crouse as far as size or physical maturity but that's short-term thinking. I think long term Connor may emerge as one of the stars from this draft." - Mark Edwards

Quotable: "He is a good skater that has that ability to kick it into another gear to split defense. He also flashes nice stick handling skills and creativity. He just seems to have a knack for scoring goals in tight, with speed, or even the greasy ones on rebounds. Everybody wants that type of player." - HP Scout Russ Bitely

Quotable: "It all starts with his speed. I love his game off the rush." - NHL Scout

Quotable: "That's a lot of points in the USHL. For whatever reason it's a tough league to get points. I wouldn't be surprised if he could've put up 100 points in the OHL or Q. He's a very good player." - NHL Scout

Conrad, Colton
RC- Shattuck St. Mary's Midget Prep (MN-HS) 5'10" 174LBS
HockeyProspect.com Ranking: NR

Conrad tore up the midget prep. Scene in 14/15 playing for Shattuck St. Mary's. Somewhat undersized for a Center at this stage but has gifted offensive ability. Conrad is a right handed shot that sees the ice well and has the ability to create space for himself and open up passing lanes in the offensive zone. Has terrific tape to tape passing ability and is able to make plays from down low or from the half wall in the offensive zone. Conrad is very good at working off the goal line and drawing defenders then seeming a pass to the weak side of the ice or to the slot.

Colton's 2-way game can be a concern, he can get caught wondering out of position and isn't overly active with his stick or along the boards in his own end. Too often he can be seen waiting for the play or puck to come to him rather than going and battling for it. Having said that, there is plenty of time for him to develop into a more complete 200 foot player and there is no teaching the offensive instincts and skill that Conrad possesses. Those aspects of his game are what could make him an intriguing potential late round sleeper pick for some team. Conrad looks to be heading to Western Michigan (NCAA) in 2015/16 however the Brandon Wheat Kings (WHL) own his CHL rights and could still be making a push for the skilled forward.

Corneil, Johnny
LC - Niagara Ice Dogs (OHL) 5'10" 190
HockeyProspect.com Ranking: NR

Johnny played a pretty limited role for the Ice Dogs this season, but was always noticeable despite the small amount of ice he received. For someone who played primarily fourth line with a little third line, 18 points is a pretty impressive accomplishment. He has a very high compete level and is speedy getting himself into corners in a hurry. Despite not having great size he has very good strength and wins a ton of battles down low. He's relentless on the forecheck and is a very annoying player to play against. He showed puck skills and intelligence under pressure to create opportunities for his linemates. He also possesses good release on his shot. Corneil isn't a player we expect to be selected at the 2015 NHL Entry Draft, but if he can maintain his competitiveness and further improve offensively when given a bigger role, he might be a player to watch in the future as he shows signs of being a sleeper.

Corriveau, Taggart
RW – Westminster (HIGH – CT) – 6'1" 181
HockeyProspect.com Ranking: NR

He skates with quick, short strides, but is graceful on the ice. His speed is impressive at the prep level. He is an agile skater who can start and stop on a dime. He makes plays happen with his ability to blow by defenders and break out of a pack, but he doesn't finish as much as he could. For as many pretty plays as he makes happen with his stick skills and skating ability, he could have scored at a higher pace.

Quotable:" I think he's a bit of a lazy player. He might be one of those high school players that gets taken late but has a really long way to go to have a chance at making it." - NHL Scout

Cotton, David
LC – Cushing Academy (HIGH – MA) – 6'2.5" 200
HockeyProspect.com Ranking: 74

He has impressive size and good feet for his size and age. For a big player, he's fairly agile and can catch and move the puck with his skates. He has a high hockey IQ and seems to let the puck find him. As impressive as his physical tools are, his smarts and vision on the ice stand out. Keeping in mind it's high school, he is strong on pucks and doesn't lose many battles, but again it is prep hockey. He has above average hands, has a quick release and can make crisp passes as well as touch passes to line mates. He was the anchor of the top line in all of prep hockey this winter. He became more of a force as he played with aggression and using his size to his advantage later in the prep season. He's destined for the USHL next season before matriculating to Boston College.

Quotable:" Good size, good skill. He was a productive player. I'd like to see more compete but I could see someone jumping on this kid early. Big kids are usually worth a long look." - NHL Scout

Coyle, Josh
LC - Peterborough Petes (OHL) 6'03" 210
HockeyProspect.com Ranking: NR

Coyle is a big centre that played limited minutes this year. Coyle is defensively responsible two-way forward and he was effective on the penalty kill, using a long reach to block passes and used his body to block shooting lanes. He is an average skater that played a simple game offensively. His physical side of the game needs to become more consistent as we've seen him be a tough player to play against, but at other times someone who needs to assert himself more.

Craievich, Adam
RW - Ottawa 67's (OHL) 6'01" 192
HockeyProspect.com Ranking: NR

Craievich was moved from the Guelph Storm to the Ottawa 67's and never really was able to advance his way up the depth chart in Ottawa. He played a bottom six role and adapted from a goal scorer to a grinder and competed for pucks down low. Ideally when it comes to the offensive game he looks to get open and utilize his excellent shot, but more towards the end of the year he accepted lower percentage, perimeter, shooting lanes. His skating is below average and still needs a lot of work to get him where he needs to be. Craievich is still a bit of a project at the OHL level and will need to further develop his game and improve before being considered for the NHL draft.

Crawford, Marcus
RD - Saginaw Spirit (OHL) 6'00" 190
HockeyProspect.com Ranking: NR

Crawford has quietly put up solid numbers as a rookie this season in the OHL. Marcus is a smooth skating puck rushing defenseman with good speed, who has pulled himself back a bit to make himself an effective two-way defender. Marcus kept it pretty simple compared to his Minor Midget play, which was very puck-rush heavy. He makes the first pass fairly consistently and advances the puck very quickly. His defensive play still has plenty of room for improvement and he tends to panic under pressure. He needs to improve his defensive positioning and be a tougher player to play against in order to maximize his potential.

Crawley, Brandon
LD - London Knights (OHL) 6'00" 197
HockeyProspect.com Ranking: 211

Crawley joined the Knights' as a free agent acquisition at their rookie camp last spring. He spent most of the season on the Knights' third pairing behind the depth of their older defenders and first round acquisition Victor Mete. Despite having good offensive tools, he played more of a defensive role this year. His season was full of lessons and "rookie" mistakes but he showed clear improvement over the course of the season.

Offensively he has an cannon shot from the point and has a great skill of finding a way to get his shot through from the point despite heavy screens. His footwork is a little clumsy but when carrying the puck he protects it well and once he gets his first few steps under him he has very good speed. He generally didn't try to do too much with the puck and as a result was pretty reliable offensively but didn't breakout either.

Defensively Crawley can be a tough player to play against down low. Despite not having massive size he handles both small shifty players and big physical players equally well. He has a gritty side and while he doesn't chase hits, he's not afraid of the rough stuff. Defensive positioning will need improvement but he showed a lot of promise as a player who made a big jump from the USPHL to the OHL in one season.

Quotable: "He's tight in the hips but I liked him tonight. I like the way his head was up and he sees the ice. He was dynamite on the PP tonight." (early in season) - NHL Scout

Quotable: "I know the kid, he's a hard worker. I saw him in camp and also early on in the season, so I may have had the luxury of seeing his offensive talents more than a lot of scouts. This kid can pass through seams and he has the hardest shot on the team. His big weakness is his feet. First few steps really hinder him and he looks a bit stiff in the hips. If he fixes his feet, his career will take off. Seventh round flier or free agent invite could pay off." - Mark Edwards

Crouse, Lawson
LW - Kingston Frontenacs (OHL) 6'03" 212
HockeyProspect.com Ranking: 8

Lawson Crouse is one of the most well rounded two-way players in this year's draft class. He plays a very sound game and is capable of playing big minutes in any situation. Crouse is a very good skater and has a good top speed. He's relentless after loose pucks, finishes his checks and is strong enough to separate players from the puck with regularity. He's very strong on the puck himself, particularly when driving the net. He's great in the cycle game and is tough to contain down low. He is very good when it comes to skating through contact as well.

Crouse is excellent defensively and is always back in the defensive zone to support. He's tough to get around in the neutral zone and regularly forces turnovers in that area of the ice. He is an excellent penalty killer and has been since early in is OHL career.

He has underrated playmaking skills and is a capable passer. Crouse has a powerful shot that is definitely pro caliber. He finds open space and gets it off relatively quickly. Crouse isn't an overly creative player with the puck and is much more of a straight-line player than a dazzler.

Crouse is low risk pick who projects to make the NHL quicker than many of his draft classmates. He will create space for his linemates at the NHL level and chip in offensively as well. Coaches will love how he excels at doing all the little things well. He will be a force to contend with in the NHL.

Quotable: "I love his game. He doesn't get enough credit for his offensive ability." NHL Scout

Quotable: "I think he can easily play on a wing in the top 6." NHL Scout

Quotable: "He might be the safest pick in the draft after McDavid and Eichel." NHL Scout

Quotable: "In his OHL draft year I mentioned to a few OHL staffers that he reminded me of lesser hitting but more skilled Tom Wilson. I think he's played a bit like that in his OHL career so far. He doesn't destroy players with his hits the way Wilson did, but he definitely plays a smarter and more skilled game. He moves the puck much better than Wilson, who simply dumped it into corners and then hunted down the D-man doing the retrieval." - Mark Edwards

Cukste, Karlis
LD – HK Riga (MHL) – 6'2" 203
HockeyProspect.com Ranking: NR

A Latvian defenseman with legit size, Cukste is a player who likes to keep it simple and can be relied upon in all situations. After bringing his steady play to his U20 national team at the World Championships Div.I in Asiago, he was able to held his own as the number one defenseman for Latvia at the top level U18 Worlds. He does nothing extraordinary well, but he can do a bit of everything. He makes good reads with and without the puck, and can complete good outlet passes to start transition.

He is not the most skilled player, so on the powerplay he needs to have open teammates available not to struggle, but he regularly chooses the safest play and is fairly effective at getting his wrister through. Even if projecting him for regular duty on a second powerplay unit at the next level might be stretching it, his play on the offensive blueline has improved along the season. We would like to see the same happen with his average skating. Karlis' chances to make an impact in the future are probably more as a defensive defenseman who can limit mistakes, block shots and move the puck efficiently while playing an unspectacular game.

Dahlstrom, John
LW – Frolunda (SWE Jr.) – 6'0" 185
HockeyProspect.com Ranking: NR

John was diagnosed with diabetes five years ago, but that didn't prevent him from developing into a legit prospect for the NHL draft. After some struggles through injuries in the first part of the season he was able to make up for the missed games in the new year, showing his scoring prowess in the Swedish junior leagues. He is a dangerous player when left open around the net and he can finish his chances using his skills and shot. He is also able to release it efficiently while dealing with opponents, the struggle for him is managing to get in a good shooting position when physically challenged by opponents.

He has good mobility with the puck and likes to stickhandle in traffic to look for shooting lanes, but his current lack of power clearly diminishes his effectiveness doing so. He shows a willingness to carry puck to the net and to work along the boards, but again, when facing top competition he lacks the energy to succeed most of the times. Also, improving his stamina would probably help his consistency throughout the game and the need of keeping his feet going without the puck. He can make good reads in the defensive zone too, but sometimes he puts himself in disadvantageous positions in open ice.
Like several other teammates on team Sweden, Dahlstrom had a disappointing showing at the U18 in Switzerland, but if he ever manages to add some explosiveness he may develop into a quality player.

Demler, Brendan
LD - Ohio Jr. Blue Jackets (Tier I U18) 6'1 170
HockeyProspect.com Ranking: NR

He is one of those sleeper players that played in scarce Tier 1 Midget league in the draft year and does not blow you away in viewings. What you do like is a defenseman with good size and mobility who can handle the puck fairly well from the back end. Again he will not put up gouty numbers offensively though he will make good outlets and keep game simple. He will need to keep filling out physically as still bit lanky though with added strength and NCAA seasons under his belt just might develop into bottom pairing at the next level. He is a project and late round flyer if anything.

Davidsson, Jonathan
LW – Djurgardens (SWE Jr.) – 5'10" 174
HockeyProspect.com Ranking: NR

Davidsson loves to score goals. He loves to score so much that he tends to forget that there are other zones besides the offensive zone. Despite the lack of defensive awareness, the impressive offensive skills Davidsson possesses make him a legit prospect. He has the ability to make it appear as though the puck is glued to his stick. He has terrific hands and is a crafty playmaker. Just when you think he couldn't pass or get a shot off, he does. Jonathan can do this while floating effortlessly around the ice, as he is a tremendous skater with a smooth stride.

He uses his body well to protect the puck, but he is not a physical player, he would pair well with a gritty, skilled forward that can get him the puck at opportune times. His shots don't pack a lot of power but they are accurate and deceptive. With all these skills though, he needs to play a more complete game. He can be too careless with the puck and turn it over and he is too much of a defensively liability. If he can learn to play more of a 200-foot game, Davidsson could turn out to be a good pick by some NHL team.

Davies, Mike
LW - Kitchener Rangers (OHL) 6'02" 195
HockeyProspect.com Ranking: NR

Davies, the former first round OHL Draft selection of the Kitchener Rangers continued to play much of the same role as he did in his rookie season as a bottom six forward but showed some improvement late in the season. He finishes checks and has a solid frame to make an impact physically. He's not afraid to take the body and grind it out down low. He wins a decent amount of puck battles and competes hard. He also has an absolute laser of a shot. He received more scoring opportunities and due to that, he more than doubled his goal total from last season.

Some of his biggest areas of concern are his skating and positional awareness. His skating did show some clear improvements late in the year but is still below average and impedes his ability to get into battles quicker and get in position for more scoring opportunities. He will also score more goals with his shot if he can find a little open ice and get available for passes in scoring areas. Davies is not a player we expect to see selected at the 2015 NHL Entry Draft.

Quotable: "Nothing to see on this team (Kitchener) for this year." - NHL Scout

Quotable: "I wasn't a fan of him in Minor Midget to start with, but he had one play in particular this year that stands out to me. It was a total lack of any effort whatsoever on a play in the defensive zone. I combine that sticking in my mind with his weak skating and those two things alone are probably enough as far as reasons why I wouldn't draft him." - Mark Edwards

Davis, Kevin
RD – Everett Silvertips (WHL) – 6'00" 183
HockeyProspect.com Ranking: NR

Davis is a smooth-skating defenseman who played in a bottom pairing role with the Everett Silvertips this year.

Away from the play, Davis has a subtlety of motion that follows him everywhere and wasted movement is reduced. Defensively, he combines using his good positioning and stick work with limiting his own mistakes in order to force opponents to earn scoring chances. Aided by good footwork he's effective in defensive transition thanks to strong poke checking ability and tremendous gap control whilst travelling in reverse. However, he can pinch at the wrong times which can put him behind the play, even for a good skater.

With the puck on his stick, Davis has very good skating and puck handling skill, but will rush his puck decisions causing him to miss his target or get picked off. He is content to keep things simple and to distribute the puck rather than trying to do everything himself. He quarterbacked the Silvertips second power play unit through much of the year. Without the puck he keeps his feet moving, consistently looking to make himself an available passing option. His viewings provided a wide range of performances from a steady secondary offensive defenseman, to one who has a lot of work ahead of him.

DeBrusk, Jake
LW – Swift Current Broncos (WHL) – 6'00" 174
HockeyProspect.com Ranking: 28

Left winger Jake DeBrusk of the Swift Current Broncos is a smart, engaged and hard-working winger with tremendous net-front presence, exceptional deflection ability and a deep gas tank. He's not the tallest forward available out of the WHL, nor is he the fastest, but DeBrusk's game oozes with competitiveness, hockey smarts and effectiveness.

DeBrusk's first stride possesses decent power but he struggles to accelerate due to some imperfections in his skating technique. Even without natural skating skills, Jake plays a powerful and physical game, most easily characterized by his ability to bowl over the opposition on his way to the net. Jake is the type of player who defends, stands up and fights for his teammates. Finally, he's a decent puck handler and effective scorer when placed around or in front of the net. DeBrusk is very effective and intelligent in timing his entry into the slot area. By doing so, he always seems to be in the right spot at the right time allowing him to produce points higher than what his raw talent ability suggests.

DeBrusk has intelligence and offensive upside that makes him an intriguing prospect. We would like to see him round out his game and further improve on his skating ability.

Quotable: "I see a really smart offensive player." - NHL Scout

Quotable: "He's solid. He's played very well in my recent viewings." - NHL Scout

Dello, Tory
RD – Tri-City (USHL) 6'0" 187
HockeyProspect.com Ranking: NR

Dello has impressed in some of our viewings throughout the year. He is strong on his skates, with a wide, solid base. He's an asset in his own zone, playing a nice stay at home game not often getting caught out of position. Has a ton of upper body strength and can separate puck from puck carrier with the best of them. His average size and below average offensive skillset will probably hold him back in the end, but the potential for him to be a good shut-down defenseman is still a possibility if he can build on this season. Dello is not currently a player we would consider drafting this season. He will be attending Notre Dame in the fall.

Dergachyov, Alexander
LC – SKA-1946 (MHL) – 6'4" 200
HockeyProspect.com Ranking: 91

A sturdy and versatile forward, Dergachyov managed to crack the U20 national team as a late '96 and was a useful piece that helped Russia to win the silver medal at the WJC. For him, the smaller rinks are certainly not a problem, as he excels along the boards and at protecting the puck. He can play in all situations and at any forward position. He battles hard for possession, blocks shots, has good hands and playmaking abilities, but he is also a legit scoring threat with his wrist shot and powerful presence in front of the net. He was in fact the top goal scorer of the MHL playoffs.

He is very strong on his skates and once he gets going his skating is fairly effective, sometimes he can even surprise defenseman by hitting another gear coming down the left side. The problem is how much time he takes to get going. That is probably what has kept him at the junior level so far, and the only real concern that might prevent him from becoming a regular contributor at the NHL level. As of now, in high paced games he struggles to keep up with the play, especially when it moves back and forth, and when he gets the puck in a stationary position he gets assaulted by backcheckers before he can complete a clean play.

Dermott, Travis
RD - Erie Otters (OHL) 5'11" 197
HockeyProspect.com Ranking: 47

Travis really progressed well this season and was given a bigger role as the year went on as a result. Dermott had good raw ability in the skating and physical department and over the course of the season improved his puck rushing ability and decision making. Too often early on this season, he would get stripped on the rush trying to do too much and not being aware of the checker approaching him. He has done a much better job of either progressing the puck or choosing a passing option before getting put into that position.

Dermott is calm under pressure and will make the right play most of the time. He played top power play minutes for Erie this season and has a great shot from the point. He also was very unselfish and moved the puck around well. Defensively he can be tough to beat, especially for a player his size. He has the stick and the physicality to take on opposing forwards. While he is very physically strong for his size, bigger forwards at the next level may pose more of a challenge for Dermott to contain.

Travis has good upside as an offensive defenseman who is reliable defensively. The only thing that probably keeps Dermott out of the first round is his lack of size. He has the pro weight and has plenty of tools to make him a successful NHL player but he will be fighting to push the six foot mark as a defenseman.

Quotable: " Really tight between him and Dunn for me but Dermott is less high risk." NHL Scout

Quotable: " Did some digging on the off ice stuff and he comes out ahead of the other undersized OHL guys." (defenseman) - NHL Scout

Quotable: " I liked this kid more with every viewing. I had Dunn ranked highest most of the year because I think his offensive potential is higher but Dermott really closed the gap between them with more consistent smart play as the season progressed. I heard good things from everyone I spoke to about Dermott as far as off ice goes. " - Mark Edwards

Deschene, Luc
RD – Charlottetown Islanders (QMJHL) – 5'11" 196
HockeyProspect.com Ranking: NR

Deschene was highly touted coming through the ranks in minor hockey in New Brunswick. We first saw him at the Canada Games in 2011 as a 13 year old playing against players two years older than him. In that year, he also played three games in major midget when he was a 1st-year bantam player. Eventually, Deschene was drafted by Victoriaville in the 2013 QMJHL draft, 50th overall, only to be traded in his first season in the QMJHL to Charlottetown.

Deschene was a very physically mature player at a young age, which explains his success in minor hockey. Right now, he's not a tall player, standing at 5'11", but he's strong on his skates. The Fredericton native is a physical defenseman in his own zone, using his strength well and ability to be a punishing hitter along the wall. He's a defenseman with decent mobility, although we would like him to refine his footwork a bit, as he can get beat by speedy forwards that try to take him wide.

Over the last two seasons he has showed flashes of his abilities as a puck rusher, but with not enough consistency to be considered an offensive defenseman right now. He has good puck skills, making good passes on the transition, but needs to make better decisions with the puck, as he's prone to turnovers. He has a strong shot from the blueline and can be an asset on the power play; his shot is very hard and already has NHL velocity to it.

Deschene is a player who hit his peak at a young age and right now sees other defensemen in the league surpassing him. He might get a look late in the draft by a team but we don't have him ranked in our top 210.

Didur, Bo
G – Langley Rivermen (BCHL) – 5'10" 161
HockeyProspect.com Ranking: NR

The first thing that stands out to you about Bo Didur's game is his pure athleticism, as he's capable of doing the splits and sliding from post-to-post in the snap of a finger. His ability to track and then stop second-chance opportunities is incredible. He plays the game well positionally, he's got great awareness, possesses good reflexes, regularly exhibits physical toughness and appears mentally strong.

Didur's stance looks fairly good. He does a good job of seeing through bodies, reading the defensive coverage and positioning himself to make a save. His superior awareness is regularly exhibited through strong positional play and really intelligent puck movement. Overall, we had a hard time finding any flaws in his positioning or his redirecting of rebounds. His upper-body reflexes are very, very good and his rebound control is better than average. Furthermore, we really like Didur's physical toughness and durability. Numerous times this year, we saw Didur get wiped out by opposition forwards crashing the net and other flying bodies; no matter how violent the initial collision, Didur would stumble to his feet, shake himself off and find a way to remain in the game.

In the end, Bo remains much smaller than the average NHL goalie and there remains a limited market for smaller-than-usual goalies.

Diffley, Brien
RD – Boston University (HOCKEY EAST) – 6'1" 176
HockeyProspect.com Ranking: NR

He doesn't have the upside that some of the other top draft eligible defensemen in the region do, but he's proven he can skate and be an impact puck carrier in transition at a higher level than some of the prep and junior guys. He's a late bloomer that had his ups and downs over the course of the college season. There is no question he can skate and help in transition. He makes a very heady, firm lead pass and skates with his head up. The question is whether or not he can maintain defensive coverage and shut down opposing forwards on a consistent basis. It was rare that BU found itself in a position where it was defending for any length of time so his defensive ability wasn't tested as often as it could have been.

Dostie, Alex
LC – Gatineau Olympiques (QMJHL) – 5'9" 159
HockeyProspect.com Ranking: NR

Dostie is an undersized centerman playing for in his 2nd season with the Gatineau Olympiques. In an eventful year for them, Dostie was one of the bright and more consistent performers for them this year.

Dostie established himself as top-2 line center in the QMJHL, finishing the season with over 20 goals and 50+ points, despite not having regular linemates to play with due to the large number of injuries the team had this season. Even at his size, Dostie has a good compete level and is tenacious. He's a smart player in possession of the puck, making smart and efficient plays with it. He's good at cycling the puck due to his quick and agile feet, and ability to make quick stop-and-go motions. He sees the ice well and is a capable playmaker; making some nice passes on the rush. He started getting more defensive assignments in the 2nd half of the season; he has a good IQ and understands how to play the game in his own end. He lacks the ideal strength right now and will need to get stronger in the next couple of years to play professionally, but Dostie won't back down from physical confrontation and won't hesitate to throw his weight around if needed. Size remains an issue with Dostie as far as NHL potential and he didn't show us enough this year to be ranked in our top 210.

Dove-McFalls, Samuel
LC – Saint John Sea Dogs (QMJHL) – 6'2" 204
HockeyProspect.com Ranking: 89

Dove-McFalls was drafted in the 3rd round of the 2013 QMJHL draft by Saint John out of the Lac St-Louis Tigres' ESPOIR program. He was the captain of that team and was a teammate of Daniel Sprong during that season. He caused a bit of surprise by making the Sea Dogs as a 16 year old coming out of the ESPOIR league, but has not looked back since. This past January, he was named assistant-captain of the Sea Dogs. Interesting note on Samuel: before playing his ESPOIR season in 2012-2013, he and his family moved to Germany due to his father's work situation, resulting in him playing one season in Germany when he was of bantam age.

He's a smart player at both ends of the ice, playing on both the power play and penalty killing units for his team. Dove-McFalls centers two of Saint John's overage forwards most of the time; they create an effective two-way line, adding depth to Saint John's lineup. The Montreal native plays a sound positional game, putting himself in the right place while supporting his defensemen and wingers well. He could be more successful if he moved his feet a little more, but overall, his skating has improved a lot since last season. Standing at 6'2", Dove-McFalls is improving his physical play role as well, not afraid to take the puck to the net. He's a vocal player on the ice and is a key player for the Sea Dogs on the penalty kill. He is also good on faceoffs for them and does a good job blocking shots and getting in the shooting lanes. Samuel also does a good job using his size to protect the puck and pays attention to the little details on the ice. His offensive upside might be a bit limited, but he does a lot of nice things that make him a valuable prospect and player on his junior club. He can surprise opponents with his creativity with the puck at times, and has a good wrist shot that can surprise opposing goaltenders.

Dove-McFalls might never be a top scorer but brings so much more to the table. He has potential as a bottom 6 forward with being very useful on the penalty killing unit.

Quotable: "Liked him in my early viewings but I cooled off on him by the end of the year." – NHL Scout

Quotable: "I have a lot of 'Q' guys ahead of him. I like him but probably won't be fighting for him on draft day." - NHL Scout

Dufek, Jan
RW – Kometa Brno (CZE Jr.) – 5'11.75" 172
HockeyProspect.com Ranking: NR

Dufek is a left shooting right winger than can be used in all situations. He can be a regular feature on the penalty kill or be the man in the slot on the powerplay He can play efficiently on a bottom six role or fill in properly on the top six if needed, at least at the junior level. He possesses decent speed and use it consistently on both sides of the rink. Can be effective on the forecheck to cause turnovers or bring some physical play. Doesn't have top skills, but no glaring weaknesses either and has the potential to become a third liner at the next level.

Dunda, Liam
LW - Owen Sound Attack (OHL) 6'04" 215
HockeyProspect.com Ranking: 186

Liam is a huge power winger for Owen Sound who the Attack acquired at the OHL Trade Deadline from the Plymouth Whalers. If Dunda was born one day later he wouldn't be eligible until the 2016 NHL Entry Draft. He has massive size and last season he played a game that is very well suited to his body as a physically intimidating player. He hit hard and punished opponents whenever possible. The problem was that was last year. This year he was MIA.

Offensively Dunda is pretty limited. He has a decent shot and even showed a few flashes of playmaking ability late in the season but all in all Liam's upside is his potential as a simple hard nosed physical player who isn't afraid to drop the gloves either.

Dunda may hear his name called later on in the draft if a team saw what we saw last season. Teams commonly take big players like Dunda later on as a re-entry pick and being the youngest player in the draft, someone may want to grab him now in case he returns to form and costs a higher pick a year or two down the road.

Quotable: "I kept waiting to see what I saw last year when I wrote rave reports on him, but I never saw it all season." - NHL Scout

Quotable: "What do you think of that Dunda kid?" - Multiple NHL Scouts

Quotable: "Loved what I saw from him last season. He struggled early this year and I was hoping the trade might spark him but if it did, I never saw it. I know that physical style is in there somewhere because I saw it multiple times last season." - Mark Edwards

Dunn, Vince
LD - Niagara Ice Dogs (OHL) 6'00" 185
HockeyProspect.com Ranking: 46

Vince is an excellent puck rushing defenseman for the Niagara Ice Dogs. Dunn is a cerebral puck mover with offensive flair. He is a very strong skater who can carry the puck up ice but also hit an ideal pass at speed. He handles and moves the puck very well in the offensive zone. He also possesses a powerful and dangerous shot. Strong for his size, he plays with an edge defensively. His ability to defend on the rush will need some improvement, as his gap, range and impatience have all been causes of concerns. Dunn doesn't possess ideal size and plays a high risk, high reward game but his upside is that of a strong puck rushing offensive defenseman at the next level.

Dunn is very dangerous when he activates himself into the rush but he needs to pick his spots better. He has a knack for creating offensively but he will need to tone down when and how he jumps into the play as he moves into the pro ranks. He has poise with the puck and makes pretty good decisions with it. His offensive instincts are very good but he lacks the same ability to think and anticipate the game defensively. Dunn needs to find a way to get excited about defensive hockey and play with the same level of passion in all three zones. If we compare him to say a Travis Dermott, he has more offensive upside but plays a much higher risk game and is not as effective in his own zone as Dermott is.

Dermott has offensive abilities NHL teams will love. He has the opportunity to carve himself out a nice NHL career if he commits to improving the holes in his game. With his ability to create offense, he doesn't need to become an absolute shutdown defender, he just needs to not be a liability in his own end.

Quotable: "He's a mess in his own zone." – NHL Scout

Quotable: "This kid can really skate." – NHL Scout

Quotable: "Wasn't great in my interview." – NHL Scout

Quotable: "This kid grew on me. He was awful in my early season viewings but I saw him a lot later in the season and I really liked him. He plays with his hair on fire at times but he creates offense. He looks to be a legit 6'0" and the kid can really skate. Play in his own zone can be a mystery from shift to shift. I think he has better offensive potential than Dermott but he probably has more bust potential as well." – Mark Edwards

Dzierkals, Martins
RW – HK Riga (MHL) – 5'11" 170
HockeyProspect.com Ranking: 195

Dzierkals is a left shooting right winger capable of bringing both considerable skills and a great compete level. He may look smaller than listed, but actually plays bigger than his limited stature. He will be the first going to the end boards battling for the puck, can throw a check when needed and often finds a way to keep possession against bigger opponents. He plays an intense game but doesn't seem to have yet the stamina to play it consistently, despite his efforts are indeed consistent. More often than not he is gassed by the end of his shifts. One of Martins' typical plays is coming through the neutral zone (or down the right side) with speed to challenge defensemen one on one, displaying his great agility and stickhandling prowess. On the powerplay he can manage the puck in tight spaces, as he keeps moving it away from defenders' sticks while he looks for options. Coming off the right side boards he is able to change angle well to find a lane to shoot on net.

One thing that has become apparent after multiple live viewings this year is that this kid is absolutely fearless on the ice. It's been impressive seeing him enter dense traffic at full speed or go after pucks without being worried by incoming opponents. Sometimes he can be at fault for unnecessary penalties, but it's difficult to hold it against a player of this kind. It's interesting to note how productive Dzierkals has been this season and at the U18 World Championships in particular. Will he be able to remain effective against men? The question is how much upside does he have, how far he is from the finished product from an offensive standpoint. If he brings off the ice the same attitude he shows during contests, he has a good starting point to improve further.

Edmonds, Ty
G – Prince George Cougars (WHL) – 6'02" 174
HockeyProspect.com Ranking: NR

Ty Edmonds was a key part in a resurgent effort for the Prince George Cougars organization and an integral component in that organization earning a birth in the post-season for the first time in four years. Edmonds came to the CHL with some decent fanfare after 15-1 record in the Manitoba Midget AAA Hockey League, but played inconsistently on a team dealing with ownership issues last year and ultimately went undrafted.

Edmonds is a left-catching butterfly goaltender who calmly and cooly makes saves from surprisingly awkward body positions. He works a lot with one knee on the ice, in a bit of a hybrid butterfly-standing position. Edmonds became adept at finding pucks amidst the chaos in front of him. He sees through screens very well and ducks, wades, pushes, stands on his tip-toes—does whatever is necessary to catch a glimpse of the puck and to stay square to the play. He's aggressive and not afraid to challenge shooters who break the line on partial or complete breakaways. He seemed to make some significant strides in the area of mental toughness from last year to this year.

Eichel, Jack
RC – Boston University (NCAA) 6'2 196
HockeyProspect.com Ranking: 2

The Eichel watch has been ongoing since age 15. There is no question he is a generational player like Connor McDavid (Erie Otter-OHL). The skating stride is exceptional. He has an explosive stride in which he can get from 1st gear to 5th gear in a hurry in an effortless manner. At times it seems he is saving the sixth gear for the NHL his stride it is that powerful. He catches players in the neutral zone like it's nothing. He is so effective carry the puck with his long reach and very soft hands and you like how he covers a vast amount of ice without the puck on the defensive as well and his strong forechecking side. His ability to create separation with explosive stride is second to none as NHL ready in the skating department for sure. He is very effectively defensively and sometimes does not get enough credit as will angle opponents out on the backcheck and will utilize his long reach effectively in passing lanes. His long reach breaks up plays and helps him keep possession as at times puck looks like yo-yo on his stick. Most people think of Eichel only on the offensive side although he plays all situations including PK and very knowledgeable in all 3-zones. He sees the ice very well as he anticipates plays with and without the puck. Eichel is an elite player with all the skill sets and hockey IQ to go along.

He shows great strength on his skates and uses his body effectively to keep puck possession. What you also like is that if he does happen to turn puck over he quickly is hard on the puck to try to gain possession back. His face-off percentage is decent though an area he could improve upon. He plays a smart game in the manner that if the play does not develop he isn't afraid to zing a shot to the net to make something happen off the rebound or using D-man as a screen. T

he coaches have great confidence in him as regularly plays the penalty kill as well, not just the power play or when goalie is pulled defensively. One aspect that sets him at the top is his shooting ability. He can fire the one-timer with great power and accuracy or he can beat goalies coming down the off-wing with a quick release. He has the ability to pull the puck to inside or outside to change the

shooting release angle to fool goalies. He has great vision and will use his strength along the wall or in the corners to find the open man or zip a pass on the tape through a seam on the power play.
You could go on and on though what ever team takes Eichel will be happy. He is not only an exceptional player on the ice but also shows great composure and leadership on the bench an din the locker room in talking with BU coaches. He is an impressive player that should make a good living in the NHL for many years. The debate now is whether heads to the NHL for the upcoming season, which he is certainly ready, or decides to take another crack at winning an NCAA Championship.

"You always hate the comparison thing yet he reminds me of today's Ryan Getzlaf with puck handle, vision, and offensive thoughts with explosive stride and speed like Jeff Carter to finish plays at the net and shooting to score. Many believe there is a big gap between McDavid and Eichel, I beg to differ." – Russ Bitely (USA Scout)

Quotable: " I have seen him one-time a shot while with NTDP-18 last season from the top of the circle on the PP as he took a pass from low to high. He released it so quick and with so much torque and power. The puck hit where the crossbar and post meet and it sounded as if the puck had spilt in two it was so loud and ringing. The puck bounced off the back of the goalie, sat spinning in the crease, and his line mate tapped it in for the goal. Let's just say he can shoot the puck NHL style for sure." - HP Scout Russ Bitely

Quotable: " Still remember an outstanding performance at the U17 in Victoriaville. He was head to head vs McDavid and played right with him. That was when I knew he ranked way up in this draft class." - Mark Edwards

Quotable: " It seems strange to feel a bit bad for a player going 2nd overall in the draft but that's where I'm at. This kid is a fantastic player and although McDavid was my clear number one, I can't stress enough how good Eichel is too. I think it was a shame how some media made it seem like he was table scraps compared to McDavid. This kid handled all his interviews and this whole situation very well in my opinion. I hope he rips the NHL apart.- Mark Edwards

Eriksson Ek, Joel
LC – Farjestad (SHL) – 6'2" 185
HockeyProspect.com Ranking: 15

Eriksson Ek has been one of the revelations of the season. Able to grab a roster spot for Farjestad before Winter, his play earned him more icetime as the months passed by. The more you watch him play, the more you understand why. He is effective all around the rink and plays a safe game.
He goes to battle in all three zones and even against men never showed signs of backing off from physical confrontations. The tough areas of the ice seem his favourite destinations. He likes to position in front of the net to look for deflections or make himself available in the slot. When he has the puck in the offensive zone if he can't shoot he tries to take the puck to the net. For how he is built he shows surprising firmness on his skates. Uses his very good reach to protect and maneuver the puck when engaged along the boards. He forechecks hard and gets physical when he really wants the puck. His passes are consistently accurate, but inside the offensive zone he is more of a shooter, which only makes sense considering his wrist shot is outstanding and definitely his best weapon. He has a short release, is able to fire from any angle with power and impressive accuracy, and he can quickly create lanes for his shot.

Eriksson Ek is an intelligent player that can make good use of his skillset and can contribute a lot on the defensive side as well. At his blueline he effectively uses his reach to negate entries into his zone. He can be effective on both special teams. It's just very difficult to find real weaknesses in his game. His skating is not pretty and has a bit of an awkward stride, but it gets him where he needs to be, and as the season progressed the situations where he didn't look quick enough to get going seemed to vanish. He may not possess 1st-line creativity or pure skills (outside of his shot), but he looks like one the safest picks of the draft.

Quotable: "He thrust himself up the rankings at the Five Nations tourney and continued his fine play right through the U18 in Switzerland. I thought he was outstanding there. His feet are his weakness for me but not enough to scare me off ranking him as high as we did." - Mark Edwards

Estephan, Giorgio
RC – Lethbridge Hurricanes (WHL) – 6'00" 188
HockeyProspect.com Ranking: 136

Giorgio Estephan is a fast moving and slippery forward with a high hockey IQ, a boatload of skill and tremendous footspeed. A confident and crafty playmaker aided most significantly by quick and speedy footwork. He is also gifted with good hands. Despite his natural skills, however, Estephan struggled in the first-half. Towards the second half, he really elevated his game, managing to double his point totals from last season.

He has really good speed both with and without the puck and is especially deceptive with it in close. He was already a good stickhandler, but added inches to his height and reach have added a new lankiness to his dangles that makes him even more dangerous than before. His footspeed hasn't suffered from the physical growth whatsoever—he can turn on a dime and receive passes expertly while in motion. An additional aspect of his game that makes him dangerous past the offensive blueline, is that he's equally skilled as both as a shooter and as a passer, making him a difficult player to predict off of the rush. Previously considered undersized, the speedy Giorgio actually grew by a few inches between last year and the 2015 NHL Entry Draft, whilst not losing much in terms of agility or speed.

Estephan's began cranking up the dials on his offensive game. Furthermore, his success-level carried over to a variety of venues—he began driving the net more consistently and winning more faceoffs, more puck races and more one-on-one battles in the offensive zone. He's no slouch defensively either, as he saw some assignments on the penalty kill and performed fairly well. As previously mentioned, he's adding size, bulk and a greater physical dimension to his game.

Quotable: Giorgio Estephan has quietly developed into a scoring threat for the Hurricanes. He has a nose for finding open ice and loose pucks and has flown under the radar since a slow start due to injury. Well worth a mid round pick. - HP Scout Scott McDougall

Falkovsky, Stepan
LD – MHK Yunost (MHL) – 6'6.5" 220
HockeyProspect.com Ranking: 158

At more than 6'6", even if still raw, this Belorussian defenseman has showed enough during the season to be considered an interesting prospect. On top of his terrific reach, Falkovsky has powerful legs and shows strength and determination in his play along the boards. His skating is adequate, can activate quickly for a big man and has a good first step. In his own end he is able to make quick decisions, can complete short backhand passes under pressure and he is not slow reacting despite his size. Occasionally Stepan can be caught going for puck battles too high, outside of the defensive zone. Not always as strong on the puck as needed when pressured, with his size and strength he should be stronger on the puck and better at protecting it when he gets possession in his zone.

He plays as a stay at home defenseman most of the time, but he seems pretty good at recognizing the right opportunity to jump on the offense and in those rare occasions he can make surprising rushes where he shows some offensive prowess. Apparently he is one of those players who look better with the puck in game action then during warm-up rushes. He has seen time on the powerplay in MHL when his towering presence has been used in front of the net. The highlight of his season has been the success obtained with his national team at the U20 Div.I Group A World Championships played in northern Italy in December, but it would not be surprising if Falkovsky could enjoy another memorable moment in late June. A late '96, with proper coaching and some needed hard work to improve his skills and puck possession play, he could develop into a serviceable defenseman at the pro level.

Fanjoy, Ben
RW – Ottawa 67's (OHL) – 6'00" 184
HockeyProspect.com Ranking: NR

Fanjoy hasn't been able to take the next step for the 67's but proved to be a valuable asset to their bottom six this past season. Ben has good work ethic and competes for pucks. He battles hard and is willing to finish his check. He is very good at the cycle game and is very fluid whenever he can get it going for his team down low. He needs to work on taking a more direct line to the puck carrier because he tends to make wide turns and circle around a little too much. He competed hard in the defensive zone and was willing to block shots. A good skater, he will need to improve his play with the puck under pressure. He showed us at the Minor Midget level that he may have some untapped offensive skill that may emerge later on as he plays a bigger role for his team. He isn't a player we expect to be drafted at the 2015 NHL Entry Draft, but is a player who does a lot of the little things right and could have some upside in him a little more down the road.

Fazio, Justin
G - Sarnia Sting (OHL) 6'01" 180
HockeyProspect.com Ranking: NR

After performing well in a handful of games last season, Fazio was thrown into the fire a little when overage goaltender Taylor Dupuis opened the season with an injury. This meant the rookie had to play 12 straight games to open the season. He served as the back-up through the remainder of this season and had a few impressive relief appearances as well. Justin displays great quickness and gets across his crease very well. He is more of an athletic goaltender than a structured one, who has made several highlight reel saves over the course of the season. He has a very strong glove. He has a tendency to have a few mental lapses that will result in a bad goal here and there. Fazio isn't among the top goaltenders in the draft class.

We don't expect Fazio to be selected in this years NHL draft.

Fellows, Patrick
LW – Erie Otters (OHL) – 6'03" 185
HockeyProspect.com Ranking: NR

Patrick is one of the more under the radar prospects caught behind a ton of forward depth but found a way to make an impact on the fourth line this season. Fellows is an excellent defensive forward and was a very reliable option when his team is holding the lead competing hard in all three zones, relentlessly pressuring the puck carrier and was excellent in the defensive zone. He has great size and will take the body to the extent necessary, but would really benefit from adding a bit of a mean streak to his game. Fellows was relied on heavily on the penalty kill and played a ton in short handed situations. He does a great job of getting into passing lanes and blocking several shots. He provides good pressure high on the point and forced turnovers. He showed a couple flashes of good offensive ability and the potential to contribute more offensively in the future but doesn't appear to have very high skillset. Fellows is a player who could get late round consideration because of his excellent defensive first game up front but the concern lies in how much skill he possesses because he was a decent offensive player at the Minor Midget level but not a big time scorer and hasn't shown much other than the occasional flash in the OHL.

Fiala, Evan
RD – Spokane Chiefs (WHL) – 6'04" 193
HockeyProspect.com Ranking: 121

After seeing a handful of games for the Chiefs' last season, Fiala played his first full WHL season for the Spokane Chiefs. Evan rose his stock over the course of the season gaining second pairing ice and playing an important role on their penalty kill.

Fiala is a big, physical, shutdown defender who plays a very safe style of game. He has a tendency to land at least one big hit early on in the game and sets the tone for his team. Good defensive zone positioning allows him to get the most out of his size and strength whether it be in open ice, or along the wall. He will need to improve on his awareness as defenders are capable of pinching behind him undetected. While he's not a big offensive guy, Fiala has shown the ability to effectively make the smart reliable play with the puck, even when under pressure.

Fiala's upside is limited to that of a bottom pairing defender. He would also be expected to see ice on the penalty kill at the highest level. Evan has the upside to be a very intimidating physical presence and isn't afraid to drop the gloves whenever necessary.

Finlay, Liam
RW – Vernon Vipers (BCHL) – 5'06" 132
HockeyProspect.com Ranking: NR

Liam Finlay is a tiny but quick and dynamic offensive forward currently playing in the BCHL with the Vernon Vipers. Finlay, an offensively charged, speedy and diminutive skater, is a curiosity to many NHL draft onlookers for a number of reasons: for one, he was by far the lightest player ranked by NHL Central Scouting, being listed at only 132 pounds. Finlay, a highly talented skater and playmaker on the man-advantage, was brought to Vernon specifically to help its woeful special teams unit and looked very comfortable carrying a heavy load for Vernon—almost singlehandedly jump-starting the power play.

Finlay is graced with tremendous hands, excellent vision and great passing skills. He's almost always a key distributor from the half-wall both on the power play and at even-strength. Furthermore, despite being easily knocked off of his feet due to his lack of size, he does a really good job of getting to the front of the net and has the skills in tight to finish as he's able to use speed and hockey smarts to dart in and out of the slot or to duck and weave through larger players and into open space. You can't help but admire how he hard he fights for positioning despite being easily overpowered and oftentimes bullied by larger opposition defenseman.

Liam is currently committed to Denver University starting in 2016-2017. At 5'6" and 132 pounds, Liam needs to set the house on fire in order to make the to the NHL. He might wind up being a late pick or a free agent invite to an NHL camp.

Fischer, Christian
RW – USNTDP (USHL) 6'1" 212
HockeyProspect.com Ranking: 49

He is a capable offensive forward with decent skating ability, passing, and shooting abilities. He is not explosive on his skates although shows decent speed and likes to wire shots as can really fire the puck in the slot or down the wing. He has good size and will create lots of scoring opportunities as he reads the play well and thinks a step ahead. He works below the dots well and has a knack around the net.

Fischer is a pretty balanced player that both sets-up plays and shows a finishing touch. Fischer is responsible in own zone too with body & stick positioning. He has the skills to eventually show his game in the pro ranks after a few years at Notre Dame in Hockey East. He will play a bit physical when needed but it's not something that comes natural to him. He takes pucks to the net, and shows finishing ability. There are times were he turns the puck over in neutral zone or on the breakout, so puck decision making outside the offensive end will need some improvement moving forward.

Quotable:" Lot's to like about him but I do think he lacks a bit in the hockey smarts department and sometimes I'm not sure he has enough compete in him. Skating could be better too, it's just ok." - Mark Edwards

Quotable:" I had a few scouts tell me that his combine interviews were very good." - Mark Edwards

Flanagan, McKay
RD – The Gunnery (HIGH – CT) – 6'0.25" 208
HockeyProspect.com Ranking: NR

A first year prep player, there is no doubt he can move the puck, help in transition and quarterback a power play. He's an aggressive player in all facets of the game. He's not afraid to join the rush and he'll step up and make a big hit in the neutral zone. He can get away with that most of the time at the prep level, but the big question remains if that will stay the case as he moves to the next level. He doesn't have the prettiest stride, but he has decent mobility and agility on his skates. He's a rugged kid who made some real noticeable hits during both the prep season and in the showcases this spring, but he needs to reel it in and be in control and play more consistently.

Fitzgerald, Casey
LD - USNTDP (USHL) 5'10.5" 185
HockeyProspect.com Ranking: NR

The younger Fitzgerald who is also off to Boston College is a solid, puck moving type defenseman. He is a bit on the smaller side for NHL D-men although he moves fairly well. He makes the outlet passes to start the transition and will make those nice stretch passes to spring his forward teammates as he sees the ice pretty well. Although not sure his game has developed at the pace of others while at NTDP as sometimes his play is a bit inconsistent with his defensive position and gets puck gazing at times. He plays steady with good defensive stick positioning, and will get pucks to the net. The offensive game is a work in progress, as he chooses to keep the game simple rather than chance on the offensive side. Like his father and older brother, his success comes from the hockey IQ.

Quotable: "He's not dynamic enough to out play his lack of size. He is a defensive D-man and 5'10" shutdown guys are not that common in the NHL. Good player but not one I would draft." - Mark Edwards

Foley, Erik
LW- Cedar Rapids (USHL) 5'11.5", 185
HockeyProspect.com Ranking: 41

High compete level would be the best way to describe Foley's all around game. He competes all over the ice, plays physical in his puck battles and if it's a 50/50 puck, more than likely Foley will out compete his opponent and come out with the puck. He likes to be first in on the forecheck and be physical on the opposing defenseman in an effort to create turnovers. Foley's not afraid to get himself and/or the puck to the net as quickly as possible. He possesses a decent release on his shot, a lot of times he will exit the boards with the puck, snap a quick shot toward the net and follow up his shot. There are times where has more time to make a play and he doesn't realize it. Foley doesn't possess that natural high end goal scorers finishing ability or elite playmaking consistently, but he shows flashes of it at times and the things he does down low and along the boards create puck possession and offensive opportunities.

Foley has a powerful, straight line skating stride that allows him to get back into the play quickly. He provides great back pressure and keeps his stick in good position. His effort and physicality in his own end help disrupt plays when his team is hemmed into their own zone; however Foley can get too focused on the puck sometimes. He will exert a lot of unnecessary energy by chasing the play and can get out of position. Foley has the potential to play in a top nine role in the NHL. He will join the National Champion Providence Friars in the fall of 2015.

Quotable: "I'm a fan. He plays hard. I liked him more with each viewing. I obviously haven't seen him live as much as some other players because of geography, but I took the time to sit down and watch extra tape on him. He plays really hard down low and like Boeser, he will go to the net with the puck. He's good on the power-play. I'll be interested to see where he comes off the board on draft day. I like his upside and think he still has room to get much better." - Mark Edwards

Fontaine, Gabriel
LC – Sherbrooke Phoenix (QMJHL) – 6'1" 197
HockeyProspect.com Ranking: NR

Fontaine, who played his first full season in the QMJHL this year, is a smart forward with a lot of speed. The Sherbrooke native was drafted by his hometown team in 2013, 29th overall, and played part of the last two seasons with the Magog Cantonniers in the Quebec Midget AAA league.

First thing you notice when you watch Fontaine is his speed; he can really fly on the ice and use his wheels in both offensive and defensive situations. He has found a nice niche with this Sherbrooke team, being used in more of a defensive role. We liked his effort playing in a checking role. He understands his role and has a good puck pursuit game thanks to his great speed. He's also a useful player on Sherbrooke's penalty killing unit thanks again to his speed and hustle.

He has struggled so far producing offensively in the QMJHL, as his hands and vision are just average. He has had some opportunities during the season to play with the highly-skilled Swiss forwards (Schweri and Wieser) but couldn't perform enough to stay on an offensive line. He's a big body down the middle with a good puck protection game but we doubt he will ever be a top point producer at the pro level. He has good qualities to become a defensive specialist down the road.

Forsbacka-Karlsson, Jakob
RC – Omaha (USHL) 6'0.75" 190
HockeyProspect.com Ranking: 61

The Swedish center has followed up his impressive first season in the USHL with a great year, moving along at over a point per game pace. Forsbacka-Karlsson, a Boston commit, is one of the most intelligent players on the ice in the USHL. He has the ability to wait for the play to come to him and not rush to make decisions with the puck. He plays a very slow, methodical game, which in turn results in him not turning the puck over often.

Jakob is an absolute beast in the faceoff circle, he rarely lost draws this year. He uses his previously mentioned elite vision to make very crisp tape-to-tape passes setting up his teammates. He definitely has a pass-first mentality but has shown off his shot on occasion this year scoring a handful of goals.

In addition to his great offensive vision and playmaking skills, Forsbacka-Karlsson works extremely hard on the back check. His defensive effort, which might go unnoticed to his offensive skillset really should not be overlooked as he has blossomed into a nice well-rounded center.

Quotable: "I think he's a solid player who wins draws and plays well defensively, but I keep expecting someone more dynamic. I have time for him, but he doesn't knock my socks off. Looks like a possible 4th liner in the NHL." - Mark Edwards

Quotable: "Love the way he plays the game. Always under control, never rushes his decisions or panics. Calm, cool, and collected in all situations." - HP Scout Justin Schreiber

Forsberg, Fredrik
RW – Leksand (SWE Jr.) – 6'0" 174
HockeyProspect.com Ranking: NR

Filip's brother didn't have a very noticeable draft season. As a '96 born he couldn't be part of the U18 national team and his play in the Swedish junior league didn't show much improvement.
Fredrik shoots right like his brother and his shot is probably the best part of his game. His one-timer in particular is very good. He also possesses good scoring instincts and a feeling for the net, but he lacks dynamism. He brings good attitude and effort to the ice, he's committed on the forecheck, but he would need better wheels to be effective at the next level in this and other areas of the game. Right now his lack of progress from last season is the most concerning reason to be down on him.

Fortin, Alexandre
LW – Rouyn-Noranda Huskies (QMJHL) – 6'1" 164
HockeyProspect.com Ranking: 197

Fortin is a player who has grown quite a bit since his midget days with the College Esther-Blondin and his style of play has changed as well. Fortin finished his first season in the QMJHL after playing the last two seasons in Midget AAA, ending up with 11 goals and 40 points with the Huskies while playing either on a 2nd or 3rd line.

Fortin was drafted in the 2nd round of the 2013 QMJHL Draft by Rouyn-Noranda, last year he missed a chunk of the season after being injured prior to the 2014 U-17 Hockey Challenge he couldn't attend. Outside of that injury, Fortin was a star in the Quebec Midget AAA league last year, scoring 72 points in 47 games (regular season and playoffs). In midget, he really did a good job using his speed and skill to make things happen offensively. Now he has gotten stronger physically and uses his size more in front of the net to win physical battles and keep possession of the puck down low. In the second half of the season, he started being used by the Rouyn-Noranda coaching staff in front of the net to screen the opposing goaltender. One of the problems with Fortin going back to his midget days was his inconsistency, still a flaw in his game. We would like to see more regularity in his effort from shift to shift; we saw games this year where he was invisible and didn't see enough effort out of him. He tends to be a bit too passive on the ice, it would serve him well to be more active on the forecheck and be more involved on the ice.

Fournier, Jordan Ty
RW – Victoriaville Tigres (QMJHL) – 6'2" 186
HockeyProspect.com Ranking: NR

Fournier is the younger brother of Dillon and Stefan who are both playing professional hockey this season. Jordan is a bit like his older brother Stefan, a rugged winger who can score goals from in close, but will eventually need to upgrade his skating.

Fournier was in his first season with Victoriaville after being selected in the 2nd round by them during the 2013 QMJHL Draft. After playing the last two seasons with the Lac St-Louis Lions, the younger Fournier made his QMJHL debut this season. Jordan is a big body and is tough to contain along the boards, he uses his strength well to power himself to the net. A bit like his older brother Stefan, he does most of his damage offensively from 5 feet to the net. His hands are average and he's not a natural goal scorer. He possesses a good hand-eye coordination to deflect pucks, and he's strong enough to win battles for the puck in front of the net. He lacks overall speed right now, and will need to upgrade his speed and explosiveness on the ice to achieve more success at the QMJHL and pro levels. Jordan plays a power-forward type of game; loves to get involved physically on the forecheck and won't back down if challenged for a fight. In possession of the puck he's a bit of an underrated playmaker; he's able to move the puck quickly to his teammates by making simple and unspectacular plays. Fournier as the size to become a power forward at the next level but not sold he has the skill level to play there, very similar to his older brother Stefan.

Fox, Trent
LC - Belleville Bulls (OHL) 6'02" 190
HockeyProspect.com Ranking: NR

Trent Fox has some tools in his repertoire and has some interesting two-way potential. Fox finishes his checks and likes to get involved physically. He wins his share of puck battles along the wall. Fox protects the puck down low and is tough to get the puck from. He's a solid skater and is confident rushing the puck up ice and into the offensive zone to try and create some offense. Fox has a good net-front presence, in particular on the powerplay. He's an in-your-face-type player and is a good agitator who is capable of chipping in some offense as well. At times he gets carried away physically though and can be prone to taking bad penalties. He also has a tendency to drift off and become a non factor for shifts at a time before re-engaging in the play.

Franzen, Gustaf
RC - Kitchener Rangers (OHL) 5'10" 173
HockeyProspect.com Ranking: NR

Franzen came over from Sweden as one of the top players selected at the 2014 CHL Import Draft. Gustaf is a two-way forward who is very mature on the defensive side of the game. He competes hard in all areas and is relentless in the defensive zone fighting to cause turnovers and taking away options from opponents. He was also a key member of his teams' penalty kill.

Offensively Franzen showed the tools to create plays but lacks in the skating and mobility department, which is so important because of his size, or lack there of. Franzen has decent hands and controls the puck well down low, despite his lack of size. He has good playmaking instincts and vision. On the rush, despite his lack of speed, he has excellent body position and can take the puck end to end, even with a backchecker all over him. Franzen could hear his name called later on in the draft. He's a bubble boy for our top 210.

Quotable: "He's like a much smaller and much less skilled, Gabriel Landeskog." - NHL Scout

Quotable: "Saw him in Lake Placid last summer listed at 6'1" or something like that. It was laughable. Other than that I knew he could help the Rangers. (who list him at 5'10") He's a reliable forward who plays a 200 foot game. He's just too small for me to draft him given what he brings to the table." - Mark Edwards

Freytag, Matthew
LW – Tri-City (USHL) 6'0.75" 195
HockeyProspect.com Ranking: 159

The physically strong winger has put together a nice season in his draft year. He buzzes around the ice as a general thorn in the side of opponents. Freytag is going to come out and compete every night, forcing turnovers and turning them into offensive opportunities. He has displayed a nice scoring touch this season and has shown flashes of playmaking skills. The Wisconsin commit has a great shot and with his work ethic, there is the potential for him to play at the next level. Freytag is worth keeping an eye on but his lack of hockey sense might hold him back for us.

Fronk, Jiri
RW - Cedar Rapids (USHL) 6'1.5" 191
HockeyProspect.com Ranking: NR

Fronk is a '94 birth year who made the jump to the United States this year to play for Cedar Rapids from the Czech Republic to increase his exposure to NHL clubs in his last year of junior eligibility. He burst on to the scene immediately impressing in the USHL preseason. As the year went on, he continued to score goals at an impressive rate and ended up in the top ten in goals in the USHL.

Fronk is a bigger guy but doesn't really use his size as much as we would have liked to see. Consistency is an issue with Fronk as well. Throughout the course of a game, Fronk would have about an even number of shifts with great effort and then half where he took a soft shift and seemed disinterested. In a game late in the season, Cedar Rapids was down three goals in the third period and Fronk looked like he not interested in finishing the game at all which was a bit concerning.

However, Fronk has a laser shot and is a fantastic offensive player. He isn't the best skater but he was at a level above most other players in the USHL and could make opportunities for himself. He sees the ice really well and sees lanes open right away. Based purely on offensive ability, Fronk is a great prospect. It remains to be seen whether or not his play this year impressed NHL clubs enough to take him as a 21 year old in his last eligible draft year.

Gabrielle, Grant
RD – USNTDP (USHL) 6'0.75" 167
HockeyProspect.com Ranking: NR

He is a decent overall D-man who moves the puck well and shows some offensive jump into his game. He isn't a dynamic type blue liner though will rush the puck and jump into the play to create offensive chances. He does not play overly physical though manages the defensive end adequately although could stand to strength up and play a little more consistent in his own end. Think the downfall in his game is at times he struggles out of the gate in games and doesn't play consistent from start to finish. At times he tries to do a little too much and leads to turnovers. He handles the puck adequately and if can simplify and make better decisions on more consistent basis his success will be that much better.

Gabrielle, Jesse
RW – Regina Pats (WHL) – 5'11" 205
HockeyProspect.com Ranking: 84

Jesse Gabrielle is a hard-nosed winger who shared his time this year between the Brandon Wheat Kings and the Regina Pats in the WHL. He is an agitating style of player who finishes his checks, works hard and skates very well for his style of game. Jesse isn't overtly tall, but he's strong and thick and difficult to knock off his feet. He has good hand-eye coordination and is able to connect on one-time opportunities, but more than that, he fights hard to get into scoring areas, has an agitating presence and has some offensive upside.

In addition to being well planted on the ice, Gabrielle has decent hands and skating ability. Even he's a good puck carrier who does a decent job of getting the puck from point A to point B. He has the ability to cut into the middle of the ice and use his skating to get past defenders. In terms of his scoring ability, he excels in close not because of slick hands—although his shot is okay—but because of an ability to fight for space in the prime scoring area. Put simply: he's a pest. Gabrielle is usually able to draw penalties in his team's favour by ignoring the insults, returning a couple of his own, playing a pestilent game near the opposition goaltender and above all, outworking the opposition.

At the end of the season, when coaches and players in the WHL's Eastern Conference were polled on who they thought the conference's "Most Irritating Player" was, Gabrielle won easily with 61 votes (Tanner Eberle finished second with 43).

Gagne, Gabriel
RW – Victoriaville Tigres (QMJHL) – 6'5" 183
HockeyProspect.com Ranking: 45

Gagne was drafted by Moncton in the 2012 QMJHL Draft, but was traded later on to Victoriaville for Philip Danault. Last season, his first season in the league, Gagne had a decent year, making his way on the top-2 lines after starting the year on the 3rd and 4th lines. This season, on a rebuilding Victoriaville team, ice time was not a problem for Gagne and he saw his goal-scoring production make a big jump.

Gagne has tremendous size and has a physical advantage over his opponents; he has a lanky frame and is still filling into it. Definitely needs to keep getting stronger as he would be eligible to play pro hockey during the 2016-2017 season. He does well in puck-protection situations, using his size and reach. Gagne skates well for a big forward and uses his long stride to generate more speed. He does a good job supporting his teammates on both the offensive and defensive sides of the game. With that size, it would be nice to see him be more physical along the boards and win more battles for the puck.

He still needs work on his consistency from game to game, he can fall asleep in some games and lack intensity. He got called out by his head coach this season for this, finding himself a healthy scratch in a game in January due to his lack of intensity. Offensively, Gagne has a nice scoring touch around the net and a very good accurate wrist shot with a quick release. With his scoring potential and size, he should attract interest from NHL teams on draft day, but his lack of consistency is worrisome. Gagne's package is very interesting but he will need to put it all together at some point. He could be an offensive winger at the NHL level if he had more consistency and jam in his game.

Quotable: "One of my viewings was versus Nick Roy in Victoriaville. Gagne easily outplayed Roy that day. He can keep up to the pace of the game so much easier than Roy. Our Q guys questioned his jam and consistency earlier in his career, but in my persoanl viewings it wasn't an issue. I like the upside." - Mark Edwards

Galipeau, Olivier
LD – Val d'Or Foreurs (QMJHL) – 6'1" 201
HockeyProspect.com Ranking: NR

Galipeau was selected by the Foreurs in the first round, 16th overall during the 2013 QMJHL Draft. He participated last summer for Team Canada during the Ivan Hlinka camp but was cut before the start of the tournament. He also played for his province at the 2014 U-17 Hockey Challenge.

Galipeau is a big boy who really enjoys playing a physical game in his own end, one of the best hitters in the QMJHL. He has shown a great ability to read the play coming towards him, also delivering big open-ice hits. He has good timing in his hits. He's also quite mobile and is able to move around the ice pretty well. He has a high compete level and will win most of his battles along the wall or in front of the net. He's at his best when he plays a physical brand of hockey.

This season, Galipeau had some health issues in the first half of the season after missing the start of the season with a concussion and he was injured again in October during a fight. Those injuries did slow his play for a period of time, but he did play solid in the 2nd half of the season. The biggest strength of Galipeau's game are his physical and defensive game, his play with the puck is still a work in progress. He has made some nice improvements during the season in that area but still not enough to consider him as a good puck mover. He makes safe outlet passes out of his zone, not trying any fancy plays with the puck.

His offensive potential is a bit limited. He's a good penalty killer, is not afraid to block shots and has a good active stick blocking passing and shooting lanes. If Galipeau ever makes it at the NHL level it would be as a bottom pairing physical defensemen, his puck skills need a lot of work.

Gardiner, Reid
LW – Prince Albert Raiders (WHL) – 5'11" 185
HockeyProspect.com Ranking: NR

Multidimensional re-entry forward Reid Gardiner of the Prince Albert Raiders is an interesting prospect to follow. Reid went undrafted last year despite good numbers, as he's only mid-sized and average in the manoeuvrability department. To his credit, he's greatly improved his acceleration speed this year, as well as his backwards skating. A decent skater with good vision and tremendous hockey sense, the word that stands out to us when considering Reid Gardiner is, "versatile." He makes tremendously smart reads in all zones and in all situations. He can pass his way to a goal or snipe the puck himself. When your team is behind on the scoreboard, Gardiner can score a goal; when your team is ahead, he can bear down on the opposition and play like a defensive specialist.

As such, he's a natural fit in all situations. He not only is a key fixture on the Raiders penalty kill, but he's also positioned at the point while Prince Albert is on the power play. Although he can play at all three forward positions and usually looks best on the wing because of a fairly traditional north-south style, he is usually entrusted with taking defensive zone draws as his faceoff skills are well above average.

All in all, Gardiner plays an honest 200-foot two-way game. He finishes his checks, blocks shots, fights hard in board battles, provides screens in the offensive zone and plays on the penalty kill and the power play. He absolutely loves dump and chase, chip and chase and all other north-south plays that allow him to shoot the puck into the offensive zone, speed past or through defenders and win the race on his own dump.

Gardiner is a good passer and a good shooter and can create offense passing off of the rush or through the cycle. On the whole, this is a player who isn't the world's greatest natural skater, but one who reads game scenarios very sharply and is versatile enough to play accordingly.

Garland, Conor
RW – Moncton Wildcats (QMJHL) – 5'8" 168
HockeyProspect.com Ranking: 100

Garland is in his 3rd season with the Wildcats after joining the team in 2012-2013 after being selected in the 6th round of the 2012 QMJHL Draft. He went undrafted in last year's NHL Draft after averaging over a point a game. This season, the Scituate, Massachusetts native led the league in scoring by a wide margin, finishing with 129 points. Garland became the first US-born player to win the scoring title in the QMJHL since Pat Lafontaine in 1982-1983.

Garland was Moncton's greatest offensive threat, playing with Ivan Barbashev all year long. They are one of the best (if not the best) duo in the QMJHL this season. Garland is undersized but still able to spin off checks and win battles. He's a very good puck-handler with elusive moves who takes good shots, creating scoring chances for his team. It seems that at times the puck just finds him on the ice, his hockey sense is that excellent.

Standing at only 5'8", Garland's size may be limited, but it doesn't show in games. Garland plays an elusive puck-control game on the wall and moves it quickly to the middle. He's an excellent playmaker, seeing the ice very well and making everyone around him better. In the offensive zone, he always keeps his feet moving, which makes him tough to defend against as he is very active. We would like to see the same effort defensively as sometimes he get caught puck-watching.

The biggest question mark with Garland is how he will make the transition to the pro level, as he will need to get stronger but Johnny Gaudreau and other small players have proven there's a place for small players like Garland in the NHL. At the NHL level Garland would be an offensive winger but also a one dimensional winger, that needs to play on an offensive line.

Gatenby, Joe
RD – Kelowna Rockets (WHL) – 6'00" 176
HockeyProspect.com Ranking: NR

Joe Gatenby is a physical two-way defenseman who played in his draft year on a star-studded hometown Kelowna Rockets club this year. At just below six feet, Gatenby doesn't come at the ideal NHL size. But he remains fairly mobile and possesses a multifaceted game. A decidedly conservative skater, he doesn't usually look like he's very fleet-footed, but can really start chugging if he needs to. Most of the time, however, Gatenby keeps his game simple, remaining calm while waiting to pounce into action with some furious first- and second-steps. In fact, his short-track acceleration in particular, was one of the biggest improvements to his game over the course of the 2014-2015 WHL season.

In addition to his physicality and slightly above-average skating, we really like Gatenby's calmness, anticipation and discipline—qualities that are all best observed while watching him play in his own zone or in the neutral zone. For instance, he's known to throw big and clean open-ice hits at the blueline that usually go unpunished because of the nonchalant manner in with which he throws them.

When defending from within his own blueline, meanwhile, he sometimes maintains a frenetic and chaotic pace when patrolling his own crease, which can make it difficult for the opposition to create plays or to find space with the puck. A fixture on Kelowna's penalty kill, he regularly collects rebounds and makes a strong backhand clearance in tight quarters.

Gatenby is a capable defender but doesn't often have lofty ambitions with the puck on his stick. His passes are simple but dependable. His shot isn't too bad either, as he can light the lamp if left in open space.

Gates, Brent
LC – Green Bay (USHL) 6'1.75" 196
HockeyProspect.com Ranking: 131

Gates season was limited due to injury in 14/15 but was close to a PPG for the Gamblers in his 33 Games. He does his best work in the offensive zone below the faceoff dots and in front of the net. Gates is a big, strong body who will play physical all over the ice. He is strong on pucks and can create scoring chances down low. Gates has a decent first few strides for a player of his build but there certainly is room for improvement in this area. Doesn't hesitate to go to the hard areas and wins a good amount of his 50/50 puck battles. Gates has a heavy shot, likes to use the defender as a screen off the rush and follows up his shot to the net.

Gates is far from a liability in his own end, he competes, blocks shots, picks his spots well to challenge the puck carrier, and has good anticipation on the penalty kill. Gates game took an impressive step forward in his second season in the USHL. He has learned to use his size to his advantage and developed more patients with the puck and it has showed in the spike in his offensive production. Gates has de-committed from Notre Dame and has since committed to the University of Minnesota for 15/16.

Quotable: "Lacks great skating and makes some questionable decisions with the puck, especially in the offensive zone." - HP Scout Justin Schreiber

Gaudette, Adam
RC – Cedar Rapids (USHL) 6'.075" 170
HockeyProspect.com Ranking: 163

A rock solid 2-way center. Gaudette played a more prominent role for the Rough Riders and gained more trust from the coaching staff as the season went along. Adam plays very sound game in all 3 zones. Has good defensive awareness in his own end and does good work on the penalty kill, getting his stick into passing lanes and disrupting plays.

Gaudette doesn't possess great skating ability. Adam is smart in the neutral zone and makes good decisions with the puck. Has the ability to play in any style of game, has the offensive skill and gets up and down the ice in an end to end game, but also can grind and battle in on the fore check in a slower dump and chase style. Adam seems to be a difference maker on a nightly basis, even if it comes to making the simple plays and executing in the faceoff circle. Gaudette will need to fill out his frame to be as effective in a similar checking role at the upcoming levels and can get muscled off the puck at times, however his willingness to battle for pucks and uses his smarts help him in those situations. Gaudette is scheduled to be off to Northeastern (NCAA) in 16/17 so he will have the opportunity to take on a more prominent offensive role in Cedar Rapids next season.

Gavrikov, Vladislav
LD – Loko (MHL) – 6'2.5" 205
HockeyProspect.com Ranking: 103

Last year we had Gavrikov ranked right at the start of the 5th round, but no NHL teams felt comfortable enough on spending a pick on this Russian defenseman. This should change this time around, as Vladislav was the leader of the Russian team at the WJC and showed what he can do under intense pressure in North American rinks. He carried his team defense and was rock solid throughout the tournament, so much that he was elected as the best defenseman of the competition. Gavrikov reads the game well and consistently makes the safe play. He works hard along the boards and in front of the net. He has improved his physical game, has added further mass to his frame and he uses his increased strength much more consistently than in the past. Bulking up might have taken away a bit from his nice mobility, but he still is above average in that department, especially for a big kid. His skating paired with his reach makes him difficult to play against, as he doesn't allow room on the defensive blueline.

During the season he made his first appearances at the KHL level in a very limited role, but even when back in juniors he didn't try to impact the game with the puck as we would like. He can use his mobility to join the offense when he sees open ice on the weak side of the defense, but if he doesn't get used to carry the puck more and transition it he will remain a one dimensional player.

Gibson, Stephen
RD - Mississauga Steelheads (OHL) 6'02" 197
HockeyProspect.com Ranking: NR

Gibson received a handful of games last season as a 16 year old but got full time duty on the Steelheads' blueline this season. Stephen has good size and is a very good skater at 6'2". He always keeps his feet moving. However, he can sometimes get a little too risky with his attempts to hold the offensive zone and needs to learn to read when it's better to get back into position. His positional awareness was a problem in most viewings. Sometimes he wasn't aware of who was around, him which had some negative results in his own end. He has size and contains decently but doesn't have much aggression and needs to utilize his size as a tool for his success. He projects as a simple shutdown defenseman but will need to improve many aspects of his game, including his decision making before having a legitimate shot at being an NHL prospect.

Gawdin, Glenn
RC – Swift Current Broncos (WHL) – 6'00" 191
HockeyProspect.com Ranking: 98

Gawdin provided secondary scoring for the Broncos on a fairly consistent basis all year long. Glenn has an attractive set of skills and a good raw package. His skating looks ugly but he gets around without issues. What we really like is his competitiveness, playmaking ability and scoring drive.

Gawdin can stickhandle through traffic very well and doesn't mind occupying space in which he has to be crashed and banged—can therefore manufacture zone entries both by carrying and dumping the puck. He can also plant himself in front of the net in order to gain second-chance opportunities. Once in the offensive zone, the staple of Glenn Gawdin's game is his playmaking skill. He's a very talented passer with excellent all-zones awareness and a good teammate when it comes to supporting others during puck battles in dangerous areas. He's especially good in competitive board battles and then calmly distributing the puck back to the point to keep the offensive alive or cycling it down low maintaining possession. In his own zone, he similarly works hard when defending down low in his own zone, where he shows a penchant for collecting loose pucks and sending them up-ice quickly.

Quotable:" I like his playmaking ability but I'd like to see him shoot the puck more. He passes up too many shooting opportunities trying to make higher risk fancy plays." - Mark Edwards

Gennaro, Matteo
LW – Prince Albert Raiders (WHL) – 6'02" 187
HockeyProspect.com Ranking: 202

Matteo Gennaro is a tall and rangy playmaking centre plying his trade with the Prince Albert Raiders. Highly touted coming into the 2014-2015 campaign, Gennaro had a tough draft year. First he had an underwhelming performance at the Ivan Hlinka Memorial Tournament, then he had a rough first half to his season—initially going six games without a point and then ten, before being relegated altogether to a bottom line centre role at the mid-season. To top it all off, he was snubbed from the World Under-18 Hockey Championships despite a significant statistical rebound at the tail end of his year. Despite all of his disappointments in his draft season, he has a unique ability to make things appear from nothing with minimal effort.

Gennaro's a bit of a one-way player, whose backchecking leaves much to be desired—even when forechecking, Gennaro doesn't accelerate to top-speed very quickly. He's lanky in the lower-body, which helps; and he has that extra gear as he'll show here and there, but he rarely puts it into motion. Where he really excels is in stickhandling. When the puck is firmly on the blade of his stick, he regularly exhibits tremendous sleight of hand abilities. For instance, he puts really good deception on an accurate wristshot, as he can pick his shots low or high and employs a number of tricky release points. He's also a good no-look passer, who makes magical looking reads in terms of vision and playmaking. Generally very well positioned and blessed with tremendous range, he has an ability to snag pucks from just about anywhere.

Gennaro tends to be a bit of a riverboat gambler—too often trying to make the impossible cross-crease pass or deke move, rather than trying to make the most simple and effective play available. His pass reception ability looked questionable at times too this season. If he can improve by making serious changes to his defensive game and consistency level, we see no reason why he isn't worth taking a chance on at some point in the draft.

Gilbert, Dennis
LD - Chicago (USHL) 6'2.25" 201
HockeyProspect.com Ranking: 104

GIlbert, a Notre Dame commit, is a guy who really established himself as the season went on and has garnered quite a bit of NHL Draft attention at this point.

Gilbert is very good skater, especially for someone of his size. His footwork and speed are at an elite level for a defenseman standing at 6'2". He isn't afraid to jump in on the rush and is calm, cool, and collected with the puck on his stick. He made the jump from the OJHL this year to the Steel and didn't skip a beat. Gilbert is an offensively minded defenseman but he plays a sound two-way game. He is far from a liability in his own zone and the coaching staff displayed a ton of confidence in Gilbert throughout the year putting him on the ice in all situations. Gilbert makes some very solid decisions with the puck as far as carrying it or making slick outlet passes to get the rush going. That said, at times he just relies more on his physical traits rather than thinking the game. He is a very confident player that did progress well throughout the year.

Quotable: "I don't think his head matches his tools." - NHL Scout

Quotable: "His footwork is incredible to watch for a junior player at his size. He has a bright future as most of his physical tools are already at an NHL caliber. He will be a fun player to watch climb up the ranks through his career." Justin Schreiber

Godla, Denis
G – Slovakia U20 (SVK) – 5'11" 176
HockeyProspect.com Ranking: NR

Godla made a strong statement at this year's World Junior Championship. He is a gritty competitor in the crease and never gives up. Despite not being over 6-foot, Denis plays a big game. When he butterflies, he remains big and doesn't slouch, allowing him to seal the ice well. He tracks the puck well into his blocker and glove. Godla can be too aggressive with his poke checks, which can open up holes on him, he needs to time them better. On quick lateral passes from his left to right, he struggles pivoting into the butterfly slide, which results in his chest flattening on the ice and him sticking his right leg out in desperation. This is unique as most left-handed catching goalies struggle with this on passes going in the opposite direction, because they fail to bring their stick with them. Coming off his post, he fills the middle well and likes to play on the top of his crease. Good skater and light on his feet, qualities that allow him to square up to pucks efficiently. Needs more seasoning and maturing, but there is potential.

Greenway, Jordan
LW – USNTDP (USHL) 6'4.75" 222
HockeyProspect.com Ranking: 72

Teams are drawn to the older Greenway because he has good size and strength to his game. There are times that he can put on dominating performance and then will go stretches whereby he looks to lack the desire to compete. He has pretty good speed, mobility for a big body as can play a physical style as well as showing offensive side. The stick skills are not high-end fashion though good as he can shoot with authority and create havoc out front, along the wall, in the corner on the forecheck, and pretty nice hands in tight for big guy. When he plays with aggressiveness and takes pucks to the net is when he is most effective, especially below the dots. If he doesn't engage physically his game is transparent. The hockey awareness is decent yet not an asset that is exceptional. Although he does show some vision with the puck to create plays. If he could put it all together he could be a dominating player as possesses great athletic ability along with size and strength. Perhaps attending Boston University will help grow his game although overall his game has taken a hit from start to finish of the season in regards to draft stock.

Quotable: " Never seems to put it all together." - NHL Scout

Quotable: " I thought Greenway was one of the top performers at the All American Prospects game. The problem, at least for me, was it was the best I saw him all year long. Greenway has tools that the NHL teams drool over but he was unable to put it all together. A few scouts told me they were a bit wary of off ice work ethic as well but I can't confirm if that's an issue." - Mark Edwards

Greer, A.J.
LW – Boston University (HOCKEY EAST) – 6'2.5" 204
HockeyProspect.com Ranking: 70

As a very young freshman for college hockey standards, he didn't have the offensive production that some scouts would have liked in his draft year. He accelerated his last year of high school to join the Terriers a year early after de-committing from Penn State. Going up against players much older than him, he proved that he was strong on his skates and had the physical maturity to hold on to pucks and win battles behind the net and along the boards even from the beginning of the season. There were flashes during the regular season, but he elevated his game down the stretch and was rewarded with a spot on the second line and more ice time. Three of his seven points were scored over the last five games of the season. He has a quick release and a hard shot. He's not a finesse type player that can stick handle and skate around opposing defensemen, but he's a bull that can get the puck and get it on net.

Quotable: " I heard some NHL Scouts say they were down on him but I think the kid needs to be cut a little slack. He probably shouldn't have been in Boston this year and he still managed to hang in there. I thought he had some good performances, especially finishing off his draft year." - Mark Edwards

Gropp, Ryan
LW – Seattle Thunderbirds (WHL) – 6'02" 187
HockeyProspect.com Ranking: 62

Ryan Gropp of the Seattle Thunderbirds is yet another of many physically mature power forwards available out of the WHL in time for the 2015 NHL Entry Draft. Like Paul Bittner, another 2015-eligible forward plying his trade with the divisional rival Portland Winterhawks, Gropp has a late-1996 birthdate and made a splash last year as a sophomore with his club, making him one of the more physically developed and well-known prospects out of the region. In his first season with the Thunderbirds in 2013-2014, Gropp put up really good rookie numbers playing on a line with Alexander Delnov and Dallas Stars 2012 draft pick Brandon Troock.

One other thing we love about Ryan Gropp is he can score from just about anywhere in the offensive zone. That's thanks to incredible speed, a strong presence, fantastic stick skills, a wonderful long-range shot that has a deceptive release. While he can strike from anywhere rather unexpectedly, you're most likely to see Ryan Gropp working hard most of the game, chugging up-and-down the wing and playing a fairly simple north-to-south game. He loves shooting while coming down the wing. If he had a bit more of a presence in the slot, a more consistent net-drive and crashed into the mesh more often, he'd almost certainly be putting up more points in the WHL.
We like that Gropp elevated his game in the absence of Matthew Barzal following the latter players' injury. On the other hand, on the whole our staff expected a bit more of a jump in terms of his statistical production and offensive consistency this year.

Grzelewski, Zach
LW - London Knights (OHL) 5'10" 197
HockeyProspect.com Ranking: NR

Despite getting cut by the London Knights in training camp and starting the season with St. Thomas Stars Jr. B, Grzelewski never gave up and posted two points per game and over a goal per game in Jr. B before being recalled by the Knights. Once called up he continued his good play providing an excellent forecheck and hard nosed play, finishing his checks whenever he could. A decent skater, he also displayed good playmaking ability and a fairly strong shot. While we don't expect Grzelewski to be selected this season, his impressive upswing this season is encouraging and if he continues this trend, he could earn himself a few looks as a re-entry player down the road.

Quotable: "Not enough to his game at 5'10" to consider him as a draftable prospect for me at this point of his career. I did like how he played at the OHL level this year though." - Mark Edwards

Guhle, Brendan
LD – Prince Albert Raiders (WHL) – 6'02" 179
HockeyProspect.com Ranking: 64

Brendan Guhle of the Prince Albert Raiders is a tall and lanky offensive defenseman who is still very raw. He is blessed with an attractive skillset with lots of room for improvement. He loves to drive down low, as his passing and shooting skills are above average and his skating is also a strength. He's very good at both giving and receiving passes. Both his slapshot and wristshot are sufficiently strong and extremely accurate. On the man advantage, usually playing from the left half-wall, he displays very good puck distribution skills and a series of shooting options that he can put high or low onto the net. A good skater with all-directional manoeuvrability, Guhle was an important part of generating offense in Prince Albert.
On the surface, Guhle brings everything to the table you're looking for in a two-way defenseman—he's big, he skates well and he has good awareness in all three zones. He can skate or pass the puck out of his zone effectively. His first passes are generally unremarkable, but he causes very few turnovers. While navigating the offensive blueline, he blasts strong slapshots from the point and accurate wristshots from down low, as he's definitely more of a shooter than a passer. He has the requisite skating chops so as to not be caught behind the play too often when roving down low, but

pinches regularly enough that he's bound to cause a few two-on-ones for the opposition here and there.

Dig a little deeper into the scouting report of Brendan Guhle and a few holes and question marks begin to appear. While he's big and tall, he appears to lack muscle-mass on his lanky frame, as he's easily stood-up on zone-entry attempts and is too easily knocked off the puck or off balance in the corners. From what we've seen, he's not one for delivering hits either. Nonetheless, there are traits to like here. It's not unusual for Guhle to lead his team in shots by the end of a game. We would like to see him improve defensive awareness and overall decision making.

Quotable: "I really liked him at the Top Prospects game but he's one of those guys that the more I watched, the less I liked him. He seems to have all the tools but doesn't get enough out of his talent. He struggles to avoid getting hammered by opposing forwards and makes some questionable decisions with the puck." - NHL Scout

Guryanov, Denis
RW – Ladya (MHL) 6'2.5" 183
HockeyProspect.com Ranking: 16

Guryanov is a left shooting right winger with an arsenal of impressive weapons at his disposal. A great skater, when the opportunity arises Guryanov showcases impressive acceleration and top speed. He likes to challenge the defensemen coming through the neutral zone and possesses a very quick release on a powerful wrister. Off the rush he becomes a double threat as he can beat defensemen wide or use his shot if given little space. His shots selection could be improved, as sometimes he seems content firing long range wristers instead of trying to attack the net like he shows to be capable of in other occurrences. Even if this season he has been showing more of a shoot-first mentality, Guryanov's playmaking skills are more than adequate, like he shows when he promptly finds from peripheral areas teammates getting open in the slot. His good vision doesn't save him from occasionally trying to get through opponents in the neutral zone when easier and safer options are available, but overall he shows good understanding of when it's time to challenge one on one or time to share the puck. What he should do more often though is circle back waiting for teammates' support when the opponents' defensive pairing his already set.

The main thing separating Guryanov from most other prospects is how fast he can move around the ice, his first step is very good for his frame and his speed paired with his reach makes him a real threat anytime there is a loose puck in the neutral zone. As he tries to maximize his offensive opportunities, Denis is frequently caught leaving his zone too early. He also shows some lazyness in his zone, when he watches the play rather using his tools to try to get the puck. Inconsistency is definitely an issue, as his efforts can look completely different from one period to the following one. Still, when he feels like giving his best he can backcheck like few other scoring wingers can do, and if an NHL team ever manages to convince him to do that on a consistent basis he has the potential to become a rare kind of two-way weapon. Guryanov is no stranger to the physical play either, he actually likes to hit with speed and his exhuberance leads to some unorthodox hits. He is a quick stickhandler and depending on how much time he has, he can use his wrister, his snap shot or powerful slapper, both off the rush or on the powerplay. Accuracy may have room for improvement, but his shots are powerful and dangerous most of the times. Guryanov has probably shown too much potential to fall in the draft because of his nationality and current shortcomings.

Quotable: " I heard really good reports on him as far as his interviews at the combine in Buffalo. Not one scout I spoke to gave him a bad review. In fact, a few raved about him. I was really happy to hear that he's a good kid" - Mark Edwards

Quotable: " I really think this kid has the talent to match-up with the top end guys in the draft. The thing holding me back from ranking him in my top 10 is some laziness in his game. The rub is that it's not consistent laziness, it just shows up once in a while but enough to scare me a little bit. His skating and shot are fantastic and he has a knack for getting himself in position to score. He's a dangerous player who can score out of nowhere. Not elite hockey sense IMO, but he's not hockey dumb." - Mark Edwards

Quotable: " Typical F****** Russian." - NHL Scout

Quotable: " For what it's worth, the typical F***** Russian quote by an NHL Scout was made after the Five Nations tourney. Made me laugh, but the kid is really good so it fell on deaf ears as far as I was concerned." - Mark Edwards

Quotable: " You know what passport he holds right? (said to Mark Edwards after he praised him for a one-timer during game action at the U18)" - NHL Scout

Hall, Austin
RD - Guelph Storm (OHL) 6'00" 190
HockeyProspect.com Ranking: NR

Hall is an above average skater who showed mobility in all directions. Reading situations faster would best help Austin utilize his skating ability. He is capable of completing good passes but sometimes doesn't read passing lanes well and gives up a turnover trying to force the puck through a lane that has been taken away. He has also been caught on a few occasions putting the puck over the glass for penalties. He's willing to take the hit to make the play and will engage physically but will need to get stronger in order to make more of an impact in this department. Austin is caught in limbo projection wise, because he's not strong enough defensively to be a shutdown defender, but lacks the offensive instincts to project as an offensive defenseman. Although this is his rookie season in the OHL and he has room to improve we currently do not consider Austin as a prospect for the 2015 NHL Entry Draft.

Halladay, Logan
G - Bloomington (USHL) 6'0.75" 194
HockeyProspect.com Ranking: NR

Halladay moved into the USHL for his first full season in the league after playing for the Janesville Jets of the NAHL the year before. While he struggled throughout the year for Bloomington, the team in front of him didn't allow him to post fantastic numbers, and there is still a lot of potential that has yet to be realized. Halladay is a really good puck handler and competes hard. It's obvious he cares a lot about the game and might even be considered too intense to the point where he lets goals against affect him too much. He will need to continue to develop next year with Bloomington in quieting his game and getting better at reacting to shots. He will head to the University of Minnesota in 2016.

Hanifin, Noah
LD - Boston College (H-East) 6'2" 203
HockeyProspect.com Ranking: 4

What draws your eyes to Hanifin besides his size is his pure skating and mobility. He has a great stride and handles the puck very well for a young defenseman. He seems to play the back end with great confidence and poise. He likes to wheel the on the patented back peddle in his own zone or to the defensive blue line and then wheel the puck up the ice, always with his head up. We can tell he likes to see the ice from this vantage point and has been doing for a while in his career with success. While this is effective, as he can lead the rush at the NHL level, he will need to train himself to be more of a puck mover at times.

He has a very good crossover and quick feet and this asset will be key for his future NHL success. We like that he leads or will join the rush to create offense. He will make the accurate outlet passes and quickly transition the puck. He also does a god job from the offensive blue line in getting pucks to the net as he quickly releases and also finds the lanes by changing position and stick, again relating back to his strong skating and agility.

While he had decent offensive success on the score sheet as a true freshman in the NCAA ranks there are times when he can finish the play more with a shot or pass that leads to a goal instead of at times not following through completely on the play. This sometimes occurs on the defensive side of the puck too as he will close the gap on opponents but needs to find that killer shut down, physicality style especially for the NHL. He will sacrifice and block shots, we'd just like to see more of total defense first mentality then quickly ready to jump on the horse for the offensive rush.

It's not that he leaves the zone prematurely, more the 1-on-1 situations along the wall and in the corners that you want Hanifin to utilize his strength more and come out with the puck. He is also a very heads up player so there are so many aspects to his game to work with and he is on the cusp of being NHL ready. Overall, another year at Boston College will not hurt the blossoming D-man to round out his defensive side and continue to gain more success on the offensive side.

Quotable: "His skating is very, very good especially the backward skating. He is probably has the best mobility for defensemen in this year's draft class. His ability to wheel and handle the puck at high speed will in itself make him successful." - HP Scout Russ Bitely

Quotable: "I think he made big strides defensively this season. Hanifin is one of those players that makes the game look easy. The way he moves on the ice and can create offense using his feet. He's a future star player, some work to improve his shot will help him on the scoresheet going forward. It's not bad but if he can make his shot more of a weapon, look out." - Mark Edwards

Hansson, Petter
LD – Linkoping (SWE Jr.) – 6'1" 187
HockeyProspect.com Ranking: 181

A '96 born defenseman that probably no NHL team considered to draft in his first year of eligibility, Hansson put his name on the map this season after a successful campaign at the U20 level earned him some SHL action with Linkoping.

Petter has legit size and nice mobility, to go along with pretty good hands. He is a puck moving defenseman who likes to carry the puck while looking for his forwards through the neutral zone. He seems better at connecting with his forwards than with his defensive partner. He has a good reach and he effectively makes use of it both defensively and with the puck. Without the puck Hansson likes to anticipate the play, which sometimes brings him out of position. Other than in those occasions, he usually does a decent job in front of his net. He makes his mark in the offensive zone during powerplay time, as he looks comfortable managing the offensive blueline and shows no hesitation when given the opportunity to shoot. Possesses a good looking and fairly personal one-timer.

His game is a work in progress, and the fact way too often he ends up falling down to the ice only adds to that feeling, but because of his progression and skills Hansson is an intriguing prospect.

Harding, Sam
RC - Oshawa Generals (OHL) 5'11" 170
HockeyProspect.com Ranking: NR

Sam was a player who looked to be on the verge of breaking out as a 16 year old for the Generals and while he did improve his goal totals, he really didn't hit the peaks he was expected to this season. Sam is a strong skating forward with good speed. He gets up and down the ice very well. He is positionally sound and can jump on opportunities in the goal area. He is also effective at deflecting the puck.

He has the moves to beat defenders one on one and can be slippery to control. He plays a full 200 foot game and even got some action on the penalty kill where he showed a willingness to block shots. Harding struggled in the face-off circle in our viewings. Sam will need to get stronger and regain the upside he showed in Minor Midget and his first season with the Generals in order to become the prospect he could be.

Harkins, Jansen
LC – Prince George Cougars (WHL) – 6'01" 182
HockeyProspect.com Ranking: 34

Jansen Harkins is a creative playmaking centre who plays an up-tempo game for the Prince George Cougars in the WHL. His game exudes competitiveness and hockey sense, as there is great continuity to his movement, accentuated by intense explosiveness and breakaway speed at unexpected but advantageous moments. He blocks shots and has an active stick away from the puck. He wins faceoffs and works hard in all situations.

As a 17 year old, Harkins really carried the Cougars' offense and helped lead them to a playoff appearance this season. He's a natural playmaker possessing a multitude of ways to create offense for his teammates. He cycles the puck well and knows where to go with the puck in the offensive zone. He also is effective going to the net taking up space and deflecting pucks on goal. He is also very strong defensively and a regular on the Cougars' penalty kill.

Harkins has good upside and skates very well with size to protect the puck with. This combination of size and skating has allowed him to possess the puck for lengthy periods of time, where he has been able to create offense and draw penalties. While he is usually pass first, his shot shows potential but will need to get the accuracy down in order to up his scoring totals. Harkins has the upside of a two-way centre at the NHL level who doesn't have high end offensive potential, but does have the potential to contribute well at both ends of the ice.

Quotable: "He's a player. Love his game. The more you watch him, the more you appreciate what he brings." - NHL Scout

Quotable: "His skating scares me a bit. I don't see separation ability." – NHL Scout

Quotable: "He's a real honest player. I see him as a 3rd or 4th liner. He's smart, I'd like him to get heavier." NHL Scout

Quotable: "Good player who I thought was kind of average in Switzerland so he finished on a bit of a downward trend for me." – Mark Edwards

Haudum, Lukas
RW – Sodertalje (SWE Jr.) – 5'11" 176
HockeyProspect.com Ranking: NR

An Austrian forward who played this past season in Sweden, Haudum certainly can't be confused with a Swede for his somatic features, but his play on the ice actually resembles the way your typical Swedish forwards play the game. Responsible, technically sound, he backchecks consistently and is most of the times very well positioned in the defensive zone. Lukas has good puck skills but is not a flashy player, even if his skating is a bit more dynamic than it may look at first glance, as he shows when he has the chance to jump on loose pucks. We would like to see him being more consistently proactive on the offensive side of the game, but when the right opportunity arises he shows that he has more to offer than just steady play. He is not someone who may lead his line offensively, more of a good complimentary player that can contribute in all areas with his smarts. He was effective in international competition this season and a strong showing in a live viewing in Asiago at the U20 Div.I World Championships helped his case. His potential needs to be tested in higher level contests, but he reads the game well and quickly recognizes opportunities.

Henderson, Jacob
RW – Omaha (USHL) 6'2.5" 203
HockeyProspect.com Ranking: NR

Henderson, a Providence University commit is a big body on the ice but tends to shy away from using his size to his advantage. Too often he tries to make the pretty play happen while lacking the skill to do so instead of using his size advantage over most players in the USHL. Skating is a big question mark at this point, his stride is a little odd and his footwork will definitely need to improve at the next level. He has average hands and an average shot but nothing that will jump off the ice at you. He is certainly an interesting prospect due to his size and offensive potential. Teams may look at him as a project and he might get a few good looks come June.

Henley, David
LD – Charlottetown Islanders (QMJHL) – 6'4" 203
HockeyProspect.com Ranking: NR

Henley was acquired last season by Charlottetown from Val-d'Or for Ryan Graves. Months earlier, Henley was picked 8th overall in the 2013 QMJHL Draft by the Foreurs. Henley also played last year at the World Under-17 Hockey Challenge for his province in Cape-Breton.

Henley is a big defenseman that usually plays on a 2nd or 3rd pairing on the Islanders' blueline. The Val-d'Or native is a defenseman who likes to play rough in front of the net and along the boards. He definitely has a mean streak and won't back down from the opposing team. Not afraid to use his stick as well to hack guys in front of the net and make their life difficult. He's more of a stay-at-home defenseman, as he struggles with moving the puck out of his zone and his decision-making with the puck is poor. He's useful on the penalty kill due to his long stick, ability to block shots and clear the front of the net. He plays with a lot of grit and uses his size to win puck battles. Henley possesses a big slapshot from the point, but lacks accuracy to hit the net on a regular basis. He's not overly creative with the puck in the offensive zone, but saw some time on the power play during the season and this was mostly to utilize said big shot from the point. He lacks agility, as quite a few times we saw him get beaten wide by quick skaters. He lacks good footwork and that has hurt him so far at the QMJHL level: not being able to contain those speedy forwards. We don't feel Henley will get drafted this year, not enough puck skills and smarts out of him.

Quotable: " If nothing else, it entertains me talking to our Q scout Jerome Berube about him. I don't think he's Jerome's favourite player." - Mark Edwards

Henley, Troy
RD - Saginaw Spirit (OHL) 5'11" 192
HockeyProspect.com Ranking: NR

After a rookie season in Ottawa last year where he struggled to get minutes, Henley was expected to play a bigger role this year. He unfortunately struggled out of the gate and was traded to the Saginaw Spirit fairly early in the season. Henley took on a depth role on the Spirit third pairing for the majority of the season and his development has seemed to stall.

Troy's skating is decent and he was noted very consistently to be very tough to beat in one on one situations with an excellent stick, not trying to do too much just shutting down the play. His positioning deeper in the zone is good, which allowed him to do fairly well along the boards. However, his reaction time can be a little hit or miss below the hashmarks which was our biggest area of concern. We saw some poor decisions resulting in scoring chances and/or goals against. One of his most admiral aspects is his willingness to block shots. He was consistently noted for blocking multiple shots and will sacrifice himself for the success for his team.

While we don't expect him to be selected at the 2015 NHL Entry Draft, Henley is a defensive first shutdown defenseman. He still has some potential and would really benefit from growing about three inches which is unlikely at this point of his development.

Quotable: " I really liked Henley in his OHL draft season and we had him ranked as a 1st rounder for that draft. I've been surprised at how poorly he has played thus far in his OHL career. On a positive note, I've heard nothing but great things about him as far as off ice goes. Hopefully he puts it all together next season." - Mark Edwards

Herbst, Liam
G - Ottawa 67's (OHL) 6'04" 195
HockeyProspect.com Ranking: NR

Herbst was given an opportunity to take over the starting role for the 67's who are very young between the pipes and he was able to take a little over 50% of the workload. Herbst does an good job of challenging the shooter and is generally in very good position for the initial shot. He rarely gets beat on the first shot of a developing play. He has a huge frame and doesn't leave much for shooters to fire at.

While he is effective at making that first save, it's what happens afterwards that gives us cause for concern. His rebound control needs improvement and it's something that got him in trouble because of his lack of recovery skills. He is also a little slow to react to freeze loose pucks in his crease. His lateral agility is still a major concern for him and hasn't improved it enough since returning from injury. He sometimes spends too much time on his knees after the first shot when he should be standing back up and getting back into position. Herbst was a high end goaltending prospect in Minor Midget, but his lateral movement and rebound control both need to see significant improvement before he can legitimately start reaching the potential he once had pre-injury.

Quotable: "He seems to be living off his Top Prospects game but he's not on my personal draft list. He can't move." - NHL Scout

Quotable: "He let in a bad goal every time I saw him." - NHL Scout

Quotable: "He's not a player I would draft. Every game I saw him play he struggled to move laterally. He simply couldn't get across to make second saves. I saw him in AAA and he was great but the injuries seemed to have taken their toll on his mobility." - Mark Edwards

Hill, Adin
G – Portland Winterhawks (WHL) – 6'03" 181
HockeyProspect.com Ranking: 154

After showing well in a handful of games last season, Adin Hill took over the starting role and has his sights set on being a re-entry selection at the 2015 NHL Entry Draft. Despite some rocky showings and some inconsistent efforts, Hill was able to steal some games for Portland with some impressive performances.

Hill stands out as a tall, aggressive and alert butterfly goaltender who is capable of making some unexpected highlight reel saves from his butterfly or when shifting wildly from side-to-side. When standing stationary—which is rare—Adin Hill is usually well positioned and extremely aggressive. Due to his size and aggressive positioning, he doesn't leave a lot of holes open in net. Those holes that are left open are quickly closed off thanks to sharp instincts—his blocker-hand is very quick and he loves flashing the leather on the side of the net.

Additionally, his size allows him to sprawl across the ice and cover a remarkable amount of the lower net. He's acrobatic and powerful enough to lift his legs far up in the air, making him difficult to beat even when he looks down and out. His puck movement is some of the best we've seen in the WHL as far as 2015-eligible goaltenders are concerned. He has a tendency to try to do too much and gets sucked out of position when he's becoming overtly excited.

His combination of size, speed, hockey sense and athleticism gives him some intriguing upside leading into the 2015 NHL Entry Draft, despite the lack of consistency in his game by game viewings.

Hintz, Roope
C-LW – Ilves (Fin elite) – 6'2" 183
HockeyProspect.com Ranking: 44

Hintz is big and smart center who has great hockey sense. Roope plays a very mature game for his age and he's already on his way physically with his bi frame. Skating is really good. his skating technique is solid. Hintz reads the game well and he can really find the right passing lanes on ice. He could use his shot more and play a more North American style hockey. Roope handles the puck well in small places and he can protect the puck very well with his good balance and size.

Hintz looks like a really good 3rd liner NHL wise with a chance to move higher in the lineup if he can develop more as far as scoring offense goes. We were a bit surprised that we didn't hear more positive reviews about him when talking to NHL scouts. The general theme seemed to be "I liked him but…". We always have a certain amount of love for players with high hockey IQ's and Roope falls into that category. He does all the little things well, taking proper angles, great stick position, solid overall positioning plus great skating ability packed in a 6'2" frame.

Quotable: "The thing that stood out for me about Hintz was that he's a very smart player, especially defensively. He understands team concepts and executes them on the ice. He reads opposing players well, anticipating developing plays and being in position to thwart the attack. Offensively he made me feel like he is on the verge of 'getting it' but it hasn't happened yet. He makes good passes, will drive the net and go to dirty areas but I haven't seen him flash that top six offensive ability you hope to see. He uses his smarts to help create offense and does make teammates better." - Mark Edwards

Quotable: "I got a couple reports from scouts that he wasn't one of their better interviews at the combine." - Mark Edwards

Quotable: "His hotel room was across the hall from me in Montreal for one night (World Junior) and I can happily report that there was no wild party or any other noise keeping me up." - Mark Edwards

Hobbs, Connor
LD – Regina Pats (WHL) – 6'00" 187
HockeyProspect.com Ranking: NR

Connor Hobbs is a two-way defenceman with the Regina Pats. He also saw some action this season with the Nipawin Hawks in the SJHL after leaving the Medicine Hat Tigers prior to a trade with the Pats. He also made an appearance at the World Junior A Championships in Kindersley.

Hobbs's footwork isn't terrible by any means, but he can get caught behind the play sometimes and looks a little clumsy and confused here and there. He can sometimes be a little too aggressive at the wrong times which gets his caught out of position. This also occurred in one on one match-up's on the rush, resulting in Hobbs giving up the inside lane to forwards a little too easily. He made a fair amount of minor mental mistakes, which sometimes lead to bigger issues.
When defending his own end, Hobbs does a great job of not giving up on plays and is really tenacious in the corners. He only wins about half of his puck battles, but you can see that he has the willingness and puck sense to potentially win more if he gets bigger. His hitting skills and physicality are very good, as he commits a lot of power and energy into his bodychecking. He's fairly good at sweeping guys out from in front of his net, a skill that should develop along with added muscle, strength and experience. Still fairly average in terms of his manoeuvrability and reach, he's an easy player to underestimate at first sight.

Hobbs shows a willingness to give 100% and leave it all on the ice. Hockey sense concerns along with decision making leaves us weary of his overall upside. Hobbs will need to continue learning when to make the smart play and when to take his chances in order to maximize his potential.

Hodgson, Hayden
RW - Sarnia Sting (OHL) 6'02" 212
HockeyProspect.com Ranking: NR

Hodgson is a big power forward who was passed over at the 2014 NHL Entry Draft. He was a player who possessed a lot of potential, however watching him closely this season, certain areas of his game simply didn't develop the way it needed to for him to be successful. He has a physical mindset and can be tough to play against because of his strength and ability to finish his hits hard. Hodgson also has an excellent release on his shot and is a very dangerous shooter. His playmaking ability has room for improvement and with good purpose, he is a shoot first player.

Defensively he backchecks hard and competes, winning battles. His skating really hasn't improved very much which was a key area for improvement for him. He is also not very positionally sound which sometimes takes away his ability to utilize his shot. He is a guy who can get visibly frustrated on the ice, which throws him off his game. He also had a habit of trying to sell penalties that players of his size aren't going to win a lot of calls on. Hodgson was an invite to Detroit Red Wings camp last season and could receive the same kind of consideration this year however we don't expect him to be selected at the 2015 NHL Entry Draft.

Quotable:" I liked him last year and if we had one more pick we may have drafted him." - NHL Scout

Quotable:" I saw him a lot late last season and he was great. I saw him in pre-season this year and he played very solid as well. It ended there. He never made me think of him as a draftable prospect again all season." - Mark Edwards

Holmes, Michael
LD - Saginaw Spirit (OHL) 6'03" 192
HockeyProspect.com Ranking: NR

After showing a lot of promise in his Minor Midget season, Holmes had a very quiet rookie season in Saginaw. This trend continued for most of the season in his sophomore year, but for the final two months or so he started to really show the promise that was seen in him in pre-OHL action.

Holmes has excellent natural size and a frame that he will be able to build onto. He is a very good skater for his size but doesn't utilize it offensively. Instead he keeps it pretty simple with high percentage first passes. He picks his spots on when to send a longer, more difficult pass and under pressure he shows the ability to chip the puck out without sending it for an icing. He has a good shot from the point but can occasionally shoot into shinpads. Holmes is not overly physical but showed a willingness to play tough down low. He's good in one on one situations while occasionally getting beat. Holmes has a high ceiling for potential but has yet to develop into a clear-cut NHL prospect so there would be some risk with the potential reward of selecting Holmes.

Quotable:" Tough player to figure out. I would just start to like him and he would do something to scare me off again." - NHL Scout

Quotable:" He was really good in a couple of my viewings. He's one of those guys with size that you want to like. He made some really awful decisions in one of my viewings late in the season. In a year where the OHL lacks depth, I was intrigued to see him play." - Mark Edwards

Huether, Kenny
RW - Oshawa Generals (OHL) 5'09" 170
HockeyProspect.com Ranking: NR

Kenny spent much of his rookie season in the OHL on the fourth line for the Oshawa Generals but did a very good job contributing in his role. He is a high energy forward who has an excellent compete level and never quit attitude. Despite his size he lands solid hits with good impact and is a very tough player to play against. Whether it's on the forecheck or the backcheck, Huether is all over his opponent forcing turnovers.

He has some decent moves with the puck and is capable of putting it in the back of the net. We don't see Huether being selected in the 2015 NHL Entry Draft. He doesn't possess a ton of upside but is a fun player to watch and one who makes life difficult for opponents. Good junior player.

Hughes, Cameron
LC- U. of Wisconsin (NCAA) 5'11.5" 175
HockeyProspect.com Ranking: NR

By looking at the stats it would be easy to come to the conclusion that Hughes development has somewhat stalled in his first year at Wisconsin and he did certainly seem overwhelmed at times early in the year. But the fact is Hughes was one of the youngest players in NCAA hockey and Wisconsin was a very young team that was lacking high end talent. Hughes spent most of his freshman year centering a 2nd line with different wingers moving up and down the lineup from week to week as Wisconsin searched for offense. He struggled early in the year to develop offensive chemistry and often was the only one on his line that was able to sustain any kind of puck possession in the offensive zone. Hughes particularly struggled against older, deeper teams where he would be going against stronger and more developed players.

Hughes plays a smart game along the wall, uses his excellent skating ability and hockey IQ to create offense off the cycle. Does a great job stick handling in traffic and protects the puck well. He possesses a pretty good release and likes to shoot off the rush. Hughes offensive game eventually developed later in the season when moved to the top line, along with that came more confidence in his game and he played some consistent hockey down the stretch. Hughes added some much needed bulk to his frame in his freshman year but still has a ways to go in that department. He is susceptible of getting bumped off the puck easily and his decision making with the puck can be slow and indecisive.

As it sits right now, Hughes projects as a solid checking line center with good faceoff abilities but until he gets surrounded with some offensive talent it's hard to tell what his ceiling is. All the skills are there for Hughes, but it's going to take some time for his game to have an identity.

Hunt, Dryden
LW – Medicine Hat Tigers (WHL) – 6'00" 199
HockeyProspect.com Ranking: 135

Dryden Hunt is an energetic and intelligent re-entry checking forward who has showed that he can score a lot of points at the major junior level while playing with the Medicine Hat Tigers this past season.

Hunt is a decent skater who is strong and sturdy and difficult to play against. His game is underpinned by above average upper-body conditioning and strong work-ethic. This list of skills makes Hunt especially difficult to contain when he's below the goal-line. In fact, teammates try to find him with the puck behind the net when playing on the power play, as he is known for making good plays from that position on the ice. When he's not streaking to his office behind the net, he makes really smart streaks in front of the goaltender to create screens and deflections. More of a passer than a shooter, he gets most of his goals off of deflections or rebounds when he's placed just outside the crease. He plays on the first line and in all situations, including four-on-four.

Especially when he's a step or two ahead, Dryden Hunt is a wide-shouldered player who is very difficult to get around or to strip of the puck. Although he plays a a top-heavy style of game, he remains incredibly balanced and difficult to knock off of his feet. Because he is so good on the cycle and at containing the puck in the offensive zone his attack-zone time is usually very high. His backchecking speed isn't always where you want it, but he's more of a scoring winger anyways.

Huska, Adam
G – Green Bay Gamblers (USHL) – 6'3" 190
HockeyProspect.com Ranking: 200

Huska spent the first half of the season playing with the Slovakian U18 National Team that competes against men in the second tier Slovakian league. In February he joined the Green Bay Gamblers, the team that drafted him 241st overall in the 2014 USHL Entry Draft, and he is set to return there next season. In April he competed at the IIHF U18 World Championship, where he was able to show some glimpses of his abilities.

Huska's biggest strength are his athleticism and competitiveness. He doesn't give up on shots and has the ability to change momentum for his team with big, timely saves. He can generate a lot of power from his legs and slides quickly across the crease, but he needs to better control such power to avoid over sliding and losing his angles. Huska finds himself scrambling outside of his crease regularly, which is inefficient. He has a great frame to fill the net but he doesn't stick to one of the foundations of goaltending, fill the middle first. Adam needs to simplify his game by filling the middle more, especially coming off the post, and pick when to be aggressive and when to be conservative. There is potential there, but Huska will need lots of seasoning and patience in his development

Quotable: "Huska had some really good stretches at the U18 tourney. Let's just say it was a big dropoff for the Slovaks when he didn't play." - Mark Edwards

Imama, Bokondji
LW – Saint-John Sea Dogs (QMJHL) – 6'1" 213
HockeyProspect.com Ranking: NR

Imama was acquired by Saint-John during the QMJHL trade period this season from Baie-Comeau, after playing the last two and a half seasons with the Drakkar.

Imama is one of the most feared players in the QMJHL, not only for his fighting skills but also his pure strength and willingness to engage physically. He's feared on the forecheck and can be very intimidating on the ice when putting pressure on the puck-carrier. He does a great job using his size to protect the puck in the offensive zone, as not many defensemen in the QMJHL can handle him physically along the boards or in front of the net. It's very tough to take the puck away from him when he's able to use his back to shield opponents away. He brings energy to his team by playing an intense physical game. Offensively, he's capable of contributing on any line for his team, but in general he's been used mostly as a 3rd liner those past two seasons. He has improved his skills over this span, but still remains average at best with the puck in offensive situations. His bread and butter will remain his physical game. His skating abilities have also improved, but there's still remains a lot of work to be done. His feet are quite heavy and he needs more explosions in his steps to keep up with speedy forwards and also be more effective on the forecheck. It would be surprising to see Imama drafted but he made some nice progress this year and few players bring his physicality to the game.

Impose, Auguste
LW – Geneve-Servette (NLA) – 5'9.75" 180
HockeyProspect.com Ranking: NR

Impose is an explosive skater that possesses outstanding agility. He can stickhandle while reaching full speed and beat defensemen wide after quick impressive shifts to the left. When coming down the right side the Swiss is often able to converge towards the slot, but his shot rarely makes the most of it. Off the rush he shows the capability to combine with his linemates and he doesn't mind sharing the puck, but his hands don't look like top 6 material and he struggles to finish his chances. He can complete good short passes, he can engage in boards battles and he had a couple of rather convincing games in the medal rounds at the U18 in Zug, but the key question mark is how much room he has for improvement. He could improve his stamina, but physically he seems quite close to the finished product, and improving on aspects like hands or finishing abilities is easier said than done.

Quotable: "This kid was all over the ice at the U18 in Zug. He worked hard every shift and contributed to his teams offensive zone pressure. His hard work led to getting himself a ton of scoring chances but he really struggled to score. He did manage to score after I left Switzerland but his lack of scoring touch left a lasting impression." - Mark Edwards

Ingram, Connor
LG – Kamloops Blazers (WHL) – 6'01" 212
HockeyProspect.com Ranking: 201

Ingram, a decent sized, wide-set goaltender came out of the blue to the Blazers. He's an undrafted butterfly goalie from rural Imperial, Saskatchewan who made it onto the team out of camp. He is positioned well and moves at a relatively quick speed to make the difficult saves. Overall, his stance and technique both look fairly good, as well.

When he's fully set, Ingram is very difficult to beat from outside the prime scoring area. He does a good job watching the puck into his glove and at controlling his stance and positioning as much as possible. The way he challenges shots varies from medium to aggressive. His rebound control could be better, as well as his second-chance save percentage, but it appears as though he's making strides in those areas. His size is key to his success as he isn't one of the more athletic goaltenders available in this draft and needs to rely on his positional play.

Despite playing on the second worst team in the Western Conference, Ingram's numbers are much better than the standings suggest and a testament to how well he kept his team in games. In his last five regulation losses this season, Ingram never gave up more than three goals. These numbers represent how well he kept his team in games, even when they weren't able to put much up on the scoreboard. Connor gave himself a chance to possibly get drafted this year.

Jaremko, Jacob
LC-Elk River (MN-HS) 5'11.25" 170LBS
HockeyProspect.com Ranking: NR

Jaremko is coming off an impressive Senior Season at Elk River where he was named "Mr. Hockey" in the state of Minnesota. Jacob Jaremko is a highly skilled center that plays the game at a high pace. He has a quick first few strides; great all around skating ability that allow him to be quick to loose pucks and can make plays in stride. His High hockey IQ and creativity allows him to make plays quickly and at times caught his teammates off guard. Jacob has another gear when entering the offensive zone that allows him to draw a lot of attention and frees up space for his teammates. There are times when Jacob could do himself better to slow the game down and take more time to read the play. His playmaking ability in open space is impressive but needs to get better along the boards and in front of the net. Jaramko is known for having a good work ethic both on and off the ice and works to improve his craft. He has finished the 14/15 season with Chicago (USHL) where he will likely spend 2015/16 before heading to Minnesota State-Mankato (NCAA)

Jaros, Christian
RD – Lulea (SWE) – 6'3" 201
HockeyProspect.com Ranking: 130

A Slovak defenseman who has been developing in Sweden for the past two seasons, Jaros was passed over at last year draft but has definitely made a good case for himself to be selected this time around. He had a strong showing at the WJC in Canada, as he was a key contributor to the surprising bronze medal captured by his national team, and earned some action with Lulea in SHL. The main improvement he made was probably in the skating department, and with his footwork in particular. His feet agility is still not ideal, sometimes he struggles to defend on quick turns and can get called for penalties along the boards, but for a big defenseman his overall mobility at this point may even be seen as a strength. He is able to transition the puck using a powerful stride and he has showed he can jump into the offensive zone without looking out of place. He will never be an offensive defenseman, but he brings a powerful right handed shot from the blueline. Jaros reads and anticipates well the play through the neutral zone, makes good use of his stick and sound decisions when he gets possession. In the defensive zone he plays a physical game, his size and strength make him effective in puck battles along the boards, he doesn't back off players and is strong maintaining position.

Järvinen, Ville
LD – Ilves (Fin jr.) – 6'4" 203
HockeyProspect.com Ranking: NR

Tall d-man who has suffered a big injury during this season. Has played only five games but he's really tantalizing prospect. Got great size and great mobility. Ville is a smart defender and he reads the game magnificently. Got great all-round tools but he have to start use his body more. Doesn't like to get rough that much what you usually expect from big guys. All in all his potential is huge but there's lot of question marks because of his big injury and toughness.

Jasek, Lukas
RW – Trinec (CZE) – 5'11.25" 165
HockeyProspect.com Ranking: 151

Even if he will be still 17 on draft day, Jasek earlier this season already saw some action in the Extraliga, something that suggests how highly considered he is by his club. At that level, however, he found himself chasing the play most of the time, rarely getting possession and the chance to show his abilities with the puck. His junior season has had stretches of strong play, but Lukas clearly struggled at the U18 World Championships, probably affecting his draft status and making even harder to get a good read on him. He can look quite different from one game to another. He certainly is a skilled individual and a sound skater, with a good first step, solid balance and some power to his stride. Looks close to six-foot tall and size doesn't seem an issue, willing to go to work along the boards, often get there first and can use his skills to deliver good passes coming off battles. He will probably take some time to develop, but despite a so-so season he has shown on occasions the potential to evolve into a legit pro winger.

Jaycox, Luke
LD - Lincoln (USHL) 6'1.5" 183
HockeyProspect.com Ranking: NR

Jaycox, a Warroad High (MN) product finished the season with Lincoln of USHL appearing in the final fifteen games of the Stars' season. It took Jaycox a couple games to get up to speed in the USHL, but ended up chipping in a goal down the stretch for Lincoln.

Jaycox is a big body who is a very good skater for his size. He showed off his offensive talent throughout his high school career and as he returns to Lincoln next year, expect him to have a central role with the Stars as they retool their roster for the upcoming season. It's obvious he sees the ice really well and will be able to put up points in his first full season in the USHL next year. He looked a little bit lost at the USHL level in his own zone in the games he played with Lincoln at the end of the year, but also showed flashes of potential. There is plenty of upside with Jaycox as he returns to Lincoln next season before heading to Northern Michigan in 2016.

Johnston, Brendan
G - Windsor Spitfires (OHL) 6'00" 198
HockeyProspect.com Ranking: NR

After spending last season with the Chatham Maroons Jr. B, Johnston appeared in over half of the games this season for the Windsor Spitfires. Johnston showed a variety of performances in our viewings this year. Sometimes he was making some game stealing saves, other times struggling to make the save to keep his team in the game.

Brendan is an athletic goaltender and has good reflexes. He is technically sound with his positioning and always seems to be in the right initial place. He is decent at making recovery saves, which is key for him because his rebound control is a key area of concern as he kicks out a lot into scoring lanes. Johnston is a goaltender who has a high ceiling in regards to his potential but consistency and rebound control needs to really improve over his next three years in junior hockey. He has numerous areas to improve just to keep getting starts in the OHL. We would be surprised if he was selected in the 2015 NHL Draft.

Jones, Caleb
LD – USNTDP (USHL) 5'11.75" 194
HockeyProspect.com Ranking: 210

We think being the younger brother of Seth Jones has some folks who have never truly evaluated his game, giving him a little more credit than he probably deserves. He does have good mobility and has shown improvement over the last couple of years, although still not sure he's draft worthy. There are times he makes good outlet passes and decisions with the puck. That's when he keeps his game simple. Then he will come back next shift and press his luck and skills that results in turnovers or a high-risk play. He will hold puck too long or think he is faster than he is.

He is just way too inconsistent in game and thinking. His hockey sense is questionable as he does not always see the ice and plays develop both offensively and defensively. There are times he will surprise you and set-up a rush but then leaving you shaking your head a shift later.

Joseph, Mathieu
LW/RW – Saint-John Sea Dogs (QMJHL) – 6'0" 164
HockeyProspect.com Ranking: 63

Joseph is a player who we have had our eyes on since his QMJHL draft year, when he played in the Midget Espoir league. We had him ranked 47th in our 2013 QMJHL Draft Guide and he was eventually drafted 51st overall by the Sea Dogs. After splitting last season between the Quebec Midget AAA league (where he amassed over a point per game) and the Sea Dogs, Joseph established himself as a full-time member of the Sea Dogs this season.

One key element to Joseph's progression over the last two seasons has been him gaining over four inches in height. He was listed at 5'8" in his QMJHL draft year and now he's up to 6'0". The skills were never a problem with him; Joseph has great puck skills and has a good understanding of the game at both ends of the rink. Back in Midget Espoir, his defensive game was non existent, but at the Midget AAA level, he was switched to center and learned a lot about playing without the puck. Now Joseph is back playing on the wing at the major junior level. He's got a great hockey sense, knowing where to be on the ice, also having great anticipation to steal pucks away from the opposing team. He has become an excellent penalty killer. He's a good skater and plays with a lot of energy and can be a pain to play against. He may not be the strongest player, but he has a high compete level. Offensively, he can create things with his speed, he's quite active and keep his feet moving. He has an accurate shot but should work on improving his velocity.

Quotable: "This is a player that started to rise quickly up our rankings early this season. I just like how well rounded his game is. I like smart players that compete they he does. Coaches can utilize his smarts on the PK and more. Some good upside." - Mark Edwards

Jutting, Tyler
RD - Shattuck St. Mary's (US Prep – Ind.) 6'4 190
HockeyProspect.com Ranking: NR

Scouts might be attracted to Jutting, as he is a big defenseman and genetically because he has a father who played NCAA Hockey. There are raw skills there, but he will be a project, as development is needed in skating and stick handling. One team just might throw the dart although we do not think it's in the cards for this go-around.

Juulsen, Noah
RD – Everett Silvertips (WHL) – 6'02" 174
HockeyProspect.com Ranking: 22

Noah Juulsen is a highly talented and lanky defenseman who played big minutes in all game situations for the Everett Silvertips. He is an effective skater, capable of taking the puck end to end. He's not afraid to pinch down low in the offensive zone when necessary. He plays big power play minutes and is very smart and consistent with the puck. He also possesses a hard point shot that regularly hits the net.

Defensively in one on one situations he is calm and effective. All while displaying a willingness to play physical when the opportunity presents itself. In his own end, Juulsen throws big hits all over the ice despite looking rather lanky—physical and equipped with a long reach. He's a difficult player to beat along the boards. Not afraid to mix it up after the whistles either, Juulsen shows good intensity. On the penalty kill, he has very low body position and likes to lay down and use his body to block potential cross ice passes. Juulsen very much prefers to be the one to make the first play with the puck out of the defensive zone, usually sending an accurate first pass up ice.

When you put together all of the talents Juulsen brings to the table, he has good upside at both ends of the ice. Juulsen will need to grow into his size and continue developing, but projects as a top four defender who can contribute both offensively and defensively.

Quotable: Juulsen really looked impressive on my end of season west coast road swing. Could always carry offensive play, but it was his improved play away from the puck that caught my attention. - HP Scout, Scott McDougall

Kalapudas, Antti
LC – Hokki (Fin 2nd pro) – 6'0" 161
HockeyProspect.com Ranking: NR

Skating is one of the easiest things to develop and that's a thing Antti really needs to improve. His offensive instincts are amazing.. got a great vision and puck handling skills and he can play very smart game but he have to develop his skating technique so that he can be also faster player. He's decent two way player considering his speed.. if he can improve that he could be a really effective player in all three zones. Average size player and can really get along in physical side of the game but it's all about his skating.

Kaprizov, Kirill
LW – Metallurg Nk (KHL) – 5'9" 185
HockeyProspect.com Ranking: 161

As an undersized 17yrs old, Kaprizov spent almost the entire season as a regular for his KHL team. Even if that is easier to do on a small club, it is still a remarkable feat that tells how much he has matured from the previous season. What, on top of his skills, allowed him to stay there is his compete level and how he went regularly to battle for the puck against bigger and seasoned players. Not obvious, his efforts and hard working attitude have remained consistent when joining his peers to compete at the U18 level, even if his performances at the World Championships has not been as brilliant as the ones offered at the 5 Nations in February.

At least at the junior level, his all-around game helps anyone playing on his line. Kirill is shifty and has a wide stance on his skates that helps his strong balance. Possesses great stickhandling ability and puck control, but perhaps the best part of his game is his capability to complete smart passes inside the offensive zone. He can upset the defense by executing the unexpected pass with accuracy, like backhanders behind the back or one touch passes on the powerplay. Kaprizov doesn't mind making plays along the boards or in traffic, and he is no stranger to the front of the net. Right now he is a real scoring threat only from in close, as his shot still lacks power. What may be more concerning for such a small player is that he lacks the top speed and straight ahead acceleration to get separation.

Karnaukhov, Pavel
LW – Calgary Hitmen (WHL) – 6'02" 194
HockeyProspect.com Ranking: 115

Pavel Karnaukhov, a Russian rookie import forward who debuted this year with the Calgary Hitmen, brings to the table a unique combination of 'subtle grace' and 'in your face.' Karnaukhov can play all three forward positions, but is usually planted at centre because he excels in the faceoff circle. His ice-time was spread fairly evenly across the Hitmen lineup, as he received assignments in virtually all situations and could be easily plugged into anywhere on the depth charts by Calgary's coaching and management staff.

Karnaukhov is a strong skater with good size and commitment to the body. His feet move fairly quickly and he can change directions seamlessly. But more importantly, he's a physical player who uses his mobility to crash and bang in all three zones. A deep knee bend and wide skating stance make him appear much smaller than he is, making him a bit like a submarine in his movements—an initially unrecognizable threat until he's suddenly fighting for body position, finishing his checks, or cutting into the slot to take a shot.

A speciality of Karnaukhov's game is his ability to fight for body position along the walls and in the corners, thereby dislodging opposition players from the puck. Another speciality is his hitting and another is his shot. We didn't see too much from Karnaukhov in the form of passing, but he got some good opportunities on net while crashing the crease and keeping his feet moving. Karnaukhov was on the ice during a lot of important defensive siuations for the Hitmen. He plays a fairly quiet game in his own end, but is definitely trustworthy in terms of his positioning and hockey sense. His game will only improve as he continues adapting to a new style of hockey, as his skills are already well-suited for North American sized rinks.

Kase, David
LW – Chomutov (CZE 2) – 5'9" 161
HockeyProspect.com Ranking: 150

Kase is a very skilled kid with impressive mobility. He plays an up-tempo style no matter if he is centering his line or covering the wing, where it's easier to picture him at the next level. He is always active and brings a good compete level on the ice. His defensive efforts as of now don't pay many dividends in his zone, he is more effective and consistent looking for pucks in the offensive zone. He has good instincts and doesn't mind entering traffic or going in front of the net looking for loose pucks or rebounds, which he can bury most of the times. With the puck he displays agility and creativity, and executes plays very quickly. These traits help him avoiding checks. His hands and feet are equally fast. On the powerplay he likes to make one touch passes from the right side boards position to surprise the defense.

His offensive numbers have been good, but you would like to see him make more of an impact at the junior level in terms of creating offense. Rarely his skill plays seem to earn him good shooting opportunities and still has to add power to his shot. If it became a legit threat, that might add a new dimension to his offensive game.

He doesn't show specific favourite plays that he could rely on when trying to make a difference at even strength at the next level. At 5'9", you have to wonder what kind of impact he could have against NHL defensemen. And if he is not good enough for a top six role, would he be able to adapt his game to the point of becoming a good third liner despite his size? The main thing that he has going for him is that he can do things fast, and can react fast enough to combine with offensive players at the next level. On draft day David might go later than his talent level would deserve, but he'll certainly hope not to fall as far as his brother Ondrej did last year.

Quotable: "Skilled player but we didn't feel like he did enough as a small guy to give us a reason to have more faith in him rankings wise." - Mark Edwards

Kielly, Kameron
RC – Charlottetown Islanders (QMJHL) – 6'1" 183
HockeyProspect.com Ranking: 145

Kameron is a late '96 birthday who's in his second season with the Islanders. He was acquired by them after his rookie season with Gatineau. This season, he was able to establish himself as a consistent performer offensively for the first time in his career in the QMJHL. Kielly, who wears an "A" on his jersey, was drafted 18th overall in the 2012 QMJHL Draft.

Kielly is a smart two-way forward who took pride of playing a strong defensive game. His game took off once he joined the Islanders and was moved back to center by coach Gordie Dwyer. He has a strong hockey IQ and a strong work ethic, understanding the game well and paying attention to the little details. Kielly was used in different roles this season and saw ice time on both the power play and penalty killing units. Centering one of Charlottetown's top 2 lines, he was able to play against the opposing top line in a shutdown role. He's a decent skater but lacks some explosiveness to make him more dangerous offensively.

Over the off-season he added mass to his frame, which made him more effective offensively, stronger on his skates and more effective in one-on-one battles. His upside offensively is limited, but he does many things well to make himself useful for his team.

Kiviranta, Joel
RW – Sport (Fin elite) – 5'10" 163
HockeyProspect.com Ranking: NR

A '96-born forward that was passed over in last year NHL draft, Joel is a speedy winger with great attitude. This season Kiviranta played in the men's league in Finland and appeared in 47 games for Sport.

He likes to join the traffic and he's reliable two-way forward. He reads the game well and can be effective in all three zones, but his size is a major concern. He's playing very tough around corners considering his size, he's a fast and smart kid so he wins quite often 1-on-1 battles. He's got average puck handling skills and vision, but he still has some potential to be a bottom six type of a players.

Knott, Graham
LW - Niagara Ice Dogs (OHL) 6'03" 180
HockeyProspect.com Ranking: 56

Graham is a big winger who played a two-way role for the Niagara Ice Dogs this season. Knott made his biggest impression in the defensive side of the game. He is a good penalty killer who is well positioned in the defensive zone. He is willing to block shots and gets into passing lanes well. He occasionally made an impact with his physical presence. When he's on he has a good compete level but he is very inconsistent. It's an area that needs to improve. Knott is a good skater with strong puck possession skills and he can force turnovers with his size and reach.

As we mentioned, he was prone to inconsistent play at times. Offensively Knott showed moments where he could get the job done, but for the most part doesn't possess any offensive abilities that suggest he could be a top six forward at the NHL level. Whoever selects Knott will be looking at a big-bodied forward who could be playing a strong defensive role while producing modest numbers.

Quotable: " I have time for the kid but he needs to start bringing it every game. Just too inconsistent" NHL Scout

Quotable: " I don't see anything there. He's not on my list." - NHL Scout

Quotable: " At times he looks like a player but I think he might be fools gold. Just when I think he might have enough to play bottom six, he plays a few stinkers and I back off again. when" NHL Scout

Quotable: " I like him, not too early in the draft but I think there might be something there. If he makes it into round three I'll start taking notice. - NHL Scout

Quotable: " Not sure what he is at the next level." - NHL Scout

Quotable: " Thought he played some of his best hockey in a Team Canada jersey both at the Hlinka and with some really good shifts at the U18 in Switzerland. In between he didn't do anything to make me think he could be a high pick this June." - Mark Edwards

Kodola, Vladislav
LC - Saginaw Spirit (OHL) 5'10" 167
HockeyProspect.com Ranking: NR

Kodola came over from Russia to join the Sarnia Sting going through some growing pains in his first season for the last place Sting. He showed flashes of brilliance this season but battled consistency issues before being dealt to the Saginaw Spirit at the OHL trade deadline. Kodola is positioned at centre but is better suited on the wing as his face-off percentage is around the 15% to 20% range. Kodola has great skating ability and is very shifty with the puck. He can be difficult to contain with quick hands but regularly gets caught trying to do too much by himself. He has shown flashes of good playmaking ability and is more of a passer than a scorer as his shot lacks power. Kodola is a small, slick puck handling forward but really doesn't project as a prospect at the NHL level and is not a player we expect to be selected at the 2015 NHL Entry Draft.

Kohn, Mason
LW - Kitchener Rangers (OHL) 5'10" 188
HockeyProspect.com Ranking: 175

Although his size provides a little concern at the NHL level, Mason's play has been a favorite with our staff. Mason is an incredibly hard working player, one of the most tenacious forwards you'll find in the 2015 NHL Draft Class. Kohn plays every shift like it's his last and plays with a desperation to win battles and get to the puck first that is extremely hard to find. He is a very good skater, but is also built solidly, which has proven very valuable for Kohn. He flies into the corner on the dump and chase and will either win the race or hit whoever does. He is a two-way forward who works equally hard in the defensive zone as the offensive zone. Mason has underrated offensive ability caught behind several veterans up front and does a great job of creating plays for his linemates, but also has some finishing ability. We don't expect Mason to be selected early but he could be a nice pickup in later on in the draft.

Quotable: "This kid could be a sleeper. High end skater/speed. Off the charts compete level, and a real pain in the ass to play against. Just wish he had a little more size." - HP Scout, Ryan Yessie

Kolesar, Keegan
RW – Seattle Thunderbirds (WHL) – 6'02" 217
HockeyProspect.com Ranking: 76

Kolesar is an intriguing power forward of huge physical proportions. Already something of a physical specimen, Kolesar plays a heavy physical style of game and can be really imposing when he's on. He's got a good shot, decent hands and can be a really agitating presence at times. Although he's a tad inconsistent from game-to-game, on his best nights, Keegan can be seen doing a little bit of everything for his Thunderbirds club—whether it be taking the puck to the difficult areas, imposing his will in all three zones, scoring or fighting—he tallied over eight fights this season.

Skating has been a main area of concern for Kolesar, however his ability to move in all directions improved immensely over the course of the 2014-2015 season. Kolesar is one of those players who gravitates towards the dirtiest areas of the ice and has the strength, toughness, agility and hockey sense to win most his battles in those areas. He won the vast majority of his one-in-one battles in our viewings of him. It helps too that, when transitioning off of the boards and into open space, he has the shooting skills to finish in close or to make plays happen in open space.

Injuries were a big impact on Kolesar's season. On the one hand, he saw increased ice-time and really elevated his game in the mid-season absence of Matthew Barzal. On the other hand, he had an unfortunate injury of his own, just at the season's conclusion. Kolesar doesn't possess much of a bust factor, although the skating needs to show continual progression. With that said he projects as a physically tough forward who opponents hate going into the corners against.

Konecny, Travis
RW - Ottawa 67's (OHL) 5'10" 176
HockeyProspect.com Ranking: 19

The former first overall pick in the 2013 OHL Draft stumbled out of the gates a bit this year but was much better in the second half. Konecny is a tireless worker with one of the highest compete levels in the draft. He possesses high end speed / acceleration and is an explosive offensive player. He has high end puck skills and quick release. His vision and hockey sense are very good and is equally dangerous distributing the puck to a teammate or finishing himself. Despite his smaller stature, he plays with a physical edge to his game and isn't afraid of anyone. With that said, his reckless play at his size may have affected his health a bit as he suffered multiple injuries this season. As much as we like the tempo at which he plays with, slowing down his pace at times could be beneficial for him instead of going at full speed all the time. That could help for one avoid injuries and be in more control and more effective as a playmaker. In October he was named captain of the Ottawa 67s, organisation showed good faith in his leadership qualities. He has represented his country at various international events, last time was when he captained team Canada last August at the Ivan Hlinka U-18 tournament. More was expected out of Konecny this season after a superb rookie season in 2013-2014 where he was the OHL rookie of the year but injuries didn't help him and playing one bad team with not much talent surrounding him didn't either. Konecny has top six forward upside at the NHL level, but he will need to overcome his size and will absolutely need to get stronger and hopefully avoid further injuries in order to reach his potential

Quotable: "He was a great interview in Buffalo." - NHL Scout

Quotable:" Loved his game in his OHL Draft season and he's kept playing the same way in Ottawa. My only concern is how his body holds up playing his game in the NHL. I like to see little guys avoid contact and he's already struggled to stay in the lineup in the OHL." - Mark Edwards

Quotable:" Hard not to like the kid given the way he plays. He's probably a top 5 pick if he was 3 inches taller." - NHL Scout

Quotable:" I don't get the hype, I haven't seen anything from him yet." NHL Scout

Quotable:" High risk pick the way he plays the game. I can't see him staying healthy in the NHL...reminds me of Fabbri the way he gets hit." - NHL Scout

Quotable:" The kid gets no respect, he's got nothing to work with, Ottawa has nothing." NHL Scout

Quotable:" He's not in my top 20." - NHL Scout

Quotable:" He won't make it to the 20th pick." - NHL Scout

Korostelev, Nikita
RW - Sarnia Sting (OHL) 6'01" 196
HockeyProspect.com Ranking: 53

A former first round pick in the 2013 OHL Priority Selection Draft, Korostelev is one of the most polarizing prospects in the 2015 NHL Entry Draft. On the positive side he is a big strong forward who has a rare combination of puck protection ability and evasiveness that is tough to find in a big forward. His shot is one of, if not the most powerful in this draft class and he has developed some intriguing playmaking ability. Nikita can crush opponents with his big frame and can be a tough player to play against at times.

On his good days, Korostelev's talent gives him the potential to be one of the top players in the 2015 NHL Draft Class. The problem is the number of times he's been completely invisible. He was a non-factor far too often in key parts of the game and sometimes for entire games. While his shot would be considered hard and at an NHL level, he completely misses the net too often. He has shown to be an effective checker but sometimes passes up great opportunities to take the body.

Korostelev is a high risk/high reward prospect. When he's at his best we think you can legitimately rank with among the top 20 players in this draft. At his worst he is barely noticeable and would be absent from the majority of NHL teams draft lists.

Quotable:" I don't see anything in him." NHL Scout

Quotable:" I saw him recently and he was the best player on the ice." NHL Scout

Quotable:" Last time I saw Sarnia, he was better than Zacha." - NHL Scout

Quotable: "He reminds me of that guy from the Mighty Ducks movie. He hits the net 1 in every 5 shots but the one that hits the net, the goalie just has to hope it hits him." - HP scout Ryan Yessie

Quotable: "I liked him a lot with the Toronto Jr. Canadiens in AAA but he's been a disappointment for me this year. His skating needs a bit of work and he's a one-trick pony way too often for my liking. His picture is beside 'boom or bust' in the hockey dictionary." - Mark Edwards

Korshkov, Yegor
LW – Loko (MHL) – 6'3" 170
HockeyProspect.com Ranking: NR

Passed over at least year draft, the still 18yrs old Korshkov brings to the table skills and speed along with his 6'3" frame (and that might be selling him short). Like he has shown more than once this season at the MHL level, he is the kind of player capable of going coast to coast after getting the puck with speed in his zone. He uses his reach to stickhandle the puck away from opponents and can pull off a toe drag here and then to find his way through. The problem is plays like that can't be often successful, especially at the next level, and are only a small part of the game. Korshkov does possess a powerful wrist shot as a more regular weapon, but the rest of his game is still lacking. Even if in his KHL appearances he hasn't looked out of place, he will have to demonstrate an adequate compete level in all areas over a longer period of time. Doesn't have a physical game despite his frame and more importantly has yet to show any capability of reacting quickly when the intensity of the game requires it, or the smarts to compensate for his lack thereof. He needs the room and time provided by the big ice to make his plays. The potential is there, but the probability of being able to exploit it one day in NHL rinks seems fairly remote.

Kotala, Jakub
LC – Mlada Boleslav (CZE Jr.) – 6'2" 187
HockeyProspect.com Ranking: NR

Kotala is a '96 born Czech forward with good size that made his debut in the Extraliga after a strong season at the junior level. His most appreciable trait is his capability to use his body to protect the puck. He is not overly skilled, but has solid playmaking abilities that he puts to work while protecting the puck or on the powerplay. Jakub shows good sense for the game and he manages to be around the puck during both offensive and defensive zone play, he is defensively responsible and helps deep in his zone. There is however a key area where significant improvement is required. He must improve his skating, he will need to become quicker in his first steps and his stride definitely needs some work.

Kovacs, Robin
RW – AIK (SWE 2) – 6'0" 172
HockeyProspect.com Ranking: 35

A late '96 coming off an underwhelming 2013/2014 season (considering his talent level), Kovacs took little time this year to reaffirm himself as a relevant prospect for the upcoming draft. He managed to crack his senior team roster, showed a willingness to backcheck and simplify his game and successfully played the rest of the campaign in the second tier Swedish pro league.

The left shooting right winger saw regular time on the powerplay, he likes to play the right half boards position to come off the boards and look for an opportunity to shoot. He possesses a dangerous wrist shot he can pick spots with, making him a threat from that position. Despite his willingness to shoot, Kovacs is a creative player with strong vision and playmaking is a big part of his game. When he is not close to the net and shooting is not an option, he can carry the puck with great speed showing his obvious stickhandling skills and skating ability. Robin likes to stickhandle keeping the puck away from the opponent and skate it where there is room while he looks for passing options and openings. Sometimes he takes unnecessary risks doing so, but his hockey sense allows him to get away with it most of the times.

When given a bit of space he can beat opponents one on one through the neutral zone, as he shifts to the left side keeping the puck wide or deke and cut inside just before. He is also very effective at making swift turns while maintaining full control of the puck, ready to execute passes right after. He can quickly change direction, his agile feet and quick hands make him very effective at picking up pucks. He is no stranger to board play and he can hold his own there. He is not easily intimidated and shows a bit of a temper, but he will need to bulk up significantly in order to keep on playing that type of game. Consistency needs to improve, he probably still lacks the energy to bring his A game for the full 60 minutes.

Quotable: " He actually reminds me a little of Kyle Connor the he way he moves around certain areas of the ice. He obviously doesn't stack up to Connor in some other areas but Kovacs is a very good player. There were times over the past few seasons where I thought Kovacs might have a chance of cracking the top 30. In the end he came pretty close to doing just that on our rankings. - Mark Edwards

Kreis, Matthew
LW - Barrie Colts (OHL) 6'00" 175
HockeyProspect.com Ranking: NR

Kreis spent most of the season on the bottom six despite being the only first round pick in the Colts lineup from the past two drafts. He got off to a shaky start this season but seems to have reinvented himself as the season progressed. Matthew was great battling in the offensive zone competing hard and winning battles for pucks. He's a good skater who drives play up ice he and regularly gains the offensive zone and can create offense off the rush. Kreis is a good passer, shifty with the puck and is effective working off the half-wall - particularly when given ice on the powerplay. He doesn't possess much finishing ability. He doesn't shy away from contact, though he's by no means a punishing forechecker.

Defensively, he back-checks hard and is almost always back to support. He should put up more points in a larger offensive role next season for the Colts, but we don't see him being selected at the 2015 NHL Entry Draft.

Kuhlman, Karson
RW – Minnesota-Dulth (NCAA) 5'10 174
HockeyProspect.com Ranking: NR

He has been bypassed a few times at the draft so perhaps third time is a charm. The knock is that he is not that big as under 6-feet though skates well and plays a 200-foot game. He has a good read on the game as anticipates plays and is able to take away scoring chances with the constant backcheck and good stick positioning. He had pretty respectable numbers this season as freshman at Minnesota-Duluth (NCHC). He has pretty good hands and offensive instincts. Kuhlman plays with good heart and will keep developing in the NCAA ranks in the coming years. He just might be a late round steal as one of those players you like in all situations on the ice and in the locker room.

Kupsky, Jake
G-Lone Star (NAHL) 6'5" 209
HockeyProspect.com Ranking: 187

Jake is a kid that pretty much came out of nowhere after being cut by USHL teams. He has the size NHL teams love and he moves really well, especially for a 6'5" kid. Lateral movement is impressive. He's raw but has a high ceiling. He has carried his team in the playoffs and outplayed Matej Tomem (another NHL goaltending prospect) in the NAHL playoffs iplaying him head to head.

Quotable: "The search for goalies never ends and the NAHL has been an extra landing spot for NHL scouts in recent years. Jake is a huge kid with raw talent who played in a lower level league. He did just about all he could do this year to help himself get drafted." - Mark Edwards

Kylington, Oliver
LD – Farjestad (SWE) – 6'0" 180
HockeyProspect.com Ranking: 29

After a couple of promising games with Farjestad early in the season, Kylington's risky play started to cost him icetime and eventually he asked to be loaned, ending up in Stockholm in the second Swedish league. As the AIK problematic season got worse, he went back to Farjestad to finish the season with the junior team. The dropping level of competition fitted Oliver's level of play, and when he had the chance to redeem his draft season at the U18 World Championships he certainly didn't take advantage. Oddly enough, international competition against youngsters was actually where he struggled the most.

His disappointing season and puzzling play make ranking Kylington a real challenge. Oliver brings rare elements to the table, blessed with elite feet he possesses outstanding speed and the agility to carry the puck around opponents with his soft hands. He regularly tries to impact the game with his skills no matter the level of the competition he is facing and has the uncommon capability of affecting and increasing the pace of a game. He usually makes good reads in the offensive zone, but that doesn't match with his overall puzzling decision making. It's one thing trying risky plays when they would make a difference, it's another one trying risky plays when there is no need for them and even no gain to be made out of them. For whatever reason, too often this season Kylington has been at fault for making those kind of plays. His careless play has led to frequent turnovers, including bad ones in the defensive zone.

A part of his game where decision making is not the cause of his struggles is when Oliver has to defend around the net and behind; especially against men he looks out of his comfort zone and even with puck on his stick he shows some junior naivety. Getting stronger will probably help his overall play in the defensive zone beyond when he is forced to engage in physical battles.

Despite his disappointing season, Kylington potential remains unquestioned. He has the poise and skills to run a powerplay, and possesses an adequate one-timer.
His wrist shot is among the parts of his game that suffer from a seeming lack of determination, too often on his rushes he misses the right split second to go for it, but on the powerplay his wrister is fairly effective. He is very good at completing long accurate passes, something he does consistently after using his speed to rapidly retrieve pucks dumped in his defensive zone. Defensively he makes good use of his stick and usually maintains good gap control.

Quotable: "He was good in our interview (NHL Combine) he did a good job with his answers and came across very honest." - NHL Scout

Quotable: "Hopefully he ends up at a spot on our list where he won't reach us. He scares me because I don't think he's a very smart player." - NHL Scout

Quotable: "Teams better not sleep on him too much because he might just come back and bite us all in the ass." - NHL Scout

Quotable: "I spoke to a few teams at the combine who told me his interviews were good. I also had one long conversation with a scout at the combine about him. We both agreed that he is a kid that could wake up one day and decide to 'flick a switch' sort of speak and play differently. If he does, he will make scouts who dropped him look bad. He is tough to rank because he flashes his ability to be top 10 kid in this draft, but it's just flashes. Hearing that his interviews were good gives me some hope he can turn it around. I didn't speak to him myself. Lot's of boom versus bust with this kid." - Mark Edwards

Laberge, Samuel
LW/RW – Rimouski Oceanic (QMJHL) – 6'2" 210
HockeyProspect.com Ranking: 141

In his first season in the QMJHL, Laberge played a depth role with the Oceanic, playing for the league top team. After being drafted out of the Midget Espoir league in 2013 (6th round, 95th overall), he played last year with Châteauguay and won the Quebec Midget AAA playoff championship, losing in the final of the Telus Cup. The Châteauguay native also played for his province at the 2014 U-17 Hockey Challenge in Cape-Breton.

Laberge is a power-forward with surprisingly good skating abilities, he has a powerful stride and agile feet. He loves to finish his hits on the forecheck, playing more of a depth role with the Oceanic as he was a bit of a sparkplug for them. As mentioned previously, Laberge didn't get much ice time this season due to the depth and high-end talent in their forward groups, but found a way to make some noise. He was arguably Rimouski's most physical forward and even got into some scraps. He found a way to score 15 times this season by playing pretty much everywhere in the Rimouski lineup due to many injuries during the season. He also scored 5 times on the power play when used there. He's a big body to move from the front of the net and understands his role well this year, looking for deflections and rebounds. He has a big and powerful shot but will need to improve the quickness of his release and his decision-making as well. He also became a very useful player on the penalty kill, not afraid of blocking shots and making good use of his stick. Laberge is an interesting prospect, might never be a top scorer but has size and a strong two-way game, which should draw interest from NHL teams.

Lackey, Michael
G – USNTDP (USHL) 6'2.5" 214
HockeyProspect.com Ranking: NR

He is a big, classic NHL size goalie that plays a blocking style with some athleticism. He sometimes has the habit of dropping first then reacting to the shots that gets him into trouble. If he would develop the athleticism more he could be that much more effective. When he stands tall in good position that's when he shows success, not just dropping into butterfly as he is big but not 6'5" monster size. He will also need to enhance the puck tracking trade instead of relying on the bigger frame in making stops just by pucks hitting him. This will be important in his long-term success. Right now he's on the outside looking in for us.

Laishram, Adam
RC - Belleville Bulls (OHL) 5'09" 160
HockeyProspect.com Ranking: NR

Adam is an undersized player, but he plays much bigger than his size. He's relentless after loose pucks, finishes his checks and he refuses to be outworked in the corners. Laishram is an above average skater who accelerates very quickly and has a good top speed. He's good skating the puck through the neutral zone and is good in terms of carrying the puck into the offensive zone with possession. He's quite dangerous off the rush, as he's shifty with the puckand possesses good vision.

Defensively, he is regularly glued to his man and is back to support whenever he can. His positioning on the penalty kill is good and you have to be weary of cross-ice passes when he's on the ice because of his closing speed. Adam won't hesitate to block shots and will do whatever it takes to win. There's a lot to like about Laishram if you forget about his size. He is pretty tiny and it will be difficult to overcome trying to reach the NHL level.

Lajeunesse, Troy
LC - Sarnia Sting (OHL) 5'09" 160
HockeyProspect.com Ranking: NR

Lajeunesse was a point of interest for our staff when watching the Waterloo Siskins Jr. B team last season and was worthy of a re-entry pick in the 2014 OHL Priority Selection Draft. He was not picked but instead went on to sign as a free agent with the Sarnia Sting. In his rookie season with the Sting he played in a third line role and did an outstanding job providing a good forecheck and being a very frustrating player to play against.

Despite his lack of size, Troy was willing to take the body and would take a hit in order to advance the play for his team. He was excellent backchecking and was very defensively sound. He was also a intrical part of the Sting penalty kill this season.

While Troy projects as an excellent junior player, his lack of size and strength is concerning at the NHL level. He has decent puck skills and offensive ability, but not something that would allow him to be a top six forward at the NHL level. He also lacks the size to project in the bottom six despite his style of play. Unfortunately if Troy was 3 or 4 inches taller he would be a player we'd be looking at in early rounds of the draft, however that is not the case and we wouldn't select Troy in this years draft.

Lalonde, Bradley
RD – Cape-Breton Screaming Eagles (QMJHL) – 6'0" 196
HockeyProspect.com Ranking: 193

The Screaming Eagles selected Lalonde in the 2nd round of the 2013 QMJHL Draft out of the Midget Espoir league. Over the last two seasons, Lalonde has proven his worth to the organization with his steady and smart plays. In 2014 he took part in the U-17 Hockey Challenge, playing for Quebec when the tournament was hosted in Cape-Breton.

Lalonde is not a flashy defenseman, but is very consistent and rarely makes mistakes on the ice. He's very steady from shift to shift and is a player that a coaching staff can trust that won't hurt them.

There's no major weakness with Lalonde's game, but nothing that stands out, either. He has a decent first pass, can be helpful on the transition game and makes good decisions with the puck. He's capable of playing on the power play but we don't view him as a power play quarterback. He can be used in a shutdown role, he's tough to beat one-on-one thanks to his good active stick and mobility. He still could improve his explosiveness, which would improve his overall skating ability. He's strong on his skates and doesn't lose many one-on-one battles. He also has a strong compete level. Over the next two seasons he should continue his strong two-way game and continue to play a bigger role offensively for the Screaming Eagles. Similar to Simon Bourque of Rimouski, does a lot of nice things on the ice but lacks a top quality.

Larkin, Ryan
G – Cedar Rapids (USHL) 6'0", 193
HockeyProspect.com Ranking: 166

Larkin is not a big goalie by today's standards at 6 foot tall, but makes himself big in the net. Larkin tries to make up for his lack of size by challenging shooters and play at the top of the crease. The knock on Larkin is that he can over challenge shooters and over pursue at times but he has done a good job improving his positioning and decision making this season. Larkin had an up and down rookie USHL season for a good Cedar Rapids squad. When he was good he was really good but certainly had his struggles at times, especially early in the season but had a healthy goalie competition which helped his development as the season wore on.

Larkin tracks the play well and is quick to find loose pucks in traffic. An athletic goalie with good lateral movement who moves post to post well and takes away the lower portion of the net. Larkin isn't overly active at playing the puck but can make the simple plays and has improved that area of his game this season.

Larsson, Jacob
LD – Frolunda (SWE Jr.) – 6'2" 191
HockeyProspect.com Ranking: 31

Larsson is a promising defenseman blessed with projectable size and impressive skating ability. At 17 he already received some icetime on a top SHL team despite his green shape, and even if there were some struggles he was already able to show some of his qualities at that level. For example, his tremendous feet. As he further develops physically Larsson has a chance to become an elite skater. He probably already is when it comes to skating backwards, something that helps him maintaining ideal gap control while he works to take the forward to the outside. He can quickly shift from defense to the offense when he gets possession and has above average hands for a defenseman, which helps him to manage the puck with poise. Likes to carry the puck exploring his options and moves very well laterally. He angles his body effectively to protect the puck while he carries it into the offensive zone and has good understanding of when joining the attack or hold back. Shows good passing on the offensive blueline and smart use of the end boards on the powerplay, already possesses a legit one-timer despite the obvious fact he has yet to fill out his frame.

Jacob will have to add a sense of urgency in his game though, with and without the puck; there is time for poise and time for resolute reactions and adjustments. The main concern right now generates from his high number of turnovers, something difficult to explain for a player with his capabilities and good vision. It's like under pressure he feels better giving away the puck rather than exploiting his tools with determination to complete a more difficult play. In the SHL that could be ascribed to things happening faster than he is still used to, but that doesn't explain why, albeit to a lesser extent, the flaw still showed up in junior international competitions. At the moment he is too soft on the puck, and only partially because of his obvious lack of strength. It seems also about adjusting his attitude. The thing here is projecting how much better he will become after adding some needed strength to his thin frame. That of course pertains his effectiveness in front of his net (needs to get tougher) and in battles in general, but also his puck possession play, as hinted above. Larsson is a guy that is probably going to be drafted higher than his actually performances along the season would warrant because of his evident talent and potential. He has the upside to become a great skater who can effortlessly play an effective two way game and log big minutes.

Quotable: "He had both some really good and really bad games in my viewings. During one bad game it reminded me of watching a stinker of a game by Hampus Lindholm in his draft year. I coincidently botched his ranking as badly as any in our 10 years...I think it was 38th or something. Ugh. My point is that Larsson has some really good tools." We will really try to remember them and his potential come rankings day." - Mark Edwards

Lauzon, Jeremy
LD – Rouyn-Noranda Huskies (QMJHL) – 6'0" 191
HockeyProspect.com Ranking: 68

Lauzon is a prospect that we liked coming into his QMJHL draft year, though he was a bit under the radar. The Huskies drafted him in the 2nd round of the 2013 QMJHL Draft and have not regretted it one bit since then. Lauzon had a strong first season in the league, mostly after Christmas where he saw his ice time increase with the injury to Dillon Fournier. This year he was again very good, and again had a real good second half of the season but unfortunately had a concussion late in the regular season and missed all of the first round of the playoffs, where the Huskies lost in six games versus Val-d'Or.

Lauzon, a native of Val-d'Or, is a solid two-way defenseman who's a strong skater with above-average top speed. He has decent mobility, but could use some upgrades to his footwork. He's active on the transition game with quality tape-to-tape passes and also loves to rush the puck in the offensive zone. He quarterbacked the Huskies' power play all year long, as he did for portions of his rookie season as well. He uses his on-ice vision and good, accurate slapper from the point to create scoring chances, and he's also quite active in the offensive zone, keeping his feet moving. The quickness of his decision-making has improved quite a lot in the past two seasons since joining the Huskies. Lauzon is solid on his skates and played tougher along the boards this year, showing that he is capable of punishing opposing players along the boards when necessary. He has become, over the course of the last two years, a good shot-blocker, and makes good use of his stick to block passes. Lauzon has chance to become a top-4 defensemen at the NHL level, he moves the puck well on the power play and has no real weakness in his game.

Quotable: "Skating is a bit knock kneed but he got around ok., Looked like a pretty smart player in my viewings although his numbers didn't match the offensive ability he showed me when I watched him. It's not like I personally saw him a ton live though." - Mark Edwards

Lazarev, Leo
G - Ottawa 67's (OHL) 5'10" 154
HockeyProspect.com Ranking: NR

Lazarev is a small, unorthodox, yet extremely athletic goalie. He uses strong anticipation and agility to make cross crease saves. Lazarev cuts off angles and challenges shooters as he comes out past the blue paint. Leo improved as the season went on but due to his small stature he struggles if his angles are off. He's a hybrid style goaltender with quick bursts to make unorthodox saves.

Inconsistent play plagued him this season; he tended to be either really good or very bad. He needs to handle traffic out front better. His aggressive style has left him hung out to dry if the opposition either takes advantage of the rebound or finds the open man staring at an open net. Lazarev will have a tough path to the NHL unless he grows; as NHL shooters will be able to exploit his weaknesses fairly easily.

Quotable: "One thing about this kid, he will never be accused of not being a gamer. He's actually a fun player to watch. Great entertainment between whistles." NHL Scout

Lemcke, Justin
RD - Belleville Bulls (OHL) 6'02" 202
HockeyProspect.com Ranking: 147

The former first round pick of the Belleville Bulls; Lemcke made some good strides this season in regards to improving his play. Last season in his rookie year he looked a little overwhelmed at times, but he stepped up his game this season. He was rewarded by getting ice in all game situations and consistently played top four minutes for his team. Justin is a big strong defender with a wide frame. Despite being a big kid, he's not an overly physical player but will finish his checks when necessary. Lemcke is good along the boards using his strength but his body positioning in these situations will need more attention to detail to maximize his success winning battles.

Justin is a pretty good puck protector, which allowed him to take the puck up ice well despite not being the smoothest skater. Without the puck he chooses the right time to jump up into the rush, which resulted in him being rewarded with some goals this season. His skating has seen improvements but he still struggles with small area quickness. He will need to get a quicker start and better mobility to be able to handle forwards at the next level. He has a powerful shot from the point, which is deflectable, but he will force it sometimes leading to blocked shots. Justin showed good upside but looks like a bit of a project at this point. He projects to be a big shutdown defender if he makes it to the next level.

Quotable: "Not a player that I was all that crazy about in AAA but he did get better this year. Skating was weak but showed signs of improvemnt this year." - Mark Edwards

Leschenko, Vyacheslav
RW – Atlant (KHL) – 5'11" 167
HockeyProspect.com Ranking: NR

Draft eligible for the third time, Leschenko this season was able to showcase himself on the big stage. He was a noticeable member of team Russia at the WJC in Canada and, albeit in a very limited role, played more than 30 games for Atlant in the KHL. He is a strong-skating right winger with a high compete level, someone who can be used in different situations. Vyacheslav is a workhorse, never quits on plays and goes with speed into high traffic areas. He can draw penalties with his speed and efforts, but his skillset better fits a bottom six role. His hands are the main area of concern, as they are certainly not first class and affect his finishing ability and offense in general.

Leskinen, Otto
LD – KalPa (Fin jr.) – 5'11" 168
HockeyProspect.com Ranking: NR

Leskinen is a smart defender with good mobility. He has a competent passing game and has showed some offensive potential in his play in domestic junior leagues. A calm skater who moves very well backwards, he can defend properly off the rush or during battles inside the defensive zone. He has average size but shows passion on the ice and never quits on plays. At the U18 World Championships Otto was forced by team's needs to play more of a pure defensive defenseman role, but didn't look out of place.

Léveillé, Loïk
RD – Cape-Breton Screaming Eagles (QMJHL) – 6'0" 220
HockeyProspect.com Ranking: 134

In his 3rd season in the league, Léveillé established himself as a premier offensive defenseman in the league after two sub-par seasons previously. Already playing for his 3rd team, Léveillé was originally drafted 5th overall in the 2012 QMJHL Draft by Baie-Comeau. During his rookie season, he was traded to Chicoutimi for Jérémy Grégoire and then the next year he was traded from Chicoutimi to Cape-Breton in the Nicolas Roy trade.

Hailing from St-Jérôme, Quebec, Léveillé is a talented, puck-moving defenseman. He's not afraid to join the rush and his passes are crisp and accurate. He excels on the power play, where he's able to show off his vision and creativity. He's very dangerous from the point thanks to his powerful shot and also moves the puck well.

This year, Léveillé was among the top-scoring defensemen in the QMJHL, finishing with 54 points in 68 games. He made some very good strides in his consistency and decision-making from last year, where he would struggle by making slow decisions with the puck and turn it over. Léveillé is really strong physically, not tall but with a very strong lower body and can pin down opponents fairly easily along the boards in the QMJHL. He's capable of playing physical in his own end by throwing some good hits, but lacks consistency in that area. He's a strong skater with good speed and footwork. Leveille chance to make it would be as a power play specialist, very good there but his defensive game needs a lot of works.

Lindberg, Brandon
LW - Sarnia Sting (OHL) 6'00" 212
HockeyProspect.com Ranking: 196

Lindberg was dealt to the Sting at the trade deadline last season and has developed well in the Sarnia program, receiving a fair amount of icetime in their top six this season. Lindberg had a high compete level but battled bringing it consistently over the course of the season. When he's on his game he is a tenacious forechecker and someone who is very difficult to play against. He does a great job of forcing turnovers and plays a pretty aggressive style of game. He competes in the defensive zone and can be tough to play against. He was a key penalty killer and excels in forcing turnovers high on the point. While Brandon showed flashes of puck skills, he would project as a bottom six forward at the NHL level who would be a key part of any teams' penalty killing unit.

Lindgren, Jesper
RD – Modo (SWE Jr.) – 6'0" 161
HockeyProspect.com Ranking: 146

A smooth skating defenseman with a good set of hands, Lindgren plays a calm game and can make plays with the puck. He has good stickhandling ability, but right now is not a dynamic presence on the blueline, making comparisons with Erik Karlsson's style look out of place. He looks particularly weak from a physical standpoint, and that might be what holds him back from making more of an impact with the puck on his stick. Obviously his lack of strength also puts him at a disadvantage in his own zone, but aside from the ensuing limitations he is not bad defensively and for his size he uses a pretty long stick.

Jesper is a good passer, something visible in his outlet attempts and when on the powerplay. He has good puck skills and can take advantage by changing angles or pulling off toe drag moves in the odd one on one situations in the offensive zone. His poise with the puck however often translates into being a bit slow to react to danger. The problem is, as of now he needs time to show his skills, when the pace of the game is slow he can do it, when it's higher pace than the average game in the Swedish junior league he keeps playing with the same low intensity level and he doesn't execute fast enough to do anything more than ordinary stuff. His play with the U18 national team on the international stage was underwhelming, as Lindgren didn't show the confidence needed to try to make more of an impact.

On a side note, moving forward to survive at the senior level he will need to do a much better job at escaping incoming checks along the end boards. Jesper has a long way to go in terms of development, but the talent is certainly there and the wait might be rewarding.

Lindholm, Max
LC – AIK (SWE Jr.) – 6'1" 195
HockeyProspect.com Ranking: NR

Lindholm is a center with notable playmaking abilities, he can complete accurate passes with both his forehand and backhand to take advantage of his good vision. Shows solid puckhandling skills and good puck protection, he doesn't mind stickhandling in traffic but sometimes that leads to avoidable turnovers. Max is fairly responsible defensively and is willing to work inside his own zone. His balance is fine and he moves his feet quickly, however his skating stride clearly needs some work, as he doesn't extend it properly and lacks straight forward acceleration. Improving his skating would definitely make him a legitimate NHL prospect.

Lizotte, Cameron
LD - Peterborough Petes (OHL) 6'02" 201
HockeyProspect.com Ranking: 198

Lizotte is an extremely physical defender whose game improved throughout the year. He has a tireless work ethic and non-stop compete level. Lizotte leaves everything out on the ice as he hits, block shots and fights. His strong anticipation and gap control skills allow him to make massive hits and break up passing lanes. He will rush the puck out of his own zone if he sees an opening and get the puck deep inside the offensive end. He would need a lot of developing offensively in order to make an impact in that area at the NHL level.

Lizotte will have to pick his spots better. He has a tendency to chase hits or get too aggressive in 1 on 1's. He struggles positionally, especially in his own zone. He tends to get too puck focused too often and he gets himself into situations where he chases rather than defends.

There is a lot to like in Lizotte's game. The kid is a gamer and would seem to go through a wall for his team. He makes are list on heart and toughness alone.

Quotable: " He's tough, he probably eats rocks for his pre-game meal." - NHL Scout

Quotable: " I really liked him in his OHL Draft year. I honestly thought he would be better at this point of his development. Having said that, I'm a fan of how he approaches the game. He's as tough as anyone in the league and (he) never saw a hit he would pass up. He's a big project, but you can't teach heart or size." - Mark Edwards

Llewellyn, Darby
LW - Kitchener Rangers (OHL) 6'01" 180
HockeyProspect.com Ranking: NR

After being regarded as a mid round pick by HockeyProspect.com in our 2014 NHL Draft Black Book, Llewellyn slipped through the entire draft. Despite a good showing as a free agent invite at the Detroit Red Wings training camp, his season started out well and he struggled to find his way to the style of play that made him so successful last season. He started coming around at about the midway point of the season and provided a strong finish to once again earn draft consideration for the 2015 NHL Entry Draft.

Llewellyn has decent size and smart positioning in the offensive zone. He is equally adept at creating plays for his teammates and finishing, but his positional play at the side of the slot has given him more scoring opportunities than anything else. He has good two-way ability and is responsible in his own end. Confidence was shown by his coaching staff putting him in more defensive situations. Llewellyn doesn't have huge upside but also possesses a low bust factor and has the intelligence and talent to contribute at the next level in a lesser role.

Looke, Jens
RW – Brynas (SWE) – 6'0.5" 180
HockeyProspect.com Ranking: 99

Looke played in a lot of different situations at a lot of different levels this season. If he wasn't playing for the Swedish U18/U20 national teams, he was playing with Brynas in the J18, J20, and SHL. All that experience this year has probably contributed to make Looke an even more versatile player, but all the changes didn't help him to carry on the strong play he showcased in the first part of the season and the injury suffered against Russia at the U18 World Championships was the final hitch of his Spring.

Jens can step into high gear quickly and is a solid puckhandler, particularly at high speeds. He can play whatever type of game is needed on his line, can find his linemates with ease but also be the shooter or the first guy going to work along the boards, as he doesn't shy away from the physical play. Even if he isn't a pure finisher, he does possess a good shot that he likes to use from the left half side boards on the powerplay. He rarely takes a shift off, consistently working hard in both zones, but despite his efforts and mobility, he often finds himself on the outside of the play. He projects as a good complimentary player, but maybe not as good as the sum of his tools.

Luchuk, Aaron
LC - Windsor Spitfires (OHL) 5'10" 183
HockeyProspect.com Ranking: NR

Luchuk who was a real offensive threat and a perennial scorer in Minor Midget has had to adapt to a lesser role in the OHL thus far in his career and has done a very good job of embracing the change. He was primarily utilized in a third or fourth line role for the Spitfires and used his strong skating ability to factor in both the offensive and defensive side of the game.

He has good speed and will challenge defenders one on one. He has good puck handling ability and was also able to create offense with a deceptive shot. He works hard on the backcheck, keeping up with opposing forwards and was usually a key part of the Spitfires penalty kill. We believe Luchuk might receive a little late round consideration. His offensive upside is somewhat untapped playing behind several veterans, so as he moves up the depth chart he will be able to show more of the offense he displayed in minor midget.

Luff, Matt
RW - Belleville Bulls (OHL) 6'02" 181
HockeyProspect.com Ranking: NR

Luff had a pretty solid rookie season in the OHL and he is receiving consideration at the 2015 NHL Entry Draft because of it. Matt was a key player for the Oakville Rangers on their 2013 OHL Cup Championship run but lacked any size or strength. However, Matt grew several inches over the past two years and now has excellent size at 6'2". He needs to learn to use his size as more of a weapon and began doing it by being a net front presence on the power play.

He has a decent shot with good power. He is also a moderately good passer. His skating will need some improvements as his first few steps are a struggle and he sometimes has a tough time with his balance. He's hard on the wall in battle but can get pushed around a little by stronger players.

Luff lacks top six offensive abilities but he also has a way to go before becoming a player who would be considered a very good role player. The positive is that with the amount in which he's improved in the last two years he is trending upwards, but still has a lot of work ahead of him to reach his professional potential.

MacArthur, Tyler
RD - Owen Sound Attack (OHL) 6'04" 179
HockeyProspect.com Ranking: NR

MacArthur plays a steady shutdown game for the Owen Sound Attack. He is positionally sound and he uses his long reach to stick check oncoming forwards and break up plays. MacArthur is effective at clearing the goal area, particularly on the penalty kill and is good at boxing opposing players out when there are rebounds. MacArthur is physical along the wall and wins his fair share of puck battles. He's also not afraid to take a hit to make a play. Offensively there isn't much to his game and he struggles with the puck on his stick. Tyler will need to improve on making the smart simple play with the puck if he wants to have a chance to advance to the next level. As he fills out he could become a very tough player to play against.

MacAdams, Eric
RW – Austin Prep (MA HS) 5'11 175
HockeyProspect.com Ranking: NR

It is actually amazing MacAdams has yet to commit to any NCAA school this late in the season as although he does not have the blazing speed and footwork he certainly plays all three zones and a very reliable 200-foot type player. He probably will not develop into the prolific scorer and numbers he has produced in the Massachusetts HS ranks, yet will play in all areas on the rink and situational plays like penalty-kill and face-offs. At the next level he probably will not fill the back of the net though does bring smarts and some offensive know-how. Not sure he gets enough credit for his vision, playmaking, and puck possession skills. We like his energy, sandpaper character, and high compete level.

Mackie, Gage
RW – Shattuck St. Mary's Midget Prep (MN-HS) 6'3" 185LBS
HockeyProspect.com Ranking: NR

The Alaska native, Gage Mackie has good work ethic and character on and off the ice. Being the first higher end prospect to head to an upstart NCAA program like Arizona State speaks to that. Mackie is at his best when he plays a north, south game and uses his large frame to get on the fore check and create turnovers. He is strong on his skates and protects the puck well along the boards and on the cycle. Does a good job setting screens in front and taking the eyes away from the goalie however, mackie's game lacks physicality and grit at times and it keeps him from being as effective as he could be. Mackie will need to develop more consistency in his physical game. There is room for improvement is some of the finer aspects of his skating but his straight line skating gets him where he needs to be.

Mackie plays a sound defensive game where he has good stick positioning on the back check and takes away cross ice passing lanes well. For Mackie, the more consistent he can become at the things he does well and simplify his game the more effective he will be.

Malgin, Denis
RC – ZSC Zurich (NLA) – 5'9" 175
HockeyProspect.com Ranking: 93

Son of former Russian player Albert Malgin who spent most of his career in Switzerland, Denis has dual citizenship but is born and raised in the Northern part of the Swiss Confederation. Malgin had little problems overcoming his small stature disadvantage at the Swiss junior level, consistently outplaying older opponents, so much that last season at 16 he was already playing regularly and producing against men in the NLB. Therefore, it was not surprising to see him play a pretty big role and producing at a PPG pace at this year WJC as an underager. It is however in the last part of the season that he may have been able to convince some NHL teams to buy into his capabilities and potential.

Expected to lead the offense of his national team at the U18 World Championships in his home country, Malgin didn't disappoint and was the engine behind Switzerland's successful campaign. Perhaps even more persuasive was how he was able to elevate his game in previous weeks during NLA playoffs, effectively contributing to his team's run to the final. Against the best players of a league that features many good skaters, Denis' speedy play through the neutral zone was very noticeable and valuable. Even if he may lack some explosiveness and his agility appears to be only average as a small player, skating is still a difference maker for Malgin. When he picks up the puck from his defensemen he usually takes several turning steps during which he chooses the open lane in the neutral zone where to quickly and progressively build his deceptive speed. Not many players can accelerate with full control of the puck like he does, and he has the rare capability of hitting another gear when he seems at top speed already. No matter how fast he is going, Malgin is still able to process the play effectively and maintain full vision of the ice. He possesses tremendous hockey sense and he takes advantage of that on both sides of the puck. Combining it with the way he can carry speed on makes him effective on the forecheck and already valuable defensively in the neutral zone, as he ends up covering more ice and lanes than most taller players. The play without the puck is probably the most underrated part of his game. Denis' effectiveness decreases the closer he gets to his own net, but he does possess a good stick defensively.

His offensive skills are obvious. He is a very good passer and puts his playmaking ability to work on the powerplay mainly from the left half side boards. His soft hands help him buying time to look for open lanes and to finish chances in tight. He already possesses a decent slap shot and a quick wrister that can surprise goaltenders, but will definitely need to add power for it to be a threat at the next level. Its accuracy may also be improved, as we have seen him miss the net quite a few times on good opportunities.

Malgin obviously needs to get stronger on the puck, but that's not the main concern with his game. Even if despite the small stature he is not unable to throw the rare check, he is largely ineffective at board play at the senior level. He will also have to learn not to carry the puck and himself into situations along the boards where he gets easily eliminated from the play. Be it in open ice or along the boards, too often Denis puts himself in vulnerable positions, and as of now doesn't possess the agility and alertness to consistently escape hits, especially along the boards. Learning to apply his hockey smarts to the board play and to better protect himself will be pivotal for his chances to successfully translate his game to the North American rinks and remain healthy along the process.

Quotable:" I liked him at the U18 this year more than I ever did in the past. I thought he had some outstanding games. One NHL scout said to me during a game that he reminded him of a poor mans Max Domi. I thought that was a pretty good comparison of some of the quick moves they both make in the offensive zone. Now that I've said that, please don't think that I'm saying he's Max Domi 2.0." _ Mark Edwards

Malmquist, Dylan
LC- Edina High (MN-HS) 5'10" 165LBS
HockeyProspect.com Ranking: NR

Malmquist was named Minnesota Associated Press Boys High School Player of the year after his senior year at Edina. The offensively skilled forward can play Center but may project better as a Winger down the road. His Combination of high end puck skills speed, offensive instincts and ability to execute at a fast pace make him dangerous in the offensive zone. Dylan has great stick handling ability and gets passes off his tape quickly. Does a very good job reading the play and knowing where the soft spots are in the offensive zone.

Malmquist game in his own end is a little bit different then in the offensive end where everything is done with decisiveness and confidence. In some viewings he seemed unsure of himself and hesitant on his defensive positioning; however the willingness to work at both ends of the ice is not any issue for Mamquist. Adding some bulk to his frame will help him be stronger on the puck and better in the faceoff circle where he struggles against larger centers. Dylan will also need some time to round out his game in his own end. Malmquist will be heading to University of Notre Dame in 15/16.

Malone, Seamus
LC – Dubuque (USHL) 5'10" 183
HockeyProspect.com Ranking: NR

Malone has taken his game to yet another level, playing at a point per game clip in 14/15 and was one of the most dominating players in the USHL all season. Malone has made strides in the style and discipline in which he plays the game in 14/15. Playing an agitating and sometimes dirty style has always been a part of Malone's game going back to his days with the Chicago Mission program. There has been a maturation and refinement to his game this year. He has learned how to be just as effective while taking fewer bad penalties. Malone plays the agitator role perfectly but has top six forward offensive skill and instincts. Often sent over the boards to relieve pressure and regain the momentum. This season it seemed he was able to get someone on the opposition to take a bad penalty almost every night. Malone has excellent vision and passing ability and has decent finishing ability with his release.

Malone has added close to 20lbs to his frame in the last year and shows great lower body strength when protecting the puck. His fluid skating stride can be deceiving and surprise defenders. Malone plays a sound 200 foot game, is equally physical at both ends of the ice. Seamus has developed into an excellent penalty killer, he won't shy away from blocking shots and does a great job reading the play and having his stick in the right position. He has quick strides to challenge the point on the penalty kill and the breakaway speed to pull away and create shorthanded chances. After spending 2 full season's in the USHL Malone's game is ready for the next level which will find him at The University of Wisconsin in 15/16 where he will likely fit into a key role for a badger team that will be looking for offensive playmakers.

Quotable: "Malone might be one of those players who needs to develop even more at the College level." - NHL Scout

Mangiapane Andrew
LW - Barrie Colts (OHL) 5'10" 170
HockeyProspect.com Ranking: 86

Last season we liked Andrew's upside and ranked him for the 2014 NHL Entry Draft, Mangiapane returned to Barrie this season as an undrafted player and responded by posting over 100 points. Though he's not big in stature, he regularly finishes his checks, goes to the dirty areas of the ice and isn't afraid to take contact to make the play.

Mangiapane is very shifty with the puck and is tough to contain, even in small areas. He is almost impossible to hit and regularly makes defenders look silly with his elusiveness. Mangiapane has a quick first three-steps, good top-speed and always keeps his feet moving. He is very good carrying the puck up ice and into the offensive zone with possession of the puck. He displays good hockey sense and knows when to pass and when to shoot. He's an excellent passer and is very dangerous off the rush.

He's a regular penalty killer and while he worries about defense first, he's always a threat to create something offensively. Mangiapane has a quick stick and closes gaps quickly, which makes him very effective down a man. His passing, vision and shiftiness are his calling cards but he's a capable goal scorer too. He has 67 goals over the last two seasons. He has an accurate shot that carries more power than you'd expect. Mangiapane will have to overcome his size but we think he has the talent, hockey sense and the skill set to give him a good shot at succeeding.

Quotable: "We had him ranked for the OHL Priority Selection Draft, went undrafted. We had him ranked for the NHL Entry Draft, went un-drafted. I really hope this is the year the kid finally gets to hear his name called at a draft. Off the charts compete level, speedy, talented and fearless. I think he could be the exception to the rule when it comes to size." - Ryan Yessie

Marcoux, Antoine
LW/C – Victoriaville Tigres (QMJHL) – 6'1" 169
HockeyProspect.com Ranking: NR

Marcoux just finished his first full season in the QMJHL after playing the last two with the Trois-Rivieres Estacades in the Quebec Midget AAA league. Marcoux got his first taste of QMJHL action last year after he was called up for good, post-Christmas break in the QMJHL. He was drafted by Victoriaville in the 10th round of the 2013 QMJHL Draft. He has good puck skills and loves to shoot; in Midget AAA he was dangerous on the power play from the half-wall position. He's a below-average skater, needs more explosiveness in his skating strides and we have not seen a lot of improvements over the last three seasons. He has decent hockey sense and can make plays offensively; but his best attribute is his puck-protection in the offensive zone. Although he's 6'1", Marcoux is not a physical player at all, but makes good use of his frame in puck-protection situations. Marcoux will be a good junior player but we don't see a lot of hope for him as an NHL player, should go undrafted at the draft.

Marino, John
RD – South Shore Kings (USPHL PRE.) – 6'0.5" 171
HockeyProspect.com Ranking: 75

The Yale commit was very good down the stretch despite playing against lesser competition. He was very impressive in the playoffs and the Beantown Spring Classic. He's a strong, smooth skater with good lateral movement and ability to rush the puck up ice. His gap control is underrated and he has a very good stick. He's a possession defender than can carry the puck, hold on to it and keep opposing forwards to the perimeter. There were times during the regular season and in the All-Star game where he appeared bored with the competition level. There is concern that he won't step out of his comfort level and head to the USHL.

Marner, Mitchell
RW - London Knights (OHL) 5'11" 164
HockeyProspect.com Ranking: 3

Marner is a player who has impressed us ever since our first viewing of him with the Don Mills Flyers. His ability to be such an impact player at just 5'6" & about 135 lbs was impossible to miss and the Knights' made him their first round pick. While he still needs to add some weight and muscle before making the jump to the NHL, he has added both height and weight since his Minor Midget days.

Marner displays high-end playmaking ability in the offensive zone and can thread the needle with impressive consistency and accuracy. While he always seemed to be more of a pass first type of forward, he has really improved his shot, which has rounded out his offensive game nicely. His 44 goals speak to that. His vision and intelligence with the puck is among the very best in the draft. Along with the high-end offensive ability, Mitch is very defensively responsible and uses his speed to apply back-pressure on the puck carrier. His improved defensive play saw him receive a regular shift on the penalty kill this season. He did a very good job putting pressure on the puck and even getting in front of some shots. Marner also created shorthanded chances due to his speed and puck skills.

If there is a concern right now for Mitch, it's is his lack of strength. He will need to get stronger in order to handle the physical toll the NHL will take on his body.

Marner should be a lock to be a top 6 pick. He played down the middle prior to the OHL but has primarily played on the wing with London. With what Marner has accomplished so far in his young career, we won't rule out the chance that he can make the switch to center in the NHL someday. Regardless, he is a skilled forward who will likely lean on his playmaking ability a little more than his scoring at the top level but is capable of doing both.

Quotable: "You don't see a player with his talent backcheck like that everyday." NHL Scout

Quotable: "One of the smartest players I've seen in past few years." - NHL Scout

Quotable: "I love watching him play. He's an extremely intelligent player who blends his creativity with high-end skill. He works his ass off in all three zones. He also creates havoc on the forecheck with his ability to change direction so quickly, he's really good on his edges. When I think ahead to when he's got a couple years of NHL under his belt playing with smart, skilled players, I see boatloads of offense being created. I think he's the 3rd best prospect in this draft and will keep Eichel on his toes once he (Marner) matures physically. I think he's either Arizona's pick at number three or the Leaf's pick when they select 4th overall." - Mark Edwards

Marody, Cooper
RC – Sioux Falls (USHL) 6'0.25" 173
HockeyProspect.com Ranking: 114

After an early season trade from Muskegon to Sioux Falls, Marody really turned it on and moved along at over a point per game pace for the Stampede and in turn made a consistent rise on the draft board throughout the year. Playing on the Stampede's first line with impressive 2016 eligible Kieffer Bellows and 2014 Maple Leafs draft pick Dakota Joshua, Marody has been able to showcase his playmaking abilities.

Marody, a Michigan commit, sees the ice very well. He's a really smart player. Sees passing lanes open up and takes them. It was nice to see his confidence grow throughout the year, especially after he joined Sioux Falls. He started taking more shots and started scoring more goals to go along with his assists.

Rising consistently up the draft board all year, Marody made a good push to get drafted in the middle rounds this year. His high hockey IQ matched with his great playmaking skills make him a guy that has a lot of potential if he continues to develop at the consistent rate he has through his two years in the USHL.

Marsh, Adam
LW – Saint-John Sea Dogs (QMJHL) – 6'0" 158
HockeyProspect.com Ranking: 123

Marsh was a player who came a bit out of nowhere this season after signing with Saint-John as a free agent. The Chicago native was undrafted in the OHL and was selected in the 2nd round by Indiana in the 2013 USHL Futures Draft.

Marsh didn't take much time to adjust to the QMJHL and had success immediately in his QMJHL career, but his play cooled off in the 2nd half of the season before he suffered a season-ending injury (high ankle sprain) late in the regular season. Marsh plays with a lot of energy on the ice and is quite active in the offensive zone. He's a good skater who uses his wheels well on the forecheck and to get open in the offensive zone. He showed potential as a sniper in the 1st half of the season, using his quick shot to score goals. He has a good compete level and gets involved physically but clearly lacks strength right now. He will need to add some mass to his frame in the next couple of years to be ready for the professional game. That would make him more effective along the boards, and he would win more one-on-one battles. Seemed to run out of gas in the 2nd half of the season, was probably not ready physically for a full season. It would be interesting to see him how he rebounds next season and if we see the same Marsh that we saw in the first half of the season.

Martenet, Chris
LD - London Knights (OHL) 6'07" 197
HockeyProspect.com Ranking: 79

After winning a Clark Cup Championship with the Indiana Ice of the USHL, Martenet made the jump to the OHL with the London Knights joining their young blueline. The OHL was trial by fire for Martenet and he had to learn from his mistakes as they occurred and he was able to improve throughout the season. He's one of the tallest players available for the draft. He is capable of playing tough down low, although his strength isn't quite where it needs to be at this point. His one on one play improved but he still got burned at times due to his lack of footwork. Playing the rush he often backed in too far, allowing a big gap, which led to giving up uncontested shots. His passing ability is a little hit or miss. He's at his best when choosing the simple high percentage, easier pass. He doesn't possess any NHL projectable offensive talent. He wanders way too deep in the offensive zone too often and doesn't possess the skating ability to always recover.

Martenet came a long way this season but in our opinion, he still has a ways to go. NHL teams will covet his size and long reach, as it screams upside. That said, Martenet is a project but has the potential to develop into a massive shutdown defender.

Quotable: " I know he's got a few flaws but I love that long stick. Compared to what's out there this year, he's got something to work with." NHL Scout

Quotable: " I full expect someone to grab him in 2nd round or the 3rd round at the latest." - NHL Scout

Quotable: " The other kid (Crawley) was better than him (Martenet) last time I was here (London)." - NHL Scout

Quotable: " He struggles with his gap control and that's hard to fix." - NHL Scout

Quotable: " He's improved a lot this year, but I've seen him give up a lot of ice playing 1 on 1's. I thought he struggled a bit with puck on his stick when he was pressured. I do like his effort level and that long reach. He got much better taking advantage of his size as the season progressed." - Mark Edwards

Massie, Jake
LD – Kimball Union (HIGH – NH) – 6'0.5" 172
HockeyProspect.com Ranking: 108

He was the defensive leader for a retooling Kimball Union squad that finished in the top eight of prep hockey. He's a dynamic talent with and without the puck. He can skate well and is exceptional in transition. He makes some high-end plays that are very flashy while not having quite the vision or hockey smarts of some of the other upper echelon defensemen in the region. He's a little reckless at times, but can step up and make big hits as well as head-turning plays with the puck. He has the highest ceiling of any prep defender in New England, but has to learn to play a simpler and more team-oriented game on a more frequent basis.

McBride, Nick
LG – Prince Albert Raiders (WHL) – 6'04" 179
HockeyProspect.com Ranking: 188

Nick McBride is a technically sound butterfly goalie who played this year with a struggling Prince Albert Raiders club in the WHL. He split the starter job with Rylan Parenteau. He had a challenging job this year in Prince Albert but still looked strong in terms of positioning, rebound control, transition technique and mental toughness. He's also NHL-sized already, standing at 6-foot-4 and still growing. A solid performance at the 2015 CHL Top Prospects Game helped raise McBride's stock in his NHL draft year.

McBride uses a fundamentally sound stance that utilizes his large frame, effectively closing off several holes. Staying in the paint most of the game, he plays a fairly conservative but relaxed butterfly style. His upper-body reflexes are a bit of a weakness at this point, as we saw him get beaten almost exclusively up high in our viewings. Long legs, however, make him naturally difficult to beat down low. His ability to cover the corners is definitely a strength, along with his ability to shift from post-to-post. This being helped along by the fact that he has such long lower extremities.

Appearing confident in the crease despite his fairly conservative style, he looks big in the net and is comfortable handling the puck. His size, stance, positioning, puck-tracking abilities and rebound control all look better than average. His lateral post-to-post mobility is very good as he is very flexible and long-limbed, giving him good shot recovery. He comes in and out of his butterfly fairly fast, but needs to show better poise, as sometimes on second and third chance opportunities he puts himself in extraneous situations that leave him down and out and too much of the net wide open—these moments are few and far between, though.

Quotable: "He moves well. I watched him go through drills at the Top Prospects game and I liked what I saw. In general terms he seems to have all the tools but at the end of the day, he's struggling a bit to get it done out on the ice." - Mark Edwards

McCool, Hayden
LW - Windsor Spitfires (OHL) 6'03" 195
HockeyProspect.com Ranking: NR

After being selected very high in the 2013 OHL Priority Selection Draft, McCool was traded from the Niagara Ice Dogs to the Windsor Spitfires in the Ho-Sang deal. The Spits' gave him every opportunity to succeed, giving him a ton of icetime and playing him in offensive situations.

McCool is a pretty simple up and down forward who does a good job of putting pucks deep and battling. He is a decent checker but would benefit from getting stronger. He doesn't possess a lot of offensive ability but will occasionally surprise you with a few flashes here and there. McCool lacks the offensive ability to become a top six player at the NHL level. There is a chance he could be drafted in a late round.

Quotable: "I didn't see anything in his game to warrant his top 10 selection in the OHL Draft and have yet to see enough in his game for me to draft him this June." - Mark Edwards

Quotable: "Not on my list." - NHL Scout

McCormick, Sam
RW – Madison (USHL) 5'10" 165
HockeyProspect.com Ranking: NR

McCormick has stayed under a lot of scout's radar so far in his young career and is a long shot to be drafted in 2015. A product of the Wisconsin High School ranks, McCormick finished up his first USHL season for the Madison Capitols. He is a smaller stature forward that has a ways to go physically to make an impact at the professional levels. However, there are aspects of McCormick's game that will give him a chance going forward. Sam is the younger brother of current Ottawa Senators prospect Max McCormick. He has high hockey IQ and work ethic. Except for his size McCormick is a complete player who brings an honest effort every night. He doesn't shy away from being physical against bigger players and doesn't quit on pucks. Has good on ice awareness, covers for his defenseman when they join the rush and comes back into his own end and gives his defenseman an outlet option when it's needed. Sam is also effective at being elusive and getting behind the opposing defenseman in the neutral zone and can get sprung on breakaways.

Offensively McCormick has a quick and accurate release. He doesn't need a lot of time to get the puck off his tape and can pick the corners nicely. He is good at reading the play and quick to loose pucks. Sam isn't shy to go after rebounds and will pay the price in front or take a hit to make a play if necessary. His skating ability allows him to avoid direct hits. One play that maybe best describes McCormick's game, he took a big hit along the boards where an opposing player caught him with his head down and he was separated from the puck, McCormick bounced back up, skated hard to back check and delivered a big hit on that same player at the other end of the ice, then proceeded to execute a pass to a teammate into the neutral zone for a partial breakaway. He was trusted to play in all situations for a Capitols squad that prided itself on a strong work ethic every night due to its lack of high end offensive talent. He moved up and down the lineup and was effective no matter where he played and had a knack for scoring big goals. Certainly how McCormick develops physically the next few years at Ohio State will determine his ceiling going forward but has a lot of good things going in his game. McCormick likely will be returning to the Capitols in 15/16 before heading to Ohio State.

McDavid, Connor
LC - Erie Otters (OHL) 6'01" 187
HockeyProspect.com Ranking: 1st Overall

We've been lucky enough to watch Connor McDavid dozens of times per season going back to when he dominated for the Toronto Marlboros, despite being a year younger than everyone else. After gaining exceptional status for the OHL Draft, he has wowed us for three seasons in the Ontario Hockey League with the Erie Otters. McDavid enters the 2015 NHL Entry Draft as our clear cut #1 prospect.

Connor possesses electrifying speed and acceleration. He gets his feet moving instantaneously and gets everything out of his stride, allowing him to pull away from good skaters quickly. At least once per game you would think he has a turbo button for his skates. His vision is outstanding and he always seems to know who's around him and what his best option is. He combines these two skills to create plays for his linemates. He is more of a passer than a shooter and is the type of player who can make anyone better. While he tends to pass more, Connor is very capable of scoring highlight reel goals on any given shift. He can blow you away with his puck handling ability. Down low with the puck he handles pressure well and uses lightning fast feet and his ever improving size to help fend off checkers. Emerging from the corner is one of McDavid's signature moves. He is so dangerous with his passing and shooting options cutting to the net, it makes him nearly impossible to stop.

Connor isn't overly aggressive or a stud defensively, but he isn't a big liability either. He seldom cheats and he spent time on the penalty kill and used his anticipation skills to force turnovers. What makes Connor so dangerous in the defensive zone and on the penalty kill, is his ability to blow past defenders in the blink of an eye anyone so much as fumbles a puck. He makes teams pay when he's given breakaways.

Edmonton won the draft lottery and will select McDavid. He will instantly make them better. Connor is a future star in the NHL and we fully expect him to live up to all the hype.

Quotable: "Is there anything left to say? I feel lucky to have been able to watch him play live so many times over the past four years. Future superstar in the NHL." - Mark Edwards

McDermott, John
LW – Westminster (HIGH – CT) – 6'1.25" 190
HockeyProspect.com Ranking: 132

He has good size, skates well and is strong on pucks, but he isn't a finisher. He uses his edges and has good lateral mobility. He projects as a bottom six player that can chip in offensively from time to time. He needs to be more assertive on a more consistent basis. Might be a player that gets selected.

Quotable: "Not much skill but a likable player. He has a good motor." - NHL Scout

McDonald, Dylan
RC - Ottawa 67's (OHL) 6'03" 178
HockeyProspect.com Ranking: NR

Dylan didn't see a lot of ice this season but when he did he was noticeable. He has great size and competes hard on the fourth line. He's a good skater and punishes opponents going into the corner. He battles hard and works for pucks. He's a tough player to play against. While he doesn't project to be selected at the 2015 NHL Entry Draft, McDonald showed he can be a tough player to play against at the OHL level. At his size, if he can show some offensive potential he could be a late bloomer.

McEwan, James
LW - Guelph Storm (OHL) 5'11" 190
HockeyProspect.com Ranking: NR

McEwan was selected out of the Chatham-Kent Cyclones program and really improved a lot from the midway point of his minor midget season through this season. McEwan is a hard working forward who competes for the puck. He is a decent checker and will take the body and take the hit to make the play. He played a bottom six role for the Storm. James will work hard and get most of his points from dirty goals. Don't expect him to be a big points guy, he plays a very good two-way game and will compete in all three zones. McEwan shows some potential as a future grinder, but isn't likely to be selected at the 2015 NHL Entry Draft.

McFadden, Garrett
LD - Guelph Storm (OHL) 5'11" 180
HockeyProspect.com Ranking: NR

McFadden, the former first round pick in the OHL Priority Selection had a decent rookie season and was expected to build on it this season. While he showed some signs of advancing his game, he didn't reach our expectations this season.

Garrett is a strong skating defenseman who is capable of rushing the puck up ice but won't do it unless he has plenty of room. His strongest asset may be his long distance passes. He often showed the ability to hit a forward near the offensive blueline from within his own zone. He has very good power in his shot from the point. He is very aggressive trying to hold the line, which led to mixed results.

Defensively he's more dedicated than a lot of offensive minded defensemen. He ties up his man in the slot very well despite commonly facing a size disadvantage. He sometimes has some mental lapses and can get caught out of position in the defensive zone. McFadden is an offensive minded defenseman but hasn't really produced in the manner we expected and still has plenty of work to get his game where it needs to be.

Quotable:" At his size I want to see a pretty dynamic defenseman and I just didn't see that from McFadden in any of my viewings these past two years." - Mark Edwards

Quotable:" I think he's just going to be a good junior player." - NHL Scout

McKenzie, Brett
LC - North Bay Battalion (OHL) 6'01" 188
HockeyProspect.com Ranking: NR

McKenzie displays above average skating and vision. He plays a strong 200' foot game competing on the backcheck. He works hard and drives the net with authority. He won't put up high point totals playing in North Bay's defensive system, but his offensive game did improve as the year went on. We thought he tried to do too much for a large chunk of the season. Brett is an effective checker and two-way forward but really doesn't possess much NHL upside at this point of his career.

McNeely, Jack
RD – Lakeville North (MN-HS) 6'2.5" 178LBS
HockeyProspect.com Ranking: 207

McNeely is a tall lanky defenseman with just an ok skating stride but needs time to full out his frame. While McNeely prides his game around taking care of things in his own end, he does posses solid puck moving skill. McNeely makes quick passes all over the ice. Jack competes hard in the corners; however he does not use his size as much as some would like to see and lacks physicality. McNeely has a heavy, accurate shot from the point that is difficult for goalies to handle. Played in all situations for a deep Lakeville North squad and was paired for most the season with Jack Sadek. McNeely finished his 2014/15 season with the Tri-City Storm (USHL) it's undetermined if McNeely will play next season in the USHL before heading to Neb-Omaha of the NCAA.

McNiven, Michael
G - Owen Sound Attack (OHL) 6'01" 207
HockeyProspect.com Ranking: 119

McNiven is a good sized goaltender who was in his OHL rookie year with the Owen Sound Attack. He got off to a hot start to his season and started seeing some 50/50 action as far as getting starts. He went through a slump after CHL Top Prospects game but rebounded to finish off his year, once again finding his consistency.

McNiven is a fierce competitor and doesn't play with as much structure as many of today's goalies. He's great with his glove hand and is quick down low taking away the bottom of the net. He uses his stick well. He takes away angles and challenges shooters. He showed the knowledge of how to direct rebounds away properly, but needs to gain consistency in that area. He will need to improve on his lateral movement. Too often he relies on his great scrambling ability to make second saves too. He needs to refine his movements from the butterfly rather than rely on highlight reel diving saves.

McNiven became an OHL drafted goaltender despite very little instruction from an actual goalie coach. He was very raw and has come miles since his Halton Hurricane days. We actually still consider him raw, but we love his progression these past two seasons. We view McNiven as goaltender who mixes his own athletic style with the structure what he continues to pickup now that he is getting instruction from an actual goalie coach. Lastly, we like the fact he stopped a lot of pucks this season and won several games on his own.

Quotable: "He has a quick glove and showed the ability to make second saves. I love his poise and how confident he seems to be. He reminded me a bit of Mason McDonald (Calgary 34th overall 2015) that way. I think if he gets better technically, he has some pretty big upside. Good kid too, I've enjoyed speaking to him multiple times." - Mark Edwards

Meier, Timo
RW – Halifax Mooseheads (QMJHL) – 6'0" 209
HockeyProspect.com Ranking: 13

Meier finished his second season in Halifax after being selected 12th overall in the 2013 CHL Import Draft. After a good first season, where he was able to establish himself as a good all-around player, he took his game to an all new level this year and was a breakthrough star in the QMJHL by being among the league-leading scorers. The Swiss forward finished the season with 90 points, which was good for 11th overall in the league scoring race. He also played for Team Switzerland at the 2015 IIHF World Junior Hockey Championship, where he amassed 6 points in 6 games.

Meier's production was a big surprise to most people. Last year he didn't get as much of a chance to play in offensive situations. He saw a lot power play time this season and played with better players this year. Full credit goes to Meier, who made very nice progression in his game, mostly with his skating which we had issues with last year. Not that it's elite now, but we don't see it as much of a problem going forward. He still needs to keep improving his starts, but once he gets going, he's very tough to handle for the opposing team. He's very strong physically, loves to take the puck to the net and loves to finish his hits. He wins a lot of battles along the boards, at the QMJHL level he's dominant in using his strength and smarts to win puck battles. Last year we saw a player who was not afraid of doing the dirty work in the corner for his teammates or taking punishment in front of the net. This year, he's still doing all of this, but he added that scoring dimension that makes him a very complete player offensively. He has a good shot and scored a lot of goals from the slot (where he likes to position himself) and also showed a very good one-timer. Clearly, playing with Nikolaj Ehlers sure didn't hurt his production either, but it's not like they were always played together this season (pretty similar to Ehlers and Drouin last year). Meier would still be considered a 1st round prospect without Ehlers on his team. He has the chance to become a very strong power-forward in the future for the NHL team that selects him in June. Meier is a complementary player and will need two good linemates at the NHL level but has potential to play on an offensive line at the NHL level.

Quotable: "Very improved from last year, his skating has come a long way since joining the Mooseheads in 2013." - HP scout Jérome Bérubé

Quotable: " I hadn't seen him since last year when I saw him at the Top Prospects game. I couldn't believe how much he improved his skating. A scout told me later that he went home last summer making improving his skating his top priority." - Mark Edwards

Meloche, Nicolas
RD – Baie-Comeau Drakkar (QMJHL) – 6'2" 200
HockeyProspect.com Ranking: 32

Meloche was Baie-Comeau's first pick in the 2013 QMJHL Draft (15th overall) out of the St-Eustache Midget AAA program. He's a player that we really like having ranked in our top 10 in our QMJHL Draft Guide. Meloche quickly established himself in his rookie season, logging big minutes and having a big impact on his team's success in both the regular season and the playoffs. This year, Meloche became one of the leaders of his team, and continued to improve his game.

Before the season started, Meloche had the chance to represent his country at the Ivan Hlinka tournament, playing on a pair with Acadie-Bathurst defenseman Guillaume Brisebois. With Baie-Comeau, Meloche plays a ton, on the top pair of defensemen and quarterbacking the power play, even finding himself on the penalty kill. Meloche is a big and strong blueliner who makes life tough for the opposing team's forwards, playing a mean game along the boards and in front of the net. He won't hesitate to drop the gloves or come to the aid of a teammate or his goaltender. Meloche is a strong boy and doesn't lose many one-on-one battles. He's very calm on the ice, nothing seems to disturb him. He's very calm in his own zone, doesn't chase players around in his zone as he always keeps strong positioning. In the playoffs against Saint John, he was clearly on the Sea Dogs' hit list and never lost his cool, letting them take dumb penalties. He has improved his footwork since last year where it doesn't seem like an issue anymore. He does a great job moving the puck in the transition game, his passes are crisp and accurate. On the power play he loves to shoot the puck, he possesses an excellent point shot and hits the net often. He makes smart decisions offensively, whether it's in his puck management or when he pinches deep in the offensive zone. He's not dynamic like a Jérémy Roy or Thomas Chabot, but he's very steady at both ends and can play any style you throw at him. We like him in the first round but he has been in constant discussion in the 25-35 range for us all year.

Mercer, Cullen
RC - Plymouth Whalers (OHL) 6'00" 190
HockeyProspect.com Ranking: 194

Mercer had a good shot in Minor Midget but didn't project that high in the OHL. After a pretty low-key rookie season, he elevated his game this season for the Plymouth Whalers. Mercer played a great two-way role rotating from the first through fourth line on any given night. He has a very powerful shot, which was a weapon for him in the offensive zone. He was more relied upon to play a solid defensive game rather than put up points.

Mercer was arguably the best penalty killing forward for the Whalers this season and was willing to block shots. He also consistently cleared the zone. Mercer is also a very physical player who loves to finish his hits whenever possible. Mercer has a chance to be selected in the second half of the draft. He projects as a bottom six forward who plays a physical role and is relied upon on the penalty kill.

Merkley, Nick
LC – Kelowna Rockets (WHL) – 5'10" 191
HockeyProspect.com Ranking: 14

Nick Merkley is a slightly undersized but gritty playmaking centre for the Kelowna Rockets. Merkley's offensive skills are high end with agility and his passing game standing out as clear specialities. Aside from his advanced passing game, he has a unique set of skills for a player of his size, as he's a dangerously physical player in open-ice and drives powerfully toward the net when its advantageous. This is a smallish offensive player, but one with a ton of intangible skills that would be silly to overlook.

Shifty on his feet, Nick Merkley finds clever ways to use his slightly undersized height to his advantage. He's a sneaky player who finds routes into scoring areas quickly, showing a fearlessness to drive into the slot with the puck. He is capable of driving underneath the point of contact on hitting attempts, or using his superior agility to move around opponents, or change speeds quickly. He utilizes tremendous edge-work to stop-and-start or turn and pivot his way out of trouble or into an open scoring lane. While he's already very good at getting himself open, Merkley's passing game is another speciality. It's a trademark of his offence, as exemplified consistently by high skilled passes, that few players in juniors can accomplish with such consistency. Not to mention a hard but easily receivable east-to-west stretch pass from below the hashmarks. He added a hitting element to his game this year as well, adding a new physical dimension to his already well-rounded list of attributes. Indeed, there are a ton of positives to Nick Merkley's game, as he has a wide array of tricks to his trade—hockey sense, passing, shooting and hitting are all clear strengths.

Size will be a concern for soome and possibly magnified a bit by his aggressive and fearless style of play against bigger opponents. He has the upside to be a top six forward who can produce and create offense for his teammates.

Quotable:" Smallish, but protects the puck well and shows good anticipation off the puck. Really like him in the 15-20 range." - HP Scout Scott McDougall

Quotable:" Might just be an amazing junior player because of his lack of size and skating issues." - NHL Scout

Quotable:" He's just a hockey player who finds a way to get it done. He can play on my team anytime. A lot of NHL scouts told me his skating concerned them, but I don't see it being a problem. He might not win awards for prettiest skater but bottom line is he seems to play though just about anything. He's a gamer." - Mark Edwards

Meyer, Jarret
RD - Owen Sound Attack (OHL) 6'09" 240
HockeyProspect.com Ranking: NR

Meyer came to the Attack after spending last season with the New Jersey Rockets of the EHL. He made the jump with the Attack primarily receiving ice as their 6th or 7th defenseman. Meyer is huge. At 6'9" Meyer is the biggest defenseman to come around in a while, especially in the OHL. With a frame like that, teams really want to be able to see some upside, but he is a player who is very much still learning how to handle the level of talent in the OHL.

He isn't close to being able to keep up to the pace at the NHL level. His puck play is hit or miss, generally only finding success when he keeps it simple with a basic pass. One on one play will need to improve and he can stumble over his own feet sometimes. Physical play is another area which will need improvement, as much smaller players (everyone is smaller) are able to push him around quite a bit.

Meyer might have some potential to be a late round flier, but it would be based solely on his huge size. He has a very long road ahead before he could play in the NHL.

Michaud, Lucas
RW – Portland Jr. Pirates (USPHL PRE.) – 5'10.5" 205
HockeyProspect.com Ranking: 170

A University of Maine commit, he projects as a third or fourth line grinder. He's strong, wins battles along the boards and competes well, but he doesn't have the offensive ability to glow over. He's a good skater that uses his edges well and is hard to knock off his feet. There are flashes where he can put the puck in the net, but his hands and stick skills are average at best. He has a quick release on a heavy shot when he's moving towards the net.

Mikkola, Niko
LD – KalPa (Fin jr.) – 6'4" 185
HockeyProspect.com Ranking: NR

Mikkola is a huge defender with above average mobility and lateral quickness who was passed over in last year NHL draft. Niko does a sound job in the defensive zone with positioning and toughness, which makes him really a tough opponent to play against. He doesn't lose many one on one battles and moves the puck fairly well. He makes good first passes out of his zone and he's got a hard shot from the point. Overall he's a smart player who doesn't try anything extra that he couldn't do, he knows his limits and plays well within them. He made some nice progression over the last year. He played this season on the 2nd highest division in Finland and look for him to be a regular in the men's league next season with Kalpa.

Miller, David
RC - Kitchener Rangers (OHL) 5'09" 185
HockeyProspect.com Ranking: NR

After two very successful seasons with the Sault Ste. Marie Greyhounds, David Miller was moved to the Kitchener Rangers at the trade deadline in the deal that sent Justin Bailey to the Greyhounds. Miller stepped in and was immediately given top six minutes and was one of the most creative offensive players on the team. Miller is a smooth skater who has great hands controlling the puck very well and is very slippery through traffic. He changes speeds well in a split second and is a strong skater. His size does affect him at times but he is moderately strong for someone of his size.

He is a dangerous offensive player because he is equally skilled at shooting and passing, keeping opponents guessing. He will need to improve his defensive game to make the jump to the next level. He projects as an offensive player at the next level but he needs to show us he can play a higher skilled game before we think he could play at the NHL level at his size.

Montembeault, Samuel
G – Blainville-Boisbriand Armada (QMJHL) – 6'3" 166
HockeyProspect.com Ranking: 102

After backing up Étienne Marcoux last year, Montembeault got plenty of starts this season with the Armada. The Bécancourt native played in 52 games and won 33 games for one of the surprising teams in the QMJHL this season. Additionally, during the season, Montembeault also played in the CHL Top Prospects game in Oshawa, but unfortunately the Armada was surprised in the first round of the playoffs against Gatineau. Montembeault is a tall and lanky goaltender, listed at 6'3" and 166 pounds. His strongest asset is attitude in his crease, we love how calm he is and how he never seems to panic. Even after a bad goal, he doesn't get rattled, he always seems to be in his little world and very focused.

One of the areas where he made some nice progress this season is in his puck-tracking, which was one of his downsides in midget and his first year in the QMJHL. He's now able to anticipate the play better and is able to react accordingly. He possesses a good glove hand and good quickness in his lateral movements. He's also very good down low, playing a butterfly style. He has long legs and covers the lower part of the net very well. He seems always in control in his movements, he's quick but rarely gets himself out of position.

Consistency is a bit of an issue with him, can give up bad goals at times. In addition, by playing with the Armada, who plays a tight system, he doesn't get as many quality shots as other goaltenders in the league faced during the season. Montembeault has the size that NHL teams coveted but we feel he's been well protected with the Armada, he was near Booth at some point this year in our rankings but not so much right now.

Moberg, Sebastian
LD – HIFK (Fin elite) – 5'11" 165
HockeyProspect.com Ranking: NR

Moberg was passed over in last year NHL draft due mostly for his lack of strength and lack of high end qualities. He's a smooth skater with good offensive talent, has good mobility and moves the puck well but his overall skill set is average. Sebastian has huge problems in the defensive zone, he's a small kid who doesn't have enough physical strength and lose too many one on one battles along the boards or in front of the net. He can compensate his weaknesses with good body and stick positioning in the defensive zone. Moberg offensive potential is the reason why some teams might gamble with him at the draft.

Moore, Ryan
LC - Plymouth Whalers (OHL) 5'07" 166
HockeyProspect.com Ranking: NR

Ryan was selected in the second round of the 2012 OHL Priority Selection Draft and he was the highest player taken in that draft by the Windsor Spitfires in that draft. He struggled a little out of the gate, as his size was a noticeable concern and after having an improved sophomore season Moore was traded twice within hours of each other first to the Oshawa Generals then to the Plymouth Whalers.

Moore is very small but has high-end skating ability. He delays well with the puck to let lanes open and also possesses a deceptively quick release on his shot. He will need to get bigger and stronger as well as improve the defensive side of his game. At this point Moore does not project as a prospect for us for the 2015 NHL Entry Draft.

Morris, Cale
G - Waterloo (USHL) 6'0.75" 195
HockeyProspect.com Ranking: NR

After a mediocre start to the season with the Chicago Steel, Morris was traded to Waterloo and something clicked. For the majority of the second half of the season Morris was a brick wall and garnered more draft attention with each passing game. A Notre Dame commit, Morris lacks prototypical elite goaltender size, but moves very quickly in the crease. Laterally he is very quick, and can get from post to post very fast.

He's an aggressive goalie who challenges shooters outside of the crease and stays square to the shooter. Consistency is something he's had a bit of an issue with and may dissuade teams from taking him in the Draft. Morris' late season lights out play in his second eligible draft year may vault him into some conversations for teams looking for a goaltender.

Morrison, Brad
LW – Prince George Cougars (WHL) – 6'00" 154
HockeyProspect.com Ranking: 69

Morrison is a speedy, skilled forward for the Prince George Cougars. Morrison impressed us this season with his flashy, skilled, offensive play. Right from our first viewing, Morrison was a guy who was tough to miss. He utilized his dynamic skating ability to consistently create offense. One of his most impressive attributes is his stick handling ability at top speed. He can make opponents look like they're moving in slow motion at times.

In addition to his puck control ability, Morrison has both great passing and shooting ability. He moves the puck well finding the open man and has a very smooth, fluid movement to his passes casually hitting difficult passes. While his shot may not be the most powerful, he does get his shot off quickly and accurately. Perhaps most excitingly, Morrison has the guts to cut into the dangerous areas to score goals—despite the fact that he's usually heavily outside and sometimes takes some heavy open-ice hits.

Our concern with Morrison at this point is to physically mature and bulk up. He takes some heavy contact at times and at 154lbs, he needs to add more muscle to his frame before he'll be able to endure the punishment of professional hockey. Furthermore, he needs to improve his in own-zone play, as our scouts caught him floating in his own zone far too many times this year. He'll need to improve his backchecking and defensive commitment, as he's not always as effective without the puck outside the offensive zone as we would like.

Murray, Liam
LD - Windsor Spitfires (OHL) 6'01" 210
HockeyProspect.com Ranking: NR

Murray made the Spitfires as a 16 year old but split the season between the OHL Spitfires and Jr. B LaSalle Vipers. Murray played full time this season, primarily playing a 4-6 defenseman role but made his presence felt, especially as the season progressed. Murray is a physical shutdown defenseman who does a decent job of pinching and delivering a good first pass. He plays tough down low and is very physical against the opposition. His positional play is a little hit or miss and will need some refinement before he can reach his potential. His skating will also need to be touched up. Murray projects as a lower end physical shutdown defenseman at the next level. He has a moderate chance at getting picked late in this draft simply based off his size and physicality.

Murray, Troy
LD – Kootenay Ice (WHL) – 6'00" 185
HockeyProspect.com Ranking: NR

Troy Murray of the Kootenay Ice is a thoughtful and smooth-skating but physically immature two-way defenseman who is one of the youngest players available in the 2015 NHL Draft. Troy is the younger brother of the Columbus Blue Jackets 2012 2nd overall selection Ryan Murray. He possesses good skating ability and likes to move the puck. While Troy didn't have the most impressive season, he is farly raw and being just 72 hours removed from the 2016 NHL Draft, there's still tons of room for growth.

Murray was at his best when making the smart pass and getting pucks deep. He has the vision and ability to find teammates other players simply don't see. However, he sometimes doesn't have the awareness to detect when those lanes are being taken away from him. This resulted in him getting picked off if he took too long to execute the desired pass. Already a tremendous straight-ahead skater with above-average agility, the added inches and pounds didn't seem to slow him down much at all. While he's probably more of a hitter than his older brother, the increased pounds didn't come with much of a mean streak.

Troy isn't much of a shooter and tends to play a safe and conservative game on the back-end. However, he is dependable and consistent. If he continues to develop, can be a reliable defender with increased ice time and get stronger, Murray would be a valuable pick later in the draft.

Musil, Adam
RC – Red Deer Rebels (WHL) – 6'03" 202
HockeyProspect.com Ranking: 82

Adam Musil is a big power forward for the Red Deer Rebels. He's a slow but skilled defenceman with a nose for the net and a good eye for details. Although a bit slow-footed by today's standards, he's nonetheless blessed with good vision and hands and is known for his finishing abilities and for playing a tough and physical game down the middle.

Skating has been a concern going back to his bantam days with the Burnaby Winter Club, but he has been able to accomplish success over the past couple seasons despite this deficiency. Thrust into a third-line checking role, Musil has embraced his assignments and has developed into an excellent shut-down centre who does a great job of asserting himself physically and collapsing down low to protect the front of his net. His puck protection ability is a spectacle in and of itself at times, even if he can be a bit selfish when playing keepaway with the puck. His vision both in his own end and in the offensive zone come very naturally for Musil and are well above average. Shooting and passing abilities are also above average and he can be very effective at both ends of the ice. While he lacks top-end speed, he shows good stamina and toughness as he was able to be a regular point-contributor to his club whilst also logging regular duty on the penalty kill.

Most definitely, he isn't going to blow you away with his speed, but Adam Musil is a limber, powerful, rangy, durable and versatile forward who can contribute to a club in a number of ways. He can score, he wins faceoffs, hits hard, blocks shots, gets the dirty areas—all of the things a coach should be looking for in a future two-way centre. But his upside at the NHL level is ambiguous at this point. He desperately needs to become faster if ever wants to be able to play a top six role at the highest level. Even when playing for his junior club, while he can make plays happen with his excellent hockey sense and good hands, most of the time he plays a rather simple game of attrition in which he wears you down with his physicality and his size.

Quotable: "Quotable:" Big kid who can really skate so you expect a lot but for me he doesn't seem to get enough done given his tools." - Mark Edwards

Mustonen, Aleksi
LC – Ilves (Fin elite) – 5'9" 165
HockeyProspect.com Ranking: NR

Third year eligible who has shown that can be productive in a pro league. Aleksis' year in Finnish elite league has been great even though he's really small kid. Powerful skater with strong lower body and can battle with grown up men. His biggest strengths are his smooth skating, vision, hockey sense and puck handling skills. Very dangerous player in the o-zone but can also play a decent game in all three zones, because he reads the game well.

Myers, Philippe
RD – Rouyn-Noranda Huskies (QMJHL) – 6'4" 188
HockeyProspect.com Ranking: NR

Myers, who is originally from New Brunswick, was drafted by the Huskies in the 4th round of the 2013 QMJHL draft. He's a player that we liked in his QMJHL draft year, especially during the 2013 Gatorade Challenge in Boisbriand, as he showed great physical tools at the event. Myers also represented his region at the 2014 World Under-17 Hockey Challenge in Cape-Breton. He even got an invitation to Team Canada's Ivan Hlinka tryout camp, but was cut.

Myers is not a flashy defenseman but has interesting tools to work with the next couple of years, starting with his size. Myers is 6'4", but still could be a lot stronger physically and more dominant in one-on-one battles along the boards and in front of the net. He likes to punish opposing forwards with solid hits and has good timing. With an extra 10-20 pounds he could become a force in his own zone in the QMJHL. He's a good skater in straight lines, using his long strides and an ability to reach a good top speed. He won't ever be known as an elite puck-rusher but showed at times this season that he's capable of doing it. The fact remains that he often keeps his play with the puck very basic with very little creativity. He will need to improve his explosiveness though, which would help in his coverage in tight spaces to make quick turns. The same goes for his overall footwork, as he can get caught flat-footed by quick forwards beating him on the outside. He had a regular shift on the PK this season, becoming a very good shot-blocker and making good use of his long reach to block passing lanes. Look for Myers to continue to evolve as a physical defensive defenseman and a key member of the young Huskies' D-corps.

Nättinen, Julius
LC – JYP Akatemia (Fin 2nd pro) – 6'2" 194
HockeyProspect.com Ranking: 42

Nättinen has been on our radar since the 2013 U17 hockey challenge where he played as an underager for team Finland. This season he was productive for the whole regular season in second highest pro league in Finland where he recorded 29 points in 39 games and also saw action in the men's league for 9 games. He also played for his country at both major U-18 tournaments this year, the Ivan Hlinka tournament in August and the U-18 world championship in April. He's a big two-way center with great hockey sense and he's good skater. He doesn't use his size perfectly just yet because he's not the strongest player in corners and you don't see him dishing out any big hits. Nättinen has the ability to make his linemates better, he sees the ice well and a great playmaker. He's very efficient in all three zones, a smart player without the puck and useful on the PK due to his anticipation and quick stick. He can also score, although he's probably not a pure goal scorer. When he gains some more experience and builds some muscle on his body he could end up being a solid player in the NHL.

Quotable: "I think he's a really smart player. He moves well and has good size. I think he can play down the middle in the NHL. He reads the ice well and supports the puck. I'd like to see him go to the net a little more, sometimes he has shifts where he plays too passive, especially in the offensive zone. He's not scared though. I don't think it's in his makeup to be physical. I think his strength is defensive hockey. While He has shown me the ability to distribute the puck, I think he really excels on the defensive side of the puck. He understands positioning, reads the play and doesn't cheat towards offense. When he gets the puck he makes quick decisions. He'll move it...doesn't over handle it. He's more playmaker than scorer." - Mark Edwards

Nielsen Andrew
RD – Lethbridge Hurricanes (WHL) – 6'03" 207
HockeyProspect.com Ranking: 83

Andrew Nielsen is a lanky two-way defender who played for the Lethbridge Hurricanes this season, doing fairly well for himself despite being on the roster of the one of the CHL's biggest underdog clubs. Nielsen is a reasonably smooth-skating defenceman who spans across the ice in fairly good timing and looks fairly powerful while doing so, despite still being a bit stringy. He plays a fairly conservative and safe game in his own end, deferring to his more experienced defence partner most of the time. Nonetheless, he showed good skill this season playing in all situations and showing good reactionary decision-making in tough situations.

In his own zone, Nielsen relies on his strong skating and smart positional play to escape with the puck when trouble arises. He uses that smart positional play to both gobble up passing lanes and to block shots, which he does fearlessly. He can be accused of being a bit stationary at times, but he does a good job of not straying out of position when his club is hemmed inside its own end. Instead of being an initiator, he generally plays more of a support role. When he does capture the puck, he does a good job of either making a quick reactionary sweep or at buying time before dishing off a safe and simple first pass.

It was when playing on the power play that Nielsen really raised eyebrows this year. In those situations, he looked like a smart puck mover and a good shooter from the blueline. In the absence of Ryan Pilon following his trade to Brandon, Nielsen saw an inordinate amount of time on the point during the power play and used that time wisely—fine-tuning his stickhandling skills along the blue paint, his passing, his shooting and his lateral mobility with the puck. In that sense, Nielsen definitely benefited from a ravaged Lethbridge Hurricanes lineup by getting significant ice-time in all situations against the WHL's most talented players. That type of experience will serve him nicely going forward.

Niemelä, Joonas
LC – Blues (Fin jr.) – 5'11" 176
HockeyProspect.com Ranking: NR

Niemelä is a good two-way player who doesn't have any big weaknesses except his size. He can play in every situation and he's valuable bottom six type player. He has a good hockey sense, decent scorer and great on faceoffs. He doesn't shine in any part of the game but he's versatile kid with great attitude. Not a big kid but can grind and be useful around corners, one problem with Niemelä as he doesn't have any standout quality that makes him standout as a NHL prospect. He does a lot of nice things on the ice but you would like to see more out of him to be drafted.

Niku, Sami
LD – JYP Akatemia (Fin 2nd pro) – 6'0" 176
HockeyProspect.com Ranking: 139

Niku is a great puck mover with great skating technique. He's an average size player who became more reliable defensively this year. Sami likes to use his speed and challenge opponents offensively, his passing game is great and he can find the open spots on the ice with ease. He's an asset for his team power play as proven in the past, he has nice poise with the puck and still keeps his game simple by getting the puck on net on a regular basis. He operates with good vision and moves the puck well to his forwards. He plays smart in the defensive zone and defends well with his stick. Not that strong right now but can handle bigger forwards good enough at this level. Will need to get stronger if he wants to compete in the pro level in North America.

We expected more out of Niku offensively this season and couldn't impress our scouts too much at the world juniors this year playing on a limited role. Niku is a late-96 born player and his development might have stalled, he has been going down in our rankings all year long.

Quotable: "Sami is a player I liked a lot in my initial viewings. Lost a bit of steam for me as I saw more of him because I questioned some decisions with the puck."
NHL Scout

Noel, Nathan
RC – Saint-John Sea Dogs (QMJHL) – 6'0" 168
HockeyProspect.com Ranking: 78

Noel was the 3rd overall pick in the 2013 QMJHL Draft, coming out of the great program at Shattuck St-Mary's. The St-John's native played in international events the past two seasons, from the U-17 Hockey Challenge to this year's U18 World Championships. He's one of the young players the Sea Dogs are building their team around for the next two to three years.

Noel is a right-handed center, and last year he didn't have much of an adaptation period coming into the QMJHL. This year, he became one of the go-to guys on his team. Since last year, Noel has been a mainstay on Saint John's top 6 forwards, also getting a regular shift on the man advantage. He's an interesting mix of speed and skills, and he's very valuable on the power play with more space to create offense. He's an excellent skater with good explosiveness in his first three steps, he works hard at both ends of the rink and plays hard.

He uses his speed well on the forecheck and is not afraid to throw some hits, and he plays bigger than his listed size. He has a great compete level and keeps his feet moving all the time, which makes him tough to cover in the offensive zone. He also happens to be a capable puck-rusher, using his great speed. He can be intimidating for opposing defensemen coming down the wing in full strides. Offensively, he's an unpredictable player, as he's as good as a shooter as he is a passer. We would like to see him make better decisions with the puck. Sometimes, instead of shooting he will make a pass and vice versa, taking himself out of a scoring opportunity. He has soft hands and good puck control. Can easily beat a goaltender in one-on-one situation and can be very creative. More was expected out of Noel this year offensively, after being such a high selection in the QMJHL draft. Look for him to take another step next season and establish himself as a top player in the league offensively. He's a player with a lot of skills but his hockey sense is limited and that will cost him at the draft.

Norman, Ryan
LW/C - Shattuck St. Mary's (US Prep – Ind.) 5'10 165
HockeyProspect.com Ranking: NR

He is a late '96 birth date that has been effective scorer at Shattuck Prep in Minnesota although the lack of high-end skill sets in shooting, stick handling, and skating although strong on his skates, will hamper his draft success. He is average in size as well and doesn't look he's added any inches to the frame over the last 12-months. He is a steady, reliable player that plays in all 3-zones. He works hard in all areas of the ice from creating scoring chances out of the corner, to winning face-offs, or playing an effective physical game. He projects to be a two-way centermen with the abilities to grind it out.

Novak, Thomas
LC – Waterloo (USHL) 6'0.5" 179
HockeyProspect.com Ranking: 58

Novak, who will be joining his linemate Brock Boeser at Minnesota in the fall, has put together an impressive USHL season. He has certainly benefited from playing with someone with the talent of Boeser all year, but Novak is a very skilled playmaking center.

Novak is an intelligent player who sees the ice very well and lets the game come to him. He is a pure playmaker who can find his teammates in all areas and put them in good position to score. To go along with his superb playmaking skills, Novak has above average hands and does a really nice job handling the puck in all situations.

While not the best skater, he does well enough. If he can develop his stride a little bit and get a bit faster he seems like a surefire bet to make it at the next level. His vision and ability to find teammates with the puck are at an elite level.

Quotable:" I liked him a lot late last season and earlier this season. I started to see more warts with him, including being a a bit of a perimeter player. Had a really poor game versus the NTDP late in the year. It's just one game but some teams had up *to eight scouts from their staff there. Never a good idea to stink out the joint on those 1130 scout nights." - Mark Edwards*

Quotable: " I have him ranked in the 80's." - NHL Scout

O'Brien, Brogan
LC – Prince George Spruce Kings (BCHL) – 6'04" 179
HockeyProspect.com Ranking: NR

Brogan O'Brien of the BCHL's Prince George Spruce Kings is a towering two-way centre with good hockey sense and a skillset that presents itself in unexpected explosions. The first thing you think when you see Brogan O'Brien is that you are looking at a player who is very, very close to being NHL-sized already. His skating needs some work, as when others are gaining speed and accelerating, he's usually lagging a bit behind. Furthermore, he's a bit weak on his feet at this point as he needs to add muscle to a really lanky frame. On the rarest of occasions, however, he can be extremely explosive and powerful in spurts of high-end skating ability, puckhandling talent, compete-level and finish.

Indeed, O'Brien's offensive game usually comes in waves at you like a tsunami. One of the difficulties containing him, is that you don't know which directions the waves are coming from. Sometimes he'll take the puck up the middle with tremendous speed and crash into the net. Other times he'll be leering outside the prime scoring area just before pouncing inside the slot and firing home a quick-release slapshot. Equipped with NHL dimensions, our biggest criticism of his game is that he didn't throw his body around nearly enough. Furthermore, we had some issues with consistency with regards to his compete-level.

O'Brien probably made his biggest splash in his draft year in an off-ice decision. He decided to remain in his hometown, but switch leagues signing with the WHL's Prince George Cougars.. O'Brien's rights were traded to Prince George for Chance Braid and O'Brien's decision to join the Cougars means that he will most likely join the wealth of 1997-born talent on the Cougars.

Ohlsson, Sebastian
RW – Skelleftea (SWE Jr.) – 5'9" 172
HockeyProspect.com Ranking: NR

Ohlsson is a little spark plug on the ice. When you see him at first, you can't help but notice he is undersized and wouldn't expect a lot from him. However, it is hard not to notice his work ethic and how he tries to play bigger than his small frame. He has a short stride and tends to hunch over too much, but that still doesn't prevent him from stopping rushes while back-checking or sneak by defenders. He has soft hands and a quick release that isn't powerful but accurate. He can score from the slot, but loves to crash the net and pick up garbage goals. Ohlsson thinks the game at a high level and is used frequently on both special teams. Not afraid to finish checks against players twice his size, when the SHL club lost players to injuries he made ten appearances in the top league and registered his first pro goal.

Okulov, Konstantin
LC – Sibirskie (MHL) – 6'0" 168
HockeyProspect.com Ranking: NR

As a '95 born, Okulov this season had his last chance to reach the big stage of the WJC, but his play at the Subway Super Series was convincing only in a couple of outings. At fault for sometimes making the odd risky play inside his zone, the smaller North American rinks may have hurt his case and he ended up being a late cut. That will hurt his chances to be drafted, but Okulov remains one of the most talented player coming out of the Russian junior leagues.

Despite his lack of power his shot is a legit threat from scoring positions, but he is first and foremost a very skilled playmaking center who needs to play with good players that can read his intuitive plays, combine inside the offensive zone and finish their chances. What he needs even more at this point to take the next step is to play regularly against better competition. He made some appearances for Sibir this season and scored his first KHL goal, but needs icetime and might be better served developing in VHL next season. On the big rink at the junior level he can slide through opponents and carry the puck into the offensive zone with ease, but he didn't make the improvements he needs in terms of becoming stronger on it and showing a consistent drive in his game.

Olund, Linus
LC – Brynas (SWE Jr.) – 5'11.25" 178
HockeyProspect.com Ranking: 117

One of the few bright spots for team Sweden at the U18 in Switzerland, Olund is a two-way centerman able to bring a calming presence to his team whenever he gets the puck on his stick. He is really good at controlling the puck while keeping it away from defensemen, using a good first step and his body very efficiently to protect it. This quality is evident on the powerplay and in board play in general. But Linus can also rush it in transition, skating is a strength and he gets up to good speed quickly. At the junior level he can carry the puck into the offensive zone with ease most of the times. He is not a physical player, he can give a hit and use his body but usually doesn't need to get physical to be effective along the boards. Doesn't play a flashy game, but he is skilled, can make turns with the puck to buy himself time.
For a player that shows good patience and good playmaking ability, sometimes he could wait a bit more and look for a second, better option, to open up. It's hard to get a good read on his offensive upside, as he still need to further develop his offensive game, but he doesn't need much time or space to release his wrister and he can get himself in good shooting positions.

Oldham, Kris
G – Omaha (USHL) 6'2.25" 203
HockeyProspect.com Ranking: NR

Oldham is a big goalie who made the jump to the USHL this year with the Lancers after playing the previous season with the Kenai River Brown Bears of the North American Hockey League. After Omaha's starting goaltender and Montreal draft pick Hayden Hawkey went down with an injury, Oldham took the reigns and posted very respectable numbers throughout the rest of the season. He sees the puck really well and can see around screens. He moves well and can get from post to post with ease. He sometimes struggles to get down into the butterfly as quick as you might like to see. There is also some concerns there about his consistency and his mental toughness to bounce back after goals. Oldham will return to Omaha next year as the probable starter and then will move on to the University of Nebraska-Omaha in 2016.

Olson, Jacob
LD- Hill Murray (MN-HS) 6'3" 210LBS
HockeyProspect.com Ranking: NR

A Big, physical, hard working defenseman, Olson keeps good gap control at his own blue line and takes away the middle of the ice well. He knows how to use his size and reach to take away time and space and disrupt plays from developing. Olson comes out of his own end with his head up and can make a decent stretch pass but is capable of missing some simple passes. Olson has decent skating agility for a big kid but doesn't have great speed which keeps him from being as effective when joining the rush. Jacob can have a bit of a mean streak at times but doesn't cross the line and keeps it within the rules of the game. He has a bomb for a shot and doesn't shy away from ripping it on the power play. On occasions it can take him too long to make a play with the puck at the offensive blue line and it can get him in trouble when pressured. He was a dominate force in the 2015 Boy's High School Playoffs and key to Hill Murray's appearance in the State Tournament. Olson joins a crowded blue line at Harvard in 15/16.

Olson, Tate
LD – Prince George Cougars (WHL) – 6'02" 174
HockeyProspect.com Ranking: NR

Tate Olson of the WHL's Prince George Cougars is a two-way defenceman with pro-level size and decent speed. He plays a physical style of game which can both help and hinder his play.

Olson's skating ability is just above-average at this point, with him ranking high in terms of backwards and side-to-side manoeuvrability as well as lane control. His backwards skating in particular showed improvement over the course of the 2014-2015 season. When he plays it properly, he became more and more difficult to beat one-on-one as the months progressed. However, he would get himself into trouble fairly regularly, aggressively looking to take out his one on one opponent physically. This resulted in a high risk, high play where he'd either land a solid open ice hit, or get beat for a scoring chance. His passing game also took a giant leap this year, as he started getting more and more ice-time on the power play and began looking like a formidable quarterback by the end of the year. With that said, he still makes some questionable puck plays inside his own zone. His shooting skills were particularly impressive, as he hammers the puck from the point with good velocity. As his skating and passing game continue to advance, Olson seems to be very comfortably growing into his frame.

Olson's best quality, without question, is his tough, durable, hard working and greasy style in his own end. Especially when defending the space in front of his net, Olson already has a bit of a reputation for quiet crosschecks, stick lifts and some borderline dirty play. Due to his physicality and the potential to improve into a reliable shutdown defender, Olson has a chance to be selected in the 2015 NHL Entry Draft.

Opilka, Luke
G - USNTDP 6'1" 192
HockeyProspect.com Ranking: 206

He actually looks smaller between the pipes than he really is although he has decent listed NHL goalie size standing above 6-feet. He is a very athletic goalie that has explosive leg strength, which allows him to get square on pucks quick. He plays position well and makes shots look easy at times. You like the composure he shows. He must continue to have a bigger presence in net although the natural abilities and reads are very good. You like the tools in the tool box for the future in this tender.

Quotable:" He is a pretty talented goalie but he always seemed to let in one soft goal in my viewings." - Mark Edwards

Orban, Ryan
LD - Ottawa 67's (OHL) 6'03" 215
HockeyProspect.com Ranking: NR

Orban showed some good promise with the Saginaw Spirit early on in the season, however a trade closer to home to the Ottawa 67's did result in a bit of a decline in ice time. Orban showed us some of the most polarizing play of any prospect for the 2015 NHL Entry Draft out of the OHL. He possesses a good compete level and his speed is pretty good for a big defender but his mobility, footwork and lateral movement needs work. He uses his long reach very well and also gets into passing lanes effectively. He showed a good first pass at times but also makes a lot of puck playing mistakes when he tries doing much more than just making the simple safe first pass. He finishes his checks effectively but doesn't have a big mean streak. Orban had some showings where he was excellent as a shutdown defender and other games where he really struggled to make a positive contribution. If the first of those two descriptions ever becomes the norm, Orban could be a solid prospect for the NHL Draft as a shutdown defender. That said, he has a lot of work ahead of him and needs to clear up a lot more of his shaky performances.

Osipov, Dmitry
RD – Vancouver Giants (WHL) – 6'04" 189
HockeyProspect.com Ranking: NR

Dmitry a former first overall pick of Amur Khabarovsk in the 2013 KHL Draft and 1st overall pick at the 2013 CHL Import Draft by the Vancouver Giants, Osipov chose the CHL. A late birthdate, he has completed his sophmore season in the WHL with the Giants, playing a much bigger role than his first season.

In addition to being built like an ox, Osipov has an attractive set of skills. Even if he has a tendency to look a bit compartmentalized and inconsistent. Skating pace ranges from fluid to furious, as he looks far smoother moving backwards than forwards, but can get going at a fairly fast pace with good acceleration. Puckhandling skills appear to be in development, as he as a bad habit of slowing way down when the puck is on his stick. Nonetheless, away from the puck, above-average skating is especially impressive when conflated with Osipov's excellent hockey sense. For instance, when travelling in reverse, he does a fantastic job at keeping good distances and maintaining proper gap control, using an active pokecheck to disrupt many zone entry attempts.

On the offensive end, Osipov has improved leaps and bounds from his rookie season with the Giants last year. In a not entirely surprising way, greater poise with the puck has coincided directly with a greater grasp of the English language. Furthermore, having never been a big-time scorer in his short career, his climbing point total is largely the result of increased ice-time and expanding responsibilities. A player whose draft status will almost certainly be encumbered by the notorious 'Russian factor,' a hot-and-cold season makes him an easy candidate for a "faller" in the 2015 draft class, regardless of his potential upside.

Paigin, Ziyat
LD – Ak Bars (KHL) – 6'6" 209
HockeyProspect.com Ranking: NR

In the third year he is eligibile for the draft, Paigin has had the chance to showcase himself in Canada, as he managed to crack the Russian team for the WJC. His play at the tournament has confimed his upside as well as the need for further development. He is still a bit of a project, on some games he shows flashes of good puck moving ability for such a tall defenseman, in others he struggles with easy plays.

This season he made the Ak Bars roster and spent almost the whole season in KHL, but he only averaged nine minutes of icetime and barely touched the ice during the playoffs. For a guy that sorely needs development and icetime, what happened this season was basically the opposite situation of what he should look for. He may still be able to improve on some things training with pro, like on the accuracy of his powerful slap shot, but his game needs to evolve rather than a finishing touch.

Paliani, Devon
RC Saginaw Spirit (OHL) 5'10" 160
HockeyProspect.com Ranking: NR

Devon was one of the great success stories coming out of OHL camps making the team after spending last season with the LaSalle Vipers Jr. B. He was quickly moved to the Saginaw Spirit and was consistently noticeable on the third or fourth lines with an exceptional work ethic. He isn't the biggest or strongest but he prides himself in being the first player into the corner. He hits hard for his size and does a great job winning battles for pucks. Considering his limited ice, especially in offensive situations his 21 points is very impressive for the first year OHL'er. We don't expect Devon to be selected at the 2015 NHL Entry Draft, but for a player who displays such great work ethic and strong skating on a consistent shift by shift basis he can't be completely counted out in the future either.

Palmu, Petrus
RW - Owen Sound Attack (OHL) 5'06" 172
HockeyProspect.com Ranking: NR

After spending last season with Jokerit U18 in the Jr. B league in Finland, Palmu made the jump to the OHL this season. Palmu is an extremely small forward with great speed and skating ability. He can fly up and down the ice and got involved offensively. He has a decent considering his size and possesses good playmaking ability. He is very shifty and makes good puck decisions in the neutral zone.

Palmu projects as a player that would need to play top six in the NHL and while he should be a good offensive player in junior, he doesn't project to have high enough offensive ability to be considered for the NHL. For that reason and the fact that he drastically needs to get stronger, we would not select Palmu in the 2015 NHL Entry Draft.

Papirny, Jordan
LG – Brandon Wheat Kings (WHL) – 6'01" 170
HockeyProspect.com Ranking: NR

Papirny is an intriguing hybrid goaltender who is able to play a bit more of a stand-up game, in combination with acrobatics and lunging saves, as a result of his excellent positioning and stance work. Because he comes out of his crease with an upright posture, a wide-footed stance, an elevated glove and a ready blocker, Papirny limits a lot of holes from the net with minimal effort. A lot has been made of his poor rebound control, but one still has to admire Papirny's recovery ability and athleticism around the crease.

In addition to all those aforementioned skills and qualities and having almost 30 games of playoff experience, there are another two qualities that speak most loudly to us about Papirny—his competitiveness and his constant desire to improve. With regards to his competitiveness, this is a highly competitive goaltender who will almost always hotly contest any goal that he deems impermissible. He excels in playoff situations. In a similar vein, he doesn't change his game whatsoever when the score changes. He's always willing to make a dangerous diving save or a lunging attempt whether his team is winning by a landslide or coming from behind. His improvements in goals-against-average and save percentage from last season to this one were both remarkable.

Parikka, Jarkko
LD - Kingston Frontenacs (OHL) 6'00" 187
HockeyProspect.com Ranking: NR

Jarkko came over to the OHL after taking an unusual path that included a year with the Des Moines Buccaneers of the USHL. He played for Finland at the IIHF U18 Championships as an under-ager last season. Parikka has good mobility. He skates well in every direction and will rush the puck a bit but sometimes chooses the wrong lanes. He knows how to contain on the wall and competes very hard defensively but lacks the strength to assert himself in these situations against bigger forwards. He keeps it pretty simple with the puck and makes good first passes, but overall his offensive skillset is below average. We don't expect Parikka to be selected at the 2015 NHL Entry Draft and he will need to get stronger in order to reach his potential, as his style of game doesn't match his physical assets.

Parsells, Adam
RD – Wausau West (WI-HS) 6'5.5" 192LBS
HockeyProspect.com Ranking: 182

Adam Parsells is a tall, lanky defenseman with a heavy right handed shot. While his straight line skating still needs to develop, he does posses pretty good mobility in the tight areas for a player of his size. His poise with the puck is impressive and can make a difficult play under pressure seem effortless. He doesn't try to do too much out of his comfort zone at either end of the rink. Adam makes a good first pass out of the zone, he doesn't skate the puck into the offensive zone often, but makes efficient plays in the neutral zone with the puck. He will need to learn to make quicker decisions, as he see's bigger and faster competition going forward. Parsells defends by using his stick and long reach advantage to disrupt plays in his own end; he's huge but not physical. He will use body positioning to defend rather than trying to deliver punishing hits. Parsells has the ability to slow the game down and get the puck out of danger when it's needed. He doesn't use his heavy slap shot very often and tends to go with a quick release snap shot or wrist shot to get pucks to the net. He can tend to try to pick corners a bit too much on the power play in a couple viewings.

There is some growth needed both on and off the ice at this stage. He's a project for an NHL team, but a 6'5" project, which can have some value. Parsells is finishing his 14/15 season with Green Bay (USHL) where he will likely return next season before heading to the University of Wisconsin in 16/17.

Quotable:" He might be a later pick. Good skater but not an overly smart player. Can be a bit soft at times which is frustrating given his size." - HP Scout Dustin Braaksma

Pavlychev, Nikita
LC – Des Moines (USHL) 6'7" 200
HockeyProspect.com Ranking: 192

Pavlychev is a really interesting prospect. The Penn State commit has the size you don't normally see in a forward, plus some above average puck skills to go along with that size. His height is certainly the first thing that you notice about him, but watching his game, he does have the offensive skillset to be a difference maker. He slashes hard to the net with the puck on his stick and it is really hard to knock him off the puck. It will be interesting to see if he can continue to be impossible to knock off the puck once he gets to college and starts playing against stronger players.

Skating is an issue, which is not surprising given that he is 18 and six-foot seven, but it certainly doesn't hold him back too much. We would like to see him be a little more physical as he tends to shy away from contact and play a more pretty game than he needs to.

Pavlychev is definitely an intriguing player that will get some attention in June. His size mixed with his decent hands will make teams take a long hard look at him.

Quotable: " He's raw but I have time for him. Reminds me a bit of Mike McCarron at the same age because of the Bambi legs. He has some upside and is a player I would probably draft him." - Mark Edwards

Pawlenchuk, Grayson
RW – Red Deer Rebels (WHL) – 6'00" 183
HockeyProspect.com Ranking: 184

Pawlenchuk is a shoot-first, physical winger who played much of this year on a line that also featured fellow 2015 draft-eligible forward Adam Musil. While the pair were a bit inconsistent when it came to the creating offense this year, in the long run the two supplied the Rebels with a dependable and energetic third-line checking unit that could score occasionally and were also leaned on heavily in penalty killing situations. For his own part, Pawlenchuk is a very good skater with breakaway straight-line speed. He uses that speed in a variety of ways to the Rebels this season, especially on the defensive end of things—backchecking with authority, hitting his opponents with tremendous force and to drive wide on the opposition defence when transitioning the puck up ice.

Pawlenchuk is the type of player who wears you down with his physicality and speed, but not necessarily with his scoring ability. Occasionally, as he showed us over multiple viewings this year, he will use that aforementioned straight-line speed and become a human-torpedo of sorts, throwing some enormous hits along the wall. Or on other occasions, he will use that speed to cut in past the blueline and will head straight to the net with the puck on his stick. His puckhandling and shooting skills are still in development and he didn't score on nearly as many breakaway opportunities as he should have. His passing game looks similarly in development—a large portion of his assists came off of rebounds that he created from shooting off of the wing. Sometimes he lacks imagination and creativity when breaking across the opposition blueline.

Pawlenchuk seems to be embracing the third line checking role he's been assigned, especially in terms of being physical and contributing to the penalty kill. He takes pride in his ability to stave off a talented power play unit with his strong defensive zone awareness. Pawlenchuk is among the best shot blockers in the WHL this past season. We like the speed, determination and energy Pawlenchuk displays, however his offensive upside and skill upside is still very questionable at this point.

Pearson, Chase
LC - Youngstown (USHL) 6'2 189
HockeyProspect.com Ranking: 153

He is a good size forward that is raw with the skills and thought process. He might have upside although there are times he just doesn't see the play develop so questionable hockey IQ. He does not seem to have the skill sets to make the little plays and passes that lead to bigger scoring opportunities. His skating and shooting are average and nothing too much really excites you enough in his game. He is uncommitted to any NCAA school and although might be some offers, not sure it might be more of lack of then deciding where.

Quotable: " I'd like to see him be a lot more physical because he lacks a bit in the puck skills department. Skating needs to be better." - NHL Scout

Pelton-Byce, Ty
LC – Madison Memorial (WI-HS) 6'1" 176LBS
HockeyProspect.com Ranking: NR

Ty Pelton-Byce was one of the best players in Wisconsin Prep Hockey all season and was rewarded by being named Wisconsin "Mr. Hockey" finalist. Pelton-Byce played in every situation for the Spartans and in some playoff games it seemed he was hardly off the ice. He was the offensive catalyst for Memorial all season so when his offensive production dried up in the WIAA state tournament, it was a contributing factor to the Spartans loss in the Semi-Finals to Wausau West.

Pelton-Byce is a strong skater who has good offensive instincts, does a good job reading the play and finding the open ice in the offensive zone. Ty has a terrific release, combined with his accuracy make him a dangerous offensive player when the puck finds his stick. Likes to play a straight ahead north-south game, doesn't try to make fancy plays, likes to use his speed to turn defenseman and get them on their heels. His two-way game still needs time to develop, not because of a lack of effort; he comes back into the play hard but can lose his positioning and defensive posture on the backcheck. He is impressive in his puck battles where he uses a combination of physicality and body positioning to get away with the puck.

While none of Pelton-Byce's aspects of his game can be labeled at the elite level, when packaged together and combined with his work ethic, it makes for an interesting prospect to keep an eye on going forward. Pelton-Byce will be heading to Muskegon (USHL) in 15/16 to continue to develop his game before heading to UMASS – Amherst (NCAA) in 16/17.

Quotable: " He's a smart player with good puck skills. He might be a kid who can sneak into our rankings late. I have time for him, he plays in a weak area as far as competition goes, that won't help him any on draft day." Mark Edwards

Peters, Collin
RC – Sioux Falls (USHL) 5'11.5" 166
HockeyProspect.com Ranking: 164

A Northern Michigan commit, Peters joined the Clark Cup Champion Stampede this year after being traded from Muskegon. A bit undersized, Peters plays a pretty solid two-way game with some good offensive thoughts. Not going to light up the scoreboard but he can chip in offensively. He is an average skater but does well enough at this level. He's not afraid to throw the body and mix it up a bit. Probably needs to put on a little weight to continue to progress with the type of game he plays. Peters is one those guys who does everything pretty well but doesn't have any particularly elite skills to jump off the ice at you. He will rejoin Sioux Falls next year before heading to Northern Michigan in 2016.

Pfeifer, Tristen
RD – Everett Silvertips (WHL) – 6'04" 180
HockeyProspect.com Ranking: 94

Tristen is one of the great success stories to enter the 2015 NHL Entry Draft. After a strong season with the Phoenix Jr. Coyotes U18 program in the USA Tier 1 Midget league, Pfeifer was invited to Everett Silvertips camp as a free agent. Not only did he make the team, he has been one of the most reliable defenders for the Silvertips. He enjoyed a lot of success in his rookie WHL season, despite being an NHL Draft re-entry player.

The rookie defender was quickly given responsibility on his team's blueline becoming a regular on the penalty kill. When it comes to puck retrieval, one thing we really like about Pfeifer. His elongated skating stride and above-average acceleration speed is also another key asset to his game. Combined with his size and strength to protect the puck when exiting his own zone. He not only has the size and the wingpsan to protect the puck, but surprisingly strong skating ability at 6'4" to go end to end is impressive. His passes tend to be hard, direct and easy to receive. While he's by no means overly ambitious with the puck, Pfeifer generally throws a strong first pass and is responsible for very few turnovers. As for his work on the penalty kill, Pfeifer does a stand-up job at blocking shots and sacrificing his body to make a smart clearance out of his zone.

Getting used to the physical rigors of the WHL resulted in a few lower body injuries suffered throughout the season. However his growth and intelligence spiked over the season as he began to really develop the little areas of the game. This is an area he will need to continue improving upon. The rate in which he has learned and adapted, along with the great physical tools he possesses makes Pfeifer a true sleeper and a potential great steal for one NHL club at the 2015 NHL Entry Draft.

Phelps, Chase
LW – Boston University (NCAA) 6'0 175
HockeyProspect.com Ranking: NR

He is a decent grinder player as the transition of his game was shown this season at Boston University after being more of the offensive output at the prep level at Shattuck. He was given 4th line duties for the Terriers as his stick sets have never been anything special and at this NCAA level he looks a step behind. The skating stride is adequate yet no break-a-way speed and the puck possession thoughts and skills are average.

Philp, Luke
RW – Kootenay Ice (WHL) – 5'10" 175
HockeyProspect.com Ranking: NR

Luke Philp is a hard-working and team-oriented re-entry centre who played with the Kootenay Ice this year. Dangerous offensively, smart and conscientious defensively, Philp can play at all three forward positions and in all situations—he was Kootenay's second line centre last year but graduated to first line wing duty this season. A better than average skater and an especially strong backwards skater, Philps keeps his feet moving. He has good speed from the outside and is beginning to attack the net more aggressively with each passing viewing. He logs power play minutes on the point and also an important part of his club's penalty killing unit. The best asset to his game is probably his competitiveness—he was a key contributor to a number of come-behind victories in Kootenay.

Luke embraces a leadership role in Kootenay and shows a consistent willingness to sacrifice his body to get his team a victory. He battles hard in all areas of the ice and seems more and more willing to mix it up in the mean and nasty spots—the corners, the walls, the front of the net. We especially enjoy how Philp manages to elevate his game in the playoffs—he was the MVP for the Ice in 2013, a key component to their upset victory over Calgary in 2014 and was the mastermind behind another near-upset over Calgary in 2015. There are obviously some criticisms to his game, as he went undrafted in last year's draft. As we noted in last year's edition of the Black Book, Philp sometimes tries to do too much, wasting a lot of energy in areas away from the puck. But his game will only get better and better along with his condition and his improved understanding of when to pull the reins back.

Size is a bit of a concern for Philip moving forward, as he will need to continue to get stronger to handle the physical punishment his style of play will inflict in pro hockey. However he has shown us that he continues to have NHL Draft potential and thus could hear his name called at the 2015 NHL Entry Draft.

Piipponen Topi
RW – KalPa (Fin jr.) – 6'0" 190
HockeyProspect.com Ranking: NR

Piipponen is a speedy winger who has produced points for the whole season playing for Kalpa in the Finland junior league. Topi has great speed and he can handle the puck well at top speed. He has decent size and does a good job in all three zones. He's got a good scoring ability and he's making good decisions with puck. He plays a very smart game and is always giving an honest effort. He's good in the corners and likes to go straight to the net which is why he has been productive all year long. His hands and stickhandling are average but he likes to play a simple game and doesn't try any fancy moves.

Quotable: "Topi is a player that Toni, our scout in Finland, has time for." - Mark Edwards

Pilipenko, Kirill
RW – MVD (MHL) – 5'10" 194
HockeyProspect.com Ranking: NR

A talented left shooting right winger, Pilipenko is coming off an overall disappointing season: struggled through some injuries early on, did get better along the Spring but didn't show much progress from last season. The late '96 born Russian created expectations for more, given his first class skills. A deadly finisher from in close, he can see his offensive options well and doesn't need much room to make defensemen pay for their mistakes. He has a dangerous wrister from the slot with an efficient release, but he is also a very good passer in the offensive zone. With his terrific puck control, he likes to play behind the net as a setup man. When on top of his game Kirill shows pretty quick feet to and he is shifty, especially while protecting the puck in the offensive zone, but his skating seems to lack an extra gear or high end acceleration to separate himself from bigger opponents.

Consistency and defensive play are clearly two areas where he needs to improve in the future. Another significant concern is that at the junior level he was on the receiving end of several huge hits. He showed good will to fight through those, but one of the first things he will need to show next year (in a season where he'll have a good chance to represent his country at the WJC) is the capability to stay healthy and better protect himself while still competing and battling through traffic.

Pilon, Ryan
LD – Brandon Wheat Kings (WHL) – 6'02" 206
HockeyProspect.com Ranking: 85

Pilon is blessed with good height, a sturdy frame and pro genetics. His father Rich played for 15 years in the NHL as a stay-at-home defenceman in New York and St. Louis. Like his father, Ryan has a pro-sized frame, good physical play and excellent hockey sense. His skating continues to improve, although it will likely never be a very impressive part of his game. He succeeds mostly by playing a more conservative and reserved style outside the power play.

Pilon had the benefit of top prospect Ivan Provorov as his defensive partner the majority of this season. This allowed Pilon to have a reliable first pass option when staggering and allowing Provorov to get his feet moving. While he often supported rather than led the rush from the back end, Pilon has improved upon his skating and has more confidence carrying the puck himself. However he likely will never win too many races. He was very patient in terms of his decision making. Once in the offensive end, Pilon is a dangerous threat from the back end. He's a good passer on simple D to D or point to side boards and generally chose those options wisely. He also has good awareness of when he needs to send the puck deep from the point which has been helpful to the dangerous Wheat Kings front end.

While he can be effective in a simple shutdown role, we saw many holes in his game over the course of the season. He will sometimes hesitate attacking a loose puck behind the net, not wanting to be the first man on the puck. This is despite having better size than the opposition most of the time. This has resulted in him arriving late, missing his check and giving the opposition an advantage in high percentage areas.

Quotable: "Ryan has never been a guy that has really floated my boat. Maybe it's because he has such pro ready size that I expect more from him when I see him. I always seemed to walk out of the rink just being kinda blah on him. Not sour, but not real high on him either." - Mark Edwards

Podluboshnov, Pavel
LW – CSKA (MHL) – 5'9" 152
HockeyProspect.com Ranking: NR

His long weird surname might be unknown, but Podluboshnov last season put together an impressive season as a 16yrs old rookie in the MHL, helping CSKA reaching the finals by scoring 15 points in 22 playoff games. Originally supposed to be eligible only for the 2016 draft, his birth date was apparently wrongly listed and he entered the new season as an interesting kid to follow for the 2015 entry draft. A prototypical small Russian winger, with agility and very good puck skills, Pavel is a deft player who entered the league playing a surprisingly advanced game. He shows sound positioning and commitment, as a righty he likes to play off the left half wall on the powerplay, is a good passer and excels at completing backhand set ups from behind the net. He can make quick decisions, one touch passes and quick turns maintaining full control of the puck.

Unfortunately his progress this season didn't go beyond an improved defensive game that earned him some time on the penalty kill, which is obviously disappointing for such a young player (who at the start of the year was supposed to be even younger). He didn't grow physically and his offensive production didn't either. A sub par showing at the Hlinka costed him a spot on the U18 national team, limiting his exposure and further reducing his chances to be drafted. As a diminutive Russian who lacks strength and sheer explosiveness he is certainly fighting against the odds.

Poehling, Jack
C/LW – Lakeville (MN-HS) 5'10.75" 164LBS
HockeyProspect.com Ranking: NR

Jack Poehling along with twin brother Nick and younger brother Ryan (1st overall pick in 2015 Phase 1 USHL Draft), were all part of a talented Lakeville squad that capped off a perfect season and the Minnesota AA State Championship this past March. In that tournament Poehling was dominate by scoring 13 goals in just 6 playoffs games. Jack Poehling is a pure goal scorer; he is dangerous anytime the puck finds his stick in the offensive zone. He can score in a number of different ways but usually they come from out working his opponent. Poehling has a nose for the net and competes for every inch in all areas of the ice. While Poehling doesn't have impressive size he is difficult to get off the puck due to his agility and elusiveness. Has a quick and accurate release on his shot. Is a terrific tape to tape passer, especially on the power play where he moves the puck quickly.

Poehling doesn't possess dynamic breakaway speed and certainly has room for improvement in the skating department; however it hasn't hindered his abilities up to this point. His decisions with the puck at times show that he believes he can make every play and at the High school level he more often got away with it, going forward he will need to learn to simplify his game and not always try to make the fancy play. Poehling finished his 14/15 season with Green Bay of the USHL and didn't look out of place in a limited role. Poehling will be off to St. Cloud St. along with twin brother Nick in fall 2015, with younger brother Ryan soon to follow.

Provorov, Ivan
LD – Brandon Wheat Kings (WHL) – 6'01" 201
HockeyProspect.com Ranking: 9

Ivan Provorov is a dynamic offensive defenceman who made his mark this year with the Brandon Wheat Kings in the WHL. Blessed with a low centre-of-gravity for his height, excellent crossover technique, powerful skating strides and tremendous puckhandling skills, Provorov is able to skate the puck from end-to-end in a quick and deceptive fashion. Fantastic edgework and turning allows him to cut quickly around the net and launch his puck rush, or set him up for a solid first pass. His hockey sense additionally allows Provorov to misdirect his opponents with highlight-reel worthy spin-o-ramas and head-fakes that leave the opposition consistently bewildered. Excellent vision, hockey IQ, passing and shooting round out an offensive game that is already in full bloom. In addition to the offensive tools, he's also a great physical player who has the ability to land crushing open ice hits on a regular basis.

Provorov is a defender who can puckhandle, pass and even shoot while skating at top speed. This makes him a difficult defenceman to predict in the offensive zone. His defensive reads are sometimes problematic as there's a lot of underlying risk in his decisions, but he has the skating skills and hockey IQ help cover some of those mistakes. Indeed, the main criticism of his game at this point is that he tries to go end-to-end all on his own a bit too much, resulting in some costly turnovers.

Provorov's defensive skillset is pretty good overall. He keeps good gaps, makes smart reads, has a strong pokecheck and a loves to hit either in open-ice or along the walls. He blocks shots, closes off passing lanes and directs traffic from the back end. Provorov is reliable on the penalty kill and played a big role for his team regardless of the situation.

Quotable:" Like just about everyone else, I like Provorov a lot. He's up with the top guys in this draft class as far as being pro ready. I think that if the right situation exists based on who darfts him, he has a chance to play NHL hockey next season."
- Mark Edwards

Radke, Roy
RW - Barrie Colts (OHL) 6'02" 200
HockeyProspect.com Ranking: 125

Radke plays a good two-way, power game. He takes care of his own end, is willing to block shots and is consistently back to support down low. He's a good skater who is effective carrying the puck up ice. Radke is straight-line player that likes to gain the line and drive the net. He has a powerful shot and isn't shy about using it, throwing pucks on net whenever he can. Radke is a very physical player who likes to finish his checks hard. He also jumps in on the forecheck and causes havoc down low. He regularly forces turnovers with good forecheck pressure and delivers punishing hits from time to time. He can be prone to forcing shots or passes that aren't there when teammates are open elsewhere.

Rantanen, Mikko
LW – TPS (Fin elite) – 6'4" 209
HockeyProspect.com Ranking: 10

Rantanen is late 96 born forward out of Finland who has made a lot of noise for a couple years now. He had an up and down first half of the season with his team but his play took off with a strong world junior where he scored 4 times and was much better in the 2nd half of the season in the finland men's league. Rantanen year was a bit hard on him because his team in Finland was really weak for the whole season. Despite that he has performed well in those though situations, he also wore the golden helmet with his team and was heavily checked by opposing teams but it didn't seem to bother him. Rantanen is a big forward with great hockey sense, he's a versatile forward who can play both on the wing and down the middle. He also can be use in every situation by his coaches.

He handles the puck very well in tight spaces and can create lot of scoring opportunities. He's a dangerous in one on one situation due to his high skill level but also his reach. He's a rough player along the board and is not afraid to get involved in the physical part of the game. He has good vision and a great shot but could work on the accuracy of his shot. It did get better after the WJC with more confidence after a great showing in Canada.

Quotable: " He wore the gold helmut for his team, the player wearing that gets a little extra attention. He played through it and got his points." - NHL Scout

Quotable: " Big, skates, hits and scores...what's not to like?" - NHL Scout

Quotable: " I liked him in Finland (U18) last year. I like way he went to the net. We put him as a mid 1st rounder pre-season if memory serves. I didn't think at the time that he would rise from that spot but he finishes up as a top 10 player on our list. Spoke to him at the NHL Combine and I liked him. He did a good job handling questions and seemed to have a good self assessment of his game." - Mark Edwards

Ratelle, Joey
LW – Drummondville Voltigeurs (QMJHL) – 5'10" 173
HockeyProspect.com Ranking: NR

Ratelle finished his 3rd season with the Voltigeurs, leading the team in goals and points. Teamwise, it was a very difficult season for the Voltigeurs, with not many wins in the 2nd half of the season. After going undrafted last year, Ratelle saw his role improve with the team. He now plays the top line at even-strength, the power play and is a leader on the penalty killing unit. He does score a lot of his goals from within five feet of the net. He's very much like a junior version of Brendan Gallagher. He plays with no fear and can always been seen around the net, battling for loose pucks and rebounds.

Ratelle is a shoot-first type of player, and likes to shoot from anywhere in the offensive zone. He lacks the vision to be an effective playmaker in possession of the puck, as he's really effective when working down low and cycling the puck. He gives his all on the ice, he can be annoying to play against as he won't back down and won't stop working. He can be a pest on the ice, and opposing defensemen don't appreciate him due to his likeliness to always charge the net and interfere with the goaltender. Ratelle plays much bigger than his size. He has a strong lower body that helps him in his physical confrontations.

Skating is still a flaw, a player of his size needs that explosiveness to succeed at a higher level and Ratelle doesn't have it now. Ratelle plays the right way but lacks speed and vision to be considered for the NHL draft, might get a look during the summer with an invitation to an NHL camp.

Reddekopp, Chaz
LD – Victoria Royals (WHL) – 6'04" 229
HockeyProspect.com Ranking: 97

Chaz Reddekopp is a big and burly defenceman with good speed, who rarely looks outsized, outmatched or intimdated. Already known as a big and sturdy two-way defenceman, Reddekopp is a player who has risen up our list this year.

His straight-ahead acceleration is powerful and fast, as evidenced when he breaks across the blueline with the puck on his stick. However his turns, pivots and general agility are his greatest downfall at this point, even if one expects those to improve with age as he is still growing into his lanky frame. After all, it is also worth mentioning that at 229 pounds, he is one of the heaviest player available in the 2015 NHL Entry Draft. Therefore, while his manoeuvrings can be a bit brutish and plodding at times, his size offers a dependable excuse and a glimpse of big-time upside at the end of his development arch. As a very good puck mover capable of making consistently effective first-passes, this upside exists at both ends of the rink. He does however have a tendency to make the occasional mental error in his own zone misreading a passing lane. He sometimes even quarterbacks the Royals power play, as his distribution skills from the blueline are very good—although his shooting skills require improvement at this point, as his wind-up can be a bit long winded at times.

Overall Reddekopp has a lot of tools and a very high upside but he is extremely raw. He can skate, pass, hit and generally play whatever role is necessary. However he still has a long way to go polishing his game and becoming a consistently reliable player game in and game out. There's little doubt Chaz will hear his name called at the 2015 NHL Entry Draft. The team who selects him will likely be one who holds his potential in the highest regard, willing to overlook the long path it will likely take him to round into the player he has the potential to be.

Richard, Anthony
LC –Val d'Or Foreurs (QMJHL) – 5'10" 165
HockeyProspect.com Ranking: 101

Richard is an ultra-fast skater playing in his 3rd season in the QMJHL, due to his late birthday. He made a name for himself at last year, scoring some key goals and also showing how good of a skater he was on a national stage at the 2014 Memorial Cup. This season, Richard finished with 91 points, centering the Foreurs' top line and finishing tenth in the league scoring race. Last year, he was playing on the 2nd line most of the time but this season Richard was the player for the Foreurs, along with Aube-Kubel. The Trois-Rivieres native was drafted 16th overall in the 2012 QMJHL Draft. Ever since then, he has shown a very nice chemistry with Nicolas Aube-Kubel. He uses his speed well to attack the offensive zone and is tough to handle due to his speed and a low center of gravity. He's a good asset on the penalty killing unit due to his quick feet and anticipation. He's extremely quick to jump on lose pucks to create offense on the PK, and he's a threat to score in those situations. His lack of size will surely affect his draft ranking and potential in the pros. Due to his lack of strength it can be tough for him along the boards or in front of the net to win puck battles versus bigger players. There are some question marks with his ability to adapt his game when not playing in an offensive role, as witnessed in his rookie season when he left to go back to his midget team because of a lack of ice time. If he can't play on an offensive line can he play in a defensive line and accept his role? He's a bit of one-dimensional forward.

Roslovic, Jack
RC - USNTDP 6'0.5" 182
HockeyProspect.com Ranking: 24

He is a player whose stock has been on the rise this season for good reason. He's a great skater and he has great skill and energy. Sure he benefited from line mates Auston Matthews and Matthew Tkachuk at the NTDP, but he has developed his game to be more of a constant scoring threat and playmaker. He has a nice set of hands as he handles the puck well and shows elusive moves especially on the 1-on-1 situations. He likes to take the puck wide in his stick handling span to create deception as he then follows with stick moves like toe drags and outside/inside moves. His speed is decent down the wing and can also create opportunities in stride. His best assets are his hands with the stick skills. He can be a little too cute at times with the puck, showing the shake-n-bake though mostly is creative with puck to set-up plays. His stock has risen with us as he seemed to continually find more confidence and it showed with performance out on the ice.

Quotable: "He was the USHL's big riser in the second half this year." NHL Scout

Quotable: "He struggles at times inside the dots but when I look at the flaws in his game compared to some other players we had in his grouping, he rated out well head to head. I liked him a lot in my late season viewings. I thought he had a strong U18." - Mark Edwards

Roy, Jeremy
RD – Sherbrooke Phoenix (QMJHL) – 6'0" 182
HockeyProspect.com Ranking: 26

Roy was the 4th overall selection in the 2013 QMJHL Draft after playing two excellent seasons with the Antoine-Girouard midget program in Saint-Hyacinthe. In his first season in the league he had the most points by a 16 year old since the late 80s, coming up 2nd all-time for goals by a 16 year old defenseman. He represented his province at the U-17 Hockey Challenge last year, where he captained Team Quebec during the event. Quebec finished 4th. At this event, he made the All-Star team with five points in six games. He was also selected to play in the 2014 World U18 Hockey Championship, but unfortunately was injured in a pre-tournament game. Over the summer, he had another opportunity to represent his country at the Ivan Hlinka Tournament where Canada won gold once again. Roy was also selected to play for Canada at the 2015 U18 World Hockey Championship this past April.

This season, things didn't come to him as easily as they did in his first season, as Roy was a marked man on the ice and was not given the free room he previously was. As an example, on the power play, he was used more as the setup man than as the shooter, as opposing teams would often have one of their players make sure Roy couldn't shoot the puck from the point. Roy is a smart player; he adjusted his game and was still dangerous on the power play, averaging close to a point per game. We would like to see Roy find shooting lanes and shoot the puck more often; he could add some velocity to his point shot in order to become a more dangerous threat from the blueline. Roy's vision is terrific; he can find open teammates in no time on the power play or at even-strength. In his zone he excels with his outlet passes, often these are tape to tape passes and very crisp as well. He doesn't waste time with the puck in his own zone; he makes good decisions and moves the puck very quickly. His hockey IQ and hockey sense are among the best of any player in the QMJHL, he thinks the game at another level. The second half of the season was a frustrating one for Roy, as he was suspended twice and was also injured, missing a good chunk of action. His ankle injury never seemed to heal and he didn't seem to be 100% in the second half of the season as well as in the playoffs.

One of the areas we would like to see Roy improve in: his skating. He's not a bad skater for any stretch of the imagination, but we would like to see him add more explosiveness. This would help him create more separation. His mobility is fine and he has good footwork, as well as a very good active stick in his zone. Roy is not an overly big player but he's very strong on his skates and wins most of his battles. He's not your typical physical defenseman, but can surprise opponents with some good hits along the boards.

Quotable: "I have been a fan of his since he played as under-ager in midget AAA in 11-12, one of the smartest defensemen in the QMJHL" - HP scout Jérôme Bérubé

Quotable: "I've liked him going back a couple of years. I didn't think he was great in some of my viewings in the second half of the season, including in Switzerland where I thought he was just ok. I think he flat-lined a bit this year compared to some of the others players in this draft." - Mark Edwards

Quotable: "I can't figure him out. One game I'll love him and another game I don't." - NHL Scout

Quotable: "I think he's one of the most overrated players in this draft." - NHL Scout

Quotable: "Everyone is talking about Chabot but I still like Roy. He's the smartest D from the Q this season." - NHL Scout

Roy, Nicolas
C/RW – Chicoutimi Sagueneens (QMJHL) – 6'4" 202
HockeyProspect.com Ranking: 67

Roy was the 1st overall pick in the 2013 QMJHL Draft by the Cape-Breton Screaming Eagles but was later traded to Chicoutimi in a blockbuster deal because of his refusal to report to Cape-Breton. The Amos native had a fine rookie season in 2013-2014 with Chicoutimi, and did very well at the U-17 Hockey Challenge. This past August, Roy also played for Team Canada at the Ivan Hlinka tournament, helping his country win gold. After the Sagueneens were eliminated in this year's playoffs, Roy was chosen again to play for his country at the 2015 U18 World Hockey Championships in Switzerland, where he did well, playing a strong two-way game.

This was a season with a lot of downs for Roy, as he struggled to find his game all year long. He had some good moments in December, where we thought he found his game for good, but then in January he went back to neutral and struggled to produce. All year he struggled to find consistency in his game. Chicoutimi was a mess most of the year with a coaching change midway through the season and a lot of injuries. This is a year where Roy needs to forget about it and start from scratch to show everyone why he was the top selection in the 2013 QMJHL Draft. He did, however, have a good showing at the U18 World Championships in April, helping boost his draft stock. Roy is extremely smart at both ends of the ice, and then you add his 6'4" frame to the mix and you see why this kid has a ton of potential. His skating is still an issue, as his top speed is just average and he needs serious work on his explosiveness. He needs to play the game at a higher tempo; he looked a step behind all year long in the QMJHL. He has a long reach and is a great stickhandler with the ability to make plays with the puck that few players can do. He has great one-on-one skills with the puck. If he's not producing offensively, Roy still can be helpful in defensive situations, as he's very good on the faceoff dot and is a smart player without the puck. Roy is not a physical player, but has good puck-protection skills along the boards, using his back and reach to shield opponents away from the puck. Since Roy is 6'4", more is expected out of him in the physical department, but the truth is that Roy doesn't have a mean bone inside of him. Roy strongest trait outside of his smarts is his vision. He is an excellent playmaker and can find his teammates with ease anywhere on the ice.

Quotable:" Offensive game didn't develop as I thought but he's a smart player and showed this year that he can play in a shutdown role. Also very good on faceoffs" - HP scout Jérôme Bérubé

Quotable:" He reminds me a bit of Freddie Gauthier at the same age. He's a really smart player who excels on the defensive side of the puck. He can struggle with the pace at but his feet looked like they were getting slightly better. He can chip in on offense but based on this year, he looks to have little chance at playing in the top six. I see him as a huge kid who can play down the middle as a shutdown guy, win draws, chip in offensively and play responsible in all three zones. - Mark Edwards

Ruuskanen, Waltteri
RD – KalPa (Fin jr.) – 6'3" 181
HockeyProspect.com Ranking: NR

Ruuskanen is a big stay-at-home d-man who's got some serious holes in his game. His skating speed and technique are big problems, he has trouble containing speedy forwards. He can play tough in his own zone and make good first passes but he could be more effective if can improve his mobility. He doesn't offer much offensively but at his best he can be great player in the defensive zone.

Rykov, Yegor
LD – SKA-1946 (MHL) – 6'1" 210
HockeyProspect.com Ranking: 144

Rykov was probably the most reliable defenseman for Russia at the U18 World Championships and one of the very few Russians to put up a legit performance in his team collapse against Switzerland in the quarterfinal.

Not necessarily as tall as listed, but fairly strong, he is a tough customer when it comes to battles inside his zones. He doesn't leave much room to forwards and engages physically as soon as he can. He is not a very physical player as for throwing checks or punishing opponents, but competes hard for the puck. His nice footwork helps him being effective in puck battles along the boards, he can keep his feet moving the right way while battling with opponents and when he is on his game he distinguishes himself for how he cap keep up with forwards that are carrying the puck around the offensive zone looking for room. Most of the time they won't get any lanes towards the net. Rykov is also hard to beat to the outside off transition and with his mobility in the defensive zone has shown the capability to play his off side too.

During possession he rarely does anything special, but shows above average puck control in motion. He can play in transition, but for someone supposed to be a two way defenseman his play with the puck this season has been rather underwhelming. Sometimes at fault for the odd bad pass, Rykov has clearly made an effort as the season progressed to cut down on turnovers, relying more on safe passes inside his zone even if he can hit his forwards in transition. He has been less effective managing the puck from the red line onward. His vision might not be the best, but has shown the mentality a defenseman requires to develop into a dependable piece. One limitation he should work on is his straight ahead skating, not nearly as effective as his lateral movement, something that affects his chances of recovery through the neutral zone.

Saarela, Aleksi
LC – Ässät (Fin elite) – 5'10" 194
HockeyProspect.com Ranking: 155

Aleksi's development has stalled and there are a lot of question marks around him. He has already suffered a lot of injuries during his young career and this has affected his game and development. He's not a tall kid but he's got a strong body and he can play very well around corners and win puck battles. He's versatile center and is capable of playing on the wing, but right now he's not shining in any part of the game.

We first saw him as a 15 years old in Drummondville playing for Finland at the 2013 U-17 hockey challenge and we notice how good of a skater he was already at that age. He was also playing very hard in his own zone and playing hard all over the ice. He can be a threat on the penalty kill due to his speed and anticipation. He has quick feet and nice burst of speed down the wing.. He got pretty good vision and he's a mature player and also got a good wrist shot with a fast and quick release, but still he hasn't been productive at the senior level. He has had concussion issues in the past.

Saarijarvi, Vili
RD-Green Bay (USHL)- 5'9 161
HockeyProspect.com Ranking: 203

Saarijarvi is an extremely dynamic defenseman whose play was a real revelation at the U18 World Championships. With a very young group of defensemen at their disposal the Finns relied heavily on Vili to carry most of the load and he sure delivered in impressive fashion. He has great mobility while carrying the puck, and that allowed him to get rid of forecheckers and start up his team's counter attack time after time. On top of his puck moving ability, he showed good vision and great execution on his passes. Saarijarvi was also particularly effective on the powerplay, where he put to work his shooting ability. On the offensive blueline however he did make some risky plays while trying to keep the puck in that were not worth the risk, as he continuously tried to impact the game as much as he could. If not for those occasions where his heart and quickness were not enough to make up for his lack of size in physical confrontations, for the most he was effective defensively, resorting to his anticipation and showing good gap control. On top of his concerning tiny frame, what hurts Saarijarvi's ranking is how underwhelming, in comparison, his play looked when on the smaller rinks of the USHL during the rest of the season. The fear is he might need the extra room provided by international rinks to be really effective. He would certainly be a good addition for a CHL team though, but he recently signed for Karpat for the next couple of seasons.

Saban, Jesse
LD - Belleville Bulls (OHL) 6'01" 209
HockeyProspect.com Ranking: NR

Saban is a big shutdown defenseman who was traded from the Erie Otters to the Belleville Bulls in the deal that sent Dallas Stars power forward prospect Remi Elie to the contending Otters. Saban had a decent rookie season where he played a lower end shutdown role for both teams. Jesse has good size and likes to land the big hit. Despite his physical side, he's moderately disciplined not going too far and taking a penalty. He showed strong defensive zone play battling hard and competing along the wall. He is also tough in front of his own net both because of his pushback. His skating will need improvement as he is a bit slow off the start and lacks mobility. He will also need to improve on his puck play, as we noticed several risky passes in his own end and an inability to read lanes that are being taken away. Making the simple, high percentage play will help him in this regard. His upside would be as a lower end shutdown defenseman with some toughness at the next level.

Saccoman, Colin
RD - Shattuck St. Mary's (US Prep – Ind.) 6'1 176
HockeyProspect.com Ranking: NR

He is good sized D-man that will only continue to gain strength while attending LSSU (WCHA) so that will even enhance his physical play more for the future. He likes to play the body and is effective in doing so. He skates decent with mobility and can handle the puck pretty well which allows him to make good outlets passes. He usually makes good decisions in moving the puck as sees the ice pretty well. He probably will get bypassed this go around yet there is game to build upon for the future.

Sadek, Jack
RD – Lakeville North (MN-HS) 6'1.5" 185LBS
HockeyProspect.com Ranking: 161

Sadek is a fluid skating, puck-moving defenseman with really good tools including a really good shot. He isn't a flashy player but he thinks the game well and makes smart plays with the puck. Has a great outlet pass and can stretch the ice using his vision and quick passing release. He has a powerful skating stride that allows him to join the rush and be effective down low in the offensive zone. Does a good job using his skating ability and footwork to buy time for himself. Sadek ran the Power Play this past season for Lakeville North, he possesses a quick release from the point and getting the puck on net is his first priority. Defensively Sadek will battle in front of his own net, opposing forwards pay a price for trying to set up in front. Sadek can get caught chasing the play at times and needs to continue to work on his defensive awareness and positioning in his own end. Sadak will be off to the University of Minnesota in 2015.

Salituro, Dante
RC - Ottawa 67's (OHL) 5'09" 178
HockeyProspect.com Ranking: NR

Salituro was a key member of the 67's offensive attack this season. He has an excellent shot and gets a ton of power out of it. He has good positioning and keeps his feet moving. He will sometimes take his shots from bad angles and lower percentage scoring areas. He has a good compete level for pucks and isn't afraid to get involved physically. He lacks the separation speed to escape opponents, which a player of his size drastically needs to be successful at the next level.

Salituro may get selected at the 2015 NHL Entry Draft but he will face an uphill battle to play in the league. His offensive skills are good but he lacks the skating and evasiveness someone his size needs to succeed at the NHL level, as his projection would be as a top six forward. He is unlikely to be able to fill a bottom six role at that level.

Quotable: " Not on my list." - NHL Scout

Quotable: " Good OHL player but he's not on my radar." NHL Scout

Quotable: " Average skater and he's small so it's not a good mix for future success in the NHL." - NHL Scout

Quotable: " I thought he was one of the top pure goal scorers in his OHL draft year back in his AAA days but he struggles to separate from checkers at the OHL level, let alone what he would be like at the NHL level." - Mark Edwards

Samsonov, Ilya
G – CSKA (MHL) – 6'3" 200
HockeyProspect.com Ranking: 21

A 6'3" goaltender that plays even bigger than that, Samsonov this season has shown more than once the capability of stealing games on the international stage. Had a memorable showing against the US at the U18 World Championships where he put together a compendium of his qualities in front of many NHL scouts, a game that will probably play a role in where he will be selected at the draft. As the Americans kept creating scoring chances and attack the net, the Russian demonstrated impressive compete level and control, without losing his composures even when hit hard by forwards crashing the net.

Samsonov has a good goaltending foundation and uses proper technique to make his saves, but can be able to come up with the extra unorthodox effort in desperate situations to save his team. His style is aggressive, knows how to fill the middle coming off his posts making the most of his size, challenges shooters in close and he seems to get better when he sees more action, apparently not bothered by traffic. He emanates confidence in most games (the quarterfinal against the host Switzerland certainly was not one of those), which probably adds to the feeling he doesn't have many weaknesses. One of them has been, in some measure, going hard from post to post, something that has looked like a work in progress along the season. At fault for over sliding more than once after strong pushes in extreme situations, he has shown better control in the Spring and in last viewings.
Still, his shoulders are not always squaring the puck and he twists his body as a result, sometimes ending up on his chest. He also tends to forget his stick when sliding right to left, exposing his five hole.

Looking for more flaws, he can be at fault for not coming out to cut the angle on shots coming from the side even if there are no other opponents anywhere close his net; his play with the puck could be better and safer, he needs to stay focused even when there isn't apparent danger (as he has been fooled more than once by unexpected turns of events) and could improve his consistency, pretty much like any other 18yrs old goalie. At the end of the day, these shortcomings are things that can be fixed, and when you consider his agility and reflexes on top of the package he brings, they pale in comparison with his pro potential, which is beyond dispute.

Quotable: "Really good goalie who might just be the best in the draft class. Has the size plus he's an athlete. He put on a show versus USA at the U18 in Finland to help out his draft stock even more. Love the way he competes. Chatted about him with quite a few scouts in Switzerland. Got glowing reviews. He might go early." - Mark Edwards

Sandberg, Johannes
LC – Djurgardens (SWE Jr.) – 6'0" 185
HockeyProspect.com Ranking: NR

There is so much Sandberg does right. An underrated and very versatile player, at the junior level he showed he can be relied upon in every situation. He can score, even from positions where is not supposed to, he can win the key faceoffs, help defending a lead or set up teammates on the powerplay. He is a crafty playmaker and is willing to take hits to make a play. He likes to set up on the half-wall to find the open teammate with a perfect, crips pass or walk out to shoot through a hole or for a rebound. He is a very intelligent player, which is why he is used in all situations. He was a penalty-killing specialist this season and logged lots of time in that situation. Even when on the PK, he would still generate scoring opportunities. Johannes doesn't have a beautiful stride, but he manages to generate enough power and speed necessary to play the game at a high level. In order for him to make the jump to the North American style of hockey, he will need to improve his physical play. Sandberg has a longer development path, but could be a dark horse pick with how versatile he is and how hard he works.

Sandstrom, Felix
G – Brynas (SWE Jr.) – 6'2" 191
HockeyProspect.com Ranking: 122

Sandstrom spent the bulk of his season playing in the J20 SuperElit splitting time with Buffalo Sabres draft pick Jonas Johansson. A member of Sweden's U18 National Team, he also made appearances at the J18 level and saw some action in the SHL this season.

Felix has a big frame that fills the net very well. He has those long legs that he can kick out quickly like paddles from a pinball machine. However, he has tendencies to leave his five-hole open. In his rare SHL appearances he had good composure and looked calm. However, at U18 Worlds he would panic easily and lose his composure. He relies on reacting to plays and struggles with anticipating threats. He has a good glove and wingspan allowing him to get a good reach and pull pucks in. He has great push lines, finding his post and filling the middle. Sandstrom has the necessary footwork at the U20 level to be successful but needs to improve on power and squareness to move up to the next level. He has the foundation to be a top goalie, but his game sense is an area that needs to improve. With more consistent game time next year, that area should see significant improvement.

Quotable: "I thought he had some ugliness at the U18 but I have always liked his potential. Samsonov stole some of his thunder in Switzerland." - Mark Edwards

Schemitsch, Thomas
RD - Owen Sound Attack (OHL) 6'04" 206
HockeyProspect.com Ranking: 111

Schemitsch is an offensive defenseman that played a ton of minutes in a two-way role for the Owen Sound Attack. He played in all game situations this season. He makes a good first pass, doesn't force plays that aren't there and possesses the ability to skate it up ice if he's given space. Schemitsch is generally calm when pressured and is composed while running the powerplay. He distributes the puck well on the man advantage and does a good job of getting his powerful shot through traffic. Without the puck he uses his long reach to knock pucks away and doesn't shy away from getting in the shooting lanes. At times he gets caught flat footed and he gets beat wide with speed but he's got better at using his stick to steer players to the outside and keep them there.

Schemitsch weakness is below the dots in the defensive zone. He has heavy feet, which hurts him with short area quickness and despite his size he struggles to win pucks. He lost far too many board battles. With the concerns around his positioning, feet and defensive zone play, we would be tempted to move Schemitsch back to forward his original position he played in AAA. We would consider trying him as a two-way forward who could play the point on the power play. He's a smart player but he is a ways from developing his defensive tools to the level it needs to be at for him to succeed at the NHL level.

Quotable: "Liked what I saw in my early viewings but the more I watched him, I saw that his feet are too far off for me to risk anything more than a late pick on him." - NHL Scout

Quotable: "He's a mess down low." - NHL Scout

Quotable: "His slow feet are what scares me most. He struggles to get around. He's a smart player but the risk associated with his foot-speed are what drops him on my list." - Mark Edwards

Schneider, Nick
RG – Medicine Hat Tigers (WHL) – 6'02" 173
HockeyProspect.com Ranking: NR

Nick Schneider is an all-around butterfly goaltender who played about one in every three games for the Medicine Hat Tigers behind overage starter Marek Langhammer. Schneider, a speedy goaltender with strong reflexes.

He has a deep-seated stance that reduces a little bit of his net coverage but allows him to quickly and powerfully change his set position and to move along the edge of the crease with relative ease. In fact, he's one of the quicker goalies available out of the WHL in this year's draft in terms of foot movement. He plays strong positionally allowing him to regularly be in preferable positioning in relevance to the play. His glove and blocker are both above average and he's able to make saves with both pieces of equipment while moving across the crease very quickly.

Although he's one of the faster and more acrobatic of the goaltenders available in this draft, he has some trouble with rebound control. We also saw him give up too many bad goals at important times that raises some concern.

Schweri, Kay
RW – Sherbrooke Phoenix (QMJHL) – 5'10" 175
HockeyProspect.com Ranking: NR

Schweri was drafted in the 2014 CHL Import Draft, 35th overall by the Sherbrooke Phoenix. He had quite an impact with the team this year. Right away he showed he had undeniable chemistry with fellow Swiss forward Tim Wieser, and both of them clicked immediately. They did very well together even if they didn't have a regular centerman playing with them during the season. Schweri is an excellent playmaker, one of the best in the QMJHL, and always looks to distribute the puck in the offensive zone. He has the ability to slow down the play and see things on the ice that few players see. Schweri played for his country at the World Juniors in Toronto and didn't have a good showing, as he was already in a slump in the QMJHL before leaving and didn't help himself with his performance. He didn't have the same success in the 2nd half of the season as he did in the first half, as teams around the league were able to figure him out.

A lot of his success comes from his passing game, as he's not the kind of player that you will see in front of the net and along the wall. He's a scientific forward who mostly stays on the perimeter and tries to find open teammates. There's no denying Schweri's passing game, but we wish he would shoot the puck more often to offer some variety to his offensive game. His shot needs more velocity so that he can be more of a threat. He has good one-on-one skills, is a good stickhandler and has the ability to beat defenders one-on-one. He's an average skater for his size and that is not necessarily good for him, as he needs to get stronger physically and improve his skating. Next year in Sherbrooke he will be without his linemate and countryman Wieser, and it should be interesting to see him perform then. Very good in open ice but struggled when the plays got tighter with less time to manoever.

Quotable: "Playmaking abilities are elite but the rest of his game is lacking" - HP scout Jérôme Bérubé

Seney, Brett
LW – Merrimack (HOCKEY EAST) – 5'8.75" 156
HockeyProspect.com Ranking: NR

There were not many players in all of college hockey that had the size the rookie from Ontario had. He excelled during the first half of the NCAA season before hitting a little bit of a freshman wall during the second half. A lower body injury helped pronate his struggles down the stretch. On more than one occasion he picked up the puck in the neutral zone and blew by a few defenders with a burst of speed to pop the puck in or dish it off to a line mate. He has good creativity and vision to go with soft hands. He has a nice touch on passes, but would benefit from being more assertive.

Senyshyn, Zachary
RW - Sault Ste. Marie Greyhounds (OHL) 6'02" 195
HockeyProspect.com Ranking: 57

Senyshyn is a hard working up and down winger who had a successful first season with the Greyhounds. During the season he commonly played second/third line receiving good opportunities with experienced players. Zachary is a powerful skater who flies down the wing and can be difficult to contain due to his speed. He will generally look to put the puck on net or make a smart, effective pass and keeps it pretty simple not trying to make a fancy play. He displayed good compete down low and will often fight for pucks winning his share of battles. He is capable of landing solid hits but is not an overly physical winger. He competes at both ends of the ice and will put pressure on the backcheck and in the defensive zone.

While he posted good numbers he gained a lot of opportunities and doesn't project as an offensive guy at the next level. Senyshyn is the type of player who could turn into a solid up and down winger who does a lot of the little things right, while providing a little bit of offense at the NHL level.

Quotable: "He 'short-arms' it too much for my liking. He's not on my list." - NHL Scout

Quotable: "I like the skating but don't get all the recent hype." - NHL Scout

Quotable: "I've liked him more every time I see him." - NHL Scout

Quotable: "This is my second viewing of him in two days...more of the same so far today. He's a late rounder for me." - NHL Scout

Sharov, Alexander
LC – Lada (KHL) – 6'2" 191
HockeyProspect.com Ranking: 160

Last year we had Sharov ranked at the end of the 4th round, but we weren't surprised to see him getting passed over at the draft. This year it would be a bit different after he made a name for himself at the WJC played in Canada. The reality is, he still has some flaws in his game that will need to be addressed before he could make a trip to North America rewarding. The main step forward to be made might be in the athletic department. As he likes to protect the puck along the boards, he needs to add power to be able to play his game at the pro level, especially in the smaller rinks. He also needs to keep his feet moving when defending, as he tends to cheat with his stick and is often at risk of getting called for hooking. His skating still looks unorthodox, and he can look like a different player in different periods of the same game.

However, Sharov has the skills, the size and the instincts to develop into a complete player if he works hard. He is able to get open without the puck or to get in front of the net at the right time, and his surgical wrist shot was on full display at the WJC. At the KHL level, despite his quick release the problem was creating for himself opportunities to use it, while for the most trying to play a safe game on the fourth line. He shoots when he sees the room to score, but he should also start doing it to get rebounds when better plays are not available.

Shaw, Austin
G - Wichita Falls (NAHL) 6'4" 205
HockeyProspect.com Ranking: NR

The Princeton University commit entered the NAHL this year for his second year as a draft eligible player as a 1996 birth year. He has great NHL goaltender prototypical size and stands very big in the net. He tends to not be able to get down into the butterfly as quickly as we'd like to see which leads to him getting beat low. However, he is pretty athletic and flexible for his size and made a few highlight reel saves throughout the year. He will spend another year in juniors before heading to Princeton.

Sherwood, Kole
RW – Ohio Blue Jackets U18 (T1 EHL) 6'0" 185
HockeyProspect.com Ranking: 205

We were chasing down Brendan Demler, who was added to NHL CS list but we ended up liking Sherwood. He played AAA all season but bumped up to play a few games in the USHL late in the season. He has really good skill with good enough size and is a strong skater. Plenty of NHL teams attended Nationals to see him, so there was some interest. Sherwood dominated at a lower level of hockey and made enough of a positive impression on us to add him to our top 210.

Sideroff, Deven
RW – Kamloops Blazers (WHL) – 5'11" 179
HockeyProspect.com Ranking: 157

Sideroff, has average size and is a quick forward who can be plugged into virtually any place on the lineup. He skates well, is a consistently hard worker and highly adaptable. Deven saw ice-time on the first forward unit right out of the gate.
Looking highly coachable, Sideroff was reliable in tough situations, as he's both versatile and dependable. His durability and attention to defensive details is additionally impressive, even if the true extent of his offensive prowess remains limited.

A two-way player who can play at all three forward positions, Sideroff is a particularly good fit on the wing because of his ability to drive wide with his speed. Indeed, Sideroff's full stride acceleration and effort on the backcheck are both much better than average. Turns and pivots are quick, as well. Furthermore, he's tough in the corners and isn't afraid to take a bodycheck to make a play. A good passer in the offensive zone and equipped with a fairly good shot, we like that he can score off of the rush or off of the cycle. But even as a good skater who wins most of his races to the puck, he has a tendency to appear a bit weak-legged in the lower extremities. And as a result of his lack of lower-body strength his gliding stance appears a bit wobbly at times and he's very easily knocked to the ground.

Nonetheless, he takes on a lot of minutes, including important assignments on the penalty kill. He endures long gruelling shifts, showing good toughness and endurance on a consistent basis. Away from the puck and especially in the neutral zone, Sideroff stands out as a very swivel-headed player with good reach and good awareness of the play around him. He excels at eating up pucks in the neutral zone with his decent size, an active stick and long desperate reaches for the puck. When playing at his best, he looks much bigger than the 5-foot-11 he's listed at. The upside of Sideroff is that he never really has a bad game. Even if he isn't clicking in the offensive zone or contributing on the scoreboard, he tends to have a consistently strong defensive game in compensation. He finished the season with an impressive plus-18, despite being on a Kamloops Blazers club that almost finished dead last in the WHL's Western Conference.

Siegenthaler, Jonas
LD – ZSC Zurich (NLA) – 6'2.5" 220
HockeyProspect.com Ranking: 38

A defenseman with legit size and strength, Siegenthaler was able to take regular shifts for ZSC Zurich as a 17yrs old throughout the entire NLA season under coach Marc Crawford. His ability to consistently play a simple game and defend in all situations made that possible. He can already hold his own in front of the net, is an effective shot blocker, doesn't mind the rough stuff along the boards where he often uses his body to separate players from the puck and overall likes to take position and cut down lanes where forwards would like to move.

Jonas is a smooth skater with good balance, and even if against the most agile forwards he could use quicker feet, he moves well in all directions and excels at quickly closing in on forwards with his reach and his considerable stick work.

Siegenthaler plays a basic game and almost always picks the first option available, but he doesn't rush plays, he can play it smart and safely move the puck most of the times; he always has his head up, which helps him to execute quick outlet passes.

This description fits his solid play throughout most of the last two seasons and certainly applies to his strong showing at the 2015 WJC in Canada, but in the last part of the season Jonas had his fair share of struggles. As the intensity of the game picked up in the last couple of NLA playoff rounds, he had some mistakes and turnovers that probably affected his confidence. Expected to be the leader of his U18 national team at the World Championships in front of the home crowd, and asked to bring more to the table than his usual standard conservative play, Siegenthaler was not up to the task.

Not only his current limitations on the offensive side of the puck were evident, he really struggled at staying away from turnovers and mistakes in general, probably hurting his draft stock as a result, with the quarterfinal against a sleeping Russian team being his only full 60 minutes of good play at the event.

Jonas has the capability to play on the poweplay as he can move the puck and properly manage the offensive blueline, but his contribution is hampered by the fact his shot is hardly a threat as of now, as it takes too long to get it off and he is unable to change angles once the lanes are shut down, which most of the times results in a blocked shot or in a shot off the target.
Even if Siegenthaler projects as a puck moving stay-at-home defenseman, he will probably need to add to his current toolset to fully succeed at the next level. There are at least three areas he should focus on: get meaner in front of his net while cleaning up the rest of his game from some unnecessary penalties, improve his shot effectiveness, learn to use more his skating to carry the puck and make plays beyond the defensive blueline. Given his solid foundation, those seem reasonable improvements to achieve as he grows up.

Quotable: "I had positive reports written up on him from last year and he continued to impress this year. He kinda finished with a few sub-par performances at the U18 in April but overall I think he's a solid NHL prospect." - Mark Edwards

Quotable: "I see some positives in his game but overall I don't like him as much as I see in some of the rankings out there." - NHL Scout

Simion, Dario
LW – Davos (NLA) – 6'3" 190
HockeyProspect.com Ranking: NR

This right shooting winger made his NLA debut as a 16yrs old, played regularly for Lugano in his draft year four season ago and with his projectable size was considered to have a legit chance at being selected (ranked 45th in CSS final ranking for Euro skaters). Simion eventually was not drafted in 2012, and probably didn't even come close in the following two seasons, during which his development stalled. But in his last year of eligibility, was it the new team with a new coach (Arno Del Curto) or was it finishing his studies and getting free of that commitment, all of a sudden something seemed to click for Dario. He enjoyed his first successful pro season, which culminated with a playoff run that saw his team claim the Swiss title and him finishing top 10 in scoring.

Despite having played only for Swiss teams along his career, the 21yrs old plays a North American type of game. He likes to go to the net or landing in front of it. Obviously doing it in NLA doesn't require to pay the same price as in North American rinks, but it's still an unusual attribute to see in a Swiss player.

His skating stride still needs some work but he is effective at getting up to speed quickly when making turns, and once up to speed inside the offensive zone he often uses it to attack the end boards fearlessly to engage in battles for the puck where he puts his size to work. In a player with that size and legit puck skills these are interesting traits. Simion can deliver solid checks and shows a good effort level from the red line on, he could however stay more active in his own zone, too often he is caught standing still watching the play and may not react as fast as required. He needs to keep moving his feet and improve his stamina to remain effective along the entire shift. The room for further improvement is there, we don't expect him to be drafted but Simion may actually be worth a pick this time around.

Shea, Ryan
LD – BC High (HIGH – MA) – 6'0.5" 175
HockeyProspect.com Ranking: 190

Shea is a good puck handler that converted to defense from forward a few years ago. The son of a big time scorer at BC, he has all the tools to be an impact player with the puck on his stick. He has tremendous vision and makes good lead passes as well shorter passes as he's moving up ice. He can also stickhandle well and join the rush in transition. He has a heavier shot than one might assume due to his relative frail frame. Whether it was the game plan or not, he seemed to try to force lead passes this season and make impossible home run passes this season. His defensive play is more inconsistent. His strength and gap control is not always there. There were a few games where he was very good at both ends, but there were other nights where his defensive play had to be questioned.

Simon, Dominik
LW – Plzen (CZE) – 5'11" 176
HockeyProspect.com Ranking: 177

Simon is a Czech winger that enjoyed a breakthrough season in his last year of eligibility for the NHL Entry Draft. The '94 born scored 30 points in the Extraliga, gaining a spot on the national team roster for the World Championships in Prague, where he was able to contribute albeit in a limited role.

The main feature Dominik brings to the table is his quickness. He is a fast stickhandler with notable agility and quick hands, he can make quick turns while keeping good control of the puck and promptly react along the boards with his fast moving feet. Despite his limited size he looks comfortable looking for pucks and opportunities in the slot, and he is able to finish his chances. Even if he is primarily a scorer, he can quickly recognize if better options are available instead of going for the net. Simon could develop into a legit complimentary player at the next level. It will be interesting to see if on draft day the interested NHL teams will feel like using a pick on him rather than waiting and trying to sign him as a free agent.

Smallman, Spencer
RW – Saint-John SeaDogs (QMJHL) – 6'1" 188
HockeyProspect.com Ranking: NR

Smallman was undrafted last year but it looks like he should hear his name called this time around. The Summerside, P.E.I. native just finished his 3rd season with the Sea Dogs and achieved career highs in every offensive category this year. Smallman was originally drafted in the 4th round of the 2012 QMJHL Draft after playing his midget hockey with the Fredericton Canadiens. He's a hard-working forward that plays hard at both ends of the ice. First and foremost, he's a player that can play in all situations for his team, who can compete with offensively-gifted players on an offensive line and can also play in a defensive role on a defensive line. He has grown up quite a bit since his midget days and now is more comfortable in one-on-one battles. He is one of his team's best players along the wall. Smallman's hockey sense is above-average, he understands the game well and is an asset to his team defensively. Smallman is one of the league's best penalty-killers due to his smarts, speed and hustle. He's not afraid to block shots as well, playing with a lot heart. Offensively, he is not a player that will take charge, but does a good job supporting his line and won't hurt you at the QMJHL level in an offensive role. When looking at the pros for Smallman, with his speed and smarts, you could see him becoming a role player if he makes it.

Smejkal, Jiri
RW – Moose Jaw Warriors (WHL) – 6'02" 183
HockeyProspect.com Ranking: NR

Born in late-1996, Jiri Smejkal of the Moose Jaw Warriors is a first-time eligible import two-way forward from the Czech Republic. Prior to arriving in Moose Jaw, Smejkal impressed scouts as an important part of the Czech Under-18 national team that left with a surprising silver medal finish. There and in the WHL this season, he established himself as a distinct defensive presence with a touch of offensive skill. While he looks a bit behind the play at times while transitioning on the offense, Smejkal nonetheless is a decent skater who plays a hard-nosed and honest 200-foot game. He showed this year in Moose Jaw that he can score, set up plays, throw some big bodychecks and even recorded his first fight.

Not the fastest skater on the ice by any means, Smejkal still possesses really strong raw acceleration technique and will almost certainly become faster and faster as he adds muscle to his lower-body. His work in the corners is good, as he has tight turning agility. More than that, his board game is punctuated by stand up upper-body strength, toughness, grit, tenacity and hard work. He's extremely active in his own zone, working hard along the walls to get the puck to safety. He transitions the play from defence to offense in a quick is sometimes haphazard fashion.

Smejkal's offensive game certainly has potential, as exhibited by his 32 points in a rookie year on a team that missed the playoffs. But his speciality is definitely his defensive abilities, as Smejkal is excellent at winning board battles, blocking shots, creating turnovers in the neutral zone, providing smart reads on offensive dumps and making splashy open-ice hits. All these skills make him well suited to a depth role at the professional level. And yet the most exciting thing about Smejkal's game is that there is indeed a larger offensive dimension that appears untapped. He's a good passer, a good shooter and has really good puck skills in tight, but he's still adjusting to the North American game and in the midst of adding strength to a skating stride that already looks technically strong.

Smith, Evan
G - Austin (NAHL) 6'6.25" 174
HockeyProspect.com Ranking: NR

Long and lanky, Smith really hasn't grown into his huge frame yet, weighing in at only 174 lbs. Smith started the year with an unsuccessful four game stint with the Victoria Royals of the WHL before being reassigned to Austin in the North American Hockey League. It is currently unclear where Smith will spend his time next season. Obviously Smith's height will make him an attractive target for NHL teams that hope he can develop further and grow into his height. He certainly takes up a lot of space in net and his size alone makes it hard for NAHL opponents to beat him. Right now, he is just a little awkward in net as it seems he doesn't have full control over his body. That said, he posted fantastic numbers for the Bruins this year and the combination of his size and potential make him worth keeping an eye on at the draft.

Smolin, Mikhail
LW – Chaika (MHL) – 5'11.5" 180
HockeyProspect.com Ranking: NR

A right shooting left winger, Smolin brings to the ice unusual elements for a Russian youngster. He likes to carry the puck with speed down the left side, but his distinctive traits are his intensity and willingness to battle for pucks. Mikhail plays a North-South game and looks right at home in high paced contests, he doesn't mind traffic or the physical play. Despite his ordinary size he is often the first one taking the body, especially along the boards. He plays bigger than his size and attacks the end boards with great speed, he is very effective at getting there first and retrieve pucks, but it's also not rare seeing him come away with the puck after hitting the puck carrier behind the net. When he has possession inside the offensive zone, he consistently goes for the net and he is a tough costumer, he stays with the play after shooting and goes for his own rebounds. He battles hard for position in front of the net, but he is better at looking for rebounds than at deflecting shots from the blueline.

Mikhail has been growing physically along the season, but will need to further develop in that area in order to play that type of game at the pro level. He is barely eligible for this year draft and could still grow. His offensive game still has to develop in terms of playmaking, but his instincts are good. He reacts and gets up to top speed quickly, even if his footwork would need some refining. His hands look still unpolished, but he can change the shooting angle with a bit of a toe drag and his shot has already good power.

Smolin backchecks hard unless he already run out of gas, he is less effective when defending in his own zone even if he doesn't mind blocking shots.
Sometimes he gets caught out of position in the defensive zone after going for checks along the boards. As he never appeared in international competition and has seen only MHL action so far, it seems unlikely to see him drafted this year, but he would certainly make for an interesting dark horse pick.

Somers, Will
LW – Hotchkiss School (NE Prep) 6'4 214
HockeyProspect.com Ranking: NR

He has the big body and physical strength that intrigues scouts. He uses the big frame to create chances in possession protecting the puck and utilizing a strong shot as well. He is not a dynamic player but long-term project if some team is willing to take a shot.

Sorensen, George
G – Herning (DEN) – 5'10" 172
HockeyProspect.com Ranking: NR

Passed over in the last two drafts, could this year be different? There is no doubt in Sorensen's ability to steal the spotlight with highlight reel saves, but his small size is a large deterrent for teams to take him. Sorensen possesses incredible, explosive power that is necessary for him to cover the crease. He has a compact stance with his gloves in tight, making him look even smaller than he is. He covers the ice down low very well with tremendous flexibility and agility. Perimeter deflections are a serious threat due his necessity to challenge more on shots due to his size. Sorensen needs to work on a consistent recovery, as he tends to get up with his dominant right leg, which slows him down. A true competitor in the crease, he has left Herning to sign a contract with Frederikshavn in the same league for next season. Even with his standout year with the Danish national team, his size will be a big factor in a team taking a chance on selecting him.

Soustal, Tomas
RC – Kelowna Rockets (WHL) – 6'03" 189
HockeyProspect.com Ranking: NR

Tomas Soustal is a lanky, curious and offensively enigmatic import forward who came into the Kelowna Rockets with a bit of hype, but then saw his draft stock fall off completely as the season wore on. He brings a number of attractive raw talents to the table—a large frame, decent full-stride acceleration, good hockey IQ and a calm nature even in chaotic situations. Stuck near the bottom of a deep talent pool in Kelowna, Soustal had trouble lighting the lamp consistently this year, even on a powerhouse Rockets club. He went 25 games straight without scoring at the end of the regular season, but was then able to tab more than a few during a lengthy Rockets playoff run.

He has good individual skills, especially when it comes to puckhandling. He does a good job of gaining zone entry through fancy stickwork and has the requisite speed and skill along the wall to be successful on the dump-and-chase as well. He's very tall and is adding weight, so you can't help but wish that he'd step up his physicality on a game-to-game basis. Although he doesn't always go into the prime scoring area as much as you'd like, he's one of those guys who has nerves of steel when he's given an opportunity from in-close.

We wouldn't be entirely surprised to see Soustal's development trajectory mirror that of teammate Justin Kirkland, who went to the Nashville Predators in last year's draft as a third round selection (). Both players are blessed with a tall and lanky build, have decent puckhandling skills and have shown an ability to score while playing in a depth role. Kirkland was also criticized for not being more physical last season. While we personally think that picking Soustal in the upper rounds would be a bit of a reach, we don't think that it's entirely out of the realm of possibilities.

Soy, Tyler
LC – Victoria Royals (WHL) – 6'00" 175
HockeyProspect.com Ranking: 106

We wouldn't be all that surprised if an NHL club takes a gamble in the first three rounds on two-way centre Tyler Soy of the WHL's Victoria Royals. Soy, who plays top-line minutes on Dave Lowry's Victoria Royals club in the WHL and scored at nearly a point-per-game pace this year, is a product of the same Cloverdale Colts Bantam A-1 program that previously produced NHL second round draft picks Tyler Wotherspoon and Jujhar Khaira. A forward blessed with equally good shooting and passing ability, Tyler's greatest exposure to scouts during this, his draft year season, was likely his appearance with Team Canada at the Ivan Hlinka tournament, where he should have silenced some critics of his defensive game, logging crucial duties as a key penalty killer for his club. He stood out there and on his Victoria Royals club this season, as a physically immature centre with good toughness, faceoff skills, shooting chops and playmaking ability.

Nonetheless, there will inevitably be some question marks regarding Soy's competitiveness and work ethic, as he has a unique but effective style of play that, perhaps unfairly, makes him ripe for criticism. A bit of a floater at times, Tyler Soy has a tendency to always look a little tired. Most definitely, it is sometimes to his advantage, as looking lackadaisical at times and invisible at others, he tends to pounce into action unpredictably in the offensive zone, which can make him a difficult player to predict or contain. His first-step explosiveness is exceptional and, again, fairly difficult to predict. His fancy footwork is additionally dangerous for the opposition, because he is capable of sniping the puck from seemingly any position—off balance, mid-stride, in tight space, or standing stationary.

See his game from afar and you might come away disappointed. But take a closer look at the ice-level and you will see that his game is full of nuance. Stick lifts, quick pivots, slight misdirections, all leave defensemen and goaltenders consistently bewildered. Indeed, superior skating skills, hockey sense and workmanship are all important qualities that Tyler Soy possesses in spades. On one viewing, our scouts saw him have a 5 point night going head-to-head against the much larger Adam Musil. However, while at this juncture he's certainly a great junior player that any junior team would love to have, at sub-180 pounds there are serious questions surrounding his ability to jump to the next level. In addition to adding greater consistency of effort to his game, he needs to get much, much bigger and add a ton of strength if he hopes to continue his success level playing against men.

Spacek, Michael
RC – Pardubice (CZE) 5'11" 187
HockeyProspect.com Ranking: 140

Spacek is a clever center who spent this past season with Pardubice in the top Czech pro league. With his senior team Michael saw time on the powerplay but at even strength he was mainly trying to take regular shifts without hurting his team, rarely creating offense. He is smart and managed to make simple plays without getting involved in physical confrontations where he had little chances to succeed. Obviously he won't have the luxury of playing that type of game in North America and his strength and capability to battle for pucks will have to improve significantly.

Spacek has good positioning in both the offensive and defensive zones, he consistently offers good puck support to teammates and shows off his stickhandling ability through the neutral zone, able to safely carry the puck inside the offensive zone.

A very good puckhandler with quick hands, he is a playmaker first but already last season showed a very good shot for his size. His skating is fine, but not an area where he can make a difference. He is effective in the faceoff circle at the junior level. After playing against men for months though, the hope was he would be able to do more than in the past against his peers. Seemed to lack some confidence and offensively we couldn't see much progress from last season.
He can also be at fault for giving up on plays too easily. Certainly has the talent to do better pretty soon, but doing it in smaller rinks will be a tougher challenge that requires strides far from guaranteed.

Spaxman, Ethan
LD – Waterloo (USHL) 6'3.5" 193
HockeyProspect.com Ranking: NR

Spaxman is a big defenseman who plays a pretty one-dimensional defensive, shutdown game. That being said, he is very good in his own zone. He is a heart and soul guy that gets on the ice and blocks shots, really sells out for the team every time he's on the ice. He's very responsible in his own zone and doesn't make a lot of mistakes in terms of turning the puck over on the breakout. He struggles a little bit with the puck on his stick, doesn't look completely comfortable.

Get beat too often on rushes and makes some mistakes on the offensive blueline keeping the puck in the zone. Spaxman is a Merrimack commit and will attend in the fall. Spaxman was a relative unknown on the NHL Draft scene to start the year and while he has made a positive impression as the season went on he's not on our radar as a draftable prospect.

Speers, Blake
RW - Sault Ste. Marie Greyhounds (OHL) 5'11" 185
HockeyProspect.com Ranking: 90

Blake was the 1st round pick of the Sault Ste. Marie Greyhounds in 2013 and was immediately given the opportunity to succeed, primarily playing a top six role for his team. While he originates as a centre, he has been moved to the wing for the majority of this season in a move that seemed to help the team because he struggled in the face-off circle.

Speers is a speedy forward who left us wanting a little more this year, especially as the season progressed. In general he's a kid with good speed and smarts but lacks skills that will dazzle you on a nightly basis. He controls the puck well in the offensive zone and makes good reads. He has some good moves one on one and has shown us the ability to deke out goaltenders and defenders. He provided a bit of a backcheck and is adequate in the defensive zone showing very good development and progress on the defensive side of the red line. He understands defensive hockey.

Speers does have some potential to be top 9 forward at the NHL level. We like a lot of things he does to contribute. He needs to bulk up to allow him to win some more 1 on 1 battles. In the past we felt like he dictated the play more. This year he seemed more of a complimentary player who relied on teammates to control pucks. We like how he's able to hold his speed when carrying the puck, but that's another area that wasn't quite as noticeable in our viewings this season. Speers can score and he makes plays. He sees things develop and reacts to it well. He's shown us good ability both on the PK and PP.

He needs to use next season and the extra ice he will gain with so many graduating Greyhounds to show what we think he's capable of producing.

Quotable: "As good as they are (Greyhounds) He's (Speers) the only player on my list from this team." - NHL Scout

Quotable: "I had a lot of time for him earlier this year and he was up pretty high on my list but he's sliding for me." - NHL Scout

Quotable: "I liked him a lot coming into the OHL. I liked the way he could do things at high speed. He was pretty solid in my first half viewings this year but looked more ordinary in my later viewings. He seemed to be more passive in the offensive zone in some of my later viewings. I always liked how proactive he played in the past. Having said that, I still think he has above average smarts and plays an NHL style of game." - Mark Edwards

Spencer, Matthew
RD - Peterborough Petes (OHL) 6'02" 201
HockeyProspect.com Ranking: 81

Spencer has a great combination of size and skating ability. Since the beginning of his OHL career, Matthew has been given a ton of ice time in all game situations and it has been trial by fire. This role has caused him to try to do too much at times and needs to pick his spots as he can get caught out of position biting off more than he can chew. He doesn't possess much of a mean streak and we would like to see more consistency in his physical game. One on one play will need improvement. He is very wild and he can go from making the perfect play one time to misreading and getting walked badly the next. His positional play will also need improvements as he can chase the play too often and be out of position in the defensive zone.

Spencer has some good tools but also has warts in his game. He makes too many mental blunders and has issues handling forecheck pressure. He's not a physical bruiser and doesn't project as having NHL powerplay ability. He was at his best at the Ivan Hlinka tournament way back in August. While at the Hlinka, he kept his game very simple and played the most mistake free hockey we have ever seen from him. His size and skating keep him in the running to be selected reasonably early in the NHL Draft.

Quotable: "I don't think he's a smart player." - NHL Scout

Quotable: "For NHL purposes I just worry how he thinks the game." - NHL Scout

Quotable: " I just saw him twice last week. He's huge and in one of the games I didn't see him make one hit." - NHL Scout

Quotable: " Struggles making reads, just not very good with the puck in general." NHL Scout

Quotable: " I think being taken so high in the OHL Draft is hurting him. Guys are expecting him to be something he isn't. I think he has good value in the mid rounds." - NHL Scout

Quotable: " I didn't have him ranked as high as he was drafted in his OHL year. I thought he dominated in his OHL Draft year because of his size and skating more than anything else. I never saw enough hockey sense to see him as a high pick. Outside of a few games where he played simple smart games, he's struggled in my viewings of him in the OHL. He doesn't have enough NHL projectable qualities for me to risk an early pick on him but his size and skating do give him some value." - Mark Edwards

Sprong, Daniel
RW – Charlottetown Islanders (QMJHL) – 6'0" 185
HockeyProspect.com Ranking: 37

Sprong has been on the hockey radar since his peewee days in Montreal, where he was considered one of the best hockey players in the province. Originally from Amsterdam, Sprong's family moved to Montreal when Daniel was 7 years old so he could continue to play a high level of hockey. The Islanders selected Sprong 13th overall in the 2013 QMJHL Draft after he dropped on draft day. During the 2012-2013 season, Sprong broke the all-time record for points in Midget Espoir, with 104 in 30 games. Sprong was not eligible to play Midget AAA due to not having Canadian citizenship. Last season, after reporting to the Islanders, Sprong had a stellar season, scoring 30 goals and 68 points and was a star in the playoffs, scoring 4 goals in 4 games against a powerhouse Halifax team. This year a lot of expectations came with Sprong and he didn't have the best beginning to the year, but found his groove in the 2nd half and posted another strong effort in the playoffs, with 7 goals in 11 games.

Sprong's stickhandling and shot are high-end in terms of this draft class. With the puck on his stick he's dynamite and he models his game after Pat Kane and Alexander Ovechkin. With the puck in the offensive zone, he can score goals without the help of his teammates, his offensive skills at this level are that good compared to the others. He can beat goaltenders from anywhere in the offensive zone with his shot, his release is among the best. He absolutely loves to play in one-on-one situations where he's able to show off his puck skills. The negative side with this skill level is that at times, he tries to do too much with the puck and can be victim of turnovers. He also could make better use of his linemates; while he has good playmaking abilities, sometime he will try an extra deke and lose the puck. He's a good skater but his explosiveness is really good and this is what he uses to beat defensemen wide on the rush. In the offensive zone, he doesn't get enough credit for his puck-protection skills, as it is really tough to get the puck away from him. He has a strong lower body and uses it well in puck-protection situations. Consistency is also an issue with Sprong's game, as not always the best effort comes out of him from game to game, but even in a bad effort he can find his way on the scoresheet. Defensively he needs to show more commitment, as he can get lazy in the defensive zone, not move his feet, and lose his man. Daniel is a strong kid, but won't be known as a physical player, rather a skill-first type of player. He made nice strides to his overall game during this season, even after a rough start (to his standard), but there's no denying that Sprong has game-breaking abilities. Sprong has been a player tough to rank all year long, he's the definition of boom or bust prospect in this year draft class.

Quotable: "He was good." (on combine interview) - NHL Scout

Quotable: "His interview (NHL combine) was fine. He was a little cocky but you expect that, right?" - NHL Scout

Quotable: "He reminds me of Ho-Sang out there. He's sliding down my list where we wouldn't get him." - NHL Scout

Quotable: "At the end of the day he's one of the most skilled players in this draft." - NHL Scout

Quotable: "His interview (Combine) was the worst one this year, reminded me of Shinkaruk a few years ago." - NHL Scout

Stadel, Riley
LD – Kelowna Rockets (WHL) – 5'10" 171
HockeyProspect.com Ranking: NR

A two-way defenseman who has been compared in the past to the Vancouver Canucks franchise defender Kevin Bieksa, the 2015 draft re-entry Riley Stadel acclimatized himself very nicely to a historical Kelowna Rockets franchise renowned for its ability to churn out NHL defenseman and defensive prospects including Luke Schenn, Madison Bowey and Stadel himself. Stadel moved to the Rockets last year, after the club selected him in the 3rd round (51st overall) in the 2011 WHL Bantam Draft out of the Cloverdale Colts A1-T1 Bantam program—that's the same bantam program that produced the Wotherspoon brothers, Tyler Soy, Jujhar Khaira and many others. Stadel is slightly undersized but looks bigger due to aggressive style, unique stance and smart gap control.

Stadel is the type of defenseman who you might never notice if not for his name being on the scoresheet. He's difficult to notice because he's so level-headed and makes so few mistakes. Furthermore, he manoeuvres around the ice in a stationary, almost robotic, action-figure-like stance that optimizes range of motion and vision but requires an odd and sometimes clumsy skating style. He's not a bad skater by any means, but extremely unconventional in terms of how precise and technical he looks in motioning from one area to another. His first steps are strong. So strong that he leans on them—even in his pivots—using them to propel forward followed by a tomahawk turn that maintains forward momentum going backwards. He maintains his lanes well, wins one-on-one battles and is a key contributor on the penalty kill.

However, one reason Stadel went undrafted last year is that he lacks offensive upside. While he's spent some time quarterbacking the Rockets second power play unit, this is not a power play defenceman at the next level in our opinion. His strongest qualities are most obvious in the defensive end, where he's quick to attack the puck and not afraid to throw his body around. He shows good focus and keeps his concentration even when slightly crossing the line; by not looking guilty he avoids earning penalty minutes that lesser defenceman probably would. There's still a lot to like here.

Stenlund, Kevin
RC – HV 71 (SWE) – 6'3" 205
HockeyProspect.com Ranking: 65

Stenlund is a hefty centerman who brings to the table an interesting package of qualities. Not too often you see players of that size featuring his versatility and puckhandling ability. Strong on his skates, he could improve his first steps but he has a powerful stride that builds up legit speed. He can carry up the puck through the neutral zone using his reach and his stickhandling ability, or share it with his wingers putting to work his solid playmaking skills, something he tends to do more inside the offensive zone. He can already cover different roles on the powerplay, either using his possession skills as a playmaker from the half side boards, or his one-timer from the blueline, or his impressive strength to take position in front of the net.

Kevin is reliable in the faceoff circle and shows a good attitude on the ice, he is responsible and willing to contribute in the defensive zone. He was only five days away from being eligible for last year draft and this season couldn't attend international events with the U18 national team, but he managed to crack the HV 71 roster and show his stuff at the SHL level, which might have helped his draft status. He was able to win puck battles against men, compete hard along the boards and effectively use his body to shield the puck. One thing he will need to improve on is his wrist shot, a bit underwhelming as at the moment its power doesn't match his physical strength. Something that made us feel not comfortable enough in assigning him an even higher ranking is the fact Stenlund has yet to show the capability to execute quickly on a consistent basis. If that will prove to be only a matter of time, his NHL future should be fruitful.

Stephens, Devante
LD – Kelowna Rockets (WHL) – 6'02" 170
HockeyProspect.com Ranking: 189

Stephens is a speedy and effective shutdown defenceman who played in this year, his draft year, with the powerhouse Kelowna Rockets. A rookie defenceman who earned a spot on the stacked club out of training camp, Stephens proved his worth as a full-timer over the course load of a full season followed by a solid playoff run. He played this year in a bit of a protege role, locked into a pairing with Washington Capitals draft pick Madison Bowey. While he struggled individually to begin the season, he gradually progressed over the long haul of the year and was well protected by the high-end talent that surrounded him.

While he's not necessarily skilled as Bowey, Stephens is a good skater and a talented puck-rusher. Very mobile with the puck on his stick and able to handle the puck with ease even at top speeds, long fluid strides propel him out of his own zone at a good speed. A confident puckhandler, he's particularly good at skating the puck out of his own zone and kick-starting the offense. Additionally, he's pretty good at both giving and receiving passes while accelerating, which gives him a ton of outlet options to start the rush.

In his own end he does a lot of things well, even though there definitely remains some room for improvement. On the positive side of things, he plays the game with a real edge, making some outstanding hits in open-ice and along the boards. We expect his physical game to grow immensely in the next few seasons in Kelowna. He will be able to add more muscle to his frame and a few more years of major junior experience to his resume. On the negative side, he has a tendency to look panicked when pressured by an aggressive forechecker.

Stephens, Mitchell
RC - Saginaw Spirit (OHL) 5'11" 182
HockeyProspect.com Ranking: 51

Mitchell was a skilled offensive forward taken by the Saginaw Spirit in the first round of the 2013 OHL Priority Selection Draft. He struggled to make much of an impact last season. Aside from a couple of inconsistent stretches, he really picked up his game this year. Stevens book-ended his season with strong performances at the Ivan Hlinka in August and U18 tournament in April.

Mitchell has great skating ability and can separate from the defender in a hurry. He has very good puck control and can make opponents look bad if they get too aggressive on Stephens. He has a good, accurate shot and is capable of picking small areas of the net. Stephens got stronger over the offseason and utilized that extra mass in the most effective way possible. He became a real physical force for his team. He loves to take the body and lands some crushing hits on bigger opponents. He generally doesn't look past any chance to finish his check. Stephens is still a little bit undersized for the type of game that he plays, which adds some risk but he has skill to produce offensively and the tenacity and two-way mindset to be a safer pick if he can't make it as a top six forward.

Stevens provides good puck support in all 3 zones and doesn't cheat by flying the O zone. He competes hard for pucks. He is a high effort player and wins his share of 1 on 1 battles despite not being the biggest of players. He is smart on the forecheck, he makes good reads and uses proper angling and stick position.

Stevens is good in his own zone. He reads the play well and is aware of his responsibilities. He is good at being aggressive at jumping on loose pucks when the opportunity arises. If he gets bigger and stronger he has the ability to become an excellent defensive player.

Stevens rose up our list as the season progressed. Although we don't see him as a top 6 forward in the NHL, he has more offensive upside than some give him credit for. We like him as smart, competitive bottom 6 forward with a high compete level, who finds a way to chip in offensively.

Quotable: "He did nothing for me in my viewings before Christmas but I've liked him in the 2nd half this season." - NHL Scout

Quotable: "I liked him in Europe and I even saw him score 4 goals in Niagara in one of my viewings this year. Stevens was always a kid with a high compete level going back to his Toronto Marlies days and that hasn't changed. He flashed a hard accurate shot in several of my viewings this year." - Mark Edwards

Stevens, Luke
LW – Noble & Greenough (HIGH – MA) – 6'3.75" 192
HockeyProspect.com Ranking: 171

The son of a former NHLer, he played through injury for some of the season, it didn't help him any, as he was already up against it for us. He's a solid checking forward with good size. His offensive ability is lacking. He skates fairly up right and has just a decent stride for a player his size but still manages speed. He has a good stick and uses his size to his advantage on the penalty kill.

Quotable: "Had a high ankle sprain and missed some key tournaments. It might hurt him a bit in the draft as far as where he comes off the board." - NHL Scout

Stewart, Chase
RD - Saginaw Spirit (OHL) 6'02" 212
HockeyProspect.com Ranking: 137

Chase was a player we really liked with Thunder Bay in his Minor Midget season and was selected in the 10th round by the Saginaw Spirit. After originally being cut by Saginaw and sent back up to Thunder Bay and the SIJHL, Stewart rejoined the Spirit in November. He became a one man wrecking crew, destroying opponents every opportunity he got.

Chase is a huge defender who loves to run over opponents. On top of his heavy physical play he showed the ability to use his stick well in one on one situations. He is tough in the slot and can be borderline dirty when taking it to an opponent. He is a very shutdown, stay at home, defensive minded defenseman who doesn't show much offensive upside but is capable of choosing smart first pass options and can get the puck out of the defensive zone effectively. He does have a powerful shot from the point that was more beneficial for rebounds than to score. His skating ability will need improvement before he can really take the next step, but for a 17 year old to step into top four minutes after getting cut in September, it's a great start and an excellent rookie season for the shutdown defender. Teams may look at him in the later rounds.

Quotable: "A project who has real sleeper potential. You'll be hard pressed to find a meaner, nastier, more physical guy in this draft. He's tough to play against in the defensive zone. If his skating and puck play improves he has pro potential." - HP Scout, Ryan Yessie

Stezka, Ales
G – Liberec (CZE Jr,) – 6'3" 179
HockeyProspect.com Ranking: 112

Stezka was the workhorse for his U20 club this year playing in over 75% of the games, he also played in every playoff game and posted some impressive numbers as well.
There is a lot to like about Stezka. He has a good frame with long legs that wall up the ice really well. Positionally he is a very sound goaltender, his nose is always towards the puck. He has good knee bend in his stance but tends to hunch over, dropping his glove. If he is facing a play on the rush he remains big, but when the play is in-zone he will hunch and drop his glove. When this happens it exposes a weakness, high glove. Laterally he has the power to get across but his chest drops forward and doesn't torque his core – making him vulnerable to shots that are just above his pads. His weaknesses are correctable though, as long as he is willing to make adjustments. He is vocal on the ice and displays good IQ, assessing threats and when he can be more aggressive. Controls his rebounds consistently and tracks the puck well. He is an intriguing prospect with lots of potential and he competes hard.

Strand, Austin
RD – Red Deer Rebels (WHL) – 6'03" 193
HockeyProspect.com Ranking: NR

Austin Strand is a tall, dependable and hyper-focused two-way defender who saw increasing ice-time over the course of his 2014/2015 campaign with the Red Deer Rebels. Still a bit lanky and adding muscle to his frame, he's surprisingly nimble and quick for a player of his size. Indeed, Strand excels in puck retrieval and at making smart keeps along the blueline and is above-average in the agility and manoeuvrability departments. As such, he wins most of his one-on-one battles with his skating rather than his hitting. While he has a really good frame for a defender, he stands out more as a rangy stickchecker than a physical hitter.

A good straight-ahead skater for the most part, Strand's first steps could be stronger, but he does a good job of staying in position and winning the important races. It appears as though he compensates for a lack of initial quickness with a long reach and some hockey sense. For instance, even though he's not electrifyingly fast, his ability to read plays and jump in just past the offensive blueline to keep the offense alive is truly exceptional. He also uses that long reach to poke pucks away and transition to the offense. Once in the offensive zone, his puck skills are fairly limited. Rangy and quick, he can certainly cart the puck around with skating skills alone, but doesn't usually shoot through the lanes he opens or produce many passing masterpieces with the puck.

Strand is one of many raw defensive talents available, being blessed with a variety of good size, skating ability and hockey sense. He could probably be a bit more physical, but he's got good range, crease-clearing abilities and an excellent pokecheck. He's a bit gun-shy in terms of his shooting and decision-making, but he's making the good reads, so it's only a matter of time until he starts pulling the trigger more often and begins making a larger name for himself. Circumstantially, he's helped along by the fact that the Memorial Cup will be in Red Deer next year and he'll have a bevy of talent surrounding him on the Red Deer blueline next year—most likely including Hayden Fleury, Colton Bobyk and Josh Mahura.

Strome, Dylan
LC - Erie Otters (OHL) 6'03" 187
HockeyProspect.com Ranking: 6

Dylan is a big play making centre for the Erie Otters who he led the OHL in scoring this year. Strome did a great job filling the hole McDavid left while he was out with an injury and away at the World Juniors. He continued to post plenty of points and help Erie win games.

Strome's best asset is his vision. He is extremely aware of the play around him when entering the offensive zone and has a rare ability to consistently find the open man. He is very dangerous as a passer, probably more so than a dynamic goal scorer. Like his brothers, especially his younger brother Matt, skating is a weakness. Dylan has improved his skating a lot since his OHL Draft season. He has always been a little bit heavy on his feet but is getting smoother than he was previously. Skating is still an area he will need to improve upon to give him the best chance to succeed at the NHL level. He plays an effective two-way game but he isn't a physical player and generally doesn't assert himself along the wall, despite his size.
While Strome's size and creative play makes him a good fit down the middle, his work in the face-off circle will need to improve. Over several viewings we tracked his face-off percentage and generally it was average at best and usually below the 50% range.

Strome has a knack at being able to get himself into position to get points, be it goals or by making a great pass. He uses patience and poise with the puck. He buys himself time to make plays with his good puck protection skills. Strome has a good compete level and is only held back at times by his feet. He has elite player hockey smarts. He makes players on his line better.

If everything falls into place as far as his weaknesses we mentioned go, Strome has a chance to play down the middle on a 1st line in the NHL. His upside is why he's being touted by some folks to potentially be selected as early as the 3rd pick in the draft.

Quotable: "Obviously his feet are his biggest weakness right now. I thought when the pace was really fast he had some issues being effective. That said, he's already improved his skating a ton since his minor midget year. I heard a lot of different opinions on him (Strome) this year. His skating definitely scared some scouts more than others. I put big value on intelligent players. He's up with the smartest players

I've seen these past few years and I think he's going to keep improving his skating. Combine the smarts with his size and vision and it explains how he led the OHL in scoring and why he's one of the most talked about players in this draft. I think the Coyotes end up choosing to go down the middle over defense with their 3rd overall pick and select Strome." - Mark Edwards

Quotable: "It seems strange to say this after he just led the OHL in scoring, but sometimes I thought that he was a bit lethargic." - NHL Scout

Quotable: "His feet really scare me, I'm not as high as some people are on him." - NHL Scout

Quotable: "I've got Marner, Zacha then Strome." - NHL Scout

Quotable: "Jason Spezza was a worse skater at the same age." - NHL Scout

Quotable: "He's a really good player. You don't take Marner if he's (Strome) still on the board. You need big guys down the middle to win." NHL Scout

Quotable: "The skating scares me because he could easily go from potential star to bust if it doesn't improve." - NHL Scout

Quotable: "I love him and the skating will get better. Big guys need time." - NHL Scout

Quotable: "Not in my top 8." - NHL Scout

Quotable: "It's tight but I've got Marner over him (Strome)." - NHL Scout

Quotable: "No way I'd take anyone at four over Strome if Hanifin is gone at three." - NHL Scout

Quotable: "Typical interview (combine) like years worth of GTHL and Burnaby players before him. They have that little sense of entitlement to them." - NHL Scout

Quotable: "Hey I'm hearing Strome could fall all the way to us at ___ so I'm ready for anything." - NHL scout

Suter, Pius
LW - Guelph Storm (OHL) - 5'11" 165
HockeyProspect.com Ranking: 120

Although Suter was on the fourth line of the 2014 OHL Champions, he always found a way to contribute. His had excellent work ethic, forecheck pressure and relentless battle that allowed him to win pucks against bigger and older players. When he moved up the lines due to other players injuries, he showed some real offensive upside and potential.

This season Pius took on a much bigger role. He used all of those hard working attributes and combined it with his skill to become a dangerous offensive forward. Suter scored over 40 goals in his second season in the OHL and although he's not the biggest guy, he's very slippery and difficult to contain. He has a very good shot and isn't afraid to go into traffic and he will commonly emerge with the puck.

Suter's biggest concern remains his size and we don't think he's as big as his listed height. That said, he has proven to us that he has very good talent and an outstanding work ethic, which may help him beat the odds as a small, talented forward. We like him as a draftable prospect this year and feel he might even be selected in the earlier rounds.

Quotable: "No way he's still on the board in the 4th round." - NHL Scout

Quotable: "There is no chance he is 5'11", that's a joke listing him at that." - NHL Scout

Svechnikov, Evgeny
RW – Cape Breton Screaming Eagles (QMJHL) – 6'3" 205
HockeyProspect.com Ranking: 17

Svechnikov was drafted 63rd overall by Cape Breton in the CHL Import Draft in 2013, and at the time it was viewed as a long shot that he would ever report to Cape Breton. After a long set of negotiations, the Russian winger reported to the Screaming Eagles this season and was nominated for rookie of the year at the end of the year. Svechnikov didn't make Team Russia for this year's World Junior Hockey Championships, after playing in the past two U18 World Championships and the U17 Hockey Challenge in 2013.

Svechnikov started the year on the injury list, but had an immediate impact when he was healthy. He's a big forward with terrific skills offensively, using his size and reach very well to protect the puck, especially down low in the offensive zone. He has a lethal shot with a quick release and a good ability to get open in the slot to fire quick shots on net. The Neftegorsk native has incredible soft hands to dangle the puck. He's not a pretty skater, his starts need some work but he's smart enough to compensate for it. He won't win a fastest-skater competition either, but gets the job done for now. He's strong on his skates and has good balance. Even at his size, Svechnikov won't be considered a physical player, but he's a strong kid who could be even stronger with added muscle to his frame. He's a good player along the wall due to his strength.

Consistency has always been an issue with his game going back to his days in Russia. It was the same story this year where he was invisible in games but still put points on the board. On draft day the Russian factor should play a role in where he gets selected, but Svechnikov did look very happy to be in Cape Breton and the QMJHL this season. Next season the Screaming Eagles should be even better and this would be Svechnikov's last season in the QMJHL—he should be one of the most dominant players in the league. We feel Svechnikov has a lot of tools to work with, his slow feet and passport might make him drop a bit on draft day but on talent along he shouldn't be too far from the top-15.

Sweezey, Bill
RD – Noble & Greenough (HIGH – MA) – 6'0" 190
HockeyProspect.com Ranking: NR

A second year draft eligible, the Yale commit plays with a mean streak. He can be very physical, landing some big hits. He is very tough to play against along the boards and in front of his own net. His skating ability is just average, but he rarely gets beat. There wasn't a better defender one-on-one in prep or high school hockey. The Boston Bruins invited him to their development camp last summer and his defensive ability is intriguing.

Szypula, Ethan
RC - Owen Sound Attack (OHL) 5'11" 170
HockeyProspect.com Ranking: NR

Syzpula didn't get a lot of offensive minutes with the Attack this season, but he has some untapped offensive potential. He accelerates quickly with the puck and does a good job of carrying the puck up ice and through the neutral zone. Syzpula is creative in space, sees the ice well with the puck and doesn't shy away from contact despite his size. He is relentless on the forecheck, regularly wins puck battles and rarely loses races for loose pucks. Syzpula puts a lot of effort into playing a 200-foot game, as he always back checks hard regardless if he's at the start or end of a shift. He is positionally sound defensively and is effective in taking away passing/shooting lanes. Syzpula doesn't have a lot of power in his shot, but it is fairly accurate and he usually gets it off relatively quick. White we don't expect to see him selected at the 2015 NHL Entry Draft, Ethan should get a lot more opportunity to show more next season.

Tammela, Jonne
RW – KalPa (Fin elite) – 5'11" 181
HockeyProspect.com Ranking: 126

Tammela is a skilled and speedy winger whose offensive potential is interesting. He's a smooth skater with great stick handling skills. He's on the small side but likes to go the traffic and can play well in the corners to retrieve pucks because of his great balance. He's efficient on the forecheck as well, he makes good use of his speed and is involved physically. He will need to get stronger to be more efficient in puck protection situations versus physically stronger player. He has good vision and likes to be creative with the puck on his stick. He possesses a powerful shot. Jonne plays a strong two-way game, he's got great attitude and is a good teammate. He's a threat to score on the PK with that great speed and anticipation. The main concern is his size but he's a smart kid, which is why he can already play with grown up men.

Tavernier, Sami
RW – HIFK (Fin jr.) – 6'0" 172
HockeyProspect.com Ranking: NR

Tavernier is a skilled winger with strong skating technique. He is a pure offensive player who has good playmaking ability and puck handling skills, but there are some issues in his game. His two-way game is quite poor and he doesn't always give a lot of effort on ice. He's got a lot of talent but doesn't perform at the level of his talent. There's a big difference between his good and bad days, which is why you don't even notice him in some games. His inconsistency is a big weakness. He's not a big kid but he's willing to get involved physically and he's good handling puck in tight places. He will have to improve his overall game if he wants to take his game to the next level. Tavernier has double citizenship, his dad is from France and his mother from Finland. He was drafted in the USHL draft by Sioux City and might be possibly looking at the NCAA.

Terry, Troy
RW – USNTDP (USHL) 5'10.5" 160
HockeyProspect.com Ranking: 168

He is one of those players that joined the NTDP late and was kind of given a back seat. Now his skating isn't dynamic nor is his overall game, although he shows very good offensive instincts as he sees the play and will utilize his strong stick skills to create scoring chances. He is not overly big so that down plays his draft stock too yet he is a sleeper type that would be a good mid-round pick. He will play at Denver under former NHLer Jim Montgomery so the development path is strong with more potential to be unleashed. He makes good, smart decisions on breakouts and sees the ice pretty well in offensive zone too though not sure he gets the credit.

Texeira, Keoni
LD – Portland Winterhawks (WHL) – 6'00" 189
HockeyProspect.com Ranking: NR

Keoni is a 'pure grit' type defenceman, he has proved a reliable fixture on the Winterhawks blueline this season. In part, this is due to his average height for a defender and slightly below-average skating ability. Yet despite lacking ideal speed and size, Keoni Texeira possesses an attractive skillset and physical package on the back-end as he possesses some offensive upside and has a sturdy frame that is low to the ice, making him really difficult to knock off balance.

Dependable and durable, he logs big minutes for the Portland Winterhawks and was entrusted in all situations to begin the 2014/2015 season. Using fairly good lateral agility and footwork, he likes to walk the line along the blueline before shooting, creating deception on his shot and opening up shooting lanes. This exibited some good hockey sense, lateral agility and hand-eye coordination. His slapshot is dangerous and he loves pulling it out of his back pocket while manning the point on the power play. He's fairly useful on the penalty kill, too, as he is good defensively with his stick and does a decent job of protecting the front of his net. However, his pure grit style can sometimes cross over, leading to disciplinary action that sometimes seriously hurts his team.

Indeed, there is some serious downside to Keoni Texeira. Most obviously, he's only middle-of-the-pack in terms of size and speed. At -6-foot, he could definitely benefit from added size and strength. When playing against bigger players he's too easily bounced off of the puck. He's not a bad skater by any means, but his struggle to keep up with quick and speedy forwards will quickly dissipate at an advanced level of play. We nonetheless think that when you account for his work-ethic, his stamina and unique offensive upside, that Keoni may hear his name called at the 2015 NHL Entry Draft

Tiffels, Frederik
LW - Western Michigan (NCAA) 6'1" 202
HockeyProspect.com Ranking: 110

Tiffels has been scouted by us previously going all the way back to a midget tournament in Quebec City where he played with Leon Draisaitl with his German team Jungadler Mannheim U18 back in 2011. Back then Draisaitl and Tiffels were the stars of that young German team. He's a great skater who can really fly with NHL speed but we question if he might be too soft. It's the knock on him for us. He can receive passes on his forehand at full speed and keep going just as fast, he has a good shot and he has proven that he can score. He has made very nice progress this season in his first season at Western Michigan under Andy Murray. He is on the radar for scouts this year and we won't be surprised if he gets drafted this season. He's a forward who likes to rush the puck down the wing and he's tough to contain due to his high end speed. He sees the ice very well and shown nice creativity and is a great passer. He's a pass first type of player and he doesn't shoot the puck enough. Tiffels is a 95-born forward who also played 2 seasons in the USHL before joining Western Michigan. If not drafted this year he could become one of those good NCAA free agents NHL teams coveted every year.

Thurkauf, Calvin
LC – EV Zug (Elite Jr.A) – 6'1" 195
HockeyProspect.com Ranking: NR

Thurkauf is a well-built forward who had a good showing at the U18 World Championships recently played in his hometown. Still 17, he is strong on his skates and finds ways to move through traffic into key areas. He shows good understanding of the game and manages to help his team in all three zones. His offensive skills seem limited but he has a good wrist shot, takes pucks to the net, likes to position himself in shooting lanes looking for deflections and is a good forechecker. In the neutral zone he is always well positioned to prevent passing lanes through open ice and his defensive game is a strength. He can contribute on the penalty kill and plays a North-South game at even strength, is effective along the boards and can throw good checks when that helps taking possession of the puck. He projects as a bottom six player and needs to improve his feet agility to react faster and be able to remain effective at the next level.

Timashov, Dmytro
LW – Quebec Remparts (QMJHL) 5'9" 189
HockeyProspect.com Ranking: 105

Timashov was drafted in last year's CHL Import Draft 95th overall by Quebec. He led all QMJHL rookies in scoring and was 12th overall in scoring in the league. Born in Ukraine, he started playing hockey when he moved to Sweden when he was 7 years old and now represents Sweden in international competition. We first saw Timashov at the 2013 World U17 Hockey Challenge in Victoriaville and Drummondville where Sweden won the gold medal. He also represented Sweden at the U18 level, playing at the 2013 Ivan Hlinka tournament.

Timashov has lots of tools in his bag. On the power play, he carries the puck in, sets up the umbrella and runs the plays. He also showed great patience handling the puck numerous times, and finds his teammates easily when he wants. He has the ability to draw more than one opponent to him in their defensive end, opening up coverage. He loves to have the puck on his stick and make plays, but has the tendency to try to do too much with it and make turnovers in the neutral zone. You will often see him carrying the puck from his zone to the offensive zone at even-strength and on the power play. He has good vision but should share the puck more often in the offensive zone to be more diversified offensively as he tends to keep the puck for a long time. Timashov works hard and with his hustle is able to create penalties in the offensive zone. He lacks the ideal size and can get outmuscled for puck battles. He's not an elite skater, and adding more explosiveness to his skating would be good for him. Timashov can create a lot of offense at the junior level but we are not sold this will translate at the NHL level. He had a lot of difficulties finding the back of the net in the 2nd half of the season and in the playoff.

Tkachev, Vladimir
LW – Quebec Remparts (QMJHL) – 5'8" 163
HockeyProspect.com Ranking: NR

Tkachev went undrafted last season but signed a contract with Edmonton after a strong showing at their training camp. However, eventually that contract was voided because of a technicality in the CBA. Last year with Moncton, Tkachev, who arrived in January, was an instant hit with the Wildcats, doing very well with fellow Russian forward Ivan Barbashev. The tiny Tkachev also had a good first round series against Blainville-Boisbriand, scoring seven times in six games. This season, in a surprising move at the time, he was traded to the Quebec Remparts after an up-and-down first half of the season with the Wildcats. In Quebec he showed some great flashes, but his consistency was lacking and he saw his ice time and role diminish as the season progressed. Tkachev's puck skills are high-end, as he can make defensemen look silly with some smooth moves one–on-one. He loves to play in one-on-one situations; he loves to challenge defensemen. He's a good skater with great agility and can make sharp turns which makes him tough to defend against. Tkachev is listed at 163 pounds, but this is more likely to be in the 145-150 range. Regardless of his real weight, he will need to add a ton of muscle to his frame before playing in the NHL. He still looks like a teenager if you see him in his street clothes. Having said that, Tkachev still competes hard when he wants to along the wall, he's not afraid to finish his hits on the forecheck. His play away from the puck will need a lot of work too, moreso in terms of his commitment in his zone. He doesn't possess a powerful shot, but it's accurate, and he has a quick release. On skills alone he should get drafted, but his size is a major concern and he has not had a very strong year either. He was also not chosen to play for Russia at the World Junior Hockey Championship which raised some eyebrows in December around the QMJHL.

Quotable: "Lots of talk about Tkachev all year long, honestly I liked his game a lot more last year than this year. All of his dekes are nice but you need more than this to make it to the NHL." - HP scout Jérôme Bérubé

Tomek, Matej
G - Topeka (NAHL) 6'2.5" 180
HockeyProspect.com Ranking: 107

Tomek is one of the latest goalies that could be drafted from the North American Hockey League. He made the jump to the United States with Topeka this year coming from Slovakia where he competes internationally. Tomek immediately made an impact in the NAHL, posting otherworldly numbers this season. He is a big, athletic goalie that is incredibly solid. Tomek is most comfortable down in the butterfly and gets down very quickly, making it very difficult to beat him low to either side. He uses his size well when he gets down cutting off all of the net and creating very few opportunities for opposing shooters to score. His footwork is fantastic, cutting down angles and staying square to the shooter. He competes in front of the net fighting through screens and does a really nice job tracking the puck. It's very hard to say anything negative about his game but on the rare occasion that Tomek does get beat, it's usually top shelf glove side. He is one of our favorite goalies in the draft and will be a great get for whoever takes him. Tomek will advance on to the University of North Dakota in the fall of 2015.

Quotable: "He impressed me at the U18 in Finland last year. This year I liked that he didn't play that 'robot like' style that so many goalies use these days. Big kid with great numbers in a lesser league. He also stopped a lot of pucks." - Mark Edwards

Trenin, Yakov
LW – Gatineau Olympiques (QMJHL) – 6'2" 179
HockeyProspect.com Ranking: 36

Trenin is Russian forward with good size that Gatineau drafted 32nd overall in the 2014 CHL Import Draft. Oddly enough, Trenin has never represented his country in top international events in the past two seasons for Russia, as he never played at the U17 & U18 levels. He came in this season as a bit of an unknown to the QMJHL and had an excellent season playing for a struggling Gatineau team. Trenin is huge, he looks bigger than what he's listed. He's very strong on the puck and uses his size very well to protect the puck and drive the net. With very underrated vision, he makes good decisions with the puck and is able to find his linemates on the ice pretty easily. He made a smooth adjustment to the QMJHL and North American game, using his size well and not being shy to play a physical game.

One of our biggest fears with Trenin is his skating abilities; he will need to improve his quickness and starts. His top speed is good enough in the QMJHL but still needs improvements there. When he hits his top speed, combined with his size, he's a bit like a freight train coming in the offensive zone and he's tough to handle for opposing defensemen due to his size and reach. Trenin had a strong postseason, playing alongside Valentin Zykov (L.A. Kings' draft pick) and should continue to progress over the next two seasons in Gatineau. Trenin has a lot going for him, skating aside he's got everything you want for a top 6 forward at the NHL level.

Quotable:" Quotable:" He's a tank. I love him below the dots. The kids a machine along the walls." - NHL Scout

Quotable:" The first time I saw Trenin this year was in a game in Gatineau versus Saint John. He was a beast down low and put himself on our map as a player to watch closely. He's really effective below the dots, despite not having great short area quickness. He looks much bigger than his listed size. I know a lot of Ontario based scouts were heading to see him the night I left for Switzerland. He was in the process of putting together a strong playoff performance." - Mark Edwards

Trinkberger, David
LD – Sioux City (USHL) 6'4.5" 207
HockeyProspect.com Ranking: NR

After not getting drafted last year, Trinkberger made the move from his German club to the USHL to increase visibility for NHL clubs. Visibility certainly isn't the issue now as he defenseman towers over most other players on the ice. He plays as one might expect, throwing the body and making his presence known. He is a very physical player.

He sometimes struggles a bit with his footwork and can get beat one-on-one with just a little bit of effort. That said, he does move fairly well for a guy of his size and can jump in on the rush on occasion. He doesn't have any elite skills but his big frame and decent mobility make him an intriguing prospect.

Tuulola, Joni
LD – HPK (Fin elite) – 6'2.5" 180
HockeyProspect.com Ranking: 128

Tuulola is a decent size all-round defender with great offensive instincts. Joni was passed over in last year NHL draft. He's got good skating technique and he can play a smart game. He makes great decisions with puck and likes to join the offense. His passing game is good as well, he makes accurate passes and also likes to use his shot which is also accurate. There's still some issues in the defensive zone, but nothing major. He's not always positioning right and he has to get stronger physically. He has shown the capability of carrying the puck inside the offensive zone and making plays from there. He's a strong skater, unfortunately he missed the WJC and the Liiga playoff due to injuries which didn't help his draft stock. This season he played 35 games with HPK of the Finland men's league scoring 5 goals and 10 points.

Vainio, Veeti
RD – Blues (Fin jr.) – 6'2" 170
HockeyProspect.com Ranking: 179

Vainio is a smooth skater with significant offensive tools. He has very good vision and playmaking skills on top of a hard slap shot and his obvious skating abilities, but he also have many flaws in his game. He's too often phlegmatic and most of the times he doesn't try his best. He's not physical despite his good size and he often tries too difficult plays with puck, generating turnovers. Sometimes he doesn't seem to know how to positioning in the d-zone. A risky player but on his good days he can be really dangerous in the o-zone. A real high risk - high reward player with a unique skating style. He floats around the ice and possesses tremendous acceleration, which helps in his recoveries

Made his Liiga debut late in the season and had encouraging performances in those first games in the top Finnish league, but his showing at the U18 World Championships was really disappointing. On top of his questionable defensive game he was overall ineffective in his play with the puck, creating more risks for his team than for the opposition.

Vande Sompel, Mitchell
LD - Oshawa General (OHL) 5'10" 180
HockeyProspect.com Ranking: 88

Vande Sompel is a small but highly skilled defender for the Oshawa Generals. He's a versatile player, as he played forward on penalty kill and at times for entire games during his first two seasons and even dating back to his Minor Midget days.
He is an excellent skater with great mobility and quick acceleration. Vande Sompel moves the puck well and makes accurate outlet passes. Dangerous on the power play with a quick hard point shot and he walks the line to open up shooting lanes. Defensively he gets caught in a lot of mismatches and generally runs around the defensive zone. He needs to improve his positioning down low because he sometimes makes it a little too easy for opponents to beat him. The team that selects Vande Sompel will probably have decided if they are going keep him at the defensive position or move him up to forward and have him play defense on the power play. If he remains a defenseman he will need to drastically improve his play in his own end.

His upside is quite high if he can improve his play in his own zone and make it as an offensive defenseman in the NHL. We're not sure if that's a realistic possibility, which is why we have him ranked where we do. It's so difficult for 5'10" defenseman to make it in the NHL. We're in the camp thinking there is probably a better chance Vande Sompel doesn't make than does make it. One thing is not up for debate. Vande Sompel is already a fantastic player at the junior level and will only bring more production going forward.

Quotable: "I like the kid and he's great junior player but I don't expect him to be the next 5'10" NHL defenseman." - NHL Scout

Vehviläinen, Veini
G – JYP Akatemia (FIN 2) – 6'0.5" 180
HockeyProspect.com Ranking: 118

Vehvilainen is not a physically dominating presence when compared to some of the other larger goalies available for this draft. However, what he lacks in size he makes up for it with superb technique. He has a great foundation, stance, skating, angles and competitiveness. He's a calm and mobile goalie. Because he is such a strong skater, he has tremendous patience and can wait till the last second before having to make a move. Veini has been very good for the whole season while competing in the second highest pro league in Finland and looks really mature already. He also completed a convincing U18 World Championship with a fantastic showing in the final against the US team.

Vejdemo, Lukas
LC – Djurgardens (SWE Jr.) – 6'2" 194
HockeyProspect.com Ranking: 173

This Swedish center took a significant step forward in his development this past season. Passed over in last year draft after playing at the U18 level, this year he was probably the MVP of the U20 SuperElit. Vedejmo has been effective in pretty much every area of the game and it will be interesting to see what kind of player he will be able to become at the senior level after an adaption period. He has good puck control and has some power to his shot, but he is not overly skilled and his projection from an offensive standpoint is far from a safe one.

However, he has a few things going for him along with his size. He is no stranger to the net, works hard, doesn't quit on the play and doesn't mind going into the corners to dig the puck to create opportunities. His strong two-way all around game makes him a candidate to develop into a 3rd liner that can bring some secondary scoring. He is not a flawless skater, his stride seems to have room for improvement, yet he can generate surprising power and use his skating as an asset, for example when chasing the puck. He can stickhandle through traffic, but he can be at fault for trying to do too much, sometimes taking too long shifts. Should further develop his physical game, as it will probably be needed to become the kind of player he projects to be at the next level.

Vela, Marcus
LC – Langley Rivermen (BCHL) – 6'02" 201
HockeyProspect.com Ranking: 132

Marcus Vela is a truculent, hard-working and talented playmaking centre who played for the Langley Rivermen this year and is committed to the University of New Hampshire for next season. Along with another seventeen-year-old rookie, the 2015-eligible goaltender Bo Didur, he shouldered a really heavy load for a Rivermen club. He played a leading role on his club despite being one of its youngest players. Logging iron-man minutes with Langley, Vela played in all situations this year, standing out as a tremendous shot blocker on the penalty kill and a tremendous playmaker on the power play. Indeed, he's one of those players who is capable of changing his mindset on a dime—the type of centre you want on the ice as much as possible and taking key faceoffs in all zones.

He was injured midway through the first round of the BCHL playoffs, which really hurt his club—which went on to lose all the remaining games. He plays in the top unit in all situations and logs a ton of ice-time. Those contributions speak out in a multitude of ways: high hockey IQ, incredible bodychecking skills, fantastic net drive, a good trash talker. Great playmaking ability, above-average faceoff skills and decent shooting ability. Beginning with hockey IQ, one thing we noticed about Vela was his incredible passing ability from the half-wall, specifically when playing on the power play. As for hitting, Vela was one of the most crushing bodycheckers in the BCHL this year—regardless of age. Fantastic net drive—especially when combined with high hockey IQ and passing skills, means that Vela is dangerous from both out wide and in-close.

He has a really high compete-level and that he loves goading the opposition into making mistakes with his agitating personality. Numerous times, we saw him trash-talk the opposition into either going way out of position or into taking a bad penalty. Once he pulls you out of position, he has the skills to make you pay. When one considers his pro-size, versatility and work-ethic, he's definitely a player worthy of serious consideration at the 2015 NHL Entry Draft.

Vladar, Daniel
G – Kladno (CZE Jr.) – 6'5" 185
HockeyProspect.com Ranking: 52

Vladar is a physically intimidating presence on the ice. Despite his size, he moves around his crease with precision and power. There is very little not to like about Vladar. A lot of what he does right starts with his stance: just enough knee bend and hands out in front. He keeps his weight balanced allowing him to move into shots and challenge when necessary. One of the best puck tracking goalies in this draft, which is why his rebounds are consistently placed in timely spots or controlled into him. He has a lot of confidence when he comes out to handle the puck and makes good decisions.

The one area Vladar needs to focus on is picking when to be aggressive and when to hang back. He is a great competitor in the crease but sometimes loses his technique when the puck is quickly moved laterally. His size is a gift and sometimes he needs to simply fill the middle instead of sliding out of the blue and into the white paint. But that will improve with maturity.

He seals the ice exceptionally well and has good flare in his butterfly. And when he is down in his butterfly, he can move efficiently, torqueing his core and staying upright allowing maximum coverage. He is a candidate to be taken fairly early in the draft despite a rather underwhelming showing at the U18 World Championships.

Quotable: "He got off to a great start in his NHL Draft year with a strong performance at the Ivan Hlinka. He's one of my fave goalies in this draft and I got glowing reviews on him from his combine interviews as well." - Mark Edwards

Vladimirov, Artem
LD - Peterborough Petes (OHL) 6'03" 218
HockeyProspect.com Ranking: NR

Vladimirov played limited minutes his first year in Peterborough. He plays a simple game but never seemed to develop throughout the year. Vladimirov must work on his footwork when pivoting, as he was beat on quick transition plays. His straight line speed is good for someone his size. Artem has good tools but is still learning how to use them properly.

He is a big physical defender who likes to assert himself and is a very capable checker. He has a powerful shot from the point but his decision making and technical game is too far off. He's about as raw as they come and would need a great deal of development to reach his potential but has the natural physical tools if he can develop the mental and positional side of the game. Vladimirov projects as a physical shutdown defenseman who is a big project and would need a lot of time and patience to develop. He isn't likely to be selected at the 2015 NHL Entry Draft.

Vorobyov, Mikhail
LC – Tolpar (MHL) – 6'2" 194
HockeyProspect.com Ranking: 148

A regular feature on this season U18 Russian national team, Vorobyov is a two-way centerman that can be relied upon in all situations because of his complete game. Is a good faceoff man with legit size, he is consistently responsible and uses his strong hockey sense on both sides of the puck. His good defensive play sometimes takes away from the offensive opportunities he is given on his teams, but he can be an effective player in the offensive zone, using his linemates to create opportunities. He sees the ice well and uses his poise to make clever plays and execute good passes. He is a good stickhandler who can slow down the play with the puck on his stick.

Perhaps the best part of his game is how he is able to cycle the puck along the end boards, he constantly shifts away from the defenseman while protecting the puck. Mikhail is a sound skater, but lacks a change of speed and his agility is average. He needs to improve the aerobic aspects of his game. He possesses an accurate wrister, but to finish more of his chances he has to become quicker.

Wagner, Austin
RW – Regina Pats (WHL) – 6'01" 178
HockeyProspect.com Ranking: 55

The Regina Pats forward Austin Wagner is a speedy and spirited winger who plays a tough, physical north-to-south game on the wing. Wagner has great speed with a strong first push and can skate at full-speed across the entire 200-foot ice surface, allowing him to go end-to-end with the puck. He has the shooting skills to finish, too. In our viewings of Wagner, he was consistent across the board in terms of on-ice performance—worked hard in board battles, backchecked well, played a good team game. We additionally like his offensive production as he had a 20 goal season with the Regina Pats—but even more, 5 of those goals were scored shorthanded.

For his height, physical dimensions and immaturity, Austin Wagner is surprisingly explosive, nimble and agile. Turns, pivots and crossover technique are all very good. At times, especially when reaching top-speed through the neutral zone, he looks like a downright thoroughbred skater in profile. Even more, he can handle the puck well while moving at top speed. He likes to drive the wing with size and speed and fire the puck on goal with power and accuracy. When handling the puck, even when under immense pressure from the opposition, he shows good protection abilities and is particularly formidable on the cycle. He put on a passing showcase a couple of times this year with the Pats.

One of his best attributes is his physical style of play. He connects with a lot of power with his checks and doesn't look off an opportunity to deliver the body on the opposition. Defensively, Wager is very proficient in puck battles. He can utilize his agility or his strength depending on the situation. One negative aspect to his game is a tendency to become frustrated and take penalties after losing the little puck battles—making a mountain out of a molehill, as it were. Nonetheless, there's a lot of raw talent and upside to be excited about in Wagner's potential and future.

Wahlin, Jake
LW – Tri-City (USHL) 5'10" 170
HockeyProspect.com Ranking: NR

Wahlin, a Saint Cloud State commit had a solid campaign in the USHL. He is a guy who buzzes around and plays a physical game while being able to chip in offensively. He is a great skater and uses those abilities to get around the ice and mix things up. His offensive skillset was definitely there but he was plagued by inconsistency throughout our viewings. He was able to contribute offensively throughout the season, especially on the power play but had a tendency to take shifts off and coast from time to time.
When he is invested and playing hard, Wahlin is a great energy guy that can score goals and set teammates up, it's just a matter of playing hard every shift and getting that consistency from shift to shift and game to game that held him back a little bit in his draft year. He will attend SCSU in the fall.

Walters, Connor
RD - Owen Sound Attack (OHL) 6'00" 197
HockeyProspect.com Ranking: NR

Connor took a little time to find his game but as the season progressed our reports became more and more positive Walters is a pretty steady defenseman who was reliable at both ends of the ice. He consistently made the first pass up the ice and while he wasn't a big offensive guy he was pretty consistent in keeping the play going and when to put the puck on the net and when to pass off. Defensively he showed a little physicality and could grind it out down low. He's a team first player who would block shots or take the hit to make the play for his team. While he doesn't have a big upside, he could develop into a solid lower end defenseman at the NHL level one day.

Warren, Brendan
LW – USNTDP (USHL) 6'0.25" 191
HockeyProspect.com Ranking: 142

He is decent sized forward that will not "wow" you with moves, skills, and high-end scoring touch though his game goes under the radar a bit and perhaps even fallen a bit since committing to Michigan a few years ago. He is a solid two-way winger who skates well though not explosive. He competes well and will go to all areas of the ice. He shows an honest north-south game up and down his wing. His upside will not be the top line scorer although he is a good compliment on the line. There is still mind and body that has potential to develop further.

Quotable" I don't see enough offense in his game to rank him very high. He has some talent, I like his compete and room for growth but he hasn't wowed me with his game." - Mark Edwards

Webster, Bailey
RD – Saint-John SeaDogs (QMJHL) – 6'5" 210
HockeyProspect.com Ranking: 143

Webster is player who came out of nowhere this season after being drafted in the 7th round of the 2013 QMJHL Draft. We first saw him during his QMJHL draft year playing for Team P.E.I. and he was not a standout player then. A bit of late bloomer following his draft year in the league, where he progressed and kept getting bigger. The P.E.I. native is a raw defender at the moment who's only scratching the surface of his potential. He has already the size of an NHL defenseman, standing at 6'5", 210 pounds and he will keep getting stronger in the next couple of years. This season he showed flashes of his potential, moving around pretty well for a kid of his stature and with nice physicality. He played mostly on the 3rd pair of defensemen with Saint John and became a key player on their penalty killing unit. He's very good at clearing the front of the net using his strength, and has become a good shot-blocker in front of his net. He got involved in a couple of scraps this season, which should increase next season as his mean streak continues to evolve. He has decent footwork and a good active stick which helps him keep pace with the opposing forwards on the rush. With the puck he's still very raw, he usually lets his defense partners who are way more skilled in moving the puck out of their zone. There's nothing fancy about his play with the puck, mostly he will try making short passes instead of trying longer passes with a higher difficulty level. Webster has a lot still to learn about the game but seems to know his limits, playing within those limits. Webster is very raw but his package is very interesting, NHL teams love projects and he's a good one. Big right handed 6'5" mobile blueliner are rare in the NHL.

Weinger, Evan
RW – Portland Winterhawks (WHL) – 6'00" 183
HockeyProspect.com Ranking: 156

Evan Weinger is an energetic and agitating winner who worked really hard to make a name for himself with the Portland Winterhawks this year as an unlikely rookie standout. A mid-sized winger from Los Angeles, Weinger's feet look really light and move really quick when at full stride. And yet he's surprisingly balanced and difficult to knock off stride. This makes him very good at driving wide with the puck and at making plays from below the hashmarks. A rookie on a lineup loaded with talent, Weinger played in a depth role but truly made the most of his limited ice-time. Whether it be by throwing big hits along the wall and in open-ice. Or by creating scoring opportunities in limited time and space. Or drawing penalties with his speed and vociferous personality, Weinger made a positive impact on his team.

As previously mentioned, he's strong on his feet, making him especially dangerous when he makes an office for himself behind the net. His passing and shooting skills are still in development, as he projects forward as a bit of an energy player, an instigator and a project for any NHL club interested in drafting him.

Weinger plays a unique pinball-type game in which he flies all over the ice and crashes into one player after another another, into one corner after another with utmost force, almost as though he were completely uninterested in scoring. This type of high energy play is Weinger's bread and butter, as it helps to absorbs opposition checks, inspires his teammates and can swing momentum in his club's favour. There were numerous games we watched, in which Weinger managed to change the tempo of a game or took the other team off-guard through his hitting game, agitating style of play or by his choice of words after the whistles.

Werenski, Zach
LD – Michigan (BIG10-NCAA) 6'2" 206LBS
HockeyProspect.com Ranking: 11

Werenski stepped right into the NCAA as a 17 year old and was instantly the top defenseman on a deep and talented Michigan squad. He puts forth an honest and consistent effort night in and night out. He already has an NHL build at the age of 18. He is difficult to muscle off the puck; some scouts feel his skating, agility and hockey IQ are as good as any defenseman in this draft. His skating strength and agility is best on display when under pressure on the breakout, he protects the puck well and uses powerful strides to elude the fore checker and get the puck up the ice. His agility and quick feet allow him to use his own net as an obstacle for fore checkers. Zach makes calm and calculated decisions with the puck and his accurate passing ability and vision allow him to stretch the ice and make seem passes up the ice quickly. He has the ability to control the pace of the game when the puck is on his stick. Werenski doesn't skate the puck deep into the offensive zone a lot, while he isn't shy about joining the rush he often falls off as the 3rd guy entering the zone. He certainly has the puck skills and skating ability to contribute off the rush but if the play isn't there for him initially he tends to return to his position at the blue line.

Werenski can play a physical or positioning defensive style in his own end. Because Zach doesn't punish guys in the corners or in front of his own net he gets labeled by some as "lacking physicality". But the fact is he uses his high hockey IQ and picks his spots well and because of that he doesn't take a lot of penalties (8PIMS in 35 games). When he is physical in the corners and plays with an edge he has the ability to take over games and control the pace at the NCAA level, however he can be just as effective using his stick and body positioning to keep players to the outside and wear them down, which will translate well to the next level.

There are very few weaknesses his Werenski's game and while 25 points in 35 games as a 17/18 year old freshman is pretty impressive, there is still some room for growth in the offensive zone. Werenski uses his agility to move laterally along the blue line in order to open up lanes. He quarterbacks the power play efficiently and distributes the puck accurately.

On occasions he passes up chances to get the puck on net in an attempt to try to setup an open back door play or one time opportunity. He is at his best in the offensive zone when he uses his agility to open up lanes and makes quick decisions toward the net with the puck. He has an elite shot from the point, whether it be a quick snap shot or a booming slap shot, he doesn't need a lot time or space to get his accurate shot off.

One more year in College wouldn't hinder his development and if Werenski were to return to Michigan for his sophomore year he would be a certain Hobey Baker Candidate. Having said that, when it comes to physically and mentally, Werenski is probably the most pro ready defenseman in this draft, depending on the team that drafts him, I don't think it would shock many if Werenski was playing professional hockey at some level this coming fall.

White, Colin
RC – USNTDP (USHL) 6'0" 183
HockeyProspect.com Ranking: 23

He is a skilled power forward style with good speed in an honest stride, nice accurate shot and hands, and decent size with strength as wins pucks battles. He shows good hockey IQ as he reads plays well and strong on puck possession by using his size and smarts. Another great asset in White's game is his shot. He can release the puck off the stick quick and accurately. He battled mono sickness in the early part of the season thus started a bit slow out of the gate though ended the season on high note at U18 World Championship scoring the OT winner for Team USA to earn a gold medal. Again he will be another player that develops well at Boston College under Jerry York and will blossom into a pro caliber player. You also like the two-way game White brings as responsible in his own end. He competes at a high level in all 3-zones and plays with bit of edge to his game. You are attracted to his game because he does a lot of things well. He probably isn't going to be a high-end producer though should amass his share of points at the next levels. White is a very respectable player that will continue to blossom.

Quotable: "This is a kid who blew up the USHL last year." - NHL Scout

Quotable: "Plenty of bad luck hurt this kids draft year." - NHL Scout

Quotable: "He will not break the scoring records at BC although he will develop into a very valuable player at Chestnut Hill and the NHL. He plays a strong 200-foot game who can score with his hard, accurate shot, win face-offs, and play physical when needed. He just might blossom into the Joe Pavlaski type." - HP Scout Russ Bitely

Quotable: "I think he's a safe bet to be a 3rd liner in the NHL. Good speed, smart player, hard worker. He always comes across looking like a pro prospect to me." - Mark Edwards

White, Colton
LD - Sault Ste. Marie Greyhounds (OHL) 6'01" 185
HockeyProspect.com Ranking: 180

Colton is an above average skater who moves up and down the ice. He has the ability to rush the puck but took on a much safer role this season with the stacked veteran Greyhounds blue line. White played tough down low and would battle for pucks but currently lacks the strength to maximize his potential in these situations. White is pretty consistent with passes up ice but when he faces heavy pressure he can sometimes freeze up. Colton was rewarded with some penalty kill time and is a strong positional defender in his own end. Colton will have a great opportunity next season playing big minutes after the graduation of most of the Greyhounds blueline where he will be able to have the icetime to show his potential.

Wilkie, Chris
RW – Tri-City (USHL) 5'11.5" 199
HockeyProspect.com Ranking: 138

After getting passed over in the 2014 NHL Draft, Wilkie has made a strong case to be selected as a second year eligible player. Amid questions about his effort last year around draft time, Wilkie has worked to prove that he is deserving of getting selected in this years draft. The North Dakota commit put on fourteen pounds from last season to this year and is putting his size to good use. Away from the puck he plays a physical game and gets involved in his defensive zone more often than not.

Offensively, the Tri-City Storm go as Chris Wilkie goes. He leads the league in goals and shots on goal by a fairly large margin. He has definitely transformed from more of a playmaker to a pure goal scorer from last season. His shot has improved quite a bit and his release is lightning quick. He'll shoot without hesitation from just about anywhere and he has the power to score from anywhere.
The biggest question mark in Wilkie's game is his decision making. He tries to do a little bit too much by myself and in result is turnover prone in the neutral zone. Tries the fancy move instead of taking what is there for him which results in some turnovers and odd-man rushes against the Storm. However, with his strong offensive play and a shift to being more of a goal scorer, there is a good chance Wilkie gets selected in his second eligible draft year.

Wotherspoon, Parker
LD – Tri-City Americans (WHL) – 6'00" 179
HockeyProspect.com Ranking: 109

Parker Wotherspoon, the younger brother of Calgary Flames prospect Tyler Wotherspoon, Parker is several inches smaller than his older brother but likely possesses a higher level of offensive pedigree. Parker's mobility and offensive abilities are the first attributes that stand out. He's a decent passer, but prefers to use his footwork to get the puck out of trouble and past the red line. Poised with the puck on his stick, he's able to weave and wind through traffic on fairly spectacular puck rushes and can make plays look easy when he gets his feet moving. He played a lot of minutes on the Tri-City power play, where he showed off a good shot. Patience, compete-level and offensive zone awareness are all areas that should undergo improvement in the next few years of his development as he had a tendency to suffer from selfishness and poor decision-making once past the opposition blueline. His defensive game, meanwhile, is generally well-rounded, even if there are a few holes here and there.

Certainly his game can be enigmatic at times, but he's very young and there's still a lot of refining to be done here, making Wotherspoon a player with good potential.

Yan, Dennis
LW –Shawinigan Cataractes (QMJHL) – 6'1" 188
HockeyProspect.com Ranking: 71

Yan is quite a story. Looking at his hockey background: born in Portland, Oregon. Moved to Russia with his family. Moved back to North America where he played his minor hockey in Sarnia and Detroit. Last season, thanks to his double-citizenship, he played for Team USA NTDP U-17 in Ann Arbour, until he chose to play in the CHL and was drafted 8th overall by Shawinigan in the CHL Import Draft.

Yan had a really good season with the Cataractes, playing on the top line most of the year and playing with fellow 2015-eligible prospect Anthony Beauvillier. They both can read each other very well, as Beauvillier likes to have the puck on his stick whereas Yan likes to find holes in the offensive zone and get into scoring position. Yan has undeniable scoring upside, and doesn't need many scoring chances to score. He's not the most active player on the ice and doesn't spend a lot of energy, but always knows where to go in the offensive zone. He is a very smart player in terms of reading the intention of his teammates. Still, we would like to see more active on the forecheck and win more puck battles, and we would like to see him play with more drive.

His puck skills are excellent, very nifty with the puck and has great one-on-one skills. Yan has good creativity with the puck and can make plays that few players can. He already has an NHL-calibre wrist shot with a quick release. He's also an excellent playmaker, seeing the ice well and making good decisions with the puck. He's an opportunistic scorer, in some games you will barely notice him and then he gets a goal out of nowhere. He has the ability to be forgotten by the opposing team in the offensive zone. Yan has nice size going forward and will need to keep add strength to his frame so he can compete better along the boards and in front of the net. Currently, it is not so much a physical game when it comes to Yan.

He's an interesting one, you seem to either like him or you hate him. His rankings have reflected this with us this year going hot and cold months after months. The skills are there but he plays too passive on the ice for our liking.

Quotable:" I didn't see him late in the year but I heard a few NHL scouts say he was playing much better." - Mark Edwards

Yetman, Bryce
RW - Plymouth Whalers (OHL) 6'01" 160
HockeyProspect.com Ranking: NR

The young winger for the Whalers missed most of what would be an injury plagued season but did leave a little impression on us in the viewings we gained. Yetman has decent size and works very hard. He finishes his checks but will need to add more muscle and gain more power for his physical play to leave more of an impact. He showed some flashes offensively and has a decent shot. While it will be tough for a team to draft him off of limited viewings this season he has shown a few glimpses of potential to get selected next year or invited to a camp.

Younan, Alexander
LD – HV 71 (SWE Jr.) – 6'0.75" 189
HockeyProspect.com Ranking: 124

Younan is a Swedish defenseman that shows good mobility and can play in all situations. He displays good agility carrying the puck when he joins the offense and can make plays with the puck in the neutral zone; with his national team he has been inconsistent in his contribution on the offensive side of the puck, but his league play suggests it's something related with his different role. Alexander looks like a far from finished product with lots of room for improvement, something needed if he wants to become a solid defenseman.

Despite a legit frame he needs to add strength and he currently lacks a bit of power in his smooth skating to get first on loose pucks. He can get beaten along the boards and his coverage of the slot and in front of the net is not always good enough. His shot is another element he will have to work on moving forward. Still, these current shortcomings do not prevent him from showing flashes of very good play, and of the player he might become. The best part of his game is probably his active stick. In the defensive zone he is often able to quickly close in on opponents to disrupt their plays with his stick work, sometimes leading to turnovers not far from the blueline, such to generate dangerous counter attacks.

Zacha, Pavel
LC - Sarnia Sting (OHL) 6'03" 210
HockeyProspect.com Ranking: 7

Zacha spent last season playing in the Czech Men's league and performed very well. He got his wish and came over to the Sarnia Sting after being selected first overall at the 2014 CHL Import Draft.

Zacha made an immediate impact with an excellent combination of size and speed. He gets up the ice very quickly and displayed excellent decision making with the puck on his stick., even under pressure. He is an excellent passer and makes hard, accurate passes on a consistent basis. As good of a playmaker as Zacha is, he's just as effective shooting the puck and possesses a laser shot. He was very dangerous firing one-timers and was a player who really capitalized on the rush. Unlike some players who make the trip over from Europe, Zacha played with a ton of physicality and did a great job finishing his checks. He's built like a man already and can crush opponents down low. He will play on the edge a bit and was suspended for some marginal hits. He will need to be better on his commitment to defense in his own zone. He got better as the year went on, but he cheated offensively too often and flew the D-zone early. He needs to be better supporting the puck, especially breaking out of his own zone.

Zacha missed a little under half the season by way of injury, suspension and World Juniors.
He projects to provide an NHL team with a great combination of size, skill, skating and physicality. While he's physically ready for the NHL, he will need to fix the minor warts in his game we mentioned before he earns minutes from an NHL coach.

Quotable: "He's number three on my list." - NHL Scout

Quotable: "He plays the right way. I actually think he would've posted better numbers if he played more selfishly. He's good enough to skate through full teams but he kept making the technically smart play of passing to his open teammate...that's where the plays died." - NHL Scout

Quotable: "Our ranking is close to yours." (HP ranking was 4th at the time) - NHL Scout

Quotable: "He's a lock to stay in our top 10." - NHL Scout

Quotable: " He was just ok last time I saw him." - NHL Scout

Quotable: "I love how fast Zacha processes the game with the puck on his stick. He's gives you everything you could want in a big guy. Toughness, speed, the talent to both score and set up goals. " - Ryan Yessie

Quotable: " Look who's he's playing with here, the kid sees a play and nobody else on his line does." - NHL Scout

Quotable: " Did you see him in Erie? (re: games 1 and 2 in playoffs) he was unbelievable." - NHL Scout

Quotable: " Loved him in Sochi (2013 U18) but I thought he was just ok at the U18 in Finland last year. Maybe I expected too much. My viewings of him in a Sarnia jersey have been really good and he played well when I saw the Czechs in Switzerland (2015 U18). He dropped slightly for me based on a few later season viewings because I'd like to see him anticipate better in order to get more scoring chances from in tight. Sometimes I thought he relied on his great shot too much, rather than pushing the play tighter to the net. Love his size, skating and nasty streak. He has a lot of the same qualities (Lawson) Crouse has, but I think Zacha has a more NHL offensive upside. I saw him create a lot of offense that didn't turn into points, so I'm betting he can post better numbers when he gets some smarter players around him." - Mark Edwards

Zboril, Jakub
LD – Saint John Sea Dogs (QMJHL) 6'2" 185
HockeyProspect.com Ranking: 25

Zboril was drafted 5th overall in the Import Draft by Saint John last June. Jakub's older brother Adam played in the QMJHL with Acadie-Bathurst two years ago. We first saw Jakub last year when he played as an underager on the Czech U18 team at both Ivan Hlinka and the April U18 World Championships. Before leaving for Saint John this season he had a strong performance at the Ivan Hlinka Tournament, scoring four goals in five games for a surprising Czech team that lost in the final against Canada.

Zboril plays a well-rounded game; he kills penalties and plays on the power play unit. He's a tough defenseman to beat on the rush because he plays the gap so well; Zboril steps up on his opponents at the right time, forcing turnovers and quick transitions. The Brno native is a very good skater and pushes the pace, jumping up in his team's rushes and skating with the puck well. He's very involved in Saint John's play, both offensively and defensively. Jakub uses his size in puck battles to win and find success defensively. Jakub usually makes a solid play under pressure, controlling the puck patiently and moving it safely but effectively to his teammates. On the power play he can be a dangerous weapon because of his big shot from the point and great puck movement. Zboril plays with a physical edge but has been called numerous times, forcing his team to kill his penalties. Unfortunately, he was hurt in early January and missed a good chunk of games in the 2nd half of the season, including the CHL Top Prospect Game. He made his return late in the season until the Sea Dogs were eliminated from the playoffs in the first round versus the Drakkar. He then left and played for his country at the U18 Hockey Championship in Switzerland. Zboril is an intriguing package of size and skills, maybe in some case it does come too easy for him and doesn't have to work hard for it.

Quotable: "*There's a lot I like about him, but one thing that keeping nagging at me when I go to slot him in my rankings is his lack of 'want to' I saw in some games.*" *- Mark Edwards*

Quotable: "*If he was a cleaner player and defended, he could be ranked as a top 15 guy based on his ability. I saw a kid who looked like he didn't give a shit though.*" *- NHL Scout*

Zborosky, Zak
RW – Kootenay Ice (WHL) – 6'00" 189
HockeyProspect.com Ranking: NR

Zak Zborosky of the Kootenay Ice is an extremely fast winger who can score off of the rush with alarming accuracy when given a sufficient opportunity, accentuating his strongest assets. He doesn't play a very cerebral or creative game and relies almost entirely on his raw physical tools of speed and shooting skills. In this sense, he's a bit of a one-trick pony, although his passing game did improve as the year went on.

Throughout the season, Zborosky perfected the skill of making quick dishes across the slot while moving at close to top-speeds. He will need to continue making improvements to his playmaking game and hockey sense if he wants to continue to produce offensively at higher levels. However, that exceptional straight-ahead speed allows him to backcheck very quickly. Which means he may end up being a fairly dependable defensive forward who can be trusted to not be a liability in his own zone.

Another aspect of Zborosky's game that is easy to appreciate is his durability. Even though he plays a very high-octane-type game, he's almost completed two full WHL seasons already without a major injury. On the other hand, he only accrued 18 penalty minutes this year, as he doesn't employ a lot of physicality in his game and leaves much of the dirty work to his teammates. He had a strong first half but really cooled off towards the end of the year after being shoved down the lineup following the returns of Sam Reinhart and Tim Bozon. Equipped with only a medium-sized build and not particularly physical, that lack of consistency in terms of offensive production might be enough to keep him off the draft board, in 2015 at least.

Zborovskiy, Sergei
LD – Regina Pats (WHL) – 6'03" 198
HockeyProspect.com Ranking: NR

Sergei Zborovskiy is a towering Russian defender who made his Canadian major junior debut with the Regina Pats this year as a rookie import.

Zborovskiy definitely projects as a simple, shutdown defender. He played a reliable game for the Pats, willing to use his size to take out opponents whenever he had the chance. He gets down low and battles for pucks but his moderately questionable skating effected him at times against speedy forwards. Although he does show flashes of offensive skill. He's not an explosive skater by any means, but he's blessed with tremendous crossover skills and is thereby able to carry the puck up ice and wind-and-weave his way around opposition forecheckers. He earned the odd cup of coffee on the Regina Pats power play this year, with most of his points coming off of his powerful one-timer slapshot from just above the offensive faceoff circle. His first-passes are generally decent, but he does throw the odd horrible turnover.

Most definitely, Zborovskiy is an entertaining player to watch when he's defending the space in front of his goaltender. He continues to show a habit for chopping, slashing and crosschecking opponents between and after the whistles. But if it weren't for his post-whistle antics—which are many here and between—you probably wouldn't notice Zborovskiy too much at all, because he plays such a simple and dependable game in his own end.

Zeppieri, David
LC - Sudbury Wolves (OHL) 6'02" 190
HockeyProspect.com Ranking: NR

After playing about 50 percent of the time in his rookie season, David was a regular for the Wolves in his second OHL season and a rebuilding one for Sudbury. David plays a steady two-way role. He is very defensively responsible and was also a regular choice for the penalty kill. He will need to apply more pressure to the puck carrier on the penalty kill and up his pace a bit, but is well positioned in his own end. He is capable of killing time off the clock if he gets his hands on the puck in a penalty killing situation. Offensively he's very limited and is more successful getting to the front of the net or battling down low than he is making a play with his hands. Zeppieri is not likely to get selected at the 2015 NHL Draft and projects as a low end two-way forward and penalty killer.

Zhukenov, Dmitri
RC – Omskie Yastreby (MHL) – 5'11.25" 169
HockeyProspect.com Ranking: NR

Zhukenov is a creative center that was a key member of his U18 national team this season, bringing consistent performances and showing off his uncommon skills. He possesses terrific puckhandling skills and he likes to slow down the game taking advantage of those while he looks for options to open up, be it to find lanes to connect with his linemates or the space to enter the offensive zone. He can see and find linemates wherever they are in the offensive zone, especially on the powerplay, but at even strength sometimes he doesn't share the puck quickly enough, even if he remains a playmaker first.

He is a nifty stickhandler who can dangle around opponents. Can show some speed through the neutral and has good balance, but he has yet to add explosiveness to his skating. As of now he doesn't look like someone who will be able to escape defensemen at the next level with his skating agility, like along the boards, and this adds to the concern of his lack of size and strength. He will have to build some needed power to be able to play and be effective in North America. That doesn't mean Zhukenov plays a soft game; he is not afraid of going into high traffic areas, is resilient and will take punishment to make a play. He is a dependable player who brings controlled play and good efforts both ways.

Zipp, Michael
LD – Calgary Hitmen (WHL) – 6'02" 189
HockeyProspect.com Ranking: NR

Left-handed rearguard Michael Zipp played in a depth defensive role for the Calgary Hitmen this year on a lineup that had a glut of skill on the back end. For his own part, we like his work as a defensive defenceman in Calgary, as he manages to keep really good gap control, directs plays well and is a fairly good puck retriever despite his limited footspeed.

You won't find too many highlight reels documenting the work of Michael Zipp, as his game tends to be very, very simple. He looks his best when making simple reads and plays to retrieve the puck in his team's corners. One thing we really like is that Zipp possesses the necessary physical tools to make a play while taking a hit and has the competitiveness to fearlessly block a dangerous shot when necessary. This makes him a valuable asset to the Hitmen penalty kill. After making a retrieval or placing himself in front of a shot, he tosses very conservative and simple first passes. On those rare occasions when he does venture beyond his comfort zone he is usually unsuccessful, so his tendency to stick within his limits is probably well-founded.

All in all, there's still a lot to like about Michael Zipp. He has a pro-size frame and an upright professional style that is dependable and predictable. His shooting from the blueline is a bit unpredictable and inconsistent, but we saw him create a few goals off of good reads in the offensive zone. We think he's a decently sized bottom pairing defender with only okay skating ability and limited offensive upside.

Zuhlsdorf, Ryan
LD – Sioux City (USHL) 5'11.25" 188
HockeyProspect.com Ranking: NR

Zuhlsdorf, a Minnesota commit, wasn't overly impressive any viewings this year, but shows potential. The inconsistency of his game is what hurts him. His decision making ability seems to vary from shift to shift. Too often we see him turn the puck over in the neutral zone leading to rushes for the opponent. On the offensive blue line he fires into shin pads and makes ill advised plays. To go along with these decision making struggles, Zuhlsdorf also shows flashes of great potential. He has the ability to make great outlet passes and a solid defensive game.

Quotable: "If he can put it all together and play a consistent game cutting out the bad decision making, it would go a long way towards giving him a chance to be a good two-way defenseman at the next level." – NHL Scout

2016 NHL DRAFT TOP 30

2016 NHL DRAFT TOP 30

RANK	PLAYER	POS	2014/2015 TEAM	HEIGHT	WEIGHT
1	Auston Matthews	RW	USNTDP U18	6' 2"	194
2	Jacob Chychrun	D	Sarnia (OHL)	6' 2"	194
3	Jesse Puljujärvi	RW	Kärpät (SM-liiga)	6' 2"	181
4	Matthew Tkachuk	LW	USNTDP U18	6' 1"	187
5	Max Jones	LW	USNTDP U17	6' 2"	190
6	Charles McAvoy	D	USNTDP U18	6' 0"	205
7	Logan Brown	C	Windsor (OHL)	6' 6"	216
8	Patrik Laine	LW	Tappara Tampere(SM-liiga)	6' 4"	209
9	Clayton Keller	C	USNTDP U18	5' 9"	165
10	Dmitri Sokolov	C	Omsk (KHL)	6' 2"	212
11	Dante Fabbro	D	Penticton (BCHL)	6' 1"	165
12	Kale Clague	D	Brandon (WHL)	6' 0"	194
13	Kieffer Bellows	C	Sioux Falls (USHL)	6' 0"	185
14	Olli Juolevi	D	Jokerit Helsinki (Jr SM-liiga)	6' 2"	185
15	Sam Steel	C	Regina (WHL)	5' 11"	172
16	Pierre-Luc Dubois	C	Cape Breton (QMJHL)	6' 1"	181
17	Mikhail Sergachyov	D	Kazan (MHL)	6' 2"	201
18	Carl Grundström	LW	Modo Hockey (SEL)	6' 0"	190
19	Brett Howden	LW	Moose Jaw (WHL)	6' 1"	190
20	Tyson Jost	RW	Penticton (BCHL)	6' 0"	194
21	Chad Krys	D	USNTDP U18	5' 11"	183
22	Alexander Nylander	LW	Sodertalje SK(Allsvenskan)	5' 10"	157
23	Taylor Raddysh	RW	Erie (OHL)	6' 0"	190
24	Victor Mete	D	London (OHL)	5' 10"	165
25	Jacob Cederholm	D	HV71 J20 (SuperElit)	6' 3"	176
26	Luke Green	D	Saint John (QMJHL)	5' 11"	174
27	Tyler Benson	LW	Vancouver (WHL)	6' 0"	196
28	Julien Gauthier	RW	Val-d'Or (QMJHL)	6' 4"	212
29	Rasmus Asplund	LW	Färjestad BK (Sweden)	5' 11"	176
30	Vitali Abramov	RW	Chelyabinsk Mechel (Slov U-20)	5' 9"	159
HM	Alex DeBrincat	RW	Erie (OHL)	5' 7"	161
HM	Tye Felhaber	C	Saginaw (OHL)	5' 10"	174
HM	Jacob Moverare	D	HV71 J20 (SuperElit)	6' 1"	185
HM	Samuel Girard	D	Shawinigan (QMJHL)	5' 9"	154
HM	Evan Sarthou	G	Tri-City (WHL)	6' 1"	179
HM	Jake Bean	D	Calgary Hitmen (WHL)	6' 0"	174
HM	Libor Hájek	C	Kometa Brno (Czech U20)	6' 2"	196
HM	Will Bitten	C	Plymouth (OHL)	5' 9"	154
HM	Jonathan Dahlen	C	Timra U20 (SuperElit)	5' 11"	168
HM	Garret Wait	LW	Edina High (USHS)	6' 1"	170

2016 NHL DRAFT PROSPECTS

Abramov, Vitaly
RW – Belye Medvedi (MHL) – 5'09" 159

A forward coming off great numbers in younger junior leagues, Abramov didn't disappoint in his first MHL season despite limited use and his small stature. Going against players up to 4yrs older than him he was a bit overwhelmed physically and athletically in the MHL, but he still found a way to produce. He can play both the center or winger position and certainly showed his stuff against his peers in international competitions. Vitaly is quick, elusive, and very skilled. He has good offensive instincts and a very good head for the game overall. He is alert defensively in his own end and shows good compete level and remarkable intensity in his play. His motor never stops and with added power he shows the potential to become an elite skater.

He likes to attack with speed down the right side and is a machine at completing passes to the slot after making quick twirls. He is very shifty and a very powerful skater. He is terrific behind the net, can find teammates or quickly take pucks to the net with both his forehand and backhand. He consistently finds lanes to converge to the net from the right side down low. Size is the obvious concern with Abramov. Inexplicably left out of the Russian team at the U18 World Championships despite other '98 born countrymen made the team, he is expected to play in the CHL next year and will be an important selection at the 2015 CHL Import draft.

Amundrud, Nik
G – Saskatoon Blades (WHL) – 6'01" 165

Nik is an aggressive goaltender who is athletic, acrobatic, agile and highly animated. While in his standing position, he bends down very low to track shots, opening areas of the net up high. He compensates for his uniqueness and unconventionality through a number of clever techniques. He has a fantastic glove hand that he can utilize when in any position. Whether it be in a standing stance or whilst doing the splits. Amundrud is an unconventional goaltender with a lot of upside for the 2016 NHL Entry Draft..

Andersson, Alexander
LD – Vaxjo Lakers J20 (SWE) – 5'10" 172

Andersson is a smart puck moving defender for the Vaxjo Lakers J20. He posted nearly a point per game relying upon his strong first pass and smooth puck rushing ability. Andersson is a smooth skater who has good hands and can carry the puck with poise and confidence. He is very calm, looking for both passing lanes and rushing the puck up ice. He controls the puck well in the offensive zone making the smart pass, distributing amongst his teammates. He is able to accurately send long distance passes from his own zone, making him a dangerous option to create odd man rushes.

Andersson is undersized for an NHL defensive prospect and can get knocked around a bit in his own end. His skating ability helps him a lot in one on one match-up's, however he can get outmatched against bigger stronger opponents. Andersson will need to add muscle and hopefully get bigger in order to maximize his upside at the 2016 NHL Entry Draft.

Anderson, Joey
RW - USNTDP U17 5'11" 189

He is a very capable winger as he skates well, handles the puck, and shoots to score. He can fire biscuit in the offensive zone from the 1-timer on the power play to zinging one as he flies down the wing. He also shows good playing making skills as well rack up his fair share of assist in seeing the ice. Not overly big in size though plays strong on the puck and is one of the better offensive threats on NTPP-17 squad this season. He is a big-time recruit for Minnesota-Duluth for 2016-17 although WHL rights held by Brandon Wheat Kings.

Anderson, Josh
RD – Prince George Cougars (WHL) – 6'03" 215

Anderson has great size already for a 16 year old wth a pro ready frame. Anderson was selected 3rd overall by the Prince George Cougars in the 2013 WHL Bantam Draft, despite needing to work on his footwork at that time. He's improved that footwork and now stands as a big and tough defender who loves to flex his muscles in all three zones. In addition to being a better than average skater, he possesses a great reach and uses it well to protect the puck and to poke it out of danger and into open space. Anderson has a powerful shot but needs to choose his options better, as he will shoot into screens that are right in front of him. Anderson will be taking a bigger role next year with a resurgent Prince George Cougars organization, as he looks to establish himself as one of the top prospects out of the WHL for the 2016 NHL Entry Draft.

Ang, Johnathan
RC - Peterborough Petes (OHL) 5'11" 153

Jonathan is a small, skilled player who's confidence and creativity grew as the as he saw more ice throughout the year. An explosive skater with an effortless stride, Ang can fly up the ice with above average hands that match his speed. Ang competed more as the year went on but must develop strength and consistency in his game heading into his draft year, as we saw performances where he didn't show up as much as we would've liked.

Allard, Frederic
LD – Chicoutimi Sagueneens (QMJHL) – 5'11" 175

Allard is a late birthday, which means instead of being eligible for this year NHL draft he's eligible for the 2016 nhl draft. The Sagueneens drafted Allard in the first round of the 2013 QMJHL draft 18th overall after playing his midget hockey in Quebec city with the Seminaire St-Francois. It was a tough season for the sags overall this year but Allard was again a bright spot for a second straight year logging tons of ice time and playing good hockey at both end of the ice. Allard is not a flashy defenseman but has a great hockey IQ and makes good decisions with or without the puck. He doesn't show much panics when he's under pressure and still makes good decisions moving the puck. He lacks ideal size to be an NHL defensemen, will need to get stronger physically to help him out in his battles along the board and in front of the net. Usually Allard will use a good active stick and his smarts to counter opposing forwards but his lack of strength will hurt him when facing bigger forwards deep in his zone. He played in all situations for Chicoutimi this year; he's a capable quarterback on the power play with good passing abilities and is useful on the penalty kill due to his smarts. Would like to see his shot improve, and could use it more often as well to not become predictable offensively. He has a good wrist shot but rarely use his slapper. He could have a bright future as a smart two way defensemen but his lack of strength is a concern.

Allison, Wade
RW - Tri-City (USHL) 6'1" 201

Allison developed nicely throughout his first year in the USHL. He already has pretty good size and after a very successful career at the U16 level with Omaha AAA, Allison made the jump to the USHL with the Storm. He certainly doesn't back down from players older than him in the league and competes every shift. He has some good offensive thoughts, but really proved his worth in his own end this past season. He will return to the Storm this coming season and will probably have a bigger role, which may allow him to showcase more of his offensive skillset. Allison will head to Western Michigan in 2016.

Asplund, Rasmus
LW – Farjestad (SHL) – 5'11" 176

Rasmus is a late '97 born who has already been a regular for Farjestad in the top Swedish league this season, usually playing on the 4th line together with Eriksson Ek. Because of this feat he was expected to make a bigger impact at the U18 in Switzerland, but was still one of the few Swedes showing some pulse in his game.

He can be used at any forward position and he is effective in the faceoff circle. Asplund brings a dynamic presence with the puck, he can stickhandle through traffic especially on the right side while he looks for lanes to the net. He shows good acceleration and strength to get first to the puck. He has been however really inconsistent in our viewings, looking terrific on some nights for such a young player, but barely visible in other games.

Badini, Jack
C/W - Lincoln (USHL) 5'10" 170

Badini joined the Stars about halfway through the year and had a limited role throughout his time in the league. He's a raw offensive talent but there is a lot potential there to be realized here. Next year will be a telling year as he will probably step into a top six role with the Stars and be expected to contribute consistently offensively. It's expected that Badini will be back in Lincoln for the next two seasons before heading to Harvard in the fall of 2017.

Bain, Maxim
RW – Irbis Kazan (MHL) – 5'09.5" 165

Maxim is a talented, undersized forward who spent the past season with Irbis Kazan of the MHL. Bain possesses excellent skating ability. He's explosive in open ice and can evade checkers very well. Tough to contain in one on one situations he has a great shot, despite his size which can sometimes decieve goaltenders. It is increasingly effective because Bain wouldn't force shots from bad areas, instead using his evasiveness to gain prime shooting areas ad fire the puck on goal.

Maxim's uphill struggle won't be in the skill department, but will need to add size and toughness to reach his potential. While he's not a big defensive player, he will block shots when he's in position in the defensive zone. Bain is a skilled forward who will look to build upon a strong season headed towards the 2016 NHL Entry Draft.

Bajkov, Patrik
RW – Everett Silvertips (WHL) – 5'11" 175

Bajkov's skating looks very good, as his first-step is sufficiently powerful and he gets going at a decent pace with minimal effort. Forward full-stride movements look elongated, but appear natural and technically sound. His ability to turn smoothly while moving at high speeds is also notable. On multiple occasions we saw Bajkov score on some talented individualistic goals. Bajkov is definitely a shoot-first type winger with a great release to his shot. Along with the offensive ability, Bajkov provided Everett with a very complete game. He already sees regular time on the penalty kill due to his defensive awareness. He has also been a solid contributor on the power play due to his aforementioned shooting skills. When on the ice killing a penalty, Bajkov has been very effective taking the body and getting the puck out of danger. We also liked his competitiveness regardless of the score. Bajkov will take on a much bigger role with his team next year and will look to establish himself as a talented, well rounded prospect for the 2016 NHL Entry Draft.

Balmas, Mitchell
LW/C - Charlottetown Islanders (QMJHL) - 5'11" 175

Selected 7th overall by Charlottetown in the 2014 QMJHL draft, Balmas was exiting his Major Midget career with a full head of steam, selected as NSMMHL Rookie of the Year and then was chosen by Hockey Canada to participate in the World U17 Challenge where he was placed on Team White and notched 2 assists in 5 games. Balmas, like most 16 years old entering the league, spent time adjusting to the game for the first couple of months trading off with other 16 years old prospects for the last 4th line positions, but after the season progressed he was seeing some regular shifts. Balmas has a strong deep skating stride and average speed for this level, but it lacks that explosive piece and the agility required to really separate himself from his opponents at this moment. We do not get a sense that he is shifty on his skates in traffic but he has very good hands and at his top speed can make a pass or stickhandle with relative ease. Balmas was used on the teams' power play unit. He proved he was effective at moving the puck in the perimeter and finding his teammates. Balmas had 11 points (in 56GP this season in Charlottetown and added 2 points in their 2 rounds of playoffs. Balmas worked hard on being defensively responsible for this season, and considering his role this season as a rookie we feel he has made some improvements here. Next season we would expect a bit of an expanded role for Balmas as his team will try and ignite the offensive fuel seen in the past.

Barron, Travis
LC - Ottawa 67's (OHL) 6'01" 198

Travis is a hard working forward selected third overall by the Ottawa 67's in the 2014 OHL Priority Selection Draft. Barron plays a high energy physical style of game and does a great job on the forecheck. He finishes his hits hard and despite being one of the younger players in the league he could compete physically against much more mature opponents. Barron doesn't show high offensive upside but he does possess a solid, powerful shot.

Bastian, Nathan
RC Mississauga Steelheads (OHL) 6'03" 195

Nathan Bastian is very strong for his age and while he doesn't possess a mean streak, he makes good use of his size. He finishes his checks and regularly wins puck battles against older players. Bastian is strong on the puck and is aggressive and assertive when it comes to forcing his way into the dirty areas of the ice. Bastian is always in pursuit of the puck and is good at forcing turnovers. He is excellent positionally and was a regular on Mississauga's penalty killing unit. Bastian uses his good skating ability, positioning and long reach to take away passing/shooting lanes. He does possess good skill with the puck, has a solid shot and good hands around the net. He scored almost 20 goals in his first full season with Mississauga and he has the potential to improve upon his offensive numbers even more in his draft year.

Quotable: "His billet family are friends of mine and they have nothing but good things to say about Nathan." - Mark Edwards

Bean, Jake
RD – Calgary Hitmen (WHL) - 6'00" 175

Jake Bean was a standout rookie defenseman for the Calgary Hitmen this year. At only sixteen-years-old, he's already standing out as a premier puck-retrieving, puck-moving and puck-rushing defenseman. It's unusual for a defenseman of this age to be the first player out on the power play and the first player out on the penalty kill, but that was the case during Bean's season with the Hitmen. Although he lacks physically maturity, Bean provides a powerful combination of tremendous skating ability, exceptional puckhandling skills and hockey sense. He is very agile in

Beaudin, Jeremie
LD – Cape-Breton Screaming Eagles (QMJHL) – 5'11" 199

Beaudin was a player we liked going into the QMJHL draft last season due to his two-way game and skating ability. We were expecting him to at least to start this season back in midget AAA but found himself starting the season with the Screaming Eagles and stayed all year long with the big club. The Eagles drafted Beaudin with the 31st pick in the draft and we had him ranked as an early 2nd rounder (23rd). Beaudin is not a player who jumps at you when you watch him; he's a player who needs more than one viewing to get a good read on. He does a lot of nice things in his zone but has no real flashes in his game offensively. He possesses a nice footwork and ability to escape pressure with one or two skating strides. He has a good first pass from his zone, he's not elite but he's an efficient puck mover from his zone and makes smart decision with the puck. Didn't get many opportunities offensively this season but still end up scoring 5 goals, one of the reasons we though going back to midget AAA was he would have got more chances to plays on the man advantage and improve his game offensively. He didn't get many chances to play on the power play this season with the Eagles. His offensive potential is still a bit unknown, should be interesting to see what role he gets next season as the eagles have already plenty of defensemen able to play that role with Leveille, Leblanc & Lalonde. Since last season Beaudin was able to add some weight to his frame now closing on the 200lbs plateau, not a very physical player but Beaudin is capable of throwing some good hits here and there when needed.

Bellows, Kieffer
LC - Sioux Falls (USHL) 6'0" 185

Not often a rookie enters the USHL ranks and posts 30-plus goals. Bellows is a strong competitor as he isn't afraid to bowl players over on the ice with physical play and goes in hard on the forecheck as he wants the puck on his stick. He is good size and solid on his skates. What you like is that he will score in a variety of ways from driving the puck hard to the net, re-directing shots in front, or getting shot out of a cannon with break-a-way speed and displaying some nice hands for the finish in tight. He plays in all zones with high compete level and willingness to score big goals. He is the son of a former NHLer, Brian Bellows, and you see the genetic talent handed down. After earning Rookie of the Year honors and helping his team to Clark Cup Championship, Bellows has lots of spotlight on him as being one of the top '98-born forwards for the 2016 NHL Draft.

Benson, Tyler
LW – Vancouver Giants (WHL) - 6'00" 196

Tyler Benson, the 1st overall selection at the 2013 WHL Bantam Draft, but had a bit of an up-and-down year with the Vancouver Giants this season. While he didn't blow us away with his offensive production this year and he sometimes struggled to make an offensive impact in our viewings. Benson has shown the capability to become a complete player. This allowed him to put together a good string of performances even when the puck wasn't going in the net for him. He was an important defensive forward, who throws big hits and is a significant part of the Giants special teams. Even though the Giants struggled mightily on several long losing stretches, Tyler Benson showed good progression in his development over the course of the season. In addition to his two-way ability, Benson is a physical player who can assert himself well against players much older than himself. He has a great shot both wrist and slap come off with excellent velocity, however accuracy needs some improvement. Benson has a lot of hype going into the 2016 NHL Entry Draft and will need to have a strong summer and show why he was selected so high in the 2013 WHL Bantam Draft.

Bilodeau, Gabriel
RD – Gatineau Olympiques (QMJHL) – 6'1" 171

Bilodeau was drafted in the first round by the Val D'Or foreurs 19th overall, but was traded this season to Gatineau in exchange for Alexis Pepin (Colorado Avalanche draft pick). Not too long after being acquired by Gatineau, Bilodeau broke his arm and missed 4 weeks of action but came back for the playoff and played in all of Olympiques playoff games. Bilodeau was chosen as well to play by hockey Canada at the 2014 U-17 hockey challenge this past November in Sarnia. The Laval native is a smooth skating defenseman who moves the puck very well; he uses his speed in both offensive and defensive situations. He's a capable puck rusher, he can skate the puck out of his zone with ease. Defensively he has good mobility and can cover opposing forwards well due to his great footwork and lateral mobility. He still needs to add strength to win more one on one battle along the board. He will need to improve his shot, he lacks velocity and that would make him more diversified in the offensive zone as he tend to always making a pass as he lacks confidence in his shot.

Bitten, Will
RC - Plymouth Whalers (OHL) 5'09" 154

Bitten enjoyed his first OHL season after being the first round selection by the Plymouth Whalers in the 2014 OHL Priority Selection Draft. Bitten is a highly skilled forward who is tough to contain. He is evasive with the puck and shifty in open space. He plays with a very high compete level, battling for pucks and chasing opponents down relentlessly on the forecheck. After contributing as a 16 year old, Bitten is expected be a key part of the inaugural Flint Firebirds season playing big minutes on the new Firebirds team.

Quotable: "One of my fave players in the 2014 OHL Draft. This kid worked as hard defensively as he did trying to score. He showed fantastic short area quickness. He will need put up big numbers in next season because he's lacking in the size department." - Mark Edwards

Bourque, Trenton
LD - Sudbury Wolves (OHL) 6'02" 178

Bourque only played about half the time in his rookie season, but when he was out there he provided a steady reliable role for the Wolves unusual for someone the age of 16 at this level, especially on a team that spent so much time in their own end. He works hard and uses his stick well to break up scoring opportunities. He had a very good compete level and battled hard for pucks. He also possesses decent mobility for his size. Offensively he has a good hard shot but was not utilized much in offensive situations. His puck play is a bit hit or miss. Bourque should take on a bigger role next year as a prospect for the 2016 NHL Entry Draft.

Bratt, Jesper
RW – AIK J20 (SWE) – 5'09" 170

Bratt is a small, speedy forward with good offensive upside. He gets really low in his stride with his chest leaning forward, but gets a decent amount of power to zoom around the ice with a great top speed. He is very capable at changing speeds to deceive defenders and give himself addition space and time. Extremely difficult player to contain. Offensively he has great hands in tight and fast paced with a quick, accurate release on his shot. He also does a good job drawing defenders in then making a pass to create high percentage scoring chances.

Bratt's body language on the ice and on the bench is tough to decipher at times. It's either just sheer confidence or arrogance, but it's noticeable. Bratt tends to drift in the defensive zone and can confuse his linemates as to who he is actually covering. He has a slender frame and could be at risk of getting hurt until he bulks up. However a defender would have to catch him first as he's very hard to hit.

Brown, Logan
LC - Windsor Spitfires (OHL) 6'05" 215

After being selected by the Niagara Ice Dogs Brown was traded to the Windsor Spitfires pre-season and immediately played an impact on their top two lines. Brown is a big forward who skates well. He protects the puck well with his size but doesn't show the aggression or assertiveness you'd like to see out of someone possessing his size. His play was a little inconsistent in our viewings, some games creating offense and possessing a strong shot but other games he appeared to drift off and not perform at the level he is capable of. If can get his consistency improved and continue to build on is rookie season, Brown could be one of the top players to come out of the OHL at the 2016 NHL Entry Draft.

Quotable: "I didn't see all that much of him in his OHL draft year. He showed big potential but lacked drive in the games I saw. This season I really liked what I saw from him in Windsor. I think he has a good chance of being a high pick next season." - Mark Edwards

Brushett, Ryan
C/RW – Lac St-Louis Lions (LHMAAAQ) – 5'11" 172

Brushett was a first round prospect going into his QMJHL draft year but with his intention to go the NCAA route slipped down to the 6th round where he was selected by Charlottetown. This season to keep his NCAA eligibility he went back for a second season with the Lac St-Louis Lions of the Quebec midget AAA league where he led the team in scoring and was one of the league best players. Brushett is a versatile forward as he can play both down the middle and on the wing. He has a high skill level offensively; a good quick accurate wrist shot and can pick corners up. He sees the ice well and can be a difference maker on the ice; consistency has been his biggest issue the past two seasons with the Lions. He has to play a more disciplined game, can spend too much time in the penalty box for useless penalties. He's an above average skater but still need to work on his explosiveness to be more dangerous offensively. He's a smart player on the forecheck where he can strip the puck away from his opponents with a good stick. He's at his best when he plays in traffic but there's some inconsistency there as well. Next year he's expected to go play in the USHL for Sioux City who drafted him in 2014, he committed after this season to play college hockey at Providence College.

Budik, Vojtech
LD – HC Pardubice U20 (CZE) – 6'01" 190

Budik is a two-way defenseman that impressed in particular at the Five Nations tournament played in his home country. He was less effective at the U18 World Championships, where he didn't show the same confidence with the puck. Vojtech can make play under pressure and moves well on his skates.

He is reliable carrying the puck out of troubles and displays strong stickhandling in transition. He has good vision, can be used in all situations and is able to quarterback a powerplay. Defensively his strength is his remarkable stickwork. Certainly an interesting player to monitor for next year draft.

Bunnaman, Connor
LC - Kitchener Rangers (OHL) 6'00" 197

Connor was a second round pick of the Kitchener Rangers in the 2014 OHL Priority Selection Draft. Bunnaman displayed maturity beyond his years quickly fitting into a penalty killing role for the Rangers instantly becoming one of their best 200 foot players and a difficult player to play against. He competes and finishes his checks hard on the forecheck. He chips in a little offensively with good puck decisions and a decent shot but isn't a big time offensive guy.

He does a great job in the face-off circle, especially as a 16 year old. Connor's skating will need improvement over the next 12 months in order for him to maximize his potential for the 2016 NHL Entry Draft.

Caamano, Nicholas
LW - Plymouth Whalers (OHL) 6'00" 170

Nicholas really got a chance early on to show what he's capable of receiving a lot of ice time on the wing. He plays hard and never looks off a chance to take the body. He isn't a flashy player but he is smart with the puck with a powerful shot and a very quick release. He is also smart without the puck seemingly always finding ideal positioning and getting himself open when he isn't directly attacking or possessing the puck. Caamano will be a player to watch heading into the 2016 NHL Entry Draft.

Campbell, Chase
RW - Sarnia Sting (OHL) 5'08" 170

Chase split this past season between the OHL's Sarnia Sting and the GOJHL's Waterloo Jr. B Siskins. He played polarizing roles on each club playing more of a depth/energy role on the Sting fourth line acclimating himself to the OHL game but in Waterloo he played more of an offensive/power play role. Campbell is very small but extremely speedy. He is tough to contain with the puck and slippery through traffic with good hands and strong puck skills.

He will be looking to take the next step with the Sarnia Sting next season but will need to get bigger and stronger to reach his potential and overcome his size.

Campoli, Michael
LD - USNTDP U17 6'2" 195

He is a Quebec native with dual citizenship as played for NTDP-17s this past season. He is also committed to Boston College already for the 2016-17 season. He is a good-sized blue liner that keeps his game simple with effective body checking in his own zone, closes gaps, and makes the initial pass to start the transition. He is just a smart, effective, poised player with minimal offensive output.

Candella, Cole
LD - Belleville Bulls (OHL) 6'01" 181

A strong skating, mobile defender; Candella had a good season as a 16 year old defender for the Bulls. His skating ability allows him close the gap quickly on opposing forwards and jumps up in the rush offensively. He is calm with the puck under pressure and usually made the right pass, although had his moments where he would have a mental lapse in judgment. Candella has high potential but needs to play more consistently and display his skills on a game by game basis.

Quotable:" Liked him less the more I saw him in his OHL draft year because of some horrible decision making. He struggled to grasp situational hockey. Thought he made some strides in his overall game this year." - Mark Edwards

Carroll, Noah
LD - Guelph Storm (OHL) 6'01" 173

Noah is a late birthdate who completed his first full season in the OHL with the Guelph Storm. He is a solid two-way defender at this level showing good composure down low competing for pucks and has a comfort level skating the puck out of trouble. He is good in one on one situations and is capable with both his stick and his body. He will need to get stronger and improve upon his consistency with the puck and with his defensive play to truly reach his potential.

Quotable:" I thought Guelph got really good value where they got him in the OHL draft. I liked him a lot in his OHL draft season. Saw him play a fantastic game late this season and proceed to follow it up with an absolute stinker in very next game. Overall I'm looking forward to watching him next year." - Mark Edwards

Cederholm, Jacob
RD – HV71 J20 (SWE) – 6'03" 176

Cederholm has a pro ready frame that will fill out and get stronger as he develops. Evidence of his physical maturity came when he made his SHL debut at the age of 16 with HV71. He is a reliable, stay-at-home defenseman that moves his frame around the ice with good mobility. In the defensive zone and neutral zone he makes excellent reads on plays. He always seems to know what's coming before it happens. Jacob is very effective at picking off passes in the neutral zone and breaking up potential rushes. He is extremely difficult to beat in one on one situations.

Cederholm doesn't have a lot of offensive skills - he is usually utilized in front of the net on the powerplay, screening the goaltender. He has shown the ability to rush the puck on occasion using his big frame to protect the puck. His passing and shooting decisions on the point leaves much to be desired. He will shoot into screens and even when that resulted in a breakaway goal, he will go back out there and make the same mistake again with his shot. Cederholm competes with great consistency and doesn't take a shift off. Jacob projects to be a highly regarded shutdown defender at the 2016 NHL Entry Draft.

Chychrun, Jakob
LD - Sarnia Sting (OHL) 6'02" 194

Chychrun is an outstanding talent who was the 1st Overall pick in the 2014 OHL Priority Selection Draft. Chychrun has everything you could ask for in a defenseman. He has size and fantastic skating to match. He's tough to beat one on one defensively and got better as this past season progressed. He has excellent vision and his hockey sense is off the charts. He knows when to rush and when to move the puck and he is capable of directly creating scoring chances with both. When DeAngelo was traded, Chychrun took over as power play quarterback and he does an excellent job directing traffic, communicating with teammates and has a pro level shot with excellent accuracy. He also displays a leadership and maturity that's unheard of for his age.

Shoulder injuries were starting to become a concern but he had surgery to fix the problem and should be healthy to start next season. Jakob has the potential to be in the discussion to fight for that #1 spot in the 2016 NHL Entry Draft but realistically will need to have a phenomenal season to unseat Auston Mathews. Regardless he is one of the best players available for next years draft.

Quotable: "I can't say enough good things about this kid. He's mature well beyond his years and maximizes his physical talents to impact that game. He did have a short adjustment period early on this season but quickly got used to the speed and never looked back. If I was picking next years draft today, he would be number two on my list.

- Mark Edwards

Clague, Kale
LD – Brandon Wheat Kings (WHL) – 6'00" 194

Clague is a top prospect for the Brandon Wheat Kings. He had an excellent rookie season and his high end lateral mobility, strong puck handling skill, vision and shooting have helped him make an impact on a contender. He likes to take off with his skating and puck handling ability by leading his own rushes through the neutral zone. Indeed, Clague is a talented and agile all-directional skater who delivers a good first pass. His shot from the blueline is definitely a strength at this point, as he hammers the puck with a quick-release slapshot that is very accurate. He has the confidence to battle down low, but lacks the strength to win enough battles at this point. Overall, his skills as an offensive defenceman look well-tuned already. He will look to use next season to show his upside as a potential first round pick at the 2016 NHL Entry Draft.

Cormier, Evan
G - Saginaw Spirit (OHL) 6'02" 198

Cormier was drafted by the North Bay Battalion but really started to show his stuff when he was traded to the Saginaw Spirit after franchise goaltender Jake Paterson was moved. Evan was selected by Hockey Canada for the 2015 U18 team, which competed in Switzerland in April. He got three starts and gave Canada some solid play. Cormier has good size and handles breakaways well. He gives up quite a few rebounds but is capable of directing them away well. Cormier's biggest concern going into next season is a lack of consistency. He's shown the ability to make outstanding saves and shut opponents down but also fights the puck some nights.

Quotable: "I thought he showed some good pro upside in my viewings at the U18. He has his warts, I'd like some better consistency with rebounds but he's young. I think he has a good foundation to build on as he enters his NHL Draft season. - Mark Edwards

Crone, Hank
C/LW - Omaha (USHL) 5'7" 150

Crone is a small forward who played a pretty big role for the Lancers this year. Although he is a small player, he is shifty and can find soft spots in the offensive zone to get shots away. Doesn't play a complete 200 foot game yet, but as his confidence grew throughout the year he got a lot more involved on the back check and played more defense. He will return to Omaha next year before heading to Boston University the year after.

Crossley, Brett
LC - Halifax Mooseheads (QMJHL) - 5'10" 153

Crossley comes to the Mooseheads by way of Shattuck St. Mary's hockey program and Captained Team NS in the 2013 Gatorade Challenge in Quebec before he was selected with the Mooseheads very first pick coming in the second round, #21 overall. Billed as a 2-way center, Crossley was given the job of pivot on the Mooseheads 4th line and was on the game sheet for 58 games and managed 6 goals and 8 points. Crossley was trusted to PK time and was used on both the 1st and 2nd unit. Crossley did reasonably well in the faceoff dot, and he was matched with some high end centers at times so it's no surprise that his faceoff wins were less than other Centers' in the league, but there were some games where he was 50/50 or better. Crossley is a very good skater fundamentally and can achieve good top speed when he pushes but we were never left thinking he had a tremendous amount of edge strength or shiftiness. His puck control was average for this level and we feel that he wants to move the puck quickly as opposed to going for a skate with it. This works in his favor at times as he has good vision for what is going on around him and is smart with puck placement if a true pass is not available. There is no feeling like he could explode through the opposition and create an opportunity with the puck, he showed he was much more comfortable at the perimeter and using his smarts to generate offence. Crossley is not an overly physical player and there are times where he does not seem comfortable in high contact situations, however there is a sense of leadership with this prospect and he could potentially turn into a player that leads his junior team in 2-3 years.

Dahlen, Jonathan
LW – Timra J20 (SWE) – 5'11" 168

The son of Ulf Dahlen, Jonathan is a pleasure to watch as his hunger and desire for the game are palpable in most shifts. He works hard in the corners, in front of the net, on faceoffs, everywhere. He attacks the net and likes to stay in front. Has a good first step, he moves fast and loves to be first on the puck. Possession is his game and when his team doesn't have the puck, he works hard to ensure they get it back.

He already shields the puck pretty well and likes to make plays from behind the net. He has a good wrister from short measure which he used to put up impressive numbers this season in Sweden at the U20 level. Growing a bit more would be ideal for his game, but if Dahlen maintains this consistent work ethic and offensive production, come draft day the family name should be called in the early rounds regardless.

Daschke, Derek
LD - Cedar Rapids (USHL) 6'2" 183

Daschke is one blue liner to get excited about as trending in right way. If he can put the whole pieces of the puzzle together on a consistent basis then he will be a good get in 2016 NHL Draft. He is a good sized body who can play physical, sound defensive game with positioning and stick. He is decent front-to-back skater although if he could improve the lateral foot speed he could really be an impressive player. He mans the blue line well as he gets good, hard shots to the net to create rebounds and re-directs. He is a Western Michigan commit that has some really good potential for the future.

Day, Sean
LD - Mississauga Steelheads (OHL) 6'02" 229

Sean had a decent sophomore season with the Steelheads. He certainly showed flashes of the potential he was projected to possess. Day is an effortless skater who can get up and down the ice incredibly well, which is even more impressive given his size. He has a very fluid stride and is poised with the puck when carrying it up ice. Day regularly jumps into the rush to help create offense and can be a little trigger happy in that regard. He gets back more often than not though because of his elite skating ability. Day isn't as physical as we would like him to be given his size. He landed some huge hits over the course of the season but is also very lackadaisical at times in puck battles along the wall.

Day usually makes a good first pass, has good power in his shot and is more than capable of quarterbacking a powerplay. His decision-making can be questionable. On occasion he seems absent minded and will force passes that aren't there. Day can be dynamic in space. He can elude oncoming checkers with ease and carry the puck end-to-end with regularity. Day has the ability to take games over when he wants to, but there are times where he doesn't seem interested. He certainly possesses huge upside and the tools of a potential high first round pick, but has a lot of work ahead of him to reach the lofty potential he possesses.

Quotable: " I've never really been a fan. In minor midget I thought he just dominated solely because of his skating ability. I didn't think he played smart hockey. Fast forward to Mississauga - he has so much talent but often his production is less than players that possess half his skill. I see laziness in his game on too many shifts. He has wowed me at times but his good doesn't happen often enough to offset the bad for me. Next June is a long way off and he has plenty of time to improve his game but right now his warts drop him down my list. I expect him to be wearing a different jersey in September. I was told he's buddies with Max Jones, could both players end up in London?" - Mark Edwards

DeBrincat, Alex
RW - Erie Otters (OHL) 5'07" 160

DeBrincat was signed as a free agent to the Erie Otters and immediately got an opportunity to play with the #1 ranked prospect for the 2015 NHL Entry Draft, Connor McDavid.

DeBrincat is a very undersized forward with excellent speed. He's tough to contain and while he has a bit of a shoot first mentality, he will move the puck around to his linemates well. Despite the lack of size, Alex is more than willing to play physical and is a very frustrating player to play against. He will take the body and if he can get in his shots or chirp the opposition, usually getting a reaction. He's a pesky player because he can agitate you with his mouth but also back it up by hurting you on the scoreboard. DeBrincat could be a very polarizing player in the 2016 NHL Entry Draft because of his drastic lack of size combined with high-end offensive ability.

Quotable: " I think it took about six viewings of him before I saw a game where he didn't score. I saw him be a player that just flat out buried his chances. Plenty of talk about him in the scout room looking ahead to next year, scouts wondering what numbers he will post without McDavid. He will have the benefit of it being year two for him in the OHL. - Mark Edwards

DeNoble, Logan
RC - Peterborough Petes (OHL) 5'09" 194

DeNoble dominated in his second year with the Lindsay Muskies (Jr. A) Which led to a mid-season signing and promotion to the Petes. He is a below average skater but makes up for it with an above average hockey IQ. DeNoble anticipates the play and was effective on the fore check and around the net with limited ice. He needs to work on skating and strength in order to make an impact every shift at the OHL level.

Dineen, Cam
LD – NJ Rockets 6'0" 176

He seems to keep physically growing and adds muscle so the trend is upward for the size. He is very mobile blue liner that handles the puck with confidence and moves the biscuit well to start the transition. He is a smart, puck mover D-man with nice potential for the next level. He is committed to Yale for 2016-17 though OHL services might just happen over the summer. He is another defenseman to keep your eye on for development this season.

Dmytriw, Jared
RW – Victoria Royals (WHL) - 5'11" 170

Jared Dmytriw is a hard-working and physical two-way forward. Skating hard in all three zones, being a dependable back checker in all situations, making extremely strong hits in the corners. He takes his shots from high percentage areas, but knows when to pass off when he doesn't have the option. He's only a slightly above-average skater for his age and physical dimensions, but his hard work, physical commitment and great shooting skills make him a significant offensive threat. Indeed, even though he'll certainly get bigger and add strength to an already fairly stocky frame, Dmytriw already does a tremendous job of fighting for space and time when his team is in possession of the puck. When he manages to create enough space for himself in the slot to make something happen, he rarely misses on a good shot opportunity. While his game tailed off a bit towards the end of this year, we really liked the promise Jared showed going forward.

Dubois, Pierre-Luc
LW – Cape-Breton Screaming Eagles (QMJHL) – 6'1" 180

Dubois was selected 5th overall in last year QMJHL draft by the Screaming Eagles and made an immediate impact with the team this season. Dubois was one of the best rookies in the league and led all 16 years old with 45 points. He also took part of the U-18 world championship as an underager this past April and back in November he was in Sarnia for the U-17 hockey challenge. Dubois grew up around QMJHL arena as his dad has been coaching for the past 10 years around the league either as a head or assistant coach. It shows when you watch Dubois as he plays a mature game and does a lot of little things well on the ice that helped his adaptation to the QMJHL. His game took a big step this year and showed he deserved to be selected in the top 5 of last year midget draft. The Rimouski native is a up and coming power forward with good speed and loves to take the puck to the net. He can control the puck at high speed and has good vision and makes player around him better with nice passes. He has an excellent wrist shot with a quick release, this year we saw him more as a playmaker with the Screaming Eagles where he showed his ability to slow down the game but makes no question about it Dubois is a capable sniper. He's a smart player on the ice, can play different type of game whether it's a finesse or physical game. Next season big things will be expected out of Dubois as the Screaming Eagles continue to improve as a team and should be amongst the league top teams.

Durflinger, Jake
RW - Sioux City (USHL) 5'7" 180

Durflinger made the jump to the USHL this year after playing the previous season for the Corpus Christi IceRays of the North American Hockey League as a sixteen year old. While he has shown some offensive skills, and an ability to occasionally chip in on the scoresheet, Durflinger's biggest contribution to his team is the energy he brings to the bottom six. Although he is short in stature, he does not back down from anyone and plays with reckless abandon. Durflinger finished second in the USHL in penalty minutes at seventeen years old. Durflinger is currently not committed to a school and it is presumed he will be back in Sioux City next season.

Eliot, Mitch
RD - Muskegon (USHL) 5'11" 174

Eliot is a solid defensive defenseman that made an impact immediately to Muskegon's lineup this year. The Michigan St. commit is rock solid, and even in his first year in the league did not get outmuscled very often. He's very strong, and presumably will only get stronger as he gets older. He wasn't afraid to mix it up and drop the gloves as a '98 in his first year in the USHL either. Eliot doesn't exactly jump off at the ice at you but is just really solid in his own zone. As the season went on and he played with more confidence, the Muskegon coaching staff started to play him in more situations and gained more minutes. Eliot will be back in Muskegon next year before going to Michigan State in the fall of 2016.

Fabbro, Dante
RD – Penticton Vees (BCHL) - 6'1" 185

A talented puck handler along the blueline, Fabbro has exceptional lateral agility and puck handling skills at the point. Which allows him to make great plays under pressure. He is also great at finding open lanes, which he uses to direct passes to teammates or the puck onto the net. His abilities on the offensive end of the puck and on the power play more than speak for themselves. Fabbro has a great pass-shot bias. His hard slapshot and quickly released wrist shot are both excellent at getting to the net creating rebound and deflection opportunities. Fabbro has shown consistency with his accurate shot all year. He's almost a specialist in terms of his usefulness as a quarterback on the power play. Playing on the power-play, he is capable of making one-time passes and one-time shots that open shooting lanes and create opportunities for his teammates. If he continues playing this type of elevated offensive game from the back-end, his options should be fairly wide open for him in the years to come. With his high end hockey sense, Fabbro is an early favourite as one of the smarter players in this draft and has good upside for the 2016 NHL Entry Draft.

Fallstrom, William
LW – Djurgardens (SWE) – 5'10" 161

A right shooting forward, Fallstrom exudes confidence with the puck and has good composure for his age. He projects to become a strong skater and he shows creativity with the puck. Fallstrom has good passing ability, even if sometimes he rushes his passes. There are situations in the offensive zone when that helps him taking advantage of openings, but in the defensive zone he could be more careful. Not afraid to go into the corners and likes being in front of the net.

Logged a lot of minutes for Djurgarden's J18 and J20 in the playoffs as he works hard every shift and gets the puck on the net, whether by creating a play or taking shots. Fallstrom needs to learn to play more consistently in the defensive zone, but he shows potential in all areas of the game. When playing on the penalty kill he has been heavily relied upon in past viewings. He is verbally committed to play for the University of Minnesota and was drafted by the Omaha Lancers in the 2014 USHL Futures Draft.

Farmer, Ty
RD - Youngstown (USHL) 5'10" 178

He is smaller D-man that developed out of the St. Louis Jr. Blues program playing a rookie USHL season with Youngstown Phantoms this past season. He is athletic type who skates fairly well and what gets you liking Farmer is his defensive smarts. He isn't going to "wow" you in the offensive zone, yet he excels by breaking up plays. He has an active stick defensively and is not afraid to block shots. He keeps his game simple, steady, and makes the initial outlet. More size and strength would do wonders along with his poised processing. He will attend Michigan State after this upcoming season.

Felhaber, Tye
LC - Saginaw Spirit (OHL) 5'11" 182

Tye is a speedy skilled forward who was taken as Saginaw's first round pick in the 2014 OHL Priority Selection Draft. Felhaber is a very speedy forward with great skating ability and can weave through traffic with the puck. He showed both the ability to move the puck to his linemates as well as flash a powerful and dangerous shot. A timest he can try to do a little too much himself. His concern in Minor Midget was not utilizing his linemates and he started to drift back into that trend as this season went on. He will need to reel himself in at times and pick his spots wisely in order to reach his potential.

Quotable: "He reminded me of John McFarland a bit in his OHL draft year because he wouldn't move the puck enough when it was the smart play. I liked him a lot more in the Saginaw jersey than I did in AAA. I thought he had a solid rookie year and set himself up well entering his NHL Draft season." - Mark Edwards

Felixson, Oliver
LD – HIFK U18 (FIN) – 6'05" 214

Oliver is a big defenseman out of the HIFK program. He possesses good hockey sense and composure. Although he has a big frame, he is capable of rushing the puck at times, protecting the puck and carrying it into the offensive zone. He sees the ice well and has good patience with the puck allowing the play to open up for him.

His forward skating ability is good for his size, but his first few steps still need improvement. His backwards skating also leaves a bit to be desired. Oliver projects as a big, solid stay at home defender, but needs to start using his size to his advantage as he can get walked in one on one situations. He isn't an intimidating presence is the tough areas where he should be dominating as well.

Fitzpatrick, Evan
G - Sherbrooke Phoenix (QMJHL) - 6'4" 203

Fitzpatrick was the first goalie chosen in his QMJHL Draft year (4th overall) and was highly touted leading up to it. He would share duties and be mentored by 3 year veteran Alex Bureau who was traded from Cape Breton in the offseason of the previous year. He was eased into the season by his team staff but by December he was getting the bulk of the starts and that did not really slow down until playoff time, showing the confidence that Sherbrooke had in him. Fitzpatrick was used against teams of all strengths and saw many different situations in his rookie year. In Midget, Fitzpatrick was best when he used his combination of great size and athleticism to deny shooters of a solution and this carried into his junior rookie year. Fitzpatrick is technically sound and this season we saw a goalie that took the time to mature and adjust to faster and more accurate shots. There were times early in the season where he looked out of position and compensating, and then the next game he would make the adjustments and come back with an amazing outing. Over time, there was more consistency and more confidence in the net and he was rewarded with more starts as a result. On more than one occasion he would make a spectacular save leaving us wondering how he saw it. Fitzpatrick is great at taking away the bottom of the net and his glove hand is above average. His deflection control is great and a lot of pucks end up unplayable. With his team on the penalty kill he is attentive and always looking for the puck and sometimes coming up big with a save. If Fitzpatrick continues his development at this pace and finds a continued consistency in his game he will be held in high consideration in his draft year.

Forsmark, Filip
LW – Frolunda J18 (SWE) – 5'11" 154

Forsmark became a popular name in Sweden after he destroyed the competition at the 2013-2014 TV-Pucken youth tournament. This year he had a good season for Frolunda J18 as he led his team in goals and points. Forsmark likes to shoot the puck, which is a good thing because he has a good sense of when a scoring opportunity is forming and positions himself in the right spot.

His skating stride seems to have room for improvement, but he shows good agility and he likes to carry his speed around the offensive zone as he looks for opportunities. In transition at the junior level he is able to challenge defensemen one on one but likes to dish off the puck with quick backhands. He will need to work more consistently away from the puck if he wants to see more success at the next level, but he has the tools to do it.

Fortier, Maxime
RW - Halifax Mooseheads (QMJHL) - 5'10" 170

This was Fortier's first full season as a Moosehead but it was with much anticipation after last year call up just before Halifax's playoff run where he showed not only was worthy of his 2013 2nd round status, but also looking to make himself a lock in the roster. Fortier buzzed for 1 goal and 2 assists in just 5 games in the playoffs that year and returned this season ready to take a permanent spot on the team. Fortier was a fixture on Halifax's 2nd line most of the season and showed some great chemistry with overager Philippe Gadoury. Fortier is a skilled and speedy player able to gain the zone with ease and can give defenders fits with his quick entry and very good hands. Indeed some of his goals are a result of his great hand-eye coordination. There is sometimes a shoot first mentality, but really he does use his linemates well when opportunity arises and is able also to use all of the ice, sometimes placing pucks in good retrieval area for linemates when a direct pass is not available, showing he has an excellent IQ in the offensive zone. With 9 goals and 21 assists in 63 games this year, Fortier ranked 20th amongst rookies in scoring, and in the playoffs he was good for 4 goals and 5 assists in 10 games. Defensively Fortier is a bit of a work in progress, we find that his anxiety to be the first guy back isn't as high as it should be in certain situations. But he has a very good overall work ethic across the ice and that coupled with his high skill set serves him well in most defensive situations and when used on the PK he understands where to be and is great at getting to his man quickly and forcing the puck. There is not a sense that he tries too much in his own end and will quickly move the puck up to his best option. Fortier sometimes shows a little lack of strength on his skates in some battles not uncommon for young prospects. Fortier is an interesting prospect to watch as he has excellent high end speed and skill and with a late birthday which makes him eligible for the 2016 NHL draft.

Fox, Adam
RD - USNTDP U17 5'10" 167

Like teammate Chad Krys he is a smooth wheeling offensive defenseman who likes to make plays from the back end by leading the rush or quarterbacking the power play. He is not gifted in size and doesn't play overly physical. He shows good offensive know-how as he sees the ice well and threads tape-to-tape passes. His defensive game is a work in progress so a few years at Harvard will certainly help round out his game.

Frederic, Trent
LC - USNTDP U17 6'2" 192

He is another upcoming product from the St. Louis, MO area. His size is continuing to grow and with that he likes to play the power forward game by taking the puck to the net, grinding out some goals.

He competes hard in all 3-zones, shows some good offensive instincts with his playmaking abilities while seeing the ice. He did not have an overly productive season so this will be interesting year on which direction Frederic takes before moving onto Wisconsin (Big 10).

Gauthier, Julien
RW – Val D'Or Foreurs (QMJHL) – 6'4" 221

Gauthier is a late 97 birthdays which makes him only eligible for the 2016 NHL draft, the Montreal native was the 6th overall pick in the 2013 QMJHL draft. Gauthier is a rare power forward from the province of Quebec, he already has NHL size and strength. Gauthier exploded offensively this season after a solid rookie season in 2013-2014, this year the sophomore forward came close of scoring 40 goals and had another extended playoff run with the Foreurs losing to Rimouski in the league semi-finals. Last year he gained a ton of experience during the season and playing all the way to the memorial cup with his team and it showed this year. He was more confident with the puck, holding on the puck longer and slowing down the play to his pace. Even if Gauthier is already a huge kid he's very good skater with good explosiveness, he has a nice burst of speed that he can use to beat defensemen wide. He's at his best when he play an aggressive style of hockey, with his frame he's excellent in puck protection situations shielding his opponent away with his back In the offensive zone and also makes good use of his long reach. Consistency is an issue with Gauthier, doesn't always play an all-out game and is not always involved like he should. He has a great wrist shot with a quick release but his hockey sense is just average, does a lot of damage in the QMJHL due to his pure strength and skill level.

Getson, Keith
LW - Charlottetown Islanders (QMJHL) - 5'11" 185

Chosen in the 3rd round of last year QMJHL Draft, Getson was coming into this season looking to recoup some of that offensive magic that made him an incredible Bantam prospect. He shared rotation on the fourth line with Balmas and Guilbault, and managed to get 56 games in and notched 1 goal and 9 assists in that time. He was used sparingly, his minutes reduced to the 4-7 range but he was given some special team time, especially some PK time. Getson had a role to play this season - to be a great forechecking winger. He still appears strong on his skates as he did in midget and as the year progressed it appeared he improved his strength and was winning more and more battles. There was really a sense he was playing with grit on every shift and we often described him as a blue collar hard working player. This is a welcome improvement and a continuation of what we saw last year in Midget as he continues to understand the importance of working well both with and without the puck and in both ends of the ice. We can only think that his coaches were happy with his execution and we are looking forward to next season to see what he could bring if he was given more offensive responsibility.

Gettinger, Tim
LW - Sault Ste. Marie Greyhounds (OHL) 6'05" 202

Gettinger was in and out of the line-up for the stacked Greyhounds this season but did well when he was able to get on the ice. He primarily played a bottom six role when he did but he showed the ability to use his size and drive the net hard. He has good positional awareness and knows how to get open with a good shot. He has the size and can be an intimidating player against the wall. Gettinger will need to improve on his skating in order to reach his potential and should be an everyday player with good ice for the Hounds next season.

Girard, Samuel
LD - Shawinigan Cataractes (QMJHL) - 5'9" 155

Girard was the 3rd overall pick in the 2014 QMJHL draft and showed why this season with a terrific rookie season with the Shawinigan Cataractes. It didn't take long for him to start quarterbacking team power play at the beginning of the season and did a great job at it all year long. Girard is an undersized defenseman who possesses high end skating abilities; he has great top speed and excellent agility. He loves to carry the puck out of his zone and can get past defender with ease, sometime he can try to do too much but as the season went on he did a good job playing a safer game. He has an excellent vision on the ice, very good at creating plays with his feet and quick to find his teammate on the ice. He acts often as a 4th forward on the ice, jumping or following the rush. Girard adaptation to the QMJHL was very quick this season and this is due to his excellent hockey sense. He took part in last November at the U-17 hockey challenge in Sarnia. Defensively due to his lack of strength, he makes sure to play smart when defending as he's not strong enough along the wall or in front of the net. He has good body positioning with a good active stick. He makes good use of his great footwork to not get beat wide and keep pace with opposing forwards. He's a big weapon on the powerplay even if he doesn't have the biggest shot, his shot is accurate but lack velocity. He's a pass first type of player on the power play but with a bigger shot he could be even more dangerous on the man advantage.

Gleason, Benjamin
LD - London Knights (OHL) 5'11" 160

Caught behind some veterans on the Knights' Gleason got into the line-up two thirds of the time and some of that action was spent playing fourth line left wing in addition to his defensive positioning. A natural defender, Gleason has excellent puck rushing upside with strong skating ability and agility to evade checkers. He moves the puck fairly well but will need to improve his defensive zone play and really needs to get stronger. At forward Gleason excelled with forecheck pressure using his speed to track down opponents.

Green, Luke
LD - Saint John Sea Dogs (QMJHL) - 6'0" 174

Drafted #1 overall in the 2014 QMJHL Entry Draft, Green was given the opportunity to start at 16 years old on a junior team that was on the rise and loaded with potential talent. Like almost every 16 years old that enters the league there were moment you could feel him adjusting to the speed and strength of the players, but by October you could see that he had started to make the small adjustments in his defensive game that were needed by him. Green is an elite skater and he continued to show a pro-ready athleticism in his stride and great poise and posture. It was obvious as the season advanced that he added strength and stamina to his skating and was hard to contain on the rush. Green has advanced puck handling ability and can do so with speed, however he used this ability a bit sparingly as he elected to move the puck quicker through the zones. He was given time on the power play and here you could see his confidence increase. He was able to find linemates with ease or he would elect to shoot if the lane was available. We felt he had confidence to quickly judge the best option available. The work in progress is always his defensive play although this did get better as the season waned and he is getting a bit better at picking his spots to pinch, although there were still times he left his partner in a bit of trouble. We wanted to see him force more battles and regain possession for his team as well. It's clear he is an offensive talent and we expect next year to be even better for him.

Greenway, James
LD - USNTDP U17 6'4" 204

He is a big body defenseman that likes to play the physical shut-down type. The hockey IQ is adequate and sometimes gets lost in own zone or tends to overplay the body though he can develop more poise in the coming year. He isn't a flashy offensive D-man but yet a tough opposing blue liner that makes life hard on opponents. He is uncommitted at the point.

Gregoire, Thomas
RD – Sherbrooke Phoenix (QMJHL) – 5'11" 152

Gregoire was the 16th overall selection in the 2014 QMJHL draft after playing for Magog in the Quebec Midget AAA league. Thomas is the younger brother of Jeremy of the Baie-Comeau Drakkar and also a prospect for the Montreal Canadiens. Thomas made the phoenix out of training camp and played a regular role with them all year and also took part at the U-17 hockey challenge in November. Gregoire is a good puck moving defensemen with a good hockey sense, he makes precise passes to his teammate and gets the puck out of his zone quickly. He has good poised as he's able to wait an extra second to move the puck for a teammate. He has potential as power play quarterback, didn't played a ton this year on the power play due to Jeremy Roy and Carl Neil in front of him on the depth chart. He doesn't possess a big shot from the point but has good accuracy and gets puck on net on a regular basis. We like his compete level, even at his size he doesn't backdown from anyone in the corners or in front of the net. He still needs to add mass to his frame to compete at a higher level but he has the right mindset.

Grundstrom, Carl
LW – MODO (SHL) – 5'11" 190

A late '97, Grundstrom managed to spend a good
of upside already receiving individual recognition at the TV-Pucken and U17 tournaments. Gustavsson has the size, talent and projectability to be one of the top goaltenders at the 2016 NHL chunk of the season in the SHL playing for Modo. It was an easier feat than it would have been on other SHL teams, but it was impressive to see how Carl could already hold his own against men at a top level. Something that surely helped him is his thick frame, as he is already able to absorb hits and compete in traffic. What makes him an impressive prospect is the agility he brings together with his powerful game.

Grundstrom can make plays at high speed and combine with his linemates, processing the play quickly enough to take advantage of his qualities. His distinctive trait, especially for a European prospect, is where he is able to go with and without the puck. The lanes he chooses are the ones that lead faster and more effectively to the net. He attacks the net with speed without the puck almost systematically, his style of play projects flawlessly at any level and perfectly fits the NHL game.

Gustavsson, Filip
G – Luela J18 (SWE) – 6'02" 172

Gustavsson took over the starting job at the World Under 17 Challenge with a series of excellent performances. Splitting the season between the J18 and J20 teams, Gustavsson was called up to the SHL at only 16 years old, however he did not appear in any game action. He has good height and a very solid frame, which really allows him to take up a lot of the net. There's really no excess movement to Gustavsson. His positioning is very tight and on the occasions where he does make a scrambling save he's quick to reset his positioning. Despite the size and the calm demeanor, Gustavsson has excellent reflexes, capable of highlight reel saves, especially with the glove hand.

Filip is always in ideal positioning on the initial shot. He does need to work on how many rebounds he gives up but he is extremely composed and quick to stop any second chance opportunities that may come his way. He has a tremendous amount Entry Draft.

Hajek, Libor
LD – Kometa Brno (CZE) – 6'01" 196

Hajek is a Czech defenseman that brings an enticing blend of qualities to the table. More of a mobile defensive defenseman than a two-way puck mover, he actually shows the tools to be able to add more consistent contribution in transition during the season that will lead to his draft. Hajek is a strong skater with pro-ready size who compete really hard in his zone. His efforts are consistent and he is a tough customer along the boards.

What makes his solid and powerful defensive game even more effective is how fast he can move the puck away from forwards once he gets possession, often killing opponents' hopes to establish sustained pressure. Libor can get caught in the neutral zone because of his aggressiveness or be at fault for the odd turnover, but he safely projects as a future NHLer.

Hanson, Bo
LD - Muskegon (USHL) 6'2" 190

Hanson was the other half of the Muskegon 2016 Draft eligible defensive pairing along with Mitch Eliot. Hanson plays a similar game to his partner as well, playing a very solid game in his own zone. He's strong on his skates, skating with a strong, wide base and doesn't lose many one-on-one battles. In addition to his skills in the defensive end, Hanson showed some good offensive thoughts throughout the season and showed some potential to grow into a very solid two-way defenseman. Hanson is still uncommitted to a NCAA school, and it is unclear at this point whether he will return to Muskegon next season or possibly join the Red Deer Rebels who hold his WHL rights.

Hart, Carter
LG – Everett Silvertips (WHL) – 6'00" 165

Carter Hart began the 2014-2015 season as one of the lesser-known goalies eligible for the 2016 NHL Entry Draft, but is quickly becoming a fixture in net with the Silvertips, overtaking the starter job from Austin Lotz several times in his 2014-2015 campaign. His game is simple and his keys to success are easy to comprehend: he's big, he's positionally solid and he's got great reflexes.

One of the most attractive qualities of the 6-foot 165-pound Carter Hart, is that he'll almost certainly continue growing and having been born in late-1998, he'll be one of the youngest goalies available on the draft board next June. His he drops down into the butterfly unusually fast. He is very quick and technically strong, which allows Hart to quickly cover the bottom of the net on one-time opportunities or cross-crease plays. He also had a very strong playoff performance for such a young player playing in several close and multi overtime games. Hart may have been a little unknown going into this season, but he has quickly shown that he has the potential to be one of the first goaltenders taken at the 2016 NHL Entry Draft.

Harvey, Samuel
G – Rouyn-Noranda Huskies (QMJHL) – 6'0" 190

Harvey was the 2nd goaltender drafted in the QMJHL draft last season and was chosen 39th overall by the Huskies. Harvey made the Huskies out of training camp and was put in a three goalies rotation to begin with but eventually got his share of starts and end up playing in 32 games for

Rouyn-Noranda. He shared the work load with 2015 draft eligible Jeremy Belisle but next season he should challenge to be the no-1 man. Harvey is not the biggest goaltender and will need to learn how to make himself look bigger in net, in our viewing this year he did look small in his crease playing too deep. Harvey is a very calm goaltender, doesn't get rattled by much on the ice and keep his composure well even when things don't go his way. He covers the lower part of the net well with his pads, he's able to track the puck well even with traffic in front of him. He's not the most athletic goaltender but has strong positioning in his crease and doesn't make unnecessary movements. He will need to play better with the puck, as he prefer staying in his crease most of the time.

Hawerchuk, Ben
LW - Barrie Colts (OHL) 5'10" 157

Ben, the son of head coach Dale, cracked the line-up as a 16 year old and played a very high energy role on the Colts' fourth line. Hawerchuk showed early on that he belonged. He had a high pressured forecheck and a great compete level. He lands some pretty hard hits considering his size and is willing to take the body, or sacrifice it in order to make the play. He doesn't have high offensive upside but he did show flashes of puck intelligence and offensive creativity. While he isn't a bad skater, we would like to see him become more explosive for him to move up the ladder at his size. He will also need to get stronger in order to maximize his potential.

Quotable: "I was really impressed with his progression this season. He earned his minutes and didn't need his father as coach to get icetime." - Mark Edwards

Hellickson, Matthew
RD - USNTDP U17 5'11" 171

Hellickson is defenseman you don't hear a lot of hype about though he just goes his business. He is a tad under the 6-foot mark though skates and handles the puck with great confidence. He makes good puck decisions and one attribute is that he sees the ice well both with and without the puck. This allows him to spring players with stretch passes and play an honorable game from the back end. He will matriculate into Notre Dame (Hockey East) after next season.

Hotchkiss, Matthew
LC - Guelph Storm (OHL) 6'01" 195

Hotchkiss was the 2014 OHL Champions' first round pick in the OHL Priority Selection Draft and despite some graduates, the Storm had a lot of players return relegating Hotchkiss to a depth role on the team. He has size and can finish his checks effectively in the corners. He kept it simple this year getting pucks deep and grinding it out. He showed some flashes of his puck skills and has a strong shot. He will need to improve his skating leading into next season to reach his potential.

Howdeshell, Keeghan
LC - USNTDP U17 6'0" 192

He is a decent sized forward developing out of Detroit with the Compuware program and now at the NTDP in Ann Arbor. His offensive game and thoughts are average although he takes care of his own end and likes to show the physical side in his game. He is off to Ferris State in 2016-17 season.

Hylland, Tyler
C/LW/RW – Blainville-Boisbriand Armada (QMJHL) – 5'9" 173

Hylland was one of favorite in last year QMJHL draft not due for his high end skills but for his work ethic and speed. He was drafted 33rd overall by the Armada and made the club out of training camp. Hylland also played at the U17 hockey challenge in Sarnia and with the Armada was a regular but also saw times in the stand rotating with the two other 16 years old rookie on the team. He's a versatile forward as he can play all three forward position, we like him on the wing more as he can use his speed better this way. He has great top speed and can reach his top speed in 3 steps. His speed and anticipation makes him a top notch penalty killer, he didn't play consistently there this year due to his inexperience but he was one of the best in midget AAA in 2013-2014. He's also a threat to score shorthanded as he's very quick to jump on lose puck and can get behind defensemen with ease. He has a good puck pursuit on the forecheck, he lacks ideal size right now and will need to get stronger physically. He's smart player with good positioning at both end of the ice that help him be more efficient. Next season he should be a regular on the Armada top 3 line and with time on both special teams. Hylland fits very well with the Armada with his work ethic, speed and two way game, he should be a favorite of head coach & GM Joel Bouchard next season

Jones, Max
LW – London Knights 6'2" 189

Many scouts like Jones because he plays tenacious with a high compete level. The likes the puck on his stick to score and plays a determined game with edge too. He just recently signed in the OHL with the London Knights. There isn't much that stops him as he will drive the puck hard to the net and also release a hard snap or wrist shot. He plays strong-minded game and with decent skills, offensive power, and grittiness too. His vision is adequate although he seems to miss some opportunities because he doesn't see the play develop or plainly just wants it himself. Many scouts will be following his path in the OHL this upcoming season.

Jost, Tyson
RW – Penticton Vees (BCHL) - 6'00" 194

Jost played a big role on a Penticton Vees club that for all intensive purposes dominated the BCHL this season. Jost is a quick-footed, free spirited and highly instinctual forward with fantastic toughness and a deadly scoring touch from the slot. The 2013 first-round bantam draft selection of the Everett Silvertips typically plays an honest and hard-working game. He is a very fast skater who usually moves up and down the ice in diagonal streaks of ferocious effort. Indeed, Tyson excels on the dump-and-chase because he's a strong hitter and wins most of his board battles. His creativity and passing skills are some of his best attributes and qualities. He scored nearly a point-per-game in his rookie year in the BCHL.

Jost loves to drive the net with his combination of speed ad puck skills. He also possesses a powerful shot. Tyson is agile and creative allowing him to make those around him better. He is very hard to knock off the puck once he takes control. Whether he goes to the highly ranked Everett Silvertips, or he continues dominating the BCHL with the Penticton Vees, expect Tyson Jost to receive serious attention at the 2016 NHL Entry Draft.

Juolevi, Olli
LD – Jokerit U20 (FIN) – 6'02" 185

Olli is a big, well rounded defenseman who doesn't have any glaring weaknesses. He has tremendous vision, making intelligent puck decisions on a regular basis. He has a good shot from the point and regularly gets it on goal through traffic. Olli has a great combination of size and skating ability, which he utilizes in both directions.

He shows good calm under pressure and wins battles in the corners utilizing his size and intelligence to come away with the puck. Juolevi has great potential going into the 2016 NHL Entry Draft and is a player who performed very well in all game situations.

Kalyayev, Maxim
G – Ibris Kazan (MHL) – 5'10" 181

Kalyayev had a respectable season spending the year with Ibris Kazan along with a trip to the World Under 17 Challenge. He split the starting job for Russia, getting the gold medal win for his team. Kalyayev doesn't give up much in terms of rebound. He plays a very scramble style of game but always finds a way to get in front of shots and consume them. He has good reflexes and is capable of making some highlight reel saves.

With all his athleticism and focus, he has his rough moments and will occasionally give up a goal that is simply unbecoming of his talent level. He moves well side to side but when the crease gets busy his size impacts him and he struggles to see through traffic. His biggest concern moving forward is his size as he's a few inches short of the ideal size for a goaltender. He will be an interesting player to watch, leading into the 2016 NHL Entry Draft.

Katerinakis, Alexander
LW – Blainville-Boisbriand Armada (QMJHL) – 5'10" 167

Katerinakis was drafted 11th overall in the 2014 QMJHL draft out of the Laval-Montreal midget program. In his first season Katerinakis played in 44 games and scored 3 times, he had a bit of hard time adjusting to the QMJHL in the first half of the season. He's an offensive player but didn't get to play in offensive opportunities as much and not scoring had some effect on his confidence. He has strong lower body and does a good job along the wall protecting the puck & winning puck battle. He's not afraid to play a physical brand of hockey as well. He can play on both wing, he's at his best when he plays with a playmaking centerman that can set him up in the offensive zone. He's a shoot first type of forward with a good scoring touch around the net and possesses a good wrist shot. He should be a lot more successful next season with more ice time and confidence in his 2nd season and extra ice time on the power play. He's a decent skater with good agility but still lacks that top gear to create separation. Defensively he learned this year that he needs to be good in his own zone to play for the Armada, in midget had tendency to stop moving his feet in the defensive zone.

Keller, Clayton
LC – USNTDP U17 5'10" 170

His hockey IQ is off the charts and he sees the ice so well. He knows when he can slash, drive to the net himself or makes a pass through the seam look easy. He is a very gifted offensive player and he shows it whether playing against older opponents or age appropriate. He skates very well as quite agile on his skates and handles the puck with ease and confidence. He put up very impressive numbers while a Shattuck and again this past season at NTDP-17 as well as fitting in quite well with the U18s. He is definitely high on the radar for the 2016 NHL Draft as slick stick skills, quick release shot, and just natural offensive instincts you can not teach. You like his unpredictable play with the puck on his stick as can beat his opponents in a variety of ways as he likes to dictate the pace of play. The downside in his game is that he will of course need to add muscle and physical as he is undersized at this point. Keller defensive play isn't bad although for the next level he will need to make more of a commitment in developing. He is supposedly off to Boston University after the draft although the Windsor Spitfires will court the high-end talent for sure.

Kilgour, Jack
LW - Kitchener Rangers (OHL) 6'02" 190

Kilgour was signed mid-season by the Kitchener Rangers after previously playing for the Strathroy Jr. B Rockets. Kilgour plays a very simplified game and was put in a very simplified role for the Rangers. Kilgour is a strong skater for his size and commonly put the puck deep and chased it. He hits hard and can be a very tough player on the forecheck putting pressure on opposing forwards. Kilgour didn't show much offensive upside this past season so the potential of an extended role with the Rangers could allow him to show a little more aside to his hard hitting forechecking game.

Kirwan, Luke
LW - Windsor Spitfires (OHL) 6'02" 213

Kirwan entered the season with a lot of potential but really struggled to get things going with any kind of consistency this season. He has excellent power forward size and protects the puck extremely well. He has a good shot and decent playmaking abilities. He is capable of getting it done in the corners but will need to further improve upon his skating as it isn't quite where it needs to be right now. We would like to see Kirwan take his game up a notch before being confident that he can be one of the top players out of the OHL for the 2016 NHL Entry Draft.

Kluuskeri, Jan
RD – Lukko U18 (FIN) – 5'09" 159

Kluuskeri is an undersized but smooth skating defenseman. He has excellent mobility from the back end and rushes the puck effectively. He walks the line well on the point with the puck and keeps his feet moving without the puck to make himself an available passing option. He has some effective offensive tools that helped him produce a little offense for his team this season

His hockey sense isn't the greatest, which can lead to mental errors with the puck, more frequently occuring the further away he is from the offensive zone. He has the speed to handle other smaller players one on one, but struggled against bigger forwards. He does have a bit of a tendency to take a bad penalty when he gets beat. Jan has some upside but has a long way to go to reach his potential.

Knierim, Willie
RW - Dubuque (USHL) 6'3" 205

He is a tough hard-nosed winger with good size that is almost like a bowl in a china shop. He plays the north-south game with physical side and hard shot or driving puck to the net. The downfall in his game is the stride as not really agile on edges and quickness will need to improve moving forward. He shows good offensive instincts, smarts, and game with grit and finish. There is some nice potential in his game. Knierim is headed to Miami (NCHC).

Krassey, Evan
RW - Niagara Ice Dogs (OHL) 6'03" 194

Despite being an 8th round pick in the 2014 OHL Priority Selection Draft, Krassey played a handful of games for the Niagara Ice Dogs. He spent the majority of the season with the St. Mary's Jr. B Lincolns. Krassey won't put up much offensively but he will strike fear in the opposition. Krassey has never seen a hit he hasn't liked and hits opponents like a truck despite only being 16. He is built solid and loves to run over opponents. He dropped the gloves against veteran players 3-5 years older than him in Jr. B and at times absolutely destroyed them. Krassey is effective on the forecheck and seems to understand his role well which has allowed him to be successful. Krassey will need to improve upon his skating but we expect to see him in the OHL next season and opponents will be keeping an eye out for when he is on the ice.

Krys, Chad
LD - USNTDP U17 5'11" 182

Krys has the rare combination among young defenseman of incredible poise and calmness with the puck which speaks to his high hockey IQ and ability to think the game quickly. Krys rarely threw the puck away in our viewings, he will either make the right play to relieve pressure or use his excellent skating ability to elude the pressure and push the puck up ice. He provides puck support for his defensive partner well. Krys can create end to end rushes by himself and has great instincts with the puck once he enters the offensive zone.

Chad does his best work running the power play at the point. He moves the puck quickly and puts passes on the tape consistently. He is great at using his skating and puck skills to move along the blue line with his head up at all times to create time and space. Krys sets the table very well as his vision is certainly above average as well as his hockey IQ. He is a very smooth operator at the blue line from starting the rush, outlet to wheeling the puck in the offensive zone or finding the open teammate for the score.

Krys isn't overly physical in the corners or in front of his own net and can be out muscled at times, however he uses his agility to get out of trouble when it's needed. Getting a stronger base and playing with a bit more grit are things he will need to continue to work on. His shot is pretty good although with added muscle he will be able to add more zing from the point regularly. His combination of skating and decision making could have him in the running with Sean Day (Mississauga Steelheads-OHL) and Jakob Chychrun (Sarnia Sting-OHL) as the best defenseman available in the 2016 draft.
Chad Krys is currently still uncommitted as far as the NCAA is concerned however the Moncton Wildcats own his QMJHL rights.

Kryski, Jake
RW – Kamloops Blazers (WHL) - 5'11" 186

Jake Kryski is a highly talented and speedy forward who played as a rookie this year with the Kamloops Blazers. Jake possesses a tremendous combination of straight-ahead speed and agility. He was utilized mostly this season to play a north-south, get the puck deep style of play, but he was willing to carry the puck over the blueline and make something happen. Not particularly big, he has a willingness to play physical. He finishes most of his checks and he does a good job of winning body position in board battles. He keeps himself highly active in terms of his work along the boards and is able to manufacture a lot of turnovers in all three zones.

Kryski's best work is in the offensive zone, as he shows nice vision and a really tremendous shot. He's not afraid to take some punishment in order to cut into the slot or on his way to the goaltender. When he gets a little space and time, he can be very dangerous. Kryski will be an interesting prospect to watch on a much improved Kamloops Blazers team where he will be able to make a bigger impact next season leading into the 2016 NHL Entry Draft.

Kunin, Luke
RC - USNTDP U17 5'11" 187

He is another of the handful of NTDP-18 players that falls after the 9/15 cut off. He is decent size although he will still need to do some filling out at the NCAA level while at Wisconsin. He can score goals as shows good offenisve know-how and smarts in the zone. He can shoot the puck and although not high-end stick skills he is still pretty crafty.

Kuokkanen, Janne
LW – Karpat U20 (FIN) – 5'11" 170

Janne is a hard working forward for the Karpat U20 team in Finland. Janne competes in all three zones, winning battles against players bigger than him. He is an excellent backchecker but is also very quick to transition into the offensive game. He possesses good speed and showed good hockey sense with the puck on his stick. He is much more of a passer than a shooter and displays skilled playmaking ability.

Kuokkanen showed patience with the puck on his stick and won't force a play that isn't there. He has a hard, powerful wrist shot but opts to look for the passing option whenever possible. Kuokkanen will need to get stronger and learn when to shoot and when to pass instead of relying on the latter most of the time.

Kyrou, Jordan
RW - Sarnia Sting (OHL) 5'11" 169

Kyrou was the second round pick for the Sarnia Sting and he received every opportunity to succeed and took advantage of it. Kyrou is a strong skater who weaves through traffic. He also has high-end hands that allow him to control the puck extremely well. Kyrou showed good ability to beat the goaltender but also set up his teammates. He possesses the puck well and shows patience with the puck and won't force a pass allowing things to open up.

There were moments where Kyrou's patience was a little too much of a good thing because there were occasions where he tried to do everything himself, resulting in a turnover and the play going the other way. He will need to get stronger to reach his potential leading into next season.

Laberge, Pascal
C/RW – Victoriaville Tigres (QMJHL) – 6'1" 160

Laberge was the 2nd overall pick in the 2014 QMJHL draft by the Gatineau Olympiques, after playing the first half of the year with the Olympiques he was surprisingly traded to Victoriaville at the QMJHL trade period. He had some issue in his first season adjusting to QMJHL and some health issues. In Victoraville he joined his midget team coach Bruce Richardsson and look to take step in his development and getting more ice time on a rebuilding Tigres squad. Laberge is capable of playing either on the wing or in the middle, he's a tall and lanky forward who has good wheels and is dangerous when he can skate freely in the neutral zone which makes him tough to handle for opposing defensemen when he's rushing the puck with speed. He has a great shot with excellent release; he's a threat in the offensive zone when he has the puck on his stick. He makes good use of his reach and size in puck protection situation to shield opponent away. He's dangerous on the power play, he has good puck skills, poise and vision. One of Laberge issue is his inconsistency; he has trouble playing a consistent game from game to game and disappeared from a long stretch of time. He still needs to add some mass to his frame, by doing that he would be more efficient in puck battle. He will never be known for his physical game but he could compete better along the board and versus physically stronger players.

Laine, Patrik
RW – LeKi (FIN) – 6'04" 209

Laine has pro size already as a 16 year old and high end goal scoring upside. Patrik's is a shoot first type of player who has a rocket of a shot. He is very dangerous whenever he gets into high percentage areas. He has great offensive skills and is able to create offense on a regular basis. After opening the season with Tappara in the top men's league, he was loaned to LeKi of the Mestis (2nd men's league) where he performed very well. He is also an effective puck handler and can work around opponents, despite lacking in the skating department.

Patrik utilizes his big frame to protect the puck, but isn't very physical. He will sometimes try to do a little too much, which kills the play. He is also a little one dimensional and isn't a fan of the defensive side of the game. Laine's upside at the 2016 NHL Entry Draft is outstandingly high. However there still remains several concerns that need to be addressed, particularly his skating and his willingness to work in all three zones.

Lajoie, Max
LD – Swift Current Broncos (WHL) – 6'01" 182

Max Lajoie is an offensive defenceman who debuted as a rookie with the Swift Current Broncos in 2014/2015 and immediately turned heads with his natural skating ability and smart puck moving ability. Lajoie is already seeing time on the top pairing in Swift Current, benefiting from a protégé-type partnership with Columbus Blue Jackets draft pick Dillon Heatherington. The two also match up on the power play where Lajoie is more likely to pull the trigger than his more experienced partner. His wristshot was one of the easier ones for Jake DeBrusk to deflect into the net this year.

Lajoie really shines in the offensive zone. Once past the offensive blueline, he regularly shows off strong footwork, good passing and great shooting ability. We didn't notice his defensive game or physical presence too much, as his defensive partner was usually the more physically imposing defender. When coming out of his own zone, he prefers to either skate the puck to safety or to make the simple pass. Already with a ton of upside, Lajoie will be looking to make an impact heading into the 2016 NHL Entry Draft.

Latorella, Michael
G - Muskegon (USHL) 6'0" 188

He hasn't yet reached that prototypical NHL goalie size though is an athletic goaltender that moves pretty well in the crease. He shows solid techniques in squaring up to shooters, lateral movements, and limiting rebounds. He is slated to enter Ohio State as an 17-year old freshman although with the London Knights (OHL) owning his rights the summer could be interesting.

Lauzon, Felix
LC – Victoriaville Tigres (QMJHL) – 5'8" 177

Lauzon is a player we had ranked in the first round for last year QMJHL draft but eventually was picked 23rd overall by Victoriaville. The most well liked attribute of Lauzon game is his smarts, he's very good at both end of the ice and understand the game very well. Defensively he supports his defense well by coming back deep and helping them retrieving pucks along the wall. He's good in the faceoff circle and be used in key moments of the game. Offensively Lauzon sees the ice well and possesses an accurate wrist shot that give fits to opposing goaltenders. He's part of the rebuilding plan for the Victoriaville Tigres with Pascal Laberge and should be an important player as soon as next season for the Tigres. He's not the biggest forward but has good lower body, which help him in puck protection situations. But at 5'8" he already has a strikes against him with NHL scouts. His explosiveness will also need to be improve, he lacks a top gear that those small player needed to be successful at the NHL level.

Leonard, John
LC – Springfield Cathedral HS (MA) 5'10" 172

He is a very good forward with lots of offensive tools along with high competitive mid-set. He skates well as strong on his edges and has the ability to cut and turn with the puck to elude defenders. He has a nice natural scoring ability as his shot is certainly above-average as well as the ability and offensive instincts to slash to the net and finish in tight with his stick skills. It will be interesting if Leonard stays home in Massachusetts or opts for the prep or USHL route for the upcoming season before heading to UMass. He has lots of attributes you look for in the next level player.

Lindgren, Ryan
LD - USNTDP U17 5'11" 194

He is a solid, thick body D-man that is tough to play against. He is not overly tall yet has a good physical side to his game in effectively using the body. He skates pretty and moves the puck in transition. He possess a good shot from the point and that's where he gets a lot of his assists off as will create rebounds and re-directs from the blue line. He was tagged early as one of the top '98-born defenseman from Minnesota although not sure if the offensive confidence has grown with his game. It will be interesting how year two at NTDP plays out before he heads to University of Minnesota.

Lindstrom, Linus
LW – Skelleftea J20 (SWE) – 5'11" 157

Lindstrom is a versatile center coming off a a very good season in Sweden. He works hard at both ends of the ice and has a quick shot that he can get off in stride. Goes into high scoring areas, showing legit scoring instincts. He has a nose for the net and for finding opportune times to get there for scoring chances. When paired with a smart passing winger, Lindstrom loves to sneak back door.

An area Linus will need to focus on to improve moving forward is his skating, and his stride in particular; he doesn't get the maximum output and extends his legs out to the side. He also needs to get grittier along the wall, but it's fairly obvious he is still far from filling his frame and he lacks strength, something that should as well help to add some needed power to his skating.

Luce, Griffin
LD - USNTDP U17 6'3" 211

He is a pretty massive body at the blue line that is intimidating to opponents as he plays with physicality in the corners and in front of the net. He does has pretty good mobility and if he can develop his foot speed even more then many teams will be calling on his services. He will probably project as a nasty, shut-down D-man although he can show some offense every now in then as he can move the puck and will jump on the play. He can shoot the puck well from the point and could improve upon handling the puck as just adequate at this stage. He will make outlets and normally good puck decisions. He is headed to Michigan in 2016-17 and his father is Scott Luce, the Director of Scouting for the Florida Panthers.

Lundh, Gusten
G – Linkoping J18 (SWE) – 6'03" 165

Lundh spent the past season with the Linkoping J18 team. While he didn't see a ton of action he did well when get got into the crease. Lundh has good size taking up a lot of the net, but is still tough to beat low when he drops down into the butterfly. He can fight pucks off at times and needs to improve on his reflexes on top shelf shots when in his butterfly.

Gusten will also need to pick his spots when playing the puck as he's a little more active than you'd like to see a goaltender who lacks puck control ability. Gusten shows intriguing upside with his size and positional play but has room to improve leading into the 2016 NHL Entry Draft.

Maher, Jordan
RC - Acadie-Bathurst Titan (QMJHL) - 5'11" 165

Maher was an exciting Midget player that brought a full set of tools and a fantastic work ethic to the rink every time. Taken in the first round 6th overall, there was the usual adjustment period for this 16 years old in the early months. Maher was used in the Center position of the 3rd and 4th lines and also on the power play. In 60 games he recorded 13 goals and 16 assists. He tied with 4 other players in being recognized with the 'Most goals per game', recording a hat trick versus Charlottetown Jan 24th, 2015. Maher has an amazing work ethic and is always looking to improve. Watching him throughout the season it was clear that as he adjusted to the league he began to find the back of the net more and also his linemates. Maher is most deadly off the rush using his speed and agility to back up and beat defenders. He also has an incredible sense for knowing where his linemates are if he is down low working the puck. He shows good patience and very good puck control in tight spaces. He has a great wrister with a fast release. There were lots of scoring opportunities generated from his ability to control the puck and then get it to the net. Maher is not afraid of contact and appears strong on his skates, although he will have to continue to get stronger if he wants to advance. Next season we expect a bigger role to be placed on his shoulders for this young Titan player. He will have to continue to exhibit a high level of speed, skill and most importantly consistency to be highly ranked.

Mäkinen, Otto
LC – Tappara U 20 (FIN) – 6'01" 176

Makinen had a great season and showed excellent two-way prowess. He is reliable in all three zones and displayed good hockey sense. He was also outstanding in face-off's every single game, nearly going perfect in some. He doesn't have much of a mean streak, but he does get the job done in the corners and the gritty areas working hard for the puck.

While he doesn't have a lot of offensive upside, he is a slightly above average skater for his size and controls the puck well under pressure. He also showed some intriguing passing ability, but offensive creativity is usually few and far between. He has a good shot but will force it at times when he has no lane. He lacks first step explosiveness and his mobility could handle some improvements, but he possesses good speed once he gets moving. Makinen has some intriguing two-way upside and plays a very mature game for his age.

Maksimovich, Kyle
LW - Erie Otters (OHL) 5'07" 160

As a 16 year old on a stacked contender, Kyle looked like he may be set for a year in the OJHL before making the jump but he overcame his size and the odds and became a strong contributor for the Otters. Kyle is extremely small but speedy and he can be tough to contain with the puck on his stick.

He is creative in the offensive zone and can exploit holes in the defense. He will need to further improve his defensive game and hopefully get bigger and stronger in order to maximize his potential.

Malenstyn, Beck
LC – Calgary Hitmen (WHL) – 6'01" 187

Already 6-foot-1 and 180 pounds, Beck Malenstyn found his way onto the Calgary Hitmen lineup after posting a strong training camp performance. The 16th overall selection in the 2013 WHL Bantam Draft continued to earn his placement on the lineup through his consistent on-ice performance as the season wore on. Dependability on the defensive side of the puck and a series of other qualities that includes good skating speed, adequate size and a high degree of competitiveness. Only slightly above-average in terms of his skating ability, Malenstyn has made a name for himself by being a big body who is physically committed and strong on the puck.

Malenstyn posted 12 points in his rookie season with the Hitmen. With increased ice and a bigger role on the team, Malenstyn will look to improve those numbers and show why he's considered a prospect for the 2016 NHL Entry Draft.

Mascherin, Adam
LW - Kitchener Rangers (OHL) 5'09" 202

Mascherin was the second overall pick in the 2014 OHL Priority Selection Draft. The Rangers played him primarily in a second/third line role depending on the night, trying not to overwhelm him while giving him plenty of opportunity to succeed. Adam has a pro level shot and is very dangerous whenever in shooting areas. He's a decent skater who is built solid and protects the puck extremely well for someone his size. Mascherin has the upside of a first round prospect but will need to become more consistent with his dangerous offensive game and continue to find good scoring areas in the offensive zone. We will want to see improvement to his game on the defensive size of the puck.

Matthews, Auston
LC – USNTDP U18 6'2" 194

There is a lot to like about Matthews game and NHL teams have been watching the 2016 Draft eligible for a couple of years now. He posted quite impressive numbers at the NTDP-18 this past season though has been playing with older aged players for some time and has not looked a step off the pace and skill. Matthews plays a strong game at both ends of the rink. For a player that is an offensive thoroughbred he certainly takes care of his own zone as well. He is a very good skater with a strong stride, edge work, balance, and agility. He changes up speed and is very deceptive especially on the 1-on-1 situations. To go along with his speed he has excellent stick skills as strong on the puck and difficult for opponents to take puck away as physically strong and smart as well. He sees that ice with and without the puck. He makes the difficult passes look easy and isn't afraid to finish plays himself as he possesses that natural goal scoring ability with his shot selection or making crafty moves to finish in tight. He will take pucks to the net or unleash a very deadly shot. He is a very good, talented all-around player many NHL teams are drooling over.

He will bring many options in the pro ranks as he has the power in his stride, shot, and thought processing. Like Eichel before him, he is a generational player that plays the complete 200-foot game. He made USA WJC U20 team as an under ager and was relied upon in key situations. His future right now is unclear as whether he'll play in Europe or head north for the WHL ranks with Everett. Regardless, he is being tabbed as the clear cut #1 overall pick in 2016. Can't say we can argue with that.

Mattson, Mitchell
LC – Grand Rapids HS (MN) 6'3" 175

He is a lanky forward that when he fills out his frame should be eve more of a force out on the ice. He moves will and can handle the puck as well as showing nice offensive instincts with the puck. You really like the potential in his game and if he can develop that finishing touch around the net this season many will after his game just as North Dakota already has for the 2016-17 campaign.

McAvoy, Charlie
RD - USNTDP U18 6'0" 205

He would have been drafted fairly early in 2015 Draft although falls with that late '97 birth date. He is decent size though plays a solid all-around game. He is a smooth skater and covers the ice well defensively and uses his stick effectively to break plays up while positioning himself well. He makes good initial outlet passes, plays poised with the puck, and uses the body checking effectively too. You like lots of the tools and thoughts of his game. He is off to Boston University for his draft year and is projected as a top 15 pick in 2016 NHL Draft.

McGing, Hugh
F - Cedar Rapids (USHL) 5'8" 157

For all of his offensive skill, McGing's best attribute might be his character and compete level. McGing plays a lead by example style, even as one of the youngest players in the USHL. McGing's 11 goals and 8 assists as a 98 birth year in the USHL was nothing to sneeze at. Scoring three very impressive goals off the rush beating a number of defenseman one on one. Hugh has excellent skating ability that allows him to generate great speed through the neutral zone and push the pace up the ice. He doesn't shy away from going to the physical areas despite his size being far from overwhelming. McGing has terrific hands and can create plays in tight area's and off the rush but is at his best when he is competing and outworking the opponent. 2015/16 will be a key season in his development as he takes on a more prominent role with the Rough Riders and to see if he hits a growth spurt. McGing is committed to Western Michigan for 16/17.

McInnis, Luke
LD – Dexter School (MA) 5'11" 170

He has lots to offer as so much potential in his game as a natural skater who can both move the puck and wheel it up himself with confidence. He makes great outlet passes as he sees the ice so well. He is very poised with the puck at the back end. You can tell his dad spent some time in the NHL and passed the gene onto his son. Sure he needs to add some size and muscle as well as tight up the defensive gap control and winning physical battles along the boards though the offensive upside and hockey IQ is quite high. He is set to attend Boston College like his father Marty in a couple of seasons.

McLeod, Michael
RC - Mississauga Steelheads (OHL) 6'01" 184

McLeod was one of Mississauga's best offensive player this past season. He's an excellent skater who accelerates very quickly and has great top-end speed as well. He makes quick decisions with the puck and is a high paced player. McLeod is shifty, elusive and regularly uses stops/starts to lose defenders. McLeod is relentless after the puck and forces turnovers frequently as a result. He is a good stickhandler and can make people miss in space. McLeod sees the ice extremely well, possesses very good passing skills and has a very powerful release in his shot. He is defensively responsible, but is also a threat every time he steps on the ice. McLeod's upside is extremely high as one of the top prospects in the 2016 NHL Entry Draft, however like in Minor Midget the big concern with him is consistency and playing this high level game on a shift by shift and game by game basis. If he can do this the sky is the limit for McLeod.

McPhee, Graham
LW - USNTDP U17 5'11" 172

McPhee possesses a little bit of a physical edge to his game and can get under the skin of opponents; however, he also possesses some decent offensive skill and instincts. His vision and quick thinking allow him to thread passes through small passing lanes. McPhee is strong on his skates, does good work along the boards. He doesn't possess high end breakaway speed but gets around the ice well and has good skating fundamentals and footwork. Certainly a long term project for any team but does a lot of things well.

Graham is slated to play for Jerry York at Boston College in 16/17, the same coach his dad George McPhee played for at Bowling Green in the 1980's.

Mete, Victor
LD - London Knights (OHL) 5'10" 165

Victor was the first round pick of the Owen Sound Attack in the 2014 OHL Priority Selection Draft but would not report and was later dealt to the London Knights before the season. Mete was a little tentative early on, struggling with the defensive side of the game and he got away from playing his style of hockey. However, he really picked up his game and by the end of the playoffs he was arguably the most valuable defender on the Knights blueline at just 16 years old.

Mete has exceptional skating ability. It's at a level we don't see every season. He moves forwards, backwards and laterally extremely well, which not only helps him with his puck rushing ability but he uses it to open up options that re not available to most defenders. He has good offensive ability and moves the puck well. He is creative in the offensive zone and packs a powerful shot for a small player. Mete will need to get stronger and continue to improve on his defensive game to reach his potential. He has the rare chance to potentially play at the NHL level despite his small stature because he is elite in other facets of his game. We would be quite surprised if he was actually as tall as his listed height. He does have a strong stalky frame.

Quotable: "He's in my top 10 for next year if the draft was today." - NHL Scout

Quotable: "It was pretty ugly early on. Dale (Hunter) threw him right into the fire and gave him a ton of minutes and Victor struggled. Dale eventually pulled back the minutes until Mete got his feet wet. There was no looking back once the minutes increased again. Mete played lights out in all my viewings from January on. He was dominant at times." - Mark Edwards

Middleton, Keaton
LD - Saginaw Spirit (OHL) 6'05" 215

Middleton is the giant younger brother of Los Angeles Kings draft pick Jacob Middleton. Coming out of Minor Midget Keaton appeared to be a player who would have benefitted from a year at a lower level but he jumped into the fire for the Spirit. The experience gave him his share of successes and failures over the course of this season.

He has NHL level size and his strength is well beyond his age. He is a tough player to play against physically, finishing his hits and engaging down low. He can also be tough in the slot for opponents to face. His skating needs a ton of improvement as he struggled to get around the ice and it did sometimes result in him getting beat one on one. He has a heavy shot from the point but will also need to improve on his puck playing ability in all three zones. The potential is there for Middleton due to his size and shutdown upside, but he has a lot of work ahead of him as well.

Quotable: "He screams potential but he was far from great when I saw him this year." - NHL Scout

Mityakin, Evgeny
LC – Avto (MHL) – 6'03" 203

Mityakin is a versatile Russian forward with very good size. He has a long reach that he uses effectively on both sides of the puck. He takes advantage of his size to protect the puck and has shown the distinguish capability of keeping control of it in a far range, preventing the opponent from making contact with it. He has a fairly quick wrister, even if not always on target, along with some playmaking abilities.

Had 23 points in 34 MHL games during this past season on a low scoring team, decent numbers for a late '97 born, but what makes the package he brings more interesting is his defensive play in the neutral zone. He backchecks consistently and he is good at taking the puck away from opponents in the neutral zone or waiting for them skating backwards. The potential seems there, but Mityakin will need to get quicker in order to better perform in more intense games. That's probably why he has not been productive on the international stage so far. Mityakin also needs to improve in the faceoff circle in order to play as a center moving forward, probably the position that fits him better.

Moverare, Jacob
LD – HV 71 J20 (SWE) – 6'01" 185

Moverare possesses an impressive skill package. He has a good, solid frame that is balanced and hard to knock around. His footwork is well polished as he transitions backwards well and shuts down attackers. Shows good compete level from the back end and is willing to engage physically. Logs time on the powerplay and the penalty kill and his goaltenders must love him because of the number of shots he blocks.

He hasn't quite mastered the soft hands yet but his one-timer is getting better. Not afraid to jump up into the play when it is safe, he can make clever plays both on the offensive blueline and in the neutral zone. He is capable making a solid first pass up ice. His biggest attributes may be however his defensive abilities, he makes very good use of his stick, often taking away the puck from his peers. His skating will need some improvement for Jacob to reach his potential.

Nauss, Morgan
LD - Halifax Mooseheads (QMJHL) - 5'10" 173

Drafted in the 5th round of last seasons' QMJHL draft, Nauss will be remembered as the consensus boom pick of the draft. Nauss was coming of a great midget year and by seasons end was a top performing defenceman in the league on a championship winning team that eventually went to the Telus Cup. The Mooseheads relied heavily on this 16 years old early in the season when they ran into some injury problems but Nauss rose to the task and was a fixture on Halifax's second pairing and the PP unit. In the end, Nauss used his talents appropriately and put up 3 goals, 18 points in 54 games played. His season shelved for a month in the middle due to an upper body injury. Nauss is a great skating defenceman, possessing a strong, agile and natural stride. Additionally, he is extremely synergistic and it's clear when you watch him he really doesn't appear to have a weak side. He has very good vision out of his own end and can deliver accurate and hard passes through zones. He is a hard worker in his own end and can be tough to play 1 on 1. Size will be a concern going forward at the pro level, at the major junior level it shouldn't be an issue as he's quit strong for a 5'10" defenceman. He isn't the type of player to run around and crush things; he is going to beat you with smarts and skill. He can unwisely choose to pinch at times and this has given opponents chances on net. We like his confidence, but this would be an area that has to be improved defensively. Nauss hungers for the offensive opportunities and has a high desire to obtain and maintain the offensive zone. He has great lateral mobility and can walk the line and funnel pucks into the net with relative ease. He could easily have captained the power play all season and we expect his role to be expanded in the next years to include this as one of his primary roles. Nauss is a quiet leader who lets his play do the talking and we look forward to watching him next year.

Neveu, Jacob
RD – Rouyn-Noranda Huskies (QMJHL) – 6'2" 194
Neveu was the Huskies 1st pick in last year QMJHL draft 10th overall, the young defenseman is also from Rouyn-Noranda. Neveu is a big two-way defenseman who was physically mature at a young age coming through the minor hockey ranks. He jumps right into the QMJHL and didn't seem out of place, didn't do much offensively during the season but was solid in his own zone and was tough to play against along the wall and in the corners. He was not intimated at all making the jump to major junior this season from midget AAA. He's a solid player one on one, he has decent mobility and a good stick which makes him tough to beat. Neveu played a regular shit on the penalty killing unit and used his size well and also not afraid to block shots in front of his goaltender. He didn't show much offensively in his first season but Neveu has some potential there, he has an excellent one-timer from the point and a good first pass out of his zone. He's a strong skater and tough to knock down but his pivots still need work. Rouyn-Noranda has a young defense corps with the two Lauzon's, Phillipe Myers and Neveu, they should all keep getting better together in the next couple of years.

Niemeläinen, Markus
LD – HPK U20 (FIN) – 6'04" 183
Niemelainen is a big puck moving defender with great offensive instincts. He has a quick release shot that he uses when walking in from the point to surprise goaltenders. He is a little indecisive on pinches, half committing to the play putting him out of position, but not far enough to execute the pinch. He has great size, but is very slender and really needs to add muscle to his frame.

Markus is a bit risky in the netural zone because of his aggressive defensive style, attempting to pressure opponents into mistakes. However, some of the more talented players will exploit this and turn it into an odd man situation. He has great positioning in the defensive zone and uses his stick effectively. Markus is a bit of a raw defender right now, but does possess upside leading into the 2016 NHL Entry Draft.

Nother, Tyler
RD - London Knights (OHL) 6'03" 188
Nother spent the season adjusting to the speed of the OHL level and was able to play a little over half the season with the Knights. Tyler is a decent skater for his size but his stride is very awkward. He plays a physical shutdown role and can be a tough player to play against but he had some rough moments getting beat one on one. His puck play needs drastic improvements going into next season as he consistently made dangerous plays with the puck in his own end. He needs to focus on making

the simple safe play with the puck right now and then grow from there. He has a powerful shot but will force it from the point.

Nylander, Alexander
RW – AIK (SWE Jr.) – 5'10" 157

Brother of Toronto Maple Leafs' prospect William Nylander, Alexander is looking to make a name for himself as a top prospect at the 2016 NHL Entry Draft. Alexander debuted with AIK's men's team in the Allsvenskan league, but spent the majority of the season posting a point per game in the J20 league. Alexander has a great ability to use his skating to create extra time with the puck to allow a play to develop. But he also possesses the straight ahead speed to exploit a flat footed defender. He has the passing ability to make beautiful cross ice passes look easy. He also possesses the hands and shooting ability to deke out goaltenders and put the puck in the net himself. Much like his brother, he can get himself into trouble sometimes trying to do everything by himself.

Nylander generally comes up big in big games, saving his best performances for the most important times. While he sometimes neglects his defensive responsibilities, he has shown the knowledge and awareness to properly position himself in the defensive zone. He is not much for the physical game as he has a small frame and will pull up going into corners when he knows he's going to get hit. Nylander is a highly skilled forward with a little bit of risk, who has a great chance at being selected in the first round of the 2016 NHL Entry Draft.

Paquette, Christopher
RC - Niagara Ice Dogs (OHL) 6'01" 174

Paquette played a bottom six role for the Ice Dogs this season and did very well providing a strong forecheck. Paquette is a very good skater and utilized his feet to chase down pucks low in the zone. He was willing to take the body when necessary. Chris has some good offensive upside and protects the puck well when going to the net. Paquette was pretty quiet in a lot of our viewings just keeping it simple and getting the job done. He will look to take a bigger role next season in his draft year.

Parsons, Tyler
G - London Knights (OHL) 6'00" 171

Parsons was a free agent pickup for the London Knights from the Detroit Little Caesars program. He jumped right into the fire of the OHL and did extremely well. He look to be a bit on the small size in net but has lightning quick reflexes and excellent lower body movement. He also possesses an excellent glove hand and can steal goals away from opponents in highlight reel fashion. He beat out the older Giugovaz as the starting goaltender in the playoffs. Parsons is expected to be the starter going into his draft year and projects to be one of the goaltenders selected in the 2016 NHL Entry Draft.

Quotable: " He is a kid who battles. He has that stop the puck at all costs mentality. Played a lot of games in front of young D-core in his rookie season and came out looking good. That's a good start towards a strong showing in his NHL Draft year. Growing an inch or two wouldn't hurt him any. - Mark Edwards

Pastujov, Nick
LW - USNTDP U17 6'0" 194

He is a very intriguing forward and has been at the '98 USA age group for a few years as has impressed since the Honeybaked days. He shows high-end skills with the puck from the thought process to the puck handling, shot and skating. He has really nice offensive knack. He was one of the top scorers this past year with U17 NTDP and look for Pastujov to continue the upward trend before heading heading for to Michigan (Big 10).

Peeke, Andrew
RD – Selects Academy 6'0" 183

He is a blooming young D-man who skates well with his directional mobility, can handle the puck at the back end, and is growing nicely in size. He will play both ends of the ice hard as can play physical, block shots as well as getting puck to the net with a strong shot. He isn't dynamic offensively though is smart with the puck decisions and can run the power play just has a steady presence on the blue line. He is a Notre Dame recruit for 2016-17 season.

Pezzetta, Michael
RC - Sudbury Wolves (OHL) 6'01" 205

Pezzetta was the first round pick for the Sudbury Wolves in this past seasons' OHL Priority Selection Draft. He played a decent role for a 16 year old getting a fair amount of ice and showing what he's capable of. Pezzetta is a highly aggressive forward who loves to take the body. All game long he finishes his checks and is a very difficult player to play against. He can sometimes get a little over the top with his hits and will make contact with the head more often than he should. Despite his physical style of game and good size he's a pretty good skater and gets up and down the ice well. He has a powerful shot and decent offensive tools making him a threat on the scoreboard as well with the body. Michael will be an intriguing player to watch leading into the 2016 NHL Entry Draft.

Quotable: "His physical game projects well for the NHL. He also has the mentality of a Tom Wilson as far as taking the body, but he's not as big and not many can punish with their hits the way that Wilson did." - Mark Edwards

Picard, Miguel
LC – Blainville-Boisbriand Armada (QMJHL) – 6'0" 167

Picard was the Armada first choice in last year QMJHL draft (9th overall) In Sherbrooke. Picard had some issues adjusting to the QMJHL this season mainly with the speed of the game. He got better as the season went on but his speed should be an area where he works hard at it over the next couple of years. Picard is a sound two-way centerman who understand the game very well at both end of the ice. Already in his first season he was getting some defensive assignment from his coaching staff and playing on the PK at times. He supports his defense well in the defensive zone and he's good at retrieving pucks along the wall. He makes good use of his size to protect the puck along the wall. Offensively Picard does a good job keeping possession of the puck in the offensive zone with a good puck protection game. He's an above average playmaker, he sees the ice well and make quick decision with the puck. He's not afraid of the rough stuff and will take the puck to the net. He's not a flashy forward but very efficient at both end of the ice. It should be interesting to see him perform next season with the Armada with more responsibilities.

Pickard, Reilly
G - Acadie-Bathurst Titan (QMJHL) - 5'11" 184

A 2nd round pick of Baie Comeau, Both Pickard brothers would get moved at the trade deadline to the Titan where they finished up their seasons. Pickard was used sparingly in Baie Comeau getting just 8 starts and twice more for relief. In Bathurst he was used more and it was apparent from his play on both teams that he began to flourish after the trade and regained a lot of confidence. Pickard relies first on great positioning and puck awareness. By the end of the season it was clear that his conditioning and reflexes were developed and a good measure of consistency was observed game to game. His season stats perhaps gloss over how he improved as the season went on - With a 0.890 SV% and 3.67 GAA and averaging almost 34 shots per game, we feel that even with the pressure of being on the weakest team in the league that Pickard performed admirably having faced the second most shots per game overall and the most shots per game average for a regular starter. As much as we like Pickard from a technical standpoint it was the unexpected saves that elevate him a little more. We observed a few athletic and second effort saves that clearly showed why he was worthy of his 2nd round pick in last year QMJHL draft. Pickard was one of the goalies selected for Canada Black at the World-U17 Championship in November 2014.

Poirier, Zach
RC - North Bay Battalion (OHL) 5'11" 186

Poirier may not be the biggest player but he plays with a lot of heart. Poirier playing a depth role for the Battalion this season, he did a good job playing a high energy game. He is a tough player to play against and will get into the face of the opposition and look to get under their skin. He has a decent shot with a quick release which makes him a threat in the scoring area. We will be looking to see more offense out of Poirier in his second season with the graduation of several Battalion forwards and has decent upside leading into the 2016 NHL Entry Draft.

Pu, Cliff
RW - London Knights (OHL) 6'01" 178

Cliff was dealt from the Oshawa Generals in the trade that sent Mermis and McCarron over to the Oshawa Generals. Pu is a perimeter style offensive player who has good instincts and is capable of creating offense for himself and others but lacks consistency in this area. Due to his perimeter style it affects his ability to have a positive impact on the game when he isn't creating offense. Cliff has upside but will need to engage and be more aggressive in order to make the impact he is capable of making next season.

Quotable: " Early in his OHL Draft season I saw him as a potential top 5 pick. He slid down my OHL Draft rankings with each of my viewings that year and his rookie OHL season continued that sliding trend. I still think Pu has potential, but he needs to start pushing the play more and take some of the passiveness out of his game. He's not without skill" - Mark Edwards

Puljujärvi, Jesse
RW – Kärpät (FNL) – 6'03" 196

Puljujärvi is a high end offensive winger with great skating ability and quick hands. He has a ton of pure offensive ability who can create scoring chances at top speed. Jesse's first few steps are excellent despite his size. His puck handling skills are also very high end and can deke around opponents despite his big size. He has a powerful shot and a shoot first demeanor, but shows the ability to set up his linemates when he wants to.

Despite the high level of talent, he will make some mental mistakes, misreading the play and turning the puck over on a bad decision. He will sometimes pass when he should shoot, and shoot when he should pass. Puljujärvi is a forward with outstanding upside for the 2016 NHL Entry Draft, but does have his share of work ahead of him to reach his potential. He will need to make better decisions and become more interested in his two-way responsibilities to reach his potential.

Raaymakers, Joseph
G - Sault Ste. Marie Greyhounds (OHL) 6'01" 180

Raaymakers played his first OHL season as the back-up for the high powered Greyhounds and got in his share of games. He was inconsistent but got his feet wet and gained experience that will help him for his NHL Draft season.

He gets to the top of the crease and takes away angles well. However, it seems like once every game he will let at least one goal get by him that he should've stopped. He has decent recovery skills and has made some impressive saves on second and even third opportunities. He also possesses decent puck playing ability. He will need to get quicker and play with more consistency in order to limit the amount of soft goals he allows.

Quotable: "I saw the good, the bad and the ugly this season. He's talented but will need to show he can play multiple games without giving up the soft goals next year. He's young, I've seen many young goalies struggle with the soft goals issue before him. I'm not crossing him off my list just yet because I saw flashes of brilliance." - Mark Edwards

Raddysh, Taylor
RW - Erie Otters (OHL) 6'01" 198

Raddysh was the Erie Otters first round pick in the 2014 OHL Priority Selection Draft and had an excellent season with the 2015 Western Conference Champions. Taylor has good size but he skates well. He can fly through the neutral zone with the puck and despite his size he can be slippery around opposing players and evade them for scoring chances. He also understands how to get pucks deep and will chase them down delivering big hits to opponents. Raddysh also has a powerful shot. On top of all his offensive tools, he's also a good backchecker and responsible defensively.

Taylor played an array of roles for the Otters at different points this season and he has shown the ability to excel regardless of what he is asked to do. He has size, puck skills, a shot, skating ability and a physical edge, which should make him one of the top picks out of the OHL in the 2016 NHL Entry Draft.

Quotable: "Showed great improvement in his game from his last AAA game to his last game this year in Erie's long playoff run. He had some really strong performances in multiple viewings for me. Taylor was even better this year than I anticipated." - Mark Edwards

Reunanen, Tarmo
LD - TPS U20 (FIN) - 5'11" 163

Tarmo is a puck moving defender who possesses very good skating ability. His footwork is very quick, giving him great mobility and acceleration, but his top speed still has a fair amount of room for improvement. He has good vision accurately making the smart pass on a regular basis. He will usually take the high percentage option rather than forcing lower risk plays making him consistently effective with the puck. He has a cannon from the point and can blast his shot for goals. However he has a tendency of shooting high and quite often puts his one-timers over the net.

Defensively he has room for improvement. He is good positionally but struggles with processing the play while moving at speed. He skates well enough to keep up but pivots too late, or reacts too late to what the opposition is doing and gets burned. Reunanen has good upside but certainly has his share of improvements to make going forward. He is an intriguing prospect with good upside for the 2016 NHL Entry Draft.

Reynolds, Keenan
LW - Owen Sound Attack (OHL) 6'01" 199

Reynolds showed a ton of potential in Minor Midget but got off to a slow start to his OHL career. There was a possibility he would play big minutes in the CCHL this year, instead he played fourth line receiving very limited ice or was a healthy scratch for the Attack.

Reynolds has good size and is a very intelligent player who reads the play well and creates offense for his linemates. He has a powerful shot and is capable of battling for the puck. He is also a defensively responsible player and showed in his limited action he can contribute as an energy player as well as an offensive player. Reynolds will need to improve on his skating and will hopefully be given more opportunity this year as his upside is high but could be hurt by the limited playing time during important stretches of his development.

Rossini, Sam
LD - Waterloo (USHL) 6'2" 181

He is a solid blue liner as tough defender with good strength already. He isn't an offensive dynamo although he skates well and can handle the puck with a good shot. He is more of the reliable D-man that is poised with the puck in his own zone, makes a good first pass, and will chip in on the offensive side every now and then. He is staying in state and will attend University of Minnesota in fall of 2016.

Rubtsov, German
LC – Russkie Vityazi (MHL) – 6'01" 174

Rubtsov is the kind of dependable two-way center that is consistently relied upon by coaches to defend leads or going up against the top offensive lines. German possesses sound technique and can keep possession under pressure using his stickhandling work, but he really distinguishes himself for his defensive work on the defensive side of the puck. He will chase the puck and his opponent through the neutral zone until he gets them. On the powerplay he doesn't look very good yet, but he does look like a good all around player in the making.

Ruotsalainen, Arttu
LC – Kärpät J20 (FIN) – 5'08" 170

Arttu is an undersized but skilled playmaking centre for Karpat's Under 20 team. He has a late birthdate and performed in the IIHF U18 championships this season. Despite being undersized, Ruotsalainen is fearless in traffic and not afraid to mix it up with bigger opponents. He willingly goes into battles but loses a large percentage due to his lack of strength.

Arttu has good vision and likes to utilize his accurate shot when he has a lane. He is a good skater and handles the puck well at speed. His size is concerning, but Ruotsalainen will be an interesting prospect to watch for the 2016 NHL Entry Draft.

Rymsha, Drake
RC - London Knights (OHL) 5'11" 175

Drake made the Knights out of camp and really became a valuable player in their bottom six. Drake does well in face-offs and is a chippy two-way forward who will get into the face of the opposition every chance he gets. He hits hard despite not having great size and battles hard on the forecheck. He has a high compete level and is a real pest to play against in all three zones. In addition to this, he shows flashes of good offensive upside and showed he can score on occasion. Rymsha shows good potential as a low risk low reward type player that may show some offensive upside along with his defensive, physical style making him an intriguing prospect for the 2016 NHL Entry Draft.

Saigeon, Brandon
LC - Belleville Bulls (OHL) 6'01" 191

Brandon was the Belleville Bulls first round pick at the 2014 OHL Priority Selection Draft. Saigeon has good size and decent strength for a 16 year old forward. He is a skilled player who handles the puck well and can create offense. He also has a decent shot and has very good positioning in the offensive zone. His opportunity to post more points should improve next season with some Bulls moving on. Saigeon will have the opportunity to raise his draft stock while playing in his hometown of Hamilton. The Belleville Bulls moved and have become the Hamilton Bulldogs.

Salinitri, Anthony
LC - Sarnia Sting (OHL) 5'11" 170

Salinitri was the first round pick of the Sault Ste. Marie Greyhounds in the 2014 OHL Priority Selection Draft but was dealt to the Sarnia Sting at the trade deadline for Anthony DeAngelo. Salinitri is a good skater with speed and can carry the puck well. He displays good puck skills and hand/eye coordination. He also shows flashes of an effective forecheck. However despite his offensive ability and his forecheck Anthony is highly inconsistent with his effort and every shift is a new adventure. Strength and consistency will be key for Salinitri heading into next season.

Sanchez, James
RW - USNTDP U17 6'2" 182

He is a power forward type that uses hockey IQ and determination to be successful. He uses the big frame in protecting the puck and driving hard to the net. He will work the walls and corners to come up with the puck. The skating stride is adequate though if he improved on his first three strides his stock would improve dramatically. Not going to be a player that puts up big numbers though has the ability to develop a nice two-way game for the next level. He will head to the Big 10 and Michigan for 2016-17 season.

Sarthou, Evan
RG – Tri-City Americans (WHL) - 6'01" 170

American goaltender Evan Sarthou appears to be next in line on a Tri-City team with a strong reputation for developing goaltenders. Evan took over the starting job temporarily when Eric Comrie left for the World Juniors then subsequently suffered an injury. Sarthou did an excellent job filling into this role coming up with big performances, helping Tri-City earn a playoff spot. Evan lead the WHL in shutouts with 7 despite only appearing in 28 games.

One of the ways he compensated for talent disparity in Tri-City was to limit rebounds. His rebound control was, in fact, some of the best we saw out of his region in 2015. He's able to anticipate shots really well because he's an upright and swivel-headed goaltender who likes to scan the offensive zone as much as possible. His butterfly technique is just okay, as it could be a little tighter, but he keeps his upper-body upright and tracks shots really well when transitioning to the standing position and back down again. Redemption rather unexpectedly came at the end of Sarthou's season in the form of an invitation to play with Team USA. at the IIHF World Under-18 Hockey Championships in

Switzerland. Despite the USNTDP goaltender Luke Opilka ready to go, Sarthou took over the starting role, leading USA to a Gold Medal performance. Sarthou will look to take the next step in his career with Eric Comrie expected to graduate to the pros, leaving Evan as the go to guy in Tri-City leading into the 2016 NHL Entry Draft.

Sartoris, Matt
LD - Gatineau Olympiques (QMJHL) - 6'5" 190

One of the biggest players in the league, Sartoris was used in a shutdown role by his team and given opportunity sparingly on the last pairing. A very good skater for his size and age, he was placed in situations he was unaccustomed to as he has some offensive tendencies in his play. In his own end he seemed to have a bit of a mountain to climb as he tried to contain the play in the corners. We found he was frequently beat as he would overplay the puck carrier and then chase the pass. There wasn't a feeling he had a great active stick in the first couple of months, but as time went on he became much better with his gap control and timings and was using his reach to an advantage. We wanted to see him explode out of his own end using his size and skating ability but he was pinned in frequently. He can have a physical edge at times but it's not as often as we would like. He suffered a broken leg and missed a substantial amount of the season - from Jan 10th to Feb 28th. When he returned he was placed back into the lineup but was only used in 2 playoff games. Sartoris will have to work hard on increasing his skating acumen and his puck control at speed in addition to ensuring he is winning all the battles in his own end.

Schaefer, Jonathon
LD - Niagara Ice Dogs (OHL) 5'09" 170

Schaefer played a handful of games for the Ice Dogs' this season but spent the majority of the season with the Milton Icehawks of the OJHL. Schaefer is a smooth skating defenseman who rushes the puck end to end very effectively. He has good power in his shot but will need to improve passing/shooting decisions. Jonathon may not be big, but he packs a ton of power into his hits. He crushes opponents down low and isn't afraid to get into it with bigger opponents. Schaefer will look to take on a regular role with Niagara leading up to the 2016 NHL Entry Draft.

Sergachyov, Mikhail
LD – Irbis (MHL) – 6'2" 200

Sergachyov will only turn 17 the day before the draft, but his remarkable play in the first part of the season earned him a stable spot on the U18 roster of his national team. He didn't disappoint at the Five Nations, and overall did well in Switzerland as well, even if he didn't show off all his tools. The Russian possesses very good hands for a defenseman, good puck protection, nice anticipation in the neutral and offensive zones, and a powerful shot already. Albeit with a personal style, he is a smooth and powerful skater. He only displays it when he sees an opening he wants to jump into, but he can surprise the opposition with impressive acceleration.

He doesn't mind joining the offense, be it on the rush or in puck possession plays in the offensive zone, where he shows more of his abilities. He brings solid size and likes to play physical along the boards, doesn't mind engaging with opponents after the whistle either. Mikhail reads the game very well and has very good poise with the puck, as his skills allow him not to panic when pressured. All in all, a very promising two-way defenseman for next year draft with first round upside.

Sevigny, Mathieu
LW – Drummondville Voltigeurs (QMJHL) – 6'0" 171

Sevigny was drafted 17th overall by the Voltigeurs in last year QMJHL after playing a year in midget with the Seminaire St-Francois in Quebec city. Sevigny dad (Pierre) was a long time veteran in pro hockey that had a cup of coffee in the NHL with the Canadiens, his dad is now assistant coach with the Quebec Remparts. When you watch the younger Sevigny it shows that he's been around hockey all of his life as he understand the game very well and is very valuable player at both end of the ice. He's always in good positioned defensively and always there to help and support his defense, he's a winger but sometime play the role of the centerman in the defensive zone by coming back deep down in his zone. Sevigny has decent size and made a quick adaptation to the major junior this year with the Voltigeurs, playing on a struggling team Sevigny made the most of it and saw his ice time jump in the 2nd half of the season after all the moves the team made during the trade period. He's tenacious on the forecheck and takes pride in playing a solid two-way game. He has a good compete level and win majority of his one on one battle. He's solid in puck protection along the wall thanks to his size and reach. He's versatile as he can play different position and can play on any line you put him out there. His offensive potential remains a question mark with him but his overall game is so good at this stage that he makes himself very valuable for his team.

Smith, Givani
RW - Guelph Storm (OHL) 6'01" 197

After being selected in the first round of the 2014 OHL Priority Selection Draft, Smith was dealt to the Guelph Storm at the trade deadline. Givani really blossomed with the Guelph Storm and by playoff time was one of their best players, playing big minutes on the top two lines. Smith is a big physical power forward who loves to finish his checks and delivered several devastating hits throughout the season and playoffs. He is very tough down low and has a great compete level allowing him to dominate along the wall at times. He has underrated offensive ability and a powerful shot. Smith will need to improve on his skating but his strong late season performance should really help him leading into his sophomore season.

Quotable: "The first time I saw Smith I was sharing a bench with Dale Hawerchuk as we were coaching against Givani in a prospects game prior to his OHL Draft season. He was both very talented and nasty that day and I feel the same way about him now. I saw him a few times in the playoffs and he was one of Guelph's best players. He was a physical force and played with a higher compete level than I had seen from him before. He's a player I'm looking forward to watching next season." - Mark Edwards

Sokolov, Dmitri
LW – Omskie Yastreby (MHL) – 6'01" 212

Sokolov entered the season as someone to look closely at, after being hyped for quite some time because of the outstanding offensive numbers he registered in all younger categories in Russia despite regularly playing against older competition. The large winger has certainly lived up to his status in this year international competitions at the U18 level, keeping up his impressive goal scoring rate.

Dmitri possesses a very good wrister for his age on top of solid puck skills. His reception of passes is flawless, he can protect the puck much better than your typical 17yrs old player can do and he certainly knows how to get himself into scoring positions. From blueline in, it's his territory. Dangerous coming off the right side boards, he is a big threat on the powerplay and possesses a bomb of a one-timer. We would like him to use more his mass and strength on his skates to take position in front of the net, but shows his scoring instincts when circling without the puck around the slot and the net. Dmitri engages in physical plays but mostly in the offensive zone, his play away from the offensive zone and in puck retrieval situations has got a little better during the season but is still an area that needs significant work. While his skating is not at all an issue in the offensive zone, his lack of acceleration in the neutral zone is concerning and prevents him from being more of a dynamic player. At the moment he is not a threat on breakaways because he gets usually catched by backchecking defensemen.

Losing some weight could help his game for his draft season. The good thing with Sokolov is he shows very good instincts and vision, he is able to combine well with his linemates despite being a pure goal scorer. He can recognize when shooting is not the best option and there is an open teammate in a scoring position. Expected to cross the ocean and bring his goal scoring prowess to the CHL next season, he should go high in the Import draft.

Somppi, Otto
LC – Jokerit U20 (FIN) – 6'00" 170

Somppi is a versatile centreman with the Jokerit U20 team. He has good size but also skates fairly well. He is a hard working player who is effective in all three zones. In addition to his 200 foot game, Somppi does a great job of finding excellent shooting lanes and can exploit those opportunities for goals. He is sneaky in the slot area and is capable of jumping on rebounds very quickly to pick up garbage goals.

While Somppi is effective putting the puck in the net, he also displays good passing skills. He struggled a little in the U20 league for Jokerit as he got relegated into a bottom six role an received limited ice under much more experienced players.

Sproviero, Franco
LD - Sarnia Sting (OHL) 5'08" 150

Sproviero enjoyed time with both the OHL's Sarnia Sting and the Lambton Shores Jr. B Predators of the GOJHL. Sproviero is an excellent skater who can take the puck out of trouble and carry it end to end. He has good composure in the neutral zone and will pass off if he doesn't have a skating lane. Offensively he moves the puck well showing good vision and accuracy. Defensively he is better than most small offensive defensemen and the use of his stick proved frustrating for opponents at times. He was also well positioned. Franco has all the talent of a 2016 NHL Entry Draft prospect but will really need to grow and overcome his size in order to reach his true potential.

Stanley, Logan
LD - Windsor Spitfires (OHL) 6'06" 210

Stanley was the Windsor Spitfires first round pick in the 2014 OHL Priority Selection Draft. He was one of the more raw players available and the Spitfires eased him in, trying not to overwhelm him right off the bat. Stanley's skating is an area of concern as he has trouble getting started. His short area quickness is an area he needs to improve. His feet can get him in trouble against speedy skilled forwards. He uses his size very well down low playing a tough game along the wall and doesn't back down from a physical challenge. Stanley showed some offensive upside at the Minor Midget level but has focused primarily on the defensive side of the game in the OHL.

Steel, Sam
LC – Regina Pats (WHL) - 5'11" 165

Sam Steel is a highly talented playmaking centre who debuted this year with the Regina Pats after being selected 2nd overall in the 2013 WHL Bantam Draft. In his rookie year in the WHL, Sam is already considered talented enough to play with Calgary Flames first round draft pick Morgan Klimchuk on the Regina Pats first line, who does most of his dirty work on the wing. Steel, meanwhile, sets up his linemates left-and-right with slick passing ability making high difficulty passes look easy. Steel seems to have a special ability to make plays way out of his peripheral vision. Both speed and playmaking ability already stand out as key qualities in the young centre.

In all three zones, his combination of quick footwork and slick hands is truly remarkable, as he spins off checks and dekes around opponents with ease. His speed allows him to skate wide on opposition defenceman and create space for himself and his teammates. He plays on both the power play and the penalty kill in Regina and is able to create a lot of shorthanded chances when he suddenly decides to turn on the afterburners. He's also a trustworthy centreman in all situations because of his above-average skills in the faceoff dots. At even strength, he can sometimes try to do too much and occasionally make a costly turnover or become a defensive liability. Steel has a lot of upside, already playing a big role with the Pats he will look to overcome his late season injury and become a top WHL prospect for the 2016 NHL Entry Draft.

Sukhachyov, Vladislav
G – Belye Medvedi (MHL) – 5'10.5" 181

Sukhachyov put up some impressive performances and numbers with Russia's U17 team this year. He is an agile goaltender that moves with ease in the crease. He has a strong core and pushes fluidly around the paint. Sukhachyov is athletic with very quick legs that allow him to get into his butterfly efficiently and fast. However, he tends to be over-active and he can get caught moving around too much while in his butterfly, opening holes and losing angles. He can also panic when there is traffic in front of him.

Not a large goaltender so he plays more aggressive, but his quick feet and good balance allow him to move back if he has too. Good competitor in the crease and plays the puck with confidence. The biggest concern for us is his rebound control, which can be absolutely atrocious at times and desperately needs refinement. There is a lot to like about Sukhachyov and if he grows more he will probably become a player to watch for the 2016 NHL Entry Draft.

Suthers, Keenan
LW - USNTDP U17 6'5" 187

Suthers joined the NTDP program after showing at strong performance at the USA Hockey Select 16s Camp last summer. He is an opposing forward with NHL size and could develop into the power forward in the pros as he has good mobility and stride for a big kid and nice set of hands too. He will need to show more finish in his draft year as tends do lots of good but leaves himself off the score sheet especially in tight. He is not the pure goal scoring type so might be a Brian Boyle style in the future. He is set to enroll at Western Michigan after next year.

Sylvestre, Gabriel
RD – Shawinigan Cataractes (QMJHL) – 6'2" 177

Sylvestre was leaning toward going the NCAA route before last year draft and was eventually drafted by Shawinigan at the end of the first round (18th overall). Finally he decided to report to Shawinigan for their training camp and the Cataractes organisation has been thrilled ever since. Sylvestre is not flashy like the other rookie blueliner Samuel Girard but so efficient in everything he does on the ice. He's a solid two way defensemen with some raw offensive attributes to his repertoire but first and foremost he likes to shutdown the opposing top forwards and did that in his first season in the league. Silvestre has good size, mobility and won over the trust of the Shawinigan coaching staff quickly and was playing in their top 4 in the second half of the season. He's strong physically and will makes life hard for any forwards skating his side of the ice and won't hesitate clearing the front of the net. He even got in scraps this year with 19-20 years old veteran, showing he has no fear. With the puck he keeps his play simple and doesn't try anything fancy, he makes a good first pass out of his zone to help the transition game. He can be helpful on the power play with his strong shot from the point. Sylvestre plays a very mature game, he should keep developing his offensive game and continue to evolve into one of the best two-way defensemen in the QMJHL in the next couple of years.

Tessier, Julien
LW – Saint-John Sea Dogs (QMJHL) – 6'1" 180

Tessier was the 15th overall selection in last year QMJHL draft after playing a year in midget with the Trois-Rivieres Estacades. This season he didn't get a lot of ice time with the Sea Dogs and might have benefited going back to midget AAA for at least half of the season. Tessier is strong skater with explosiveness down the wing, he can create room on the ice with his speed. In the last two seasons he has really become a sound player defensively by making better reads in the defensive zone and be more involve. He at time this season at some defensive assignment playing on the PK for the Sea Dogs but again his ice time was limited this season. Tessier is a solid all-around player and remind some of former QMJHL Michael Bournival. He works hard at both end of the ice, a good skater with a decent scoring touch. It should be interesting where he fits in the Sea Dogs lineup next season and keep track of his development.

Thierus, Lucas
LW – Sherbrooke Phoenix (QMJHL) – 5'10" 170

Thierus split last season between Sherbrooke and his midget team in St-Eustache and also played at the U17 hockey challenge in November in Sarnia. Thierus was drafted 28th overall by Sherbrooke in June of 2014. Thierus is a prolific scorer in midget last year scoring 28 goals in 40 games which was amongst the best of any draft eligible player in that league. He has a lethal wrist shot and can score from anywhere in the offensive zone. He's a powerful skater and likes to challenge opposing defensemen one on one. He's tough to knock down off his skate and excel in puck protection skills. This year with Sherbrooke he had a tough time finding good quality ice time in an offensive role, he had a tough time playing a different role on the team that he's not use to. He did start playing a more physical game this season, he's a strong kid along the board and it show this year. His primary role on a team should be for his goal scorer abilities, he's sniper and he likes to shoot the puck from anywhere. He could make a better job of using his teammate on the ice, tend to try a bit too much on his own. Another area of his game that will need to be improve for next season will be his defensive game, just a better overall effort will be needed.

Timleck, Adam
RW - Peterborough Petes (OHL) 5'08" 157

Timleck made an impact with limited ice time in his rookie season. A smart player; Timleck showed offensive creativity which led to an occasional promotion on the second power play unit. He has quick hands and puck possession skills and a real nose for the net. Although he is small, he plays a fearless style of game and was very willing to engage opposing players who were much bigger than him. Timleck will need to get bigger and stronger in order to maximize his potential.

Timms, Matthew
LD - Peterborough Petes (OHL) 5'09" 181

Timms is an undersized defenceman with offensive upside. He has quick feet and jumps up in the rush. He really started to show his skill the last quarter of the season and in playoffs, where Timms was much more confident rushing the puck and made better decisions. He sees the ice well and on the power play finding open teammates with a pass or cutting backdoor. With his size, Timms plays a physical game and likes to get into it with opponents but needs to continue getting stronger in order to win more battles down low and in the slot.

Tkachuk, Matthew
LW – London Knights (OHL) 6'1" 187

His game has taken tremendous strides in the last few years not that the hockey IQ wasn't there but the skating department. His stride was very choppy years ago although he skates fairly well now, not explosive or high-end speed yet agile enough to make plays. You like how Tkachuk reads plays with high anticipation as he will pounce on the puck on the forecheck by picking off passes and thinking steps ahead. The vision with the puck is quite good as he sees the ice and he has that ability to make those soft, little passes whether it be on the breakout along the wall or from behind the goal line. He shows those genetics like his father, Keith, ex-NHLer as nice, natural goal scoring thoughts and abilities. He thinks the game well. The young Tkachuk has a nice set of hands and plays well below the dots creating space and finding the open man, or potting the goal himself with a slippery move or well placed shot. He will be one of the top American born players chosen in 2016 as late '97 birth date. Watch for him to post up impressive numbers in the OHL this season in London.

Tufte, Riley
LW - USNTDP U17 6'5" 190

He is another big name signing for Minnesota-Duluth along with Joey Anderson for the 2016-17 season. You immediately are drawn to his large frame and inability to moves pretty well for a big guy and also handle the puck. He has very good stick skills and offensive know-how yet he lacks putting it all together on a consistent basis. There are times when you see him dominating while being the play maker and then his performance lacks. If he could add more physicality, nasty side to his game along with the ability to finish on the score sheet more consistently he will be a heck of a hockey player.

Tuulola, Eetu
RW – HPK U20 (FIN) – 6'01" 209

Eetu is a huge prospect with excellent scoring ability. He knows where to go in the offensive zone, whether it be in front of the net or getting open to unload his cannon of a shot. He's great around the corners and in front of the net. He displayed good puck handling skills for a big guy. He has a very shoot first mentality, but the velocity and accuracy of his shot gives him good reason.

His skating is currently his biggest weakness. He lacks any first step quickness and his technique and speed still needs work. He can look a bit clumsy out there in open ice with a lot of end to end action going on. He showed some physicality, but we've also seen him dive trying to sell an injury then celebrate on the bench afterwards when a penalty is called. Tuulola has a lot of upside but his skating must improve in order for him to reach his potential.

Verbeek, Hayden
LW - Sault Ste. Marie Greyhounds (OHL) 5'09" 180

Verbeek is a hard working energetic forward for the Greyhounds. He played a limited role this season primarily on the fourth line. Verbeek is a strong skater with a very high compete level. He hits hard for his size and is a relentless forechecker. Verbeek is tough to play against and is a chippy player who will get his shots in when he can. His size will be his biggest thing to overcome heading into the 2016 NHL Entry Draft, as he has shown talent and offensive upside leading into his jump to the OHL.

Wait, Garrett
LW – Edina HS (MN) 6'1" 170

He is a rising player and probably does not get a lot of the hype as attends public HS in Minnesota instead of playing in the USHL or for NTDP. He is a player that certainly has impressed in the years and Minnesota (Big 10) is getting a good one in the recruiting trail. He is good size who skates well and handles the puck. He shows great vision and has the ability to create offense with the puck. He can cut or slash the puck to the net, shoots extremely well, and can seam a pass through for the assist. He will garner lots of attention this draft season.

Walker, Zach
RW - USNTDP U17 6'0" 185

He's not the offensively gifted player but yet plays a more straight-up north-south game, with compete, and determination. He will fit into the role type player as soon as he sets foot onto Boston College after next season with NTDP-18. He owns a nice skating stride, likes to get speed down the wing and drive to the night from the outside, as the stick skills are average. He is also not afraid to play the body.

Weissbach, Linus
RW – Frolunda J20 (SWE) – 5'09" 148

Weissbach is a speedy, offensive forward who spent his season split between Frolunda's J20 and J18 teams. Weissbach has a high end top speed and strong skating ability. He has excellent hand speed and is one of the best pure stickhandlers heading into the 2016 NHL Entry Draft. He has a quick release on his shot and can use his puck handling ability to get himself into high percentage scoring areas. Despite his size, he was willing to engage physically but greatly lacks strength.

Weissbach will need to get stronger, as he can get knocked off the puck once he isn't moving at his top speed. His size is also a bit of a concern, but there is no questioning his offensive upside. He is expected to be one of the most skilled players to come out of Sweden for the 2016 NHL Entry Draft.

Wells, Dylan
G - Peterborough Petes (OHL) 6'02" 187

Wells is a big athletic goalie that got the opportunity early in his OHL career to start. He is calm in the net and deflects pucks to the outside, eliminating opportunities for rebounds. Wells plays on top of his crease challenging shooters and can play the puck very well. He has very quick lower body movement and his reflexes allow him to make highlight reel saves. His playing time was reduced after the acquisition of Matthew Mancina, but he still possesses the upside of a high end junior goaltender and legitimate NHL prospect. Wells has a tendency to let in some soft goals unbecoming of his talent and will need to improve on that leading into the 2016 NHL Entry Draft.

Woll, Joseph
G - USNTDP U17 6'2" 190

He is good size and brings great athleticism and extremely explosive laterally and with movements. He does a very good job getting square to pucks as sharp and crisp in movements and reads. He works hard and the game is continuing to trend upward. He is a Boston College recruit for Fall of 2016.

Yakovenko, Alexander
LD – Belye Medvedi (MHL) – 5'10" 157

Yakovenko is an undersized Russian defenseman who managed to play with the U18 national team despite being a '98 born who doesn't look physically ready for top competitions yet. Even if Alexander struggles in battles in his zone because of his size limitations, he doesn't shy away from the physical play and can even deliver the odd open ice hip check. His short skating stride doesn't look good, but he is actually effective when he needs to carry the puck up quickly. Defensively he makes good use of his stick, but it is the powerplay the situation where he can better showcase his qualities.

He can move the puck, can change the angle to find lanes with his wrister and possesses a beauty of a slap shot, surprisingly hard for his body and accurate too. Hopefully Yakovenko will grow some more leading up to next year Entry Draft.

Zelenak, Vojtech
LD – HC Sparta Praha U20 (CZE) – 6'05" 214

Zelenak had a solid season with HC Sparta Praha U20 team while playing internationally on multiple occasions for Slovakia. Vojtech is a massive defender, who utilizes his size very well. He was a dominant presence along the wall winning battles with ease and pushing opponents out of his way. Some opponents took their time getting to the corners when sharing a puck pursuit with Zelenak. On the wall he contains very well against large forwards. He makes smart simple plays down low, not trying to do too much.
He showed the ability to carry the puck on occasion and uses his frame intelligently to bring the puck up ice. He is actually a very good skater considering his size. On offensive rushes he can sometimes get a little too ahead of the play and doesn't support his defensive partner the way he should. He has a very powerful shot that he keeps low and easy to deflect. Zelenak shows great upside as a shutdown defender who has a touch of offense but will need to be adjusted on some of his fundamental issues. These are generally things that can be resolved through good coaching.

2017 NHL DRAFT PROSPECTS

Aucoin, Yan
LD – Albatros du College Notre Dame (LHMAAAQ) – 6'0" 202

Aucoin is a big defenseman with a fluid skating stride with good lateral mobility. This mobility allows him to cover a lot of ice and be quickly involved in one-on-one battles. At the beginning of the season, he lost the majority of his battles along the boards but made big improvements over the course of the season. He used his body and stick better and got his ice time increased from the mid-season. In past years he was always taller and bigger than his opponents, but this year he was forced to adapt, as for the first time, this was not the case for him. His transition game is good enough; he makes quick, accurate passes. He's capable of creating offensive scoring chances, he's quick at moving on the blue line and has a good wrist shot. He's good at finding shooting lanes and getting his shot through to the net. He was chosen to play for Team Quebec at the Canada Games and logged a ton of ice time. He was able to show off his consistently and reliability during the tournament, which gave the coaching staff the ability to trust him.

Baribeau, Dereck
G – Blizzard du Séminaire St-François (LHMAAAQ) – 6'4" 171

Baribeau is a goaltender that already has great size and is most impressive thing about him is his agility in his crease. He's very athletic, has strong legs and his pushes from side-to-side are powerful. He's calm in his crease and likes to challenge opposing shooters. He has a sound control of his rebounds, he redirects low shots well and with high shots he's able (most of the time) to not give any rebounds. He's comfortable with traffic in front of him as well and thanks to his height he's always able to track the puck. He had a strong year with the Blizzard, where he was dominant in the 2nd half of the season. He finished 1st in save percentage and 2nd in goals-against average in the Quebec Midget AAA league. He was also part of the Canada Games with Team Quebec, where he did very well, and the Gatorade Challenge in May. He's without a doubt the best goaltender of this QMJHL draft class and only worry with him has been his work ethic. It remains to be seen if it will improve in major junior.

Boudrias, Shawn
RW – Phenix du College Esther-Blondin (LHMAAAQ) 6'2" 176

Boudrias is a tall player with a good skill level, allowing him to be a dangerous player offensively. He has good size and does a good job protecting the puck. He is able to skate in different areas of the ice, even though he doesn't keep the puck on his stick too long. His long stick allows him to break up many plays in the neutral zone and he covers a lot of space on the ice. He's a player who is careful in terms of not turning the puck over in the neutral zone, and this is what makes him an efficient player. He's reliable defensively, always working hard on the backcheck. Also, he's not afraid to get his nose dirty in the front of the net and is able to jump on rebounds to score some goals. He will need to work on his footwork and his acceleration if he wants to become a more complete player, because right now he's lacking in those areas. Boudrias is not the type of player who will run over his opponents, but will finish his hits smartly so he can win back possession of the puck.

Bowers, Shane
LW/C –Halifax McDonalds (NSMMHL) - 6'0" 162

After a showcase Bantam season and helping lead his team to an Atlantic title, all eyes shifted to Bowers as he joined 'The Macs' for the season. After a couple of games of feeling things out, he began to exude increased confidence with each passing week of the season and certainly finished the year on a very high note for a 15 year old, amassing 23 goals, 29 assists, 24 penalty minutes in 34 games. In the playoffs, he turned it up again and in 17 games, he tallied 15 goals and 18 assists. He won the regular season scoring title and was first in scoring in the playoffs. These numbers are not surprising, considering the set of tools he has at his disposal every shift. His skating is high-tempo and athletic, and he can be extremely shifty while in full flight. His top speed was extremely hard to contain through the neutral zone or in the perimeter of the offensive zone and his vision at these speeds was elite. He also possesses a great set of hands and has an excellent feel for the puck while in motion. He can use this to be the playmaker, the finisher, or whatever the situation calls for. Bowers is the type of player that could beat you everywhere on the ice, both with and without the puck, and regardless of his current slight frame, he has room to grow and get stronger and was not shy about giving or taking body contact at any time. Bowers has an on-ice presence that shows leadership and a high compete level not frequently seen at this level. He seems to thrive under pressure and when the stakes are raised, so does his game - he is constantly making adjustments to make sure he matters and can help his team. Bowers was used in every situation and understood his role. There is no question in our minds that Bowers can compete at the next level and if he continues to develop at this pace the upside could be very high indeed. Bowers was drafted in the 3rd round of the USHL draft by Waterloo in May.

Bulitka, Shane
LW - Elgin-Middlesex Chiefs (MHAO), 5'10.5" 158
Bulitka was drafted in the second round, 28th overall by the Sudbury Wolves in the 2015 OHL Priority Selection Draft. Shane was one of the smartest players available for the 2015 OHL Priority Selection draft which helped lead him lead all of the Alliance area in assists this season. Bulitka is a cerebral offensive talent who has excellent vision and sees plays that not many players his age can visualize. He can create offense for his teammates but also has the puck skills and finishing ability to put the puck in the back of the net. He plays a bit of a perimeter game and is more likely to stay on the outside and exploit a hole in the defense, rather than going full speed up the middle. His defensive coverage is good for a skilled player and consistently gets back and makes good plays on the back check. While his skating ability isn't a flaw, he doesn't possess that top gear you'd like to see in high skilled players and does affect him at times.

Burt, Robbie
RW - Mississauga Rebels (GTHL), 5'11" 193
Burt was drafted in the first round, 11th overall of the 2015 OHL Priority Selection Draft by the Kingston Frontenacs. Robbie is a big winger who we liked early on potential wise but leveled off as the year went on. He moves well for a player of his size and is able to generate a good head of steam with space to skate north and south. He is good at getting into solid positions in the offensive zone and using his size as an advantage in front of the net. He displays a good hard shot, but needs to work on his accuracy as he often misses the net or puts it into the goalies crest. He showed at times that he can play with an edge and be a physical force but he didn't get involved enough physically for our liking. He is very effective at getting the put out of his own zone when the puck gets wrapped around the boards to him. Burt would benefit from improving the consistency of his compete level and strive to bring it every shift instead of taking the occasional shift off. When Burt is on his game he is extremely difficult to defend, and has the capabilities of providing a momentum swing for his team.

Cardinal, Tommy
RW – Commandeurs de Levis (LHMAAAQ)- 5'9" 175
Tommy is, without a doubt, one of the most physical players in the Quebec Midget AAA league and this, at only 15 years old. He often looks for the big hit and at times can go over the legal limit. Without a doubt, Cardinal can change the momentum of a game with one of his big hits. He's solid on his skates and his speed helps him a ton to deliver those big hits. He does tend to put himself out

of position when trying too hard to focus on hitting. He also has trouble keeping his emotions intact and can get off his game plan. Cardinal is not only a player capable of playing a physical game; he has very good skills with the puck. His wrist shot is quick and he is able to release it in no time. He spends most of the year on the 2nd power play unit with Levis this season. He's very good at creating spaces for his linemates and is not afraid to play in traffic. He's also quick at putting pressure on opposing defensemen, which keeps the puck in the offensive zone longer. He's not the leader of a line but is very good at supporting his linemates. He also can play different roles on a team.

Chainey, Jocktan
LD –Estacades de Trois-Rivières (LHMAAAQ) – 6'0" 195

Chainey is a big defenseman with good mobility who possesses good abilities with the puck. He has a wonderful shot from the point, the best among any defensemen from Quebec, and is also very good on the transition game. He's good at controlling the puck and is capable of getting out of danger with his puckhandling. His hockey sense is not his strongest point, but he always found a way to make the good play with the puck because he's able to skate with it or find open teammates quickly. He's very strong physically and is tough to contain for the opposing team. Defensively, he was well surrounded with Trois-Rivieres and improved this part of his game. He's capable of cleaning the front of the net. He needs to improve his bodychecking technique, because at his size, he should have more impact along the wall. He uses his size when he's in possession of the puck in order to protect it and take advantage of his opponents. He played a big role on the power play for Trois-Rivieres this season and when he was out because of injuries, it showed in the team's performance. He played at the Canada Games and had a tough tournament because of his poor defensive game, but was still able to show off some skills with the puck.

Chmelevski, Sasha
RC - Honeybaked U16 (HPHL), 5'10" 170

Chmelevski was selected first round, 10th overall by the Sarnia Sting in the 2015 OHL Priority Selection Draft. Sasha has decent size mixed with a good combination of skating and puck control ability. He creates opportunities with strong a north-south style. He can score with his shooting ability or he will take the puck hard to the net and show finishing touch in $ght around the goal. He protects the puck well and maintains good puck possession. He recently led Honeybaked in scoring at USA Hockey U16 Nationals. When acquiring puck control he likes try and take control of the offensive game. He slick with the puck and can handle it well in tight and splits well going outside to inside creating deception. If he develops his skating stride it would really help him maximize his potential.

Comtois, Maxime
LW –Grenadiers de Chateauguay (LHMAAAQ) – 6'0" 176

Comtois is our top-rated prospect from the province of Quebec, much like he has been all year long, and already has good pro potential. He's a gifted goal-scorer: he scored a combined 49 goals this season in 73 games this year. Comtois is very dangerous in the offensive zone; he possesses a great, accurate wrist shot with a quick release and likes to shoot the puck from anywhere in the offensive zone. He has good puck skills and can beat defenders with good one-on-one stickhandling, a skill he employs with ease at this level. He has a really good sense of finding holes in the opposing team's defense to position himself in scoring opportunities. All season he scored big goals for his team, he's proven to be clutch in big games. He's the kind of player you want on the ice when you need a goal; he always seems to find a way to score those key goals this past season. One aspect of his game that Comtois might not receive enough praise for: his playmaking abilities. He sees the ice very well and makes quick and smart decisions with the puck. He plays the point on the power play with his midget team and has good puck distribution skills from there. He's tough to defend against for the opposing team, as he can hurt you with either his shot or passing abilities. Comtois already has good size at this point and will only continue to get stronger as he matures physically; he does a fine job protecting the puck and makes good use of his reach. He's capable of playing a physical game but can be immature and lose his cool, causing penalty troubles when things don't go his way. We would like to see him working on his speed a bit, as he is not a bad skater, but with more explosiveness, he could be more of a threat off the rush. He's a decent player in his zone due to his excellent hockey sense, but does tend to stop moving his feet on the backcheck at times. Comtois should have an impact at the QMJHL level next season—he's definitely ready for a new challenge.

Côté, Louis-Filip
LW – Commandeur de Lévis (LHMAAAQ) – 6'0" 165

Louis-Filip is among the elite forwards of this draft class when it's time to talk about pure offensive talent. He has exceptional puck control and is able to make plays that few players can achieve. He also possesses a great on ice vision, which allows him to make passes in tight spaces and also position himself well to finish plays. His skating abilities are among one of his strongest features. He's a fluid skater and has good overall skating technique. He's able to change directions quickly in tight spaces and is a capable puck-rusher. Defensively, his hockey sense helps him anticipate plays from the opposing team and break them up. However, he can get caught out of position by trying to leave too quickly in the offensive zone. He also can get beat when he plays the puck too often in defensive situations. He can become invisible when the game gets physical, when he doesn't have as much space to work with on the ice. Nevertheless, he possesses good size and needs to learn how to use it better. Côté was unfortunately injured in the playoffs and was forced to miss the Canada Winter Games, where he would have been a key player for Team Quebec. His lack of competitiveness and consistency hurt him a bit during the playoffs and late in the regular season, where he was invisible.

Crête-Belzile, Antoine
LD – Blizzard du Séminaire St-François (LHMAAAQ) – 5'11" 165

Crête-Belzile is without a doubt the best defenseman of this draft class. He had a tough beginning to the season while battling injuries. He grew and became stronger this season; he had a big impact on his team and on Team Quebec at the Canada Games, where he had a ton of ice time. He played in every situation and had a wonderful tournament. He possesses an excellent skating technique and a powerful skating stride. He moves around with good fluidity and is always in good position wherever he is on the ice. His hockey sense is elite, his decision-making very often allows him to find the right play and he is able to anticipate the play very well. He also possesses very good puck skills. He controls the puck very well and is able to rush it in the offensive zone with ease. He has a good slapper from the point and is able to read the play quickly to make good and quick transitions. Even with an average size, he wins the majority of his battles with good body positioning and a strong stick. He's as good offensively as he is defensively. Crête-Belzile is the type of defenseman that every team would like to have on their team. He missed the Gatorade Challenge in May due to another injury. There are some concerns about his durability going forward with him at the QMJHL level.

Davis, Hayden
RD - Hamilton Huskies (MHAO), 6'01" 166

Davis was selected first round, 13th overall by the Niagara ice Dogs in the 2015 OHL Priority Selection Draft. Davis is a big, smooth skating puck rushing defenseman for the Hamilton Huskies. Davis really showed his talent early before falling victim to an injury that kept him out for over two months. After returning it took him a little time to get going and never seemed to regain quite where he was at in the first few weeks of the season. Davis is a big puck rushing defenseman who has an excellent combination of size and skating ability. He is capable of rushing the puck but also has an excellent first pass and moves the puck extremely well from the back end. He has a knack for firing perfect long distance passes to send his teammates on breakaways. He walks the line effectively on the point and has been great on the power play. He also has a good shot from the point. Defensively, Davis will need some work. He gives too much space on his gap and forwards can push him deep into the defensive zone allowing for a higher percentage shot. He's decent in the corners, but his aggression is a bit hit or miss. He will need to play a little tougher during the game and maybe take it back a few notches after the whistle as he took too many undisciplined penalties in between whistles that hurt his team. Davis has a very high upside and has the offensive tools that could make him a good OHL player next season, but his defensive game will be a work in progress.

DiPietro, Michael
G - Sun County Panthers (MHAO), 6'01", 193

DiPietro was selected second round, 23rd overall by the Windsor Spitfires in the 2015 OHL Priority Selection Draft. Michael was one of the top goaltenders out of the entire 2015 OHL Priority Selection Draft class. Which is what caused the Spitfires to jump at the opportunity to add him early in the second round. He is extremely athletic and has exceptional reflexes. Even in the butterfly he's extremely quick when opponents try to go upstairs on him, and he's very difficult to beat low. He always seems to be in the ideal positioning and is rarely ever beaten by the first shot. He is very technically sound covering his angles effectively and intelligently. He is not a very flashy goaltender and is very composed under pressure. Michael's rebound control is decent, it isn't a standout feature of his game but he doesn't struggle with it either. His biggest area of improvement will be the transition from the first save to the second safe. He can be a little delayed when reacting from the initial shot and getting into position for the rebound. Most of the goals we have seen him allow this year has come from these plays.

D'Orio, Alex
G – Cantonniers de Magog (LHMAAAQ) – 6'2" 193

D'Orio is a big goaltender who catches the puck with his right hand. He covers a lot of room in front of his net and moves well. His legs are powerful and he is fast to move in his crease. He has good rebound-control and plays well with traffic in front of him, as he challenges shooters and gets hit by a lot of pucks. He's also a sound puckhandler outside of his crease. With Magog this season, D'Orio shared the workload with veteran Xavier Potvin. He had a great season with a goal against average of 2.36 and a save percentage of .916, which were both good enough for top-five in the league. He was part of Team Quebec at the Canada Games and was also part of the Gatorade Challenge in May for the QMJHL Draft Combine. He brings a lot of confidence to his net and there is no doubt that for teams looking for a goaltender at the draft, he's going to be an excellent choice. There is a very good chance we will see him in the QMJHL next season.

Durandeau, Arnaud
LW/RW – Lac St-Louis Lions (LHMAAAQ) – 5'10" 167

Durandeau had a very successful first season in the Quebec Midget AAA league with the Lac St-Louis Lions, scoring 25 goals and 51 points in 42 games and adding 8 goals and 19 points in 16 playoff games. He's very dangerous in the offensive zone; one of the most dangerous forwards from this draft class in possession of the puck in the offensive zone. He's the type of player that doesn't need a ton of scoring chances to get on the scoresheet. Durandeau has an excellent wrist shot with an excellent release that can beat goaltenders from anywhere in the offensive zone. He's a good setup man as well, making him a tough player to get a read on for the opposing team. He's a decent skater but lacks an extra gear. With that, he could create more space for himself and be more dangerous when he rushes the puck. Without the puck, his effort is a bit inconsistent. Sometime he works hard, showing good commitment, and at other times he will stop moving his feet in the defensive zone and lose his man. Durandeau played at the Canada Game for Team Quebec, often being paired with fellow Lions Veleno and Capannelli. He finished the tournament with 8 points in 6 games. He's a big weapon on the power play, where he takes advantage of the extra space. Durandeau plays more of a finesse than a physical type of game.

Eder, Tobias
LW – EC Bad Tölz U19 (DNL) – 5'11" 165

Eder represented Germany at the U18 as an underager and was the youngest skater on the squad. It was easy to see why he made that team. Showing good feet and speed, he brought a high compete level and his smart play in all three zones. Eder has good instincts to go along with legit skills, and as his numbers on the season confirm, he can put the puck in the net. He could make for a good pick at the Import Draft.

Gadjovich, Jonah
LW - Owen Sound Attack (OHL) 6'02" 198

Gadjovich played a limited role on the Attack on the third or fourth line but did very well when he was on the ice. He plays with a lot of energy and drives the net hard. He forechecks and showed a high compete level. Gadjovich displays good positioning in the offensive zone making him available for scoring chances. Jonah will benefit not only from extra ice next year but the late birthdate that should ensure he is playing a top role with the team by the time he is eligible for the 2017 NHL Entry Draft.

Gallant, Zach
LC - Mississauga Rebels (GTHL), 6'02" 175

Gallant was selected first round, 5th overall by the Peterborough Petes in the 2015 OHL Priority Selection Draft. Gallant has been a player who has really improved his play as the year has gone on. His big frame and quick skating make him a force each game. Being first on the puck in the offensive zone allows Gallant to use his body effectively to shield off defenders and create offence. He has been a reliable player for the Rebels as he is used in all situations and shows his ability to win face-offs on a consistent basis. He is extremely effective on the penalty kill and is willing to sacrifice his body for the betterment of the team. Gallant has gotten himself into penalty trouble at times this year and sometimes lets his emotions get the best of him. We have seen some laziness creep into his game throughout the year which also have led to untimely penalties. Gallant shows he has a high hockey IQ and plays a very reliable role for his team but his potential will benefit if he can add more of an offensive flair to his game. Gallant is the type of player who won't put up big points at the next level but is the type of player you win with because of the way he plays the game beyond just putting points on the board.

Gilmour, Brady
LC - Quinte Red Devils (ETA), 5'09" 156

Gilmour was selected first round, 6th overall by the Saginaw Spirit in the 2015 OHL Priority Selection Draft. Brady is a top talent with high end hockey sense. His skill set, and work ethic make him a constant threat and standout among his peer group. Brady has excellent vision and a tremendous ability to anticipate the play in all three zones. At his best in possession of the puck, Brady has proven to be an outstanding playmaker. Outstanding puck skills, including the ability to make quality saucer passes on both the forehand and backhand make it very difficult to limit his options in the offensive zone. His shot is very accurate and he has a sneaky quick release. Gilmour's first two steps are very good and his compete level is extremely high. He isn't going to out-muscle opponents, but his craftiness and elusiveness allow him to play in the high traffic areas. Finding the open ice with or without the puck is a definite strength to his game. Never quitting on a play, his passion, understanding of the game and on-ice leadership is evident at all times. Brady has a very good chance to make an impact in his first season in the OHL if he can improve on his skating ability.

Hawel, Liam
RC - Ottawa Valley Titans (OEMHL), 6'01.75" 152

Hawel was selected first round, 22nd overall by the Sault Ste. Marie Greyhounds in the 2015 OHL Priority Selection Draft. Liam combines good size and mobility with an excellent skill-set. Liam is at his best when he's using his size to protect the puck and take it to the net. He has a repertoire of moves including an effective inside-outside move that allows him to create plenty of offence. Liam skates well, especially for his size and often likes to carry the puck through the neutral zone and gain the offensive zone himself. He is also not afraid getting involved on the penalty kill. He is a very good playmaker and effectively finds the open ice in possession and his patience with the puck allows for his team mates to find space as well. In terms of his physical game, Liam is willing to hit but does show some inconsistencies in this area.

Hischier, Nico
LC – Bern (SWI Jr.) – 5'11" 163

Hischier is a Swiss kid that has been destroying the competition in his country's junior leagues as an underager. He brings hockey smarts that are rarely seen in a 16yrs old, something that helped him to make his national team for the U18 World Championships despite his current lack of power. He was the only '99 born player attending the event. Nico displays very good vision and hockey sense, most of the times he recognizes the right play to do before getting the puck and he moves in the right places without it. He is also a master at taking away the puck from his opponents. A very interesting player to watch develop whilst he adds some needed strength.

Hoyt, Peyton
RW – Fredericton Canadiens (NBPEIMAAA) - 5'9" 154

Hoyt was selected as an underage player to play in the NB/PEI Major Midget League last year and even then it was apparent he would be one to watch this season. It does not take too many viewings to realize that he has an arsenal of weapons at his disposal and sometimes it's hard to predict what you will see next. This is player that wants to get the puck on net - his 29 goals and 9 assists in 30 games are a testament to what we have seen as a willingness to do what it takes to get the job done. He is a powerful skater that cuts deep but also has decent footspeed. His agility is raw, and he will elect to get right in your face instead of peeling off. He can be an aggressive player that can play with an edge, delivering punishing hits to opponents willing to accept them. Hoyt's skills are all very well developed - his passing, shooting and IQ are all what we have come to expect from players in the top tier of this league. His puck control at high speeds was very good as well. If he can demonstrate everything we have seen in him thus far at the next level, then he could be a very effective player in any situation that his coach may place him in. Hoyt was also very good at the Canada game playing for him province, showing off his skills level but also his hard hitting style during the tournament.

Hughes, Aidan
G - London Jr. Knights (MHAO), 6'02.5" 238

Hughes was selected second round, 34th overall by the Sarnia Sting in the 2015 OHL Priority Selection Draft. Aidan Hughes is a big bodied goaltender who was one of the top goaltenders selected in the 2015 OHL Priority Selection Draft. Hughes numbers are staggering, however that is the case with most goaltenders playing for a top team. However, he has progressed throughout the year to be one of the best big game goaltenders in this class. He struggled early on with catching pucks and rebound control, however both have improved throughout the year to the point where they can be considered strengths. Hughes can drop into the butterfly and still cover most of the net. His upper body reflexes are impressive to the point where he can stop a puck point blank in that position when they go upstairs. He's extremely difficult to beat and doesn't really have one glaring weakness. Ideally we would like to see him get quicker, however his positioning more than compensates for average speed. The only time anyone seemed to get to him down the stretch was when they crashed the net and started making contact with him.

Jones, Ben
LC – Toronto Marlboros (GTHL), 6'00" 165

Jones was selected first round, 7th overall by the Niagara Ice Dogs in the 2015 OHL Priority Selection Draft. Jones was relied upon to play in all situations for the Toronto Marlboros this season. He played a vital role in the overall success of the team and proved to be one of the best two-way centers in the GTHL. He has great instincts and uses a strong understanding of the game to get into good positions in both the offensive and defensive zones. He shows strong skating abilities and carries the puck up the ice with confidence. He is very effective on the penalty kill and is willing to sacrifice himself for the team by blocking shots. He moves the puck very efficiently on the power play and shows the willingness to drive the puck to the net off the rush. Jones has shown that he possesses one of the most lethal shots in the GTHL, but he often waits to long to release it which results in his shots being blocked or deflected. He looks to pass before taking a shot which allows defenders to get on top of him in a hurry. Jones has very good leadership qualities and always puts the team before him. For Jones to reach his full potential he will need to find a way to chip in more offensively and find ways to utilize that terrific release.

Keating, Austen
LC – Guelph Jr. Gryphons (SCTA), 5'11" 161

Keating was selected first round, 16th overall by the Ottawa 67's in the 2015 OHL Priority Selection Draft. Austen is a skilled offensive center for the Guelph Jr. Gryphons. He had a very productive season as he led the SCTA in scoring with 60 points in 36 games. He was relied upon heavily to carry the load offensively and he did an excellent job getting his team a 2nd place finish in the SCTA regular season. In our viewings Keating displayed a high hockey IQ and was always creating offense for his team. He has excellent vision in the offensive zone and can make very difficult passes to set his line mates up for easy goals. He also displayed a very hard, accurate shot that proved to be deadly when he was given a little bit of space. He's a good skater and can protect the puck very effectively when taking the defenseman wide. He isn't afraid to go into the dirty areas but he doesn't do it on a consistent basis as he would float around the top of the zone some shifts and wait for the puck to come to him. He helps out a fair amount in the defensive zone but he could use some improvement with his compete level defensively. Austen has a lot of tools that project him to become a very good offensive center, but he will need to get stronger and work on his willingness to compete for an entire game as he has been prone to take several shifts off throughout a game. Keating has the ability to take over games and we would like to see him bring that ability every night.

Krief, Alexander
LD – Lac St-Louis Lions (LHMAAAQ) – 6'2" 178

Krief is a good-sized defender from the Lac St-Louis Lions, who skates very well for an almost 6'3" defenseman who just turned 16 years old recently. His combination of size and skating abilities is among the best in this draft class. It was an up-and-down season for Krief, who showed some good promise earlier in the year but had some struggles in the 2nd half of the season, where he played as a forward in some games. He was chosen as an injury replacement with Team Quebec at the Canada Games, where he was used mostly as a forward on the 4th line during the tournament. He was also part of the Gatorade Excellence Challenge in early May in Boisbriand, with all the best draft-eligible prospects from each province. Krief will need to add some mass to his frame in the next couple of years, so he could become tougher to play against along the wall and in front of the net. Krief can skate the puck out of his zone with ease and can get out of danger with just one or two strides. He's a powerful skater with those long strides. He has a fine first pass out of his zone; he's at his best when he keeps it simple on the ice. He struggles when he tries too much with the puck and makes bad decisions. His play in his own end will need some improvement, and the same goes with his reads and defending one-on-one. He's capable of playing on the power play, with a big shot from the point that he likes to use (he will need to work on his accuracy, though).

Lacombe, Charlie
RD – Vikings de St-Eustache (LHMAAAQ) 6'01.5" 182

Lacombe is a defenseman with great efficiency in his own zone. He's very consistent, which makes him a popular defenseman in this draft class. He works hard in his own zone and he's strong along the wall and in front of the net, where he uses his size to win battles. He loves to play a physical game and is afraid of nothing. With the puck, he makes simple outlets to his forwards, but tends to get rid of the puck when he's under pressure. His positional game will also need some work, as he can get caught out of position in his own zone and this can allow the opposing team some scoring chances. Offensively, Lacombe started the year a bit slowly, making errors in possession of the puck or making bad passes. As the season progressed, Lacombe gained confidence and his offensive game improved. It's one of the reasons he was chosen to play for Team Quebec at the Canada Games. He was a key player for Quebec and showed that he could be a strong two-way defenseman in the future. He does lack consistency in his offensive game, and this is the area he will need to work on to become a top defenseman in the QMJHL. Depending which team drafts Lacombe in June, it is very possible to see him make the jump to the QMJHL next season.

Lefebvre, Simon
RW – Rousseau-Royal de Laval-Montréal (LHMAAAQ) 6'01.5" 184

Lefebvre is a big power forward that played for the Rousseau-Royal of Montreal this season. On November 16th, he had a serious injury following contact along the boards, and didn't play again afterwards. He fractured his left fibula and also had ligament damage. He's strong physically and that allows him to put himself in front of the net and jump on rebounds that are free. It's exactly what he does on the power play, and this works for him. He can deliver big hits and work well deep in the offensive zone. He lacks a lot of consistency; in some games Lefebvre was invisible, like many players on his team. His top speed is not bad, but he needs to work on his explosiveness, which would allow him to go wide on opposing defensemen and cut to the net while protecting the puck, which he does well. With a good stride, he could be one of the most dangerous forwards in Midget AAA. Lefebvre possesses good puck skills and is able to beat defensemen in one-on-one situations. It's a good asset for him, since he can create scoring chances in many different ways, which put his opponents in doubt as to what he will do with the puck. Moreover, his long reach allows him to keep the puck the farthest away from the opposing defensemen and also enables him to take the puck away from them.

Lefebvre could start next season in major junior due to his physical maturation but with the big injury he had, it wouldn't surprise us to see him play another year in Midget AAA.

Martineau, Vincent
RD – Phénix du Collège Esther-Blondin (LHMAAAQ) 6'00" 201

Martineau is one of the best right-handed defensemen from this draft class; he played for the Collège Esther-Blondin Phénix this past season. He lacked a bit of consistency in his game, as in some games he would lose the puck and create turnovers. Other than that, Martineau is a defenseman with a lot of talent. He plays well in one-on-one situations by closing his gap quickly. He rarely leaves a forward alone in the defensive zone, and brings them along the wall, where he's able to retrieve the puck often. In transition, Martineau keeps his game simple by making quick, simple passes, but when he has free space in front of him he won't hesitate to rush the puck in the offensive zone. He has good footwork; some improvements could be made in his acceleration and his top speed, but nothing major in his case. Martineau can play different roles on a team. He can play on the penalty-killing unit like he can on the power play. During the season, Martineau showed enough progression that we think he's among the best 15 year old defensemen from this draft class. It will be interesting to see if he's back in Midget AAA next season, all depends on which team selects him during the QMJHL Draft.

McGregor, Ryan
LC – Burlington Eagles (SCTA), 5'11" 140

McGregor was selected second round, 24th overall by the Sarnia Sting in the 2015 OHL Priority Selection Draft. Ryan was the offensive leader for the Burlington Eagles, putting up 37 points in 32 games. He was consistently involved in the offense for his team and showed excellent vision with the puck. He shows a high compete level for the most part but he has been prone to coast through a few shifts each game. He excels in the give and go game as he looks to win puck battles, dish it off to his line mate then he drives the net hard looking for the return feed. This has proven to be effective in our viewings and he consistently created scoring chances for himself. He is an above average skater but he will benefit from becoming more explosive to gain that extra step on defenders when taking them wide. He doesn't play a physical game but he doesn't shy away from contact as he is always on puck pursuit. McGregor showed us some excellent vision in the offensive zone and some creativity that can allow him to produce offensively at the next level. He will need to get stronger to help him win puck battles and become more explosive.

Meireles, Greg
RC - Ottawa Jr. 67's (OEMHL), 5'10" 170

Meireles was selected first round, 12th overall by the Kitchener Rangers in the 2015 OHL Priority Selection Draft. Greg has incredibly quick feet, and explosive strides that make him one of the fastest players in minor midget. Meireles has very good hands that match his explosive skating that can easily fly by or stick handle through opposing defenders. Meireles has a hard accurate shot that he can get off quickly while mid stride on the rush using an opposing defenceman as a screen. He has high hockey IQ and vision and will look to set up his team mates off the rush. He is smart along the wall with the puck and will make the smart simple play to keep the play going and maintain puck possession for his team. He has a great compete level and will battle very hard for pucks. He's tough on the fore check taking away time and space from the opposition. Defensively and on the penalty kill Meireles is dangerous as he anticipates the play well and can break up passes and pressures the opposition with his speed often forcing mistakes. Meireles needs to work on making better decisions for when to go wide by a defenceman or try to go through them. He also has tendencies of holding onto the puck too long.

Morand, Antoine
LC – Grenadiers de Châteauguay (LHMAAAQ) – 5'9" 156

Morand has been one of our favourites since the start of the regular season, finding himself paired with Maxime Comtois all year long and leading Châteauguay all the way to the finals of the Telus Cup. Morand finished as the 6th-leading scorer in the LHMAAAQ, one point behind his teammate Comtois. He also shone at the Canada Games, where he led Team Quebec in scoring with 11 points in 6 games. Morand is one of the best skaters in the draft, and likes to rush the puck as he has the speed to beat opposing defensemen wide. He also uses his speed very well on the forecheck by always putting pressure on the puck carrier. He plays a fearless game despite not being the biggest player, but gets involved in the tough areas of the ice. He will need to get stronger at the major junior level with bigger and stronger opponents, but his compete level remains excellent. Offensively, Morand is a gifted playmaker, seeing the ice very well and possessing the ability to find teammates quickly. For most of the first half of the season, he played the point on the power play with Comtois when the Grenadiers used five forwards on the ice. In the second half, he was moved back to his forward position, playing the half wall on the man advantage. Morand is more known for his playmaking abilities but he can score as well, he possesses a very good wrist shot with an excellent release. From the beginning of the season to the end we felt his shot was vastly improved, finding that he added more velocity to it. Already Morand plays a smart game at both ends of the rink, doesn't quit on the backcheck and is a good penalty killer due to his speed and anticipation.

O'Grady, Reagan
RD - Sudbury Wolves (OHL) 6'01" 191

Reagan was selected in the first round of the 2014 OHL Priority Selection Draft by the Kingston Frontenacs but was quickly delt to the Sudbury Wolves at the trade deadline. O'Grady has good size from the back end and plays a more defensive role for his team. His offensive game is still developing and with his late birthdate he has plenty of time to become more consistent with his outlet passes and choose better shooting lanes from the point. Going from a playoff team to the last place team in the OHL, O'Grady got some extra opportunities which included a little power play time for the Wolves.

Paquette, Jacob
LD - Ottawa Jr. 67's (OEMHL), 6'02" 195

Paquette was selected second round, 31st overall by the Kingston Frontenacs in the 2015 OHL Priority Selection Draft. Jacob is a skilled, intelligent two-way defender for the Ottawa Jr. 67's. Paquette reads the play as good as anyone in this draft class. He has incredible gap control skills; he also plays with a physical edge and will choose his timing wisely when to step up and deliver a punishing check at the blue line. Paquette anticipates the play very well and has the vision to make excellent outlet passes. He is also a good skater for his size and capable of carrying the puck and knows when to rush and when to pass. Paquette has excellent positional play in his own zone and angles shots to the outside and will win battles in the corners. He is patient with the puck on his stick and is calm under pressure, having the ability to curl back and find open players for outlet passes. Despite being so reliable on the backend, Jacob was great on the power play making smart puck decisions, good passes and has a very powerful shot from the point which he gets through on a pretty regular basis.

Pataki, Brady
RW - Sudbury Wolves (OHL) 6'02" 217

Pataki was a question mark going into this season coming out of the Chatham-Kent Cyclones program as to whether he will need a year of Jr. B before making the jump to the OHL. Brady impressed in camp and earned a spot playing on the Wolves' bottom six forward group. His skating is his biggest need for improvement but has progressed since the previous season. He is a huge forward who loves to play physical. He hits with a ton of power and looks for any excuse he can find to take the body. Pataki will look to improve and continue to adjust to his huge body but with his late birthdate he has two years before becoming eligible for the NHL Entry Draft.

Pettersson, Elias
LC – Timra (SWE Jr.) – 5'9" 123

Watching Elias stepping onto the ice for the first time in a J20 contest you might have thought he was his team's mascot. Barely over 120 pounds, as soon as he touched the puck that thought would however vanish away. His tremendous puck skills are immediately obvious. Probably because of his apparent lack of strength his skating had been holding him back till the most recent months, but it wasn't the case anymore in the very last part of the season, allowing him to better showcase his skills. Pettersson is very advanced at reading the play, his hockey IQ appears to be off the charts. He can complete one-touch passes as he knows where to put the puck before he gets it, or delay the play to open passing lanes when needed, as he has the skills to buy time for himself. He is just an outstanding passer overall. He already shows that puck protection will be a strength after filling out, as he angles his body perfectly. He is the kind of player that can get involved in puck battles with much bigger opponents, look overwhelmed and still find a way to let his team come up with the puck. Elias has a knack for positioning himself in lanes and intercept opponents' passes. On top of all of this, he possesses an accurate shot whose impressive velocity is difficult to explain looking at his diminutive size.

His brother Emil has been a Nashville draft pick in 2013 and is 6'2", Swedish hockey fans will be keeping their fingers crossed hoping for this 16yrs old kid to grow to an average size at least. If that starts to happen along the next two seasons, his name will be a very popular one by the time the 2017 draft comes around.

Phillips, Markus
LD – Toronto Titans (GTHL), 5'11" 204

Phillips was selected first round, 9th overall by the Owen Sound Attack in the 2015 OHL Priority Selection Draft. Markus is a smooth skating defenceman for the Toronto Titans. He moves with ease up and down the ice and can go from standing still to full speed very quickly. Phillips uses his exceptional skating ability to get himself out of trouble and often turns it into leading the rush up ice. He carries the puck with confidence and isn't shy about leading an offensive rush starting from his own zone. Always keeps his feet moving. He was relied upon to play significant minutes on the backend for the Titans and played in all situations. He does a sufficient job quarterbacking the power play, he often looks to pass before shooting but when he has the open lane he gets his low hard shot through from the point. His strength and work ethic often has him on the winning side of puck battles in front of his own net or in the corners. He is not afraid of getting into shooting lanes and blocking shots and has a very good stick when defending two-on-ones. Throughout the season Phillips has shown improvements to his defensive game and his gap control, as he was a big part of the Titans early success in the post-season. While his defensive game improved we saw a decline in his offence, he took on the role of being a steady defender late in the year but stopped being the offensive threat that he showed in the early stages of the season.

Popugayev, Nikita A.
RW – CSKA (MHL) – 6'4" 192

Nikita A. should not be confused with the other '98 born Nikita Popugayev (Nikita O.), as they are pretty much polar opposite players. Nikita A. is a lanky kid, and looking at his frame skating up the ice with the puck on his stick it's easy to see the potential. Popugayev can stickhandle, can finish his chances, and might develop into a strong skater for his size. He is however still a project of a player at this stage, the next step will be starting to produce in the MHL after his encouraging numbers at the U17 level.

Poulin, Anthony
LC – Commandeurs de Lévis (LHMAAAQ) – 5'8" 180

Anthony is a small centerman that plays well at both ends of the ice. He has nice offensive flair. When mixed with his hustle and acceleration, he's a constant threat when in possession of the puck. He's as good playing as a shooter as he is a passer. He's very quick when changing directions and in puck-protection; which makes him tough to contain. At 15 years old, he was playing on his team's 2nd power play unit and 1st penalty killing unit. This says a lot about his versatility and involvement on the ice. Poulin has a very high hockey IQ, with or without the puck, making him very efficient on the ice. Even with his small stature, he's tenacious, and this often helps him in his one-on-one battles versus bigger players in both offensive and defensive situations. He has good hand-eye coordination, which makes him very good at stealing pucks away from opponents in defensive situations. He's also well-known as a leader both off the ice and on the ice in the way that he plays. He was named assistant-captain with his Midget AAA team and was named captain of Team Quebec for the Canada Games last February. He went through a cold streak at the end of the season and in the playoffs. He looked like he lost some confidence while in possession of the puck, and was lacking his typical energy. He was also very involved defensively despite this, and remains an important part of his team because of his versatility.

Proner, Robert
LD – Toronto Titans (GTHL), 6'01.5" 210

Proner was selected second round, 30th overall by the Saginaw Spirit in the 2015 OHL Priority Selection Draft. Robert has excellent size, and played a strong and dependable role for the Titans this season. He skates well for a defenseman of his size and can protect the puck effectively. He showed a willingness to rush the puck at times and carried it into the offensive zone. Proner has an effective shot from the point as he often uses a short windup to get the puck through and on the net. He battles hard on the walls and often uses his size and strength to punish players when battling for the puck. He has an active stick and is generally able to keep opponents to the outside when entering the offensive zone. He makes strong tape-to-tape passes and is good at leading his teammates with passes through the neutral zone. Proner occasionally makes questionable decisions with the puck trying to force passes and make fancy plays. He will benefit from keeping his puck movement simple at the next level. Although he is a good skater for his size, there is room for improvement with his lateral footwork, which would make movements easier when keeping defenders on the outside. Proner also struggled this season with his discipline from time-to-time as he would get frustrated when things weren't going his way and often took penalties that put his team in a tough position.

Ratcliffe, Isaac
LW - London Jr. Knights (MHAO), 6'03.5" 171

Ratcliffe was selected first round, 15th overall by the Guelph Storm in the 2015 OHL Priority Selection Draft. Ratcliffe is a big power forward with big upside. He has excellent size and skates surprisingly well for such a big forward. His technique is a bit stiff but once he gets moving he can generate good speed. He has also shown the ability to evade checkers with his hands in combination with his skating when he enters the offensive zone. Ratcliffe started the year passing a little too much if anything, looking off good shooting opportunities to feed his teammates. As the season ended he was shooting the puck a lot more. He has an absolute cannon of a shot and is very dangerous with the puck, however he does miss the net a little too often. Ratcliffe is a smart player and is very adaptable to any situation. He will even play the point on the power play. Ratcliffe has a big body and has improved throughout the year in regards to playing a more physical style, however he still needs to be a little more aggressive and assert himself. Ratcliffe is a project who has huge upside if he can grow into his size and develop into the star player he has the potential to be.

Roberts, Elijah
RD – Toronto Marlboros (GTHL), 5'08" 151

Roberts was selected second round, 32nd overall by the Kitchener Rangers in the 2015 OHL Priority Selection Draft. Elijah played a two-way role for the Marlboros this season seeing a lot of ice in all game situations. He is small in stature but is very strong on his feet which make him very tough when battling for pucks along the wall. He combines strength and positioning to win a ton of battles, and often comes away with the puck. Roberts has very good gap control and is tough to beat in one-on-one situations as he uses his exceptional skating to stay on the opposition. He has been very hit or miss with the puck, capable of both excellent puck movement and some real mental errors with the puck. We have seen him make some very good stretch passes down the ice, but we have also seen him fumble the puck in his own zone causing him to turn the puck over. He does a good job eluding fore checkers and skating himself out of trouble in his own zone. Roberts is a player who has some intriguing potential as he is very athletic, and if he can grow and get stronger he can be a very good player at the next level. Improvements to his decision making, physicality and shot from the point will allow him to make the jump quicker.

Stevens, Liam
LW – Hamilton Jr. Bulldogs (SCTA), 5'07" 181

Stevens was selected second round, 27th overall by the Guelph Storm in the 2015 OHL Priority Selection Draft. Liam is an undersized stocky forward for the Hamilton Jr. Bulldogs. Despite playing on a weaker team Stevens managed to win SCTA Player of the Year as he recorded 51 points in 34 games during the regular season. He has very quick feet to go along with his quick hands, which make him a handful for defenders in one-on-one situations. He has really good speed which allows him to rush the puck effectively, and he has the ability to slip past defenders when carrying the puck down the wall. He plays a pretty physical style of game and loves to lay big hits on the oppositions biggest players. He does a good job of driving to the net off the wing and has scored some highlight reel goals. He didn't have much talent surrounding him but he still shared the puck and found a way to put up numbers and keep his team in games. We would like to see a little more consistency in Liam's game as he is unbelievable on some nights and just average on others. He will also benefit from growing which will help him continue to play a physical game against bigger opponents in the OHL. Stevens' projects to be a very talented player at the next level we just need to see the same compete level each and every game.

Strome, Matthew
LW – Toronto Marlboros (GTHL), 6'02" 181

Strome was selected second round, 8th overall by the Hamilton Bulldogs in the 2015 OHL Priority Selection Draft. Matthew captained the Toronto Marlboros this season and utilized his size and excellent hockey IQ to be an effective player for his team. Being the younger brother of New York Islanders forward Ryan and a future top NHL draft pick Dylan, Matthew has been shown the ropes as to what it takes to be successful. He possesses one of the highest hockey IQ's in this draft which allows him to play an effective role each and every game. Although Strome isn't blessed with the effortless skating like his teammate McLeod he makes up for it with his strong positional play. He plays in all situations and provided some excellent penalty killing during the GTHL Playoffs. He shows good leadership on the ice as he is always engaging in conversation with his teammates about what is expected on the upcoming shifts. For him to become an effective player and follow in his brothers footsteps he will need to work on his explosiveness and overall speed when rushing the puck up the ice. He has decent puck skills but there is room for improvement in both his stick handling and shot. We feel Strome will benefit from working his way up through the lower levels where he will be able to get stronger and work on his skating to be able to play at the fast pace of the OHL.

Suzuki, Nicholas
RC - London Jr. Knights (MHAO), 5'09.5" 180

Suzuki was selected first round, 14th overall by the Owen Sound Attack in the 2015 OHL Priority Selection Draft. Suzuki is a dynamic skilled forward for the London Jr. Knights. Few prospects in the OHL draft carry the level of flash and skill that Suzuki has put on display this season. He has the talent to score highlight reel goals. He has a high end shot that makes him a threat to score every time he has the puck in the offensive zone. He has good speed and is a very shifty skater. He also possesses good hands and is hard to take the puck away from. His defensive game is a work in progress and while he has shown some improvements in this area, he will need to continue to work on it. He was able to capitalize on some of the weaker teams piling up 4-5 goal games against some of the non-playoff teams in Alliance, while needing to be a little more consistent against teams with stronger and more talented defenders.

Teasdale, Joel
C/W – Gaulois d'Antoine-Girouard (LHMAAAQ) – 5'11" 184

Teasdale is a player who we have heard about for quite some time in Quebec, who didn't exactly have the start of the year we had hoped for, with 4 points in his first 11 games. He found his game the rest of the year, averaging close to a point per game and also had a nice showing at the Canada Games, playing for his province. Teasdale was slowed down by injuries during the year, including one at the end of December which made him miss over a month of action. Teasdale, who hails from Sainte-Julie, is a player with a high hockey IQ who understands the game very well at both ends of the ice. He's good on the penalty kill, with a sound positional game and good anticipation. We also saw him blocking shots on the PK, which is always a good sign coming from an offensive player. Offensively he was challenged this year, playing on the worst team in the league, without a lot of help. He can play either at center or on the wing, showing good versatility. He has good puck skills with a good arsenal of dekes to beat defenders one-on-one; Teasdale has quick and soft hands that help him. He's strong on his skates and does a good job protecting the puck along the boards and retrieving pucks in the corners. Teasdale is not overly flashy, but he's very efficient all over the ice for his team. We like his poise with the puck, as he has the ability to wait an extra second to make a pass to a teammate. We also like his vision, as he makes players around him better. One of our concerns with Teasdale has been his health going back to his bantam days. Here's hoping he stays away from the injury bug at the next level to fulfill his potential.

Thomas, Robert
RC - York-Simcoe Express (ETA), 5'08.5" 158

Thomas was selected second round, 26th overall by the London Knights in the 2015 OHL Priority Selection Draft. Robbie is a slick-skating centre with very good offensive instincts. He finds the open man well and his soft hands allow him to receive both good and bad passes very well. In possession, he has the unique ability to slow the pace of the game, avoid checks and create quality offense chances. While he is comfortable using his accurate wrist shot, Robbie is more of a playmaker thinking pass first. Robbie is also one of the more effective and crafty face-off centres in his peer group. At times, Robbie has a tendency to skate by the traffic areas without stopping and competing. While he won't overpower anyone defensively, his high hockey IQ enables him to read the play and use a good stick to break up plays.

Tippett, Owen
RW – Toronto Red Wings (GTHL), 5'11.25" 175

Tippett was selected first round, 4th overall by the Mississauga Steelheads in the 2015 OHL Priority Selection Draft. Owen is an elite offensive talent who played on a team that struggled all season. He often was the reason why they stayed in games and he proved that in his first round playoff performance against Don Mills. He is an exceptional skater with long powerful strides and can beat nearly any defender when he is on his game. Tippett does an excellent job using his size to either protect the puck or separate opponents from the puck. He has elite puck skills and excels at winning one-on-one situations before beating goalies with either his elite level shot or quick dekes. What makes him so dangerous is the NHL ready shot he possesses but also his high end passing ability, which makes him so unpredictable sometimes. He doesn't shy away from contact and is relentless when battling for loose pucks in the corner. Early in the year he struggled with consistency over a full game, but was able to be a game changer at any moment. Early on he showed selfishness in his game, but that came with being on a team where he was relied upon to provide all of the offense to keep his team in games. He loves to walk off the side boards to get a hard shot on goal, but needs to look to make back door passes to his teammate so he doesn't become predictable. Tippett has all of the tools to be very successful at the next level.

Vilardi, Gabriel
RC - CIHA Voyageurs (OEMHL), 6'02" 175

Vilardi was selected first round, 2nd overall by the Windsor Spitfires in the 2015 OHL Priority Selection Draft. Gabriel is a high end forward prospect playing with the CIHA Voyageurs. Gabriel has great size and uses it well to protect the puck. He always finds a way to get his shot off and gets good power in it. When controlling the puck, Vilardi does a great job of finding the open man. At times playing for CIHA this didn't result in a goal, but the number of scoring chances he could create over the course of a game was sometimes staggering. Vilardi competes at both ends of the ice and really just needs to get his skating improved upon to help him keep up better when the pace ramps up.

Voyer, Alex-Olivier
RC – Cantonnier de Magog (LHMAAAQ) – 6'1" 179

A big forward who plays very well at both ends of the ice, Alex-Olivier is a player with a lot of potential. He's a strong skater with a good mix of fluidity and speed for his size. He has a quick shot; he's the prototype power-forward. He's very efficient on the forecheck, he likes to play in traffic in the offensive zone. His hockey sense is well-developed and he makes good decisions when in possession of the puck. If he's not able to find an option, he's capable of protecting the puck for a long time in the offensive zone. He doesn't possess the best offensive upside, but his hockey sense and involvement make him a complimentary player to an offensive line. He even played some games this season on the point on the power play. What is the most liked in his game is his versatility; he can play on the wing or at center and be involved all the time in the play. He's often the first to get back defensively on the backcheck. His compete level is really high and he works hard in the defensive zone: he backchecks, he blocks shots, gets involved deep in his own zone, he anticipates plays in the defensive zone well and takes care of other little details that few players do. For this reason, he was one of the most utilised players on the penalty killing unit of his Magog team. More was expected out of him offensively this season, but he's such a complete player on the ice, and with his potential, he should not wait too long before hearing his name called.

Webb, Reilly
RD – Toronto Titans (GTHL), 6'02" 188

Webb was selected second round, 33rd overall by the Hamilton Bulldogs in the 2015 OHL Priority Selection Draft. Reilly has excellent size, and played a physical role for the Toronto Titans this season. He skates well for a player of his size and has shown his versatility playing both defense and right wing for his team. When playing forward Webb made his presence as a physical fore checker who took the body every chance he had. When playing defense he would play more of a stay at home style. He battles hard on the walls and punishes opposing players. At times Webb would go a little over the line, and take penalties, which we'd like to see him improve on by walking the line between physical and obstructive. Although Webb showed his ability to play anywhere in the lineup we see him as becoming more of a defensive defenceman who plays an assertive physical game at the next level.

Willms, Jason
LC - Kitchener Jr. Rangers (MHAO), 5'11.25" 179

Willms was selected third round, 43rd overall by the Sudbury Wolves in the 2015 OHL Priority Selection Draft. Jason has been a tremendous two-way player for the Kitchener Jr. Rangers this past season. Spending his second year in minor midget, he excelled despite missing time on multiple occasions for injuries. When you think of the type of player teams win with, Willms style of play comes to mind. He is a tenacious fore checker, his skating isn't perfect but it's effective and with the urgency he plays with, he forces a ton of turnovers. He is very intelligent in transition and quickly gets into excellent positioning. He doesn't possess high end skills, but is skilled enough with the puck to create plays and can pass and score equally well. Jason is one of, if not the best defensive forward in the Alliance area. He is willing to block shots, gets his stick in lanes and has excellent awareness in his own end. He's a tough player to play against and does a great job of shutting down the oppositions' top line. Jason projects to be a player who can provide secondary offense and play against the opposing teams' top line. He also is the kind of player who would be a great candidate to be a captain one day in the OHL. His style of play made him a favourite with our staff.

SCOUTS GAME REPORTS

White vs Red, Ivan Hlinka Canada U-18 camp, August 3rd 2014

WHT #3 RD Roy, Jeremy (2015): Didn't have his best game today, was not a threat offensively and Team White's power play was a non-factor. He had a solid game defensively with no glaring mistakes. Liked his work on the PK in the 3rd period, blocking shots despite the score being 6-0 for Team Red. Started to see the Jeremy Roy of last season late in the game with a couple of real nice shifts.

WHT #34 RW Merkley, Nick (2015): Merkley did a whole lot of nice things for Team White in a losing effort today. Loved his speed, and he uses it well on the forecheck. Created scoring chances using his speed on the outside, where opposing defensemen couldn't contain him. Showed good hands, creating a scoring chance for himself after a nice in/out move in the offensive zone in a one-on-one situation.

WHT #10 RD Spencer, Matt (2015): Spencer's play was decent today. He showed some good puck movement and at times showed good speed, rushing the puck from his zone. Made some good reads at both end of the ice, threw a nice open ice hit on Anthony Beauvillier in the 3rd period. Good release on his shot from the point.

WHT #22 LW Crouse, Lawson (2015): The big power forward was just okay today. He didn't get much going offensively, but showed strong puck-protection skills, using his big frame to shield opponents away. Down low, he's tough to knock down and handle. However, he was the victim of a turnover that led to a Team Red goal.

WHT #23 C Barzal, Matthew (2015): Not the best effort out of Barzal today, as he tried to do too much with the puck. He loves to have it on his stick, but never gave it back after he received it, electing to try the extra move, which caused turnovers.

WHT #16 C Harkins, Jansen (2015): A good game overall for the WHL prospect, who did some good work along the boards and was able to create some scoring chances with his hard work and strong forechecking presence. He was strong on the puck, was tenacious and didn't quit. His skating during the game was cause for concern, as he didn't have much explosion and just an average top speed.

WHT #14 C Konecky, Travis (2015): Loved his physical game today, as he threw many hits including one early in the game on Marner (one of the top players on Team Red). Although he's not a big kid, he did a fine job protecting the puck along the boards and using his back to shield opponents away from the puck. He's tough to knock off his skates.

WHT #5 LD Galipeau, Olivier (2015): Loved his aggressiveness to hit and make life tough for the opposing team, one of the most physical defensemen in this game. Galipeau was used in power play situations and struggled to move the puck quickly, making some bad decisions with the puck.

WHT #4 RD Bear, Ethan (2015): Similar to Galipeau, Bear is a tough player to play against and he showed that in today's game. Not tall, but very strong on his skates. He battles hard in his zone along the wall and in front of the net. Made some nice plays with the puck and was active in the offensive zone at times, trying to make plays.

WHT #2 LD McFadden, Garrett (2015): An undersized defenseman from the OHL, McFadden showed some quick feet in this game and a good burst of speed to get away from the opposing forecheckers.

He's shifty on the ice; he loves to rush the puck and have it on his stick in offensive situations. Can be risky at times trying to do too much, as he got caught pinching and that led to Team Red's 3rd goal.

WHT #40 G Tremblay, Olivier (2015): An undersized goaltender, Tremblay was down on his knees early today on some sequences. Played half of the game, letting in three goals, but I wouldn't blame him too much on any of them, as the Team White defense didn't have a good game at all. Loved his battle level in the crease and his very quick reflexes.

WHT #42 G McBride, Nick (2015): A good-sized goaltender who covers the net well. Came in relief to Tremblay and gave up three goals in the first ten minutes of action he saw. Didn't get much help from his defense, but could have had at least two of those goals back. Didn't seem confident in the 2nd period after coming in cold from the bench, but did come back strong in the 3rd period, not allowing a goal in the last 20 minutes.

RED #28 LW Beauvillier, Anthony (2015): He was one of the better players for his team today, bringing a lot of energy to his line with his speed and being able to contribute offensively. Finished a nice pass from Mitchell Stephens on a two-on-one, scoring the game's opening goal by sliding the puck under Olivier Tremblay. He made a great pass to Nicolas Roy for Team Red's 5th goal of the game. Took a bad offensive-zone penalty, but that's about the only bad thing he did today. Worked hard all game long.

RED #34 RW Marner,Mitchell (2015): Marner showed superb puck skills today, showing great patience and excellent puck control. He loves to have the puck on his stick and was dangerous every time he had possession. He's a super smart player and makes everyone around him better. He's a good skater that was able to go wide on Team White's defensemen today, showing a nice burst of speed. He's not afraid; he took some big hits today but got back right up immediately. He was very impressive without the puck as well, backchecking hard and also making a real nice play on Team Red's 6th goal, stealing the puck from a Team White player and beating McBride with a low blocker shot.

RED #16 C Roy, Nicolas (2015): Showed off his strong two-way game today, including some great moments on the PK, putting pressure on the forecheck with his long reach and active stick. A smart player who takes his man out when backchecking and blocks shots. Offensively, he was a little quiet in the first half of the game but came alive in the second half, scoring his team's 3rd goal after receiving a pass from Beauvillier in the slot, where he was able to get open. Looks like his skating has improved since last summer, and he also looks stronger, which helps him be more efficient at protecting the puck along the boards.

RED #21 C Stephens, Mitchell (2015): Loved his work ethic today. He made good use of his speed and made a great pass to Beauvillier for the game's opening goal. He was efficient on the forecheck and finished his hits.

RED #23 C/W Bethune, Jarred (2015): Loved his work ethic and how he was very tenacious on the forecheck. He scored his team's 4th goal by jumping on a rebound in front of the net. He did a good job most of the game driving the net. He may not be the biggest guy, but he was very good in front of the net at screening the goalie or making life hard for the opposing defense.

RED #5 RD Meloche, Nicolas (2015): Threw a big hit along the boards early in the first period, showing that he is strong on his skates. He does not have the quickest of feet, but moves the puck well from his zone. Made some good pinches in the offensive zone, as it helped keep pressure on Team White's defense.

RED #6 RD Myers, Philippe (2015): Not a flashy performer, but uses his size well in the defensive zone and in front of the net. His decision-making was on and off today, as he got caught taking too much time to make a play and turned the puck over right in front of his net. He is at his best when he stays within his limits, when he has the puck on his stick.

RED #13 LW Musil, Adam (2015): He is a strong kid along the boards and he's also capable when it comes to protecting the puck nicely in those situations. Not a speedster; got smoked while skating with his head down, but got his revenge with a good hit on #4 Ethan Bear later on.

RED #15 RW Knott, Graham (2015): A big kid who played a real smart game today. Scored the Reds' 3rd goal with a nice shot on a breakaway, showing impressive confidence taking his time before taking his shot, not bothered by an opposing player catching up to him. He made an unselfish play, taking a hit to make a play and keeping the pressure in the offensive zone. Didn't play a real physical game, but was smart at just separating opposing players from the puck thanks to his good size.

RED #11 C Strome, Dylan (2015): Scored a goal by winning a battle in front of the net. Strome is a strong kid on his skates. His skating seems to be a weakness, but he's a smart player and knows where to be in the offensive zone to be effective.

RED #31 G Sawchenko, Zachary (2016): Only faced five shots in 30 minutes of action today and didn't allow a goal. He was not tested at all by Team White in the first 30 minutes of the game. Not the biggest goaltender, but showed some good technique and composure in his crease. Tough to evaluate in a game like this.

RED #30 G Booth, Callum (2015): Booth is a good-sized goaltender who also shut off Team White today, blocking 14 shots in 30 minutes of play. He was more tested than his teammate Sawchenko in this game, mostly in the 3rd period when the game was out of reach. Liked his competiveness, as he didn't quit on 2nd and 3rd rebounds.

RED #10 C Estephan, Giorgio (2015): Showed some interesting flashes during the game. He is a good skater who is not afraid to rush the puck from his own zone, creating scoring chances for himself. He has good hands, and showed some nice dekes in one-on-one situations. Elusive on the ice, was able to see hits coming his way in time to get out of the way.

White vs Red, Ivan Hlinka Canada U-18 Camp, August 4th 2014

WHT #10 RD Spencer, Matt (2015): Made life hard for opposing forwards in his zone, played physical on them and didn't give them a lot of room to manoeuvre down low. Spencer was active in the offensive zone, pinching and keeping the puck deep in the Reds' zone and also getting open on the blue-line to receive passes. Also showed off a strong and accurate slapshot from the point.

WHT #16 C/LW Harkins, Jansen (2015): Showed good poise with the puck on his stick, making some good passes and making good decisions with the puck. Strong on the puck; it's tough to take the puck away from him. He does good work along the boards and around the net. His skating could use an upgrade, as he doesn't have good top speed and won't blow by anyone.

WHT #2 LD McFadden, Garrett (2015): Better puck management from him today than yesterday, as he chose to make the simple play with the puck rather than forcing it. He's a good skater and I saw him use that great speed by jumping into the play to create some offense. Got outmuscled in his own zone, as he is not the biggest kid, and Adam Musil got the better of him on one sequence.

WHT #8 C/W Noel, Nathan (2015): Worked hard during the game, but couldn't get things going offensively with his line. Loved to rush the puck in the offensive zone, and he does it pretty well thanks to his great skating ability. Can reach great top speed if he goes untouched in the neutral zone. Although he's undersized, he does a fine job protecting the puck versus bigger players.

WHT #9 C/W Speers, Blake (2015): A better effort from last night, but similar to his linemate Noel, couldn't achieve much offensively today. Competed harder tonight with some good hits, and he had the puck on his stick more often in this game.

WHT #22 C/W Crouse, Lawson (2015): Worked hard in all three zones and was really tough to handle for any defenseman due to his strength and size. Scored a goal from being around the net and jumping on a rebound. Played physical along the boards and was a beast on the forecheck. He doesn't lose many one-on-one battles. Once he has installed himself in front of the net on the power play or even strength, at this level he's tough to move from there.

WHT #6 LD Reddekopp, Chaz (2015): He got caught flat-footed in the offensive zone and didn't have enough speed to get back, taking a hooking penalty in the process. Some questionable plays with the puck tonight, and he was slow at making his decisions as well. Love the size, but his footwork needs work and puts him in trouble versus quicker forwards.

WHT #13 LW Soy, Tyler (2015): Good, quick feet, showed some flashes in the offensive zone with the puck but not enough to really leave a mark. Liked his burst of speed down the wing and how he can beat defensemen wide, and although he lacks strength, he's not afraid to take the puck to the net.

WHT #23 C Barzal, Matthew (2015): Love his skating ability. He loves to rush the puck in the offensive zone and does it well. He can get away from defensive coverage easily with one or two quick, short strides or just by changing directions. At his best on the power play, where he has more space and time to make plays. Played too much on the perimeter in the offensive zone and held on to the puck too long at times, trying to do too much on his own.

WHT #5 LD Galipeau, Olivier (2015): Once again, loved his aggressiveness in his zone and how he punished any opposing forwards coming into the zone. Had some struggles with the puck today; a turnover led to Team Red's first goal of the game. With the puck in the offensive zone, he was not very good, as he struggled and looked nervous with it. He missed some easy passes in his zone with no pressure on him.

WHT #14 LW Konecky, Travis (2015): Loved his compete level in this game. Konecky goes all out all the time, and at both ends of the ice. He gave the Team Red defense some problems on the forecheck, thanks to his quick stick, and he also loves to dish out some good hits along the boards. Scored Team White's 2nd goal with one second left in the game from a laser one-timer from the blueline.

WHT #40 G Tremblay, Olivier (2015): Fought hard to track the puck with traffic in front of him, as he is a small goaltender. Loved his compete battle in his crease, though his rebound control could have been better.

WHT #42 G McBride, Nick (2015): A better performance from him today than yesterday as he covered his net well with his big frame and didn't go down on his knees too early. Moves okay laterally, showing a sound rebound control today.

WHT #4 RD Bear, Ethan (2015): Liked Bear's game today, as he made some good decisions with the puck and some good reads. He has a quick release on his hard shot from the point, and he showed some upside in the offensive zone today. One negative in his game today was one sequence where he lost the puck behind his net, leading to a great scoring chance for Dylan Strome.

WHT #34 RW Merkley, Nick (2015): One of the best players on his team today, showing once again that he's one of the fastest skaters in camp. Finished every hit on the forecheck, and defensemen will get rid of the puck quickly when they know he's on the ice. Drives the net every chance he gets. Showed off some good agility as well; he was able to avoid getting hit while carrying the puck. Showed some good on-ice vision tonight, making some pretty passes in the offensive zone.

RED #8 LD Davies, Kevin (2015): With his effortless stride, he can rush the puck out of his zone with ease. He is not overly big, and it can be difficult for him versus bigger players in his own zone. He has a good first pass and some qualities in him to make him an offensive defenseman.

RED #28 LW Beauvillier, Anthony (2015): Scored the Reds' 2nd goal from the side of the net, finding a hole in his 2nd attempt. He has a nice scoring touch around the net and he showed why with this goal. Not as good as in game one, but did work hard at both ends of the ice and played the role of sparkplug once again.

RED #34 RW Marner, Mitchell (2015): Marner showed once again his superior puck skill in this game, though maybe at times he got too cute with the puck. Again, he showed some impressive work without the puck and was able to make a couple of steals, with one almost ending up being a goal for Team Red. His passes are precise, and he's very imaginative with the puck. Few players at this camp can think the game like he does.

RED #30 G Booth, Callum (2015): Booth tracked the puck very well in this game, even with traffic in front of him. Very good in 2nd and 3rd rebound saves, doesn't quit on a puck and can make some highlight reel saves with his attitude. Didn't give up a goal in 30 minutes of play—he has not allowed a goal so far in camp in 60 minutes.

RED #6 RD Myers, Philippe (2015): Laid out Crowse with a big-time hit, which was a rare time we saw Crouse take the worst of a hit. Did a good job clearing the front of the net with his size and stick work. Nothing flashy about his game offensively, but he makes smart plays with the puck. His footwork can be an issue versus quick forwards. Used his reach well in defensive situations.

RED #16 C Roy, Nicolas (2015): A good overall game out of Roy at both ends of the rink. He was very strong on the puck and it was tough to take it away from him. Used his reach and size well to help him protect the puck in the offensive zone.

RED #21 C/W Stephens, Mitchell (2015): Great game from Stephens today, who scored a beauty of a goal firing a shot from the faceoff circle after getting out of the corner. Did a good job protecting the puck and worked hard along the wall with his line cycling the puck. He has a good burst of speed down the wing and surprised the opposing defensemen, going wide on them and driving the net. Strong effort on the forecheck as well.

RED #23 RW Bethune, Jared (2015): Liked his speed tonight, as he used it well at both ends of the ice. Made some good hits tonight on the forecheck and was tough to play against. Did a great job in front of the net screening the goaltender, he battled hard and was tough to deal with there.

RED #11 C Strome, Dylan (2015): Not a real flashy player but always seems to be at the right place at the right time. Scored a goal after receiving a pass from Marner who created turnover behind the team WHITE net found him in front of the net for team RED first goal.

RED #31 G Sawchenko, Zachary (2016): He showed quick reflexes, covering the lower part of the net very well. Although he's not big, he does track the puck well even with traffic in front of him. He made some real good saves in the 3rd period, keeping the lead for Team Red.

RED #5 RD Meloche, Nicolas (2015): Not a fan of his footwork and of how he got beat wide on a couple of occasions. He's a big, strong kid that can hold on to big players along the wall, but could be meaner in certain situations. Moves pucks quickly out of his zone, but his passes were lacking a little bit of accuracy today.

Canada vs. Sweden, 2014 Hlinka Memorial Tournament, August 12th, 2014

CAN #25 W Musil, Adam (2015): He was not very noticeable in the first 50 minutes of the game, though he did some good work in front of the net for Canada's 4th goal. He's a big kid and he's tough to move up from there.

CAN #12 C Harkins, Jansen (2015): Solid game from Harkins, who was able to create some scoring chances for himself by working hard in the offensive zone. Liked his work on the PK unit blocking shots and having an active stick. Scored Canada's 5th goal on a penalty shot, which was not a pretty goal but the puck still found its way behind the Swedish goaltender Sandstrom. Harkins lacks explosiveness in his strides, and overall lacks quickness at the moment.

CAN #27 RD Spencer, Matt (2015): Made some good decisions with the puck and some strong pinches to keep pressure in the offensive zone. Even deep in the offensive zone he showed some good puck control and was poised. He showed good speed when rushing the puck from his zone, playing most of the game paired with Jeremy Roy. Threw some good hits also, mostly on the PK.

CAN #15 LW Soy, Tyler (2015): Soy played well today, making things happen even if he didn't have the puck. A good active stick by him led to a great scoring chance for his line after he stole the puck from a Swedish defenseman. Liked that he kept his feet moving and kept working hard which led to a penalty for Team Sweden. Nice pass to Stephens for Canada's 3rd goal.

CAN #23 C Stephens, Mitchell (2015): Though Stephens was not very noticeable other than the two goals he scored, both goals were from near the net. The first one was from a rebound and the 2nd came when he jumped on a loose puck. Other than those two goals, I didn't notice Stephens a whole lot in this game.

CAN #16 RW Marner, Mitchell (2015): Marner showed elite stickhandling and puck control today but it didn't show in terms of results for him. He skates well and he's very smart both with and without the puck. Sometimes, he tried too much with the puck to create some offense for his line.

CAN #7 RD Roy, Jeremy (2015): Did a lot of nice things on the power play today, showing nice patience with the puck, waiting until the last second to find some open teammates. Moved the puck nicely from the left point on the power play today, as he was paired with Matt Spencer. Lots of his shots were blocked from the point in the first period, as he was clearly part of Sweden's game plan. Nice play rushing the puck from his zone and getting away from pressure which led to Canada's 3rd goal by Mitchell Stephens.

CAN #18 LW Konecky, Travis (2015): Played a lot today, mostly with Barzal on every shift. Strong forecheck presence; gets his nose dirty along the boards and in front of the net. Made some real good passes today that were both hard and accurate.

CAN #14 C Barzal, Matthew (2015): Showed off his great speed all game long, and his quick hands in tight. Liked his effort on some shifts without the puck, some impressive backchecking moments as well including one where he stopped a great scoring chance by not quitting on the backcheck. Held on to the puck a little bit too long at times, waiting too long to make a pass and the scoring opportunity either disappeared or the teammate was no longer open.

CAN #22 RW Knott, Graham (2015): Nothing flashy from him today, but most of the time he was keeping the play simple and making smart plays. Not a bad skater for his size, moves around well enough and he's tough to either knock down or strip the puck from. Did the dirty work for his line today.

CAN #31 G Sawchenko, Zachary (2016): Canada was all over the Swedes most of the game today, so Sawchenko didn't get a lot of work. Not much of a chance to stop Sweden's first and only goal, after a nice tip right in front of him. Liked his level of calm in his crease and how he did a fine job with his rebound control.

CAN #2 RD Bear, Ethan (2015): Loved his compete level in the defensive zone. He's tough to play against even if he's not the biggest guy out there. He's strong on the puck and can make some nice plays in the offensive zone, but can be slow at times in making a decision with the puck and his shots get blocked as a result.

CAN #17 LW Crowse, Lawson (2015): Not many players at this level can contain him in front of the net. He scored Canada's 2nd goal jumping on a rebound. Can hold onto the puck for a while; excels in protecting and cycling it. On the power play, Team Canada uses him in front of the goaltender to create some havoc in front of the net and possibly tip in shots from the point. He has a good skating stride for a big kid and works hard at both end of the ice. Loved seeing his smarts on the penalty killing unit.

CAN #16 C Roy, Nicolas (2015): Loved how he supported his defenseman very well in his zone, acting like a 3rd defenseman at times. Saw some good shifts on the forecheck with Merkley, using his long stick to give the Swedish defense headaches, leading to Canada's 2nd goal. Used his long reach and size well to protect the puck, showing nice poise with the puck and how he can be a very creative playmaker.

CAN #10 RW Merkley, Nick (2015): One of the best from Team Canada to put pressure on the forecheck; loved his speed and how well he used it. He loves to hit and he's strong on his skate. Showed nice creativity with the puck and was able to set up his teammates on a couple of occasions. Makes a lot of things happen with his speed; he has a non-stop motor and he's tough to contain.

SWE #11 LW AHL, Filip (2015): Played a power game, using his size well to protect the puck and drive the net. Could be quicker, but once he gets that big frame going, he's tough to stop. Showed some nice flashes, but not enough to really make an impact in the game.

SWE #1 G Sandstrom, Felix (2015): Gave up five goals today, but I felt as though his defense didn't really help him out today. His rebound control was a bit off, which led to the 2nd and 3rd Canadian goals. One could make the case that he could have had the penalty shot goal back, but overall, the Swedish defense didn't look good today versus a much better Canadian team. I like his poise and demeanor in front of his net, doesn't seem to get rattled by much.

SWE #6 LD Kylington, Oliver (2015): Real quick and agile skater from the back end, and without a doubt the most skilled player on Team Sweden at this tournament. Can rush the puck in the offensive zone with ease thanks to his skating ability, quarterbacking Team Sweden's power play and moving the puck well. He's also quite active in the offensive zone. Loves to have the puck on his stick, and as shown tonight, he has some real good puck skills but can be risky at times when trying to do too much.

SWE #20 RW Looke, Jens (2015): Showed some interesting flashes today; a good skater with a nice burst of speed that he uses if he wants to go wide on a defensemen or create separation between him and the defenders. Showed some good puck skills and was able to pull off one or two good dekes in one-on-one situations.

SWE #17 LW Grundstrom, Carl (2016): The youngest player on the Swedish team, Grundstrom showed some jam in this game, not backing down versus a top Canadian team. Didn't mind getting hit and had some good hits of his own. Didn't back down after whistles as well. Didn't do a whole lot in term of offense, other than creating a penalty after a good scoring chance in the slot.

SWE #4 LD Younan, Alexander (2015): Made a nice pass/shot to #23 Magnusson, who made a nice tip for the lone goal for Team Sweden, a real smart play as he kept the puck low which made it easier to tip in. Good sequences in his zone as well, blocking shots in front of the net. Overall, he played a decent game at both ends of the rink, is a decent skater and capable of rushing the puck at times if he doesn't try too much.

SWE #29 LD Karlsson, Gabriel (2015): Played in all situations of the game with #6 Kylington; I liked his frame and long reach he has to work with in defensive situations. Needs some work in terms of mobility and agility, but he does play a smart game. Needs to be more polished, but on the power play, I did notice he made some smart decisions with the puck. At that size he could have been more physical today, playing versus a rugged Canadian team.

SWE 3 LD Alftberg, Philip (2015): Played on the 2nd power play unit, moved the puck okay in this game. He made some good passes, but could stand to make quicker decisions with the puck. Needs some work on his shot from the point. In his own end, he was overmatched physically versus bigger and stronger Canadian forwards. Lost pucks in his zone after being pressured, which led to #17 Crowse's goal in the 2nd period.

Owen Sound Attack at Barrie Colts – Preseason, September 1 2014

C Ethan Szypula (2015) – Szypula made an impact early in this one beating Daniel Gibl blocker side from the top of the circle. The shot was a little weak, but it was accurate and he did a good job getting it off quickly. He wasn't afraid to battle in the corners against bigger players, and didn't shy away from the dirty areas.

D Thomas Schemitsch (2015) – Schemitsch played a steady game for the Attack in this one. He consistently made accurate outlet passes, which allowed Owen Sound to safely exit the defensive zone. Some of his outlets could have used a little more power, but they were still effective for the most part. His positioning defensively was solid, and he used a good stick to disrupt oncoming forwards. He was calm when pressured by forecheckers and generally made good decisions with the puck. On the powerplay he did a nice job distributing the puck and getting shots through. Schemitsch scored on a wrist shot that found its way through traffic.

D Tyler MacArthur (2015) – MacArthur also played a pretty sound game on the backend. He made smart reads with the puck, and did a good job getting it out of danger areas. He pinched into the play to help create offense a couple times, but he ensured he was quick to get back and really picked his spots before doing so. MacArthur was willing to take hits to make a play, and did a good job clearing the front of the net; especially when shorthanded.

D Rasmus Andersson (2015) – Andersson absorbed contact well and powered through several checks. Andersson consistently hit teammates right in the tape with passes regardless of the difficulty, and was accurate with his shots as well. He was able to get good power on most of his shots, and got them through traffic and on goal in most cases. He was very fluid, poised and never panicked in the defensive zone. His positioning was solid, and he sealed off oncoming forwards well.

D C.J. Garcia (2015*) – Garcia continues to look like a new player. He took a couple hits to make plays, and didn't retaliate to a knee-on-knee collision. Garcia used his good speed and skating ability to take the puck out of danger, and made good outlets throughout the game. He used his stops/starts to lose oncoming players, and showed a lot more poise than we saw last year. Garcia was physical, but didn't take himself out of position to lay the body. He sealed players off well, and his positioning throughout the game was solid.

W Roy Radke (2015) – Radke made an impact in a variety of ways during this game. He was physical, consistently finished his checks and had a few huge hits. Radke skated through hits on occasion, and regularly knocked opponents off the puck. He won battles in the corner, which helped him create a few chances, and he showed nice hands in tight going forehand-backhand before scoring the eventual game-winning-goal.

C Matthew Kreis (2015) – Kreis continued on what has been a strong training camp and preseason. He showed good speed through the neutral zone and safely carried it into the offensive zone on several occasions. Kreis made a couple nice plays in the defensive zone to break up Attack rushes, and was committed to a 200-foot game. Offensively, he showed good vision and distributed the puck well leading to a few good chances. Kreis was able to win some battles along the wall, and didn't shy away from contact. He wasn't dominant, but he was effective and contributed in all aspects of the game.

September 1, 2014 - Saginaw Spirit at Sarnia Sting

OHL Exhibition Game

SAG #5 RD Crawford, Marcus (2015) - Marcus displayed a good stick in one on one situations but will give too much space at times. He showed very smooth mobility and good skating ability, able to carry the puck. He rushed a puck clearing attempt when he had time which resulted in a chance on goal, but recovered by clearing the second chance.

SAG #27 RC Stephens, Mitchell (2015) - Stephens was very composed when using his speed to carry the puck into the offensive zone. He scored by jumping on a loose puck in the slot. In the shootout he was able to deke out the goaltender but lost the handle on the puck.

SAG #62 LC Felhaber, Tye (2016) - Felhaber looked a bit tentative in this game, but it did address his biggest concern going from Minor Midget, which was puck distribution. He was doing a very good job making smart simple passes to advance the play and wasn't trying to do too much. He was very apprehensive around physical play and appeared to grip his stick a little too hard on a scoring chance in the slot.

SAG #1 G Murdaca, Joseph (2016) - Joseph played one period plus overtime and the shootout. He didn't face much action during his 25 minutes of action but did an excellent job in the shootout making huge saves before eventually getting beat for the winning goal on his last shooter.

SAG #39 G Ovsjannikov, David (2015) - David does a good job of coming out and cutting down angles quickly. He was capable of making the second save on rebounds. He really struggles handling the puck making bad reads on when to come out and play the puck and also made questionable decisions when he had the puck on his stick.

SAR #3 LD Black, Alex (2015) - Alex struggled today struggling to make the play with the puck out of the defensive zone despite multiple attempts. He blindly threw the puck away at one point which resulted in a scoring chance against. He was capable of playing a physical game but was penalized at one point for jumping ahead to land a hit.

SAR #5 LD Chychrun, Jakob (2016) - Jakob made a great end to end rush with the puck and was steady defensively, but didn't do too much beyond that.

SAR #6 RW Bushnell, Noah (2015) - Loves to play a physical game. He looked for every possible opportunity to finish his check. His skating still needs a fair amount of improvement.

SAR #9 LW Lajeunesse, Troy (2015) - Troy was effective early on providing a steady forecheck and causing turnovers. He set up one of Sarnia's goals with a strong forecheck to cause the turnover, then followed it up with a quick pass into the slot. He seemed to get a little exhausted as the game went on.

SAR #12 LC Lindberg, Brandon (2015) - Lindberg showed excellent work ethic and forecheck as he created chances in the offensive zone.

SAR #13 LW Ciccarelli, Matteo (2015) - Matteo was effective in finishing his checks and even forced some turnovers. He mishandled the puck in the scoring area.

SAR #14 LC Zacha, Pavel (2015) - Pavel has great size and good strength. He was willing to use it by playing physical, taking the body multiple times. He has a laser release on his shot but missed the net a few times. He got a chance on the shootout but was stopped by the goaltender.

SAR #20 LD Schlichting, Connor (2015) - Connor is making plays quicker showing progression in his puck playing ability. However he got walked one on one.

SAR #26 LC Kodola, Vladislav (2015) - Vladislav showed flashes of skill and skating. He beat the defender late in a tie game for a chance but took the low percentage shot instead of the higher percentage pass. He mishandled the puck in the defensive zone which maintained the opponents zone pressure. Kodola struggled drastically in the face-off circle losing virtually every draw, many of them cleanly.

SAR #27 RC Kyrou, Jordan (2016) - Jordan had a very good game today showing great skating and puck control ability. He drew a late penalty in a tie game with his puck handling skills. He is able to open himself up for shots evading defenders and creating enough space to get his shot off. He was forcing his shot a little bit on the power play. In the shootout he made a great play with quick hands to beat the goaltender and win the game in the shootout.

SAR #33 G Fazio, Justin (2015) - Justin displayed great quickness. He gets across the crease very well with fluid movement. He made a great cross ice glove save.

Final Score: Sarnia Sting: 3 - Saginaw Spirit: 2 - OT/SO

Erie Otters at Barrie Colts, Sept 4, 2014

Score: 7-6 Barrie in a shootout

C Connor McDavid (2015) – McDavid put on one of the best individual performances I've seen in a very long time. With 11 Erie regulars out of the lineup due to rest before NHL camps or injuries, as well as several others graduating, McDavid singlehandedly kept Erie in this game and gave them a chance to win. After Barrie took a 5-1 lead, McDavid took a bad offensive zone penalty and seemed flustered. Then he simply took the game over. He used his explosive stride to gain high-end speed through the neutral zone and gain the line with possession. He always managed to slip through seams and get open, and displayed a quick release getting several good shots off in the slot. McDavid had several beautiful end-to-end rushes that lead to goals for his team. He thought the game at a high speed, showed great creativity and was able to hit teammates regularly. Whether he threaded the needle through some feet, bounced it off the boards or used a saucer pass through traffic, he found open teammates frequently. McDavid played some penalty kill and wasn't afraid to get in the shooting lane to block shots. At one point he blocked a Jonathan Laser slap shot, grabbed the puck and took it the other way before scoring a short-handed breakaway goal. He regularly took defenders wide with speed and took it towards the danger area after gaining a step. He scored a power play goal, even strength goal as well as a short-handed marker while tallying two assists to boot. McDavid also showed off his great hands on numerous occasions, including in the shootout when he made Daniel Gibl look foolish.

D Cole Mayo (2015) – Due to some injuries, Mayo was given the opportunity to play on Erie's top defense pairing. Mayo finished his checks whenever he could, and had good gap control throughout the night. He sealed off oncoming forwards a couple times throughout the night, was positionally sound and wasn't afraid to block shots. Mayo blocked a shot, left the game for a minute or two and his first shift back he didn't hesitate and blocked two more shots. One area Mayo did struggle with was his outlet passing. His outlet passes weren't accurate, as he missed several open teammates with breakout passes throughout the game.

G Daniel Dekoning (2015*) – Dekoning got off to a dreadful start in this one. His positioning was off, he was overcommitting, and as a result a lot of pucks were getting by him. He allowed a weak goal low blocker, and was beat with a couple poor shots when there was little to no traffic. His rebound control was poor early on as well. Dekoning did get much better as the game went on, though. After allowing five goals in the first period or so, he settled in and allowed one goal the rest of the way. He made some big saves, and allowed Erie to stay in the game to get back in it. It certainly wasn't his best performance, but there were some positives.

Barrie

D Rasmus Andersson (2015) – Andersson had a good game for the Colts, and was quite good offensively. Andersson consistently was able to get pucks through, and got good power in his shots while doing so. He did a nice job of holding the line and keeping pucks in the offensive zone, which lead to several scoring opportunities the Colts otherwise wouldn't have had. Andersson's gap control was good, particularly with McDavid, but McDavid did manage to beat him clean in open ice at one point. Andersson's defensive work was good, especially on the rush. One play in particular an Erie forward tried to hit another player over the middle to stretch the defense and Andersson rubbed him right off the puck before retrieving it and making a good outlet pass. Andersson jumped into the rush a few times to help create some offense, and he was able to make oncoming Erie forwards miss in open ice.

W Matthew Kreis (2015) – Kreis played a solid two-way game in this one. He had a good stick in the neutral zone, which caused some turnovers and forced Erie to reset offensively on several occasions. He was able to carry the puck into the offensive zone with possession with regularity, and set up shop on the half-wall before making a play with the puck to create offense. He managed to lose defenders and find open ice, which helped him generate some scoring chances in tight. Kreis was dangerous coming off the wall, as he had some good shots and also distributed the puck well in those situations. Kreis knew where to be on the ice, and always seemed to be in the right place to pounce on rebounds. He earned himself a couple second chance opportunities by doing so. He was always back to be an outlet for the defense, he was creative in open ice and scored a nice goal going five-hole in the shootout.

W Roy Radke (2015) –He had a couple chances throughout the game, but wasn't much of a factor. He wasn't as physical as I've seen in games past, and struggled to get anything going offensively. Radke broke up a couple plays in the defensive zone and finished his checks when he could, but was pretty quiet in this one.

C Cordell James (2015*) – James was quite effective in this game. He won several battles for loose pucks, and did a very nice job defensively. His positioning was good, especially on the penalty kill, as he took away shooting lanes, broke up passes and made it difficult for Erie to create offense. On the other side of the puck, James was creative offensively and productive. He had a beautiful saucer pass to hit a trailing Nick Pastorious, which turned into a goal. He also showed good hands eluding two Erie defenders before sending a cross-ice feed to Justin Scott for an empty net tap in.

Sep. 7, 2014 – Kamloops Blazers v. Victoria Royals (WHL Pre-Season)

KAM #3 LD Maier, Patrik (2015) – A talented backwards skater with sharp awareness in reverse. Needs to work on his puck skills. Passes were often way off course, and the same goes for shots. Turned the puck over a couple of times in the offensive zone after making a few foolish passing attempts. Nonetheless, strong skating skills and decent gap control meant that he was on the ice a lot and stood out as a fairly dependable minute munching defenseman who excels in his own zone.

KAM #10 RC Revel, Matt (2014) – Looked like a very talented playmaking centre with decent skating skills, good energy and excellent passing abilities. In terms of passing, he is better at giving than receiving, but there is still a lot to like. Good along the walls and in the corners. He was on the ice for two of Kamloops even-strength goals, including providing the screen for a Brady Gaudet rocket overtime winner.

KAM #24 RD Rehill, Ryan (New Jersey 2014) – Looking bigger and badder this year than last, Rehill was a scary player to be up against in this game. An attitudinal puck moving defensemanwith size, grit, and a smatter of skill. Hits hard and delivers a steady if unspectacular first pass. His game was a bit frantic at times, as he had issues with discipline and came plummeting to the ice on his own command on a couple of occasions.

KAM #34 RW Sideroff, Deven (2015) – Stood out as a useful plugger in the neutral zone, constantly disrupting passing efforts. I really like his full stride and effort on the backcheck. Consumes space and eats up pucks in the neutral zone with decent size, an active stick, and long, desperate reaches for the puck. Looks much bigger than the 5-foot-11 he's listed as. Looked especially effective on the penalty kill, where he made a number of good checks on defenceman. Had a couple scoring chances, too.

KAM #41 RG Kehler, Cole (2014) – Kehler only played half of the game, but he was excellent in my opinion. First and foremost, he already comes equipped with NHL size. Furthermore, his angles, rebound control, and poise all look very good for a player of his age. I liked how he tracked the puck amidst the chaos and how he followed opposition shots with his eyes. Seems to have a tendency to look behind himself a lot on shots, erring on the side of caution and choosing to be safe rather than sorry.

VIC #2 LD Hicketts, Joe (2014) – Using a stick much higher than usual for a player of his height, Hicketts had tremendous gap control while skating backwards, and is very difficult to beat one-on-one. As for his slapshot, much has been said of it elsewhere. But one area that might go understated, is Hicketts' ability to find or open shooting lanes through lateral movement up high. In this game, I think he took 5 or 6 shots, and all of them reached the net. This was an excellent performance.

VIC #6 RD Brown, Travis (Chicago 2012) – Steady and sturdy on his skates, he transitions from north-to-south in good timing. Made a few really good plays for the Royals on the power play, working the quarterback position in tandem with Joe Hicketts. Though he didn't score, he got a few good shots on net, including one that led to a goal by Tyler Soy at the beginning of the second period.

VIC #7 LD Kolhauser, Jake (2014) – Employed a smart puck possessing game, looking much more agile and comfortable with the puck this year. Made really strong passes in all three zones, and was difficult for the opposition forecheckers to get around. Played more minutes than is typical for a third pairing defenceman, receiving dutiful time at even strength, penalty kill, power play and four-on-four situations.

VIC #9 RD Walker, Jack (2014) – His ability to shield the puck along the high wall is one of his best assets in my opinion. Not particularly big or intimidating, Walker is pretty fearless and headstrong with the puck, unafraid of taking it into dangerous areas and virtually unperturbed by physical play or altercation. It's somewhat difficult to read his nonchalant attitude at times; he can be regularly seen lip-synching to the arena rock music while sitting on the bench.

VIC #17 LC Soy, Tyler (2015) – Stride looks much, much longer and each kick more powerful than they did in years previous. A good passer, Soy is an even better pass receiver, who is capable of almost instantly steadying even the most wobbliest of pucks or adjudicating for the poorest of passes. He potted a quick goal in the first off of a sweet rebound set up by Travis Brown. Also of note, Soy won the majority of his faceoffs in this one.

VIC #18 LC Hannoun, Dante (2016) – Despite having great speed and generally good awareness in the offensive zone, his lack of size really limits him at the major junior level. Looked outsized and overmatched, getting beaten by a streaking Luke Harrison, who is typically a depth checking player. Did, however, look ahead of the curve in terms of his faceoff abilities and general maneuverability. Hannoun's development might just be a waiting game for the Royals.

VIC #29 LD Reddekopp, Chaz (2015) – Tonight, he played side-by-side almost entirely with captain Joe Hicketts. Reddekopp was poorly positioned and suffered from slow footspeed in this one. Puck handling skills can also reveal warts at times, further limiting his abilities on both ends of the ice. Too often was pulled out of position and didn't possess sufficient agility or footspeed to get back in time. Only played even strength, and took occasional shifts on the penalty kill.

Sep. 8, 2014 – Kamloops Blazers at Vancouver Giants (WHL Pre-Season)

KAM #2 RD Fora, Michael (2014) – Played a simple and steady game full of all the "nuances" and "intangibles" that scouts and coaches really like. A smooth skater with great size, who spans the ice quickly and retrieves pucks gracefully, he left the tilt with a goal and a +1. This is a player, who on first viewing, seems swivel-headed, calm-headed, and equipped with good hockey IQ. I liked that he took a physical approach to the game.

KAM #7 RW Kryski, Jake (2016) – Jake Kryski, who I noted on my scoresheet in the game previous for having a really nice wristshot, played yet another really strong game in which he was afforded opportunities to show off his shooting skills. On my first viewing, I assumed he was an overager based on his play. Strong skating, passing, and shooting all stand out. Kryski scored a beautiful goal while streaking down the wing in the first period.

KAM #14 RC Needham, Matt (2013) – Needham stood out from the pack early in this one as a powerful skater and thoughtful two-way pivot. He surprised me with his physicality and hitting. He formed a really strong line alongside Sideroff and Nathan Looysen that was dangerous all night long. He was on the ice for two of the Blazers' goals.

KAM #23 LD Gaudet, Brady (2013) – Fluidity in motions and solid stickhandling underpin the game of this two-way defensemanwho has a bevy of puck moving options—part skater part passer he can either outlet the puck with ease or make a rush with his skating abilities. Add to that list of abilities a booming slapshot, and you wind up with a pretty attractive package here, regardless of age or size.

KAM #34 RW Sideroff, Deven (2015) – Continued where he left off the day earlier, proving himself as a dependable two-way forward for the second game in a row. A decent skater with better reach than his size suggests. Strong positional play translates to effective cycling technique in the offensive zone, whereas strong positional play led to good shot blocking in the defensive end. A Don Hay-type player.

VAN #8 LC Baer, Alec (2015) – This was an underwhelming game for Alec Baer, who looked so promising during the Giants pre-season camp. When playing on the power play, he could look a bit "puck-hog"-ish at times, and made a couple of errors that led to turnovers. Didn't show a lot of hustle or bustle and lacked work-ethic in his board and corner battles.

VAN #11 LW Stukel, Jakob (2015) – Fights almost too hard for his space and might over-think things a bit, as he had to jump a number of enormous hurtles to have any success in this game. A fantastic skater with the puck, he once again made a couple of nice individualistic plays that almost led to a goal. Mysteriously isn't scoring, but is still shows great puckhandling ability, deking skills, hand-eye coordination and passing traits. Scored with just seconds remaining in the third.

VAN #17 LW Benson, Tyler (2016) – Didn't score any points but played a pretty good game on all sides of the puck. One of the fastest, strongest, and most difficult players to contain, he does a good job of streaking to the front of the net quickly and getting opportunities there. Plays a physical game and has a ton of hustle. It's hard to believe he's also one of the youngest players on the ice, too.

Sep. 8, 2014 – Kelowna Rockets vs. Victoria Royals (WHL Delta Pre-Season Invitational)

KEL #3 LD Stadel, Riley (2014) – Played a comfortable game in which he looked far more fluid in his motions than he did last year. Looking less robotic and more agile, he's still not as explosive on his skates as I would like. Nonetheless difficult to remove from the puck. Manufactured some effective first passes, but was ultimately limited by a lack of effort and discipline from his teammates up front. Later, wound up in the box on a holding call that came after falling a few steps behind his check.

KEL #10 RC Merkley, Nick (2015) – Coming off of the recent Ivan Hlinka tournament and a pre-season game the night before in which he exerted much energy, his ice-time seemed heavily limited in this one, as did his compete level. Looked "pumped" in the warmup, showing strong skating skills accentuated by powerful pushes and a deep knee bend, but started the game with little fire. Seemed tired and frustrated. Lost a number of important board battles in all zones and was no better in the faceoff circle.

KEL #23 LW Kirkland, Justin (Nashville 2014) – I don't know if it was tiredness, rink rust, or lack of motivation, but he lacked speed all game and came across as rather feeble when pressured for the puck. Effort on the backcheck and his own end looked particularly lackadaisical. On the other hand, he showed decent puck moving skills, a decent wristshot, and wasn't ever a lone liability on the ice as it was a fairly sloppy team effort tonight.

KEL #24 LW Baillie, Tyson (2014) – Didn't have a lot of puck support, so his hard work often went unrewarded. Physical proportions aren't ideal, but he appears to have a strong lower body and is an excellent skater. Lacks seriousness at times, but he wore an 'A' through much of last season, and so one can't help but conjecture that he has at least some leadership qualities.

VIC #19 RC Hannoun, Dante (2016) – One of the more interesting contrasts you may ever see in a hockey game is watching the 5-foot-6 Dante Hannoun play on the same line as the 6-foot-6 Axel Blomqvist. Skating alongside each other in full gear, you almost get the sense you are watching a father-and-son game. Despite size limitations, Dante made good passes and a good compete level all game long, getting a couple of good chances off a quickly released wristshot. Very good at faceoffs.

VIC #23 RW Blomqvist, Axel (Winnipeg FA, 2013) - Had a really strong outing in this one. At 6-foot-7 and 213 pounds, he looks as tall as a GMO steroid-induced beanstock that was grown in nitrogenous soil next to the nuclear plant. While turns, pivots and general agility leave something to be desired, his stance is unusually wide and strides unusually long and powerful for his dimensions. He had a nice goal on a beautiful feed from Tyler Soy in the first period that was scored through crashing the net.

VIC #2 RD Hicketts, Joe (2014) – Utilizes the boards to formulate beautiful breakout plays, showing that he has a number of crafty pass types. On the defensive end, he showed really impressive escapability in the corners and decision making when pressured. Scored yet another goal off of his thunderous slapshot from the point. I firmly believe that, injury's considered, if he were three or four inches taller, he would have been drafted in the first round last year.

VIC #9 RD Walker, Jack (2014) – Versatile, as he seems to be able to alternate between positions so fluidly and instantaneously. Arrives with a 'tried-and-true' formula for success: jumps into plays quickly looking just like a speedy forward and makes a good pass to keep the play alive, then he sneakily retrieves back to his set position; wash, rinse, repeat. In this game, he saw playing time in all situations—even strength, penalty kill, power play and four-on-four. Left the game with only a secondary assist but looked much better than the stats suggest.

VIC #17 LC Soy, Tyler (2015) – Had a productive, efficient and impressive game. Made really nice passes all over the ice, and continues to show an eagerness to get into tight spaces or dangerous areas in order to make a play. Continues to show great pass perceptibility and a quickly released wristshot that is very accurate. Had an assist on a nice dish to Axel Blomqvist in the slot.

VIC #24 RW Nagy, Regan (2015) – Propelled by really furious footwork, good knee and hip placement and subsequently strong forward momentum, plays a game more reminiscent of a 5-foot-9 player. Moves down the ice at a really quick pace, whether he's holding the puck or not. Furthermore, this is a player who hits hard, shoots hard and plays hard. A bit gun-shy at times and his upside might have some limitations, but I does a good job of keeping his feet moving away from the puck, thereby making himself useful in all situations.

VIC #27 RW Dmytriw, Jared (2016) – Another small, quick and skilled forward for the Royals was Jared Dmytriw. A diminutive but talented player who excels at finding open space and letting off a quick wristshot. A fast but quiet skater who moves all over the ice without garnering the attention of opposition defenders until he throws a big hit out of nowhere.

VIC #29 LD Reddekopp, Chaz (2015) – Showed a modicum of improvement in this one. Passes were much better, crisper, more clearly delivered, and more easily received. I thought he still looked a little slow-footed, but overall played a much better game. Received some time on the power play and looked decent.

Sudbury Wolves at Barrie Colts, Sept 11, 2014

Score: 4-2 Barrie

Sudbury

LW Ivan Kashtanov (2015) – Kashtanov was pretty quiet in this one. He was able to elude defenders and oncoming checkers in open ice several times throughout and had a couple nice carries up ice, but was never a consistent threat in this game. He was late to several rebounds in front, and missed a couple chances he did manage to create. Defensively he was a bit of a roamer. If the puck was near he'd try to make a play for it, but he was all over the ice in his own zone and was almost never in position.

D Austin Clapham (2015) – Clapham played a sound game on the backend. He took several hits to make plays – either outlet passing or simply shooting it up the boards to get it out. He did a good job of holding the line in the offensive zone, and his holds led to several chances. He won his fair share of puck battles along the wall, and made good outlets after he retrieved the puck. He also made good D-to-D passes in the offensive zone, and was calm patrolling the line on the powerplay. A couple times he lost his man in the defensive zone, but for the most part he was good positionally.

D Chase Hawley (2015) – Hawley was very physical in this game. He was aggressive on the wall, and always made sure he gave out more than he took. He was overly aggressive at times, which led to a bad penalty in the neutral zone. He dropped the mitts with Nick Pastorious late in the game and was beaten easily.

G Troy Timpano (2015) – Timpano was extremely confident handling the puck, which turned out to be a fault. He made several good passes with it, but he was caught early in the game behind the net and had to take an interference penalty to prevent a goal. Later in a 3-2 game he mishandled the puck while well out of his net and that led to the dagger goal. When he stayed in his net, he was actually quite good. His positioning was good; he squared up to shooters, didn't over commit and was very calm in the crease.

Barrie

D Rasmus Andersson (2015) – Andersson did a good job of clearing the net front in this one. He skated away from forecheckers and carried the puck out of his zone and up ice on several occasions. He stickhandled around defenders a few times, and simply dumped it in when met at the line by a couple defenders. Defensively he had a good stick and used it to break up a few rushes. He was able to get shots through traffic, especially on the powerplay, and that led to some juicy rebounds. He kept his gaps small and didn't give oncoming forwards an inch. He drew a penalty after the whistle and made a beautiful slap pass the ensuing powerplay to set up a glorious chance in front. He moved the puck very well on the man advantage, and played a nearly perfect game. One negative was he flipped the puck out of play in the defensive zone when the Colts were already shorthanded.

LW Matthew Kreis (2015) – Kreis continues to impress me in the preseason. He had a nice net drive on the opening goal, and showed quick hands finishing the chance in tight. He had some creative stretch passes, and was able to hit open targets a variety of different ways. He was strong on the backcheck, and always there as an outlet for the defense. He was excellent on the half-wall on the powerplay, showing good vision and creating offensively. Kreis showed a quick release coming off the wall, and processed the game at a high pace. Once again he gained the line with control of the puck regularly, and didn't back down physically.

RW Roy Radke (2015) – Radke had nice stick work on the penalty kill to force plays and take passing lanes away. He pressured the puck carrier on the powerplay ferociously and caused a couple turnovers. In the offensive zone, he was effective in the cycle game and finished his checks whenever he could. Radke had several chances on the doorstep, and scored a nice one-time goal in the slot. Radke showed good bursts at times, as he went wide with speed before gaining a step and taking it towards the net. He had a couple turnovers from forcing passes, but overall played a good game.

Rouyn-Noranda Huskies vs Drummondville Voltigeurs, September 12th 2014

RN #5 LD Lauzon, Jeremy (2015): Played a lot tonight, and in all situations of the game. He played on the right side tonight, even if he's a left-handed shot. Lauzon has decent footwork and tried to rush the puck many times from his zone. On occasion I thought he took too much time to make a decision with the puck on his stick. On the power play, he's very good at getting pucks to the net, even with heavy traffic in front of the net.

RN #3 RD Neveu, Jacob (2016): A good, steady performance from the 16 year old defenseman. He didn't wow anyone, but made smart plays with and without the puck. A very strong player physically, and he is not intimated by older players at the junior level. Neveu made a real nice pass to Mathieu Lemay in front of the Drummondville net for the lone goal for his team.

RN #13 LD Lauzon, Zachary (2017): The younger brother of Jeremy played on the 3rd pair of defensemen tonight and didn't get as much ice time as the other 16 year old D on the team (Neveu). Both he and his partner had issues getting the puck out of their zone on a shift that lasted for a while. Unlike Neveu, the younger Lauzon is physically immature and it showed in some battles along the boards. Did have some shifts with his brother, and that seemed to calm him down. He played more of a puck movement game, which is a strength of his.

RN #18 C Boucher, Mathieu (2015): Rookie who was a high-scoring forward with Amos in the Quebec Midget AAA league last season. He showed some good speed on the forecheck and in puck pursuit. He couldn't generate a lot of offense in general in this game. His lack of size hurt him in the offensive zone, and he had a hard time versus bigger and stronger players. He showed a good compete level, and was not afraid to get his nose dirty in front of the net.

RN #1 G Harvey, Samuel (2016): The young Harvey was pulled from the game after allowing four goals to the Voltigeurs. He didn't get a lot of help from his defense tonight, and two of those goals were scored while the Huskies were on the power play. Of the four goals, he might want to have the 1st and 3rd ones back. The first one went through him and the 3rd one he went down on his knees too quickly, which opened up the upper part of the net. I did like his composure, even if things go well he didn't seem to be rattled. His rebound control was just okay in this game. He's capable of much more, as he showed last year in Midget AAA.

DRU #4 LD Gagne, Benjamin (2017): Still 15 years old, Gagne played a decent game tonight. He's at his best when he keeps things simple with the puck and doesn't try too much. In general, he played a safe game and took care of things in his own zone. Still needs to add mass to his frame as he can be overmatched physically at the moment, but he's a smart defender and uses his stick well to defend.

DRU #11 LW Ratelle, Joey (2015): Undrafted in 2014, Ratelle played a strong game tonight. He's effective in all three zones and is still a pain to play against, much like he was last year. Scored two goals tonight, blocking shots on the penalty kill unit and finishing every hit he could. Ratelle's skating is still just average, he's very tenacious on the puck carrier and on the forecheck. He was the top Voltigeur tonight.

DRU #22 C Sevigny, Mathieu (2016): Sevigny played a very smart game tonight. Despite it being his first game in the league, he looked like a veteran out there. He made good decisions with and without the puck, supporting his defensemen well by coming back deep in his zone. Already plays on the penalty kill unit, and he is quite useful there. He got his first QMJHL point by making a quick pass to Ratelle on the Voltigeurs' 4th goal. Strong on the forecheck as well, giving fits to the puck carrier.

DRU #95 LW Golovkovs, Georgs (2015): Like Ratelle, the Latvian forward was undrafted last season. Thought he looked stronger on his skates tonight than he did last year, his puck protection was better and his play along the boards was good as well. Didn't generate a lot of offense tonight, I thought he stayed too much on the perimeter in the offensive zone, even on the power play.

DRU #98 LW Doucet, Justin (2015): Huge kid who's still very raw, lots of work needs to be done with regards to his skating this season. Tends to chase the puck too much on the ice. Works hard every shift and loves to finish his hits with impact. Got into a scrap in the 2nd period. Doucet creates a lot of room on the ice for his linemates, and he's an interesting prospect to watch this year and see how he develops. Made some very nice strides in terms of his overall game since the beginning of last season.

Sep. 12, 2014 – Kelowna Rockets at Vancouver Giants (WHL Delta Pre-Season Invite)

KEL #10 RC Merkley, Nick (2015) – Crafty, creative, and explosive with the puck on his stick, he's an extremely difficult player to predict 1-on-1. In this game, it looked like the puck was attached to his stick by a string at times, as he managed to make a number of clever dekes around the opposing defenders. Played in all situations in this game, looking particularly good on the penalty kill. Can stickhandle his way into any area of the ice, but he looks most dangerous when he's aggressive and nearest to the net.

KEL #28 LD Gatenby, Joe (2015) – After flopping on the pass, instead of giving up on the play, turning, falling a step behind and chasing, he opted to stand tall and bodycheck the opposing forward away from the loose puck allowing his teammates to re-group and re-position themselves. The play showed great anticipation and a clever form of discipline, as it stood right on the precipice of being an interference call. In the moment, he looked like a defenceman's defenceman, recognizing his options and strengths to arrive at the right decision at the right time. Still somewhat limited in terms of his ice-time, I'm still trying to pin-down the rest of Gatenby's game.

VAN #8 LW Baer, Alec (2015) – An above average skater with decent size and a high degree of skill, I think his best attribute tonight was his vision in the offensive zone. Because he's a good shooter and likes to wind up his wristshot, goalies usually challenge him aggressively giving him excellent passing opportunities. He had a real knack for finding guys who were open. His defensive work wasn't outstanding in this one, but it wasn't terrible either.

VAN #11 LW Stukel, Jakob (2015) – A surprisingly dynamic offensive player and a natural winger, as I don't think I've ever seen him play a game without getting at least one good offensive chance and I don't think I've ever seen him take a faceoff either. In any case, he played an intriguing role on a line scored a collective total of 4 points even though Stukel himself left the game with 0. Has a weird habit of doing a lot for very little.

VAN #20 RD Atwal, Arvin (2014) – I can't help but mention Arvin Atwal, who I consider an under-appreciated part of this Giants team. Shows good lateral speed along the blueline, hustles to make good keeps in the offensive zone, and has incredible hand-eye coordination when defending in one-on-one or puck retrieval situations.

VAN #22 RD Osipov, Dmitry (2015) – With increased ice-time, looks increasingly confident both with and without the puck. Will never blow you away with his acceleration or top-flight speed, but he's strong on his skates, agile in all directions, quick-footed in reverse, and impossibly difficult to beat 1-on-1. Some refinements still need to be made to his offensive game, particularly in the realms of passing and shooting, but his defensive game is really, really strong.

VAN #35 LG Porter, Cody (2016) – While I didn't see him face a ton of shots, there were a number of things to really like about Cody Porter. He has decent size at 6-foot-1, 181 pounds and good movement to go along with his frame. Looks athletic and like an early expert in the butterfly technique. An excellent communicator with his defensemen and other teammates. His voice reaches the back end of the rink. Not all of his play action calls were the right ones, but it seemed like the pure bravado in his voice gave every player on his team a bit of jump and an extra step.

September 12, 2014 - Erie Otters at London Knights

OHL Exhibition Game

ERI #10 LC Bily, Shaun (2016) - Shaun showed good compete level in his own zone. He can evade checkers with puck skills and speed. He was 50% in the face-off circle tonight.

ERI #12 RC DeBrincat, Alex (2016) - Alex is fairly undersized for a potential NHL prospect but he displayed excellent skating ability. He has great hands and controls the puck very well. His hard work and compete allowed him to create scoring chances for his team.

ERI #13 LD Saban, Jesse (2015) - Constantly going for hits. Hard point shot.

ERI #19 LC Strome, Dylan (2015) - Dylan's skating is still heavy but much smoother than it was before. He showed strong puck patience and created a few chances tonight.

LON #14 RD Nother, Tyler (2016) - Multiple bad turnovers early on in this game. Skating for his size effective but a bit of an awkward stride. Got pressured in his own zone and sent the puck over the glass for a penalty.

LON #21 LD Gleason, Benjamin (2016) - Competes in the slot but he lacks strength. Very smooth skater on the rush. He made a few bad decisions with the puck in his own zone.

LON #52 LD Crawley, Brandon (2015) - Brandon is very smart with his shot choosing the right times and got the puck through. He also pinched at the right time retreating when he wasn't going to be able to make the play but quickly stepped up and got the job done when necessary. He was penalized for a huge, textbook hit. He showed the capability to rush the puck on a few occasions but when he's in the offensive zone he doesn't need to take the big wide turn that he had a tendency of doing. Crawley was effective at clearing the defensive zone.

LON #55 LD Mete, Victor (2016) - Outstanding lateral movement to open up passing options that aren't available to most players because of his skating. Moves side to side faster than some can skate forward. Victor struggled defensively against good puck protecting forwards. He tried to side step a check which resulted in a scoring chance against.

LON #93 RC Marner, Mitchell (2015) - This wasn't Mitchell's best game. He showed flashes of his skill but would sometimes try to do too much on a play when the simpler option was available after he made a great evasive move. He was still able to create chances for his team but a bad turnover lead to Erie's first goal of the game. He was about 50% on face-off's tonight.

LON #1 G Parsons, Tyler (2016) - Tyler can get drawn out of position by a patience shooter. He displays outstanding quickness, but also displayed too much extra movement. Rebound control will need improvement as it cost him at times in this game.

Final Score: Erie Otters: 4 - London Knights: 0

Sep. 12, 2014 – Quebec Ramparts at Sherbrooke Phoenix

QUE #30 G Booth, Callum (2015) – Gets into his butterfly and closes the gap in less than the blink of an eye. Looks extremely controlled when he is fully set in the butterfly position. His leg pushes are quick, but also subtle and nuanced. After two goals from behind the net plays, you have to question Booth's 360 awareness just a little. Indeed, almost always looked most vulnerable in this game when dealing with wraparound attempts or pucks coming from behind his net. Puckhandling skills also look like they could use some work after a couple of tough giveaways. Had some good second-chance saves.

QUE #88 LW Timashov, Dmytro (2015) – Definitely not a straightline skater by pure intuition, as exhibited by an almost comical turnover on his first shift that resulted from him stupidly circling around in his own zone. Later, back on the attack during the same tired shift, he forced a pass to a teammate in the slot and caused another turnover in the opposite end. The crowd in Sherbrooke whistled at those plays. He scored a goal in the second, but rest of his game was butt ugly.

SHE #1 G Fitzpatrick, Evan (2016) – Began the game playing backup to Alex Bureau, before he hurt his arm in the second period. A weird coincidence, given that on the day the Sherbrooke Phoenix celebrated the long and storied career of Jocelyn Thibeault, as Thibeault makes a decent comparison. After all, on first sight, he seems like more of a hybrid goalie than the butterfly specialist across from him. Plays a bit of an old-school style, aggressively standing up when challenging shots. He was perhaps a bit too aggressive and far our of his net on the first Quebec goal by Dmytro Timashov, however.

SHE #89 LW Schweri, Kay (2015) – Wow, oh wow. The first goal in the game is set-up on one of the most beautiful behind-the-net passes you'll ever see, courtesy of Sherbrooke's Swiss import Kay Schweri. Schweri's edgework in shifting from side-to-side and fooling Callum Booth—not to mention everyone in attendance—was a thing of beauty. Made another beauty assist in the second. This was 'all-world' type playmaking performance in a memorably impressive debut.

SHE #97 RD Roy, Jeremy (2015) – Played a lot of minutes in all situations—skating very smoothly and efficiently from shift-to-shift throughout. The main quarterback of the Phoenix power play, he was the default pass when players were looking for someone to send the puck to. May tend to over-estimate the abilities of his teammates, making fanciful reverses or breakout passes that only he really possesses the skating ability or puck handling skills to reach or handle. A fantastic passer off his backhand, he has a multitude of options when skating on the rush or left in open space.

September 19th 2014 USHL Fall Classic West Lincoln Stars v. Sioux Falls Stampede

LIN #8 Klack, Chris LC (2015) – Very impressive vs. Sioux Falls, was probably the best player on the ice for Lincoln today. He's undersized but super shifty in open space, almost impossible to hit. He displayed great vision today, sees the open passing lane and hits it, great set up guy. Probably won't see him score a ton of goals this season, but did pot a rebound goal in front of the net today.

LIN #10 Fidler, Miguel LW (2014, Florida 5th Round) – Pretty solid game for the Panthers draft pick. Had a nice stretch pass up ice to set up Lincoln's first goal. Little concerned if his offensive skillset will make the transition to the USHL. Still has the physical aspect to his game but seems to be more disciplined. Will be interesting to see if he can score consistently at this level.

LIN #15 von Ungern-Sternberg, August LC (2015) – Scored a beautiful breakaway goal in the first period, stole the puck in the neutral zone and took off. One dimensional player. Good in the offensive zone, controls and protects the puck well. Undersized but plays with heart.

LIN #17 Hoff, Ludvig LW (2015) – Developed a definite edge to his game over the offseason. Works hard in every area of the ice, really get after it on the backcheck. Really quick player as well.

LIN #18 Kalynuk, Wyatt LD (2015) – Really nice hands for a defenseman, can control the puck well at the blue line. Just a really solid, dependable player. Never really saw him out of position at any point during the game. The Lincoln coaching staff utilized him in all situations of the game. Solid showing.

LIN #20 Ausmus, Tye RD (2015) – Had an assist on the Lincoln in the third period. Not super flashy with the puck, but does his job and isn't a liability. Sees the ice very well, doesn't telegraph his passes.

LIN #21 Bethune, Jared LC (2015) – Very impressive young player. Super patient with the puck on his stick, high percentage shooter. Knows how to buy time with the puck to get his shot. Very aware of his surroundings and the situation of the game and does well reacting. Will not be with the Stars all season as he will return to Warroad High School to play his senior high school hockey season.

LIN #23 Ward, Keegan RW (2015) – His game has come along nicely since last season where he was used sparingly by Lincoln. Has not lost his physical presence. Still needs to make huge improvements in his offensive skill and skating. Dropped the gloves in the second period and more than held his own in the fight.

LIN #24 Lee, Cam LD (2015) – Very offensive minded defenseman. Occasionally tries to do too much with the puck coming out of his own zone leading to a number of turnovers. Great skater. Good shot release. Needs to be smarter with the puck if he is going to continually jump in on the rush. Offensive skillset is superb.

SF #4 Nanne, Tyler LD (2014, New York Rangers 5th Round) – Played a really solid game in both ends. Offensively he showcased his skills, great skater, sees the ice very well. Scored a nice goal on the power play in the first period. Just as good in his own zone. Never saw him get caught out of position or puck watching. Impressive showing.

SF #8 Joshua, Dakota LC (2014, Toronto 5th Round) – Has the size to dominate at this level. The puck always seems to find him. Dominated in the face off circle today. Fed his teammates in front of goal with a couple of nice passes. Great vision. Saw a couple of issues with his mobility but it's early in the season. Had a good assist on a Stampede goal in the first period.

SF #18 Warpecha, Daniel (2015) – Seemed to still be finding his way at the USHL level. Tended to look a little lost at points in the game. Needs to work on his skating, lateral mobility, sometimes gets stuck flat footed. Assisted on goal in 2nd period.

Scouts Notes: This was a fun back and forth game that allowed me to see Sioux Falls' two NHL draft picks and well as Lincoln's stockpile of young talent. The two teams traded goals one after another until Lincoln finally came out on top with a goal in the early stages of the third period. The game finished 4-3 in favor of the Stars.

September 19th 2014 USHL Fall Classic West Muskegon Lumberjacks v. Fargo Force

MUS #2 Eliot, Mitch RD (2016) – The 1998 born Michigan State commit impressed against the Force. Easy to see what MSU sees in him. Great on his skates, skates with a really good base. Not the flashiest with the puck but he has the ability to play it. Committed a few neutral zone turnovers and took a lazy hooking penalty, but those were really the only two negatives in a pretty solid performance. Tons of potential here along with his 2015 eligible D partner, Bo Hanson.

MUS #3 Cecconi, Joseph RD (2015) - Has that elite size that teams are looking for in defensemen. Combine that size with his skating ability and you have a really good player. Uses his size well, threw a couple huge hits in the game. Really good spacing when skating backwards, never really gets beat outside. Just really solid defensively. Offensive skill has come along since last year and Muskegon is using him on the power play, but still some work to do in that department going forward. Will be interesting to see how his offensive skills develop throughout the year.

MUS #9 Hanson, Bo LD (2016) – Played alongside the other 2016 eligible defenseman Eliot for most of the game. Made some mistakes you'd expect to see out of a 16 year old playing his first year in the USHL: turnovers, looking lost, etc. However, he showed flashes of really inspired play throughout the game. Has a lot of potential that will come to fruition once he grows into his 6'3" frame.

MUS #11 Iacopelli, Matheson LW (2014, Chicago 3rd Round) – As expected, tended to be the best player on the ice today. At 6'2", 200 pounds has a physically imposing frame that he uses quite well which is an improvement from last season. Threw around his body and knocked players at this level off the puck with ease today. Tough to gauge how far his defensive game has come going against players at the USHL level. Great release on his shot. Played tons of minutes in every situation. NCAA Clearinghouse issues landed him back in Muskegon to start the year but he may find his way to Western Michigan for their second semester.

MUS #12 Marody, Cooper RC (2015) – Had two points in the game. Scored on a back door pass streaking to the net on the power play and also assisted on a power play goal in the third period. Had a pretty solid game offensively. Turned the puck over more that a few times which will be an issue that needs to be fixed heading into his draft year.

MUS #17 Keefer, David RW (2016) – Muskegon's first round pick in the 2014 USHL Entry Draft played limited minutes today vs. Fargo but looked like he fit right in. Didn't really look lost or make a lot of mistakes that you usually see with young guys at this level. Got some time with the power play unit so it appears like the Muskegon staff is expecting big things out of him this year. Will more than likely earn more minutes as the season progresses.

MUS #20 Paulovic, Matej RC (2014, Dallas 5th Round) – Projects as a prototypical power forward. Has the size and knows how to use it. Battles in the corners, did not shy away from contact in any situation. Works very hard in the defensive zone and creates turnovers. Great team player.

FGO #17 Smirnov, Denis LW (2015) – Played a pretty good game today v. Muskegon. Small guy who is quick on his feet. Very aware of his surroundings and the situation he's in, especially in the offensive zone. Scored a nice goal in the third period, in front of the net.

Scout's notes: The game started off pretty ugly for Fargo as it took them nineteen minutes to register their first shot on net. In the second period, Fargo seemed to come to life and it was a little more back and forth. The game ended up 3-2 in favor of Muskegon.

September 19, 2014 – Penticton Vees at Surrey Eagles (BCHL Showcase)

PEN #1 LG Barry, Brendan (2016) – Didn't get off to the greatest start, letting in 2 early goals. Seemed inspired after taking a big check from a Surrey forward and didn't let in another goal thereafter. At 5-foot-11 and 175 pounds, a lanky upper body and upright stance make him seem much larger than he actually is. I like the way he follows shots with his eyes, and the way he anticipates both shots and plays. Showed good durability and poise.

PEN #2 RD Fabbro, Dante (2016) – A highly skilled puck rushing defenseman with a great first pass and an even better shot. A talented puckhandler along the blueline. Possesses exceptional lateral agility and puckhandling skills at the point, making a number of wondrous keeps in difficult situations. Additionally great at finding open lanes, which he then used to direct passes to teammates or the puck onto the net. Hard slapshot and quickly released wristshot are both excellent at hitting the goalie's pads and creating rebound opportunities. Looked like a wizard while quarterbacking the power play.

PEN #4 RD Bast, Gabe (2016) – A very good straight-ahead skater and a strong first passer. Made a number of nice keeps and passes from the opposition blueline, but what I really liked about Bast was his simplistic but effective first-pass capabilities. Particularly good at passing with his defensive partner—Mike Lee—in all three zones. Something of a puck-possession defenseman, he made a couple of nice defensive plays, too, looking fairly strong one-on-one.

PEN #10 RD Gendron, Miles (Ottawa, 2014) – Having played both forward and defence before arriving to the BCHL, he shows great puck-moving abilities when it comes to both giving and receiving passes. Shooting skills are there, as he lets off a quick and accurate wristshot and also holsters a strong slapshot that is known for creating rebounds. His defensive commitment and awareness can be a bit temperamental at times, but his offensive game more than compensates for said inconsistency in reverse. I really liked the enthusiasm and effort-level.

PEN #27 LD Hilderman, Jarod (2015) – Not flashy but a good skater in all directions. dependable in reverse, but capable of springing the offence into action, too. Possesses a really good pokecheck and a really good set of shots from the point. In a sense, it was a bit difficult to get a full read on his defensive game because of how good his team was playing—he made a couple poor pinches that went largely unnoticed and were virtually inconsequential because teammates recovered on his behalf.

PEN #28 RC Newsome, Mitch (2015) – Playing on a line that included Demico Hannoun and Patrick Sexton, the read on Newsome is that he's a speedy playmaking centre; however, watching him tonight I got almost the exact opposite impression. I thought he did a good job of gliding slowly into open areas and getting off good shots. He made some good passes too, but I was more impressed with his positioning, pace and presence than I was with his speed or passing game.

PEN #67 LC Finlay, Liam (2015) – A dynamic offensive player, he is a guy who doesn't keep the puck on his stick for very long, preferring to get rid of the puck and into jump into new, open, advantageous areas. Indeed, a quick decision maker and a good reader of the game, he's able to make passes or shots happen very quickly and in deceptive timing.

PEN #71 RW Jost, Tyson (2016) – Has that typical Western Hockey League "Oh, please come and hit me"-type style, in which he's regularly handling the puck through the corners and along the half-wall. Well balanced, and thereby really difficult to knock off of the puck. In fact, one of the Eagles players hit Jost so hard that a pane of glass got knocked out of place and into the second row. From thereon, he looked a bit like a force unleashed. Dangerous on the power-play, he set up two goals on the man advantage within two minutes at the end of the second period.

PEN #77 RW Zerter-Gossage, Lewis (2013) – Named the first star of the game and scored a hat-trick. Some of his goals were gifts from linemates Tyson Jost and Liam Finlay, and one was an individualized wraparound goal that was simply a thing of beauty. On that goal he showed tremendous footwork, hand-eye coordination, and shot accuracy.

SUR #27 RC McMurphy, Chase (2012) – A highly vocal player who inspires his teammates both by example and by regular on-ice lecturing. He scored a great slapshot from the point on the power-play, and actually gave the Eagles a glimmer of hope before things fell apart completely in the third period. I liked his effort and commitment in all three zones and how strong his determination was regardless of the score.

September 20th 2014 USHL Fall Classic West, Tri-City Storm v. Fargo Force

TC #3 Dello, Tory RD (2015) – Notre Dame commit had a solid first period. When he had the puck you never really saw him panic. He blocked a few shots and has really stepped up as a leader in the Tri-City defensive corps despite being the youngest defenseman on the team. Unfortunately Dello did not return to the game after the first period.

TC #15 Freytag, Matthew LW (2015) – Flew around the ice today hitting nearly everything that moved in blue. Super solid on his skates. Didn't display much offensively in this game but has been a noted goal scorer in the past. Would be worth keeping an eye on to see if his goal scoring ability transfers to the USHL level.

TC #20 Wahlin, Jake LW (2015) – Put on a passing clinic. Showcased great vision on the ice finding open teammates left and right in the offensive zone. Super smart with the puck, rarely turns it over. Was finally rewarded for his efforts with an empty net goal late in the game.

TC #30 Dillon, Alec G (2014, Los Angeles 5th Round) – Had a great showing in his second USHL game. Dillon has elite size at 6'6", and has the ability to move post to post very quickly. Made a highlight reel glove save late in the second period. Fargo didn't get a shot until eleven minutes into the first period but ended up testing Dillon through the last two periods. Made 23 saves on 24 shots faced.

FGO #4 Baudry, Justin LD (2015) – Good puck moving defenseman. Sees the ice well on breakouts and offensive situations. Needs to pick up his game in his own zone. Wouldn't go as far to call him a liability in the defensive zone but his awareness and physicality needs improvement.

FGO #7 Stevens, Brody RW (2015) – Did not play a lot of minutes until midway through the 3rd. When he was on the ice he looked solid. One of those guys that always wants the puck on his stick. Willing to shoot from just about anywhere. Scored a goal late in the game to bring Tri-City within one goal.

FGO #11 Cakebread, Christian LC (2015) – Can be described in one word: feisty. He's got a high motor, zipping around the ice getting physical. Pretty strong player, solid on his skates. Impressive on the penalty kill. Will fit right in at North Dakota. Not going to create a lot of offense at the next level, but is high energy in every part of the ice.

FGO #17 Smirnov, Denis LW (2015) – Small guy who can flat out skate. He would benefit from better players around him, he currently has to create all his opportunities by himself. Soft hands. Finds pockets of open space on the ice and gets to them. Biggest knock on him is his size (5'11" 170).

FGO #31 Beydoun, Robbie G (2015) – Came in about halfway through the second period. Played pretty well to keep Fargo in the game. Only got beat on a 2 on 1 rush where he got hung out to dry by his defense. Games will be tough to come by this year with Israelsson in front of him.

Scout's notes: Another rough start for the Force today as it took them 11 minutes to get their first shot on goal. The last two periods were highly spirited with Fargo almost making a comeback late in the third. Final score was 3-1 Tri-City.

September 20th 2014 USHL Fall Classic West Omaha Lancers v. Des Moines Buccaneers

OMA #9 Jordan, Zach RW (2015) – Was very involved in offensive zone. Played with Washington draft pick Steve Spinner and 2016 draft eligible Hank Crone. He's a big kid that plays up to his size. Pushes guys off the puck and uses his size well. Shot is far from accurate, needs to hit the net to be effective. Skating needs work but potential is definitely there, needs to progress throughout the year to improve his draft stock.

OMA #25 Spinner, Steven RC (2014, Washington 6th Round) – Fed Hank Crone on his goal in the second period. Saw the ice well. Finds his open teammates with the puck. Very strong in the faceoff circle, doesn't lose many draws.

OMA #26 Forsbacka-Karlsson, Jakob RC (2015) – Had a great game finding his teammates with the puck. Had four assists on the night, setting linemate Shane Gersich up for all three of his goals. More apt to shoot from last year from what I saw. Didn't see him lose a faceoff all night. Can see him improving his draft stock throughout the year playing with Gersich.

OMA #29 Crone, Hank LW (2016) – Scored a nice goal on a feed from Spinner. Still pretty small, 5'8", 145ish. Seemed very hesitant to go into the corners and in front of the net. Hasn't yet found his groove at this level. Will be sure to improve throughout the year if he sticks on the 23 man roster.

OMA #61 Gersich, Shane LW (2014, Washington 5th Round) – Super fast skater. Great shot that jumps off his stick. Had a hat trick in this game and probably should have had at least one more goal that hit the post. Had an assist in the 2nd period. In for a big year in 2014-15.

DSM #17 Pavlychev, Nikita LC (2015) – It cannot be understated how big this guy is. He looks like a man amongst boys on the ice at 6'7" 210. Played a lot of minutes on the PK and had a nice assist on a short handed goal in the second period. As is an issue with a lot of big guys at this level, skating is an issue but he showed some wheels taking a loose puck in the neutral zone and streaking to the net to score in the third period. Lots to like here with the intangibles, just needs a little refinement.

DSM #11 Zajc, Miha RW (2015) – Pretty physical guy. Plays a lot bigger than 6'0", had a pretty quiet game offensively in a 9-7 game. Really good on the penalty kill. Very little there offensively in terms of shot and passing skills in this game. Looking forward to future viewings to see how he progresses throughout the year.

Scout's Notes: Pretty sloppy defensive game on both sides, ending in a 9-7 score line. Was nice to see the offensive abilities of the players involved but overall a really sloppy game on both sides.

September 20th 2014 USHL Fall Classic West Lincoln Stars v. Muskegon Lumberjacks

LIN #10 Fidler, Miguel LW (2014, Florida 5th Round) – Quiet game from Fidler against Muskegon. Very strong on his feet. Can take a beating and hold on to the puck extremely well. Took a bad penalty late out of frustration. Played on Lincoln's top line and played a lot of minutes. Average showing, left something to be desired in terms of offensive ability.

LIN #15 von Ungern-Sternberg, August LC (2015) – Didn't get to showcase his offensive abilities in this game. Stars were on the PK most of the game so he didn't play a whole lot. Protects the puck well from poke checks when he has it. Size is an issue. He plays with heart but struggles to hold his own.

LIN #17 Hoff, Ludvig LW (2015) – Displayed a nice touch to his passes today. Got many opportunities to showcase his ability on the penalty kill, which he has a lot of. Speedy little guy who is willing to hit. Has some offensive ability, did a good job of getting the puck on net.

LIN #18 Kalynuk, Wyatt LD (2015) – Turned in a below average performance today after a pretty impressive game yesterday. Had a horrible turnover that led to a Muskegon breakaway. Got caught flat footed watching the puck a handful of times leading to a couple Muskegon odd man rushes. Has been pretty solid in previous viewings, but the entire Lincoln team was bad today.

LIN #20 Ausmus, Tye RD (2015) – Really didn't do a whole lot in the game, good or bad. He is just a solid player, doesn't do anything flashy, but he's not a liability at all. He's a solid skater with a good wide base. Took at 10 minute misconduct for unsportsmanlike conduct late in the game.

LIN #21 Bethune, Jared LC (2015) – One of the few bright spots from an otherwise very poor Lincoln performance. He's good in both ends, creating turnovers and finding open teammates. Great skater, elite straight line speed. High hockey sense, very aware of what's happening on the ice, does not turn the puck over.

LIN #23 Ward, Keegan RW (2015) – Regressed back into his form from last year when Lincoln went down by a few goals. Took runs at opposing players, took a high stick and roughing penalty in the same play late in the game. Just wasn't very smart when Lincoln fell behind. There's no doubt he's a strong guy and hard to knock off the puck but he needs to be smarter and keep his emotions in check if he's going to play at the next level.

MUS #2 Eliot, Mitch RD (2016) – Another solid performance out of the 1998 born defenseman. Stayed at home and was very good in his own end. Was out on the PK often which shows how much trust the coaching staff already has in him. Got caught puck watching a few times. Very promising player.

MUS #3 Cecconi, Joseph RD (2015) – Extremely calm with the puck. Sees the play developing and then makes his decision. Scored a goal early in the second period. Didn't get beat one-on-one once throughout the game. Good showing, needs to keep improving throughout the year.

MUS #9 Hanson, Bo LD (2016) – Used his size well in the game. Was very physical today. Skating needs to improve. Decision making is still an issue, was trying some to do too much coming out of his own zone, resulting in a few turnovers. Fought Lincoln's Angus Scott in the second period.

MUS #11 Iacopelli, Matheson LW (2014, Chicago 3rd Round) – Best player on the ice. Scored on a nice give and go two-on-one with Mason Jobst. Had two more good scoring opportunities that hit the post. Not much left to prove at this level.

MUS #12 Marody, Cooper RC (2015) – Had a really good showing against Lincoln. Assisted on two goals and then scored one of his own in the 3rd period going glove side off the post and in on Stars goaltender Peyton Jones. Struggles with getting bit by the turnover bug random places in games leading to questions about consistency. Had a really good tournament with five points in two games.

MUS #17 Keefer, David RW (2016) – Great game for the late 97 birthdate winger. Got big minutes in this game, especially on the power play. Took full advantage of his opportunities, scoring two goals, tipping a shot from the point in and then taking it into the dirty area in front of the net himself and finishing. Great awareness for a player his age, always seems to know where the puck is going and gets there. Tons of potential here for the Michigan State recruit.

MUS #31 Latorella, Michael G (2016) – It's pretty rare to see a 16 year old goaltender in the USHL and even more rare to see them perform at the level Latorella did in this game. He made save after save on the breakaway. The two negatives of the performance were it seemed like he had a problem with rebound control in the game and then he did get beat short side on a great shot. However, the positives out of this performance by the young netminder far outweigh the negatives. Made 34 saves on 36 shots faced.

Scout's notes: Not a great game to watch, the game was marred by ill-advised Lincoln penalties and an onslaught of Muskegon's offense. Final score was 7-2 in favor of Muskegon. It's too early to tell anything definitively but Muskegon looks dominant thus far.

Sport U20 – Ilves U20, sep 21, 2014

#18, Ilves, LD, Ville Järvinen (2015) – Ville had a great game today. He's big all-round D-man with great slapshot. He really likes to participate offensive game and he's doing it well. Great vision and decent passing game. He's good in all three zones. His slapshot is great but not very accurate. Ville is a great skater for his size: backwards and forwards with good technique. He was good in the D-zone: especially good without the puck, uses his sticks very well and win battles with that. He's big guy and he should be meanier in the front of his own net and around the corners. Likes to play hard and give hits but doesn't really do it well. When he add some muscle and get his balance better, he will be a really good D-man. Looks like good late round pick at the moment.

#25, Ilves, RD, Jesper Mattila (2016) – Jesper is a undersized D-man with good offensive tools. He's really smart with puck and gives always easy first passes well. Smooth skater with great mobility and always knows where to be in the D-zone. Not the strongest game today but did succeeded well. He's small and doesn't even try to play physical game which is his biggest problem. There's lot of situations where he's in troubles because the lack of strength. He really got the tools but he needs to be a lot tougher in the D-zone.

#4, Sport, LD, Robin Salo (2017) – Robin played his second game in U20 league and was a beast. Already great player in all three zones and was his team best D-man today. Scored 2 assists and +3 in a 7-4 victory and showed great efforts during the whole game. Great hockey sense and did always right decisions with the puck. He's only 15 year old but played really physically and succeeded at it. Was really good in the D-zone and won his battles usually and then gave accurate passes to forwards. He already got good frames: lot of power in his legs and in his upper body and he's pretty fast skater. His technique isn't the best but when he got that right, he will be a amazing skater. Robin is a smart player who has taken big development steps during the summer. He will be eligible in the Import Draft and coming over would be a great decision for him. His game style fits in the smaller rink better than the european rink.

Shawinigan Cataractes vs Blainville-Boisbriand Armada, September 21st 2014

SHA #3 RD Sylvestre, Gabriel (2016): Played a regular shift and got limited ice time on the 2nd power play unit. Threw some hits along the board. Beginning of the game is decision making with the puck was slow but got better as the game got along.

SHA #8 C Phelan, James (2015): Showed good speed during the game on the forecheck, tenacious and tough to play against. Good work on the PK with a good active stick, almost scored after creating a turnover on the penalty killing unit.

SHA #11 LW Yan, Dennis (2015): Showed some flash in the offensive zone with a big time shot but overall his effort was lacking a bit. He's good at finding space in the offensive zone and getting open for his teammate. Never far from the net on the power play. Would have like to see him more involve in the game.

SHA #28 RW Gignac, Brandon (2016): Lots of speed from this guy, can really fly on the ice. Didn't do a whole lot offensively but opposing defensemen knew when he was on the ice because they were backing up because none of them could contain him with his outside speed. He's a bit undersized and struggle versus bigger player along the board or in front of the net.

SHA #77 LD Welsh, Nicholas (2015): He's good at getting puck on net from the point. Played on the first power play unit tonight with #94 Girard. His passing game was a bit off today, his passes were lacking accuracy and it hurt the transition game for the Cataractes. Undersized d-men, struggle in his zone versus bigger and stronger forward.

SHA #91 C Beauvillier, Anthony (2015): Got good ice time today, played in all kind of situation. Use his speed well on the forecheck, carrying the puck and on the PK. Possesses a good shot, like to shoot on the powerplay. Has a shoot first mentality. Like his effort on the backcheck and use his stick well in defensive situation.

SHA #94 LD Girard, Samuel (2016): Tons of poised with the puck already for Girard, doesn't look like a 16 years old rookie. Played a ton on the power play where he's at his best. Makes good & quick decisions with the puck on the power play. Will rush the puck at will when he has space, not many players can keep up with his speed. Shot is just average. Can be overmatch in his zone versus more physically mature players.

SHA #98 C Aucoin, Emmanuel (2015): Didn't play a lot but had a real good shift were he had 2 huge hits on the forecheck. Skating lacks a gear. Played on Shawinigan 4th line.

BLB #18 RW Hylland, Tyler (2016): Already Hylland is playing in different role for the Armada, today he was use on the power play in front of the net and on the PK as well. His speed and anticipation are what makes him a good player on the PK. Works hard all over the ice, one of the few players who can keep up with Samuel Girard when he's rushing the puck from his own end. Could have tie the game late but was robbed 2-3 times by the Shawinigan goaltender. Hylland is not overly big he goes in the tough area of the ice.

BLB #22 RW Katerinakis, Alexander (2016): Still young but Katerinakis is very strong on the puck and not afraid to go to the net looking for tips or rebounds. Hustle hard to win puck races and effective along the board. Missed a penalty shot late in the game to tie the game.

BLB #57 C Picard, Miguel (2016): Picard played a smart game overall, without the puck he knows where to go and has a good active stick. Doesn't put himself in trouble on the ice and did a fine job on the PK. With the puck in the offensive zone he lacks some confidence compared to his teammates Hylland and Katerinakis at the moment. Skating will need an extra gear as well.

Oshawa Generals at Barrie Colts, Sept 25, 2014

Score: 5-2 Oshawa

Oshawa

C Sam Harding (2015) – Harding played a complete 200-foot game in this one. He created several chances offensively and was in good position to bang in a rebound on the power play on what was the game-winning goal. In his own zone he was positionally sound, especially on the penalty kill, and he used good positioning to get in the lanes and force Barrie into passes they didn't want to make. He also used an active stick to break up several pass attempts. He was relentless on the forecheck, and his puck pursuit was excellent.

W Anthony Cirelli (2015) – He played limited minutes in this one. He was effective on the forecheck and good along the wall, but really didn't play enough to make an impact.

D Stephen Templeton (2015) – Templeton played a physical game, but was overly aggressive at times. He took himself out of position trying to land a hit, and took a bad penalty retaliating to a hit from Michael Webster. He did a good job clearing the net, especially on the penalty kill, and for the most part he was defensively sound, but he needs to keep his emotions in check.

D Mitch Vande Sompel (2015) – Early on Vande Sompel was a bit of a mess in his own zone, but he got better as the game progressed. He used his excellent skating ability to close caps effectively, and won several races to loose pucks. He lost his man in the defensive zone a couple times and was soft in front of his net as he wouldn't engage in net front battles, but when he got the puck he was excellent. Vande Sompel made effective outlets consistently, and skated the puck out of trouble whenever necessary. In the offensive zone he created quite a few scoring chances, and did a nice job holding the line. On one occasion he did a spinerama drop pass off the boards that landed right on the tape of a teammate on the halfwall. Defensively he showed a mixed bag, but offensively he was quite dynamic.

Barrie

LW Matthew Kreis (2015) – The Colts were missing three top-9 forwards in Brendan Lemieux, Roy Radke and Givani Smith so there wasn't as much competition, but Kreis may have been their best forward in this game. He gained the line with possession of the puck on several occasions and did a nice job of finding open teammates in the offensive zone. He was effective on the power play coming off the half wall, and showed good vision hitting teammates all over the ice. He forced a couple passes, but always backchecked hard, especially after a turnover, and nothing he did resulted in a goal against. He wasn't excellent, but on a night when many Colts were mediocre he was quite good.

D Rasmus Andersson (2015) – Like Kreis, Andersson was good but not great. He made some good outlet passes throughout the night and was calm when pressured. He used the boards to get the puck to teammates whenever necessary, and showed good creativity with the puck on several occasions. His backhand passes had excellent power in them and were accurate. Andersson got pucks through for the most part, too, but there was almost always someone in his face so he didn't get many good looks. Defensively he was beat a couple times, but for the most part his positioning was good and he was willing to engage physically with anyone; including Hunter Smith.

G Mackenzie Blackwood (2015) – Blackwood started well, but really tailed off as the game went along. His positioning was good, he didn't cough out many rebounds and he showed good lateral movement. That said, his glove was pretty weak throughout. Blackwood bobbled a couple easy shots, and allowed a gloveside goal to Brad Latour. After he allowed a couple he started to unravel, lose confidence and started to allow goals he probably could have stopped. He wasn't the reason they lost, but he certainly didn't do as much as he could have to keep them in it.

September 26, 2014 - Plymouth Whalers at London Knights

PLY #13 LW Dunda, Liam (2015) - Liam was effective keeping it very simple delivering big hits. In the third period he came off the wing unchallenged by defenders and wired a hard shot top shelf just under where the crossbar and post meet.

PLY #17 RW Yetman, Bryce (2015) - Working hard and finishing his checks. Needs to get stronger in order to maximize his potential in the style of game in which he plays. Bryce was a consistent presence on the forecheck.

PLY #19 RC Mercer, Cullen (2015) - Cullen showed a great work ethic consistently from a shift by shift basis. He made things happen out there by finishing checks, driving the net, and keeping his feet moving opening things up for himself. He wasn't a huge impact when it came to the scoresheet, but never quit working.

PLY #41 RC Bitten, Will (2016) - Will showed off his excellent hands in this game particularly in the offensive zone. He was immediately given top minutes on the Whalers' power play and showed smart puck movement with the ability to control the puck and be patient.

LON #6 LD Gleason, Benjamin (2016) - Benjamin played right wing on the Knights' 4th line tonight. He provided a good forecheck pressure taking time and space away from opponents. He stole the puck for a partial break, but when he needed to beat the defender one on one he made an attempted pass that went astray.

LON #14 LD Crawley, Brandon (2015) - Brandon thrived with his first pass in this game and consistently completed it, even when heavily pressured by forecheckers. When he had space he showed a comfort level to carry the puck but quickly passed off when pressured if an option opened up. He did a good job on the penalty kill handling Plymouth's big forwards in the slot area and down low. His physical game picked up late, landing a few very solid hits.

LON #23 RC Rymsha, Drake (2016) - Drake finished checks in the offensive zone. His work ethic was consistent and he kept his game simple, but hard working.

LON #79 RD Nother, Tyler (2016) - Tyler had a very shoot first mentality from the point and while a few made it through, he would shoot when it was not his best available option or the shooting lane was covered. He made some dangerous puck decisions in his own zone and needs to improve on his puck protection ability as he is too easy to strip off the puck for such a big player. He made some solid defensive plays in his own end using his reach and keeping his feet moving.

LON #93 RC Marner, Mitchell (2015) - Excellent puck movement on the power play. He was able to identify and exploit passing lanes, even small ones so well. He was extremely dangerous on the power play creating chances but his linemates couldn't finish on this night. He played all game situations, but his compete level was a little hit or miss on the penalty kill.

LON #1 Parsons, Tyler (2016) - Tyler showed outstanding reflexes but gave up lots of rebounds. He made some huge point blank saves. Despite giving up five goals he played great for London and the score could have been much worse. The first two goals he had no chance on, two were perfectly placed shot and on one goal he overcommitted on a deke putting him out of position.

Final Score: Plymouth Whalers: 5 - London Knights: 0

Sep. 26, 2014 – Portland Winterhawks at Vancouver Giants

POR #25 RW Weinger, Evan (2015) – Skating was just slightly above average, even if his arm fluction appeared a bit awkward, as he looked sharp on his edges and possessed good agility in tight spaces. Utilized his long reach to take away passing lanes. Moving efficiently in reverse, he did a stand-up job at limiting entries by the opposition with a good stickcheck. His passing game was generally good.

POR #43 LC McKenzie, Skyler (2016) – Despite being very short and looking rather light on his feet, moving like a torpedo, he punishes guys with huge hits along the boards. Playing fourth line minutes, I didn't get a chance to see a whole lot of McKenzie in terms of on-ice action, but I liked his enthusiasm on the bench and willingness to become involved physically. He also showed some decent shooting skills when in the offensive zone.

POR #44 RD Texeira, Keoni (2015) – Decently positioned for most of the game and was capable of throwing his body around in the corners and along the half-wall. After gaining possession of the puck he made a couple of nice outlet passes to spring the rush, but also threw up a couple stinkers. Carries an active stick and uses it in a slashing style when he is attempting to gain puck possession. He scored a goal while walking the line and then went over the line, getting ejected after a questionable hit.

VAN #1 LG Lee, Payton (2014) – One knock on Payton Lee's game from last year was his mental toughness, which I thought he had lots of tonight. After going up 2-0 on Portland in the first half of the first period, there was a bit of a letdown for the Giants as they gave up three goals losing the lead entirely before the end of the first frame. Lee bounced back from this disappointment beautifully, and despite letting in one more goal, was more than proficient enough in net to garner the victory for his squad.

VAN #22 RD Osipov, Dmitry (2015) – Osipov's night wasn't pretty. When being pressured down low in his own zone, he didn't so much pass the puck as much as he threw it up ice haphazardly, causing a couple of icing calls. And then, he took a really foolish roughing penalty in the first period in the form of a punch to the face in open-ice nowhere near the puck. He found himself benched for almost the entirety of the last two periods.

VAN #11 LW Jakob Stukel (2015) – Stukel, my 'Player of the Game' tonight, remains a difficult player to assess. Created scoring chances from within and beyond the prime scoring area throughout all three periods. A tremendous playmaker, he makes a lot of 'eyes in the back of his head'-type passes. Seems to be playing scared less and less with each passing contest.

VAN #17 LW Benson, Tyler (2016) – The first goal of his Western league career was one worthy of the highlight reels, as he went coast-to-coast with the puck before scoring a backhand beauty. After scoring his first WHL goal, he had a bit of offensive tunnel-vision, probably related to the excitement. For instance, a few shifts later he created a couple of really nice chances playing with Popoff and Houck before forgetting about his backchecking responsibilities and allowing a goal against in transition.

VAN #47 LC Bobylev, Vladimir (2015) – This is not your typical Russian forward. A player who clearly takes pride in finishing his checks, Bobylev has a bit of a unique hitting style—he will rush into the boards with speed, looking like he's about to crush you, but then takes a tactful approach and lightly bumps players off of the puck rather than obliterating them. Bobylev's wristshot is very powerful, even if it lacks accuracy at times.

September 27, 2014 - Sudbury Wolves at Belleville Bulls

SUD #2 LD Bourque, Trent (2016) - Trent had a strong performance tonight. He worked hard early and often and used his stick effectively to break up plays. He competes and showed good mobility down low. He has a good hard point shot with a limited amount of power play time. He did make his share of puck mistakes but was good overall in this game.

SUD #3 RD Clapham, Austin (2015) - Austin was very physical on the wall and finished his hits every chance he got. Took a holding penalty in the slot early in the second period.

SUD #11 RW Paliani, Devon (2015) - Devon showed a good compete level and anticipation to take away passing options

SUD #13 C Pezzetta, Michael (2016) - Michael was very aggressive all game long playing a very physical game and finishing his checks. He took a head checking penalty in the second period getting a little too high with his hit.

SUD #18 RW Kashtanov, Ivan (2015) - Ivan possesses good speed and utilized this speed to draw a penalty going wide on the defender and getting taken down. He made a great play late in the game trailing 2-1 coming out of the penalty box after serving Jacob Harris' penalty causing a turnover then making a great play down low to create a scoring chance to try and tie the game.

SUD #23 LD Capobianco, Kyle (2015) - Kyle made an impact right away drawing a power play the first shift of the game while protecting the puck around the net. He assisted on Sudbury's only goal of the game fanning on a one timer which went to Schmaltz who scored. Kyle is a good skater who always keeps his feet moving. He made smart pinches and always made it back into position. He did however take a few long shifts tonight and got beat one on one. He was very effective playing top power play minutes making smart passes with the puck under pressure and a very good shoot/pass selection on the power play. He was great with the puck under pressure all game long. He made a great play in the final minute of the game saving the offensive line and kept the play going and nearly scored the tying goal. He made quick decisions in the final minute and gave his team a chance to tie the game.

SUD #44 LC Zeppieri, David (2015) - David gets around somewhat alright but his skating is very awkward. He played quite a bit on the penalty kill but didn't put nearly enough pressure on the puck carrier. He did make a good play drawing in all five Belleville players into the corner and against the wall to kill time off.

BEL #5 RD Lemcke, Justin (2015) - Lemcke is a big strong defender who played in all game situations tonight. Despite his size, he needs to be more physical and using his great size when he's got an opponent lined up. He showed flashes of good puck protection when he got his feet moving. He has good power in his shot and when he gets it through he provides a good deflectable shot. However, he will force his shot at times. He lacked small area footwork to get from his position in the zone to the wall losing some races and battles due to slow footwork in transition and direction changes. Shifty forwards down low eluded him. He showed a good stick in some situations but needs to improve on his puck decisions. His puck movement did improve on the power play as the game went on.

BEL #22 LD Hanley, Jack (2016) - Jack got his first OHL point when his shot hit the crossbar and was finished by Cramarossa to give his team the lead and was the eventual winning goal.

Final Score: Belleville Bulls: 2 - Sudbury Wolves: 1

September 28, 2014 – Victoria Royals at Vancouver Giants

VIC #17 LC Soy, Tyler (2015) – Has a tendency to always look a little tired, but pounces into action quickly thanks to a good first step and sharp instincts. Tonight, he made a couple of nice reads to intercept wayward passes and kickstarted the offence for his team. His best skill continues to be his passing creativity, as exhibited by a chip-pass play that set up teammate Austin Carroll for a tuck-in goal at the outset of the second period.

VIC #19 LC Hannoun, Dante (2016) – Had a strong game, although he continues to look very, very small. A very good skater with a quick hop, and his hockey IQ and all-zones awareness is very high.

Lacks the reach at this point to take full advantage of his best skills. Often looks just a few inches short of making a great play happen. Most dangerous with the puck on his stick in the offensive zone as he is capable of making some really nifty plays from behind the net.

VIC #24 RW Nagy, Regan (2015) – A north-south player with strong east-west manoeuvrability, skates up and down the ice very quickly, finishes his checks religiously, and does a good job of getting a decent shot onto the net. First step or two are fairly powerful, although his full-stride acceleration could benefit from elongation and better arm fluction. Nonetheless, remains hard working and plays an admirable team-oriented game.

VIC #27 RW Dmytriw, Jared (2016) – Best qualities are without question his agility, quickness, speed, and determination. This is a player who can take off like a rocket or turn on a dime depending on what's needed in the moment. A very difficult player to track in the corners or to keep to the outside because of his elusive footwork. Still very, very small, he's blessed with a very low centre of gravity, and so he is well balanced on his feet and very difficult to knock off of the puck with physical pressure alone.

VIC #29 LD Reddekopp, Chaz (2015) – Straight-ahead acceleration is powerful and fast, as evidenced when he breaks across the blueline with the puck on his sticks; and yet his turns and general agility are his greatest downfall at this point, though one expects those to improve with age as he is still growing into his lanky frame. Manages to lay the body without taking himself too far out of position. Good at smothering pucks in the corner in order to kill time when playing a man down. Puck movement was really, really good at times as he makes a good hail-Mary pass out of his zone.

VAN #8 LW Baer, Alec (2015) – Baer can skate. Moving his feet very quickly and at an optimum width apart for the purposes of acceleration, elongation and balance, he has a fantastic full stride, and can continue accelerating comfortably with the puck tied to his stick. Can stickhandle while moving quickly too, but at one point he got caught with his head down going east-west in the neutral zone and was absolutely demolished by Austin Carroll. Baer not only returned to the ice, but also scored a beautiful goal as a sweet revenge.

VAN #17 LW Benson, Tyler (2016) – Skating, physicality, hockey sense, and offensive skills make him a master technician on the ice in terms of creating opportunities for his teammates. Big for his age and looks sturdy on his feet, he's a good two or three inches shorter than most other players in the league at this point; and yet, despite his somewhat diminutive nature, players already seem to fear his hitting skills and don't respect his time or space while he's handling the puck. Scored 2 points tonight.

VAN #22 RD Osipov, Dmitry (2015) – Once again, his backwards skating looked fluid and he played a game that was swivel-headed and conscientious. He does a tremendous job of limiting space in front of his net on the penalty kill, though he isn't a punisher by any means. His first passes were decent, but nothing to write home about. In reflection of his quiet, unspectacular but nonetheless efficient game, Osipov left the contest with no points, but a plus 2.

VAN #47 LC Bobylev, Vladimir (2015) – Fast, powerful and amusing in this one. Once again looking like he had an extra jump to his step, it was evidenced on the scoresheet for the second game in a row with Bobylev picking up his first ever WHL goal off of a Tyler Morrison deflection. Very enthusiastic after scoring. Does a lot of things behind the play and off camera that had me chuckling to myself in the corner of the arena—throws a lot of jabs, rabbit punches, and needless sticklifts when the referees aren't warching.

Sherbrooke Phoenix vs Drummondville Voltigeurs, September 28th 2014, QMJHL

SHE #2 Gregoire, Thomas RD (2016): Like his puck movement tonight, quick decision and a good first pass out of his zone. Joined the rush a couples of time tonight trying to create some offense. In his zone he lack strength to compete along the board or in front of the net right now, not shy but gets pushed too easily.

SHE #21 Thierus, Lucas RW (2016): Scored his first 2 career goals in today's game the same way, with some good speed down the wing and quick and accurate shot blocker side. Doesn't look overly fast but has a strong and powerful stride which he used well to beat defensemen wide. Didn't get a lot of ice time but took advantage of his opportunity.

SHE #26 Poulin, Nicolas LW (2015): Big kid who use his size well in the offensive zone to win battles and protect the puck. Good on the forecheck and plays a good role on the bottom 6 of the Phoenix. Skating need some work, lacks speed and agility. Made a nice pass to Lafontaine on Sherbrooke 4th goal,but overall his play with the puck was below average. Could make his decision more quickly when he has the puck. Son of former NHLer Patrick Poulin.

SHE #71 Deslaurier, Vincent C (2015): Made a real good pass to Daniel Audette for a chance on a breakaway. Played center on a line with a the 2 swiss forwards Wieser and Schweri, does the little things well at both end of the ice. Good job at retrieving puck along the board but let the two swiss forward work their magic in the offensive zone.

SHE #89 Schweri, Kay RW (2015): He showed off his excellent vision tonight with some real good passing plays, his passes on the5th & 6th goal were ridiculous. He think pass first all the time and always look to find his teammate open and is patient enough with the puck to wait an extra second or two to find them. Didn't work hard enough when he didn't had the puck in his zone, was waiting in his position to get it back. In the offensive zone he stayed mostly on the outside and didn't get really involve in traffic.

SHE #97 Roy, Jeremy RD (2015): Roy had a good game, nothing flashy but could have been better. His passing game which his usually great was off a bit today with some accuracy issues. On the power play he made some good read but had trouble finding a shooting lane, credit goes to Drummondville forwards for not giving him much space on the point.

DRU #4 Gagne, Benjamin LD (2017): Strong game in one on one matchup for Gagne, doesn't get big matchup yet but was solid one on one when he needed. Compete hard and is a strong kid along the wall.

DRU #6 Carignan-Labbe Julien RD (2015): Strong kid, love to get physical in his own zone and his tough to play against. Didn't do a good job at moving the puck today, decision were slow and his passes were lacking accuracy.

DRU #11 Ratelle Joey LW (2015): Ratelle was the best forward for Drummondville today, work hard in all three zones and was strong on the puck. Scored 2 goals today, was able to beat Jeremy Roy wide and then going high on the Sherbrooke goaltender and the2nd goal he made a nice tip at the side of the net for a power play goal. Still not the best skater but always found a way to contribute offensively for his team.

DRU #19 Barre-Boutet Alex C (2015): Good skater with a good burst of speed which help him create separation between him and opponents. Good pair of hands and tried to dangle the puck on a couple of occasions. Lack strength and can be pushed easily off the puck, see the ice well and he's a good passer. Didn't create much today offensively but showed some flashes.

DRU #22 Sevigny Mathieu C (2016): Involve in all three zones, backcheck hard and a strong forechecker as well. Goes to the net and had a good scoring chance after a rebound in the slot. On a couple of occasions with possession of the puck didn't see an open teammate who would had a great scoring chance. Makes good use of his stick in the defensive zone and is able to block passes and steal puck.

DRU #98 Doucet, Justin (2015): Big kid and love to finish his hits on the forecheck. Lacks overall speed and agility, was used during the game in front of the net where he's tough to move from there.

October 3, 2014 - Barrie Colts at Sarnia Sting

BAR #19 RD Andersson, Rasmus (2015) - Rasmus kept pretty quiet in this game overall, not having any big moments good or bad. He was his strongest in regards to puck movement making an excellent breakout pass while shorthanded to create a breakaway chance. He always takes a look at his options and consistently made the smart decision. A lot of intelligent, simple plays on the ice both exploiting open ice and distributing the puck properly in the neutral zone.

BAR #22 RW Radke, Roy (2015) - Roy was very effective for the Colts' and opened the scoring picking up a lose puck in the slot and fired it past the goaltender. He moved the puck effectively and took up space in the slot using his size very well.

BAR #29 G Blackwood, Mackenzie (2015) - Mackenzie showed good patience on a shorthanded breakaway early on to keep his team on pace. He made quick reads to be able to make the second save, however he shows a little too much extra/unnecessary movement. He allowed two goals in this game, neither were goals he had much chance on. The first was a rebound off a one timer he stopped and the second was a screened/deflected point shot that found it's way through.

SAR #5 LD Chychrun, Jakob (2016) - Jakob struggled a bit tonight in his teams' home opener. He was rushing a lot of plays resulting in several puck playing mistakes. While his skillset is very visible, he needs to get comfortable at this level and get his timing down in order to succeed as he is capable of.

SAR #9 LC Lajeunesse, Troy (2015) - Troy was very slippery along the wall and won several battles despite his lack of size due to his work ethic and determination.

SAR #11 RW Hodgson, Hayden (2015*) - Hodgson has an extremely powerful shot which was on display, including a laser that went off the post, but his only goal of this game came off a great deflection of a point shot. While he's more of a finisher he did a good job moving the puck in the offensive zone and even created a few scoring chances. He also played physical and while not over the top like he can be, he was effective in this area.

SAR #12 LW Lindberg, Brandon (2015) - Lindberg was effective playing big minutes on the penalty kill and finishing every check.

SAR #14 LC Zacha, Pavel (2015) - Pavel made a great impression right off the start playing very physical. He showed excellent poise with the puck in the neutral zone. He was very confidennt with the puck making smart, accurate passes continually. He also has the skating to take the puck through to the offensive zone showing a great first few steps, especially for his size and overall strong skater for a huge forward. He showed the capability of being a playmaker creating multiple chances including assisting on the first goal with a nice pass to Korostelev who's one-timer created the rebound goal.

SAR #35 RW Korostelev, Nikita (2015) - Registered an assist on Sarnia's first goal with his powerful one-timer that created a rebound that was quickly put behind Blackwood.

Final Score: Barrie Colts: 4 - Sarnia Sting: 2

Oct. 3, 2014 – Swift Current Broncos at Vancouver Giants

SWI #15 RC Gawdin, Glenn (2015) – Can stickhandle through traffic very well and doesn't mind occupying space in which he has to be crashed and banged—can therefore manufacture zone entries both by carrying and dumping the puck. Look good along the boards and when defending down low in his own zone, where he showed a penchant for collecting loose pucks. Won several faceoffs cleanly. Shooting skills were put on display, when he scored in the second period.

SWI #19 LW DeBrusk, Jake (2015) – Main speciality, aside from incredible net crashing abilities, is a one-time scoring touch that he showed off numerous times, including a streaking goal early in the first. Drives the net very hard and is difficult for defensemen to contain. His presence in front of Ryan Kubic was a major factor in the first period game tieing goal. Later, he showed off his tremendous passing skills by setting up a goal with a nifty pass from behind the net. When he had a hand in three of the games' goals, it would be hard to say he had anything but a fantastic game.

VAN #8 LW Baer, Alec (2015) – Alec Baer had a very good game, if not a one-dimensionally offensive showing. Tends to take some ambitious shots off stride that hurt his shooting percentages. Stickhandling and finishing capability both stood out as specialities in this game. Blessed with quick hands, good acceleration ability, and better than average range of motion in his upper-body.

VAN #22 RD Osipov, Dmitry (2015) – Dmitry Osipov had a fairly average game tonight, as he didn't stand out too prominently. In this game he logged long minutes on the power play and showed a penchant for limiting the opposition's time, space, and scoring opportunities. He's very good at racing down pucks in the corners and offering support in board battles.

VAN #31 G Kubic, Ryan (2016) – Just a few days after being named to one of the three Canadian World Under-17 Hockey Championships squads, Ryan Kubic made his WHL debut as a starter tonight. Has a wide butterfly stance that he goes in and out of very, very quickly. While he let in a few suspect goals right around his crease, I thought that his positioning, mechanics, decision making and competitiveness were all better than average. His first start wound up as a loss, unfortunately.

VAN #47 LC Bobylev, Vladimir (2015) – He was missing that "jump in his step" I saw in the last two games, and it led to one of his less memorable performances. Despite increased ice-time, he looked average at best out there and downright tired at times. Playing with less physicality, he looked tentative with and without the puck and was responsible for a number of untimely offsides. I've come to learn that when Bobylev comes out of the gate slow, he tends to play the whole game a bit slowly.

Ottawa 67's at Barrie Colts, Oct 5, 2015

Score: 9-3 Barrie

Ottawa

C Travis Konecny (2015) – Early on in this game Konecny was a little soft in the defensive zone. He cheated a little and had one-hand on his stick while trying to step around a Colt, which led to a turnover and a shot against. He showed good speed in his first three steps, and generated good speed through the neutral zone. Konecny did a good job of attacking throughout, and really put the pressure on the Colts defense. He was able to make players miss in open ice, as he danced around defenders on several occasions. Konecny had a good stick on the PK, and was effective playing that role. He blew past the defense on one PK and showed off his exceptional release beating Blackwood glove side. He was creative with the puck, and was a constant threat throughout the game. Konecny showed good hands, and looked comfortable playing the point on the powerplay, though I think he'd be more effective with his shot coming off the half-wall. He was relentless after the puck, and forced several turnovers by applying pressure. Konecny didn't shy away physically, either, as he had a few hits, and was involved after the play several times.

C Dante Salituro (2015) – Salituro didn't have his best game, but he did show some flashes. He regularly gained the line in the offensive zone with possession, and was creative off the rush. Salituro displayed good hands and passing ability, though he did force several throughout the night that resulted in turnovers. He was creative with the puck, avoided several oncoming checks, and made one beautiful backhand saucer pass that landed right on the tape for a scoring chance. For the most part he provided good support along the wall in all three zones, and his positioning was OK. He bobbled a puck in the defensive zone early on that led to a couple shots against.

RW Artur Tyanulin (2015) – He showed creativity with the puck, and displayed good hands throughout. On one occasion he was knocked to his knees but still made a beautiful cross-ice saucer pass to setup a shot. At times he was too fancy with the puck, and had a few poor turnovers. Tyanulin used his shiftiness and quick feet to stretch the defense, though a couple times he cheated up too far. For the most part he backchecked hard, and was pretty reliable defensively. He did take a bad penalty at the end of the 1st that the Colts converted on.

RW Jeremiah Addison (2015) – Addison won several puck battles in the offensive zone, and distributed the puck well. He played at a high pace, and showed good vision finding open targets with regularity. Addison showed high hockey IQ when feeding a teammate, and quickly slipping through a gap to try and capitalize on a give-and-go. He showed good speed throughout, and was responsible in his own zone.

D Troy Henley (2015) – Henley struggled in this one. He looked lost at times in the defensive zone, and struggled to stay with his man in front of the net. Henley failed to clear it on several occasions, and was caught watching in front of the net. He blocked a couple shots, but really wasn't sound in his own zone. On the other side of the puck, Henley was able to get his shots through, and did a good job of holding the blue line.

Barrie Colts

RW Roy Radke (2015) – Radke was strong on the wall, and used his body to finish checks when he could. He wasn't afraid to go to the dirty areas of the ice, and scored a nice powerplay marker on a net drive play. He had some effective shifts cycling the puck as well. Radke struggled off the rush, as he couldn't gain a step and was forced wide and behind the net several times.

C Matthew Kreis (2015) – Kreis played a solid 200-foot game. He back-checked well and was able to force some passes from behind. Kreis also served as a good safety outlet for his defensemen. He showed good speed, kept his feet moving constantly and drew a penalty while cycling by doing so. Kreis liked to go wide with speed, gain entry to the offensive zone and look to distribute from there.

D Rasmus Andersson (2015) – Andersson missed the net a few times, but did a relatively good job of getting pucks through. One shot he got through ended up being deflected by Lemieux for a goal. When a clear passing lane wasn't available Andersson did a nice job of using the boards to get the puck up ice. His gap control was good, though on one occasion his ankles were broken in open ice and it led directly to a goal. His net front awareness wasn't great at times, either, as he'd go to get in the shooting lanes and would leave a man open in front without looking to see if a teammate had picked him up. He only pinched on a couple occasions, and did a good job ensuring someone was covering for him in case he was caught.

G Mackenzie Blackwood (2015) – Blackwood did a nice job of staying square to shooters, not over-committing and ensuring he was in good position to make stops. His rebound control was good, and when he coughed them out he used his athleticism and size to sprawl and make the next stop. He tracked pucks well, and was able to find several loose pucks through feet. Blackwood also showed good leg strength when holding the line while several 67's hacked away in the crease. One area that continues to be a bit of a concern is his glove. He allowed two goals there in this contest, one of which he probably should have had.

October 5, 2014 - Sarnia Sting at Mississauga Steelheads

SAR #5 LD Chychrun, Jakob (2016) - Strong puck decisions on the power play. Good patience and had the ability to know when to shoot and when to pass. Used his size to muscle opponents off the puck. Got hurt blocking a shot but was able to return after a few moments. Made a great rush on the power play exploding up the middle splitting the defenders then got a great scoring chance. Chychrun launched a rocket top shelf to score the first goal of the game and of his OHL career. About a period later, Jakob would fire a wrist shot past the goaltender for Sarnia's second goal of the game and the game winning goal. Both wrist and slap shot were excellent. Was utilized in the final minute of a one goal game.

SAR #9 RW Lajeunesse, Troy (2015) - Troy showed great compete all game and forced turnovers. He got a partial break at one point but got leveled going one on one with an opposing defender. He moved the puck fairly well creating a few scoring chances for his team. Played final minute of the game with a one goal lead.

SAR #10 LW Kodola, Vladislav (2015) - Vladislav showed some good flashes of speed and puck skills but tried to do too much at times with the puck.

SAR #12 RW Lindberg, Brandon (2015) - Great move on shorthanded scoring chance but was stopped. He played a ton of minutes on the penalty kill tonight. Didn't identify Korostelev coming out of the penalty box, which would have been a clear cut breakaway. Brandon was utilized in the final minute of the game but took a checking from behind penalty putting his team shorthanded for the final 30 seconds.

SAR #14 LC Zacha, Pavel (2015) - Zacha made some great give and go passes but has some teammates who wouldn't give it back to him. Displayed an outstanding inside out move to create a scoring chance for his team. Great puck movement displayed in this game.

SAR #25 RC Kyrou, Jordan (2016) - Jordan played a lot of minutes tonight and was notable at both ends of the ice. He provided a great backcheck to force the turnover. He got involved on a couple big rushes but was unable to follow through including a 3 on 1 where he attempted to do it himself but lost the handle on the puck.

SAR #35 RW Korostelev, Nikita (2015) - Nikita opens himself up well in the offensive zone to utilize his shot. He engaged physically throughout this game finishing several checks. His skating is OK but certainly has room for improvement. He could stand to get more out of his strides as he has power but doesn't gain as much ice as he could. Protects puck well going up ice using his body and hands.

SAR #32 G Fazio, Justin (2015) - Did a great job staying square to shooters. He also did a good job controlling and not allowing many rebounds. He was playing a little too deep in his crease at times. He only allowed one goal but it was a soft one. Overall a very good game for Fazio.

MIS #4 LD Day, Sean (2016) - Able to protect the puck well when activating from the point and makes some good moves at the blue line to ensure offensive zone control. Effortless skating ability. Lacked compete at times in the defensive zone.

Final Score: Sarnia Sting: 2 - Mississauga Steelheads: 1

October 5, 2014 - Kitchener Rangers at Oshawa Generals

KIT #15 LC Franzen, Gustaf (2015) - Great play on backcheck to break up play. Gustaf played in all game situations and was effective in creating offensive plays and maintaining good positioning in the defensive zone. Wasn't afraid to get involved physically when necessary. Gustaf was around 50 percent in face-off's today.

KIT #17 RW Kohn, Mason (2015) - Excellent forecheck pressure throughout this game. However when he gets his hands on the puck he can sometimes try to do too much. Got plenty of time on the penalty kill.

KIT #18 D Blaisdell, Doug (2015) - Doug had a pretty steady first period, consistently made the right first pass however as the game went on he lost his positioning in the defensive zone a few times. He made a good play with his stick to break up a big scoring rush. Blaisdell was utilized in the final minute of the game with a tie score and he got caught being a spectator on the rush and drifted too far away from his man and got walked before he could recover for the winning goal. Overall not his best performance.

KIT #23 LW Mascherin, Adam (2016) - Adam picked up the puck in the slot in the second period and quickly fired a shot to score Kitchener's second goal of the game, and his first career OHL goal. Minutes later he found a hole in the goaltender while holding the post to slip in Kitchener's third goal of the game. Mascherin would have two of Kitchener's three goals this game. He received good time on the power play.

KIT #74 LC Bunnaman, Connor (2016) - Connor moved the puck well on the offensive rush. He was very composed when under pressure with the puck.

OSH #26 LD Robertson, Daniel (2015) - Daniel provided some physicality in a somewhat minimized role for Oshawa tonight. He does a very good job containing on the wall.

OSH #58 LD Vande Sompel, Mitchell (2015) - Good movement on power play to continuously open himself up as a passing option without the puck. When he has the puck he generally moves it quickly. Mitchell played top power play minutes. Slow recovering after turning puck over in the offensive zone created a three on one rush for Kitchener and a scoring chance against. Overall he did a better job in the defensive zone than previous viewings.

OSH #89 RC Harding, Sam (2015) - Sam possesses good speed and got up and down the ice well. Good deflections in the slot. Sam really struggled in the face-off circle only winning around 20 percent this game.

Final Score: Oshawa Generals: 4 - Kitchener Rangers: 3

Oct. 5, 2014 – Prince George Cougars at Vancouver Giants

PRI #2 LD Ruopp, Sam (2014) – Moved up the depth chart from last season and is making the most of his increased ice-time with the Cougars [post-op edit: Ruopp was later in the month named captain of the Cougars]. A fairly good skater for his size who sometimes had difficulty maintaining his lane control last season, he's made improvements to his positioning game. Outlet passes were generally strong, even if he didn't create a whole lot of action offensively speaking. A physical punisher in his own end.

PRI #9 LW Morrison, Brad (2015) – Coming off of a long road-trip game in Spokane, looked rather tired and uninspired in a game in which he saw limited ice-time. While skating technique is far from perfect, his feet move quick like the blades of a lawnmower when accelerating to full speed. Even when tired, he cleverly in and out of prime scoring areas, looking ready to pot in a rebound, although luck wasn't really on his side in this game. A bit invisible in his own end, he was a contributing factor to a bad giveaway in the first period that led to a premium scoring the other way.

PRI #12 LC Harkins, Jansen (2015) – He did a good job of handling the puck while moving at a decent clip. First steps come off with a lot of power and he is very quick skating backwards. Also difficult to knock off the puck once he has it, as he appears very balanced. Can deke or pass his way out of trouble if necessary, as he has exceptional stickhandling and passing skills. Plays in all situations and is active in his own zone.

PRI #13 RW Babych, Cal (2015) – The son of Vancouver Canucks defensemanDave Babych skates at a decent if not slightly below-average clip and is good at winning board battles. Keeps an active stick, that when conflated with a generally physical style, allows him to force a lot of turnovers. Instincts are good, as he created a few turnovers in the neutral and offensive zones, even if his skillset looked only average upon first viewing.

PRI #25 LD Olson, Tate (2015) – Possesses impressive skating skills and manoeuvrability on the ice. Strong on his edges and blessed with quick feet, has shockingly good escapability that allows him to buy time and make good plays out of his own zone. Shows really good hockey sense by utilizing the boards cleverly on breakout passes. Echoed that showing of high hockey IQ with some brilliant keeps and pinches in the offensive zone, really impressing me with his instincts and first-step capabilities. His game was not without mistakes. Left some of his checks acres of space at times and it cost his team.

PRI #28 RD Josh Anderson (2016) – Tall and sturdy, blessed with tremendous leg strength—they were tree-trunk, like. Skating in all directions was phenomenal in consideration of both his size and immaturity. Threw his body around, blocked shots, made good first-passes and was swivel-headed in all three zones. Saw a fair bit of ice-time and looked highly dependable despite being so young.

VAN #12 RC Brumm, David (2015) – An excellent energy forward who brings a cool combination of skating, skill, hitting and stick skills to the ice. He has played much of the year already with Vladimir Bobylev and the two appear to have tremendous chemistry as they bring similar qualities to the table. Continues to do a good job of finishing his checks, creating turnovers and manufacturing scoring opportunities for he and his linemates.

VAN #17 LW Benson, Tyler (2016) – Returning from a one-game suspension following a huge open-ice hit on Jesse Lees in a road game against Kelowna, Benson didn't look tentative at all as he skated hard, finished his checks hard and clean, made strong plays, and put up points on the scoreboard. A force in all situations—on the penalty kill, power play, with the lead, a goal or two behind, in tough situations, or at any other time you need him. Has tons of versatility.

VAN #22 RD Osipov, Dmitry (2015) – Not proficient enough to quarterback his team on the man advantage, but makes some great plays from the point and has really improved his shooting skills. He scored an assist on a one-timer slapshot from the point that was deflected high by Jackson Houck and into the net; interestingly, Osipov and Houck attempted to score using the exact same play just a few minutes earlier.

VAN #26 RD McKinstry, Ryely (2016) – Looks mature beyond his years. First passes are excellent and his shooting abilities are coming along very nicely. A beautifully simplistic wristshot from the point hit the net and then came out in the slot and landed on the stick of Joey Hamilton and went into the net shortly thereafter. Later, with Foster parked in front of the net, he let off a beautiful wrister that went past a screen and into the net, tallying his first ever WHL goal. He also won a fight tonight. Left the game with a Gordie Howe hat-trick.

VAN #47 LC Bobylev, Vladimir (2015) – Has a great puck protection ability to shield the puck in all areas of the ice—whether it be behind the net, in the corners, in mid-ice or anywhere else. Surprisingly agile for a player of his size, he does a good job of using his powerful upper-body to shield the puck and his nimble lower-body to spin off checks. Has a hot-headed nature during scrums after the whistle. If he wants to acclimatize himself to the North American game, he'll have to become acquainted with those type of post-whistle situations and learn how to engage in them without going penalized.

October 10, 2014 - Barrie Colts at London Knights

BAR #14 LW Smith, Givani (2016) - Smith was noticeable using his size to play physical.

BAR #19 LD Andersson, Rasmus (2015) - Only defenseman to get time on Barrie's top powerplay unit, Rasmus has a good shot from the point but hits the net about 50% of the time. He has the patience to allow shooting lanes to open up and can put a hard low shot on net. He jumped up on a short-handed rush displaying a good wrist shot. He utilized his wrist shot from the point on the powerplay and found it's way through to give Barrie their third goal of the game.

BAR #22 RW Radke, Roy (2015) - Skates well for his size. He was noticeable for making a few very strong passes. Needs to be more aggressive with his size.

BAR #26 RW Mangiapane, Andrew (2015*) - Andrew was able to make an impact in this game creating plays out of nothing.

BAR #29 G Blackwood, Mackenzie (2015) - Made a huge save early on stopping the initial shot then robbed the rebound to keep the game scoreless at the time. Made an excellent 150ft. pass on the powerplay to keep pressure on the Knights. Flashed the glove on numerous occasions. 1st goal no chance. Same with second goal as he made the first save on a deflected shot, rebound banged in.

LON #14 D Crawley, Brandon (2015) - Cannon shot from the point that is very accurate and gets on goal virtually every time. Good gap control in the neutral zone. He needs to hustle more to the offensive line once the play has progressed up ice, didn't get to the line in time on a few occasions. Won battles on the wall against older forwards. Generally made smart pinches from the line but on one pinch late in a one goal game he took too long getting back into position resulting in a 3 on 1 chance for Barrie.

LON #86 D Martenet, Chris (2015) - Couldn't contain forward going to the slot despite his size advantage. Instead he hooked him which gave Barrie a powerplay which resulted in Barrie's tying goal.

LON #93 RW Marner, Mitch (2015) - Mitch opened the game with an excellent scoring chance on his second shift but was absolutely robbed by Blackwood. He was consistent throughout this game utilizing his evasiveness and puck skills to create scoring chances. He made an outstanding pass up to Dvorak sending him in on a breakaway chance. On London's first goal he made an excellent play massing the puck instead of jamming at it like most players would have. It directly resulted in London's first goal of the game. He crashed the net hard late in the game helping London score their third goal of the game as well. In addition to his offensive play, Marner received ice on the penalty kill as well.

LON #98 D Mete, Victor (2016) - Chased play down low going well out of position resulting in Barrie's first goal of the game. Made an excellent long distance pass from deep in his own zone. Willing an capable of blocking shots when playing on the penalty kill. Mishandled puck in his own zone on the power play resulting in a scoring chance against.

LON #1 G Parsons, Tyler (2016) - Tyler comes well out to cut down angles on incoming forwards. He plays very aggressive against shooters. He follows the play very well on the penalty kill when the team is spreading the puck around.

Final Score: Barrie Colts: 4 - London Knights: 3

October 10th 2014, Muskegon Lumberjacks v. Lincoln Stars

MUS #2 Eliot, Mitch RD (2016) – The '98 born defenseman played a solid game tonight. Was used as a seventh defenseman so he didn't get a ton of playing time but certainly made an impact when he was on the ice. Fought LaDouce of Lincoln halfway through the first and held his own. Very encouraging to see him mix it up with players much older than him. Tons of potential here.

MUS #3 Cecconi, Joseph RD (2015) – Played a really solid game. Not going to wow you but is a super reliable defensemen. Did a great job tonight using his stick in his own zone breaking up passes, deflecting shots, etc. He's very calm and relaxed on the ice, with and without the puck on his stick.

MUS #5 Trinkberger, David LD (Undrafted 2014) – Big body. Very solid on his skates. Best while in his own zone. Lock down, stay at home kind of player. Wasn't afraid to jump up and join rush although at some points he would have been better served to give the puck up to a teammate. The 6'5" defensemen could make a push to be drafted this year.

MUS #11 Iacopelli, Matheson LW (2014, 3rd Round Chicago Blackhawks) – Best player on the ice as he has been in every previous viewing. Scored a goal five hole in third period on Lincoln's Peyton Jones. Really nothing left to prove at the USHL level.

MUS #12 Marody, Cooper RC (2015) – Works as a set up guy for Iacopelli on top line and power play unit. Going to rack up the assists this year. Did shoot the puck a few times, but the concerning thing was the amount of shots he took from low percentage areas. He's a very smart player, but he needs to lay it off to teammates instead of taking those ill-advised spots.

MUS #17 Keefer, David RW (2016) – He is more impressive in every viewing. He's not afraid to get into the dirty areas and throw his body around despite his lack of size. He sees the ice really well. Fed a great pass to Iacopelli on his goal in the third period.

MUS #25 Marchin, Tommy LW (Undrafted 2014) – Very hard worker. Great player in his own zone. Skating definitely needs work, below average first few steps and acceleration. Physical player. He's what I would consider a late bloomer in terms of offensive ability, but his offensive game is definitely coming along. Kind of a what you see is what you get player, very raw but has the physical tools and the offensive game is coming along.

MUS #29 Schierhorn, Eric G (Undrafted 2014) – Allowed two goals on twenty-two shots. Moves slow and relaxed. Struggled to get set on more than a few shots faced, resulting in him ending up on his backside. Tons of potential with his athletic ability. If he gets out quicker and gets set before the shot starts coming in his game could improve a lot. Got beat both times by being too deep in his crease and not being able to see around the screen. Biggest thing is him ending up on his backside scrambling a lot.

LIN #10 Fidler, Miguel LW (2014, 5th Round Florida Panthers) – Very strong on the puck, extremely hard to knock him off the puck. Strong skater. Will the play the body and does so effectively. Smart player, sees the ice well. Is still lacking an effective offensive skillset since making the jump to the USHL. Projects as a bottom six type player at the next level.

LIN #15 vonUngern-Sternberg, August LC (2015) – Plays a solid game, not going to jump off the ice at you. Lacks that killer instinct when he has someone in his sights. Seems to be afraid to shoot at times. One-dimensional player. Good skater, passes the puck well and finds his teammates.

LIN #18 Kalynuk, Wyatt LD (2015) – Used in all situations tonight. Skates with a good solid base. Pretty solid in his own zone, doesn't really get caught out of position. Uses his stick well, breaking up passes and creating turnovers. Pretty underrated player in my opinion.

LIN #24 Lee, Cam LD (2015) – Scored a great goal top shelf from the point to beat Schierhorn in the first period. Smooth skater, can really move the puck. Leads the rush every time he has the puck in his zone. Tries to do too much at times and ends up turning the puck over in the neutral zone. Tends to be weak in his own zone, not really willing to play the body.

Sport vs. Ilves, october 10, 2014

Ilves #28 RW Hintz, Roope (2015) - Hintz had a great night today in 4-3 victory. Scored a 1+1 and formed a amazing duo with Aleksi Mustonen. Hintz is a big kid with great offensive instincts: good passing skills, great vision and decent wrister. Roope likes to play around corners and he's good at it. Knows how to play in small places: protecting and handling the puck. He has played as a winger in his first pro season but he's really a centerman. He's really smart in the o-zone, for example in a one shift he shot a low and weak wrist shot which led to a rebound and he did it on purpose. The biggest problem is his skating ability: his first steps and mobility are quite bad. Definitely a long-term project and he got the tools but really needs to improve his skating and two-way game.

Ilves #21 C Mustonen, Aleksi (2015) - Mustonen had also a great night and scored 1+1. He has went undrafted two times but now he has truly showed his skills. Mustonen is a small center man but plays like a big one. He got lots of power in his lower body and he's a fast skater. Great hockey IQ and really good playmaker. Eventhough he's small, he likes to play physically and that makes him potential late round pick. There's still some "young guy problems" in his game: in a one shift he got 2-in-1 situation and he tried to shoot which is fine but the shot went straight to the goalies chest. Aleksi also knows how to play two-way game because of his smartness and speediness.

Ilves #5 D Mäkelä, Aleksi (Drafted by Dallas Stars 2013) - Aleksi had a subpar game. He's a stay-at-home d-man and he's doing it fine. He's a big kid and he really likes to play rough but that's it. He didn't showed any puck or passing skills which is a huge problem. He did a couple of bad decisions with puck and a one situation led to a opponents breakaway. He's good in front of his own net but that's not enough. He needs to be better with puck. Simple passes etc.

October 11th 2014, Chicago Steel at Tri-City Storm

CHI #10 Laczynski, Tanner RW (2015) – Pretty quiet game from Laczynski. Doesn't really do anything offensively to jump off the ice at you. Had a couple bad turnovers in the neutral zone as well as the offensive zone trying to get too cute with passes. Lost a few battles in the corners and getting outworked going one on one with guys trying to get to the net.

CHI #23 Jackson, Robby LW (2015) – Assisted on the game tying goal and then scored the game winning goal in the third period potting the puck home from a scrum in front of the net. Obviously very offensive minded player, would go as far as to say he is a one-dimensional player at this point. He's got great hands, loves the puck on his stick, can make opportunities out of nothing. Not the strongest skater on the ice but has the uncanny ability to kind of float into soft spots in the defense and get the puck. He sees the play develop really well. Can anticipate where the play is leading and where he needs to be and he can get there.

CHI #28 Olofsson, Freddie RW (2014, 4th Round Chicago Blackhawks) – Fairly quiet game out of Olofsson tonight offensively. Plays a really solid game. Very good skater, smooth stride and can really move. Very smart player, sees the ice well. Has improved even more in his own end coming from last year and is continuing to develop a nice two-way skillset.

TC #3 Dello, Tory RD (2015) – Played a really good game. Not flashy by any means, but he gets the job done, and more importantly he gets the job done consistently. Have seen him a handful of times now and he has consistently turned in good, solid performances. Dello skates with a really strong, solid base. It's almost impossible to out muscle him and beat him one on one. Made a great play with an empty net behind him to catch up to a streaking Steel player and knock him off the puck before he could pot the empty netter. Absolutely great showing in his own zone tonight. He might be undervalued by some because of his lack of an elite offensive skillset, but he is capable of moving the puck. Really nice game tonight.

TC #20 Wahlin, Jake LW (2015) – Showed off some of his speed tonight. Willing to shoot from just about anywhere. Super quick release on his shot. Good hands. Starting to develop more of an edge to his game. Had two good scoring opportunities in the slot that he couldn't quite finish.

TC #30 Dillon, Alec G (2014, 5th Round LA Kings) – Allowed two goals on 31 shots. Didn't get much help on the first goal. He uses his massive frame (6'5") to his advantage, not coming out too far from his crease. Tracks the puck really well. Fundamentally sound. Can move post to post really well for a guy his size.

TC #44 Wilkie, Chris (2014, Undrafted) – I have been really impressed with Wilkie so far this season. In the past there has always been some questions about his compete level and if the desire was there. This year it seems that he out on a mission and he is showing his real skillset which may have been overshadowed by effort concerns in the past. He is a great skater, and he has the ability to create something out of nothing. The skill has always been there, it's just been a question of compete level. So far from the viewing I have had, it looks like all the pieces have finally come together for Wilkie this season and his name might be one to keep an eye on around draft time as a second year eligible.

Scout's Notes: This was a really good game of hockey. Although it was a low scoring affair, there were tons of offensive chances for both teams so really credit the goalies, Alec Dillon from Tri-City and John Lethemon of Chicago. After a period and a half of scoreless hockey, Tri-City scored to make 1-0. In the third period, Chicago got goals from Connor Murphy and Robby Jackson to make the final score 2-1 in favor of Chicago.

Oct 12. 2014 Sport U20 VS. Lukko U20

Sport #5 D Salo, Robin (2017) - Salo had again a great night. He's really mature player for his age and always doing great decisions with the puck. Calm allround d-man who's already physically grown up. Salo always gives easy first pass and got a great vision. He's good skater, especially backwards but needs to improve his technique which isn't bad but not perfect. He got lots of power in his legs which is why he's strong skater. Could be even better if he develops his technique and then he would be one the top D-men in his age group (in Finland). he showed also some of his powerplay skills today: great passes and accurate shots. In 5vs3 powerplay he played in front of the net and was a beast. Also lot of great penalty kill shifts: knows how to block shots and always shoots the puck out of d-zone safely. He's an interesting name in the Import Draft and would definitely success in the CHL in next season.

Sport #61 RW Vähäkangas, Verneri (2016) - Vähäkangas played in the fourth line today which is wrong place for him. He's an offensive player with great puck-handling skills and needs a big role. He's small winger but got a great speed and vision. He's got great first steps and good mobility but his biggest asset is his offensive skills. Sees the ice very well and really knows how to dangle. Showed today lot of attitude but didn't got any help from his linemates. Physically weak and usually lost his one-on-one battles but there's great offensive tools which makes him really interesting prospect.

October 13, 2014 - Kingston Frontenacs at Mississauga Steelheads

KGN #13 LD Parikka, Jarkko (2015) - Jarkko has good mobility and skates well in all directions. However on one rush he took the wrong route and ended up turning the puck over for a scoring chance. He knows how to contain on the wall but lacks the strength to execute against bigger forwards.

KGN #26 RC Nichol, Ted (2015) - Ted was a regular on the penalty kill and played with a ton of energy. Made a great pass in the third period of a close game to set up a scoring chance.

KGN #67 LW Crouse, Lawson (2015) - Lawson's speed has improved considerably over the past twelve months. Good forecheck pressure creating turnovers and scoring chances out of his pressure. Consistent work ethic, competed every single shift. He needs to add a mean streak because his physicality was non-existent in this game.

MIS #4 LD Day, Sean (2016) - Sean played in all game situations but he had a very mixed performance in today's game. Sean showed smooth skating ability and carried the puck with ease. He had his best rush in overtime giving his team a partial scoring chance. He showed good vision to accurately move the puck at a high speed. He made a good delay on his shot during a power play and showed his puck patience to allow the lane to open up before shooting the puck. However on the power play he mishandled the puck on multiple occasions. He will at times try to hold the offensive line too aggressively in low percentage circumstances then would lack urgency on the backcheck. On the penalty kill he didn't pressure the puck carrier at all, on one occasion he got walked around off the wall when he didn't pressure which resulted in a scoring chance against.

Final Score: Kingston Frontenacs: 3 - Mississauga Steelheads: 2 OT/SO

Oct. 15, 2014 – Surrey Eagles at Langley Rivermen

SUR #12 RW Westgard, Ty (2016) – Saw a lot of ice-time tonight. A decent skater with better agility than speed, his specialty is probably his strong and accurate wristshot coupled with clutch scoring abilities. Game that went to overtime after a Westgard wristshot that found its place in the top corner for a game-tieing goal. Blessed with relatively quick feet, Westgard stands out as a natural offensive winger who likes to drag the puck out wide and is good at splitting the defence.

SUR #27 LC McMurphy, Chase (2013) – Once again, I thought that the Surrey Eagle's captain offered a lone bright-spot on an otherwise lackadaisical Surrey Eagles effort. Possesses strong fourth, fifth and sixth stride acceleration speed. Saw him starting out the backcheck from deep in his own zone, far behind several other players, only to beat those players across the opposition blueline with his outstanding full-stride capabilities. Looking like a true captain and leader for his team, he combines such skating acumen with a physical style and strong commitment to team defence.

SUR #35 Christian Short (2014) LG – Playing on a rather weak Surrey Eagles club, I thought Christian Short did a fantastic job of keeping his team in the game despite a heavily one-sided shot differential after two periods. It's a bit oxymoron, but Short is a fairly tall goaltender who I feel plays a bit too deep in his net. Other than that, I think his game is generally very strong. Able to play deeper in his net as he tends to play more of a stand-up game than is conventional for goalies these days. Looks equally strong on his glove and blocker, and does a good job of redirecting rebounds into the corners.

LAN #30 Bo Didur (2015) LG – By all accounts, Bo Didur's specialty is competitiveness and a "never-say-die" attitude that really came directly to the forefront in his performance tonight. A head-on-head collision with teammate Marcus Vela knocked Didur down. However, he continued playing, putting up a more than decent performance and an overtime victory. Upper-body reflexes are very, very good and I also like his ability to slide from side-to-side quickly. Rebound control is better than average, and I have a hard time finding any flaws in his positioning. He is far from NHL sized, but he has been consistently impressive in both of my viewings.

LAN #4 LD Masellis, Dominic (2015) – Offers an attractive, if not extremely raw, example of a pure combination of size and skating abilities. Turns, pivots and the speed of his footwork all look highly advanced for a player of his age and size. All other important attributes to a two-way defenceman, however—passing, shooting, awareness, etc.—seem like a work in progress. While he makes a decent first pass, I wish he had a bit more poise with the puck as he has a tendency to blindly shoot it up the ice when placed into tight quarters or when put under pressure by the opposition.

LAN #12 RC Vela, Marcus (2015) – Had a fantastic game punctuated by hard work down low at both ends of the rink. In fact, he was so committed to defending his own crease, at one point he came into a head-on-head collision with his goaltender, Bo Didur. A slightly better than average skater, he maintains a robust first step even if his top-speed is not elite. Though he was left off the scoresheet, he manufactured a couple really nice screens on teammates' scoring opportunities thanks to good drive and net-front presence. Insanely committed to finishing his checks.

October 15, 2014 - Erie Otters at London Knights

ERI #12 RW DeBrincat, Alex (2016) - Alex is undersized but has very high end skating ability. He is also a three zone player and has a great backcheck. He competes hard in all zones and isn't afraid to get involved along the wall. DeBrincat scored twice for Erie tonight showing the ability to both score and create scoring chances.

ERI #19 LW Strome, Dylan (2015) - Dylan had a rough first half of the game and took two tripping penalties in the first half. Strome got better as the game went on. He showed good positioning at the side of the net on the power play and got a tap in goal due to positioning. He made a great shootout move to score Erie's only goal on the shootout.

ERI #97 LC McDavid, Connor (2015) - Connor had a pretty quiet game for someone of his stature. He did register an assist on two of Erie's three goals, but really didn't get to play his game. He displayed the flashes of his elite vision, skating and puck skills, but couldn't get too much going consistently. His frustration became visible when he was hip checked in the third period when trying to make a move one on one and instead of getting up and backchecking, he sat on the ice, yelled at one of the officials, then got up and as he was skating back to the defensive zone yelled at the other official. Connor made an absolutely outstanding shootout but hit the goal post. Connor had an excellent day in the face-off circle winning approximately 75-80 percent of his draws tonight.

LON #14 LD Crawley, Brandon (2015) - Brandon contained forwards along the wall effectively in the defensive zone. When the puck is deep in the offensive zone he needs to show more hustle to the offensive line. When he gets there he has done a good job showing mobility and patience with the puck, not forcing his shot option for smarter passing lanes or sending the puck deep. Kept icing the puck under pressure.

LON #25 RC Rymsha, Drake (2016) - Drake was very effective at agitating the opposition and getting involved along the wall. Excellent forecheck pressure all night long.

LON #93 RW Marner, Mitchell (2015) - Mitchell was pretty quiet in the first half showing his puck control ability down low in the offensive zone, creating a few potential chances. His play really picked up in the third period opening by stealing the puck in the defensive zone and going end to end with it creating a scoring chance. In the shootout he showed his puckhandling ability and went five hole, but it wasn't there.

LON #98 LD Mete, Victor (2016) - Great play on the line to keep a play going in the offensive zone. He struggled getting outmuscled in the slot which resulted in a big scoring chance against. However, along the wall forwards struggle to evade him due to his skating ability.

Final Score: London Knights: 4 - Erie Otters: 3 OT/SO

October 17, 2014 - Niagara Ice Dogs at Guelph Storm

NIA #4 LD Dunn, Vince (2015) - Vince was very smooth skating up ice with the puck. He is patient and can slow things down and make the proper play in the neutral zone whether it be accelerating with the puck or making the proper pass. He played on the top power play unity and possesses an above average shot with an above average slap shot and a quick release on the wrist shot. He was very comfortable finishing his hits and landed an excellent open ice hit. Despite the physical play he struggled a little at time in battles along the boards.

GUE #13 RW Craievich, Adam (2015) - Craievich still needs to improve his skating a fair amount. When he accesses the offensive zone he focuses on getting open in the slot area and will look to open himself up in scoring position.

GUE #14 RC Boston, Tyler (2015) - Good speed to enter the offensive zone with the puck and created a few chances. Without the puck he went hard to the bet and scored the opening goal. Despite his size, he's not afraid to crash the crease.

GUE #27 LD McFadden, Garrett (2015) - Garrett sent smooth, hard, accurate passes up ice all game long. It seemed almost every pass from McFadden was hard and on the tape of his target. He is a very smooth, quick skater and can skate the puck out of trouble. On the power play he did a very good job distributing the puck and making quick decisions when pressured.

GUE #28 LW Rapp, Aleks (2015) - Aleks was effective finishing his checks hard.

Final Score: Guelph Storm: 3 - Niagara Ice Dogs: 2

Oct. 17, 2014 – Kamloops Blazers at Vancouver Giants

KAM #7 LW Kryski, Jake (2016) – Multifaceted game continues to impress me on many levels. Blessed with a tremendous combination of straight-ahead speed and agility. Acclimatized well to the Don Hay coaching regimen, playing a simplistic but effective north-to-south dump-and-chase game that is easy to admire. Not particularly big, he finds ways to be physical. He finishes most of his checks and he does a good job of winning body position in board battles. Made some nice feeds into the slot.

KAM #14 RC Needham, Matt (2013) – A good skater, he showed that he is capable of quarterbacking the power play in the game tonight, not looking out of place in the least while navigating the left point on the man advantage. A player with good defensive awareness, he looked like indistinguishable from a defensemanat even-strength, too, working hard to win board battles behind his own net on a number of occasions tonight.

KAM #18 LW Winther, Mike (Dallas 2012) – Spent most of the game on the wings, where he typically uses his speed to drive defenders wide and his passing to open up space in the offensive zone creating scoring opportunities for teammates. He shows good strength and speed, as his initial steps are better than average and he utilizes a quick and compact skating stride. A tough and strong player who is difficult to knock off the puck.

KAM #34 RW Sideroff, Deven (2015) – Had a fairly average outing tonight. A good skater who wins most of his races to the puck, he has a tendency to appear a bit wobbly-legged at times. Acceleration remains impressive and turns and pivots are very quick. Utilized in all situations, looking particularly useless on the power play and particularly useful on the penalty kill. Didn't look dangerous offensively, but didn't have a bad game per se either, because he did a lot on the defensive end of the puck tonight.

KAM #35 LG Kehler, Cole (2016) – A tall and strong goaltender already blessed with NHL-quality physical dimensions who shoots left and catches right. Tall and well-postured, his first shot positioning is very good and he does a good job of spitting rebounds into the corner and away from the slot. His blocker-side stopping abilities appear to be his best at this point; the other side of the net he has a tendency to drop his glove a little low. Legs come out very wide on his butterfly, exhibiting strong flexibility and coordination. On the negative end, his cross-crease agility and skating movements look a little sloppy and under-developed at this point as he has some difficulty staying in the paint while tracking the puck and changing position.

KAM #37 LD Maier, Patrick (2015) – This guy seems like a total pain in the ass to play against. Stands out at first sight as a fluid and wide-stanced defensive rearguard with really heavy hitting potential, but there is much more to his game than just his physicality and skating ability. Seems to get into a lot of arguments with just about everyone—whether it be opposing players, teammates, coaches, or above all, referees. Game was defined by several penalties and a few bad turnovers.

VAN #8 RC Baer, Alec (2015) – Normally very fast and agile, looked slow in his turns and pivots tonight. Must have been tired, as when defending up high he looked slow as molasses moving in reverse. Stickhandled his way through what seemed like all five Blazers while in the neutral zone but didn't score. Playing on the outside, he showed off an impressive slapshot that can now be officially added to an already stocked repertoire of shots. Threw a few big hits tonight too, which is nice to see.

VAN #17 LW Benson, Tyler (2016) – Plays in all situations and regularly exhibits fantastic durability and stamina as he manages to move around the ice very quickly and to play a physically engaged game for the vast majority of his shifts. Fast feet allow him to win the vast majority of puck races he's involved in. Shows a consistently competitive drive, looking like his team's hardest worker when it comes to board battles. Excels on the cycle, where he uses his quick feet and hands to emerge into the slot unexpectedly with the puck on his stick. Scored a goal using this methodology tonight.

VAN #22 RD Osipov, Dmitry (2015) – Showed a lot of improvements in this game, as his shooting, stick placement and discipline all looked much better tonight. A smooth-skating pass-first defensemanby nature. Has shown an ability to get both wristshots and slapshots on net with a tremendous amount of consistency. While his shots aren't particularly powerful, he's really good at reading the play and getting them through traffic and onto the net. A beautifully placed wristshot was a rover from the point and really seemed to elevate his teammates. He remains a smooth backwards skater, but his arm fluction is very awkward in his forward movements and he can look like a bit of a 'runner' at times. In his own end, he did a really great job using a strong cross-checking method to contain opposition forwards outside of the slot, and did so without being penalized.

VAN #26 LD McKinstry, Ryely (2016) – Still a little slow-footed for this level, but makes up for his lack of speed with tremendous hockey sense, awareness and anticipation. His passes are clear, direct and easy to receive. His shots are accurate, powerful and intelligently placed. Playing alongside Arvin Atwal, McKinstry covered a lot for his much older defensive partner tonight.

VAN #47 Vladimir Bobylev (2015) LW – Had one of his more average and forgettable games tonight. Has an explosive first step, but he has a lot of girth to carry around with him and his stride recoveries are a bit arduous. Springs forward quickly and has an intimidating presence straight off the hop, but tends to slow way down after his first three or four strides. Shots are much better than his passes, largely because they are very, very powerful. Took some bad penalties.

Windsor Spitfires at Barrie Colts, Oct 18, 2014

Score: 7-4 Barrie

RW Ryan Foss (2015) – Foss started the game on the 4th line and played limited minutes in the first 40, but seemed to get more ice in the 3rd. For the most part he was quiet early on and didn't do much besides finish a couple checks and get pucks in deep, but he was more effective in the final frame. Foss cycled the puck down low well, and went hard to the net on a few occasions. He also scored a late goal on a wraparound to keep Windsor in the game and give them a chance.

C Aaron Luchuk (2015) – Luchuk played a very good two-way game. He was effective on the penalty kill, winning several faceoffs, getting pucks out and ensuring he took away the passing/shooting lanes. He blocked a couple shots, was positionally sound and showed good awareness looking up ice as a penalty expired to try and create a chance for his team. Luchuk displayed quick feet, and drew a penalty in the offensive zone by keeping his feet moving and using his shiftiness to make himself difficult to contain. Luchuk also won several battles and didn't hesitate to throw his weight around at much bigger players.

D Andrew Burns (2015) – Burns didn't register a point, but I thought he did a nice job of creating offensively in this game. He consistently made good outlet passes, and was creative off the rush. He didn't hesitate to jump into the play to give his team an advantage, and because of his fluid stride he was always able to get back defensively. Burns wasn't physical, but he used an active stick to make it tough for oncoming forwards to get by him. On the powerplay he did a nice job of getting shots through. Burns did have a bad turnover in the neutral zone that led to a couple chances against, but for the most part his passing ability and creativity was a positive for the Spits.

C Logan Brown (2016) – Brown was one of the best players on the ice in this one. He consistently gained the Barrie line with possession of the puck, and was able to set up shop and create offense once doing so. Though he wasn't physical, he used his big frame well to protect the puck. A few healthy runs were taken at Brown throughout the game but he was strong on his skates and was never knocked off the puck. Brown made good passes on both his forehand and backhand, and displayed good vision finding small seams in the defense and taking advantage of them.

LW Matthew Kreis (2015) –On his first shift of the game he carried the puck up ice and through the neutral zone before sliding the puck through an oncoming defender's legs and dancing around him and generating a scoring chance. He had good speed throughout which made him tough to defend. He isn't physical and doesn't have a large frame, but he won several puck battles throughout the game and scored a beautiful backhand goal from the slot on a net drive.

RW Roy Radke (2015) – Radke was effective on the forecheck and created a couple turnovers while finishing his checks in the offensive zone. He was effective cycling the puck, and drew a penalty in the offensive zone while doing so. Radke took a hit to make a play in the neutral zone and it led directly to a Barrie goal. He was strong on the puck, and skated through a few checks during, which allowed him to get by defenders and generate a scoring opportunity.

D Rasmus Andersson (2015) – Andersson may have played the best game of his young OHL career. He tracked his man well throughout the game, and didn't get caught going through traffic to stay with his guy on the cycle. He pinched into the high slot early in the game before beating Alex Fotinos far side with a quick, accurate wrist shot. When an easy lane wasn't made available, Andersson used the boards to get pucks by Spitfires defenders and to open teammates. On the powerplay he distributed the puck well, as he moved the puck quick, the passes were accurate and he didn't force any plays that weren't there. He was calm when pressured with the puck, and held the line in the offensive zone consistently all game long. Andersson was also physical in this one, as he had a few big hits, was involved in some post whistle activities, and was very tough to deal with in the corners. On two occasions Andersson faced an oncoming forward in a one vs one situation, and both teams Andersson forced them wide and they ended up with a weak shot or none at all.

Note: Mackenzie Blackwood did not dress due to a lower-body injury.

October 18, 2014 - Plymouth Whalers at Peterborough Petes

PLY #29 G Bowman, Zach (2015) - Doesn't over extend himself which helped him make quick direction changes getting in front of the puck. He's quick to freeze the puck. Generally a moderately good performance tonight.

PLY #10 LW Caamano, Nicholas (2016) - Got hit hard but went to the net afterwards and quickly put away a rebound for his first career OHL goal. He made smart simple plays with the puck throughout the game.

PLY #19 RC Mercer, Cullen (2015) - Blcked shots on the penalty kill. Great compete in the defensive zone. Peterborough goalie lifted his leg up on a rebound and Mercer quickly slipped it behind him for Plymouth's third goal of the game. Cullen was slightly above 50% in the face-off circle tonight.

PLY #41 RW Bitten, William (2016) - Drew a power play in a tie game in the third period using his speed to fly past a defender, causing him to be obstructed on the way to the net. Used his speed and quick puck skills to move the puck intelligently.

PET #35 G Smith, Scott (2015) - Good size, gets to the top of the crease, but gives up a lot of rebounds. Made a mistake on Plymouth's third goal of the game lifting up his leg with the puck in front making it easy on the goalscorer.

PET #3 LD Lizotte, Cameron (2015) - Struggled early on with the puck, but made a great long distance pass later on. Got caught flat footed one on one then no hustle after.

PET #11 LD Vladimirov, Artem (2015) - Artem had a contrasting review on this game. He has good tools but struggled in his performance. He is a big defenseman, strong and more than willing to play physical. He skates fairly well for a defender his size. However he mishandled the puck down low and displayed a low panic threshold rushing plays. He miscalculates how much time he has with the puck taking too long to make a decision and gets stripped. Walked in one on one match-up's. He started having a little more success when he simplified his decisions and chose only high percentage puck plays.

PET #17 LW Betzold, Greg (2015**) - Betzold had one of his best performances to date. He showed good positioning in the slot on the power play, which lead to a good deflection on Peterborough's first goal. Smart puck decisions and can protect the puck very well. Good power in his shot, got a few scoring chances later on in the game hitting the goal post on one play, and was absolutely robbed by Bowman on the other.

PET #22 RW Ang, Jonathan (2016) - Great speed, used it on the forecheck, not so much on the backcheck. He is very confident and smooth skating with the puck on his stick but is too easy to knock off the puck at this point.

PET #27 RD Spencer, Matt (2015) - Matt showed smooth skating ability and was capable of rushing the puck out of trouble. However he needs to choose his spots, because he tried to do this too much and got caught and stripped a couple times. He showed a willingness to play physical and finish his check, but doesn't have much of a mean streak to him. Top minutes in all game situations. He likes to jump up in the play as much as possible. Made some very good first passes but was inconsistent in this area as he also made some bad reads. Walked in one on one situation and lost a couple battles down low. Chased a forward well out of position leaving his man alone in the slot who almost scored.

Final Score: Plymouth Whalers: 4 - Peterborough Petes: 3 - OT/SO

October 18th, 2014 Cedar Rapids vs Madison Capitals MADISON CAPITOLS

CDR - #27 F-Erik Foley (2015) – After a slow start to the season Foley has started to pick up his play the last couple of games. Had his motor running all night, skates hard at both ends of the ice and hunts the puck well. Made a great play skating into the zone which lead to his goal, pulled up at the hash marks, fed a great pass to the F3 then found some open ice down the middle, got the puck back in his tape and made a skill move to score on the backhand. Would like to see him use his size a bit more and take the puck to the net but shows great patience with the puck when he does pull up and usually makes a solid play with it. Will also play a physical game along the boards and does not shy away from contact.

CDR - #7 LD-Charlie Curti (Undrafted) – A tad undersized at the moment at just 5'11" but has a solid build and used great positioning on opposing players along the boards to win battles and clear pucks. Has good gap control and knows when to close on players and take away time and space. Makes sound plays with the puck in the D-zone and will join the rush when it's permitted. Good skating ability with and without the puck. Did try to do too much with the puck a couple times, passed up clearing opportunities to try to skate the puck out of the zone. Logged a lot of minutes and played in all situations.

MDC - #14 LD-Tommy Muck (2015+) – Impressive skating ability both with and without the puck. A tad undersized but is sound fundamentally and uses good stick position to disrupt passing lanes well. Can get beat by quick powerful forwards on the edge because of lack of strength, has trouble with Foley (CDR) a couple of times. Shows great patients with the puck on the point and if under pressure will make the smart play and take what the Ice gives him. On scoring play he got the puck at the right point, instead of instantly putting the puck on the net with no screen in front, he used the space the

CDR player had given him at the point, moved in from the point, waited for a screen in front of the goalie and fired and great wrist shot under the bar. Is off to a great start to the year with 3 goals, 2 assists in 6 games, is the teams 2nd leading point producer and is a team best +6.

MDC - #6 D-Cooper Watson (2015+) – Big Physical Defenseman, will step up on players and battle forwards in front of the net and win most of those battles. Moves the puck well on the point but lack of foot speed is a bit of a concern if he mishandles the puck on the point, a forward would likely be off to the races, however did make good plays with the puck on the point and did a good job getting shots past traffic and to the net.

Game Notes: Cedar Rapids carried the play for most of the night which caused Madison to take some penalties which ultimately cost them the game. Madison was able to feed off their home crowd in their Organizations Inaugural home opener and keep the game close but it seemed Cedar Rapids took their foot off the gas a bit late in the 1st and into the 2nd period which allowed Madison to stay in the game. When Cedar Rapids wanted to, they were able to lean on Madison make them play in their own end and dictate the game. CDR eventually added an empty netter at the end for the 5-3 win however Madison had its chances in the final moments to tie it up. Not a lot of draft eligible players on MDC roster but the team does have some talented players who all work hard each shift and good goaltending which will keep them in a lot of games this year. Just a matter of time before they will learn how to pull out these close games.

HIFK U20 - Sport U20, oct 18, 2014

HIFK #12 RW Tavernier, Sami (2015) - Sami was a really dangerous player today but couldn't score in a 3-2 victory. He's really skilled winger with great playmaking ability. Smooth skater with great technique and he's good around the corners: good puck-handler in small places and can make quick turnovers. The problem is that he creates lot of great opportunities but he's inefficient. Sami needs lot of muscle but he's a great long-term project.

HIFK #38 LD Rautanen, Juho (2015) - Juho played an average game today: he's good and calm d-man in the d-zone. Gives good first passes and doesn't try to do anything special with the puck. He knows where to be in the d-zone and Juho is a good defensive d-man but got nothing to offer in o-zone.

Spo #4 LD Salo, Robin (2017) - Played again great game even though his team have been awful for the whole season. Robin showed again strong performances during the whole game in all three zones. Calm d-man with great hockey IQ. He's doing great decisions in powerplay and his slapshot and wrister are quite accurate. Good in shorthanded also: block shots and covers passing lines. Really versatile player with good physical ability.

KalPa U20 – Lukko U20, oct 18, 2014

Kal 8# RW Piipponen, Topi (2015) – He had a decent night today. Topi is a strong skater especially his maximum speed is great. He likes to play straightforward game and he's doing it well. Always trying to get in front of the net and he got great scoring sense. Today he showed lot of great attitude and willingness to play physically. Not the smoothest puck-handler and he needs a playmaking center beside him. Got good potential and he fits better in the North American rinks than Europes.

Kal 2# LW Tammela, Jonne (2015) – Jonne played really good game tonight and scored the winning goal in the last minute of the game in a 5-4 victory. Small but incredible skilled player with great playmaking ability. He's fast and smooth skater and he got lot of power in his legs which effects his fastness and also his balance. Likes to play around cornes and gives decent hits for his size. Doesn't really like to shoot the puck and always looking for chance to pass. He should be more straightforward so that he could play in NHL. He's small kid but that really doesn't bothers him.

Kal 26#, RD Ruuskanen, Waltteri (2015) - Waltteri has suffered injuries and played his second game of this season. He's a big kid and got a great hockey sense. Always doing easy decisions and plays very well in the d-zone. He's really tough in front of his own net and likes to play physical. His skating is good for a big kid and he's smart with the puck puck and good in all three zones. His slap shot is pretty accurate but not that strong. Great game for him today.

Kal 28# LD Leskinen, Otto (2015) - Otto had a good game today. He's remarkable skater: great technique and really smooth first steps. He's great offensively and doing great decisions in the o-zone. He's kind of allround d-man eventhough there's some question marks: Otto is a small guy which is why he isn't the strongest player around the corners. He's good battling in one-on-one situations but the problem comes when he needs to battle with grown up men. Got great tools to be an amazing player in the future.

Kärpät U20 vs. Jokerit U20, oct 18, 2014

Kär #10 RW Aho, Sebastian (2015) - Aho was a little disappointment today. He's played with men and now he's back in the juniors. Aho is definitely skilled player with great passing ability and he's outstanding offensively but his two-way game is quite bad. Great skater with good technique and his wrister is pretty powerful. Not that physical and losses battles around the corners. He's remarkable puck-handler but his comprehensive game is big problem.

Kär #24 C Ruotsalainen, Arttu (2016) - Arttu had a decent night. He's skillful player with good hockey sense. Great playmaker and quick hands. Arttu is a pure offensive player who's really weak two-way center. He's really small and doesn't got any kind of physical tools. Fast and smooth skater with great offensive instincts and he could be a interesting player in the Import Draft.

Kär #8 RW Mäenalanen, Saku (Drafted by Nashville Predators) - Great skater, smooth hands and good scorer but he shouldn't play in juniors. There's no room for him in the pro team and that's bad for Saku. Amazing tools and he's too good for juniors. Gave couple of beautiful passes today and was surprisingly motivated.

Jok #8 LD Juolevi, Olli (2016) - Olli was one of the best today. Young guy but plays like a veteran. Really mature d-man who plays great in all three zones. Olli is a really calm player and gives great short and long passes. Great blueliner with accurate shots and he looks like a perfect player because he's also physically gifted. There really isn't weaknesses.

Jok #24 C/RW Somppi, Otto (2016) - He's versatile forward whose already physically great. Good hockey sense and great two-way game ability. Otto is really good with the puck and he got great speed and technique. Powerful first steps and smooth skater. He's doing everything pretty well but hasn't yet showed anything outstanding.

October 18th 2014, Green Bay Gamblers at Tri-City Storm

GB #8 Gates, Brent LC (2015) – Was left pretty unimpressed with Gates' performance tonight. In the back end of the road trip, Gates took a handful of shifts off and didn't look to be playing with much urgency. Negatives aside, Gates did display some offensive upside, creating some opportunities for himself. Showed decent hands at times and showed he could be effective in his own zone if he made the effort to. He isn't going to pot a ton of goals but can chip in. I would lean more towards the idea that he had an off night in my first viewing of him this season.

GB #10 Wegwerth, Joe LW (2014, 4th Round Florida Panthers) – Big guy that likes to throw his body around. Great on the Gamblers' penalty kill, getting down to block shots and buzzing around hitting anything with a pulse. Offensive ability has come along a little bit this year as he makes some offensive minded plays with the puck and driving to the net, but his role is much better served as defensive forward. Could be a good bottom six guy for the Panthers in the future.

GB #15 Smith, Ryan RW (2015) – Scored a great goal patiently outwaiting Tri-City goaltender Alec Dillon and beating Dillon high blocker side. Showed fantastic vision not only on the goal but throughout the entire game. Sees the play develop really well and knows where he should be. Great release on his shot. Showcased some good hands and puck handling ability. Strong skater. Really impressed with Smith's game today, look for him to move up rankings as the year progresses.

GB #17 Brown, Chris RW (2014, 6th Round Buffalo Sabres) – Has really burst onto the USHL scene this year coming out of Cranbrook High School last year. The Boston College commit scored a highlight reel unassisted goal from the right circle in the second period. Really impressed with his game, creating scoring opportunities for himself.

GB #20 Saarijarvi, Vili RD (2015) – The undersized, speedy Finnish defensemen had a really solid game tonight in his role. He's got great foot speed, very quick. Sees the ice really well and can find his teammates. Quarterbacked Green Bay's power play and did a really effective job, with a couple really nice outlet passes to get the rushes started. Scored top shelf on Alec Dillon in the third period, showing off his shot and great release. Defensively, his size is really holding him back. He got out-muscled one-on-one more than a few times. He is a very complete offensive defenseman, but in his own end he's just not there. At 5'9", 160 pounds his size and physical tools are what's really holding him back.

GB #28 Miletic, Sam LW (2015) – Miletic is Chris Brown's teammate from Cranbrook High and the Gamblers coaching staff reunited them on the same line with Brent Gates centering the two wingers. Miletic had a pretty quiet game tonight, not really doing much to jump off the ice at you. That being said, he's a pretty fundamentally sound player that skates with a good base. He's a big body standing at 6'2" and he does get after it, although I would have liked him to see him use his size to his advantage a little bit more and play with a bit more of an edge.

TC #3 Dello, Tory RD (2015) – Another solid performance by Dello who consistently turns in good performances in my viewings. Really strong guy who isn't going to get beat one-on-one. Doesn't get phased, always calm under pressure. Assisted on Jake Wahlin's game tying goal in the third period.

Dello, a Notre Dame commit, isn't going to do anything spectacular to wow you, and I think he's a bit underrated because of that. He's just a good solid defenseman that takes care of business in his own end first, and you can always count on him to do that.

TC #15 Freytag, Matthew LW (2015) – Freytag is a high motor guy who buzzes around in all three zones putting pressure on puck handlers and creating turnovers. Cuts hard to the net with the puck on his stick. Is decent in all categories, but isn't elite at any one thing. Not going to see many guys out hustle or out compete Freytag on the ice.

TC #20 Wahlin, Jake LW (2015) – Scored the game tying goal in the third period on an assist from Tory Dello for his first goal of the year. Had a really nice cross ice pass to Chris Wllkie that he just couldn't finish on the play. I was really impressed with how smart Wahlin is on the ice, he sees everything really well and it's pretty rare to see him give the puck away. Has a good release on his shot and it would benefit him to start shooting a little bit more.

TC #30 Dillon, Alec G (2014, 5th Round Los Angeles Kings) – Allowed three goals on twenty-three shots faced. Probably should have had the first two as he cheated and gave space blocker side and just couldn't get his arm up to stop the shot. Struggled to get into a rhythm early as he only faced two shots through the first fifteen minutes of the game. He's a big body that takes up a lot of space in the net; he knows that and uses it well. Was beat high on all three goals he allowed.

Scout's notes: This game ended 4-3 after Green Bay won in the shootout. Tri-City outshot the Gamblers 57 to 24 but Green Bay goaltender Jason Pawloski shut the door on the Storm leading Green Bay to the victory.

October 24, 2014 - Belleville Bulls at Sarnia Sting

BEL #5 RD Lemcke, Justin (2015) - Lemcke's puck play was very hit or miss, particularly struggling with his outlet pass. He made a good play jumping up in the rush, driving the net and fired home Belleville's third goal of the game. Went out of position a bit to chase the play in the defensive zone.

SAR #10 RW Kodola, Vladislav (2015) - Lightning quick moves but not effective around contact. Good backhand pass set up 3-2 goal. Will rush passes sometimes

SAR #11 RW Hodgson, Hayden (2015*) - Good physicality throughout game. Delivered undisciplined hit from behind with 57 seconds left in regulation in a 3-3 game.

SAR #14 LC Zacha, Pavel (2015) - Great work in his own zone to force turnover then very quickly identified an option up ice and made a great pass. He then went full speed to the net and picked up the puck and quickly finished for Sarnia's first goal.

SAR #25 LW Kyrou, Jordan (2016) - Jordan showed good patience on Sarnia's first goal taking the puck around the net when there were no options then made a good pass when it opened up setting up the goal.

SAR #35 RW Korostelev, Nikita (2015) - Needs to win more battles down low. Has a high end shot but needs to hit the net a little more.

Final Score: Belleville Bulls: 4 - Sarnia Sting: 3 - OT/SO

North Bay Battalion at Barrie Colts, Oct 25, 2014

Score: 4-3 North Bay

North Bay

C Brett McKenzie (2015) – McKenzie played a solid 200-foot game in this one. He was always in position defensively, and made it tough for Colts defensemen to get shots through. McKenzie was strong on the backcheck and disrupted a couple odd man rushes throughout the game with backside pressure. He did a nice job of generating scoring chances down low, and wasn't afraid to go to the paint to try and bang one in. He finished his checks, and was effective cycling the puck as well. McKenzie mishandled a couple passes during the game, which led to missed scoring opportunities. He also lost some races for loose pucks.

LW Zach Bratina (2015*) – Bratina may have been the best player on the ice. He showed great hockey IQ reading the play and jumping in to intercept a breakout pass before undressing Daniel Gibl in tight for an early goal. He showed good hands throughout the game, as he was able to step around defenders with regularity. Bratina showed good speed in his first three steps, and really attacked through the neutral zone, which forced the D to back off. This allowed him to set up in the offensive zone and create several scoring opportunities. He was relentless after the puck, and forced a turnover behind Barrie's net that led directly to a goal. Bratina also took care of his own zone, and used an active stick to knock the puck off the stick of a Colts' defender before moving the puck up ice to create a 2-on-1.

D Zach Sanker (2015) – Sanker was physically engaged all night, and did a nice job of forcing attackers to the outside before finishing them off. His positioning was good, he always knew where his man was in front and defended the cycle well. Sanker played a 2-on-1 perfectly where he forced a bad angle shot while also taking away the passing lane. He also blocked a couple shots, and didn't force any outlet passes.

Barrie

RW Roy Radke (2015) – Radke started slow but seemed to improve as the game went on. As usual, he was good on the forecheck and creating off the cycle. He showed good hands stepping around a couple defenders, but generally when he tried to get fancy it resulted in a turnover. Radke was very good killing penalties, as he pressured puck carriers in all three zones and forced quick plays, which led to a couple turnovers.

RW Matthew Kreis (2015) – Kreis was good carrying the puck through the neutral zone, and showed good vision hitting open teammates coming off the half wall. He forced a couple turnovers and didn't shy away from puck battles or going to the net, but didn't show any scoring touch in this game. Kreis had three or four Grade A chances around the net and failed to convert on all of them, which was the difference in this game. His speed and puck skills allowed him to generate chances, but he just couldn't finish them.

D Rasmus Andersson (2015) – Andersson did a nice job of leaning his body with his stick to fake a pass, which opened up lanes for passes or shots to get through in the offensive zone. He also showed his big shot, as Cormier couldn't handle a point blast and a big rebound bounced out for a Joseph Blandisi goal. Andersson pinched down the wall to keep several plays alive, and held the line in the

OZ several times. He made smart decisions with the puck, was perfect with almost every pass, and never broke stride while accepting them. Andersson also blocked two shots to keep the Colts alive with the net empty, showing good special awareness.

Notes: Mackenzie Blackwood did not play due to injury...Jake Smith was the back-up...Brendan Lemieux did not play due to suspension...Draft eligible defenseman Riley Bruce did not play...Nick Paul played a complete 200-foot game, scored, and was dominant down low...Joseph Blandisi was one of a few players able to consistently generate scoring chances.

October 25, 2014 - Ottawa 67's at Sarnia Sting

OTT #5 LD Mercer, Matt (2015) - Struggled a bit in this game, particularly when it came to handling the puck. Struggled under pressure.

OTT #13 RW Tyanulin, Artur (2015) - Showed flashes of puck handing ability but for the most part he was very uninvolved in this game. He fired the puck top shelf in the third period when the game was over, a fairly good shot to score Ottawa's fifth goal.

OTT #17 RC Konecny, Travis (2015) - Travis generates great power with his skating strides. He was keeping it pretty simple in this game, not challenging defenders, not nearly as aggressive on the puck carrier. He is playing like he hasn't completely recovered from the big hit he too last week.

OTT #91 RC McDonald, Dylan (2015) - Dylan was noticable playing on the fourth line providing plenty of physical play. He competed hard and finished all his checks asserting his size against some big opponents on the wall. Heavy first few steps.

OTT #96 RC Salituro, Dante (2015) - Explosive quickness and extremely fast. He tries to keep his feet moving at all times because the second he slows down he gets knocked around. Picked up a loose puck and caught the goaltender going the other way to score, then later in the game he won a race to the puck then made a great pass to set up their fourth goal, playing a direct impact in 2 of Ottawa's first four goals in this game.

OTT #37 G Lazarev, Leo (2015) - Extremely small but very quick. His side to side and leg quickness is excellent. He struggles catching the puck and dropped several shots that should have been in his glove, instead wound up in potential scoring areas. He is extremely aggressive playing the puck skating out to the blueline twice to race for the puck. His puck playing ability is not very good and some of the high risk puck plays nearly backfired on him. Despite all of this he didn't face much in terms of scoring chances and nearly recorded a shutout if not for a highlight reel goal by Korostelev.

SAR #5 LD Chychrun, Jakob (2015) - Made some excellent passes including one notable long distance pass that created a partial break. Showing flashes of the player he has the potential to be and while he's still making some rookie mistakes, he appears to be learning from mistakes that were made in early October and seems to be improving every game.

SAR #10 RW Kodola, Vladislav (2015) - Has trouble handling hard long distance passes. Very hit or miss with his passing ability, would make some fantastic plays with the puck but then in clear passing situations he would freeze up and take the puck into the corner. Has the ability and vision to make some great plays, but has some mental letdowns at random moments.

SAR #14 LC Zacha, Pavel (2015) - Reads passing options and makes decisions extremely quickly for a player of his age and at this level. Strong skating ability, especially for his size and didn't ease up when forechecking and backchecking. Not afraid to finish his hits whenever he could.

SAR #20 LD Schlichting, Connor (2015) - With starting goalie already injured, Connor crosschecked an Ottawa player on top of their other goaltender while in the butterfly taking a penalty and nearly injuring his teams only other OHL goaltender. He struggled all day long making mental mistakes of some simple, basic hockey plays.

SAR #25 RC Kyrou, Jordan (2016) - Surprisingly ineffective based on previous viewings, did a lot of floating around and wandering out of good positioning.

SAR #35 RW Korostelev, Nikita (2015) - Took a puck in the face early in the game and continued with his shift. He was pretty quiet in this game, but scored an absolute highlight reel beating two defenders and the goaltender to break the shutout with 12.3 seconds left.

SAR #32 G Fazio, Justin (2015) - Fazio showed good quickness but was completely left out to dry on a few goals by his defense. The other looked to be a simple mental lapse, which may have been from playing 12 straight games with Dupuis out. Either way, he made a few saves showing flashes of his ability, but for the most part was not on his game tonight.

Final Score: Ottawa 67's: 6 - Sarnia Sting: 1

Quebec Remparts at Saint John Sea Dogs, October 26, 2014

QUE #30 G Booth, Callum (2015): Played a solid game making big timely saves keeping his team in the lead/tie. Booth has good size, limiting the amount of movement he needs to make. Booth has… good rebound control knocking them down close and covering up. Saint John had numerous power play chances in the second and he shut them down 5 on 4 and 5 on 3. In the third, overtime and shootout; Booth stopped numerous odd man rushes, breakaways and chances in close.

QUE #88 LW Timashov, Dmytro (2015): Timashov has lots of tools in the bag. On the power play he carries the puck in and sets up the umbrella and runs the plays. Timashov showed great patience handling the puck numerous times and finds his team mates easily it seems. He has the ability to draw more than 1 opponent to him in their defensive end, opening up coverage. When Timashov is under pressure he outworks his opponents, pushes the pace and draws penalties. Timashov has toughness with his skill, being able to take a hit and make a play; as seen in this game when he assisted Quebec's second goal.

SNB #5 LD Chabot, Thomas (2015): Chabot finds himself on Saint Johns second D pairing and second power play unit. Chabot plays solid in his own end and has success retrieving the puck and making a play in pressure situations. He doesn't mind physical play and is successful in winning battles on the boards; fighting off checks as well. Chabot has a quick stride making him dangerous offensively too. Chabot set up Saint Johns second goal, displaying his ability to win battles and make good plays.

SNB #10 C Noel, Nathan (2015). Noel had a quiet game with some scoring chances but Quebec took away his time and space. Noel is a speedy forward with good hands but he doesn't over handle the puck. Noel uses his speed to beat opponents instead of trying to stick handle around them. Noel is a good positional player and is able to support his team/line mates with his speed.

SNB #38 LD Zboril, Jakub (2015): Plays a well-rounded game. Zboril kills penalties and plays on the first power play unit. Zboril is a tough D man to beat on the rush because he plays the gap so well. Zboril steps up on his opponents at the right time forcing turnovers and quick transitions. Zboril became more involved offensively as the game progressed. Zboril is a very good skater and pushes the pace jumping up in his teams rushes and skates the puck well.

Oct. 29 – Brandon Wheat Kings at Vancouver Giants

BRA #6 LD Pilon, Ryan (2015) – Showed a high degree of skill in all three zones and appeared dangerous from end-to-end. A little slower in transition than his pairing partner, he's still a smooth skater. Outlet passes and offensive puck movements are fantastic. Decision-making looked very good, manifesting itself most obviously in safe and reliable first-passes to his teammates. Shooting skills were also on display, as he put a number of good wrist and slapshots onto the Vancouver net, including a goal from the hashmarks during a brilliantly timed pinch in the second period.

BRA #9 LD Provorov, Ivan (2015) – A mid-sized, smooth-skating, swivel-headed defenseman with a fantastic skating stride and ideally low centre of gravity that makes him very difficult to knock off the puck or to place off balance. Paired with Pilon, Provorov played on the right side, utilizing his fantastically strong one-timer slapshot. Didn't make an impact with his shot tonight, breaking three sticks by my count. Terrific at identifying weak spots in coverage and recovering after his own or his teammates' mistakes. Stick was very active when in pursuit of the puck and he did a great job achieving advantageous body position on his opponent when engaged in the corner.

BRA #12 LW Gabrielle, Jesse (2015) – Battled hard and showed good competitiveness when he was on the ice. A tenacious skater, he wins most races to the corners and the majority of his puck battles. I liked his toughness and willingness to crash the net in the offensive zone, and he wasn't a slouch in his own end by any means either. Best quality might be his hand-eye coordination, as he was able to score on a beautiful one-touch scoring play while hiding-out just a skate blade away from the top-right of Payton Lee's crease.

BRA #33 LG Papirny, Jordan (2014) – He's grown a bit since going undrafted last year, now standing at a taller-than-average 6-foot-1 and a half. But more then just his dimensions, he's also improved his stance and positioning, so that he looks much taller than he appears on the scoresheet. His ability to track the puck in traffic was excellent tonight, as he was able to make some desperation scrambling saves. His glove-hand also looked impressive tonight.

VAN #8 LW Baer, Alec (2015) – Baer stands out as a fleet-footed sniper with speed to kill. He had a couple scoring opportunities tonight in close, as he can shoot the puck in very close quarters. Deking skills are supernatural at times, but weren't on display tonight. The Brandon defence should be given some credit for containing Baer to the outside, but in all fairness, the Vancouver forward lacked competitiveness in front of the net and made some weak passes in the offensive zone for an altogether underwhelming game tonight.

VAN #22 RD Osipov, Dmitry (2015) – Passing out of his own end is pretty good, but he needs to break the habit of delaying with the puck behind the net for an interminably long time when his team is losing. On the defensive end, I thought his skating and anticipation looked good as always tonight. And while he had improved discipline, going un-penalized in this game, I thought he sacrificed some of his physicality in return. He looked a bit outmatched when playing against Brandon's best players and ended the night with a negative-2.

Sarnia Sting at Barrie Colts, Oct 30, 2014

Score: 7-1 Sarnia

C Pavel Zacha (2015) – Zacha had a quick first three steps, generated top speed in a hurry and attacked the neutral zone with speed on a consistent basis. He had a few powerful net drivers where he gained a step on Colts' defenders and took it right to the paint. Zacha was strong on the backcheck, and had a few takeaways in the neutral zone catching Colts players from behind. He displayed high hockey IQ, as he always picked up his assignments defensively and knew where to be on the ice. Zacha consistently got good power in his shots, and scored a beautiful slapper in the 1st period. He won the majority of his faceoffs, and was an absolute beast on the puck. Zacha was always back to support the defense, and had no problems engaging physically.

RW Nikita Korostelev (2015) – Korostelev showed good hands and puck skills throughout. He was able to make people miss in open ice, and showed off a nice release getting shots off quickly. He had a few good shots throughout, and was dangerous from afar because of his shot. Korostelev gained the Colts line with possession regularly, and was able to generate several quality chances from his controlled entries. On the other side of the ice, Korostelev made a couple nice defensive plays. He won some puck battles, and was back in the zone to recover loose pucks or any floaters around the slot. He didn't shy away from contact, and mixed it up a bit with Jonathan Laser after he was really hard on Zacha.

LW Vladislav Kodola (2015) – Kodola played some center and wing in this one, and was effective in both situations. Like Korostelev, he continually gained the opposing line with possession of the puck, and was creative off the rush. He showed off a quick release on several occasions, and had plenty of scoring chances throughout. Kodola shied away from contact on occasion, but he did win some puck battles and scored a rebound goal in tight, so he wasn't afraid of going to the dirty areas of the ice. Kodola set up his teammates for a few good chances, and made good passes on both the forehand and backhand.

C Troy Lajeunesse (2015) – He wasn't flashy, but he played an effective two-way game. He generated good speed in his first few steps, and forced the D to back off because of his speed. Lajeunesse was relentless after loose pucks, and battled with players much bigger all night. He was also very effective on the penalty kill, though he had a few chances there that he probably should have converted.

RW Noah Bushnell (2015) - Bushnell played a very good two-way game. He finished his checks, was strong on the forecheck, and won plenty of battles along the wall. Bushnell had a good net front presence, and was tough to move in tight. Bushnell took hits to make plays, and provided good support along the wall in all three zones. He did take a bad offensive zone penalty, but played a good game overall.

RW Matthew Kreis (2015) – Kreis was relentless after loose pucks, and won plenty of battles along the wall. He was shifty with the puck, and eluded a few checks. Kreis was very pacey and made quick passes to open teammates in the offensive zone. He had a couple really good chances but couldn't finish.

RW Roy Radke (2015) – Radke won plenty of puck battles and applied good pressure on the forecheck, which forced some bad passes that led to turnovers. He played in front on the power play with Brendan Lemieux out of the lineup, but struggled to maintain position in front when he tried to screen Taylor Dupuis. He missed a couple passes to open teammates and failed to convert on a breakaway, but he did a good job putting himself in position to get these chances. Radke played his man loose in the defensive zone, and was on for a handful of goals against.

D Rasmus Andersson (2015) – Andersson looked about as good as you can in a 7-1 loss. He was on for just one goal against, and did a good job of keeping attackers to the outside. Andersson finished players off several times, and drew a retaliation penalty after laying a big hit. He used his big body to shield off Sarnia players, and once again made good outlets with regularity. He didn't force plays that weren't there – either shots or passes – and had no problem skating the puck up ice if nothing was available.

October 31, 2014 - Sault Ste. Marie Greyhounds at London Knights

SSM #9 RW Senyshyn, Zachary (2015) - Competes very hard in the slot screening goaltender. Finished his checks hard.

SSM #37 RD Bouramman, Gustav (2015) - Recovers quickly when a turnover occurs in his own zone. He is a decent skater, capable of rushing the puck and brought the puck up ice on a few occasions. He made a good play on the draw to evade forechecker, but then made a horrible pass after right onto the stick of the same forechecker. He got the first assist on the Greyhounds first goal making a quick pass over to Darnell Nurse off the draw who beat Giugovaz with a point shot.

SSM #17 C Miller, David (2015) - Miller is a strong skating forward who competed all game long scoring two goals. His first goal, second for the Greyhounds was scored when Miller picked up a loose puck and quickly scored. He then scored Greyhounds fourth goal going to the net and finishing a good pass on the rush.

SSM #18 RW Speers, Blake (2015) - Blake played a good two-way game tonight. He always keeps his feet moving and showed good hands. He made smart decisions with the puck in all three zones and has a very high compete level. He does a good job in the neutral zone, getting his stick into passing lanes. Wasn't a critical offensive player in this game but he did create a few scoring chances.

SSM #38 LW Verbeek, Hayden (2016) - Excellent speed and agility. Got hit hard down low and was slow to get up and get off.

SSM #32 G Raaymakers, Joseph (2016) - Raaymakers played in relief of Halverson after he allowed 3 goals on 5 shots. Made a mental error on London's fourth goal, the first he allowed in this game as he got across well but kept his glove hand down leaving a big hole to shoot at. He gets to the top of the crease well to take away angles on shots. Showed decent puck playing ability through the game.

LON #14 D Crawley, Brandon (2015) - Was good physically, pivots late.

LON #93 RW Marner, Mitchell (2015) - Good creative pass to set up London's first goal. He used his speed on dump and chase to strip defender of the puck creating chance. Poised passes in offensive zone under pressure. Made a few mistakes with the puck when trying to make fancy passes, one of which directly resulted in a Sault Ste. Marie goal.

Final Score: London Knights: 8 - Sault Ste. Marie Greyhounds: 5

October 31st 2014, Waterloo Black Hawks at Lincoln Stars

WAT #12 Boeser, Brock RW (2015) – Huge game for Boeser tonight. He is impossible to knock off the puck. Seemed to do whatever he chose out there against Lincoln. Scored hat trick, on three really nice goals. On the third goal he forced a turnover against Lincoln's powerplay, turned on the jets and finished with a slick move. Very intelligent with and without the puck. Hockey sense was off the charts tonight. Super impressive performance.

WAT #15 Novak, Tom LC (2015) – Really impressive game from Novak. Showed off his elite hockey sense. Saw the ice really well, finding linemate Brock Boeser for a goal with a nice cross crease pass. Biggest thing I can say is he is a very smart player. Strong on his skates, tough to get off the puck. Hard to find many negatives with his performance tonight.

WAT #62 Montour, Brandon RD (2014, 2nd Round Anaheim Ducks) – Scored a nice goal in the second period, taking it coast to coast and beating the Lincoln goaltender one on one. Great skater mixed with slick hands make him really tough to deal with for the opposition. Very solid at the offensive blue line and doesn't make mistakes with the puck.

LIN #8 Klack, Chris LC (2015) – I continue to be impressed with Klack even in the limited role he plays with Lincoln. Buzzes around all 200 feet of the ice and forces the issue. Not elite in any facet of his game but he works hard to make up for the talent deficiency. Hard to play against. Great energy guy.

LIN #10 Fidler, Miguel (2014, 5th Round Florida Panthers) – Fidler was invisible all night tonight excluding two hits he laid. Continues to struggle to adjust to the pace of the USHL in the offensive zone.

LIN #18 Kalynuk, Wyatt (2015) – Solid performance turned in by Kalynuck tonight. Didn't chip in offensively much but he was not a liability. He makes smart decisions at the offensive blue line and doesn't take unnecessary risks in his own zone. Has emerged as Lincoln's best defenseman in my eyes.

LIN #24 Lee, Cam (2015) – Not a good performance by Lee tonight. He consistently made poor decisions not only in his own zone but also at the offensive blue line. Tries to do too much at times: takes the puck into the zone by himself and turns it over leading to odd-man rushes, taking the shot straight into shin pads over and over, etc. The offensive talent is there, but just doesn't make good decisions.

Tri City Storm vs Madison Capitals (11-1-2014)

TC - #3 D- Tory Dello (2015) – Communicated well with defensive partner and goalie, always directing traffic vocally or with his hands and makes sure all bases are covered when defending a rush. Dello showed great skating ability, very much a straight line skater with an effortless stride. He creates separation from the fore-checker by skating hard back on puck retrievals. Made solid tape to tape outlet passes. Will join the rush if that is the play but showed good patients with the puck in waiting for forwards to get open for an outlet pass.

TC - #15 LW- Matt Freytag (2015) – Defensively responsible forward who covers for a jumping D-man well. Displayed good patients with the puck in both ends, doesn't panic with the puck and will slow the game down, sometimes to a fault because at times he leaves you wanting more dynamic plays with the puck on his stick, but he seems to think the game well and very rarely makes a poor play with the puck. Had the primary assist on Tri-City's 2nd goal after getting in on the fore-check, creating a puck battle behind the net and getting it out to Mason Appleton in the slot. Is a big body and uses it well along the wall protecting the puck. Ended the game with 2 assists, plus 2 and 2 shots on goal.

TC - #44 LW – Chris Wilke (2015+) – Had a solid game despite not showing up on the score sheet. Had 6 shots on goal, most of anyone on Tri-City, was a -2, however sometimes a players +/- doesn't reflect their game that night. Wilke showed his talent as a north/south forward who skates equally hard whether it's heading into the offensive zone or getting back into the play to pick up his check. Displayed great skill in being able to shoot in stride using the defender as a screen. Opposing goalie made a couple great saves on situations such as those.

TC - #22 C – Mason Appleton (2015+) – Had a dominate night with 2 goals and missed a couple other good scoring chances due to great saves by the opposing goalie. Appleton played a physical, gritty game which saw him get called for a checking from behind, slashing as well as an unsportsman like conduct penalty.

TC - #20 LW – Jake Wahlin (2015) – Was able to do some good things despite being limited to the 4th line for most of the night. Usually was his line that was sent out to get some energy going. Did however see some time on the Power play and had the primary assist on Chris Wilke's Power play goal to take the lead in the 3rd period. Needs to add some strength in order to win more 50/50 puck battles.

MAD - #14 D – Tommy Muck (2015+) – Has moved up onto the top Defensive pairing for Madison and doesn't look out of place playing in all situations. Very active on the power play, always moving trying to create or find passing lanes for his teammates and jumps down for a backdoor pass often on the PP. Continues to show great skating ability and good decisions with the puck. Muck still needs to fill out his frame to be more effective along the boards and win puck battles. He uses his skating ability to get out of tight situations with the puck. Makes the simple tape to tape passes on the outlet.

MAD - #17 RW – Sam McCormick (2015) – Small forward but always plays with high energy and high compete level. Tonight scored the Overtime winner after Tri-City turned the puck over in their own end and found himself alone in the slot with the puck after a pass from Mitch Hultz which he wasted no time one-timing it past the Tri-City Goaltender. Plays with a lot of grit despite his size of 5'9" 160LBS. Continues to get more and more confident with his play in each viewing.

MAD - #7 RW – Will Johnson (2015) – Johnson is one of those players that doesn't really stand out but plays a simple game that results in showing up on the score sheet in most games. Was able to net the game tying goal late in the 3rd period. Will go to the gritty areas either in the corner or in front of the net for loose pucks without fear.

November 2, 2014 - Team Sweden vs. Team USA

World Under 17 Championships - Preliminary Round

SWE #2 LD Andersson, Alexander (2016) - Smart puck movement in his own zone. Patient, calm and composed both looking for passing lanes and rushing the puck up ice. Great fake and go on the rush causing forwards to hesitate momentarily giving him a lane to skate through.

SWE #3 RD Cederholm, Jacob (2016) - Good passing and rushing options, he has a big body but protects the puck well on the rush. Tries to force his shot through from the point. At one point it got blocked by a defender five feet away from him into his shinpads. USA took the puck up ice and scored 2-0 goal. Cederholm went back out on the power play and tried to force the exact same shot with a defender five feet away clearly not learning after the costly mistake.

SWE #12 RW Bratt, Jesper (2016) - Great skating ability, capable of changing speed and has a great top speed. He is very agile and can beat defenders one on one quite frequently.

SWE #13 RC Fallstrom, William (2016) - William succeed in all game situations, on the power play he quickly banged home a rebound to score Sweden's first goal. He was also a regular on the penalty kill and was even utilized on a five on three situation.

SWE #16 LW Nylander, Alexander (2016) - Uses skating to create time with puck in neutral zone and defensive zone when no option was available. However he tried to do too much himself on a few occasions today. Good cross ice pass by Nylander helped set up Sweden's first goal of the game. He pulled up going to the wall after a puck if he knew he was going to get hit.

SWE #17 LC Olsson, Oliver (2016) - Oliver got involved on the offense a few times. He scored Sweden's third goal with great positioning and a tip in. He then got another great scoring chance beating two defenders one on one then made a great move on the goaltender but got robbed. He delivered a huge hit but took too many steps for a charging penalty. Bad turnover in his own zone on the power play created a short handed chance for Team USA.

SWE #18 LW Davidsson, Marcus (2017) - Scored Sweden's second goal driving wing, the rebound came right to him and he quickly put it away. Made a no look through the legs pass in his own zone created a great scoring chance for Team USA

SWE #19 LC Sethsson, Albin (2016) - Albin was used as the lone forward on a five on three penalty kill. Was very effective on the PK killing time off the clock and clearing the zone.

SWE #23 LW Weissbach, Linus (2016) - Great top speed and quick hands. Had breakout pass opportunity but couldn't see it and got leveled instead.

SWE #26 RW Andersson, Lias (2017) - Set up Sweden's second goal with a low shot off the pads causing a rebound to go directly to his linemate. Outstanding play stripping Khorodenko of the puck then instead of forcing his shot made a very intelligent pass which set up an easy tap in for Sweden's third goal.

SWE #30 G Lundh, Gusten (2016) - Gusten has good size and is tough to beat down low. He was fighting the puck a bit tonight and gave up a lot of rebounds. He struggled at times handling the puck and directing rebounds away.

USA #37 LC Keller, Clayton (2016) - Keller was arguably the best player in this game. He possesses great speed and works hard in all three zones. He played in all game situations and he showed good evasiveness on the penalty kill to take time off the clock. He remains calm even with pressure around him. He made a great diving play to clear the defensive zone then got up quickly to take the puck in for a breakaway chance. Later on he controlled the puck through the offensive zone, fending off defenders then while protecting he fired a laser shot to score USA's fifth goal.

USA #42 LC Khorodenko, Patrick (2017) - Patrick displayed excellent offensive zone passing in this game. He was effective in all three zones in this game, making a great shot block then took it back for a breakaway. While he was stopped, the rebound would not be resulting in a goal. He showed good anticipation all game in the defensive zone high on the point picking off passes. He made a horrible play in his own zone turning the puck over which immediately resulted in Sweden's second goal. He redeemed himself later on walking in off the wall and firing a powerful shot past the goaltender on what would be the winning goal of the game.

USA #43 LD Greenway, James (2016) - James has excellent size and uses it very well imposing himself constantly against Sweden's forwards. While his first few steps need work he skates fairly well for a big defender and protects the puck with his long reach. He made a great long distance pass setting up a breakaway, but he made some puck playing mistakes in his own zone.

USA #44 LD Krys, Chad (2016) - Strong skater and skillset, but multiple own zone turnovers.

USA #45 LC Howdeshell, Keeghan (2016) - Keeghan played a very good game today showing speed to beat defenders resulting in scoring chances. He also picked the pocket of a Sweden defender early in this game, walked in and fired home the opening goal of the tournament for USA.

USA #49 LW Jones, Max (2016) - While playing high on the wall on the power play he fell but showed great presence of mind to make a great play with the puck to keep the play going. He possesses a hard shot, and kept it low when shooting from a distance on the power play for deflections. He played very physical looking for the big hit and landed a few solid ones. Went hard to the net on turnovers, one in particular he was able to bang home the rebound for USA's second goal.

Final Score: Team USA: 6 - Team Sweden: 3

November 2, 2014 - Team Russia vs. Team Canada Black
World Under 17 Championships - Preliminary Round

RUS #5 D Sergachykov, Mikhail (2016) - Mikhail showed good puck rushing ability and made intelligent passes. He is quick to activate from the point and get involved offensively. He delivered an excellent open ice hit tonight.

RUS #11 RW Abramov, Vitali (2016) - Vitali is a powerful skater with great speed and very shifty. He created offensive chances with his passing ability but also his ability to beat defenders one on one in outstanding fashion. Abramov created Russia's fifth goal by delaying with the puck against a sprawled Canadian defender then fired a hard shot that went off Mesheryakov and in.

RUS #25 F Mesheryakov, Mikhail (2016) - Mesheryakov played a huge role in his teams victory tonight. He made a great play to pick up a loose puck and quickly make strong pass to set up Russia's first goal. He then fired a laser top shelf to score their third goal, then finally he deflected home Russia's fifth goal.

RUS #26 F Bain, Maxim (2016) - Maxim scored Russia's first goal of the game with good positioning and a great finish. Excellent skating ability.

RUS #27 RW Sokolov, Dmitri (2016) - Possesses an excellent shot. He scored twice, once by blasting a perfectly placed shot past the goaltender, the other on a good deflection for the eventual game winning goal.

RUS #30 G Sukhachyov, Vladislav (2016) - Vladislav showed good quickness and skating ability but gave up plenty of rebounds in tonight's game.

CAB #4 D Clague, Kale (2016) - Kale showed good evasiveness with the puck and was capable of carrying it up ice. He made very good long distance passes, but in the offensive zone got caught trying to force the pass on multiple occasions. Excellent play with his stick on the backcheck to break up a partial breakaway.

CAB #7 LW Volcan, Nolan (2016) - Good skating ability. Despite being listed at 5'8" Nolan delivered an exceptional amount of hits in this game. He delivered a few massive hits on much bigger opponents all throughout this game.

CAB #23 D Girard, Samuel (2016) - Samuel had a few puck control mishaps in the defensive zone which hurt his team but overall he had a very good performance and got better as the game went on. Girard is a capable puck rushing defenseman who is quick, shifty and changes speeds at the right time and will find passing options.

Chicago Steel vs Madison Capitals (11-2-2014)

CHI - #10C-Tanner Laczynski (2015) – The first thing that stands out is his skating ability and effort. Very fast to pucks and closes in on defenders quickly. Always had his feet moving, you won't see him coasting very often. Has the knack for finding the open ice, knows where he needs to go or where the puck is likely to end up. This showed on his goal where he read the shot from his teammate went to the area where the rebound was likely to go and found the puck on his stick and buried it for the game's first goal. Didn't play an overly physical game but has decent strength and can win battles against bigger strong players.

CHI - #28RW Freddie Olofsson (2013- CHI) – Kept off the score sheet which is a rarity so far this year but made some good plays on the Penalty Kill, getting his stick in passing lanes and disrupting passes. Won't be overly physical which can cause him to lose some puck battles, if he ever develops a mean streak, with his size would be difficult for anyone to handle giving his skill set.

CHI - #23LW Robby Jackson (2015) – Displayed a strong work ethic all night, battles hard for pucks and was first on the fore-check all night. Has a quick release with his shot but didn't convert on any of them due to some solid saves. Doesn't hesitate to try to beat defenders 1 on 1 with the puck and can turn them quickly with his speed and agility. Provides good back pressure defensively allowing his defenders to maintain good gap control to the oncoming rush. Always aware of where his stick is and tries to have it in a good position at all times. A couple of times he could have chose the simpler play with the puck, whether it be just chipping the puck into the corner or making the simple pass rather than trying to beat the defender or trying the thread a pass through traffic. Very strong on his stick in puck battles.

CHI - #3D Zach Osburn (2015) – Moved the puck well, makes great tape to tape passes and can get pucks through to the net but needs to work on getting the puck off his stick quicker rather than a long winding wrist shot. Assisted on Chi. First goal by getting a shot from the point to the net.

MAD - #30G Garrett Metcalf (2015+) - Big goalie who takes up a lot of the net at 6'3" 181LBS, does a good job moving his head to look around screens and search for pucks. Battles hard in the net and made many amazing saves to keep Madison in the hockey game. His play the last few games may have wrestled the starting job away from Darren Smith. Doesn't seem to get rattled, even after giving up a goal, he tends to make a big save shortly after. One of those goalies that the more action he sees the better he is.

MAD - #17RW - Sam McCormick (2015) – Continues to improve with every game. Played a simple game, if nothing was there he would just put the puck towards the net into high traffic areas. One thing for sure when you watch McCormick is the effort is always there, doesn't take a shift off or coast during a shift. Feet are always moving, very effortless skater.

November 3, 2014 - Team Finland vs. Team Russia

World Under 17 Championships - Preliminary Round

FIN #3 D Felixson, Oliver (2016) - Despite his size Oliver provided a good puck rush up the ice carrying it into the offenisve zone. He showed good patience to make the right play with the puck. He showed great awareness after a play to force a turnover while back peddling, stealing the puck which lead to Finland's third goal.

FIN #8 D Reunanen, Tarmo (2016) - Tarmo has a powerful shot which at one point was deflected from the point for a goal. He showed quick footwork but struggles with longer distances. He got beat pretty bad in this game in one on one match-up against a skilled forward.

FIN #9 D Kluuskeri, Jan (2016) - Jan has a big shot from the point. He made a bad spin and blind pass resulted in scoring chance against. Took a bad interference penalty on the power play after losing a puck race.

FIN #18 LW Kuokkanen, Janne (2016) - Janne was a player who was effective and hard working in all three zones today. He provided an excellent backcheck to break up plays, but he is also quick into transition when forcing a turnover. He has good speed and is very smart on the rush with the puck. He can carry and pass very effectively making good decisions. He has a hard, powerful shot but is at his best when creating offense with his passing ability.

FIN #21 RW Nurmi, Markus (2016) - Not a strong skater but contains well on the wall.

FIN #22 C Rasanen, Aapeli (2016) - Excellent cross ice pass to set up Finland's first goal.

FIN #24 C Somppi, Otto (2016) - Good finish on a cross ice pass to score Finland's first goal of the game. He also scored Finland's third goal of the game picking up a rebound in the slot and slipping it past the goaltender.

FIN #28 D Vaakanainen, Urho (2017) - Great long distance pass to create a breakaway opportunity for his team. Urho was tough to beat defensively in one on one situations.

FIN #30 G Laakso, Leevi (2016) - Didn't have to make many saves but was excellent when called upon for the majority of the game. Very quick side to side and quick pads. Good patience on breakaways. Russia scored a few goals late but held strong in the shootout stopping 4 of 4 for the win.

RUS #5 D Sergachykov, Mikhail (2015) - Mikhail fired a rocket over the shoulder of Laakso, which really sparked Russia's four third period goals.

RUS #12 RW Popugayev, Nikita O. (2016) - Great one on one move to beat the defender but got robbed by the goaltender. Scored a big goal in the final minutes of the game banging home a rebound to bring the game within one goal late.

RUS #27 RW Sokolov, Dmitri (2016) - Great vision in the offensive zone around passing and shooting decisions, reading his options quickly. He scored with 1.0 left on the clock blasting a one-timer to tie the game. He took two of Russia's four shootout attempts but was stopped both times.

Final Score: Team Finland: 5 - Team Russia: 4 - OT/SO

November 3, 2014 - Team Sweden vs. Team Canada-Red

World Under 17 Championships - Preliminary Round

SWE #6 D Moverare, Jacob (2016) - Jacob made some good passes up ice in this game. Showed some physicality in this game but gets too high with his hits at times.

SWE #8 D Thilander, Adam (2017) - Very physical in his own zone. Puck play struggled at times and he even almost threw the puck into his own net.

SWE #12 F Bratt, Jesper (2016) - Jesper showed good speed and excellent hands to score Sweden's first goal of the game on a breakaway. During a line change, Jesper's puck skills and evasiveness really showed as he was able to help his team complete a full line change going one on five in the offensive zone with the puck evading checkers which directly lead to a scoring chance. He played in all game situations and provided a powerful forecheck.

CAR #5 RD Fabbro, Dante (2016) - Consistently made intelligent decisions with and without the puck all game long. Reads plays well and makes smart accurate passes. Very capable of rushing the puck up the ice. Made quick accurate passes on the point.

CAR #6 D Day, Sean (2016) - Day had one of his more impressive performances in recent memory. He was moving the puck very well on the power play making quick decisions under pressure. His defensive game wasn't great but offensively he was a key part of his teams' success.

CAR #11 LW Mascherin, Adam (2016) - Walked in and fired a wrist shot top shelf to give Canada a 2-0 lead. Keeps his feet moving and keeps finding ways to get open in the offensive zone.

CAR #15 RW Bitten, William (2016) - Explosive acceleration. Very good compete level on the walls despite his lack of size. Battles for pucks, once he has the puck on his stick he's very evasive and difficult to contain.

CAR #18 LW Smith, Givani (2016) - Good drop pass entering zone, set up scoring chance. Good power in his shot.

CAR #19 C Patrick, Nolan (2017) - Great one on one move on wing with size and skill to get scoring chance.

CAR #22 C Brown, Logan (2016) - Fired a quick wrist shot on a pass during the power play for the first goal of the game. He displayed good skating for a forward of his size. He uses his size to box out opponents well in puck races.

Final Score: Team Canada-Red: 4 - Team Sweden: 2

November 4, 2014 - Team USA vs. Team Canada-Red
World Under 17 Championships - Preliminary Round

USA #37 C Keller, Clayton (2016) - Scored a hat trick tonight showing off his skill and his quick finishing ability, although one of the three was a little soft. He competed very hard in all three zones.

USA #43 LD Greenway, James (2016) - Dangerous turnover at the offensive line. Great control on the wall on the wall with the puck and opponent on him.

USA # 44 LD Krys, Chad (2016) - Great evasive skating and puck skills to shake checkers off when he controlled the puck. He also possesses good speed and moved the puck well tonight. Hit teammate in the leg with his shot which went in for USA's sixth goal.

USA #48 LW Suthers, Keenan (2016) - Took up space in the slot well. The puck hit him in front and went in for USA's sixth goal.

USA #49 LW Jones, Max (2016) - Max provided a great mix of talent and physicality. He opened the scoring firing a quick shot past the goaltender. He landed a few solid hits and is always ooking to physically punish opponents.

USA #51 RD Fox, Adam (2016) - Adam was particularly strong with the puck when taking it up ice showing good patience to find the right lanes and exploit them quickly.

USA #53 LD Hellickson, Matthew (2016) - Overcommitted to puck handler in a two on one making the passing lane easy for Canada's second goal.

USA #55 RW Yamamoto, Kailer (2017) - Good finish in the slot for USA's third goal crashing the net.

USA #35 G Woll, Joseph (2016) - Made several great saves in the first period and continued his strong play throughout the game. He covers a lot of net while not giving up many rebounds at all.

CAR #5 RD Fabbro, Dante (2016) - A little risk vs reward with aggressive defensive play. Very high level hockey sense with his positional play and ability to read the play. Carried the puck up ice comfortably

CAR #6 D Day, Sean (2016) - Sean did well in the offensive zone on the power play distributing the puck, but when used on the penalty kill he struggled to apply pressure and gave opponents all the time in the world to make decisions.

CAR #11 LW Mascherin, Adam (2016) - Jumped on a rebound in the slot to score Canada's first goal of the game

CAR #12 C Felhaber, Tye (2016) - Good pass 2 on 1 to set up Canada's second goal of the game. Good creativity during his shift but at the end of his shift he needed to show a little more urgency getting off the ice, displayed negative body language on these occasions.

Final Score: Team USA: 7 - Team Canada-Red: 3

November 6, 2014 - Team Slovakia vs. Team Finland

World Under 17 Championships - Quarter-Finals

SVK #3 LD Matejovic, David (2016) - David has excellent size and moved the puck up ice consistently in this game. His first few steps are not very good but generates decent speed over time. He is a bit uncoordinated with his hands and feet in small areas and will go out of position.

SVK #7 LD Zelenak, Vojtech (2016) - Vojtech has excellent size and uses it well. He was very effective in battles along the wall winning battles and containing forwards effectiely. He also protects the puck very well when rushing the puck and is a very good skater considering his size. He made smart, simple plays down low, not trying to do too much. Vojtech can get a little ahead of the play and doesn't support his defensive partner once he starts skating forward with the puck and needs minor fundamental changes to how he approaches transitional play. He has a powerful and deflectable shot shot which was tipped in for Slovakia's only Quarter-Final goal. Took a penalty hitting an opponent chasing the puck carrier. Overcommits to shooter on odd man rush.

SVK #11 RW Roman, Milos (2018) - For a player just under four years away from his NHL Draft eligibility Milos put on a very impressive performance. While he was by far the youngest player in this event there no backing down from Milos. He played an exceedingly high energy game, showing relentless compete in all three zones. He was very effective in the defensive zone putting pressure on the puck carrier and forcing several turnovers. His strong defensive play gave him a role shorthanded and probably the best penalty killer for their team blocking shots and taking away time from the point. He displays good speed along with vision to make smart passes. He also possesses good hand/eye coordination and handled bouncing pucks very well.

SVK #17 LW Bucek, Samuel (2017) - Samuel showed good puck control on a short handed rush taking time away but also opening up potential chances. He does a good job of opening himself up for passes the second puck control is gained by his team.

SVK #25 LC Solensky, Samuel (2016) - Skilled passing ability was displayed on the power play by Samuel. He contributed offensively, primarily with creating a few chances but also deflected in Slovakia's only goal. Took a bad hit from behind penalty.

FIN #3 LD Felixson, Oliver (2016) - Very calm and composed when rushing the puck into the offensive zone. However at times he will rush his puck decisions.

FIN #9 RD Kluuskeri, Jan (2016) - Jan displayed good mobility on the point and a good skater who always keeps his feet moving. He can also control the puck while under pressure but made some bad puck decisions, particularly on the power play.

FIN #10 LW Vesalainen, Kristian (2017) - Jammed home first goal midway through the first. He also made an excellent pass to create Finland's second goal. Fired a powerful shot top shelf to score Finland's fourth goal. Kristian was very effective getting the job done for his team and was arguably the best forward on the ice this game.

FIN #19 RW Tuulola, Eetu (2016) - Eetu was very physical in the offensive zone today. He was used on the point during Finland's power play and displayed a cannon of a shot. He also has the size to take up penalty of space in the slot.

Final Score: Team Finland: 5 - Team Slovakia: 1

November 6, 2014 - Team Sweden vs. Team Canada-White

World Under 17 Championships - Quarter-Finals

SWE #23 RW Weissbach, Linus (2016) - Linus has high end speed and very quick hands. He is highly skilled but was also willing to play physical despite size. He was evasive but once he slowed down he was somewhat easy to knock off the puck.

SWE #1 G Gustavsson, Filip (2016) - Very composed on second chance opportunities. Great reaction time, maintains good positioning, little to no extra movement. Made some excellent saves

CAW #1 G Harvey, Samuel (2016) - Samuel made some key saves to keep Canada in this game. He was very aggressive challenging shooters, especially on breakaways and was tough to beat.

CAW #3 RD Green, Luke (2016) - Struggled with turnovers in all three zones. Skates well with good evasiveness, made some nice simple plays in neutral zone.

CAW #4 LD Middleton, Keaton (2016) - Massive size but his mobility struggles which is most evident against smaller speedy players. He was able to make the simple pass without pressure but struggled when under heavy pressure turning the puck over multiple times and fired the puck over the glass for a penalty as well. Fired point shot into screen.

CAW #6 RD Hague, Nic (2017) - Excellent size and lots of strength. He gets good power in his shot. He was extremely reliable today for his team breaking up several plays in the defensive zone using not only his size, but a good stick.

CAW #7 RD Quenneville, David (2016) - Good neutral zone puck control, skates well and evades defenders when challenged on the rush. Struggled with a few offensive zone turnovers.

CAW #10 LW Jost, Tyson (2017) - Great agility and puck control. Created multiple scoring chances for his team today.

CAW #19 LW Barron, Travis (2016) - Travis made himself very noticeable tonight delivering some hard hits and playing with good energy.

CAW #22 LC Howden, Brett (2016) - Howden displayed excellent compete along the wall and won a ton of battles. He was really a leader for Canada and gave them their best chance to score in this game. He made great puck decisions in the offensive zone and processed options quickly. He had the ability to read where the play was going and would get to where he needed to be before the puck got there. Took an undisciplined penalty on the forecheck.

Final Score: Team Sweden: 2 - Team Canada-White: 0

November 7, 2014 - Team Sweden vs. Team Canada-White

World Under 17 Championships - Semi-Finals

SWE #3 RD Cederholm, Jacob (2016) - Good size, has confidence to take the puck up ice as well as the puck skills and knowledge of how to use his size to do so.

SWE #6 LD Moverare, Jacob (2016) - Jacob provides good compete level from the back end. He won battles and was tough to beat in the defensive zone. His skating needs improvement.

SWE #16 LW Nylander, Alexander (2016) - In the biggest game to date Nylander put forward his best performance. He was creating offense all game long. He used his speed and puck skills on the rush to set up a scoring chance early. He showed quick finish on a different rush again using his speed to execute the play. He had good defensive positioning to steal the puck and get it deep after a very long shift of being pinned in the defensive zone. Great creativity and skill.

SWE #20 RW Steen, Oskar (2016) - Oskar was willing to take the body despite his size. He showed great anticipation to predict the passing lane, steal the puck and turn it into a scoring chance.

SWE #1 G Gustavsson, Filip (2016) - Extremely composed in the net and is always in great position for the initial shot.

USA #52 LD Luce, Griffin (2016) - Puck movement very inconsistent, uses wall effectively but was hit or miss on getting puck to targeted man.

USA #35 G Woll, Joseph (2016) - Woll got off to a very shaky sart fighting the puck and struggled catching the puck. Despite looking off of his usual performance he still got in front of shots and aside from an early goal shut the door for his team.

Final Score: Team USA: 4 - Team Sweden: 1

November 7, 2014 - Team Russia vs. Team Finland

World Under 17 Championships - Semi-Finals

RUS #30 G Sukhachyov, Vladislav (2016) - Very quick pads but gives up a multitude of rebounds.

RUS #4 LD Yakovenko, Alexander (2016) - Alexander made effective first passes up the ice and was effective on the offensive line keeping the play going.

RUS #11 RW Abramov, Vitali (2016) - Showed good speed tonight and made a great move to beat defender then score for Russia. Later on he made a good pass dirivng the net to set up Russia's sixth and final goal.

RUS #27 RW Sokolov, Dmitri (2016) - His skating is a bit clumsy and lacks explosiveness but has an excellent shot. He finished on the rush to give Russia their fifth goal.

FIN #3 LD Felixson, Oliver (2016) - Got walked on Russia's third goal. Held stick awkward during pressure when puck came back he mishandled it.

FIN #6 LD Niemelainen, Markus (2016) - Bad turnover in his own zone. Half commits to offensive zone play putting him too far out to make the play, but far enough that he's out of position defensively.

FIN #8 LD Reunanen, Tarmo (2016) - Quick hands and a smooth skater but his pivots need improvement and resulted in him getting beat. Very short steps in his skating. Offensive line mistake resulted in turnover.

FIN #14 LC Makinen, Otto (2016) - Smart play in close to break up clear attempt and keep power play pressure. Scored on possession and got assist. Forced shot with passing options.

FIN #18 LW Kukkanen, Janne (2016) - Excellent pass to sent up Finland's only goal. Great playmaking ability

Final Score: Team Russia: 6 - Team Finland: 1

U of NORTH DAKOTA vs U. of WISCONSIN – (11-7-2014)

WIS - #33G - Joel Rumple (FA - SJ) – Like most nights so far this season Rumple kept Wisconsin in the game by making a number of great saves. Despite facing 28 shots in the first 2 periods, his team had a 2-1 lead going into the 3rd period. Showed the ability to battle to find pucks in traffic and was quick to cover loose pucks, takes away the lower part of the net well which allows him to be so good in traffic. Has a terrific glove hand which UND challenged a lot. Very calm and collected demeanor but played a confident game on the top of his crease all night.

WIS - #28D - Kevin Schulze (FA) – Was one of Wisconsin's best and most consistent defenseman all night. Schulze is a bit undersized by today's standards at 5'11" but has terrific skating and puck moving ability. Will need to add bulk his frame to be more successful in puck battles and defending more powerful forwards. Displayed high hockey IQ with his decisions with the puck, reading the play in the defensive zone and knowing when to clear the puck off the glass or when to possibly move the puck to a forward or his partner. His skating ability allows him to have good gap control when defending the line rush, even against some of UND's top skilled forwards. Makes a good outlet pass and has the ability to hit forwards in the neutral zone with a stretch pass. Played in all situations tonight while being paired with Jack Dougherty (NSH). Played the point on a struggling Wisconsin Power play but made some good plays with the puck, Passes always tape to tape and gets a quick shot off toward the net. Not overly physical in the dirty area's and will need to learn to use more body positioning to win more battles in those areas.

WIS - #4RD - Jack Dougherty (NSH-2014) – Playing big minutes for Wisconsin all season long. Not an overly offensive player tonight but played a very solid defensive game. Can create chances with his puck skills but being paired with Schulze who has good puck skills as well, Dougherty plays the more stay at home role in that pairing. Uses his big frame to seal off the opposition and used great positioning to win puck battles along the boards. Played with a lot of emotion and competes until the final horn. Still a lot of room for growth in his game but is Wisconsin's best defenseman early on this season.

WIS - #12RW - Grant Besse – (ANA-2014) – High Energy forward, skated hard and battled for pucks. Was quick to be in on the fore-check and played physical on the UND defenseman. Besse created some good scoring chances by driving the net both with the puck and without. Didn't shy away from sacrificing his body and blocking shots. Had 2 Assists tonight.

UND - #8C - Nick Schmaltz (CHI –2014) – Was the most dangerous player offensively on the ice all night despite not showing up on the score sheet. Created offensive chances on almost every shift it seemed like. Even when he doesn't have the puck he was able to create space for his teammates because of the attention he draws. Used his skating ability well to jump into lanes and get open for the puck and can get his shot off quick and in tight spaces. Had one shift where he seemed to have the puck on his stick in the offensive zone the entire time, even when he passes it and there was a shot toward the net it would end up right back on his tape and he would just continue to circle the zone with it. On a couple occasions he found himself leaving the defensive zone a bit early, looking for a outlet pass in the neutral zone where a more 2 way center would have stayed back and got open for a simpler outlet pass with less risk. Didn't play a particularly physical game, despite it being a rivalry game where it seemed there were physical plays flying everywhere.

UND - #15RW - Michael Parks (PHI – 5th Rd.) – 2 goals, first the go ahead goal early in the 3rd on the Power Play and eventually the GWG shorthanded after blocking a play down the boards, then using his speed to beat the defender to the loose puck in the neutral zone and scoring on a breakaway. Will battle hard along the boards and in front of the net for loose pucks, played a physical gritty style.

Nov. 7, 2014 – Everett Silvertips at Vancouver Giants

EVR #3 RD Juulsen, Noah (2015) – A little slow in his start-up, but he's not afraid to pinch and rove down low in the offensive zone. Can spring the rush through strong passing technique and great vision. His first passes are strong and direct but easy to receive. On the defensive side, he does a good job of staying in position and containing his checks, regardless of how chaotic things are becoming around his goaltender. Throws a nice low-lying wristshot on net from the point.

EVR #8 RW Bajkov, Patrik (2016) – Skating looked very good, as his first-step is powerful and he gets going at a decent clip with apparently minimal effort. Forward movements look technically sound. Scored a couple of goals and a few were fairly individualistic efforts. Granted, his first goal came on a beautiful feed from Scherbak. But on his second goal, he simply skated down the left side and picked his shot far-side high on Cody Porter. Played on the penalty kill a lot, where he's not afraid to take a big check to make a smart clearance. I liked his competitiveness, as he showed a willingness to take punishment regardless of the score.

EVR #38 RD Davis, Kevin (2015) – Has a deceptively powerful first-step and terrific crossover capabilities, allowing him to move very quickly and very suddenly in all directions. His best quality might be his Niedermeyer-esque ability to move jump from his traditional defensive lane to another lane in just two or three steps, effectively cutting off a passing option, gaining possession for himself, and quickly transitioning the puck up ice. Feet are only quick when the situation is advantageous, however. Away from the play, Davis has a subtlety of motion that follows him everywhere, and wasted movement is reduced. A strong defensive effort; safe when it came to creating offense.

EVR #70 G Hart, Carter (2016) – While he was helped by an excellent defence in front him, Hart never looked perturbed by action in front of his crease and did a really good job of tracking the puck in midst of the chaos. Lower net coverage was exceptionally good, as he has good agility and flexibility. Does a really good job of getting his pandle down low to the ice when appropriate, and then smothering the puck with his glove hand after making the initial stop. Showed good anticipation, by making a few desperation saves and by knowing when to correctly go into the snow-angel.

EVR #77 LW Cochrane, Carter (2015) – Normally plays defense, but was moved up to forward in this one. A fast forward-moving skater and a physical hitter, he did a good job of engaging himself in board battles and killing time to protect his team's lead. While he had a quiet night in terms of pure offensive production, he did a lot of good things in his own end that would be easy to miss, including backchecking hard and making sure he was covering his man at all times.

EVR #95 RW Scherbak, Nikita (Montreal 2014) – Appears a lot larger on the ice than his listings suggest. He likely looks larger than expected because he has long limbs, an elongated skating stride and moves at torpedo speed at all times. Ability to carry the puck without challenge through all three zones is really breathtaking, as opposition players simply move out of his way. They don't want to be bulled over. A very good passer who plays a bit of a perimeter game. Shooting skills were also very good, as his wristers continuously hit the net and created second-chance scoring opportunities for his teammates.

November 8, 2014 - Team Russia vs. Team USA

World Under 17 Championships - Gold Medal Game

RUS #4 LD Yakovenko, Alexander (2016) - Yakovenko made an impact at both ends of the ice. He made some great defensive plays in the slot to clear away chances and break up passes. He also was willing to block shots. He scored the gold medal winning goal firing a hard shot through a screen into the back of the net.

RUS #5 LD Sergachyov, Mikhail (2016) - Mishandled puck in his own zone resulting in scoring chance. Hard shot from the point. Does a great job getting his stick in passing lanes.

RUS #7 LD Ryzhenkov, Pavel (2016) - Pavel was hit or miss defensively before making what could have been a championship game altering move. He made some great plays down low containing offensive chances, but also taking too much risk trying to hold the offensive line nearly giving USA an odd man rush. With just minutes left in the game up 2-0, Pavel took a penalty. However he was hurt on the play and went to the dressing room as a teammate served his penalty. A minute later he returned to the bench and eventually the play, landing a big hit from behind giving USA a 5 on 3 power play, taking a total of six minutes in penalties between his two penalties (also receiving an ineligible player on the ice penalty). USA would score once on the power play and his team held on, but this play could have cost Russia the gold medal.

RUS #11 RW Abramov, Vitaly (2016) - Great work down low in the offensive zone showing consistent work ethic and determination. He would do this on one particular play where his persistence directly resulted in a turnover and he took the puck and set up Russia's first goal of the game. He provides excellent puck protection ability for a small forward. Very shifty and very hard to contain.

RUS #17 LC Rubtsov, German (2016) - Rubtsov saved his biggest game for last at this event. He showed good hands and agility to beat defenders and create scoring chances. He did this several times including making a very smart pass to set up the gold medal winning goal. He also contributed defensively playing as the only forward on a huge 5 on 3 penalty kill in the final minutes of the game. He also finished his checks.

RUS #26 LW Bain, Maxim (2016) - Quick finish on a turnover to score Russia's first goal of the game. He uses his speed and evasiveness very well offensively, but was also willing to block shots.

RUS #27 RW Sokolov, Dmitri (2016) - Dmitri made a factor in this game using his hard shot to create scoring chance, but also blocking shots in the defensive zone getting in front of everything he could.

RUS #29 G Kalyayev, Maxim (2016) - Maxim doesn't get up much in terms of rebounds. He plays a bit of a scrambly style of game but always found a way to get himself in front of shots. Made an excellent hand/eye save to keep a shutout for 58:30 of this game against a high powered USA offense. The one goal that got past him kinda caught him napping on the play, it was a little soft but overall his performance was excellent. Handles cross ice passes well but struggled with traffic.

USA #36 LW Pastujov, Nick (2016) - Strong skating ability and covers ground quickly. No hesitation to get involved in the play. Showed puck skills to create offense.

USA #37 LC Keller, Clayton (2016) - Put the puck over the glass early on to take a penalty. He took another penalty after two failed power play attempts drilling the goaltender Kalyayev taking another penalty. Down two goals in the third, he spent too much time talking to officials and needed to put his focus on helping his team get back in the game.

USA #41 RW Lockwood, William (2016) - Lockwood much like the rest of the tournament played a high energy, physical game finishing every check he could. Didn't show much offense, but very good work ethic.

USA #43 LD Greenway, James (2016) - Greenway struggled tonight, mishandled puck twice behind his own net, the second of which directly lead to Russia's first goal. Mishandled puck on the penalty kill which resulted in another chance. Took a hooking penalty when a Russia forward beat him one on one down two goals with eight minutes left. Despite his struggles Greenway still has great potential, excellent size, good strength and can be tough to handle along the wall for opposing forwards when they have the puck.

USA #44 LD Krys, Chad (2016) - Used speed to o end to end carrying the puck and creating chances in the offensive zone, but has the skating to get back defensively.

USA #49 LW Jones, Max (2016) - Used size to protect puck well in the offensive zone. Played with a ton of determination and looked for the big hit and landed a few huge ones. Scored a bit of a soft goal with a hard shot catching the goaltender sleeping, it was stoppable but Jones' took advantage.

USA #51 RD Fox, Adam (2016) - Excellent stick in the defensive zone. Can skat ethe puck out of trouble. Generally made the smart, simple play with the puck in the neutral zone taking skating lanes when they were available, otherwise taking the high percentage option. Good puck movement playing on USA's top power play unit.

USA #52 LD Luce, Griffin (2016) - Played plenty of minutes on the penalty kill. Made smart simple plays with the puck, didn't try to do too much with it. Tough to beat one on one and handled speedy forwards well.

USA #55 RW Yamamoto, Kailer (2017) - Great pass to set up scoring chance. Banged home a loose puck but the goal was called off. High compete level, won puck races and made smart decsions with the puck on his stick.

Final Score: Team Russia: 2 - Team USA: 1

Charlottetown Islanders vs Blainville-Boisbriand Armada, November 8th 2014

CHA #10 C Kielly, Kameron (2015): Kielly played a sound two-way game today, supporting his defensemen well in his own end and making some nice plays with the puck in the offensive zone. Showed good vision finding Sprong on a couple of occasions in the offensive zone, scoring his goal by going to the net with his stick on the ice and receiving a perfect pass from Sprong from the corner. Worked hard in all three zones, and while he is not a speedster and doesn't have the best shot, I like his smarts.

CHA #11 RW Sprong, Daniel (2015): Sprong was playing in front of his friends and family for this game, and did both real good and real bad things tonight. Loved his speed and how he likes to attack the defense with the speed he generates in the neutral zone. With his speed and skill level, he can be intimidating for an opposing defense. He can control the puck extremely well but tonight, on occasion, he was trying too much with the puck and trying too much by himself. Can create a lot of chances offensively, and is also tough to knock down off his skates as we saw in a breakaway early in the game where he had a defenseman all over him. Showed flashes of how good his hands are after almost scoring a highlight-reel goal after a nice deke versus a Blainville-Boisbriand defenseman. When he decided to share the puck, he made some real nice passes for quality scoring chances, such as that pass to Kielly for Charlottetown's 2nd goal, which was a thing of beauty, very accurate and extremely quick off his stick. Could make more efforts in his own zone, as he can be immobile at time there.

CHA #13 C Getson, Keith (2016): Played mostly on the 4th line today and I didn't really notice him out there until the third period. He had a couple of great shifts, including one where he almost scored off a great rush from the neutral zone, where he used his speed very well. Getson brought some good energy to his team with those early 3rd period shifts.

CHA #14 C Chlapik, Filip (2015): Chlapik, who has been good for the Islanders all year, was quiet today. He's a smart player and even in a game where he doesn't play well, he doesn't get into trouble. The only bad play from him came when he lost the puck in the slot in his own zone, which led to Nikita Jevpalovs' 2nd goal of the game (but the puck was bouncing a bit). Nothing stood out offensively for him today, even with power play time on the first unit.

CHA #2 RD Deschêne, Luc (2015): Solid game from him, as he kept his game simple with the puck. Made simple plays when rushing the puck out of his zone, if he didn't have an option, he just chipped it by the boards. His skating is good enough to skate the puck out and get away from pressure when needed, but he could work on his footwork a bit though. He's not a tall player, but is real strong and protects the puck well. Liked his composure tonight and thought he played a solid game overall.

CHA #4 RD Thompson, Will (2015): In the first half of the game in the defensive zone, he had a tendency of not moving his feet, which got him into trouble, but he was much better in the 2nd half of the game. Made some strong plays in one-on-one situations and took his man out when needed. His decision-making with the puck needs to be quicker; saw him rush the puck more in the 2nd half but his lack of decision-making hurt him. Overall I thought his passing game was off a bit today as well.

CHA #27 LD Henley, David (2015): Loved his aggression in his own end today, as he didn't mind finishing his hits and protecting his goaltender. He can be taken out of position in his zone when he tries to be too physical. Showed his big shot from the point early on in the game, and as he doesn't get much power play time, he doesn't get many opportunities to use it. Henley's play with the puck was not really good today, as he missed a lot of easy passes that hurt the transition game of the Islanders.

BLB #33 G Montembeault, Samuel (2015): Overall, Montembeault was not often tested in this game; making 15 saves on the 17 shots he faced. He was calm and relaxed in his crease, even after allowing a goal, he kept his focus in the game. He has good size and can track the puck well, even with heavy traffic in front of him. Covered his angles well and let the puck hit him, and doesn't waste a lot of energy as he has a strong technique. The first goal he allowed was on the power play, where the puck hit his defenseman's skate before going behind him. On the 2nd goal, he had no chance, after a great pass from Sprong to Kielly at the side of the net.

BLB #17 RW Hamelin, Brendan (2015): Played on a line with Jevpalovs and Martel, the team's top two forwards. Did a nice job on the first Jevpalovs goal, protecting the puck along the wall and making a one-hand pass to Martel, who then found Jevpalovs in front of the net. With his line, he had some good shifts with a strong forecheck, causing problems for the young Charlottetown defense. Worked hard in all three zones and did well in a supporting role to Martel and Jevpalovs on the team's top line.

BLB #21 LW Mongo, Yvan (2015): A smallish forward that is strong on his skates and can fly out there. Plays a bottom-six role with the Armada and is used to bringing energy to the team. He does it well, with some strong forechecking. Not afraid to finish his checks, does a good job protecting the puck along the boards, cycling it. Good active stick in the neutral zone where he stole the puck, which led to a scoring chance on a breakaway but saw him denied by McDonald.

BLB #71 LW Jevpalovs, Nikita (2015): The overager passed over in the last two NHL Entry Drafts had a strong game, scoring a hat trick. His first goal of the game was a real nice goal, deking Mason McDonald in front of the net. His 2nd goal was from a quick shot after a turnover in the slot, and the third goal was in an open net on a two-on-one after a great feed from Danick Martel. He probably could have scored five to six goals tonight, but McDonald made some great saves on him. He worked hard all game long, his line was very strong on the forecheck and was able to pin down Charlottetown in their own end.

BLB #85 LD Walcott, Daniel (NYR 5th round pick 2014): Walcott was solid, his skating abilities are excellent and he can be everywhere on the ice. Very strong on his skates; made some good hits and was also a target but got the better of hits he received. Got a ton of ice time today, rushed the puck with ease out of his zone. Didn't lose many battles out there, a favorite of mine last year who is playing great again with a "C" on his jersey this year.

November 9, 2014 - Saginaw Spirit at Kitchener Rangers

SAG #5 RD Crawford, Marcus (2015) - Good skater, moves the puck up ice quickly and effectively. Dangerous play with the puck in the slot.

SAG #6 LD Orban, Ryan (2015) - Good compete level, skates well for such a big defender. He will finish his checks but doesn't play a mean game. He gets his stick into passing lanes on a consistent basis. Needs to get stronger on his skates as he got knocked off balance a little too easily when opponents made contact with him.

SAG #12 LD Holmes, Michael (2015) - Decent shot, forced it when its blocked

SAG #27 RC Stephens, Mitchell (2015) - Good finish on a two on one to score Saginaw's first goal. Uses his speed very well in the defensive zone. Took a retaliatory penalty off the face-off when whacked off draw he took it up a notch and was penalized for it. He was about 66.7 percent on the face-off tonight.

SAG #55 LD Middleton, Keaton (2016) - Middleton had one of his better games in our viewings making several smart plays with the puck both at the offensive line, and in his own zone. He moved the puck up ice to set up Saginaw's third goal of the game. He got time in every game situation playing on Saginaw's second power play and penalty killing units. He landed a very high percentage of his passes this game and played a pretty reliable and effective game tonight.

SAG #62 LC Felhaber, Tye (2016) - Good work in the defensive zone to force turnover. Moved the puck effectively and moved it well when entering the offensive zone. He was rewarded for his unselfish play with a great pass fed in the slot and quickly finished with a good shot for Saginaw's fourth goal. Went down very easily on a two on one drawing a power play. He struggled in the face-off circle with his winning percentage around the 20% range.

SAG #88 RW Artemov, Artem (2015) - Made very good passes, one of which set up Saginaw's first goal of the game. His skating is satisfactory but not great and is a little slow going up and down the ice. He protected the puck well on the power play playing on the second unit, but got caught trying to do too much himself.

KIT #15 RC Franzen, Gustav (2015) - Good hustle on the backcheck. Will hang back even after puck is gone if a defenseman jumps too far up on the rush. Good compete in the slot defensively breaking up a scoring chance. Excellent defensive zone compete. Lacks that extra gear of explosiveness which is so important for a player of his size. Did not contribute much offensively. Franzin was excellent in the face-off circle winning 75% of his draws.

KIT #18 LD Blaisdell, Doug (2015) - Let forward get behind him on the rush too easily early on. He contained very well along the wall. He made some smart pinches from the point to keep the play going without much risk. He didn't force his shot if he doesn't see a shooting lane. Game looked more simplified than previous viewings making a good first pass and more simple puck decisions. Contained forwards in the slot well and prevented a potential goal.

KIT #74 LC Bunnaman, Connor (2016) - Good hustle on forecheck. Good face-off's

Final Score: Saginaw Spirit: 5 - Kitchener Rangers: 4 - OT

Cape Breton Screaming Eagles at Acadie-Bathurst Titan, November 9th, 2014

AB #55 LD Brisebois, Guillaume (2015): Brisebois is Acadie-Bathurst's team captain. Brisebois is very offensively involved but also defensively responsible. Brisebois sets up the Titan power play; carrying the puck and setting up in zone. He moves the puck quick and efficiently. His quick decision making and skill allows him to be involved offensively and keeps his team on offense as he does not turn the puck over. He does a good job using his size to protect the puck and win battles. When the forwards are rushing the puck, he does a good job joining the rush creating another offensive threat and confusion in opponents back check.

AB #25 LW Truchon-Viel Jeffrey (2015): Truchon-Viel is not an overly flashy player, but he does a good job using speed to beat defensemen on the outside of a rush. He has a good quick release and hard shot. He also does a good job offensively finding himself open in the offensive zone. He was 3rd star of this hockey game because of a hard working effort and timely assist on a late goal to tie the game.

AB #11 LW Boivin, Christophe (2015): Boivin is a very active player that has lots of speed. Unfortunately at 5'7" his size causes him issue at times. Boivin wins races to pucks and often uses his speed to beat players but in physical battles he is at a disadvantage. He is a smart player that plays his position well, but also uses his speed and quick feet to support his teammates.

CAP #4 LD Bell, Jason (2015): Bell is a solid defenseman who takes care of his own end and plays physical. He gets lots of ice time and also spends time on the power play. Bell also does a good job joining his team on the rush offensively. A couple times Titan players caught him flat-footed 1 on 1 beating him wide, causing him to take a penalty and giving up a good scoring chance.

CAP #12 RD Lalonde, Bradley (2015): Lalonde is a defenseman who soaks up a lot of ice time. He plays big minutes even strength, and also plays power play and penalty kill. He had a fairly quiet game with a nice assist setting up a nice goal on the power play.

CAP #37 RW Svechnikov, Evgeny (2015): Svechnikov is a big forward that has an impact whenever he is on the ice. He set up 2 of the Eagles goals in the game using his size to pressure opponents and win battles. He does a good job controlling the puck in tight spaces under pressure. He is very dangerous offensively as he has a lot of skill. A couple times in this game he was guilty of doing too much with the puck. He over handled the puck once in the defensive end, and turned it over leading to a Titan goal.

CAP #26 RD Leveille, Loik (2015): Leveille finds himself on Cape Bretons bottom D pairing but still sees lots of ice time. Leveille kills penalties and was on a lot in the 3rd period protecting a lead. He makes good plays under pressure and makes solid body checks. He does not play passive in the neutral zone, he pinches at the right time and closes the gap well between him and his man.

CAP #23 LW Lazarev, Maxim (2015): Lazarev plays both wings well. He is another very skilled and dangerous player offensively. He has good speed and uses it to get open and find himself with the puck. He also makes good quick passes. He is not very physically involved and avoided battles in this game. It was a quiet game for him.

Nov. 10, 2014 – Russia at WHL (Subway Super Series, Game 1)

RUS #6 LD Gavrikov, Vladislav (2014) – Ice-time was mysteriously down from last year's event, and Gavrikov was not paired with teammate and usual partner Rushan Rafikov. When he was on the ice, he was hemmed in his own zone on a number of occasions, but did a good job of reserving energy and containing opponents to the outside. Playing head-to-head against Greg Chase on many shifts, he won just about every one-on-one battle between the two. Ability to quietly smother opponents in dangerous areas is an easy one to understate.

RUS #7 RD Rafikov, Rushan (Calgary, 2013) – Appears to have added an extra dimension to his strong defensive game, as he looked more comfortable roving down low in the offensive zone than he ever has in my past viewings. In addition to looking dangerous in the offensive zone with good forwards and backwards skating and nice passing skills, Rafikov did a good job of winning puck races, making simple outlet passes and working hard to create smart clearances.

RUS #17 RW Scherbak, Nikita (Montreal, 2014) – It was an interesting night for Nikita Scherbak, who was returning to Saskatoon after having been dealt from there just weeks ago—going from the hometown Blades to the Everett Silvertips in a curious trade at a curious time. Scherbak was playing a decidedly Western-style dump-and-chase game. In some respects, this made him a bit of a misfit in tonight's game as his team as trying to play more of a 'run and gun'-type style.

RUS #22 LD Provorov, Ivan (2015) – A deep knee-bend offers extra power in his first-stride propulsion. The unusual gliding stance doesn't hinder his agility whatsoever, as he still looks powerful and controlled on his edges and can spin, turn, or pivot as fast as anyone else on the ice. Loves to start the rush from behind his net when on the power play or when at even strength, as he can lead the rush by skating, passing or shooting the puck into the attacking zone. Wins races to the puck and throws a really intriguing and old-school swivelling hipcheck in the corners. Ice-time grew as this one went on.

RUS #25 LW Dergachev, Alexander (2015) – Tall, reasonably fast, finishes his checks, and plays an honest two-way game. Looked really active, aggressive and effective on the penalty kill, fighting like a starving bull for the puck in the slot and then making a couple crucial clearances to get his team out of danger. Does a fantastic job at rushing players at the point and manufacturing turnovers. A few harmless steals and chips out of his zone led to breakouts for his teammates. Shooting looked fairly good on a partial breakaway opportunity while killing another penalty. Stamina was a bit of an issue, but he kept his shifts short.

CAN #4 RW Bowey, Madison (Washington, 2013) – It's interesting that Bowey has ties to the game of football, as his hitting style is more reminiscent of an American football-style stiff-arm than it is to a traditional hockey hit. In fact, he earned a penalty for stiff-arming his opponent in the first period. Used the same motion to absolutely eliminate an opponent and a scoring opportunities without being penalized. A good skater who passes and shoots the puck well.

CAN #15 LW Virtanen, Jake (Vancouver, 2014) – If you're a fan of Jake Virtanen, than this was a game that probably had your heart palpitating from start to finish. From taking a hard hit to his recently surgically repaired shoulder and being carried to the team dressing room, to scoring a game-tieing goal for his team and then throwing an even harder hit to his opponent in return, this was an eventful contest for this Vancouver Canucks prospect.

CAN #20 LW Point, Brayden (Colorado, 2014) - One has to love the continuity in his game, as it seems like Point's feet are always moving. His brain also seems to process the game very quickly. Speed and deking skills were put on display a couple of times, including on one occasion in which he shook himself free for a partial breakaway opportunity on Shesterkin. Speed was shown off again when he went wide of Yudin to create a two-on-one chance.

CAN #23 LC Reinhart, Sam (Buffalo, 2014) – Wearing the 'C' for Team WHL and coming into the game as a returnee from last year's World Junior squad, Sam Reinhart played a typical 'Sam Reinhart game' tonight. He won draws, showed tremendous awareness and anticipation, and created scoring opportunities for himself and his teammates on a consistent shift-to-shift basis. Likes to post-up high and in the middle of the offensive zone, and is great at making plays from that position.

Nov. 12, 2014 – Tri-City Americans at Vancouver Giants

TRI #17 Braden Purtill (2015) LC – Playing at both centre and wing, Braden Purtill had a good game showing off better than average skating skills and a decent wristshot. He played limited minutes in a third line role. He showed good speed and decent strength while hustling in his backchecking effort. Even when he isn't scoring, Purtill rarely seems like a defensive liability. He takes draws, finishes his checks, works hard in the corners, provides screens, and can play in all situations if necessary.

TRI #36 Brandon Carlo (2015) D – He has good footspeed, agility and hand-eye coordination for someone of his stature. He has the ability to skate from one end of the ice to the other with the puck on his stick. Carlo attempted it on a couple of occasions in this game, and threw out some really terrible giveaways in important areas. Otherwise, his passing game was okay and his shots were decent as well. Later in the game, he showed signs of fatigue and disinterest when he was joking with Parker Wotherspoon during a pivotal situation. If he can get a grip on those unforced turnovers and improve his competitiveness, the upside here is tremendous.

TRI #37 Parker Wotherspoon (2015) D – Even though he wasn't solely responsible for any of his teams most egregious errors, I thought that this was a poor showing for Parker Wotherspoon. Wotherspoon looked slow and plodding in his foot movement and struggled playing the puck. He scored on a fairly quickly released slapshot from just beyond the right-side faceoff circle. The shot didn't initially beat Cody Porter, but eventually squirmed over his pads carried by its own power and momentum. Away from the puck, Wotherspoon lost his man on a number of occasions, and lacked seriousness in his on-ice communication and general body language.

VAN #22 Dmitry Osipov (2015) D – A smooth but not necessarily speedy skater, Osipov has good mobility, reach and hustle. When he appears fully focused, his positioning can be. He manages to do nothing because players avoid streaking up his side of the ice. An upright skater with good posture and upper-body strength, he stands tall and offers an intimidating presence at his own blueline and has excellent gap control in the neutral zone. Once trapped in his own end, he wins short-area races, absorbs hits well, boxes out opposition forwards with ease, and limits zone entries with a strong pokecheck. Discipline has been an issue in the past, but wasn't one tonight.

VAN #26 Ryely McKinstry (2016) LD – Ryely McKinstry contributed at both ends of the ice tonight with a goal and a plus-2 differential. I really like the chemistry McKinstry has developed with Arvin Atwal thus far. In their search for a quarterback power play with good shooting skills and vision, I think the Giants have somewhat settled on McKinstry. His shooting skills speak for themselves, with McKinstry having scored several goals over my last few viewings of the Giants. And his passing game isn't bad either. He delivers a decent first pass and, if necessary, he can skate the puck across the opposition blueline himself. Perhaps the best part of McKinstry's game is his defence—as he is constantly improving his skating and own-end awareness. His hitting skills are way ahead of where they should be for his age. His ice-time is gradually increasing in his rookie season.

Nov. 13, 2014 – Russia at OHL (Subway Super Series, Game 3)

RUS #6 LD Gavrikov, Vladislav (2014) – Again looked like a really dependable and important part of Russia's penalty kill tonight. He's a leftie, but he plays on the right side when down a man, because he's known to make a nice slapper clearance. While on the penalty kill, he continues to do a good job of collapsing quickly to the front of the net, and tying up the opposition in front of the net whilst also getting into passing lanes. The ways in which he contains his checks can often be extremely frustrating for the opposition, as shown by the number of chippy battles he has after the whistle.

RUS #25 LW Dergachev, Alexander (2015) – Looks surprisingly agile for a player of his height and girth, as he does a fantastic job of spinning off checks. Did a good job of positioning himself in front of shots on the penalty kill, even making a few daring shot blocking attempts. I again thought that his stamina could be called into question, as he looked far less enthusiastic and hard-working the longer he was left out on the ice.

OHL #6 D Spencer, Matthew (2015) – Did a good job of living up to his name as a traditional defensive defenceman—insofar that he didn't do anything noticeably good or noticeably bad in this game.

However, given that it's his only tryout for Team Canada in terms of the World Juniors, and that he was playing in his hometown Kingston arena, I left wanting a little more than I got.

OHL #58 D Vande Sompel, Mitchell (2015) – A highly agile, highly intelligent, and relatively quick-footed defenceman, Vande Sompel does a good job of spinning off checks and getting the puck out of trouble when retrieving. In the first period, Vande Sompel looked a bit reluctant while playing on the man-advantage and too often deferred to his defensive partner while in his own zone. In the second period, he stayed on the ice for longer than he should have on one shift, and got sucked out of position by Tolchinsky, leading to a goal against.

OHL #23 C Garlent, Hunter (2013) – A dynamic offensive forward who has been passed up previously in two NHL drafts. Small but quick and agile, Garlent's game is resmiscent of a homeless man's Patrick Kane. He likes that Kane-esque stop-short move at the blueline after gaining zone entry, and is a talented enough stickhandler and passer to make things happen from that area of the ice. His vision is very good as he threaded the needle with a few passes in this one.

OHL #26 RW Konecny, Travis (2015) –Had a decent game that was characterized by tremendous work-ethic. Typically looked like one of the hardest workers on his team and skated very quickly. Beaten in a few key board battles and looked a bit tentative in key situations. Got stung in a knee-on-knee incident that followed from a poorly timed side-step. On the one hand, I liked how daring and electric he was regardless of the score; but on the other hand, I think it's fair to say that he needs to do a better job of protecting himself if he wants to have long-term success at the next level.

Scout's Notes: A dominating 4-0 victory for the Russians, this was not a good showing for the 2015-eligible OHL prospects being showcased tonight—namely, Matthew Stephens, Travis Konecny, Hunter Garlent, and Mitchell Vande Sompel.

November 14, 2014 - Owen Sound Attack at London Knights

OSA #4 RD Schemitsch, Thomas (2015) - Schemitsch has a good shot from the point. He gets it through and doesn't force it when the lane isn't there. He has excellent size for a defenseman. He played physical a few times on the point but got his stick up when doing so. He struggled a little in the offensive zone making some bad passes on the power play and tries to hold the line at times when he should be getting back. His skating stride is a little awkward and lacks acceleration. He lost a battle down low when he went way out of position then while recovering the open man scored for London.

OSA #9 RC Szypula, Ethan (2015) - Ethan has explosive speed and skating ability. He created a few zone possessions for his team with his skating ability and speed but didn't do much offensively aside from that until the third period when he made an excellent one on one move on the defender then made a great play to get hit shot off hitting one post, then the other, then out.

OSA #17 RD Meyer, Jarrett (2015) - Meyer is a massive, towering defender who surprisingly was able to get up and down the ice fairly effectively. He moved the puck pretty well, usually choosing the simple passes. He got knocked around pretty easily by smaller opponents considering his size. He was walked on one play by speed.

OSA #20 RD MacArthur, Tyler (2015) - Decent skating for big guy, with team down 4-0 he dropped the gloves and landed some big bombs dropping his opponent.

OSA #21 LW Gadjovich, Jonah (2017) - Jonah's ice was exceedingly limited, gaining lass than a handful of shifts in the first 40 minutes of the game. However, as a few fights occurred , Gadjovich was given a little time to start the third period and made the most of it. He provided a ton of energy. He drove the net hard every chance he got, competed for loose pucks and finishing his checks. He jumped on a rebound scoring Owen Sound's fourth goal bringing them within one with less than six minutes remaining. It was an odd situation where Gadjovich was holding a broomstick for the vast majority of the game but every time he stepped on the ice he made an impact for his team and was the best player for Owen Sound not named Platzer or Nastasiuk.

LON #14 LD Crawley, Brandon (2015) - Good containment on the wall vs speed and also vs size. However, he needs to get stronger to be even more effective in these situations. He jumped up on the rush a few times under pressure with the puck and showed some evasiveness. He had an excellent shift late in the game controlling a big forward down low, steals the puck then skated it out of trouble with ease getting the red line and putting it deep.

LON #86 LD Martenet, Chris (2015) - Struggled to keep puck in offensive zone. Ejected after Owen Sound's fourth goal hitting opponent after the goal.

LON #93 RW Marner, Mitchell (2015) - Played in all game situations. He has excellent speed and moved the puck well on the power play. Blocked shot on the penalty kill. He made some high end passes to teammates at top speed. He scored a great goal with 1:09 left to seal the victory finding an open lane and quickly finished beating the goaltender.

Final Score: London Knights: 6 - Owen Sound Attack: 4

North Bay Battalion at Barrie Colts, Nov 15, 2014

Score: 3-2 Barrie

North Bay

LW Zach Bratina (2015*) – Bratina generated good speed in his first three steps and used it to fly through the neutral zone with regularity. Defenders continuously had to back off, which allowed him easy access into the offensive zone. He drew a penalty early, and setup several good chances with his creativity. He played with the puck on his stick a lot, and was the playmaker on his line. He finished his checks when he could, and didn't shy away from battles in the corner. He did, however, take three penalties in the game, though a couple of them were questionable.

C Brett McKenzie (2015) – McKenzie didn't do much offensively, but he was good defensively as usual. He did a good job of reading the play, and intercepted several passes on the penalty kill throughout the game. He was always back to support in the defensive zone, and liked to engage physically when he could. McKenzie did a good job of getting the puck to Bratina in the neutral zone and letting him create.

D Zach Shankar (2015) – Shankar played very limited minutes in this one, even when Brendan Miller was serving a 2 and a 10 for getting into it with Brendan Lemieux midway through the game. Shankar did have a couple rough shifts, and was absolutely walked by Kevin Labanc late right before Labanc sniped the eventual game winner.

Barrie

LW Matthew Kreis (2015) – Kreis did a lot defensively for a winger, and when he caused a turnover he liked to carry the puck up ice. He was relentless after pucks in all three zones, and when he couldn't carry the puck into the offensive zone he dumped it in and used his speed to win the race for loose pucks. He drew a penalty in the offensive zone, and was good in seal and support situations.

RW Roy Radke (2015) – Radke was good on the forecheck and played a big role on the penalty kill. He drew a penalty while shorthanded, and was effective on the cycle, especially late in the game when Barrie was defending the lead. Radke had a couple good drives down the wing and in one situation he eluded a check from a defender before centering it for a good scoring opportunity.

D Rasmus Andersson (2015) – Andersson defended well in 1-on-1 situations and was reliable in his own zone throughout the night. He was engaged physically, involved in a couple scrums after the whistle and did a nice job clearing the net throughout. Andersson found some space near the front of the net (on the PP) and had Jake Smith down and out, but couldn't convert on his chance. He consistently got his shots through, and was able to get good power in his shot while doing so. One was deflected in front by Lemieux for a goal on the man advantage, and he added another assist later on top of that. His gap control was really good, and he didn't allow anyone to get the inside on him. Another thing he did well was flick pucks high at Smith so the Colts would force an offensive zone faceoff and get fresh bodies on the ice.

G Mackenzie Blackwood (2015) – Blackwood was exceptional in what was his 1st game back from injury. He made several big stops early in the game to keep the Battalion off the board, and gave the Colts a chance to get their feet underneath them. His positioning was good, he was square to his shooters and used his big body well to take up a lot of the net. Blackwood made a few nice glove saves, and showed great lateral movement stretching out to make some Grade A saves throughout the night. He stopped 30-32 in the win.

Scout notes: Nick Paul scored two goals, including one off a beautiful give-and-go, and was arguably the best player on the ice throughout...Brendan Miller and Brendan Lemieux went toe-to-toe all game long and were involved in several big scrums...Miles Liberati (while sitting on the bench) hit Garrett Hooey when he skated by North Bay's bench and started a big scrum on the bench...Kyle Wood played a very steady game, eating up a lot of tough minutes and adding two assists in the process.

Tappara vs. Ilves 15.11 Nov, 2014

Ilv #28 RW Hintz, Roope (2015) - Roope had decent night. His hockey sense and puck-handling skills are great. Really smart kid who got size. He's average skater and his technique is fine but he needs lot of power in his lower body to be much better in the corners and to be a faster skater. Especially the first steps. He plays with pretty big confidence and his passing game is stunning.

Ilv #21 C Mustonen, Aleksi (2015) - Aleksi showed tonight his amazing skating ability. Quick feet with great technique. He's undersized but that doens't mind him: likes to go to the traffic and really can battle against grown up men. Smooth hands and great vision.

Ilv #5 D Mäkelä, Aleksi (Drafted by Dallas 2013) - Aleksi had a pretty good game. Really good in the d-zone and plays always steady defensive game. Big kid who's first passes are quite accurate. Nothing showy but have shown some development during the summer and the fall.

November 16, 2014 - Sudbury Wolves at Kitchener Rangers

SBY #3 RD Clapham, Austin (2015) - Smart first pass up ice. Decent backwards skating. Great play on a two on one to break up a scoring chance. Got special teams action on the second penalty kill unit.

SBY #8 LD Masters, Jonathon (2015*) - Provided an excellent forecheck pressure as a defenseman playing forward in this game. He competed extremely hard and forced turnovers in all three zones. Dropped the gloves with big power forward Brent Pedersen and dropped him. Excellent game for Masters, especially considering his limited play.

SBY #18 LW Kashtanov, Ivan (2015) - Kashtanov saw very limited ice, but made an outstanding move on the shootout to extend the game.

SBY #23 LD Capobianco, Kyle (2015) - Capobianco was moderately effective offensively, playing top power play movements, moving the puck very well in the offensive zone and making a solid first pass up ice. However he really struggled defensively turning the puck over in his own zone and having multiple defensive breakdowns. He would benefit from being a little tougher down low against opposing forwards. He received an interference penalty for playing the body too late in a one on one match-up.

KIT #15 RC Franzen, Gusfaf (2015) - Franzen made a few very good defensive plays but wasn't much of an impact beyond his side of the redline. He made a great play while on the penalty kill to steal the puck and bring it in for a short handed scoring chance. He has decent skating ability but relay lacks that top gear and that explosiveness someone his size needs. Good evasiveness while on the wall on the power play to keep the play going. Below 50% on face-offs

KIT #17 RW Kohn, Mason (2015) - Mason has a very high compete level and works hard consistently. First shift of the game he used his speed to blow by the defender on the outside and create a scoring chance. He has good power in his shot but missed net a little too much.

KIT #18 LD Blaisdell, Doug (2015) - Blaisdell consistently made the smart simple play with the puck either passing off or exploiting holes to skate through and get the puck deep. He took the hit to make the play with the puck and didn't back down from the physical game, while not being all that overly physical himself. He played pretty smart in the defensive zone on a consistent basis. He effectively contained forwards along the wall. His footwork and speed is decent and fairly smooth for the speed he has, but still has room to improve. He got called for a bit of a weak tripping penalty when he got his stick in the opponents skates, but later on, early in the third period he got beat one on one then rammed the opponents' head into the wall and was miraculously not called for it. He was utilized on a big 5 on 3 penalty kill moments later.

KIT #23 LW Mascherin, Adam (2016) - Mascherin played on the second power play unit. He created and took advantage of every shooting opportunity but tried to force his shot a few times on the power play and resulted in turnovers. Bad turnover with pressure when he needed to pass instead of trying to do too much himself. Needs to utilize his linemates a little better. He got a chance in the shootout and chose to use his shot but was stopped.

Final Score: Sudbury Wolves: 3 - Kitchener Rangers: 2 - OT/SO

Sport u20 vs. tps u20 16 nov, 2014

TPS #8 D Reunanen, Tarmo (2016) - Tarmo showed today lot of great plays. Smart kid with great vision. He's really skilled d-man whose power play ability is an amazing. Great skating, especially his top speed. Accurate long and short passes and great hockey sense. He's quite small but he plays smart in the d-zone and that makes him pretty good all-round D.

TPS #48 RW Nurmi, Markus (2016) - Nurmi scored a one nice goal today. He's tall kid who's quite good battling in the corners. likes to play rough and his scoring sense is pretty good. Obviously he needs lot of more muscle and he have to be much faster to be a pro. He got the size and hockey sense but there's lot of work to do with his physicality.

TPS #18 C Vähätalo, Julius (Drafted by Detroit 2014) - He plays great two-way game even though he isn't that fast. Big center and he's really good around the corners. Didn't show anything special with the puck today. He have to work with his feet a lot or otherwise he won't ever play higher than finnish elite league.

Spo #4 D Salo, Robin (2017) - Robin had a horrible game. He played just couple of shifts today and was pretty lost in the D-zone. He have been top d-man in his team at this fall and there might have been some problems with his health today.

Victoriaville Tigres vs Acadie-Bathurst Titans, November 16th 2014

VIC #27 RW Gagne, Gabriel (2015): Gagne has tremendous size and a physical advantage over his opponents. Gagne skates well and uses his long stride for speed. Gagne does a good job supporting his team mates and plays his position well. One time Gagne did a good job back checking and helped support his D, but then he made a costly D zone turnover. Gagne could use his size more as he seems physically uninvolved at times. Gagne has a good shot and quick release.

AB #55 LD Brisebois, Guillaume (2015): Brisebois continues to impress with his play. He could use a little more strength and size as he is sometimes outmatched physically. But, other times he shows the work ethic and ability to beat opponents and separate them from the puck. Brisebois shows great patience with the puck and makes great plays. He is able to be patient with the puck because he controls it so well under pressure. Brisebois is an effective D man on top of his teams power play set up and breaks the puck out effectively.

AB #11 LW Boivin, Christophe (2015): Boivin is a small forward at only 5'7". But, he plays like his size is a non-factor thanks to great skill and speed. Boivin's speed makes it possible for him to control play when he has the puck. He works hard in the corners and battles and wins them with his elusive skating and speed. He has skilled hands and good passing skills; making him very dangerous in the offensive end. He set up nice goals in this game on the power play.

AB #20 C Kerr, Aaron (2015): Kerr played a very solid game impressing in all areas. Kerr plays of the Titan power play and penalty kill. Kerr is not always the most skilled player on the ice, but he is usually the hardest working. His hard working play drew penalties on opponents more than one time in this game. Kerr has good speed and uses his body well to protect the puck. He had a multi-point night assisting and scoring goals.

November 21, 2014 - Erie Otters at Sarnia Sting

ERI #13 D Saban, Jesse (2015) - Strong defensive play battling hard/successfully along the wall, using good body positioning. Cleared zone very well on the powerplay. Really struggled bad with the puck struggling to visualize the pass and turning the puck over multiple occasions.

ERI #19 C Strome, Dylan (2015) - Dylan put up good numbers in this game starting with Erie's second goal, picking up a loose puck on a scramble during the power play giving Erie a 2-0 lead. He was rewarded with a phantom assist on the third goal, but made up for it on the fourth goal with an excellent pass to set up his teammate. Strome is a very defensively responsible forward with a steady and consistent backcheck. His skating still has it's concerns but has shown clear improvement. He showed good patience with the puck on the power play, delaying and letting lanes open, but sometimes still made the wrong decision. He struggled to win face-off's in this game.

ERI #21 RW Fellows, Patrick (2015) - Patrick was noticeable on the penalty kill. Excellent defensive play competing in his own zone, getting into passing lanes and blocking shots. He put good pressure high on the point to force turnovers.

ERI #44 D Dermott, Travis (2015) - smooth skater with good lateral movement. Moved the puck up ice well on a consistent basis, making quick decisions.

SAR #3 D Black, Alex (2015) - Alex played a team first game with the puck taking the hit to make the play on multiple occasions. He is a decent skater but his turns are not great. Got walked one on one a few times, taking a penalty after one of the times.

SAR #6 RW Bushnell, Noah (2015) - Got some time on the powerplay and was utilized in front of the net using his huge frame to impact the goaltenders ability to see the play. Pretty quiet outside that and his physical play, doing a good job separating opponents from the puck.

SAR #10 LW Kodola, Vladislav (2015) - Great use of speed to make plays happen. Very slick on open ice with the puck, difficult to contain. Created a great scoring chance displaying vision and puck moving ability.

SAR #11 RW Hodgson, Hayden (2015*) - Short, choppy strides. Good move to beat defender and create scoring chance.

SAR #14 C Zacha, Pavel (2015) - Extremely comfortable under pressure. Great speed and changes directions well. Made some high level passes in this game. He was ejected for delivering a devastating check from behind in his own zone.

SAR #35 RW Korostelev, Nikita (2015) - Nikita has an exceptionally hard shot but couldn't hit the net. This occurred several times this game as Korostelev would get open but kept shooting the puck high or wide. Could have scored 3 or 4 tonight if accuracy was better. Played physical in this game using his size on multiple occasions. Made a very skilled pass to a teammate but they missed on the one-timer.

Note: Zacha was suspended 6 games by the OHL for the hit.

Final Score: Erie Otters: 7 - Sarnia Sting:1

Nov. 21, 2014 – Portland Winterhawks at Kelowna Rockets

POR #7 LW Bittner, Paul (2015) – Created a few scoring opportunities alongside Chase De Leo, with De Leo repeatedly setting up the big bodied Bittner from behind the net. Bittner is a difficult guy to move from the slot, so he stays there a lot. Especially on the power play, he loves to occupy space directly in front of the opposing goaltender. Normally looks a bit tentative, but showed good toughness and durability in this one by remaining in front of the opposition goaltender even after being chop-blocked awkwardly by Gatenby.

POR #21 LD de Jong, Brendan (2016) – Receiving rave reviews from his coach, I thought that 16-year-old Brendan De Jong had a very good game. He makes really good reads in all three zone and appears to have exceptionally high hockey IQ for his age. In his own end, he does a good job of transitioning the puck up ice with smart, simple and easy to receive passes. In the neutral zone, he gets a really hard stick onto hard dumps, that more often than not, go around the boards and out to his wingers.

POR #44 RD Texeira, Keoni (2015) RD – Had a good game in which he made a lot of "stupidly simple" plays. He's not an electrifying skater, but he is efficient in his movements. His backwards skating is particularly good, as he is difficult for opposition players to beat wide. Fairly strong, he's also difficult to power through—making him the winner in most one-on-one situations. A fantastic penalty killer, he does a good job of checking forwards in the slot and lifting their sticks so as to prevent deflections and rebound opportunities. Can play on the power play, too, where he's not the greatest passer but holsters a really good shot that is fairly accurate and extremely powerful.

POR #3 Ethan Price (2015) RW – Passing was enigmatic. To put it into Dickinsonian terms, it was his best quality and it was his worst quality. He created some nice give-and-go plays with Nicolas Petan, but he was also responsible for some really ugly turnovers on careless pass attempts. Looked just okay on the power play, as he lacked hustle and will when it came to tracking pucks in the corner.

KEL #10 LC Merkley, Nick (2015) – A small but hard working forward, with unique footwork and skating abilities—every stride exudes competitiveness and creativity. Passing ability is his calling card. Has that 'eyes in the back of his head' quality so many scouts are on the look for. Not stunningly fast, he's great on his edges. His ability to turn on a dime and distribute the puck simultaneously is exhibited with stunning consistency. Using this method, he received a second assist on a nice passing play goal in the first period.

KEL #21 Stephens, Devante (2015) D – A way better than average skater with good forward momentum, but one who is plagued by a few deficiencies that are difficult to overlook. Backwards skating could use a little bit of work, specifically. In the offensive zone, he's far from a pinpoint passer or playmaking machine, but he does a decent job of getting the puck into open ice, where—largely because he plays on such a fantastic club—his teammates can usually reach it and do something with it.

KEL #28 Gatenby, Joe (2015) RD – The story of the game might be that of Joe Gatenby versus Paul Bittner. Normally the deliverer of a good first-pass, a bad giveaway led to a scoring chance by Bittner. Later, he got the better of Bittner by getting into his passing lanes and by poking the puck off of his stick. Finally, late in the game while on the penalty kill, Gatenby chopblocked Bittner—whether or not it was intentional is not exactly clear—effectively taking him off the ice for the rest of the game. Later through a big open-ice hit on Skyler McKenzie. This was a physical outing for Gatenby.

GREEN BAY GAMBLERS vs MADISON CAPITOLS (11-21-14)

GB - #17C – Chris Brown (BUF - 2014) – Had a solid game with 2 assists. Brown worked hard at both ends of the ice. Made simple but good plays with the puck on the power play and did a good job creating space in the offensive zone by drawing defenders to him. Did a good job back checking by picking up the 3rd forward into the zone and eliminating scoring chances. Didn't shy away from contact in what was a very physical game at times. Was strong on the puck at and was able to draw penalties because of it.

GB - #11C – Aaron O'Neill (2015) – Left off the scores sheet but created some scoring chances with his speed, especially around the edges with the puck by making defenders turn and taking the puck to the net.

GB - #20 D – Vili Saarijarvi (2015) – Has a heavy right handed shot from the point, displayed good one timer ability and was able to get shots through traffic and toward the net. Not overly physical when battling opposing forwards in front of his own net.

GB - #10LW – Joe Wegwerth (FLA - 2014) – Big winger at 6'3" who will take the puck to the net and can be difficult to handle with a head of steam. Needs to work on his first couple strides, his foot speed was an issue when trying to get to loose pucks. Has decent hands but needs to use his size better in puck battles, lost too many 50/50 pucks to smaller albeit greasier players. Was used effectively as a screen in front of the net on the power play, and did battle hard for positioning in that area. Had a couple good scoring chances in overtime.

GB - #15RW – Ryan Smith (2015) – Creates his scoring chances by being in the right position and reading the play well, has a good idea where the puck is going to end up. Played a physical, up tempo style and seemed to get under some players skin at times.

GB - #8C – Brent Gates Jr. (2015) – Displayed good vision, can make quick passes through lanes in the offensive zone. Knows where he is likely going next with the puck before it arrives on his tape. Led the team with 7 shots on goal.

MAD - #7RW – Will Johnson (2015) – Has good speed, got in on the fore check quickly and pressured D-man to move the puck quickly. Beat defender to a puck retrieval and fed a quick pass to the slot for a goal by #18 Richter. Had 3 assists on the night including a great feed on the Power play for the game tying goal in the 3rd. was easily Madison's best forward tonight.

MAD - #37 LW – Haralds Egle (2015) – Made strong plays with the puck by taking it to the net hard which drew attention from the opposing defenseman on a number of occasions. Has a powerful skating stride and can get going at a high speed quickly. Used defender as a screen and can get his shot off quickly and followed up his shot looking for a rebound. Scored on a shot from the goal line which caught the goalie off guard and beat him short side over the shoulder?

MAD - #17 RW – Sam McCormick (2015) – Plays a bigger game then what showed on the score sheet (1 Assist) or what shows by his physical stature. Plays with a high hockey IQ, always knows where he needs to be. Used in all situations. Doesn't seem to panic, will take the extra second to make the smart play with the puck which was displayed on his assist where he could have thrown the puck to the net where there was traffic, instead made a great feed to the defenseman jumping into the slot who beat the goalie with a snap shot.

MAD - #14D – Tommy Muck (2015+) – Had a couple turnovers at the blue line which resulted in scoring chances but displayed his smooth skating ability and continues to create offensive chances. Passes D to D well in the defensive zone, uses the boards well if needed. Moves the puck well on the Power play and remains Madison leading point producer from the back end despite not showing up on the score sheet tonight.

Game Notes: A very physical contest, as most rivalry games are. Both teams wanted to play a dump and chase game and be physical on the fore check. In result forced some players to take some penalties. Both teams penalty kill was pretty good. A back and forth game where both teams carried the play for large chucks at a time. Chris Brown (GB) and Will Johnson (MAD) were the most effective players offensively but also made contributions at both ends of the ice. Like most games, both goalies would likely tell you they let a couple in they shouldn't have but both made some great saves late in the game to keep it tied.

Nov. 21, 2014 – Regina Pats at Vancouver Giants

REG #2 LD Zborovskiy, Sergei (2015) – Isn't explosively fast, but with each long-legged step he lunges from point to A to point B in fairly good timing. Showed good puck distribution skills and a willingness to rove down low into the offensive zone. Utilities as a defensemanwere most apparent on the penalty kill. Plays a fairly dirty game but does so subtly and doesn't get penalized as much as he should.

REG #27 LW Wagner, Austin (2015) – Surprisingly explosive, nimble and agile. Turns, pivots and crossover technique are all very good. Especially when reaching top-speed through the neutral zone, he looks like a downright thoroughbred skater in profile. Can handle the puck well while moving at top speed. Scored a goal in the second period in which he gathered the puck off of a faceoff and then took off completely with it, going from west-to-east and south-to-north all by himself. Shows good protection abilities and is particularly formidable on the cycle.

REG #29 LC Hunt, Dryden (2014) – Scoring two goals tonight, it would be difficult to overlook Dryden Hunt's contribution. Plays an intelligent and hard working game. Appears to have good shoulder strength, as he is able to easily control the puck and shake off checks simultaneously. A frustrating player to contain when defending against the cycle. His attacking zone time was extraordinarily high tonight.

REG #39 LC Steel, Sam (2016) – Foot movement and agility are both well above-average and I expect his straightahead acceleration to improve immensely with increased leg strength and muscle development. Does a decent job of gaining proper body position in board battles and is good at smothering guys off of the puck. Can relax on the perimeter at times, as he is still able to make plays and be dangerous from there, as well. A fantastic passer.

VAN #17 LC Benson, Tyler (2016) – Scored a goal when he crashed the net and closed in quickly on a rebound just outside the crease with a blink-of-an-eye wristshot. Aside from his penchant for execution in close, backchecking speed, full-stride acceleration and agility remain his best qualities, as he is already a stand-out as one of his team's best penalty killers. On the penalty kill he does everything—he rushes the point, makes good reads, gets shorthanded chances, blocks shots, absorbs hits, and makes great clearances.

VAN #32 RW Bobylev, Vladimir (2015) – An easy player to notice on the ice because of his size. Continues to bring energy to his shifts by playing a robust and physical game and by consistently crashing the crease. His backcheck lacks effort at times, but he appears to have added shot blocking abilities to his array of skills as he does a good job of getting his big frame into shooting legs and using his thick legs as blocking apparatuses.

Peterborough Petes at Barrie Colts, Nov 22, 2014

Score: 4-3 Petes

Peterborough

LW Josh Coyle (2015) – Coyle played limited minutes in this one. He was effective on the forecheck at times and finished his checks when he could, but didn't make much of an impact. He showed good power in his shot on a couple occasions, but missed the net both times.

D Matt Spencer (2015) – Spencer didn't get on the scoresheet, but he played a real good two-way game. He used his speed to close gaps quickly, and was positionally sound throughout. Spencer consistently won races for loose pucks, and drew a penalty in the 1st period while doing so. He had a good stick in the defensive zone, and was able to break up a few attempted passes because of it. Spencer made a good first pass, and made easy outlets regularly. He did a good job of keeping everything to the outside, and sealing off oncoming forwards. Spencer was confident carrying the puck up ice, and jumped deep into the offensive zone a couple times to keep plays alive. While Spencer was very good, he did take a tripping penalty that led to a Colts goal and allowed them back in the game. Spencer didn't shy away from using his body, and at one point stirred it up pretty good while standing right beside five Colts when they were huddling up to discuss their powerplay plan.

D Cam Lizotte (2015) – Lizotte played a simple game but was effective doing so. He was very physical and finished off his guy whenever he could. He cleared the net effectively on the penalty kill, got pucks out and was always on his man. Lizotte had a few big hits in this game, and played the same rugged stile for 60 minutes.

D Artem Vladimirov (2015) – Vladimirov had a real good stick in the defensive zone, and broke up countless pass attempts and odd-man rushes throughout the game. He certainly wasn't afraid to be physical, and laid the body whenever he could; especially on Brendan Lemieux. For the most part his passes were accurate, but he did miss a couple outlets he probably shouldn't have.

Barrie

RW Roy Radke (2015) – Radke had a very quiet first 40, but got going in the 3rd. He had some good shifts cycling down low and sustaining pressure in the offensive zone. Besides a couple hits he was hard to notice early on.

RW Matthew Kreis (2015) – Kreis did a nice job eluding checks and creating in the offensive zone. He used his speed to gain a step on opposing defenders, but if there was not a clear lane to the net he'd go wide and behind the net which at times defused the play and ended it altogether. He had a couple good chances in tight, but couldn't finish a play off. Kreis was very aggressive on the forecheck, and didn't allow any easy breakouts or outlets, which led to some turnovers.

D Rasmus Andersson (2015) – Andersson was not at all intimidated by Nick Ritchie in their head-to-head battle. They traded hits, slashes, etc. throughout the game and it was a battle that lasted a full 60. Andersson was very physical in front of his net and in the corners. He pushed opposing players off the puck regularly, and was able to consistently make good outlets to push the play up ice. Andersson made great passes through the neutral zone and nearly every pass was on the tape. He pinched into the offensive zone several times to keep the play alive, and did a nice job of holding the line in Peterborough's end. He was able to get pucks on net, and showed great vision finding creative ways to get open teammates the puck with regularity. In the defensive zone, Andersson defended the cycle well and did a nice job of not losing his man in traffic.

G Mackenzie Blackwood (2015) – Blackwood wasn't at his best in this one, but after the Petes went up 4-1 he locked it down and gave the Colts a chance to come back. He tracked pucks well, and was effective in taking away the bottom of the net. Though his numbers weren't great, a couple goals were scored on the powerplay and another one he had a defensemen as well as Nick Ritchie completely blocking his lane, so there's not much he could have done. Blackwood was confident playing the puck when given the opportunity. He wasn't afraid to mix it up, either, as he joined a scrum in front of the net after the whistle, and gave Nick Ritchie a pretty good shot on another occasion.

November 23, 2014 - Saginaw Spirit at Sarnia Sting

SAG #3 RD Stewart, Chase (2015) - Showed a good stick on multiple one on one plays against both small skilled and bigger stronger forwards. Very tough and competitive in the slot. Landed a big hit on a bigger opponent, but later penalized for sticking the knee out on a hit.

SAG #13 LW Webb, Mitchell (2015) - Finished every check hard landing nearly 10 in this game. Doesn't like being hit and will retaliate even at risk of a penalty,

SAG #14 RW Paliani, Devon (2015) - Excellent work ethic, high compete level and finished checks hard. Didn't force passes in the offensive zone and remained patient with the puck.

SAG #27 RC Stephens, Mitchell (2015) - Used his speed to drive the net and his body to protect the puck effectively when going to the net if he gets a step on the defender. Got some penalty kill ice but wanders out of position. He struggled to create much offensively tonight. Played the last shift of the game down a goal.

SAG #55 LD Middleton, Keaton (2015) - Able to use size against smaller forwards, but got knocked off balance far too easily and struggled to contain opponents down low.

SAG #62 LC Felhaber, Tye (2016) - Tye has very good speed and uses it effectively. On one play he got hit hard, he showed some pushback then was able to fly down the ice to get in position to finish a cross ice pass for Saginaw's second goal of the game.

SAG #39 G Ovsjannikov, David (2015) - Much better at playing the puck than previous viewings, moving it well and clearing it away from trouble. Struggled going side to side getting beat twice. He also struggled catching shots glove side.

SAR #3 LD Black, Alex (2015) - Black has decent strength and an effective checker but doesn't check his man well in the slot. Will chase play out of position. Beat one on one.

SAR #11 RW Hodgson, Hayden (2015*) - Will block shots and finishes checks hard. Tries to embellish but is not very good at it

SAR #25 RC Kyrou, Jordan (2016) - Scored Sarnia's second goal of the game with good positioning then quick reception of the puck then quick release for goal. Flashed speed and puck skills on a few rushes while on powerplay.

SAR #35 RW Korostelev, Nikita (2015) - Made a great inside out move then excellent pass to set up Sarnia's second goal of the game. He used his size well on a few occasions protecting the puck and playing physical. Good, hard one-timer to score third goal for Sarnia.

Nov. 25, 2014 – Prince Albert Raiders at Edmonton Oil Kings

PRI #4 Brendan Guhle (2015) LD – He's big, he skates well, and he has good awareness in all three zones. While he's big and tall he appears to lack muscle-mass on his lanky frame, as he's easily stood-up on zone-entry attempts and is too easily knocked off the puck or off balance. In the offensive zone, Guhle does a really good job finding open space and widening passing lanes for good opportunities. I like his decision making with the puck, as he has a good habit of keeping things simple. His first passes are generally unremarkable, but he throws very few turnovers. This is a player who knows his own limitations. When trying to make long bomb passes, he is usually unsuccessful. While navigating the blueline, he blasts strong slapshots from the point and accurate wristshots from down low, but always has plenty of passing options, as he is a very good puck distributor from beyond the blueline. His wristshot technique is particularly clever, as he doesn't put hard shots on net, but finds places to shoot that create second-chance scoring opportunities for his teammates.

PRI #19 Reid Gardiner (2014) RW – Gardiner is a very good skater with strong first-steps who does a good job of staying firmly in his lane, thereby maximizing his speed and limiting his distances from scoring opportunities. Gardiner plays an honest 200-foot two-way game. Gardiner finishes his checks, blocks shots, fights hard in board battles, provides screens in the offensive zone, and plays on the penalty kill and the power play. He absolutely loves dump and chase, chip and chase, and all other north-south plays that allow him to shoot the puck into the offensive zone, speed past or through defenders, and win the race on his own dump.

PRI #21 Matteo Gennaro (2015) LC – Gennaro's a bit of a one-way player, whose backchecking speed leaves much to be desired—even when forechecking, Gennaro doesn't accelerate to top-speed very quickly. He is a bit slow-footed, but he is a conjurer with the puck on his stick, is generally very well positioned, and has tremendous range. There is a mentalist element to Gennaro's skating, as his turns are wide and slow, but he nonetheless has a penchant for always turning in the right direction. Indeed, Gennaro doesn't have to do a whole lot to create turnovers, as the puck often just magically ends up on his long stick. When the puck is firmly on the blade of his stick, he continues to show off tremendous sleight of hand abilities. He puts really good deception on an accurate wrist shot, as he can pick his shots low or high, and employs a number of tricky release points. Tonight he showed some good skills but didn't score or create many chances for his teammates.

EDM #21 Tyler Robertson (2015) LW – Tyler Robertson took a tough spill to the ice and returned to the bench limping; he came back to the ice for the second period and showed good toughness and durability by playing a serviceable if unspectacular game for the Oil Kings. Robertson is a good neutral zone player who does a good job of converging on players with the puck and causing turnovers. Furthermore, he's a better than average skater and good passer who excels at wheeling around the ice with the puck on his stick, and is therefore capable of transitioning the puck up ice very, very quickly. I would've liked to have seen greater backchecking speed and attention to detail when it came to Robertson's defensive game tonight, but it would be difficult to criticize a player for skating and hustle issues when he's returning to a game after being injured. He received lots of minutes despite being hurt, which shows how important he has become to this Oil Kings club.

Nov. 26, 2014 – Prince Albert Raiders at Calgary Hitmen

PRI #4 LD Guhle, Brendan (2015) – Loves to rove down low, as his passing and shooting skills are well above average and his skating is also a strength. Passes tend to be easily receivable, and he has a high accuracy rating on his shots. Pokechecking ability is better than average, as he was able to disrupt several zone entry attempts in this game. Most impressively, he blocked a shot at the end of the game by diving head-first into it.

PRI #19 RW Gardiner, Reid (2014) – Scored a goal early in this one. Once in the lead, Gardiner's positioning and demeanour changed completely, as he suddenly transformed into a mature and conscientious defensive forward who played his check very closely and disrupted several scoring opportunities for the opposition.

PRI #21 LC Gennaro, Matteo (2015) – Played in a depth role and saw limited even strength ice-time. Naturally big and strong with a long wingspan. He was defeated by a couple of defensemen on poor deke attempts and even poorer zone-entry attempts. Good on the cycle as he showed during a brief cup of coffee on the power play this evening. Wristshot and backhand both look decent. He saw some time on the power play, where he looked like a good passer. Was a defensive liability at times.

CAL #9 LC Karnaukhov, Pavel (2015) – A deep knee bend and wide skating stance make him appear much smaller than he is, making him an unrecognizable threat when he's finishing his checks. Does a good job of fighting for body position and dislodging opposition players from the puck. He takes faceoffs and won the majority of his draws in this one. To my surprise, he was trusted a lot in important situations tonight, including being double-shifted at the end of the third period.

CAL #2 LD Bean, Jake (2016) – An above-average skater for his age, who looks a bit awkward at full-speed acceleration but generally moves well in all directions. As a sixteen-year-old, he already plays regular minutes on the penalty kill and quarterbacks the second power play unit. Appears to have great offensive awareness and distribution instincts. Looked a bit vulnerable at times in his own end at times and lost a few key battles in the corners.

CAL #4 LD Zipp, Michael (2015) – An alright skater who navigates his own end smartly and with limited wasted motion. His work along the walls and in the corners is very good, as he won the majority of his board battles tonight. Does a good job of working the puck to centre ice with a serviceable first pass. He's a stalwart on the penalty kill, where he makes reads the play well, responsibly block shots, throws big body checks, and makes important clearances.

CAL #32 LD Sanheim, Travis (Philadelphia 2014) – Skating ability in all areas is miles ahead of anyone else on the ice, allowing him to play keepaway with the puck and to rove down low into the offensive zone with complete impunity. When travelling with the puck below the hashmarks, he becomes even more dangerous thanks to a tremendously accurate wristshot, which he used tonight to score Calgary's only goal. Stickhandling skills at top speed are phenomenal. Stamina also appears very good, as he plays a ton of minutes and looks completely energized from whistle to whistle.

November 28, 2014 - Erie Otters at London Knights

ERI #19 LC Strome, Dylan (2015) - Skating still a bit choppy but it has progressed over time. Phantom assist on the Otters' first goal. Good forecheck pressure and strong on the backcheck. Shot is slightly above average despite being a bit of a pass first type of forward. He was slightly below 50% in the face-off circle.

ERI #44 RD Dermott, Travis (2015) - Dermott was pretty consistent with his puck decisions making good passes up ice. He uses his skating to open options up most of the time when there are none. Good power play ice displaying a hard point shot but did get caught behind the play on one power play which resulted in a short handed chance for the opposition. He plays a tough chippy game and takes an extra shot when he can to try and get under the skin of opposition but generally chooses smaller or younger opponents and avoids bigger, tougher or high skilled players with the extra curricular stuff.

LON #14 LD Crawley, Brandon (2015) - Good point shot, made great rush using good speed to beat forward and drive the net for a chance.

LON #86 LD Martenet, Chris (2015) - Martenet's puck movement has shown a little improvement, particularly on one play where he made a good move to protect the puck past a defender then made a smart accurate pass up ice. However he is still getting caught making no look passes for turnovers and choosing the wrong lane at times. Will benefit from making the more simple option. Good move to protect puck up and out of the zone with a good pass. This also applies to the rush as he made a good rush on one particular play, but instead of making the safe option he tried to beat three Otters to turn the puck over. His skating is OK for his size but will need a fair amount of progression before making a professional jump.

LON #98 LD Mete, Victor (2016) - Good puck rush early to calmly navigate the neutral zone. He uses his skating and vision to effectively rush the puck into the offensive zone several times throughout the game and is very tough to contain with the puck on his stick due to excellent quickness.

LON #23 RC Rymsha, Drake (2016) - Made some good passes in his own zone early on and went hard to the net to score London's second goal.

LON #93 RW Marner, Mitchell (2015) - Marner made a key defensive play early on to check an opponents stick in the slot to prevent a scoring chance for Erie. Unfortunately the puck went off his skate and in for Erie's first goal later on in the period. He was overpowered in the slot on the power play to negate what would have been a great scoring chance. Marner played on the top power play unit and was on the second penalty kill unit as the Knights' are giving Marner more defensive responsibility, where he is showing clear improvements on his side of the red line.

Final Score: Erie Otters: 3 - London Knights: 2 - OT/SO

Blainville-Brosbriand Armada at Saint John Sea Dogs, November 28, 2014

BLB #33 G Montembeault, Samuel (2015): Montembeault is a solid goaltender that put forward a good performance in this game. Standing at 6'3" Sam uses this size and makes himself look big in the net. He moves very little, stays quiet in his crease making big saves look simple. He does a good job soaking up rebounds preventing second chances. Sam also helps his team out by making good moves handling the puck. The one goal allowed in this game came off a great shot from the wall on the power play when the winger was allowed to walk in close and shoot. In the shootout it took 6 rounds for Saint John to score.

SNB #38 LD Zboril, Jakub (2015): Jakub Zboril is very involved in Saint John's play both offensively and defensively. Jakub uses his size in puck battles to win and find success defensively. Jakub uses his solid skating ability to play a tight gap pressuring his opponents on the rush and in D zone play. Jakub usually makes a solid play under pressure controlling the puck patiently and moving it safely but effectively to his team mates. Zboril plays with a physical edge but has been called numerous times forcing his team to kill his penalties.

SNB #5 LD Chabot, Thomas (2015): Thomas Chabot is another very involved dangerous defenseman on Saint John's second D pairing. Chabot is not as physically involved as he could be, but he uses his skill and speed to beat opponents. Chabot makes good decisions on his team's pressure breakouts and works hard to get the puck out of his D zone. Chabot likes to jump up in on his teams offensive rushes but works hard to get back defensively. There were a couple times he rushed the puck himself and over handled the puck leading to turnovers.

SNB #10 C Noel, Nathan (2015): Nathan Noel is a great offensive threat for Saint John. Noel's speed creates a lot of offense for Saint John. Noel is a very fast skater with a smooth quick stride. Noel also show defensive responsibility, working hard and finding his man on the back check shutting down opponents puck movement on the rush. As mentioned Noel has great speed, that he could use more to beat opponents while doing less with his hands handling the puck. Noel is out to take most of Saint John's big face offs.

SNB #12 LW Marsh, Adam (2015): Adam Marsh is good well-rounded player for Saint John in both ends. Marsh took a bad penalty in the first that lead to Blainville-Brosbriand's first goal. Marsh had lots of scoring chances in this game, and he made good when it counted most scoring on the power play late third to tie the game. Marsh is a player who gets a lot of ice time for Saint John with their top players.

SNB #16 C Dove-McFalls, Samuel (2015). Samuel Dove-McFalls is Saint John's first line center, playing on both the power play and penalty kill. Dove-McFalls centers two of Saint John's overage forwards. They create an effective two way line.

Ferris State vs U. of Wisconsin (11-29-2014)

FSU - #6 C - Kyle Schempp (NYI-2014) – What has been a knock on Schempp (defensive play) didn't look that way tonight. Played a solid two way game, had a very active stick, disrupted passing lanes both on the penalty kill and on the back check. Schempp didn't create a lot in the offensive zone tonight but made up for it with his 200 foot game.

FSU - #9RW- Chad McDonald (FA) – Was Ferris State's most effective forward in the offensive zone. Has a quick release which was on display on his goal from the left hash marks that beat Rumple on the glove side. Battled for pucks hard and was physical when he needed to be.

FSU - #30 G- C.J. Motte (FA) – Wasn't his best performance but a couple of the goals that he let in were great scoring opportunities by some top notch players. Like most nights Motte battled throughout the night, made some nice saves. He is able to know when his team is chasing the puck and makes a save and holds on for a whistle. Is very quick in getting back into position if he gets swimming in his crease, which did happen from time to time.

UW - #7D- Keegan Ford (2015) – Not a big defenseman at only 5'8" but forwards should always be aware where he is on the ice. Plays a Physical style, stepped up on a couple forwards at the blueline with punishing body checks. Won his puck battles by simply being more physical than the other player.

UW - #19C – Cameron Hughes (2015) - Has a quick first few strides. Good skating ability with the puck. His effectiveness did not translate to the score sheet but was one of Wisconsin's best forwards all night. Won a lot of his one on one battles and did a good job buying time when outnumbered until support arrived.

UW - #12 RW – Grant Besse (ANA. 2014) – Played a gritty but yet skilled game tonight. Showed off his NHL caliber shot by scoring from the top of the circle on a rocket wrist shot to beat Motte over the glove. Won puck battles and created scoring chances when he was physical along the boards. When he got speed through the neutral zone he was difficult for the Ferris State Defenders to handle.

UW - #33G – Joel Rumpel (FA-SJ) – Made 3 point blank saves in the second period to keep the game tied. Showed great flexibility by getting the pad over to the post to make the saves. Quick glove hand and was quick to cover loose pucks in the crease. Another solid performance from Rumpel.

UW - #4D – Jack Dougherty (NSH-2014) – Scored the eventual game winner on the power play in the 3rd period with a slap shot from the high slot. Played physical and is hard to get off the puck. Takes good angles on puck retrievals and moves the puck out of his own end quickly. Doesn't join the rush a lot, most of that duty is done by his partner #28 Kevin Schulze but is effective with the puck. Showed decent gap control on the few occasions where Ferris State would enter to the zone on the rush, takes away time and space well.

UW - #37D- Kevin Schulze (FA) – Created a few chances by joining the rush and picks his spots well. Good vision and showed ability to make a stretch pass when it's there. Made quick plays with the puck on the power play. Did a good job moving with the puck and opening up shooting lanes from the point. Schulze is progressing into a solid puck moving defenseman for Wisconsin.

Game Notes: When you look at Ferris State's roster you don't see a lot of high end skill. Most of their forwards play a similar style of game and they all play within their team structure. Very few line rushes into the offensive zone and rarely do the defenders join the rush. But it's very effective, they dump the puck and they grind on your Defenseman and try to wear you down and frustrate you into turnovers. Wisconsin was able to counter that by having good puck retrievals by their defenseman with good puck support and getting the puck out of the zone quickly. It was a very back and forth game with each team holding pressure on the other for stretches before a boarding penalty in the 3rd period put Wisconsin on the power play where Jack Dougherty (NSH-2014) was able to bury the eventual game winner for Wisconsin.

Charlottetown Islanders vs Moncton Wildcats, November 30th 2014

CHA #14 C Chlapik, Filip (2015): Filip Chlapik complements the Islanders by giving them a good offensive threat on their second line. Chlapik has decent size and competes hard for pucks. Chlapik wins puck battles on walls and usually is in good position when not having to compete. Chlapik sees lots of ice time especially on special teams.

CHA #11 RW Sprong, Daniel (2015): Daniel Sprong is the Islanders most offensive player. Sprong has great speed and puck handling skills. Sprong pushes the pace of the game when he is on the ice because of his quick feet controlling the puck and perusing. Sprong also has great puck moving skills because of his great vision and hockey sense. Sprong sometimes over controls the puck taking himself away from the easy play into a difficult one on a couple of occasions.

CHA #27 LD Henley, David (2015): David Henley is a big defenseman that soaks up a lot of the Islanders ice time. Henley is a safe bet as he is patient and positionally strong. Henley is not usually involved in the Islanders rush play or offense. Henley is a great penalty killer because of his long stick. Henley's size helps him in all puck battle situations.

CHA #19 C Goulet, Alexandre (2015). Alexandre Goulet is another good all round threat for the Islanders on the second line. Goulet is a player that sees a lot of ice time. He is hard on pucks for checking and defensively sound. Goulet has a short but very quick stride possibly limiting his speed.

CHA #10 C Kielly, Kameron (2015): Kameron Kielly is the Islanders first line center and a very involved players. Kielly is on the Islanders first power play and penalty kill units. Kielly is positionally strong and he support his team mates well all over the ice. Kielly does a good job with Sprong's speed feeding him the puck and finding ways to get open and dangerous himself. Kielly works hard in face-offs and battles to win draws.

MON #19 C/RW Askew, Cameron (2015): Cameron Askew is a big first line forward for Moncton. Askew is positionally strong and finds himself in the right position usually. Askew has a good quick shot and creates numerous scoring chances with his skilled play. Askew has a pretty good stride for a bigger forward. He also fought the Islanders biggest player in the 3rd period showing a lot of toughness standing up for his team-mates.

MON #8 RW Garland, Conor (2015). Conor Garland is Moncton's greatest offensive threat. Garland leads Wildcat scoring by a lot and it shows with his play. Garland is very under sized but finds himself able to spin off checks and battles. Garland is a very good puck handler with elusive moves and takes good shots creating Moncton scoring chances.

Nov. 31, 2014 – Swift Current Broncos at Red Deer Rebels

SWI #15 LW Gawdin, Glenn (2015) – A very fast 200-foot player with excellent all-zones awareness, good backchecking speed and sharp playmaking instincts. Continues to show exceptional awareness and anticipation. Despite being slightly slower than usual in his turning and pivots, he transitions easily and quickly from one end of the ice to the other. Shooting remains a work in progress, as he needs to do a better job of identifying open shooting lanes.

SWI #19 LW DeBrusk, Jake (2015) – A bit slower than usual without the puck, he's nonetheless exceptionally fast when handling the puck, as having the puck on his stick does not hinder his footspeed in the least. That ability to handle the puck at surprising speeds makes for many easy and uncontested zone entries. His unique knack for handling the puck on his backhand remains strong. Played keep-away with the puck several times tonight. Also got several nice deflections on the net, as his hand-eye coordination is elite.

SWI #27 LD Lajoie, Max (2016) – A good straight-ahead skater with fairly average agility. While playing on the power play, he wasn't able to make up for a Brett Lernout's turnover and got caught a step behind on a second period goal-against. Otherwise, decision making appears strong. First passes are safe and conservative but generally mistake free. Shooting ability and vision from the point is very good, as he managed to get one of his wristshots into the net by way of a Jake DeBrusk deflection.

SWI #31 G Child, Travis (2015) – It wasn't a good start for 2015-eligible goaltender Travis Child, who let in the first shot he faced after a Conner Bleakley wrister ripped the mesh. He mishandled the puck a couple of times too to make for a fairly poor first period showing. A second period five-hole goal-against on an unscreened slapshot from Austin Strand spelled the end of his night early in this one.

RED #2 RD Strand, Austin (2015) – His footwork is very quick, his hand-eye coordination is extremely strong, and his agility is shockingly good for a player of his size, as his lower-body motions with and without the puck look very fluid in all directions. His feet shuffle properly in a poetry of motion during the directional transfer from forwards to backwards or vice-versa. Superior weight transfer technique gives Strand a very good shot, as well.

RED #7 RD Grman, Mario (2015) – Grman does a good job of identifying worthwhile board battles to engage in and was able to step up in the neutral zone without taking himself too far out of position. I didn't always agree with his decision making, but when in trouble Grman did a good job of calmly getting himself out of danger. He had the fight of the night and perhaps one of the fights of the year with WHL veteran Colby Cave during a third period all-out brawl.

RED #16 LW Pawlenchuk, Grayson (2015) – Turns are a bit slow, but his straightahead speed is very good and his top speed is very high. Creates a lot of turnovers through good hockey sense, hard work and an active stick. Passing and playmaking vision were both noteworthy, as he set up teammate Austin Strand with a nifty cross-ice pass on a second period goal from the blueline. Appearing brave and determined can be relied upon for getting into dirty areas and for providing screens in front of the opposition goaltender and likewise for blocking shots on the penalty kill.

RED #25 RC Musil, Adam (2015) – Through the first half of the game, Adam Musil put in a disappointing performance in which he saw limited ice-time at even-strength. Speciality appears to be above-average strength in the faceoff circle and along the boards. His footspeed appears a bit slow and his forecheck lacks effort at times. A few unforced turnovers also marred his night.

Mississauga Steelheads at Barrie Colts, Dec 4, 2014

Score: 5-3 Barrie

Mississauga

C Michael McLeod (2016) – McLeod's high-end puck skills were on full display as he showed good hands and creativity with the puck generating chances on a consistent basis. He used his quick first steps to generate speed quickly and was very good skating the puck through the neutral zone. He was relentless going after loose pucks, and was effective on the backcheck throughout. McLeod also did a nice job of eluding defenders in space and was a threat on the rush.

RW Nathan Bastian (2016) – Bastian played a very good two-way game. He showed good chemistry offensively with McLeod, and did a good job of taking care of his own zone. He always picked up his defensive assignments, and took a regular shift on the penalty kill. Bastian was effective along the wall, finished his checks and didn't shy away from going to the dirty areas. He also made some skill plays with the puck and drew a penalty coming off the wall in the offensive zone.

Barrie

RW Roy Radke (2015) - Radke took a bad penalty early when the Colts were already shorthanded, but made up for it with good PK work throughout. He also drew a penalty on a net drive, and generated several chances around the paint. Overall he played a good game but he struggled to go wide as he couldn't get a step on opposing defenders and it led to several dead rushes.

D Rasmus Andersson (2015) – Andersson continues to be a horse on the backend for Barrie. He did a great job of sealing guys off all night long, and muscled opposing players off the puck on numerous occasions. He made a good first pass consistently and moved the puck around well on the powerplay. Andersson also did a good job of getting pucks on net, and several attempts caused big rebounds around the crease. His positioning was good defensively, and Andersson broke up a couple plays with a good stick, too. He's not pinching as much as he used to and did a better job of picking his spots, which makes him a more reliable 200-foot player.

G Mackenzie Blackwood (2015) – Blackwood wasn't tested a ton, especially early, but he had a pretty good showing. For the most part he did a good job of controlling his rebounds, and didn't give out many 2nd chance opportunities. At times he was more focused on the guy standing in front of him than the puck.

Scouts notes: 2015 eligible Matthew Kreis and 2016 eligible Sean Day were not in the lineup.

Mississauga Steelheads at Barrie Colts, Dec 4, 2014

Score: 5-3 Barrie

Mississauga

C Michael McLeod (2016) – McLeod's high-end puck skills were on full display as he showed good hands and creativity with the puck generating chances on a consistent basis. He used his quick first steps to generate speed quickly and was very good skating the puck through the neutral zone. He was relentless going after loose pucks, and was effective on the backcheck throughout. McLeod also did a nice job of eluding defenders in space and was a threat on the rush.

RW Nathan Bastian (2016) – Bastian played a very good two-way game. He showed good chemistry offensively with McLeod, and did a good job of taking care of his own zone. He always picked up his defensive assignments, and took a regular shift on the penalty kill. Bastian was effective along the wall, finished his checks and didn't shy away from going to the dirty areas. He also made some skill plays with the puck and drew a penalty coming off the wall in the offensive zone.

Barrie

RW Roy Radke (2015) - Radke took a bad penalty early when the Colts were already shorthanded, but made up for it with good PK work throughout. He also drew a penalty on a net drive, and generated several chances around the paint. Overall he played a good game but he struggled to go wide as he couldn't get a step on opposing defenders and it led to several dead rushes.

D Rasmus Andersson (2015) – Andersson continues to be a horse on the backend for Barrie. He did a great job of sealing guys off all night long, and muscled opposing players off the puck on numerous occasions. He made a good first pass consistently and moved the puck around well on the powerplay. Andersson also did a good job of getting pucks on net, and several attempts caused big rebounds around the crease. His positioning was good defensively, and Andersson broke up a couple plays with a good stick, too. He's not pinching as much as he used to and did a better job of picking his spots, which makes him a more reliable 200-foot player.

G Mackenzie Blackwood (2015) – Blackwood wasn't tested a ton, especially early, but he had a pretty good showing. For the most part he did a good job of controlling his rebounds, and didn't give out many 2nd chance opportunities. At times he was more focused on the guy standing in front of him than the puck.

Scouts notes: 2015 eligible Matthew Kreis and 2016 eligible Sean Day were not in the lineup.

Dec. 5, 2014 – Portland Winterhawks at Vancouver Giants

POR #44 Keoni Texeira (2015) LD – Keoni Texeira had a great game on the back end tonight even though he didn't contribute too much offensively. It's difficult to get a good read on his skating, as he is highly conservative in his motions and prefers to support rather than lead the rush. He can jump into the play if necessary—as he did tonight in a great 2-on-1 one-timer opportunity during a four on four situation—but does so fairly uncommonly. Going backwards, he doesn't necessarily win foot races with his speed, but he does a fantastic job of keeping pace and is very good at limiting breakout chances with an active stick, fantastic defensive awareness, and good discipline. He negated several 2-on-1 breakouts for the opposition tonight by hustling to make a pokecheck or to wipe out a passing lane. He is a bit undersized and bounces a bit off of the boards when absorbing bodychecks—easily dislodging him from the puck. He is a capable stickhandler, has a great pokecheck, and thinks the game at a very high level during tricky situations.

POR #7 Paul Bittner (2015) – Paul Bittner had a bit of a roller coaster game tonight. For his size and height, his agility and turns are actually very good and he has a surprising amount of spring in his step. Bittner cheats a lot in terms of his positioning. On the power play he can be seen comically wandering way, way beyond the opposition blueline and then emerging back onside suddenly during an attempted zone entry, making the slightest contact with the defender, and creating a lane for the puck carrier. During one such play, he was given an interference penalty for his efforts. Once in the offensive zone, he tends to hang out right in front of the opposition goaltender at the top of the crease, being ready for rebound chances and providing screens. He's very good at absorbing punishment here and is an agitating presence. Because of his positioning on the ice, he gets a ton of scoring chances. While he was in good position to get his chances, tonight he had terrible puck luck and couldn't execute on a number of great chances near the net, hitting the crossbar twice.

VAN #11 Jakob Stukel (2015) RW –Very fast in transition, Stukel is an excellent F-1 forechecker as he presses opposition defensemanhard with speed, agility, and active stickwork. He has a nice wide skating stance, changes direction on a dime and has good range of mobility. A fantastic passer with tremendous vision and creatively, he stands out as a pass-first playmaker rather than a finisher, as his shot lacks top-end power and he tends to place his shots directly at the goalie.

VAN #22 Dmitry Osipov (2015) LD – Dmitry Osipov did a tremendous job on his assignment of checking Paul Bittner tonight. As with Bittner this evening, he's generally able to box the opposition out very wide because of his superior mobility and strength. His size, reach, and work along the walls make him a very difficult defensemanto get the puck around in the offensive zone. He didn't play on the power play but he did appear regularly on the penalty kill. Playing on the top defensive pairing with Mason Geertsen but less minutes overall, he looked far more comfortable than he has in the past, and didn't appear to be thrust into a situation he wasn't ready for. He's beginning to shoot the puck more, and it paid dividends tonight, setting up the first goal of the game with a rebound out front.

VAN #26 Ryely McKinstry (2016) LD – Ryely McKinstry continues to be one of Vancouver's most dependable defenceman, playing on the team's second pairing alongside Arvin Atwal. He's playing the puck with a ton of confidence right now, making head-fakes and opening up passing lanes like an experienced overager. His slapshots and wristshots from the point are strong and accurate, and he does a really tremendous job of being patient and waiting for shooting lanes to open.

Dec. 6, 2015 – Saskatoon Blades at Vancouver Giants

SAS #8 Nikita Soshnin (2015) LW – I thought Nikita Soshnin played well and had an impact on the game tonight. He scored only his third goal of the year off of a faceoff chance and rebound off of Payton Lee. His wristshot and aggressiveness looked good as he was able to get the puck off with a very quick release after pouncing on it quickly. He's really small but he does a good job of using his lack of size to his advantage, by ducking under checks and using his agility to weave into opportune areas. This skill presented itself repeatedly when Soshnin would sneak underneath two tied up players on the faceoff to steal away the puck.

SAS #9 Cameron Hebig (2015) LC – Cameron Hebig had a physical game tonight in which I really liked his compete-level and defensive play. In his own zone, he did a fantastic job of keeping tight gaps with his checks, rushing the puck carrier, and creating turnovers. He's a really good body-checker, too. Because he holds all the requisite defensive skills, he is something of a utility player for Saskatoon in that he logs a ton of minutes on the penalty kill, where he does a really good job of blocking passes and sacrificing his body to block shots. In the offensive end it was a fairly quiet night on the whole but he made some nice passes into the slot to create opportunities for his teammates.

SAS #35 Nik Amundrud (2016) G – Nik Amundrud, really frustrated the Giants faithful tonight by keeping their favourite team off of the score clock until midway through the third period. While Amundrud is typically an aggressive and acrobatic goaltender known for crazy and unconventional saves—and there were certainly a few of those tonight—he actually looked very relaxed, well positioned, and technically sound in this one for the most part. Despite being reasonably tall, this is a goalie that untypically tracks the puck down low rather than up high, He has incredible second-save ability as he seems to always keep an eye on the puck no matter how awkwardly his body is positioned after the initial save.

VAN #8 Alec Baer (2015) LW – I really like Baer's skating game, even as he continues to add muscle and weight to his frame. At times he fights hard for the puck and takes it fearlessly to the net, at others he looks like a perimeter player who tries to rely on his superior shooting skills alone.

VAN #11 Jakob Stukel (2015) LW – Getting faster and looking more comfortable with the puck since returning from an injury, I continue to really like Jakob Stukel's game as a key playmaker for the Giants. He looked great and especially creative tonight playing alongside centre Thomas Foster. He fed numerous centring feeds to Foster throughout the game, many of which fooled the Saskatoon defence. Definitely more of a passer than a shooter, Stukel's speed and vision are a good compliment to straight-ahead players like Foster.

VAN #17 Tyler Benson (2016) LW – It's not uncommon for Benson to make 3 or 4 great plays on a thirty second shift as he has the foot speed to be all over the ice in short order. While he certainly hasn't disappointed too many folks in the offensive department, I think the biggest improvement Benson has made to his game this year has been to his hitting. Put bluntly, Tyler Benson is as physical a 16-year-old forward you'll probably ever see at this level.

VAN #22 Dmitry Osipov (2015) LD – While he's not much of a puck-rusher, his short-area skating and stickchecking abilities continue to improve with increased responsibility and ice-time under new coach Claude Noel. His offensive remains limited but I like his consistency level. He doesn't stretch the play too far with his passing, but he can be relied upon for a dependable outlet out of his zone.

December 7, 2014 - North Bay Battalion at London Knights

NBY #8 RD Bruce, Riley (2015) - Bruce played a solid stay at home game for the Battalion tonight. Good plays down low to get into passing lanes. Uses his size and strength in the slot to clear traffic. Calm and composed positionally. Huge open ice hit but generally wasn't a punishing defender. Played second unit penalty kill.

NBY #12 LC McKenzie, Brett (2015) - Physical off the start and consistently finished his checks throughout the game. Didn't show much offensively in this game but plays the defensive forward role well. Can chase the puck instead of establishing position.

NBY #16 LW Sherman, David (2016) - Sherman made an impact with a strong forecheck and an excellent work ethic. He battled hard, just needs to get stronger. He was relentless every time he stepped on the ice and was able to create several turnovers.

LON #86 D Martenet, Chris (2015) - Martenet was effective in using his long reach to make things more difficult for forwards trying to get past him. He made some good first passes in this game but also unnecessarily iced the puck. Can stand around a bit in the defensive zone.

LON #93 RW Marner, Mitchell (2015) - Marner was outstanding tonight moving the puck. He displayed his exceptional vision and puck skills to make difficult passes look easy. He made an excellent pass to set up London's first goal. He also fired a deflected pass for a one-timer goal, London's second. Marner also played on the penalty kill doing a decent job in his own zone. At one point he stole the puck and made a great move to turn it into a scoring chance. Marner's lack of strength was evident on the backcheck.

LON #98 D Mete, Victor (2016) - Not forcing the rush, making smart passes off early when necessary.

Final Score: London Knights: 5 - North Bay Battalion: 4 - OT

December 9, 2014 - Erie Otters at Kitchener Rangers

ERI #17 RW Raddysh, Taylor (2016) - Played on the top line tonight and provided an excellent work ethic forcing turnovers and creating offensive chances with smart puck decisions.

ERI #44 D Dermott, Travis (2015) - Tough for his size and a strong skater with good puck movement. His ice was limited in this game as he was hurt when colliding with Brent Pedersen.

KIT #18 D Blaisdell, Doug (2015) - Playing more physical in his own zone. Good compete in slot. Good clear on PK.

Final Score: Kitchener Rangers: 7 - Erie Otters: 4

USANTDP U18 at U. OF WISCONSIN (12-12-2014)

USA - #7 LW - Matthew Tkachuk (2016) – Showed good hands can stick handle and make plays in traffic. Did some good work on the fore-check and wasn't shy about taking the body. Tkachuk doesn't have the dynamic speed and skating ability so there is room for improvement in that area. Showed good hockey instincts in pursuing the puck. Scored by following up the play toward the net, RW Jack

Roslovic passed up a 1 on 1 opportunity with the goalie and left a drop pass for Tkachuk who finished it into the open net at the back door.

USA - #19 C - Auston Matthews (2016) – Matthews could step into NCAA hockey tomorrow and be one of the best players in the country. Still uncommitted, However Everett of the WHL hold his CHL rights if he decides to go that route. Auston had a dominate game by not only scoring 2 goals (1 EN) but also got 10 shots on goal, many of them from terrific scoring area's either between the hash marks or in close to the crease. Has terrific instincts, knows where he needs to be to find the loose pucks, once he gets to the puck it was almost impossible to get him off of it. Showed great patients with the puck when it was needed but most of the time he makes quick smart plays, seems to have a pretty good idea where he wants to go with the puck prior to getting it on his stick. One play he found himself skating east to west through the slot with the puck, the Wisconsin defender was able to get body contact on him and get him down to the ice, but Matthews never lost control of the puck, stick handling from his knees, eventually getting back to his feet, separating himself from the defender and feeding the puck back to the slot for a scoring chance. He has a very quick and powerful release with the snap shot. Was responsible defensively as well, skated hard on the back check and uses his hockey IQ in the defensive zone to disrupt plays. If there was a knock on Matthews game tonight is he was 8-10 on face-offs.

USA - #12 LW - Jordan Greenway (2015) – Didn't use his size to his advantage as much as he could. Was out muscled and outworked to loose pucks by smaller players on a couple occasions. Didn't work as hard on the back check as I'd like to see, he coasted back into the play on a couple occasions. Greenway did play better in the 3rd period which resulted in 2 assists. Used his size and battled in front of the net later in the game. Has all the tools to be an effective power forward but just didn't put it together for a full 60 minutes tonight.

USA - #25 D - Charles McAvoy (2016) – Needs to work on his decision making with the puck in his own zone. Had one turnover where the outlet pass from behind the goal line ended up right on the Wisconsin forwards stick and ended up in the back of his own net. Has good puck skills and skating ability and can make a lot of plays with the puck seem effortless, however on a few occasions he could have made the simple play to clear pucks off the glass and tried to make a pass instead.

USA - #28 RW - Jack Roslovic (2015) – First thing that stood out was his passing ability. Makes quick decisions with the puck in all 3 zones and passes are tape to tape and in stride. Moved the puck well on the power play, using one-touch passes nicely to keep the defenders chasing the play. Passed up a terrific scoring chance one on one with the goalie to use a drop pass to #7 Tkachuk for an open net at the back door.

USA - #17 RW - Jeremy Bracco (2015) – Has elite puck skills as well as skating ability. Was able to get the edge on the Wisconsin defenders all night but didn't take the puck to the net very often, liked to slow the play down, circle the zone with the puck, creating space for his teammates. Wins a lot of puck battles despite being one of the smaller players on the ice. Uses his hockey IQ, agility and puck skills to win battles, rather than physical play.

USA - #4 D - Casey Fitzgerald (2015) – Played in all situations tonight. Made solid outlet passes and has well enough skating ability to join the rush if permitted. Didn't shy away from the physical play either. Defends the rush well, uses good gap and active an active stick to disrupt line rushes. Got turned by a Wisconsin forward a couple of times but uses his skating well to get back into the play and disrupt the play.

USA - #3 D - Caleb Jones (2015) – Didn't provide a lot offensively and didn't join the rush a whole lot tonight but played a solid game in his own end. Made a couple nice stretch passes to forwards in the neutral zone. Did a good job holding pucks into the offensive zone on a couple occasions.

USA - #24 D - Steven Ruggiero (2015) – Uses his size well along the boards, sealing off opponents and buying time until support arrives. Was physical in front of his own net, abused forwards who try to set up there. Didn't do any incredible offensive plays but made solid simple plays with the puck. Used the boards well to move the puck to relieve fore-check pressure.

USA - #29 G - Luke Opilka (2015) – Did a good job with rebound control all night. Showed very quick pad movement. Can play a little deep in his crease at times but battles to see through screens and find loose pucks. Takes away the lower part of the net well.

UW - #19 C - Cameron Hughes (2015) – High hockey IQ, worked hard along the boards, won a lot of 50/50 puck battles. Saw a lot of good things in his game for a team that got outplayed for most of the night. Great skating ability, did good work cycling the puck and shields the puck with his body well. Was a prolific scorer in the AJHL last season, putting up 74 points in 70 total games, it's only a matter of time before he figures it out at the NCAA level. Has time to add some muscle to his slender 6'0" frame.

Kitchener Rangers at Barrie Colts, Dec 13, 2014

Score: 4-1 Barrie

Kitchener

LW Mike Davies (2015) – After playing limited minutes in the 1st period, his role seemed to increase as the game went on. He had a couple good chances in the slot area, and won his share of puck battles along the wall. One battle in particular he outworked two Colts and centered it for a great chance. He took a bad penalty in the offensive zone, but also drew one later in the game. One thing I didn't like about his game was he hit the ice way too many times. He was weak on his skates and was knocked over pretty easily on occasion.

C Gustaf Franzen (2015) – Franzen's game was a mixed bag. He created some good chances in the offensive zone and made some nice passes throughout, but he made some bad reads with the puck, too. One play in particular he forced a brutal pass while on a 5-on-3 powerplay and it went the other way for a Kevin Labanc breakaway goal. He missed a few shifts after that. He did backcheck hard throughout and was always back to support the defense.

D Doug Blaisdell (2015) – Blaisdell was one of the best Rangers on the ice. He read plays quickly and made smart, simple plays with the puck. His outlets were good, and he took several hits to make plays. Blaisdell held the line in the offensive zone several times, and did a good job of getting pucks through. He didn't panic defensively, and intercepted several pass attempts on odd-man rushes, which led to play going the other way. He skated hard for line changes, and always hustled to get involved in the play. His gap control was very good, and he seemed to have a calming influence on the ice. On his first shift he fanned on a shot and it went the other way for a chance, but he was very good besides that.

Barrie

LW Matthew Kreis (2015) - Kreis showed good vision early finding creative ways to hit open teammates all over the ice. He made a gorgeous pass through a seam that gave Justin Scott a mini-breakaway, though he didn't convert. Kreis also used his speed well to put pressure on the back check. He didn't generate much offense overall. I didn't see if he was injured at some point but he wasn't on the bench for the 3rd.

RW Roy Radke (2015) – Radke played a simple but effective game. He finished his checks, won puck battles, drove the net and caused havoc in front. Radke blocked a couple shots on the penalty kill and did a good job of getting pucks out.

RW Andrew Mangiapane (2014 +1) – Mangiapane was very dynamic in this game. He used quick stops and starts to lose defenders, and was always attacking. He distributed the puck very well, especially on the powerplay, and was a threat almost every shift. Mangiapane did a nice job slipping through seams and finding open ice in dangerous areas. He was relentless after the puck, forced several turnovers and didn't shy away from contact. He also had several chances while playing on the penalty kill, and scored a nice PP marker on a one-timer in the slot.

D Rasmus Andersson (2015) – The Rangers had a couple 5-on-3's in this game and Andersson was a big reason why they were unable to convert both times. He used his size well to box out in front, and did a nice job of clearing out loose pucks. Andersson consistently made good outlet passes, and in the offensive zone he put pucks on net if no options were available. He was able to show his big shot on the powerplay on a couple occasions, but Greenfield was able to fight them off. Andersson shot for deflections several times throughout, and they gave Greenfield trouble at times. On one play Andersson skated end-to-end, made Iafrate miss a hit attempt in open ice, danced around the other defender and put the puck in front for a good scoring chance. Overall it was a very good game.

G Mackenzie Blackwood (2015) – Blackwood didn't face a ton of shots early but his workload really picked up as the game went on. The Rangers tested him with several deflection plays and he was always up to the task. Blackwood tracked pucks very well, and made some very good stops high glove. He showed good lateral movement, and was quick moving post-to-post. Blackwood was confident playing the puck and helped jumpstart a couple rushes by coming out to play it.

December 13, 2014 - Saginaw Spirit at Niagara Ice Dogs

SAG #3 RD Stewart, Chase (2015) - Stewart played a pretty reliable, steady, shutdown game tonight. He got his stick on shots deflecting them away from the goal. Delivered a huge hit one on one forcing the forward outside then finished the check hard. Didn't show much offensive awareness, was unable to identify breakout pass opportunity on a line change with a forward way up ice. He did get an assist firing a shot on net which deflected off a teammate and in for Saginaw's second goal.

SAG #27 RC Stephens, Mitchell (2015) - Stephens starred tonight scoring four of Saginaw's seven goals in their route over Niagara. The first goal came from a great forehand/backhand move to beat the goaltender. His second goal was scored when the puck went off him and into the back of the net.

He did a great job all game opening himself up on the power play. He would score his hat trick goal through this ability and used a strong shot on a downed netminder to score. He would score his fourth by going to the net and scoring while falling. Aside from his four goals he hit the post opening himself up on the power play and easily could have had five. He was willing to hit and finish his checks, but lacks strength. Was driving the net when he got nudged and hit the ice hard and was subsequently penalized for diving.

NIA #4 LD Dunn, Vince (2015) - Dunn saw many successes and failures in this game. He has excellent puck control and did a great job down low carrying the puck up ice shaking checkers and smoothly transitioning to the offensive zone. He made some very good plays in the offensive zone but he is a high risk high reward defender who takes big risks to keep the play going at the line. He got burned one time trying to hold the line, which resulted in a Saginaw goal. He ends up too far out of position in the defensive zone too much.

Final Score: Niagara Ice Dogs: 7 - Saginaw Spirit: 1

December 13th, 2014 Youngstown Phantoms at Tri-City Storm

YNG #7 Letunov, Max C (2014, 2nd Round St. Louis Blues) - Played a nice game, was very involved in the game on both sides of the puck. He had an assist on Melnick's game tying goal in the third period. Very solid two-way player, good with his stick breaking up passes and uses his size well to knock opponents off the puck. Offensively fired a ton of shots on goal and creates chances by himself. His skating, specifically foot speed has developed nicely since I saw him last year. Developing right on track to play a big role at the next level.

YNG #10 Conley, Kevin LW (2015) – Pretty quiet game from Conley. Took a sort of bone-headed penalty in the second period and made a few questionable decisions throughout the game. Did not see a ton of ice time, but was involved offensively when he was out there. Overall came away scratching my head a bit after his performance. It looks like he has the tools to be a good player but some of his decisions are questionable.

YNG #22 Pearson, Chase C (2015) – Pearson had a chance to play big minutes centering the Phantoms' top line this weekend with Kyle Connor being loaned to USA Hockey for the World Junior A Challenge. Unfortunately, he didn't do much with his chance, and didn't really ever look comfortable out there tonight. He is a big body, and definitely looks bigger than most of the other guys on the ice. He plays a good, solid game in his own zone, and is very aggressive on the back check. However, it would have been nice to have seen him be more involved offensively.

YNG #33 Birdsall, Chris G (2015) – Came away very impressed with Birdsall after this one. He's very fundamentally sound, which is pretty much required with his fairly average size. He gave up two goals on thirty-three shots and eventually suffered the loss in the shootout. He played a solid first period, then gave up two goals in quick succession in the middle of the second period. I thought he bounced back well from these two goals and refocused mentally to finish the game strong.

YNG #56 Farmer, Ty RD (2016) – Didn't play many minutes at all, used as a seventh defenseman. In the time that he was out there, he didn't look out of place, often matched up against players a couple years older than him. However, he did make some of the mistakes you might expect with a guy his age playing in the USHL.

TC #3 Dello, Tory RD (2015) – Was impressive as usual in my viewings of him. Just impossible to beat one on one and truly looks like a man amongst boys on the ice. Very strong on his skates, and throws his body around, but doesn't chip in much on the offensive end. Great decision maker. Was probably the smartest player on the ice tonight.

TC #19 Allison, Wade RW (2016) – This was my first viewing and I was really impressed with Allison. He flew around the hitting everything that moved. Great energy guy. Looked great on PK and on the back check. Could be a force in the USHL if his offensive game develops.

TC #20 Wahlin, Jake LW (2015) – Probably the best performance he's had that I have seen this year. He is very fast, and gets going on a straight line skate quickly, getting up to top speed fast. He scored a goal from a weird angle in the corner banking it off the goalie and in. His game seems to be inconsistent, showing up some nights, but taking others off.

Scout's notes: Very exciting game with the Kyle Connor-less (loaned to USA Hockey for the World Junior A Challenge) Youngstown scoring two goals in the third period to tie the game and send it to overtime. It was goaltending battle til the end between Birdsall and Rutledge of Tri-City. Final score was Tri-City taking the games 3-2 in a shootout.

Dec. 13, 2014 – Tri-City Americans at Everett Silvertips

TRI #17 LW Purtill, Brayden (2015) – Played at centre in a bottom six role tonight and looked fairly average. Lost the majority of his draws, looking outmatched by a variety of opponents in the faceoff circle. A good passer with above-average vision who made a couple nice drop passes tonight. He called for the puck a lot, but was ultimately left unrewarded by his teammates who chose to cycle the puck instead.

TRI #36 RD Carlo, Brandon (2015) – When leading the rush through the neutral zone, he is often respected with time and space because he's a huge head's up skater who would likely bowl over anything in his way. Streaked across the neutral zone and entered the offensive zone, skating wide past the hashmarks before dishing off a brilliant assist into the slot. Shots were simple but good. Unfortunately, he had some issues with positioning and discipline in this one.

TRI #37 LD Wotherspoon, Parker (2015) – A dynamic and powerful skater who can lead and then join the rush in quick succession. Zone entry capability is very good thanks to quick feet, a head's up approach, and great puckhandling moves. Upon making good keeps on the blueline, he typically delivers both a low wristshot and a hard slap pass with velocity and accuracy. In his own end he plays a greasy and masochistic game that translates into blocked shots, frozen pucks in the corner, and many a post-whistle antic.

TRI #31 G Sarthou, Evan (2016) – Poor rebound control led in part to the fourth goal against—the other contributing factor was Brandon Carlo not closing the gap on his man. This wasn't the best game for the young Evan Sarthou who appeared a bit erratic in the paint tonight and a bit slow in the reflex department. To be fair, it was a high scoring affair at both ends of the ice.

EVR #3 RD Juulsen, Noah (2015) – Stood out tonight as a big and sturdy defensemanwho plays in all situations. A considerate and conservative decision maker, prefers to deal with the breakout pass as patiently as possible, often deferring to his defensive partner multiple times, drawing forecheckers out of position, and then making a first pass after much deliberation. A decent puck mover and holsters an accurate and effective wristshot from the point. In a few cases he was too easily beaten into the corners during short-area races.

EVR #8 RW Bajkov, Patrik (2016) – Continues to play on the Silvertips' top line, usually alongside the Russian pair of Ivan Nikolishin and Nikita Scherbak. Fits well into the role of scoring winger as his top-speed acceleration, hustle, and shooting skills are all high-grade. For instance, he used that hustle to follow up on a Juulsen shot from the point and tucked away a low wristshot in this one.

EVR #38 RD Davis, Kevin (2015) – An excellent skater who is dependable thanks to strong pokechecking ability and tremendous gap control whilst travelling in reverse. Dangerous on the power play due to a very strong one-timer slapshot that is delivered in quick release time. Advanced lateral mobility add deception to shots. Can be a bit overzealous in terms of his outlet passing, as he often shoots for the stars when easier simpler options are available.

EVR #70 G Hart, Carter (2016) – Does a good job of tracking the play and covering the upper and lower portions of the net equally, making good saves tonight with both his upper and lower body. Butterfly technique is good as he adjusts his body well mid-shot and transfers his weight in meaningful and non-extraneous ways. Stand-up positioning was a bit off in one instance when he was caught off balance and off stride coming out aggressively on a seemingly harmless wristshot that found the back of the net during a first period power play. Otherwise this was a good night for him.

EVR #77 RD Cochrane, Carter (2015) – A good skater but a little distracted in terms of his positioning, as there seems to be a lot of unnecessary adjustments and wasted motion in his movements. Unique in terms of his first pass styling, as he makes a bit of a squib pass that hops over sticks and goes from blueline to blueline. It's not pretty but it works for him. Saw a smidgen of power play ice time in this game where he didn't look entirely out of place in the quarterback position. A quiet night aside from a really nice play he made from his stomach after taking a big hit.

EVR #89 LC Nikolishin, Ivan (2014) – Nikolishin took the majority of the draws for his line where he performed admirably. He looked like a heck of a playmaker on a series of opportunities he set up for Scherbak, usually feeding the Montreal draft pick while he was streaking through the slot. Nikolishin can shoot too, however, as he showed with a booming slapshot that hit the post a number of times.

EVR #95 LW Scherbak, Nikita (Montreal, 2014) – Moves like lightning through centre ice when leading the rush and can do all things at top speed—deke, pass, shoot, dump and chase, and more. Keeps his head up and avoids oncoming bodycheck attempts whilst moving at top speed. Looked fantastic at retrieving passes from Nikolishin whilst streaking into the slot through various bodies. Quarterbacks from the right point on the power play, where he looks like a good passer.

December 14, 2014 - Peterborough Petes at London Knights

PET #22 RW Ang, Jonathan (2016) - Great work ethic in this game putting consistent pressure on the forecheck. Forced multiple turnovers in this game with his pressure. Took a bit of a beating in this game as he got hit hard seemingly every time he touched the puck.

PET #26 LC Coyle, Josh (2015) - Coyle did an excellent job defensively in this game. He made several great plays short handed to make sure the zone was cleared. He had a few good short handed rushes as well. He also blocked shots.

PET #27 RD Spencer, Matthew (2015) - Spencer was given a ton of ice time for the Petes in all game situations, especially the power play. He has a hard shot which created a scoring chance. He made the right play the majority of the time on the power play. Spencer played it pretty safe on the offensive blue line and picked the right times to be aggressive. He was caught flat footed on London's third goal and stopped skating after he was beat taking him out of the play. He was out of position again not long after but London missed on an open net on the 2 on 0 rush. When his team was building momentum he grabbed Yakimowicz and threw him to the ice taking what should have been a clear penalty.

PET #35 G Smith, Scott (2015) - Faced a ton of action in first an got in front of every shot he faced, but was beat give hole on all three goals. Lost track of puck multiple times, quick 1 turnover 4th not much chance, out of position on scramble and scored on fifth goal.

LON #89 LW Grzelewski, Zach (2015) - Zach showed good compete and made the best of a limited role. He made an excellent pass to set up London's fourth goal. Also has good positioning in the offensive zone.

LON #93 RW Marner, Mitchell (2015) - Marner had a very good game creating scoring chances with his passing ability as well as strong hand/eye coordination He scored London's fifth goal slipping the puck past an out of position goaltender. He flipped the puck over the glass for a penalty in his own zone.

Final Score: London Knights: 5 - Peterborough Petes: 2

December 14, 2014 - Oshawa Generals at Guelph Storm

OSH #8 RW Pu, Cliff (2016) - Good compete battling for puck, made smart decision in offensive zone, showed good puck control and patience.

OSH #22 LC Cirelli, Anthony (2015) - Great backcheck, high compete in defensive zone, good pass on rush, good skating ability.

OSH #25 RW Huether, Kenny (2015) - Small but very pesky player who plays hard, finishes checks. Controls opposition on wall very well for his size, every shift is non stop, hurries on the back check.

OSH #58 LD Vande Sompel, Mitchell (2015) - Vande Sompel got into a little trouble with the puck early on turning the puck over in his own zone and on the rush multiple times on his team's first power play. On their second power play he moved the puck a lot more effectively. He also received ice on the penalty kill as a forward. Couldn't handle opponent in the slot which resulted in a scoring chance against. However he was able to suck him into taking a penalty afterwards.

OSH #89 RC Harding, Sam (2015) - Picked up rebounds in slot to score 2nd Oshawa goal on PP. Also played PK

OSH #35 G Appleby, Ken (2015*) - Excellent size and used it well taking away angles. Technically sound holding post with play below the line and pushing off the post to the top of the crease. Has a bit of a weakness five hole and can be exploited by one timers.

Final Score: Oshawa Generals: 3 - Guelph Storm: 2

Barrie Colts at Mississauga Steelheads, Dec 14, 2014

Score: 6-1 Barrie

Mississauga

LW Nathan Bastian (2016) – Bastian played a pro-style game in this one. He finished his checks, was effective cycling down low and made smart plays with the puck. He backchecked hard with regularity, and did his best to play a north-south game. Bastian made some nice defensive plays while killing penalties, and won his fair share of puck battles along the wall. He didn't create much offensively, though.

C Michael McLeod (2016) – There were a lot of powerplays in this game and McLeod doesn't play special teams (or didn't today) so he saw limited ice. He took a few big hits to get pucks out and backchecked hard but wasn't really a threat offensively. Pretty quiet game from him.

D Sean Day (2016) – Like most Steelheads, he wasn't at his best. On the first shift of the game he had a couple bad giveaways in the defensive zone and that kind of set the tone for his game. A couple rushes he turned it over trying to dance around defenders, and he was also caught pinching deep in the zone at times. Even with his great skating ability he couldn't get back before Barrie had a couple chances the other way. It wasn't all bad, though, as he did make some nice passes and created offensively during a few shifts while playing forward, but overall it was not a great game from him.

Barrie

RW Roy Radke (2015) – Radke might have played his best OHL game in this one. He was strong on the puck, created several chances off the cycle and drove the net with purpose. He made a great feed to Hooey in the high slot for one goal, and scored a pair of his own as well. Radke was a regular on the PK, which was perfect on the day, and overall played a sound 200-foot game.

D Rasmus Andersson (2015) – Andersson played another steady game for the Colts. His defensive positioning was good and he did a nice job of closing gaps and sealing players off. He defended well on the cycle game and broke up a couple of them by anticipating the passes. Andersson had a few nice rushes with the puck and had no problem carrying it up ice if nobody was open for an outlet. Andersson was great on the penalty kill, and on one occasion he rushed it up ice, flipped it into Mississauga's zone, picked up the puck and pinned it against the boards killing almost 10 seconds of time.

G Mackenzie Blackwood (2015) – Blackwood played the puck with regularity and rushed out of his crease on a couple occasions to get loose pucks before a Steelhead reached it for a breakaway. He was calm in his crease, squared up his shooters and ate almost everything up. On the rare occasion he coughed out a rebound he used his long legs and quick reflexes to stop the 2nd chance opportunities. Blackwood made some very good post-to-post saves, and played a very good game stopping 33-34 in the win.

Notes: Givani Smith played well on the top line in place of the suspended Brendan Lemieux...Matthew Kreis did not play due to injury.

Dec. 16, 2014 – Everett Silvertips at Vancouver Giants

EVR #3 RD Juulsen, Noah (2015) – Already plays on the top pairing and quarterbacks both power play units for the Silvertips as a seventeen-year-old. From the top of the point, he holsters both a strong one-timer and a deadly accurate but low-lying wristshot. Did a good job of keeping his puck movement quick and simple tonight. I especially enjoyed a couple of chip passes he made high off of the glass to get the puck out of trouble.

EVR #8 RW Bajkov, Patrik (2016) – A good passer already, Bajkov's speciality appears to be a high wristshot that he manages to get onto the goaltender with an alarming accuracy. He didn't score tonight, but he continued to look dangerous in the offensive zone thanks to confident puckhandling and superior vision. His effort in the defensive end wasn't bad tonight, either.

EVR #38 RD Davis, Kevin (2015) – Skating all begins with the stance, and Kevin Davis has a perfect skating stance. With a 90-degree knee bend and an upright upper body position, he moves quickly and fluidly in all directions. Fantastic crossover technique, superior lateral agility and full 360-degree mobility allows Davis to easily dance into passing lanes or disrupt zone entries. On the negative end, he was a responsible for a couple turnovers and mishandled the puck a few times tonight.

EVR #70 G Hart, Carter (2016) – Normally shows good lower net coverage but was beaten low by Tyler Benson early. Otherwise, I like his calmness, but I think his game could benefit from a bit more speed and tenacity when the puck is in tight, as he looked a bit stationary and predictable in his movements. Another easy criticism to levy at the young Carter Hart is that he still looks very young and a bit small standing in the net.

EVR #77 RD Cochrane, Carter (2015) – Had a good if not forgettable game tonight, as he was back on defence after a brief tenure at forward. He looked more comfortable on the back end, making a few good first passes and disrupting several plays in his own end through use of some traditional board play. Logging the most minutes I've seen him play this season, he was dependable but unspectacular. A couple bad turnovers in his own end spoiled an otherwise quiet evening.

EVR #95 LW Scherbak, Nikita (Montreal 2014) – Nikita Scherbak is big, quick, and talented, but he was kept in check excellently tonight by Mason Geertsen, who later almost took Scherbak's head off with a high cross-check after Scherbak slashed the Giants defensemanbehind the play. He showed good toughness by returning to the game, and looked fairly effective throughout. The 'poor man's Galchenyuk' comparison doesn't seem entirely out of line.

VAN #11 LW Stukel, Jakub (2015) – A a threatening presence on the half wall during the power play, as he he's able to 'thread the needle' with ease, and plays with linemates who can execute on his plans. Furthermore, he is beginning to develop two other qualities that are worth monitoring—hitting skills and shooting capabilities. He continues to add power to both his hits and shots as the season progresses.

VAN #17 LW Benson, Tyler (2016) – Did what he does best tonight—contributed in all zones and in all situations, and put the puck in the net by virtually skating into it. Shifts tend to be very short and efficient. He's almost always a buzz-saw when he's on the ice and rarely gears down or gets tired. Difficult to knock down or off of puck, possessing tremendous "yards after contact" ability.

VAN #21 RD Menell, Brennan (2015) – After a fairly good venture at the forward position, Brennan Menell—whose number was changed from 3 to 21 to help scouts recognize him on the wing—is now mysteriously back at the blueline and playing defence again. I like him better at forward, personally, as his strengths are definitely his straight-ahead speed and passing abilities off of the rush. His wristshot isn't bad either, as he'll show you repeatedly on the power play.

VAN #22 LD Osipov, Dmitry (2015) – I continue to really like Osipov's game as it is in a constant state of upward momentum at this point in the season. His skating, hitting and containment abilities have all come to full fruition under the early tutelage of new coach Claude Noel. Logging a ton of minutes with Colorado Avalanche draft pick and stud d-man Mason Geertsen, on many nights I leave feeling that Osipov was in fact the more impressive and dependable defensemanamongst the pairing.

VAN #32 LC Bobylev Vladimir (2015) – Even though they rarely contribute much on the scoresheet, in terms of providing the Giants with energy, physicality and offensive zone time, Bobylev's fourth line is generally one of the most effective lines from night-to-night. Tonight's game against Everett was no exception. He was really inconsistent at the beginning of this season, and he hasn't put up a lot of points in his rookie season, so bringing energy to his club from game-to-game is crucial.

Blues U20 vs. HIFK U20 17th dec, 2014

#45 Blu RD Vainio, Veeti (2015) - Veeti had a pretty subpar game. He's a tremendous offensive D-man whose vision is great. Great blue liner with great puck handling and always doing good decisions with the puck in the o-zone. His slapshot is an average level but they're pretty accurate which is why there's plenty of times lot of rebounds. Veeti is a smooth skater with great technique but he got lot of problems in his defensive game… He's trying lot of risky passes and he's not ready to play physically. He's pretty good to defense with his stick but he really needs to start use his body in front of his own net.

#36 Blu W Björkqvist, Kasper (2015) - He showed today lot of great things. This kid likes to play straightforward and he's doing it well. Tough kid with great attitude and he's doing lot of work on ice. Great around corners and can challenge defenders with his speed. He's a decent puck-handler also which makes this kid pretty interesting.

#91 Blu C Niemelä, Joonas (2015) - Scored a one beauty goal today with an accurate wristshot. He's smart center who's pretty good playing on short-handed. Reads the game well and got pretty good vision. He's not big or physical which is a huge problem. Likes go to the traffic but he's not the the best battling around corners or in front of the net. Decent puck handler but he's more of a bottom six type of player but if he wants to make it NHL, he really have to improve his physicality.

#12 HIF RW Tavernier, Sami (2015) - Had a another bad game. He really got some skills and his vision is great but it seems like he doesn't know how to use his gifts. At his game he showed great motivation and he's trying to play tough even though he isn't a big guy. He just couldn't to create scoring chances which is kind of his job. He's a smooth skater and he got all the tools to be a great player but there's lot of work to do.

Plymouth Whalers at Barrie Colts, Dec 18, 2014

Score: 4-2 Plymouth

Plymouth

LW William Bitten (2016) – Bitten used his quick first three steps to generate speed through the neutral zone and consistently carried the puck into the zone with possession of the puck. He battled hard, finished his checks and wasn't afraid of going into the corners with much better players. He was relentless after loose pucks and drew a penalty after winning a puck battle. Bitten did a nice job of finding open ice and he scored the eventual winner just outside the crease. On Plymouth's first goal he knocked Rasmus Andersson off the puck, collected it and fed Campagna in front. One negative in Bitten's game was that he turned it over in the defensive zone and it led to one of his teammates taking a penalty.

RW Cullen Mercer (2015) – Mercer played an exceptional two-way game in this one. Offensively he showed good vision with the puck finding open targets all over the ice, and consistently won puck battles. He accelerated quickly through the neutral zone, was hard on the forecheck and his puck pursuit was excellent. Defensively he was always in position, covered his points and back checked hard with regularity. On the penalty kill he did a great job getting in the shooting lanes and used an active stick to make pass attempts difficult, too. He blocked a couple shots, consistently got pucks out and was on the ice late defending the lead. Mercer was rewarded for all his efforts with an empty-netter.

D Tyler Sensky (2015) – Sensky kept things very simple in this game. He was physical when he could be, but didn't go out of his way or take himself out of position to lay the body. He made smart decisions with the puck, and always took the easy outlet to get the puck out. Offensively he didn't create much, though on one play he drove the middle of the ice drawing a couple defenders his way before dishing the puck to Jacob Collins for Plymouth's 2nd goal.

G Zack Bowman (2015) – Bowman was tested early and often in this one and did a great job between the pipes. It was all Barrie for the 1st and he made several big saves to keep the Whalers within one and give them a chance to get their feet underneath themselves. He showed good athleticism, and made several good stops on 2nd opportunities. Bowman played the puck several times, too, and did a nice job making it easy on his defense whenever he could help.

Barrie

RW Roy Radke (2015) – Radke was rather ineffective in this game. He tried to drive the net a couple times but couldn't get a step on the defender and was forced to stay on the outside. He finished his checks when he could, but didn't do much in the offensive zone. On one occasion Joseph Blandisi was cross-checked down to the ice, then several more times while he was laying down and Radke didn't step in or do anything to prevent it. Perhaps he didn't want to take a penalty, but when you're 6'2, 200 pounds and people are taking liberties with the captain you expect him to do something.

D Rasmus Andersson (2015) – Andersson was a mixed bag in this game. Offensively he was a threat almost every time he was on the ice. I counted six shots on goal from him, including an absolute blast on the powerplay late to get the Colts within one. He also set his teammates up for several good scoring chances. Defensively, he was pushed off the puck prior to one of the goals, and lost his man in front on another. For the most part he was good defensively, but the couple mistakes he did make were costly. He was pretty physical in the corners and in front, though, which I liked and consistently made good outlet passes, including some three zone stretch passes to jump start the rush.

G Mackenzie Blackwood (2015) – Blackwood's numbers weren't great, but he played better than they'd indicate. Of the three goals he allowed, one was a bardown snipe over his shoulder, and on another it was a cross-ice pass where the Whalers' forward was left wide open. For the most part he tracked pucks well, and did a good job squaring up to shooters. He did cough up a few big rebounds throughout. Blackwood played the puck regularly and came out to break up a few potential chances for the Whalers.

HIFK U20 - KalPa U20 19th december, 2014

#2 Kal RW Piipponen, Topi (2015) - Scored his team first goal today. He challenged a d-man and won his battle and then shot an accurate wrister which ended up to the net. He got great power forward ability - great speed, good technique, got the size and he likes to join the rush. He plays very well in all three zones and he usually win his battles. He's playing smart and his vision is pretty good which makes him really versatile player. Speedy and dangerous winger. Would be even better in the small rink.

#8 Kal RW/LW Tammela, Jonne (2015) - Jonne had a decent night. Showed his amazing skillset again but didn't got any points today. Skilled dangler who's pretty straightforward player. He's not the biggest kid on the ice but he likes get physical and his balance is great. Smooth skater, almost perfect technique but his scoring ability is an average. He's not a pure scorer and he really isn't a typical playmaker but he's there somewhere in the middle. Smart kid whose potential is huge.

#28 Kal D Leskinen, Otto (2015) - Otto had an average game. Great mobility, he see the ice very well but his passes wasn't the that accurate today. His skating looks great and he really know what to do with the puck. Likes to join to offense and he's also doing pretty well in the d-zone. Not the biggest guy but he's trying play tough. Great defensive position. The best thing is his motivation and attitude. Always protecting his own goal with passion and u can really see how pissed off he is after a bad shift.

#12 IFK RW Tavernier, Sami (2015) - Smooth skater, good playmaking ability and quick hands. Dind't really show those skills today and was lost like the whole game. There seems to be a big difference between his good and bad day. He was benched almost whole third period - played just two shifts there. He needs to work with his all-round game a lot.

Dec. 19, 2014 – Russia at Canada (World Junior Hockey Championships, Exhibition)

RUS #3 LD Yudin, Dmitry (2013) – Plays top pairing minutes, makes a tremendous first pass, and holsters a good shot from the point. When stuck in his own zone or fighting for pucks in the corners he isn't always as calm as most scouts would probably like, but he gets the job done frenetically if he needs to.

RUS #25 LC Degacheyev, Alexander (2015) LC – Good positioning and stick work while on the forecheck, as he presses the opposition hard with his unique combination of size, speed, range, and puck sense. Ability to both give and receive passes is very good, even when moving at a decent clip through the neutral zone. Can handle the puck effectively on both his fore and backhand and likes using the back-pass as an option, especially when working on the cycle.

RUS #29 LD Provorov, Ivan (2015) RD – For the most part he wasn't really noticeable—first passes were good, he got a couple shots near the net—but on at least a few occasions, Ivan Provorov had some rough shifts tonight. On one instance, he fanned on a one-timer, spilled over the puck to a rushing forward, got caught flat-footed in reverse, was hemmed in his own zone for what felt like an eternity, and then got absolutely steamrolled by Nick Paul.

CAN #12 LW Crouse, Lawson (2015) – Didn't score but looked dominant in all areas of the game—offensively, defensively, physically, and with the puck on his stick. Showed off tremendous puck protection abilities with his stickhandling in the corners, drawing a penalty at the conclusion of the first period. Sneaks into passing lanes very quickly and has the reflexes and range to pounce on dangerous turnovers. His slapshot also appears impressive.

CAN #20 RW Nick Paul (Ottawa 2013) – Looked aggressive, physical, provided a net-front presence, and was dangerous with the puck on his stick. He can deke, he can pass, and he can shoot. Plus, he's huge. His game tailed off a bit towards the end, as he started to look tired after being given several long shifts and assignments, but otherwise, I thought that this was a fantastic showing for Paul.

Ottawa 67's at Barrie Colts, Dec 20, 2014

Score: 3-1 Barrie

Ottawa

C Travis Konecny (2015) - Konecny showed some good bursts of speed through the neutral zone, and created some good chances in the offensive zone. His high-end release was on display on a couple occasions, and he showed nice hands in tight stickhandling around a defender before making a nice move just outside the paint. He backchecked hard, was consistently back to support and always took care of his defensive responsibilities. He made a couple nice passes waiting for the trailer and hitting him in space, but offensively he didn't create as much as we've grown accustomed to seeing.

C Dante Salituro (2015) – Salituro generated great speed in his first three steps and was effective skating the puck up ice, but he struggled to create offense throughout. It seemed like he was trying to do too much and one of those nights were nothing would go right. He closed gaps quickly while killing penalties and did back check with regularity, but his effectiveness was very limited in this one.

RW Jeremiah Addison (2015) – Addison gained the blue line with possession of the puck regularly, and used his speed to back defenders off. He took a couple hits to make passes, one of which led to a great scoring chance, and battled for loose pucks. Addison did have a few turnovers in the offensive zone, though, which led to clears and/or odd-man rushes for Barrie.

Barrie

RW Roy Radke (2015) – Radke had a couple nice hits and was effective in the cycle game at times, but he was certainly not at his best. He struggled to create his own lane and couldn't get his shots to the net. Radke had a glorious chance in front and couldn't finish that. He also had a couple turnovers in the defensive zone that led to chances against.

D Rasmus Andersson (2015) – As is always the case almost every pass he made was on the tape. He moved the puck effectively on the powerplay, and did set up several chances in that regard. He was calm while walking the line, and played with a lot of poise in his game. He struggled getting shots through early, but got pucks on net late, and Brendan Lemieux's game-winner was scored on a deflection play from an Andersson shot. He was caught running around in his own zone a couple times but generally he was good defensively as well. He played pretty well, but wasn't himself on this night.

G Mackenzie Blackwood (2015) – Blackwood wasn't tested a ton, but was good when called upon. He showed good lateral movement stretching from post-to-post to stuff a wraparound attempt, and made some good glove saves throughout. At times high shots gave him some trouble and he coughed out some rebounds on those occasions, but was always there to make the 2nd save if the puck wasn't cleared out by his defense. The only goal he allowed was on a back door play where Bell was left uncovered.

Dec. 21, 2014 – Sweden at Canada (World Junior Hockey Championships, Exhibition)

SWE #4 LD Kylington, Oliver (2015) – He's a left handed defenceman, but he switches sides with his partners a lot and so finds himself on the right side a fair bit, successfully finding time and space, opening up one-timer opportunities. straight-ahead skating speed looks amazingly fast, as he is able to win races from a mile behind. Passing game looks only decent at this point, as there were a few cases of poor communication in this game. Not a terrible games by any means, but he's also had much better I imagine.

CAN #28 LW Crouse, Lawson (2015) – Tonight he played left wing with Frederik Gauthier at centre and Jake Virtanen on his opposite wing. Like a true pro, he responds well to physical pressure, looking energized when defensemanhit him in the corners. He didn't do a lot in terms of adding to the offence tonight, but threw some really nice hits out there, and he has the professional and intimidating presence that scouts are looking for in a prospect.

CAN #17 C McDavid, Connor (2015) – His exceptional skating ability allows him to buzz around the offensive zone endlessly. And his passing below the hashmarks is second to none. From that position on the ice, I particularly like his ability to make passes back to the point. He missed a wide open net after being stickchecked by Adrian Kempe in the third period.

Dec. 26, 2014 – U.S.A at Finland (World Junior Hockey Championships, Round Robin)

USA #2 LD Hanifin, Noah (2015) – A seemingly effortless skater who keeps his head up almost the entire game. Appears to have a dual speciality—cross-ice passing ability and amazing crossover technique in his footwork—meaning he can at all times choose to either pass or skate the puck to greener pastures at all times. Excellent in retrieval and makes a good head's-up first pass. Paired with Ian McCoshen, Hanifin was the offensive counterpart to McCoshen's "steady hand."

USA #9 RC Eichel, Jack (2015) – A thrashing skater who has breakaway acceleration that he puts on display from shift-to-shift, as he appears to have a bottomless gas tank. Vision, passing, and shooting abilities are all elite, even when travelling at full-speed. A very dangerous player coming out from behind the goal-line, as he explodes out of the gates and is fearless about entering the prime scoring area with the puck. Made a nice pass from the behind the net for an assist in the first. Looks uber competitive at all times, whether it's competing for space in the offensive zone or taking a faceoff in his own end. Effort on the backcheck is quite often just as good as his effort on the forecheck, which is truly an amazing feat if you've ever had the pleasure of witnessing Eichel's forechecking ability.

USA #23 LD Werenski, Zach (2015) – Superior skating skills were on display tonight, as I saw him surge past his own teammate in, Noah Hanifin, of all skaters, to collect a few loose pucks. As fast handling pucks as he is chasing after them. Leads the rush on the power play, makes his own zone entries, and then quarterbacks from the point, where he shows excellent vision, passing, and shooting abilities. Keeps his feet moving more than most quarterbacks, opening up space in the offensive zone, creating shooting lanes, constructing playmaking options and opportunities. Slapshot is outstanding.

USA #26 RD Carlo, Brandon (2015) – Has a lot of confidence when handling the puck through the neutral zone, as he makes good passes, dumps, head-fakes and other clever moves to gain zone entry for his club. Forced his shots a bit in the offensive zone, but had few mistakes otherwise. A fixture on the penalty kill, where he used his big body and strength to limit opportunities for the Finns in the slot. Possesses good crease-clearing abilities, especially in terms of how he handles rebounds in the slot—he's becoming known for his hand-eye coordination and ability to strongly swat loose pucks off of the ice and out of danger.

USA #34 LC Matthews, Auston (2016) – This was actually a highly disappointing performance from 2016-eligible Auston Matthews. There were tunes he looked like the youngest and most immature player on the ice far too many times this afternoon. Seemed over-ambitious in one-on-one situations tonight. Needs to show better poise, as he looked far too beaten up over routine missed opportunities.

FIN #13 RW Puljujarvi, Jesse (2016) – You can't help but be stunned at his quickness and his skating ability and his edgework. Has a really nice hands too, but can be a loosie-goosie with the puck at times. Without the puck, meanwhile, his hockey smarts and instincts in terms of getting himself open are absolutely phenomenal. He'll likely become a total force of nature when this tournament comes back around next year, as the tools are all there and he just needs added strength and conditioning.

FIN #16 RC Rantanen, Mikko (2015) – Scored almost immediately with a clever shot. As he appeared in that situation, this is a player who usually looks effective, dangerous and opportunistic in the offensive zone. Has really good stickwork and takeaway skills too—it was stripping Noah Hanifin of the puck that set up the early goal. He might suffer from a lack of stamina, as he drifted away from the productive areas in the later, but I still came away liking his size, speed, vision and creativity.

FIN #22 RC Hintz, Roope (2015) – Looked fast, skillful, powerful, and physical. Drew a couple penalties by keeping his feet moving and driving the net with passion and confidence. Showed really good passing skills and hockey IQ on a couple cross-crease passes that almost set up Jusso Ikonen—a player whom I thought showed excellent and instantaneous chemistry with Hintz. A power forward who bulls his way across the blueline before ripping off a strong shot or sending a pass into the slot for a streaking teammate.

FIN #26 LW Aho, Sebastian (2015) – Made things happen tonight, whether it was off of the rush, on the cycle, or by providing a strong and sturdy net-front presence. Game is still open to interpretation, though. After all, Aho generated a few "oohs and ahhs" off of driving wide, but didn't produce anything meaningful on any of his skating or stickhandling heroics.

December 27, 2014 - Team Switzerland vs. Team Czech Republic

2015 World Junior Championships - Preliminary Round

SUI #18 LW Schweri, Kai (2015) - Small but slippery on the wall with quick hands. Assisted on fourth goal.

SUI #25 D Siegenthaler, Jonas (2015) - Good stick in one on one situations. Calm under pressure with the puck and protects it very well .Skates very well for a big defenseman and can skate the puck out of trouble confidently. Will take the hit to make the play with the puck. Supports his defensive partner well. He was utilized in all game situations and has a good shot from the point finding ways to get it through. Penalized in the third period for putting the puck over the glass.

SUI #28 RW Meier, Timo (2015) - Timo made a very high skilled pass to set up Switzerland's first goal. Great composure with the puck throughout this game and makes excellent passes. However on one play he had a great chance two on one and mishandled the puck negating the play. He showed some toughness landing a good open ice hit in the third period. He also got involved in scrums after the whistle. Lets up on the back check.

CZE #14 C Zacha, Pavel (2015) - Zacha made a good move on the power play to create scoring chance. Made one great play where he split the defenders but was robbed by the goaltender. He worked hard in the defensive zone winning battles for pucks. Was a little less noticeable as the game went on.

Final Score: Team Switzerland:5 - Team Czech Republic: 2

December 28, 2014 - Team Switzerland vs. Team Russia

2015 World Junior Championships - Preliminary Round

SUI #16 LW Malgin, Denis (2015) - Good positioning playing on Switzerland's second power play unit but passed in high percentage shooting situations and shot in low percentage shooting situations.

SUI #25 D Siegenthaler, Jonas (2015) - Caught his opponent with their head down and landed a massive open ice hit one on one. Good stick both one on one and in odd man situations to knock the puck off the stick and break up passes. Great diving play when he was recovering in transition to break up the play. He has good defensive positioning and doesn't chase the play. Consistently made smart decisions with the puck whether it be a smart pass up from deep in his own zone, in the neutral zone or just keeping the play going at the line. Very high level hockey sense.

SUI #28 RW Meier, Timo (2015) - Good move to split the defenders using his acceleration and hands to create a great scoring chance. He mishandled the puck in the slot on a few occasions, he also had a puck mistake that lead to Russia's sixth goal.

RUS #25 C Dergachyov, Alexander (2015) - Dergachyov was used primarily in defensive situations playing big penalty kill minutes and was the only fowrard used at one point on a key 5 on 3 penalty kill. Made some mental errors with the puck around the offensive zone. Not an offensive player.

RUS #29 D Provorov, Ivan (2015) - Consistently strong with the puck providing good puck rush out of zone with pressure. Very strong skating defenseman who played with a physical edge and finished his hits hard.

Final score: Team Russia: 7 - Team Switzerland: 0

Dec. 28, 2014 – Russia at Switzerland (World Junior U20)

RUS #3 Dmitri Yudin (2013) D – The scouting report on Dmitri Yudin is that he's an aggressive and agitating defensemanwith some offensive skill—he showed off all these characteristics in a good performance against the Swiss. Yudin got under Fiala's skin in the first period, drawing Switzerland's best offensive player into the penalty box in a double-minor for roughing.

RUS #25 Alexander Dergachyov (2015) C – As with the Subway Super Series (his first coming out party), Dergachyov is seeing increased ice-time from game-to-game thanks to his size, endurance, and consistency of effort. The fruits of his efforts finally came to be with a late first period goal to put the Russians ahead 2-0. A quick wristshot from the top of the offensive faceoff circle fooled Gauthier Decloux, who was playing excellent up until then.

SWI #25 Jonas Siegenthaler (2015) D – Normally plays in the Swiss leagues, splitting his time GC Küsnacht in the NLB and Zürich in the NLA. He got caught flat-footed and fell behind on a play in the first period, but used hustle and range to poke the puck away from an opposing forechecker that sprung free on a 2-on-1. He co-quarterbacked the power play along with Yannick Rathgeb, looking fairly dangerous thanks to good vision, passing and shooting skills. His wristshot lacks strength, as it was too easily swatted away by smallish Russian forwards.

SWI #28 Timo Meier (2015) RW – Normally plays for the Halifax Mooseheads of the QMJHL. Timo Meier was a wrecking ball early in this one, as he crashed and banged everything in sight, and then looked dangerous after gaining possession of the puck. He started the game on a line featuring Kevin Fiala and #18. A big body with a nose for the net, he looks dangerous in all situations, getting a couple chances on goal during his penalty killing duties tonight. He used his speed and big body to draw a penalty on Rinat Valiev in the first period.

Dec. 28, 2014 – Seattle Thunderbirds at Vancouver Giants

SEA #12 LW Gropp, Ryan (2015) – A ball of energy tonight, as he kept his feet moving all over the ice—looking constantly dangerous in the offensive zone and highly disruptive in the defensive end. A fast straight-line skater with a well-rounded and multifaceted game—he can make plays happen with his passing, his shooting, or his hitting. Even though he didn't record a point on the play, I thought that Gropp's physicality and aggressiveness was the offensive catalyst on the game winning goal.

SEA #15 C Pederson, Lane (2015) – Lacks top-end speed and skill, but I still love his mobility and his hockey knowledge. Additionally, his subtle but effective movements in the offensive zone opened space and created opportunities for his teammates tonight. He isn't the fastest guy in the world, but his first-step explosiveness is good enough that he'll get his fair share of chances if he continues pouncing on loose pucks and firing them home. I also really like his faceoff and passing skills.

SEA #25 LD Bear, Ethan (2015) – Had a great game tonight, highlighted by a fantastic slapshot goal from the blueline. Turns and pivots can be a bit clumsy sometimes, but skating aside, he's generally dependable in his own end and logs a ton of minutes in all situations. A tremendous puck mover and even better first passer, he doesn't have to have the quickest feet in the world because he has a plethora of outlet options—saucer passes, flip passes, backhand passes, they were all put on display tonight.

SEA #28 RW Kolesar, Keegan (2015) – He's big, he's physical, he's dangerous with the puck, and he plays well in all situations. Skating ability, however, is left to interpretation. First few steps leave much to be desired, which is understandable given the amount of mass he needs to move with just his legs. But after five or six strides, he's absolutely flying down the ice, looking like one of his team's fastest players. Upper-body strength appears well-developed already, as wide strong shoulders and a strong grip on his stick make Kolesar a very difficult and frustrating player to pry the puck away from. There's also a bit of an agitator element to him, as well.

VAN #8 LW Baer, Alec (2015) – Finally rewarded in this one, showing good instincts on a goal that compensated for an otherwise average game. Movements with the puck are best when he's being unselfish as he's got underrated vision and playmaking skills. Needs to get away from the sniper designation and become more dangerous off of the rush by better utilizing his teammates. Suffers from tunnel vision a bit. Too often gets the puck on his stick near the net and commits himself to a predictable wraparound play when there are many better options more easily available.

VAN #17 LW Benson, Tyler (2015) – It was a Tyler Benson showcase tonight in the offensive zone, as there are times when he looks like an unbridled elite talent—stickhandling, passing, and shooting are all phenomenal and well ahead of development. On one memorable play in the second period, he dangled danced between, past, and around almost every Seattle Thunderbird player on the ice, all before dishing the puck off to a teammate for an easy goal. His hitting game is additionally remarkable.

VAN #22 RD Osipov, Dmitry (2015) – Game is beginning to level-out again after a run of several stellar performances on home ice. He was just average tonight as he struggled a couple of times with regards to discipline—a running theme throughout his draft year. He's an intimidating presence going into the corners at this level because of his size and meanness, but I don't know if his 'just above average' quickness and grit will carry him to the same levels of success when playing against bigger and more skilled competition.

December 31, 2014 Plymouth Whalers at Windsor Spitfires

PLY #10 LW Caamano, Nicholas (2016) - Caamano looked for every opportunity to hit and finished every check. He had great positioning in the offensive zone which lead to multiple offensive opportunities. He found his was on the scoresheet making a great play when entering the offensive zone with the puck, drawing in the defender then passed over to set up Plymouth's third goal. He then scored Plymouth's fourth goal quickly getting into position on the wing on a turnover then a well placed shot for the goal.

PLY #13 LW Dunda, Liam (2015) - Dunda's focus this game was strictly physical looking for and landing some huge hits. Was an overpowering player on the wall. Dropped the gloves in the second period with Liam Murray but didn't fair too well.

PLY #19 RW Mercer, Cullen (2015) - Mercer played an excellent two-way game for Plymouth today finishing every check with power. Good play defensively early to read a pass and lift the stick to negate a high percentage scoring chance. He also played on the top penalty kill unit and made some big shot blocks and zone clears. Assisted on Plymouth's first goal winning the draw back to the defensemanwho shot for goal.

WSR #3 D Murray, Liam (2015) - Murray recorded the Gordie Howe hat trick less than 35 minutes into the game when he pinched in from the point and quickly scored the first goal of the game. He then assisted on Windsor's second goal. He also dropped the gloves with Liam Dunda and faired very well.

WSR #40 RW Moore, Ryan (2015) - High end skating ability. Deceptively quick release on shot. Controls puck well on the powerplay. Delays to let lanes open up. Scored Windsor's second goal, a bit of a weak one finding a hole with his shot on the wing. Got hit hard a few times.

WSR #51 D Chatfield, Jalen (2015*) - Competed hard for pucks and won battles. Activated from the point as frequently as possible. Struggled to move the puck at speed. Lost race to puck and took down opponent for penalty.

WSR #91 LC Luchuk, Aaron (2015) - He shows slick moves with his hands and skating ability taking the puck from the neutral zone to the offensive zone. Used speed to beat the one defender but then instead of engaging other defender he took a low percentage shot. Covers for defender who jumps up in play. Great behind the back pass set up scoring chance. He was around 50% in the faceoff circle tonight.

Final Score: Plymouth Whalers: 6 - Windsor Spitfires: 4

January 2, 2015 Sarnia Sting at London Knights

SAR #5 LD Chychrun, Jakob (2016) - Chychrun had a great game at both ends. He gets his shot off quickly from the point and blasted a laser through for Sarnia's second goal of the game. He was in on Sarnia's sixth goal firing the puck from the point with a minute left to reduce their deficit by one. He then made a huge play in the neutral zone with the goaltender pulled to keep his team in the game. He has a good stick and displayed this both one on one and with coverage in the defensive zone getting in passing lanes. He lost the puck on London's third goal when the official interfered with his ability to play the puck and his skating route. Calm under forecheck pressure and had some impressive end to end rushes on the power play. Without DeAngelo in the line-up Chychrun was utilized as a big puck rusher and quarterback on the power play. However he was also relied upon to come up huge for his team defensively as well.

SAR #8 LD Sproviero, Franco (2016) - Tonight was Sproviero's OHL debut and he put together a very strong performance. He is an undersized defenseman with strong skating ability. He was capable of rushing the puck and did so very well on multiple occasions. He drew a power play at one point with his puck rushing ability. He was surprisingly calm under pressure with the puck and could skate the puck out of trouble from deep in the defensive zone. He made a good first pass consistently not trying to do too much. He gets into passing lanes well and showed a good stick in one on one match-up's with the skating ability to keep up but wouldn't engage beyond using his stick.

SAR #11 RW Hodgson, Hayden (2015*) - Hodgson made a good deflection to score Sarnia's first goal. He was a little hesitant on the back check and got a little too casual with the puck a few times. He showed a little passing ability making some good set up's through traffic when he was focused.

SAR #12 LW Lindberg, Brandon (2015) - Lindberg had a big first period seemingly creating a scoring chance every shift. He uses his physical play to knock opposing defenders off the puck then makes a strong pass to create a chance. He did this in each of his first few shifts to give Sarnia some good chances early. He provides a high compete level. When he has the puck entering the offensive zone he likes to drive the net with it.

LON #14 LD Crawley, Brandon (2015) - Crawley was effective in one on one match-up's against some bigger opponents not letting them get inside on him and maintaining strong enough body position to keep opponents on the outside. He won some battles along the wall and was also capable skating the puck out of trouble, protecting the puck well and gained a few very good puck rushes. Smart, poised passes up ice. Pinched at the right time to keep the play in the offensive zone.

LON #89 LW Grzelewski, Zach (2015) - Zach played a high energy game and competed hard for pucks. He fired a rocket top shelf for London's second goal. Drastically improved since September.

LON #93 RW Marner, Mitchell (2015) - As usual, Marner got involved on the offense registering a point on six of the eight goals for the Knights. He came up big late in the game showing great patience behind the net and set up London's sixth goal to give them the lead. He then scored London's seventh goal with a great move and a good shot. After Sarnia bridged the gap to one, Marner sealed the game up with an empty netter. He also made some great plays to get scoring chances but was robbed. His defensive play is continuously improving. He made a great play on the backcheck then took the puck end to end. He forced turnovers on the penalty kill then took plenty of time off the clock. He even showed a little physicality finishing his check on a bigger opponent.

Final Score: London Knights: 8 - Sarnia Sting: 6

Jan. 2, 2015 – Prince George Cougars at Vancouver Giants

PRI #12 Jansen Harkins (2015) C – Jansen Harkins had a good game tonight in which he played an important role in all three zones. Strong on both ends of the puck, he was a key contributor in all situations. A fantastic playmaker who sees the ice very well, he was very good at getting the puck to his teammates in opportune areas tonight, as exhibited by his 3 assists. Although he's considered a 'natural playmaker,' he possesses a bottomless bag of tricks when it comes to creating offense, as he has several ways besides passing to create opportunities for his teammates, whether it be cycling, his shooting abilities, or something entirely different and unexpected like a deflection or a sneaky back-door set-up.

PRI #9 Brad Morrison (2015) LW – Finishing the game with no points, no shots, and 2 penalty minutes, I didn't see the speedster Brad Morrison do anything too spectacular or noticeable in this game, other than make a few nice plays from tough positions on the ice. A quick-footed winger who plays a bit recklessly at times, he has a habit of getting knocked hard with big hits, but finds ways to make plays from his back, his knees, etc.. His game waned at times.

PRI #21 Jared Bethune (2015) LW – Jared Bethune had a rocky evening. Even though he put some points up, he was plagued with consistency and discipline issues all night long. Appearing frustrated at various times, his skating was very spastic as he was a bit 'all over the place' on the fore-check—wayward hands and feet aside, showed good third and fourth stride power on the forecheck and good hitting skills. Unfortunately, I didn't see that same type of skating velocity on the back-check. He was the last man back on more than a few goals against. His physicality was good, but otherwise I thought his game seemed a bit out of control.

PRI #25 Tate Olson (2015) D – I thought Tate Olson was quietly Prince George's best player tonight, as he played a fantastic shut-down game in which he limited chances close to the net and made smart decisions to retrieve pucks and quickly send them up ice. His pokechecking skills are well above-average as he does a good job of calmly digging pucks free from chaotic environments. He showed some skating and puckhandling skills, too. When in possession, he funnelled the puck to the net smartly from the blueline; off the rush, he skated the puck up centre ice and made some nice passes after gaining entry into the offensive zone.

VAN #8 Alec Baer (2015) LW – Earning an assist on a soft and flat pass through the high slot that set up a Mason Geertsen one-timer, it was nice to see Alec Baer get on the scoresheet as he's been on a bit of a dry-spell lately. His skating game remains very good, as he has good feet and hands to match—but he's lost some of his offensive mojo as of late, as he hasn't been taking the puck hard enough to the net and fallen into a perimeter role. It was especially nice to see Baer get on the scoresheet with an assist, as his passing game needs to be unearthed again if he hopes to turn his season around.

VAN #21 LD Menell, Brennan (2015) – At even strength, Brennan Menell plays on a second pairing with Arvin Atwal that had its struggles tonight with unforced turnovers and fumbled retrievals. But on the top power play unit, Brennan Menell is beginning to see top pairing minutes alongside stalwart Mason Geertsen and is making the most of his opportunity. His offensive numbers are rising rapidly as his confidence and offensive skills are finally coming to a boil. I especially like Menell's shooting abilities from the point, as he holsters a wristshot that is a seeing eye missile at times.

VAN #35 Cody Porter (2015) G – Coming into the game to relieve Payton Lee, who let in 4 goals before the game's midway points, Cody Porter had an absolutely brilliant showing in which he showed off his tremendous mental toughness. A tough situation to be placed in on home ice, Porter's positioning, composure, and rebound control were all fantastic. Kept the Giants in the game long enough for them to escape with a victory.

London Knights at Barrie Colts, January 3 2015

Score: 10-3 Barrie

RW Mitch Marner (2015) – Marner generated good speed in his first three steps and accelerated quickly through the neutral zone. He was able to gain the line with possession on a consistent basis, and showed good creativity with the puck. He didn't record a point for just the 2nd time since Mid-October, but he did create some chances for his teammates and easily could have had a couple. Marner did force some passes when the Knights fell behind and looked like he was trying to do too much at times. He also turned it over on the powerplay, which led to a short-handed goal.

D Brandon Crawley (2015) – He was a minus-3 on the night, but I think that was a result of poor goal-tending as much as anything else. Crawley used an active stick in the defensive zone to disrupt some plays, and for the most part his positioning was good. Crawley had a couple nice rushes with the puck and seemed confident carrying it on his stick. He did get caught trying to do too much in his own zone on one occasion and it led to a turnover that ended up in the back of his net.

D Victor Mete (2016) – Mete played a pretty good game given the circumstances. He made good outlets throughout the game and was confident carrying the puck up ice if necessary. He jumped into the rush to help create some offense, and used his fluid skating ability to get back if he was ever caught up ice. There were a couple defensive breakdowns and he took a bad boarding penalty late, but for the most part was pretty good.

RW Roy Radke (2015) – He was effective on the forecheck and his offensive zone pressure forced the Knights to reset their breakout several times. Radke scored an absolute snipe off a forced turnover, and back-checked hard throughout. Tait Seguin took a healthy run at him in the neutral zone and Radke sent him flying after bracing himself.

D Rasmus Andersson (2015) – Andersson played one of the best games of his young OHL career. His outlets and D-to-D passes were consistently accurate, and he set up his teammates for countless chances. He had no problem getting shots through traffic, and showed excellent release and power on his 1st period goal. He defended well against odd man rushes, and was physical in the corners and around the net. His puck movement on the powerplay was exceptional, as he made quick decisions with the puck and distributed it well. He pinched a couple times where he probably shouldn't have, but generally he was able to get back whenever he decided to do so.

G Mackenzie Blackwood (2015) – Blackwood showed great lateral movement stretching out to make a few big saves, and he came up big when the Colts were killing off a 5-on-3 early in the game. He did allow a weak goal late in garbage time, but he was good throughout. He stopped 26-of-29 in the win.

MICHIGAN TECH vs U. of WISCONSIN (1-3-15)

MTU - #10C - Tanner Kero (FA) – Tanner Kero was MTU's leading scorer going into this series. Tanner used his stick skills and ability to read the play to win his puck battles. Is aggressive on the fore check and will battle hard for pucks but didn't play with much of a physical edge in those 50/50 puck battles, but still won his fair share of them. One of the best skaters on the MTU team did a good job jumping into lanes and getting into position for scoring chances. Had a team high 7 SOG, and if it wasn't for some terrific goaltending he could have had at least a couple goals. Played in all situations and did a good job picking his spots and challenging the point on the Penalty Kill.

MTU - #30 G –MTU – Jamie Phillips (WPG-2012) – Phillips wasn't challenged much tonight but was solid. He didn't give up much for rebounds or second opportunities. He made the saves he was suppose to make. Phillips is a big body in the net; he stays very square to the shooters and stays on top of his crease. What I liked most about his game is he was always into the game even though he didn't see a lot of pucks, when the puck was in his end he was active, looking around screens, trying to find pucks in traffic. Was never caught off guard.

MTU - #23 -Alex Petan (FA) – Petan isn't an overly physical player but will go to the hard areas for pucks without hesitation. Liked to setup beneath the goal line with the puck and used his vision and playmaking ability to find the open man. Played more of a rover position on the Power play, sometimes would setup on the half wall, sometimes below the goal line and did spend some time at the point. Showed more of a pass first mentality tonight but does have a quick release when he did use his shot. Used his skating ability to break up a couple plays on the back check.

UW - #19 - Cameron Hughes (2015) – Hughes played a solid 200 foot game. Showed some good technique on face-offs, often tying up the opposition until support arrived. Hughes showed good ability to protect the puck along the boards with his body and good cycling ability. On a couple occasions he wanted to get a cycle going but had no puck support so the play fizzled. Would like to see him play with some better offensive forwards to see if he can get his offensive game going. Hughes has a quick first couple strides but his speed seems to taper off at times.

UW - #33G - Joel Rumpel (G)(FA-SJ) – After getting pulled the night before Rumpel responded with what might be the best game of his career, a 47 save shutout, many of them were high end saves on great scoring chances. Rumpel took away the lower part of the net well all night and was quick to recover rebounds. Had great rebound control on shots coming through traffic, kept MTU's second chances to a minimum. His ability to bounce back after possibly his worst outing of his college career tells me a lot about his mental toughness.

UW - #28D – Kevin Schulze (FA) – Schulze has become a very consistent contributor on the backend for a Wisconsin team that has been lost for most of the season. Schultze made good clean first passes out of his zone. Almost sprung a forward behind the MTU defense on a couple occasions but the pass was mishandled. Always had his head up and isn't afraid to bring the puck up the ice on his own. Showed some good hands on some dump ins to the opposite corner which allowed his forward to retrieve the puck first. Was better tonight at protecting the puck along the wall and knowing when you may have to kill it along the wall until support arrives rather than trying to skate it out of a situation.

Game notes: Michigan Tech carried the play for most of the night and showed they were the better team but Joel Rumpel stole a game for Wisconsin; one they really had no business winning. Wisconsin scored the eventual game winner UW's #24 Jedd Soleway (Phx 7th Rd.) found #9 Morgan Zulinick (FA) on the weak side of the defense right after coming off the bench for a partial breakaway and beat MTU Goalie Jamie Phillips (WPG). Wisconsin eventually sealed the win with an empty netter in the final minute.

January 3, 2015 Fargo Force at Sioux City Musketeers

FGO #7 Stevens, Brody RW (2015) – Scored a nice goal top shelf from the circles to open the scoring for the Force. Can be a force if he wants to. Had a couple soft shifts. Big frame but didn't play the body as much as I would have liked to see.

FGO #19 Eyssimont, Mikey LC (2014 Undrafted) – Game has come along since last year. Saw the ice well tonight moving the puck around the offensive zone and finding open teammates. Not really a force in all three zones but shows effort in his own end. Not sure if his play this year will get him a look in his second year of draft eligibility but he is progressing well year to year.

SC #13 Durflinger, Jake RW (2016) – Kind of a rollercoaster game for the 16 year old. Shows flashes offensively of why he's playing at this level as a 16 year old at times but also shows his young age in mistakes often. He complicated things tonight, made easy plays harder than they should have been. Plays small, gets outmuscled easily. Will need to get bigger.

SC #15 Ryczek, Jake RD (2016) – Smooth skater. Tries to make the tough play at times instead of taking what's given to him. Gets sucked out of position from time to time in his own zone. Showed great speed twice when his partner turned the puck over at the offensive blue line to beat his opponent back and knock him off the puck.

SC #19 Kurker, Sam RW (2012, 2nd Round St. Louis Blues) – Had a hat trick tonight. Was a force all night. Big body, uses it well. Goes to the dirty areas and does what it takes to score.

SC #55 Zuhlsdorf, Ryan LD (2015) – Shaky performance tonight. Made a few questionable decisions on and off the puck. Wasn't very responsible on his own blue line: not having his stick on the ice and the puck getting out of the zone, firing multiple shots into guy's shin pads, not holding the wall well and losing possession. Probably just an off night, but raises a few question marks for me. Does a lot fundamentally well, but decision making is a question mark at this point.

SportU20 vs. BluesU20 4 Jan, 2015

Blu #45 D Vainio, Veeti (2015) - He was benched half of the game and showed again some worrying features.. He got huge problems in the D-zone and he's making lot of mistakes without puck. He's not a big kid and he hasn't shown willingness to even play physically. He's got tremendous puck skills and he's great blue liner with accurate and hard shots. Veeti handles the puck very well and finds great passing opportunities. He's average skater but could definitely be better because he got a good technique. Top speed is good enough but first steps need to better.

Blu #36 LW Björkqvist, Kasper (2015) - He didn't show anything spectacular today but had a decent night. He got great speed and he likes to play straightforward. He's not a magician with puck but he win battles with his attitude. He see the ice very well and always doing right decisions like dump the puck to the o-zone and not trying some fancy move. Kasper is decent in the all three zones and he really got some scoring sense.

Blu #91 C Niemelä, Joonas (2015) - Joonas is a smart center who usually do the right decision with puck. Not that great puck-handler but reads the game well and he got a great hockey sense. Scored a one goal today which was due to his smartness on ice. He's good on wheels but his biggest problems are in the physical side. Undersized kid who really need to add some muscle but he likes to join the traffic and not giving up there.

Spo #4 D Salo, Robin (2017) - Showed again how mature he can be. Already playing tough and he doesn't afraid anyone. Robin reads the game well and his passing game is just great.. long and short passes are accurate. His positioning in the D-zone is good and doesn't loose his one-on-one battles. He's great all-round d-man but he have improve his shot and start to use it more.

Niagara IceDogs at Barrie Colts, Jan 8, 2015

Score: 5-2 Niagara

LW Graham Knott (2015) – Knott showed good strength skating through checks and using his body to protect the puck. He used his powerful strides to gain a step on defenders, and had a couple breakaways in the game. Knott failed to convert both times, but had a good shot on both occasions, and on the 2nd breakaway the trailer was there to bang in a rebound. He was very tough to control coming from behind the net, and was good in the cycle game. His passes were accurate for the most part, and he always seemed to know where to be on the ice. Knott was effective on the PK and used his stick to break up several plays. He used his strength to push Colts players off the puck, and overall played a strong 200-foot game.

D Vince Dunn (2015) – Dunn used his skating ability to rush the puck up ice on several occasions, and wasn't afraid to jump into the rush to help out offensively. He made a few good pinches to keep plays alive, and moved the puck well in the offensive zone. He was confident walking the line, and for the most part his shots got through. Dunn didn't shy away from contact, either, and was involved in a very spirited fight with Colts tough guy Nick Pastorious where Dunn fared surprisingly well. The one negative in his game was that he took a couple unnecessary minors.

RW Roy Radke (2015) – Radke didn't do much offensively, but he did a good job taking care of his own zone in this one. He took a regular shift on the penalty kill and was able to clear the puck a few times. His positioning was good, he blocked a couple shots and he also saved a goal by clearing a rebound from just outside the crease. Offensively he had a couple turnovers at the opposing blue line and forced a couple passes that weren't there.

RW Andrew Mangiapane (2015*) – Mangiapane was one of the best players on the ice in this one. He showed good anticipation intercepting a bank pass early in the game, and made a good read centering it for Barrie's 1st goal. He forced a couple turnovers by heavily pressuring the puck carrier, which led to some good scoring chances. Mangiapane regularly gained the opposing line with possession of the puck and was very good in regards to zone entries. He was elusive in open ice, and drew a penalty after eluding an oncoming defender. He continues to show why he should be drafted as a re-entry.

D Rasmus Andersson (2015) – His first pass was almost always on target, and whenever nobody was open he skated the puck up ice without problem. It won't show up on the scoreboard, but he set up his teammates for several Grade A scoring chances, and easily could have had a few points in this one. Andersson also was able to get a handful of shots on net, and shot for a few nice deflections that led to 2nd and 3rd opportunities in front. He also had a couple end-to-end rushes, and did a great job using his big frame to shield the puck and prevent it from being taken away. Defensively, his position was decent and he blocked several shots at both even-strength and on the penalty kill.

G Mackenzie Blackwood (2015) – Barrie certainly wasn't at their best tonight and if it weren't for Blackwood it wouldn't have been close. Midway through the game the shots were 26-10 Niagara yet the game was tied at two. Blackwood tracked the puck very well and didn't seem bothered from traffic in front of him on the PP. He was composed in his crease and didn't overcommit to any shots. Blackwood also stopped a few breakaways and made some great saves extending his legs to cover up the bottom of the net. Blackwood made several 2nd and 3rd chance saves when his teammates left him hung out to try, and ended up with 35 saves in the loss. He doesn't look like a guy who has started almost 20 games in a row.

January 9, 2015 Erie Otters at London Knights

ERI #19 C Strome, Dylan (2015) - Strome made some good plays on vision and awareness, one of which resulted in Erie's third goal when he deflected a hard pass in. He is effective in outwaiting the defender and getting his shot off. Mishandled the puck on the power play a few times resulting in a clear. When the pace picks up he can sometimes take too long to make a decision and his skating affects him in these situations.

ERI #21 RW Fellows, Patrick (2015) - As usual Patrick was excellent on the Otters penalty kill. He does a great job of getting his stick in passing lanes effectively. He showed some offensive skill in this one displaying patience with the puck then a smart, accurate pass to set up Erie's fifth goal.

ERI #44 D Dermott, Travis (2015) - Travis looks smooth rushing the puck. He evades checkers well but sometimes isn't aware of backcheckers and can take too long to make a decision, which resulted on multiple occasions resulting in him getting stripped on some of these rushes. Has puck skills but needs to be more consistent with them. Great shot from the point. Gets stick in the passing lanes well on PK.

ERI #97 C McDavid, Connor (2015) - Connor made an impact immediately in this game using his speed and acceleration to force London to take a penalty 15 seconds in. He played on both the first and the second power play unit for the Otters on most occasions. He also plays secondary penalty kill minutes. He can sometimes try to do a little too much on his own on the rush, which at one point lead to him getting stripped leading to a breakaway which resulted in a penalty. He made a great move to fake out the goaltender then wrap around putting it off a London skate and in. Exceptional level acceleration and speed. Not physical but did assert himself a few times when he needed to; doesn't play scared.

LON #86 D Martenet, Chris (2015) - Martenet has excellent reach and used his stick effectively down low. He was caught flat footed one on one and was walked for Erie's second goal. He lacks footwork and mobility but is able to make up for it in some situations with his stick/reach.

LON #93 RW Marner, Mitchell (2015) - Mitchell was much quieter than usual, especially on the power play playing the point and wasn't able to create what he usually does on the man advantage, despite playing about 75% of the time on the power play from the back end. The only time he created offense was when he pinched down and used his puck skills deeper in the offensive zone. His shot from the point was put in for London's second goal. He made a great defensive play one on one don a shorthanded rush to break up the play.

Final Score: Erie Otters: 6 - London Knights: 2

January 10th, 2015 Waterloo Black Hawks at Tri-City Storm

WAT #3 LD Spaxman, Ethan (2015) – Big body, plays big and throws his body around in his own zone. Very responsible in the defensive zone. Gets down and blocks a ton of shots. Really sells out for the team. Made a few questionable decisions at the offensive blue line and in the neutral zone. Panicked with the puck when there was any sort of pressure on him. Was pretty one-dimensional tonight.

WAT #12 RW Boeser, Brock (2015) – Strong showing. More I see him play the more I love his game. Creates offensive opportunities for himself and just skates circles around defenders. Didn't find himself on the score sheet tonight but still made an impact on the game. Once he has the puck it's almost impossible to get it off of him. Super strong skater. Very smart with the puck, doesn't try to do too much, takes what they are giving him and turns it into instant offensive. Very impressive performance.

WAT #15 LCNovak, Tom (2015) – Had two points (goal and assist) tonight. Showed his playmaking skills multiple times. Very smart, offensive minded player that knows how to find the open man. Had a couple soft shifts in the midst of a very close game which is worrying. Offensive talent is absolutely there it's just a matter of working hard every shift.

WAT #20 LD Rossini, Sam (2016) – Big 16 year old. Huge frame. Very raw player. Potential to be a shut down defenseman is there just needs a little bit more refinement.

WAT #22 LW Sheehy, Tyler (2014 UD) – Had two really nice assists on both Waterloo goals. He sees the ice well, makes smart decisions. Doesn't turn the puck over. Knows where to put the puck on shooter's sticks. Really benefits from playing with Novak and Boeser.

TC #3 RD Dello, Tory (2015) – Continues to be impressive in every viewing. Always poised, never really panics. Model of consistency - what you see is what you get every time. Strongest player on the ice, possibly the strongest the player in the USHL. Outmuscles anyone who tries to get by him. Had some great battles with Boeser tonight. Nothing he does is flashy but he's the kind of guy you can trust to do his job and not screw up.

TC #19 RW Allsion, Wade (2016) – Skates with a purpose. Gets to the dirty areas and outworks guys. Buzzes around causing problems and being a general pest to the opposing team. Scored a nice goal top shelf from the right circle to seal the game for the Storm in the third period.

TC #20 LW Wahlin, Jake (2015) – Skated hard to the front of the net and was rewarded with a rebound goal in the first period. Really an enigma to me. During some viewings he jumps off the ice and others he is completely invisible. Consistency is an issue.

TC RW #44 Wilkie, Chris (2014 UD) – Continues to come along nicely after the disappointing year last year. Willing to shoot from just about anywhere. Would consider him selfish at times taking the shot on odd-man rushes when the passing lane is open. Now leads the USHL in goals. Might be a guy to keep an eye on in June as a second year eligible.

Acadie-Bathurst vs Saint John Sea Dogs, January 7th 2015

AB #55 LD Brisebois, Guillaume (2015) – Brisebois is the Titan leader in all areas of their game. Brisebois is the team Captain and leads his team in offensive and defensive situations. Brisebois is a good puck handler and shows confidence and patience with the puck. On the power play he controls the puck high and low; moving it around with great passes and also putting himself in a good place to receive it back. Brisebois takes risks offensively and his team mates usually cover for him well when he vacates his defensive position.

AB #8 RW Popov, Egor (2015) – Popov saw a lot of ice time through this game. Popov is quick skater with strong but not very smooth stride. Popov works hard to keep pucks deep in the O zone. Popov is also usually in a good position defensively and gets in a good place to receive a pass.

AB #20 LW Kerr, Aaron (2015) – Kerr is a fast forward that really gives the Titan some offensive punch. Kerr's speed gave Saint John's D trouble all game, quickly closing on them forcing turn overs. Kerr scored a great goal using speed and strength on the rush taking the puck wide, beating the d man cutting to the net putting the puck top corner.

AB #11 LW Boivin, Christophe (2015) – Boivin is a very crafty winger with lots of skill and a great set of hands. Boivin is limited by his size and is beat off pucks easily. He relies on his ability to beat opponents using elusive skating and dekes. He often finds ways to get the job done controlling the puck well and making smart plays.

SNB #26 LD Bell, Jason (2015) – Bell was recently acquired by Saint John from Cape Breton. Bell is an offensive defenseman with a great shot. Bell's shot is heavy and he has a good quick release. Bell is always offensively involved. In the O zone; Bell takes risks and jumps in offensively often. Bell stays aware defensively and is usually in proper position. In the first Bell lost a puck battle off the wall that lead to a goal against

SNB #10 C Noel, Nathan (2015) – Noel centers Saint John's most offensive line. Noel has great speed that often controls the tempo of the game during his shifts. Saint John has his line of the ice as much as possible it seems. When Noel has the puck he makes good passes showing off his solid vision. Late in game a Noel was in position to cover a D man caught pinching and quit on back check leading to a Titan goal.

SNB #12 LW Marsh, Adam (2015) – Adam Marsh is a well-rounded player for Saint John; he is a smart back checker and aggressive fore checker. Marsh plays a safe game for his team by making responsible plays in all zones. Marsh is offensively dangerous low in the O zone. Marsh works hard to keep pucks low and puts the puck to the net when possible. A couple times Marsh made a very skilled move to create time and space but then made a bad pass.

SNB #16 C Dove-McFalls, Samuel (2015) – Dove-McFalls adds depth to Saint John's line up centering their third line. Dove-McFalls plays a sound positional game usually, putting himself in the right place supporting his D men and wingers well.

SNB #5 LD Chabot, Thomas (2015) – With Zboril out of Saint John's lineup; Chabot is on the ice often with a heavy workload. Chabot is calm and patient with the puck, but can sometimes over handle it. Chabot sees a lot of time on the power play and penalty kill. Chabot is a great skater that always keeps his feet moving keeping him involved at all times. A good example of his quickness was a time he pinched a weak side rim off in the O zone and carried low to set up a goal.

SNB #18 RW Smallman, Spencer (2015) – Smallman has great size and a good nose for the net. Smallman had 2 goals in this game; the first he put himself back door off a cycle play for a tap in and the second he drove the net hard on a rebound to bang it in. Smallman's skating has improved through his junior career and he has become one of Saint John's go to guys offensively. As mentioned Smallman has great size and he uses it well playing a strong game physically.

SNB #51 LW Imama, Bokondji (2015) – Imama was recently acquired from Baie-Comeau before the trade deadline. Imama had an impact in his first game as a Sea Dog playing a solid power forward role on Saint John's top offensive line with Smallman and Noel. Imama is big solid forward that battles hard plays a skilled game with lots of physical play. Imama has a great shot getting pucks to the net and also does a good job setting up Smallman and Noel.

Moncton Wildcats vs Saint-John Sea Dogs, January 8th 2015

MON #19 C/RW Askew, Cameron (2015) – Askew plays a big role on Moncton's top line with Barbashev. Askew has good hockey sense and skates himself into good position to usually be an offensive threat. Askew has a good accurate shot he showed off receiving a pass low on a bad angle and shooting it top shelf to score a power play goal for Moncton. Askew has good size (6'2" 205lbs)- he can be dominant physically and other times not so much.

MON #8 RW/LW Garland, Conor (2015) – Garland currently leads the QMJHL in points. Garland has great speed and skill. It seems at times the puck just finds him. When Garland has the puck, he moves it really well and creates a lot of offensive threat. Garland makes Moncton's top line with Barbashev and Askew dangerous every time they're on the ice. Standing at only 5'8" Garlands size may be limiting but it doesn't show in games so far. Garland plays an elusive puck control game on the wall and moves it quickly to the middle.

SNB #26 LD Bell, Jason (2015) – Bell played a more responsible game than the previous night in this one. Bell is always involved offensively, but his quick feet help him get back and cover for himself. Bell always looks to jump in offensively on the rush. Bell scored a nice goal jumping in as the 4th man late on a 3 on 2 and put a nice shot past Dubeau. Saint John uses Bell on most of their power play time and also their penalty kill.

SNB #10 C Noel, Nathan (2015) – Noel is a very speedy center that pushes the pace every time he is on the ice. At times Noel could work a bit harder for pucks, but when he has the puck Noel spins off checks and can be very elusive. Noels speed allows him to push the opposition D back quick creating space on the rush. Since Noel's line is Saint Johns top line, he is on taking most of the important draws.

SNB #12 LW Marsh, Adam (2015) – Marsh is winger that adds skill with responsibility to Saint John's line up. Marsh does a good job in his end being in position and making a good outlet pass. In the O zone he works hard to get pucks deep or to the net. On the line up card, Marsh is on the 3rd line, but as the game progresses he is a minute eater playing with all lines.

SNB #16 C Dove-McFalls, Samuel (2015) – Dove-McFalls played a more physical game than usual in this one. Dove-McFalls was hard to play again in all zones, finishing hits. He could be more successful if he moved his feet a little more. Dove-McFalls is on for some of Saint John's power play time, but always on for the PK.

SNB #5 LD Chabot, Thomas (2015) – Chabot is very smooth skating, skilled and well rounded defenseman. Chabot takes care of his own end and also ramps up Saint John's offense every time he is on the ice. Chabot directs play when he is on the ice directing the back check as play comes towards him. Chabot also quarterbacks the offense. Chabot's smooth speed allows him to lead the rush for Saint John carrying the puck wide on the rush. Chabot protects the puck well on his backhand using his body to carry the puck where he wants.

SNB #18 RW Smallman, Spencer (2015) – Smallman is a big forward that continues to improve night in, night out. Smallman works hard to create offensive for him team and he also works hard to get back on the D side of the puck. Smallman has grit and can get things done that way, but he also has decent speed that allows him to carry the puck. Smallman works hard to get the puck low and find his teammates for offense.

SNB #51 LW Imama, Bokondji (2015) – Imama played a better game the night before. Imama plays on Saint John's top line with Noel and Smallman and works hard to create success this line. Imama showed patience at times in this game controlling the puck and making nice passes on the rush, high in the O zone. The night before it seemed he tried shooting a little more and working pucks low.

BOSTON UNIVERSITY at U. OF WISCONSIN (1-9-2015)

BU - #2 RW - Ahti Oksanen (FA) – Gets looked over a lot because he plays on Jack Eichel's left wing but Ahti is a solid power winger with good size and finishing ability. Oksanen played defense last year but was moved to forward this season has added offense to BU's top 6 forwards. Wasn't overly physical on the fore check but still has time for that to develop. Scored both BU goals late in the 3rd to force overtime.

BU - #9 C -Jack Eichel (2015) – Didn't have his best game. I didn't see a lot of physicality to his game, either with the puck or without. This was Eichel's first game back since the world juniors so there may have been a little rust there. Eichel was just as elusive with the puck as he always was but didn't generate a lot of scoring chances with it. He did however almost score on the first shirt of the game when he drove the net, out muscled the defenseman for position and tipped the centering pass just wide of the goal. Eichel did get out muscled on the back check by #28 Schulze that resulted in a short-handed goal against.

BU had Eichel posted below the goal line on the power play, and while he showed good passing skills and puck retrieval, the only play he made most of the night from that position was a bad angle shot from along the goal line. Would have liked to see him take the puck to the paint from that position.

BU - #26 LW - AJ Greer (2015) – Has good size and skates well for a big guy but didn't see a lot of consistency in his compete level tonight. Got out worked and out muscled in many 50/50 puck battles, sometimes against much smaller Wisconsin players. Was quick getting out to the point and challenging the play.

BU - #10 RW - Danny O'Regan (SJ-2012, 5th Rd) - O'Regan was BU's most dynamic forward for most of the night. Was left off the score sheet but created a lot of chances by using his speed and taking the puck to the net. O'Regan battled hard for loose pucks and was first on the the fore check most of the night.

BU - #25 RD - Brandon Fortunato (2015+) – Fortunato was passed up in last year's NHL entry draft, mostly to do with his lack of size. Fortunato showed a good compete level all night. Didn't shy away from the corners or play against larger players. Has a great first pass, it wasn't always the homerun pass into the neutral zone, sometimes it was a solid 10-20 foot pass to relieve pressure. Scored on a Rebound from a point shot that fell on his stick as he was moving in from the point on the power play. Fortunato picked his spots well when jumping in from the point, didn't take unnecessary risks at either blue line that I saw. No doubt Fortunato needs to add some bulk to his frame but possesses all the skating, puck moving ability and hockey IQ that you would want from today's defenseman.

WIS - #19 C - Cameron Hughes (2015) – Played a physical game. Hughes came to the defense of a teammate after a questionable hit. Probably would have fought the BU player if fighting was permitted in college hockey. Seemed to play with an attitude all night. Didn't miss an opportunity to finish his hits, didn't create a lot offensively 5 on 5 but did make good passes on the power play, seemed to find a seem through the middle of the ice and was able to find a teammate on the other side of the rink. Passed up some shots at the net, would like to see him take those opportunities when they are there.

Game Notes: BU was fortunate to tie this game with 2 late goals in the 3rd with the goalie pulled. BU looked dominate at times but the combination of timely saves by Wisconsin goalie, Joel Rumpel and the inability to keep the pressure on Wisconsin Consistently forced them to have to poor it on late, luckily for BU it was enough to get the tie.

BOSTON UNIVERSITY at U. of WISCONSIN (1-10-2015)

BU - #9 C - Jack Eichel (2015) – Played with more of a physical edge tonight. Was throwing hits and stopped on a lot more pucks then the previous night where he did a lot of circling and coasting. Came out of the penalty box, created a turnover by pressuring the puck, eventually found the puck in the slot, used his reach and patients to slide through the middle of the slot and found the goalie not in a position to make a play on the puck and scored. BU also moved Eichel to the point position on the Power play where he was much more effective then he was down low the night before. Flicked a quick snap shot from the point that found the top shelf for his 2nd goal of the night. Had one more similar play that was tipped in front by O'Regan on the Power play. Eichel also found him with a 2-1 in the third with an opportunity to score his 3rd of the night and made a great feed over to O'Regan who tapped it into the open net. Eichel ended up with 2 goals and 1 Assists and was dominate all night long.

BU - #27 D - Doyle Somerby (NYI-2012, 5th Rd.) – Big Hulking defenseman showed good agility being able to keep up with shifty forwards like Besse and Hughes along the boards. Showed a good stick, being able to disrupt passing lanes and poke check with his long reach. Looked like he still has a ways to go with his skating before the next level but provided good shutdown ability.

BU - #10 RW - Danny O'Regan (SJ-2012, 5th Round) – O'Regan has 2 goals and 1 Assist tonight, his line of Eichel and Oksanen was dominate in all 3 zones. Did a good job defending and creating turnovers. O'Regan was especially good providing back pressure on Wisconsin's forwards. O'Regan's first goal was on a mid-air deflection on a point shot from Jack Eichel, the 2nd was shorthanded on a 2 on 1 also assisted by Eichel.

WIS - #33 G - Joel Rumpel (FA) – Despite giving up 6 goals Rumpel did make some fantastic saves 5 on 5. The game got away from Wisconsin in the 3rd due to penalties and poor defensive zone coverage, but Rumpel did show the ability to battle until the end of the game.

Quebec Remparts vs Drummondville Voltigeurs, January 11th 2015

QUE #21 RW Tkachev, Vladimir (2015): Showed elite stickhandling in the offensive zone on some shifts but overall, the young Russian was rather quiet today. Played on the Remparts' 2nd offensive line and got regular power play ice time.

QUE #88 LW Dmytro Timashov (2015): Played on a line with Adam Erne and Anthony Duclair today, but didn't do a whole lot in the game. His line couldn't get much going offensively; lots of individual play from all three. Caused quite a few turnovers trying to be too fancy in zone entries with the puck. His lack of strength was evident in one-on-one battles in the offensive zone. Worked hard overall, but tended to stop moving his feet in the defensive zone.

QUE #30 G Booth, Callum (2015): Had a tough 1st period, including a softy on the Drummondville first goal. Seemed to battle the puck all the time in the first period and his control rebound was off. He got better as the game went on, and made quite a few good saves to keep his team in the game, as they were able to steal one point from Drummondville. Even if things didn't go well in the first half, he kept his cool, which is a trait I like about him.

DRU #19 C Barré-Boulet, Alex (2015): Loved his game today, playing in an offensive role now due to recent trades by the Voltigeurs. Made quick decisions with the puck and sees the ice well. He played the point on the power play which is new for him this season. Liked his patience with the puck and he's a smart player, scoring two goals in the game.

DRU #22 C Sevigny, Mathieu (2016): Scored the game's opening goal on a weak shot from the point that Callum Booth would like to have back. Sevigny is a consistent performer, already plays a mature game at both ends of the ice and did it again tonight. Played physical and was strong on the forecheck with his line. Worked hard and supported his defense well by coming down low in the defensive zone to help them out.

DRU #4 RD Gagne, Benjamin (2017): Late '98-born defender played a mature, steady game. He made good use of his stick breaking up rushes with a quick active stick. Good gap control. He played big minutes for the Voltigeurs today, showing good mobility with good feet.

DRU #6 RD Carignan-Labbé, Julien (2015): Good physicality in his own end. This strong kid can protect the puck well in his zone. Cleared the front of the net fairly well and has some mean streaks in him. Struggled with the puck tonight, had trouble getting the puck to his forwards and his lack of vision hurt him with his play selections.

Jan. 13, 2015 – Culver Military Academy at Cushing Academy (Watkins Tournament Championship Final)

CUL #8 C Bachman, Karch (2015) – Showed off tremendous skating skills, good playmaking vision, and serious faceoff chops. I love his game in the offensive zone, as he uses his quick feet to buzz around the net while keeping a keen eye for open teammates. Ability to pass the puck while confined to tight spaces was remarkable. Won most of his faceoffs. Backcheck lacked effort at times, while his shooting looked a bit premature at times.

CSH #3 D Dillon, Matt (2016) – Showed decent manoeuvrability and good passing ability in a game that was mired by turnovers and costly mistakes. While he has good hands and feet, he has a tendency to get too confident with the puck at times and is a bit insensitive to oncoming pressure. Didn't make bad decisions, but took too long to make the good ones.

CSH #35 G Daccord, Joey (2014) – Standing at 6-foot-3, Joey Daccord possesses the requisite size of an NHL goalie prospect, and it was easy to see why in a game in which Culver continuously tried—unsuccessfully—to beat Joey Daccord up high. Excellent reflexes properly accompanied his champion size, allowing him to deflect rebounds out of danger areas. I generally liked his positioning, as I thought he looked aggressive at the right times and big in his net at virtually all times.

CSH #11 C Cotton, David (2015) – Not the fastest skater on his club, but he possesses the vision and playmaking skill to be a highly effective and dependable F-3 forechecker. Didn't play a ton on the penalty kill, but attention to detail and hard work stood out as strengths in terms of his defensive-end play. Utilized his size and his big body to shield the puck well, but I would've like to have seen him dominate the game more given his advantage in that department.

Jan. 16, 2015 – Tri-City Americans at Vancouver Giants

TRI #11 LW Comrie, Ty (2015) – Had a great game tonight in which he scored a goal. His lone tally came off of a quickly released wristshot from his off-side. Pouncing on a loose puck, he showed really good straight-ahead acceleratiopn by taking off with it after turning on the afterburners. His speed and hands are both terrific, but he could definitely stand to improve his defensive game as he looks a bit uninvolved with the puck in his own zone.

TRI #31 G Sarthou, Evan (2016) – Posting a shutout performance, I would be hard-pressed to see Evan Sarthou as anything but an MVP for his Tri-City club tonight. His butterfly technique was near perfect in this one. But he seems to specialize in aggressively challenging shots from the top of his crease and handling the rebounds with ease.

TRI #36 RD Carlo, Brandon (2015) – A quiet but effective night in his own end. His skating is just fluid enough and his size more than sufficient enough for him to almost always keep his lane and form a formidable defender to beat one-on-one. His one-on-one work in the corners and in front of his net were both exceptional. On the offensive end, he kept it very, very simple in terms of puck movement tonight. In fact, if anything, he has a tendency to keep things 'too simple' at times.

TRI #37 LD Wotherspoon, Parker (2015) – Greasy and unbridled nature of his defensive game came to the forefront, as he was a monster at clearing his crease of pesky screen attempts and an absolute warrior in the corners and along the boards. He proved very difficult to gain position on in front of the

Tri-City net. His offensive game also showed some razzle-dazzle as he made several neatly timed entries into the Giants offensive end.

VAN #17 LW Benson, Tyler (2015) – Had yet another good performance tonight, even if he's had better throughout the year. His quick feet allow him to emerge quickly into the opposition's prime scoring area, where he rips off a quick and accurate wrister. Even though he didn't play badly by any means, tonight was one of his quieter performances. He will likely see a leap in scoring next year as his shot's accuracy improves.

VAN #21 RD Mennel, Brennan (2015) – Had a good game tonight, playing top line power play minutes alongside Mason Geertsen. I like Mennel's passing ability, which he showed off tonight by working the puck back-and-forth along the blueline with seeming impunity. His quick-turning wheels also allow him to rove down low in the offensive zone, where he's already gaining a reputation for making good reads with the puck. He took a couple bad penalties, but otherwise looked good.

VAN #22 LD Osipov, Dmitry (2015) – Continues to improve as a defender, playing on the Giants' top pairing alongside Mason Geertsen. While Geertsen plays a more stationary game in front of the net, Osipov is a bit of a rover as he has really good small area ability and is good at chasing down pucks and retrieving them out of the corner.

January 16, 2015 - Charlottetown Islanders at Sherbrooke Phoenix

CHA #11 RW Sprong, Daniel (2015) - Daniel showed great hands in traffic and played top offensive minutes for Charlottetown. He has a quick release on his shot but also displayed passing ability making a nice pass to set up a one-timer on the Islanders' second goal.

CHA #14 C Chlapik, Filip (2015) - Showed a decent release to score Charlottetown's second goal of the game on a two on one. He showed evasiveness and quick hands but does get stripped trying to do a little too much by himself. Made a skilled pass on the power play that set up a big chance for his team. He had a fair amount of negative body language in this game following battles, which he struggled in.

CHA #27 D Henley, David (2015) - Henley moved the puck well without pressure showing the ability to consistently make good passes under these circumstances, but whenever there was pressure and he had to rush those plays resulted in turnovers quite often. At his best with the puck when he made simple plays out of the zone. He has excellent size and engages in physical battles on the wall. He has the backwards skating to keep up with the play and made a few solid plays on two on two and one on one rushes. Decent skater for size. Very late questionable hit gave Sherbrooke a power play.

SHE #89 LW Schweri, Kai (2015) - Kai has outstanding quickness and speed and utilizes it to put pressure on the puck carrier. He changes directions extremely quick and is very hard to contain. Possesses a hard shot but needs to work on the accuracy.

SHE #97 D Roy, Jeremy (2015) - Jeremy is an extremely smooth skater. He moves very well laterally and is as fluid as they come in this draft. He is poised on the rush, very smooth carrying the puck and can fend off checkers very well, then separate. He has an outstanding ability to read plays and react accordingly so quick and intelligent, it's a tough skill to find. His hockey sense is extremely high. Among the smartest players in this draft. Consistently makes the right play. Smart shot to find a hole to put it through resulted in scoring chance. Played top minutes in every situation for his team. Good stick one on one. Not a physical player but doesn't play scared either.

Final Score: Charlottetown Islanders: 2 - Sherbrooke Phoenix: 0

January 17, 2015 - Saint John Sea Dogs at Gatineau Olympiques

SNJ #2 D Webster, Bailey (2015) - Bailey has excellent size and uses his body to force opponents off the puck when the situation calls for it. He plays opponents tough and punishes when he gets the opportunity. He made a defensive mistake letting his man get into the slot which lead to Gatineau's second goal. He won races to the puck, surprisingly for a player his size. Was able to outmuscle a big strong power forward despite the forward having a step on Webster. Moved the puck very well for a shutdown defender knowing when to move the puck to his defensive partner and when to send it deep for the cycle. Shows raw ability but a ton of upside.

SNJ #5 D Chabot, Thomas (2015) - Chabot is a smooth skater and always keeps his feet moving. He has excellent mobility and looks extremely smooth moving in every direction. He has an excellent stick defensively using it to break up plays, break up passes and it makes him very tough to beat one on one. One of, if not the best defender in this draft when it comes to using his stick. Shot selection from the point needs to be better. Showed good puck skills and made intelligent decisions. Played in all game situations and received top minutes for Saint John.

SNJ #10 C Noel, Nathan (2015) - Good skater with excellent speed but has a very slender frame. He didn't have a huge impact on this game but showed flashes of real puck skills evading checkers and using his hands to beat defenders. He is pretty smooth with the puck in the offensive zone and made some nice plays to create scoring chances. Did an outstanding job in the face-off circle winning almost every draw in this game in regards to draws won by centremen.

SNJ #12 LW Marsh, Adam (2015) - Has a small frame but possesses good separation speed on the wing. He consistently gets in great scoring position and has a great skill for constantly getting open for scoring chances. However he struggled to pull the trigger a few times despite his posiitoning. He made some good plays with the puck in all three zones under pressure.

SNJ #16 C Dove-McFalls, Samuel (2015) - Samuel showed excellent two-way ability tonight. He blocked a ton of shots, at one point getting up and making a diving play to follow it up to clear the zone. He played in all game situations and was effective on the power play as well moving the puck well creating chances. He is a strong skater for someone with such a big frame.

SNJ #55 D Green, Luke (2016) - Green is a high risk, high reward defender with excellent skating ability. He's almost impossible to beat outside in one on one match-up's but did get beat when opponents would fake out and go in on him. He is capable of rushing the puck and can be an effective passer on the point. Unfortunately he tries to force a lot of shots from the point, many of which get blocked. In the final minute he made a costly mistake trying to do too much himself with an empty net giving up an easy turnover and an easy empty netter to seal his team's loss.

GAT #32 LW Trenin, Yakov (2015) - Trenin has a huge frame and finishes his checks hard. He plays a bit of a power forward game but did show puck skill in this game. He fired a good one timer on a bouncing puck. He made smart passes playing on Gatineau's top power play unit.

Final Score: Gatineau Olympiques: 4 - Saint John Sea Dogs: 2

Rouyn-Noranda Huskies vs Blainville-Boisbriand Armada, January 17th 2015

RN #3 RD Neveu, Jacob (2016): Big, physically-mature kid played a regular shift at even-strength and on the PK. He's strong along the boards and didn't back down when challenged physically. On the PK, he forgot to cover Danick Martel at the side of the net which led to the Armada's 2nd goal. Didn't do much offensively during the game but showed great speed rushing the puck from his own zone in the 3rd period.

RN #6 RD Myers, Philippe (2015): Got involved physically in his own zone during the game, using his size and reach well to defend in his zone. Has decent speed skating forward due to his long strides. He can get into trouble versus quick players going wide on him, as he doesn't possess the quickest footwork. Moved the puck fairly well to his forwards, kept his game simple.

RN #1 G Harvey, Samuel (2016): Some issues with his rebound control today, fought the puck most of the game. Didn't look big in his net and played deep, which didn't help either. Liked his compete level; he didn't quit even though he didn't have his best game. Would have liked to have the 4th goal back after his team scored two quick goals and had the momentum going for them.

RN #16 RW Beaudin, Jean-Christophe (2015): Played on the wing on the 2nd line and played on the point on the power play, got caught being too cute with the puck on the power play and lost it to Philippe Sanche, who scored the Armada's 3rd goal after Beaudin's turnover. On the power play, he had a tough time getting his shot through, as he couldn't find a shooting lane. Showed some nice things in the 3rd period, including good speed on the wing when he had time and space in the neutral zone. Almost scored late in the 3rd into after hitting the post at the side of the net.

RN #13 LD Lauzon, Zachary (2017): Younger brother of Jeremy who was not in the lineup, Zachary played on the 3rd pair with basically no ice time on special teams. Liked his feet, saw that he can get away from pressure pretty easily and moves the puck well. Struggled in physical battles in the game as he lacks strength right now. He's been up and down all season between his midget AAA team and the Huskies.

RN #24 LW Fortin, Alexandre (2015): Plays on an offensive line and got quality ice time on the power play, as the Huskies played with five forwards on the first power play unit. Made some good plays in the neutral zone, with a good active stick knocking pucks down. On the power play he was used at the side of the net, where he was able to flash his playmaking abilities, including a real nice cross-ice pass to Julien Nantel for a great scoring chance (robbed by Montembeault). Decision-making with the puck in the neutral zone was a flaw with his game today.

BLB #33 G Montembeault, Samuel (2015): Made some good saves in the game, really tough to beat down low, quick legs and covers a lot of space. He moved well in his crease, making a couple of nice saves with a quick post-to-post movement. Liked how calm he is in his crease, and his good rebound control. On the PK, he did a good job tracking pucks with traffic in front of him, his height is useful there.

BLB #57 C Picard, Miguel (2016): The first-round pick from last year's midget draft centered the 4th line. Nothing flashy but did the little things well, was good on the forecheck and cycled the puck well with his linemates. Good along the boards and made smart decisions with the puck. Didn't have much ice time today, good active stick in the neutral zone.

January 18, 2015, Barrie Colts at Oshawa Generals

BAR #19 D Andersson, Rasmus (2015) - Andersson shows good offensive tools but can sometimes get way ahead of the play, one situation resulted in a 3 on 1 down low. He had a great breakout option on the penalty kill but didn't see it and fired it down the ice instead. Played his man well in two on two match-up's. Plays big minutes for the Colts.

BAR #26 RW Mangiapane, Andrew (2015*) - Mangiapane's skating is absolutely effortless. He's not afraid to go into traffic and plays with a really gritty edge and when he carries puck into traffic, he usually comes out the other side with it. Played top unit on the penalty kill and power play as well as five on five. He spent a little time on the point on the top power play unit. On the penalty kill he came through clearing the zone in a few key moments.

OSH #22 C Cirelli, Anthony (2015) - Cirelli provided good energy for the Generals. He forechecks hard and forced several turnovers in this game. He also finishes his checks. Showed some flashes of puck skills but didn't do too much today.

OSH #35 G Appleby, Ken (2015*) - Did a great job recording the shutout. Made some very good point blank saves. Uses his size to take away angles very well.

Final Score: Oshawa Generals: 1 - Barrie Colts: 0

Kärpät vs. Frölunda 20th Jan, 2015

Kär #9 RW Puljujärvi, Jesse (2016) - He was benched for the two first periods but got some ice time in the third period. Showed great speed and great offensive instincts couldnät do anything special. Great back checking and showed willingness to play rough.

Kär #8 LW Mäenalanen, Saku (Drafted by Preds 2013) - Saku had a decent night... Great speed with good puck handling skills but wasn't that effective. He's hard-working kid with great attitude but hasn't yet find his best at pro level.

Frö #7 D Larsson, Jacob (2015) - Jacob showed he's ready to play with men. Mature kid with great vision and mobility. Likes to join the offense and he got quite accurate shots. Wasn't playing that much managed his role perfectly.

Frö #62 LW Lehkonen, Artturi (Drafted by Habs 2013) - Hard-working winger with great hockey sense. He's not the most skilled player on ice but he's very versatile kid with great attitude. Doing great in all three zones and he's really reliable two way player.

Frö #9 LW Görtz, Max (Drafted by Preds) - Didn't show anything with puck but you can noticed his offensive skills. Big kid with great skating and likes to go the traffic.

Frö #88 Johnson, Andres (Drafted by Maple Leafs 2013) - Speedy forward with amazing offensive tools. Not a big guy but can play rough around corners because of his good balance. Great vision and puck-handling skills... Always dangerous in the o-zone but needs to work with his two way game.

Jan. 20, 2015 – Seattle Thunderbirds at Prince George Cougars

SEA #12 LW Gropp, Ryan (2015) – Played physically, mirroring the size and hitting ability of his linemate Keegan Kolesar. A better skater than Kolesar despite being taller and larger. Gropp is very difficult to contain due to his combination of size, speed and physicality. Able to put the puck in the net from in close or out wide, he scored on a wristshot from just a foot away from the crease.

SEA #13 LC Barzal, Matthew (2015) – Looks fully recovered from a cracked kneecap, as he was able to absorb an early hit in the corner that looked dangerous. Returned to the game after the hit looking fast and motivated. Pulled out a whack of wild passing tricks, setting up Robert Lipsberg on 2 goals and racking up 4 assists in total. A flashy performance.

SEA #25 RD Bear, Ethan (2015) – Has a 'fire-hydrant' frame that makes him difficult to knock off balance. Made some nice chip passes off the boards to spring the offense. Creative when it comes to outletting the puck and extraordinary calm when he has foreheckers bearing down on him. Made a couple nice keeps and showed off a powerful shot.

SEA #28 RW Kolesar, Keegan (2015) – Played in a bit of a complimentary role on the opposite wing of Ryan Gropp. Footspeed lags at times, but he possesses enough strength to make up for it. He has good offensive zone awareness and excels at pinning and protecting pucks along the boards or wearing the opposition down with checks of his own. Scored on a funky backhand that was unconventional but well timed.

PRI #9 LW Morrison, Brad (2015) – Morrison is a small, speedy and shifty player who creates a ton of offense from the back-door area. Scored from that area tonight after receiving a great pass from Harkins. Loves making fancy individualistic moves with the puck as he showed on a couple nice toe-drags tonight. Creates a ton of space on the ice by being hard to beat one-on-one and absorbing checks. There was a bit of selfishness to his game as he dipsy-doodled with the puck a bit too often.

PRI #12 LC Harkins, Jansen (2015) – Skating stride continues to get longer and more powerful. Passing and vision continue to improve even though he was already advanced in those areas. Delivered a terrific 'seeing-eye' pass through three Seattle sticks to set-up Brad Morrison for an easy tap-in goal. Because his game is underpinned by a 'snap decision'-type style, he makes the odd bonehead play. Shot blocking continues to be a strength.

PRI #25 Olson, Tate (2015) D – Seems to have added an extra step to his skating and improves his decision making with each game. Offensive production and efficiency on the power play continues to improve. His shot looks more accurate but the windup is still a bit long. Playing with greater confidence and poise, his passing and general breakout game have come along really nicely.

PRI #21 LW Bethune, Jared (2015) – This was a bit of a disappointing effort tonight. I still like the raw attributes Bethune brings to the table, however. A strong and powerful player, even though skating could use improvement. Easily wins board battles against smaller players, but lost several one-on-one battles against Keegan Kolesar tonight, which doesn't reflect well on his projection at the next level.

LINCOLN STARS vs MADISON CAPITOLS (1-21-2015)

LIN - #12 LW – Walt Hopponen (2015+) – Would have liked to see him use his build to separate people from the puck but still won a good amount of battles. Doesn't have the high end skill set but gets up and down the ice well and can make a good pass. Had a shoot first mentality when he got the puck on his stick in the offensive zone.

LIN - #16 RW– Michael Gillespie (2015+) – First thing that stands out is his skating ability, smooth skater and can squeeze and jump through holes you don't see there. Was an aggressive fore checker and pressured the Defenseman all evening. The stars leading goal scorer up to this point in the season wasn't able to find the back of the net tonight, but his play away from the puck created chances.

MAD - #17 LW- Sam McCormick (2015) – Showed a high compete level all night long. Was the victim of a huge hit in the corner in the 3rd period, got right back up and delivered a big hit at the other end of the ice against a larger player. His size doesn't detour him from playing a physical game. Battled hard in front of the net. You can see a progression in his game from the start of the season. The effort was always there in McCormick's game but tonight he looked to play with more confidence both with and without the puck.

MAD - #14 D – Tommy Muck (2015+) – Made good outlet passes, always has his head up looking up ice. Did a good job eluding fore checkers and showed the skating ability to pull away from them when he needed it. Didn't show a lot in the way of creating offense but had good gab control for most of the night and made good decisions with the puck at both bluelines.

MAD - #2 C – Ryan Lohin (2015) – Played a solid game, Picked up an assist. Handled himself well in the faceoff circle. Can get up and down the ice well and works hard getting back and was in good defensive position most of the night. Had an active stick in the defensive zone, disrupting plays and taking away space quickly. Took the puck to the net strong on a couple occasions.

Soo Greyhounds at Barrie Colts, January 22, 2015

Score: 4-3 Greyhounds

Sault Ste. Marie

RW Zachary Senyshyn (2015) – Senyshyn finished his checks with regularity, and went to the dirty areas of the ice. He had a couple strong net drives, and used his size to protect the puck while crashing the crease. He used his big, powerful strides to generate good speed through the neutral zone, and showed good hands dancing around a pretty steady defenseman in Jonathan Laser. He was regularly back to support in the defensive zone, and played a solid 200-foot game. He did have one bad turnover that led to a mini-breakaway for Joseph Blandisi, but he was unable to capitalize.

D Medric Mercier (2015) – Mercier was poised carrying the puck up ice and through the neutral zone, and on occasion went on the forecheck chasing down his own dump in. He read plays very well and didn't allow easy entries into the defensive zone. Mercier's gap control was excellent, which allowed him to seal players off effectively. He laid a big hit into Stephen Nosad as he tried to slip by, and finished guys off whenever he could. Mercier didn't panic when oncoming forecheckers got in his face, and made good outlets throughout the night. He also scored on a slapper from the point that powered through Daniel Gibl's glove.

D Colton White (2015) – White did a nice job poking the puck off oncoming players and made quick, simple outlets after forcing a turnover to turn the play around and move up ice quickly. If there weren't any easy plays he would bank it off the glass and out. White was physical along the wall, and was positionally sound tracking forwards through the defensive zone. White did a nice job of sucking in forecheckers and taking them out of the play before advancing the puck up ice at the last second. He took a tripping penalty, but besides that he played a very good game.

D Gustav Bouramman (2015) – Bouramman made good outlet passes with regularity, and also had a couple good rushes with the puck. He showed good poise carrying it, and moved it very efficiently on the powerplay. He wasn't afraid to jump into the play, and came down to the halfwall on several occasions to help out in puck battles and keep plays alive. He looked very calm, and because of his good skating ability he was able to get back whenever he was in trouble.

Barrie

LW Matthew Kreis (2015) - Kreis did a good job generating speed through the neutral zone and carrying the puck safely into the offensive zone, which allowed Barrie to set up offensively. He backchecked extremely hard, and his backside pressure forced several turnovers throughout the night. He had a few good shots from the scoring area, and overall played a good two-way game.

RW Andrew Mangiapane (2015*) – Mangiapane was very dangerous coming off the wall, as he could see the entire offensive zone, read the defense and either find an open target or take a good shot. He puts pucks on net with regularity, and wasn't afraid to drive for rebounds. He did a good job accepting some poor passes in his feet, and played the game with great pace. He consistently carried the puck into Soo's zone with possession, and was very good off the rush. Mangiapane was very disruptive on the forecheck and he caused a couple turnovers with his pressure.

Note: Rasmus Andersson, Mackenzie Blackwood, Roy Radke and Blake Speers were all out of the lineup for their respective teams.

U. of MICHIGAN VS U. of WISCONSIN (1-23-15)

MICH - #10 LW - Justin Selman (FA) – Was a key part of Michigan's 7-4 comeback win after being down 4-1 in the 2nd period. Selman had 3 goals and 1 assist tonight. Was active in front of the net on the PP, has a very active stick and works to get open in front. Selman's line along with Zach Hyman (FLA '10) and Dylan Larkin (Det '14) was dominate in the offensive zone all night and eventually took the game over in the 3rd period.

MICH - #19 RW - Dylan Larkin (Det. 2014) – Pursued the puck hard all night long. Won a lot of his puck battles and once he retrieved the puck he was difficult to move off of it. He created a lot of chances in the offensive zone, both off the rush and on the fore check.

MICH - #13 LD - Zach Werenski (2015) – Showed the ability to slow the game down when it was needed. Made solid outlet passes and liked to stretch the ice. Didn't skate the puck up past center ice very much but made crisp clean passes in the neutral zone. Showed a quick stick in the defensive zone. Didn't panic or get chasing the play in the defensive zone. Did have one assist on a power play goal and did create some chances in the offensive zone with his quick decision making at the point.

Note: Werenski Night 2, 1-24-14 vs UW – Showed a lot more offense then the previous night by shooting the puck more and scoring 2 goals. First goal was a wrist shot from the slot that was just over the goalies pad and under the glove. His second goal was on a shot from the faceoff dot that beat Goaltender Rumpel short side over the blocker.

WIS - #19 C - Cameron Hughes (2015) – Had a few good shots off the rush that created rebounds and scoring chances in front. Showed the ability to circle the offensive zone with the puck and make a good play with the puck. Didn't force shots or passes through traffic and continues to progress and gain confidence at the NCAA level.

WIS - #33 G - Joel Rumpel (FA-SJ) – Had quick pads all night, made a couple nice saves with the pad on deflected shots from the point through traffic. Worked hard to look through screens and found rebounds. Gave up a couple ones late in the game that he would probably want back but gave his team a chance to win early with some big saves.

WIS - #28 RD - Kevin Schulze (FA) – Best viewing I have had on him all season. Shower great patients with the puck on the offensive zone, very agile and was able to move the puck down low and found Grant Besse in the slot for a goal. Showed great speed getting back and catching Dylan Larkin on a partial breakaway to disrupt a scoring chance.

January 23rd 2015, Omaha Lancers at Tri-City Storm

OMA #10 Henderson, Jake RW (2015) - Big body who is a physical presence on the ice. Threw his body around and made the Storm think twice about going into corners with him. Not a great showing offensively, couple bad neutral zone turnovers. Started to look disinterested as the game started to slip away.

OMA #18 Angello, Anthony RW (2014, 5th Round Pittsburgh Penguins) - Didn't play too many minutes tonight, played on Omaha's fourth line for the majority of the game and got very little power play time. Created some matchup problems as Tri-City's bottom six guys had trouble containing him but didn't end up making the Storm pay.

OMA #25 Spinner, Steven RW (2014, 6th Round Washington Capitals) - Another guy on Omaha who had a below average showing. Is very creative and intelligent in the offensive zone but struggles to play a 200-foot game and put in the effort in his own zone.

OMA #26 Forsbacka-Karlsson, Jakob RC (2015) - Probably the lone overall bright spot for the Lancers in this game. Like his game the more I see it. Controls the faceoff circle, and although he didn't get on the score sheet tonight he sees the ice really well and possesses a very high hockey IQ.

OMA #29 Crone, Hank LW (2016) - Wasn't on the ice much through the first two periods but role expanded in the third. Assisted on Omaha's lone power play goal. Smaller than pretty much everyone he's going up against but doesn't show it. Really like his potential going forward.

OMA #35 Oldham, Kris G (2015) - Never really looked comfortable tonight and was pulled after allowing two goals on five shots.

OMA #61 Gersich, Shane LW (2014, 5th Round Washington Capitals) - Not a bad game but not a great outing either. Showed off his speed as he often does, using those quick first couple strides and he is gone. Shot early and often on the rush but couldn't beat Tri-City goaltender Rutledge.

TRI #3 Dello, Tory RD (2015) - Solid performance. Nothing flashy as always but just a solid game. Near impossible to beat one-on-one and did a pretty good job of containing Gersich tonight as that was his match-up for most of the game.

TRI #15 Freytag, Matthew LW (2015) - Scored a nice goal in the second period from the left circle. Quick release on his shot. Pretty speedy player. Showed good effort on the back check. A lot to like about his performance tonight.

TRI #44 Wilkie, Chris RW (2014 Undrafted) - Solid performance, really ran the show for the Storm tonight despite only scoring once. Makes some questionable decisions with the puck going through the neutral zone trying to do too much by himself. Scored an unassisted tally in the second period.

Saginaw Spirit at Barrie Colts, January 24, 2015

Score: 3-1 Barrie

Saginaw

LW Jesse Barwell (2015) – Barwell used his speed to close gaps quickly, get in on the forecheck and was effective on the penalty kill. He accelerated quickly and carried the puck through the neutral zone and safely into the offensive zone for several controlled zone entries. Barwell was poised under pressure, and was effective moving the puck coming off the half-wall on the powerplay. He showed his quick release sniping one off the bar and in early, and had several quality shots throughout the game.

C Mitchell Stephens (2015) – Stephens back-checked hard and showed commitment to a 200-foot game right from initial puck drop. He was almost always in position in the defensive zone, and was relentless after loose pucks. Stephens used an active stick to disrupt several plays, and was effective on the penalty kill. He had a couple rushes where he carried the puck up ice while generating good speed before driving the net for a chance. He didn't shy away from a physical game or the dirty areas of the ice. Stephens showed good power taking a couple strong shots, and made a nice play setting up Barwell for Saginaw's 1st and only goal.

C Tye Felhaber (2016) – He was certainly the driving force on his line. He accelerated extremely quickly, and used his speed through the neutral zone to attack defenders and push them back, allowing easy zone entries. He was confident carrying the puck, and was creative off the rush. Felhaber embraced contact, but certainly was on the worse end of several collisions. Felhaber was pushed off the puck easily a few different times, and he took a penalty early in the game for some stick work in the corner.

D Marcus Crawford (2015) – Crawford was a mixed bag in this game. His puck movement on the powerplay was pretty good, and he did make some defensive plays, but there were a lot of mistakes in his game. He pinched in to try and keep a play alive while on the PP and missed the puck entirely, which allowed a clear-cut breakaway for Joseph Blandisi. Crawford's passing was good in close, but he missed several outlets and stretch passes throughout. There was a lot of bouncing pucks, high passes, etc. off his stick. Crawford also forced some passes to forwards who were covered, showing questionable decision-making. Defensively, he lost his man a couple times in the defensive zone but was OK in his own end. He's not an overly physical player, but he does like to use his stick a lot; both to disrupt plays and rough up opposing players.

D Keaton Middleton (2016) – Middleton was extremely physical in this game. He did a nice job clearing the crease, especially on the penalty kill, and was a body mover throughout. He pushed players off the puck regularly, and seemed capable of making good outlets to get the puck out of the zone after forcing a change in possession. Middleton did a nice job getting in the shooting lanes, and blocked a couple shots. Middleton took a delay of game penalty late, but played a solid game for Saginaw.

Barrie

C Matthew Kreis (2015) – Kreis played one of his better games this season. He did a nice job driving the net and pulling defenders to him, before feeding the points for wide-open shots. He backchecked hard throughout the game, and forced a couple turnovers in the neutral zone. Kreis played with good pace, was creative in space and made several passes that resulted in either a scoring chance or a drawn penalty.

LW Roy Radke (2015) – Radke went to the net consistently in this game, and put as many pucks on Cormier as possible. He finished his checks, was effective in the cycle game and had several nice net drives. His forecheck pressure forced two Saginaw defenders to shoot the puck out of play trying to rush a play.

D Rasmus Andersson (2015) – Andersson was strong on his stick, and did a good job powering through stick checks and contact. He made a bad turnover exiting the zone, which led to Saginaw's only goal, but he really settled down after that. His outlet passes were accurate, and he had no problem jumping into the play. Andersson made a couple defenders miss in space throughout the game, and on one play eluded a defender before going upstairs on Cormier for what turned out to be the game-winning goal. Andersson won several puck battles, and used his body to shield the puck/box out attackers. He also showed good awareness and instincts reading the play and jumping up to intercept several outlet passes and keep plays alive.

G Mackenzie Blackwood (2015) – Blackwood looked good in his first game back from illness. He was beat high glove early, but made some nice glove saves after. He was square to his shooters, his positioning was good, and he did a nice job looking big while hugging the post and cutting off angles. Blackwood made two or three excellent saves going side-to-side to stop the back door play.

January 24, 2015, Windsor Spitfires at Sarnia Sting

WSR #91 C Luchuk, Aaron (2015) - Hit hard down low, went off slowly but returned next shift with good speed and hands on the rush. He then took a bad penalty after losing the puck. Generally plays top penalty kill unit.

SAR #5 D Chychrun, Jakob (2016) - Has taken over powerplay quarterback role with loss of DeAngelo. Makes quick decisions. Good shooting/passing decisions. Quickly goes to good scoring areas.

SAR #8 D Sproviero, Franco (2016) - Naturally a defenseman, Franco played forward tonight. He provided a solid forecheck, won races to puck battled in corner and on the wall and forced several turnovers.

SAR #11 RW Hodgson, Hayden (2015*) - Hodgson cleaned up the garbage in the slot to tie the game 2-2. Absolutely crushed DiGiacinto on the wall. Took two penalties in the first period, first was bad and complained second was legit.

SAR #28 D DeFarias, Josh (2015) - DeFarias, usually a defender played forward today and made some impressive skilled plays with the puck to create scoring chances for his team.

Final Score: Windsor Spitfires: 3 - Sarnia Sting: 2 OT

Cape Breton Screaming Eagles vs Saint-John Sea Dogs, January 26th 2015

CAP#12 RD Lalonde, Bradley (2015) – Lalonde is an offensive defenseman who creates lots of scoring chances for Cape Breton. Lalonde plays a solid two way game. Lalonde does a very good job finding shot lanes from the point and gets good pucks on net. In some cases Lalonde is out muscled from the puck can be physically out worked by opponents.

CAP #37 RW Svechnikov, Evgeny (2015) – Svechnikov plays on his off hand wing and is usually looking for a pass to shoot on the rush. Svechnikov scored a nice goal on the power play setting up on the week side wall, moving back door for a tap in cross ice pass; showing off his nose for the net. He also assisted a goal passing the puck to the point and screening the goaltender as the point shot went in. He shows off his skill all game when he has the puck, making good passes, patiently handling the puck and making nice plays.

CAP #23 LW Lazarev, Maxim (2015) – Lazarev also plays on his off hand wing on a line with two of Cape Bretons over agers. Lazarev also has good skill and worked hard in the d zone this game. On a couple occasions Lazarev slid to block shots. Lazarev has a good set of hands and the skill to control the puck well under pressure in tight spaces.

CAP #27 RD Leveille, Loik (2015) – Leveille is often paired with Lalonde on the point. Where Lalonde is a shooter, Leveille is more of a set up man and passer. Leveille controls the top of Cape Breton's power play umbrella. Leveille has is a speedy skater with a nice smooth stride.

SNB LD #26 Bell, Jason (2015) – With Zboril being out of Saint John's lineup Bell must play a bigger defensive role. But when Bell has the opportunity offensively he doesn't waste any time jumping low in the O zone or in the rush; often carrying the puck himself. Bell makes good passes and also shows good hands and vision.

SNB #10 C Noel, Nathan (2015) – Noel is a scoring threat almost every time he is on the ice. He turned it up on the 2nd period of this game; creating lots of scoring chances and setting up Saint John's one goal, making a nice reverse pass to Smallman set up on the post. Noel often uses his speed to control the puck circling the O zone until his finds an open man. Noel lost a big draw late in a 1 goal game with their goalie pulled in the O zone, which then lead to a Cape Breton empty net goal.

SNB #12 LW Marsh, Adam (2015) – Marsh plays a responsible defense first style of game usually. In this game Marsh was paired with Noel and Smallman. Marsh creates offensive opportunity for his line mates on a few occasions in the game.

SNB #16 C Dove-McFalls, Samuel (2015) – Dove-McFalls usually plays on one of Saint John's checking lines. Standing at 6'2" Dove-McFalls is improving his physical play role. Dove-McFalls kills penalties and also moves up and down Saint John's lineup soaking up ice time.

SNB #5 LD Chabot, Thomas (2015) – This was one of Chabot's quieter games offensively, as he played more of a defensive role for Saint John. However, on the power play it usually revolves around Chabot carrying the puck on the break out and setting up on the O zone. Chabot makes great passes and shows great vision doing so.

SNB #18 RW Smallman, Spencer (2015) – Smallman is a big, skilled player for Saint John who continues to impress with his improving play. Passed over in last years draft; Smallman is making it hard for scouts to over look him this season. Smallman played a big part killing penalties for Saint John as he laid down to block 2 slap shots in a row, showing commitment to team first play. Smallman also scored the lone goal for Saint John in this game. Smallman uses his size to win battles and also shows good bursts of speed.

SNB #51 LW Imama, Bokondji (2015) – Imama appears to be working hard every shift. Imama takes good shots, showing a good quick and hard wrist shot he often gets on net through traffic. Imama shows good power forward potential getting in on the fore check and winning puck battles.

Oshawa Generals at Barrie Colts, Jan 29, 2015

Score: 5-1 Generals

Oshawa

C Anthony Cirelli (2015) – Cirelli showed a commitment to a 200-foot game right from the get go. He backchecked hard, and stayed tight to his man in the defensive zone. He went to the dirty areas in the offensive zone, and did a nice job finding soft spots in Barrie's defense throughout. Cirelli finished his checks when he could, and had an assist in the game.

C Sam Harding (2015) – Harding didn't get a lot of playing time, but was effective when he had an opportunity. He played a good two-way game and consistently made smart decisions with the puck. Harding was positionally sound in the defensive zone, and was regularly back to support the defense. He did have one bad turnover, but besides that played well.

D Mitch Vande Sompel (2015) – Vande Sompel had a very good game. He showed great explosiveness in his first three steps and accelerated quickly through the neutral zone. He had a few controlled zone entries as well. Vande Sompel was poised when being pressured by forecheckers, and he eluded several check attempts in space. He walked the line very effectively in the offensive zone and did a nice job moving away from sticks/bodies and creating lanes for his shots to get through. He consistently won races for loose pucks and made a good first pass so he didn't have to spend much time in his own zone. Vande Sompel was effective playing forward on the penalty kill, too, as his closing speed took away passing/shooting lanes quickly.

Barrie

C Matthew Kreis (2015) – Kreis started the game on the 4th line, but took several shifts in the top-9 as the game went on. He used his speed effectively skating through the neutral zone to back off the defense before safely carrying it into the offensive zone. He was effective in the cycle game, and hit several open teammates in the scoring area coming from behind the net. Kreis came back regularly to support and his backside pressure did disrupt some Oshawa rushes. Kreis assisted on Barrie's lone goal.

LW Roy Radke (2015) – Radke was strong on the puck, and looked like a man possessed at times through this game. He had a couple thunderous hits, and some nice net drives as well. He was good cycling down low, though a couple times he threw the puck away by passing it where Colts players were not. Radke did create some chances, though, and hit Hooey with a beautiful cross-ice pass that Hooey couldn't convert. Defensively Radke was always back covering his man, and his pressure forced several turnovers throughout.

D Rasmus Andersson (2015) – The Colts didn't convert on any of their powerplays, but they had a ton of chances, and Andersson was a big reason why. His puck movement on the man advantage was very good, as he was moving it quickly and hitting open teammates all over the ice. He also got several good shots through. He played with some physicality in this one, as he finished guys off whenever he could, and was involved in several scrums on different occasions with Michael McCarron and Michael Dal Colle. For the most part he stayed with his man and tracked well while defending the cycle. Andersson blocked shots throughout, and broke up a couple odd man rushes as well. His outlet passes were regularly on target, and he also put a few stretch passes on the tape. He lost a battle with Matt Mistele in front of the net, and it led to directly to a goal. He'll need to continue working on boxing out attackers in the danger zones.

G Mackenzie Blackwood (2015) – Blackwood was certainly not on his game in this one. He seemed to have trouble tracking pucks, and he was coughing out a lot of rebounds, especially up high. He's normally very good handling the puck, but even there he struggled tonight. Blackwood bobbled a couple pucks, and couldn't seem to get anything to go his way.

Jan. 29, 2015 – Prince George Spruce Kings at Langley Rivermen (BCHL)

PRI #21 LC O'Brien, Brogan (2015) C – Already very, very close to being NHL-sized. Straight-ahead and backchecking speed needs some work, as do turns and pivots. Lacks balance and remains bit weak on his feet. Showed offensive promise in this one, however, producing from just outside the slot with an explosive stride onto a loose puck and finishing with a quick-release slapshot. Also won most of his faceoffs tonight.

LAN #12 LC Vela, Marcus (2015) – Showed a different side of himself tonight as he was a physical punisher who threw a ton of weight into every bodycheck. Left the game with no points and 4 penalty minutes, but created a lot of chances. Stickhandling well off of the half-wall from that position, we love his one-touch passing ability and drive to the crease. Skating continues to improve with added strength to his second and third strides. One of its youngest players, he stands out as perhaps the quickest backchecker on his club.

LAN #19 LW Kehler, Colton (2015) – Hasn't seen the sort of production increase he might have been expecting, coming off of a move from the lowly Cowichan Valley Capitals to the division lead-contending Langley Rivermen. Played in a support role tonight. A good but not great skater, who comes down the wing with good speed and physicality. Wasn't afraid to agitate to draw a stiff crosscheck and subsequent penalty. While aggressive, his game would benefit from greater net drive.

LAN #30 G Didur, Bo (2015) – I've yet to see Bo Didur have a "bad game" or an "off night" this year, and tonight was simply more of the same. The Rivermen blocked a ton of shots tonight, but he still did a really great job of seeing through bodies, reading the defensive coverage, and positioning himself to make a save. Rebound control was exceptionally good tonight as he did a fantastic job of jumping on and smothering pucks when they bounced off his chest protector and into the slot. Despite being a bit short, he's got good ability to cover the upper-half of the net thanks to strong reflexes.

Niagara IceDogs at Barrie Colts, Jan 31, 2015

Score: 6-3 Barrie

Niagara

LW Graham Knott (2015) – Knott was effective on the forecheck and had a couple heavy hits to separate Colts players from the puck. His positioning in the defensive zone was good – in particular on the PK – and he had several clears. Knott was strong on the puck, and made some nice power moves towards the net. He showed good vision making accurate passers to teammates all over the ice, and set up some nice chances. He backchecked very hard throughout, and had a couple takeaways in the neutral zone. At times he would dump and chase when it wasn't necessary, and he didn't create much offense for himself.

D Vince Dunn (2015) – Dunn was making crisp outlets and accurate passes all night, and it showed up on the scoresheet with him registering an assist on all three goals. His puck movement in the offensive zone was very good. Dunn was excellent carrying the puck up ice, through the neutral zone and into the offensive zone for controlled zone entries, but he relied too heavily on that at times. There were a couple occasions where he could have dished it off to open teammates, but kept it himself and ended up getting caught in the offensive zone. Due to his good skating ability he was able to get back most times, but there were a couple times where his questionable decision making allowed Barrie to generate scoring chances.

Barrie

C Matthew Kreis (2015) – Once again Kreis centered the 4th line, but did move up for a couple shifts here and there and he did play special teams. Good cycling down low led to Barrie's 1st and 5th goal. Kreis was able to skate away from oncoming checkers, and lost several of them with stops/starts. He did a nice job avoiding stick checks carrying the puck up ice, and on one occasion he stickhandled around three defenders before getting a good backhand off.

LW Roy Radke (2015) – Radke did get a few good chances in this game, but he struggled to create his own shot in one-on-one situations. He pressured well on the forecheck, and had a couple big hits on the night. Radke was effective down low in the cycle game, especially late killing clock, and was very responsible in his own zone. He made smart decisions with the puck, and didn't try to force anything that wasn't there.

D Rasmus Andersson (2015) – Niagara's players were taking runs at Andersson all game, but he maintained a calm presence and didn't force any outlet passes knowing he was about to get hit. He moved the puck well on the powerplay, and regularly got shots through. He didn't carry the puck up ice regularly, but did have two nice end-to-end rushes, both of which led to scoring chances and sustained offensive zone time for the Colts. Andersson used a good stick in the defensive zone and broke up a couple pass attempts on odd-man rushes to as well. He played physical around the net, especially with Josh Ho-Sang, and wasn't afraid to mix it up in the corners. On one play Andersson accepted a pass at the point, toe-dragged around the defender before walking in and rifling a shot off the cross bar. The lone stand out mistake from Andersson was on one play where he was exiting the defensive zone he had the puck poked off his stick and Niagara's forward ended up picking it up and getting a shot off, though Andersson recovered well and ensured it was from the outside.

G Mackenzie Blackwood (2015) – It wasn't Blackwood's best game, but he got the job done. He was very good down low and his side-to-side movement was excellent, especially stopping back door plays on the penalty kill. He made a couple nice glove saves, but did struggle with rebound control on high shots. Blackwood also allowed a bit of a squeaker early in the game, though he did recover well after.

Saint John vs Blainville-Boisbriand, January 31st, 2015

SNB #5 LD Chabot, Thomas (2015): Chabot was decent for a struggling Saint John team today, using his smooth skating strides well to rush the puck in the offensive zone. Made good reads in the offensive zone on the power play, played the role of the playmaker more than the shooter on the power play. His excellent footwork helped him go back and forth between offense and defense with ease. He played more often on the PK today than he did in previous viewings, due to the Sea Dogs playing shorthanded quite often in this game.

SNB #10 C Noel, Nathan (2015): Despite playing three games in three days, Noel really worked his butt off today (mostly in the first half of the game, when his team was still in it). Used his speed well on the forecheck and was physical all over the ice. Worked hard at both ends of the ice and made some nice backchecks as well. When he was able to get his speed going from the neutral zone, he was a dangerous player offensively and tough to stop for opposing defensemen.

SNB #2 RD Webster, Bailey (2015): Webster was kicked out of the game in the 3rd period after he delivered a big hit in front of his net and subsequently fought Nikita Jevpalovs after the play. Overall, this was not a great game for him, as he made some questionable decisions in his zone. Lost his stick and decided to go get it in the corner, leaving his man wide open in the slot for a great scoring chance. Other than his big hit in the 3rd period, I felt that Webster could have been meaner in front of the net and along the boards. I did like the shot-blocking abilities he showed on the PK in this game, and saw that he was used often on the Sea Dogs' penalty-killing unit.

SNB #12 LW Marsh, Adam (2015): Didn't have a lot of jump today and was barely noticeable out there. Looked tired playing in a 3rd game in as many nights. Played a regular shift, but I also noticed him on the power play in the 2nd half of the game where he had trouble handling the puck around the faceoff circle.

SNB #55 RD Green, Luke (2016): Like Chabot, Green is a fantastic skater and is very confident when he carries the puck. Only 16 years old, Green already plays on the Sea Dogs' first power play unit and doesn't look at all like a rookie. Defensively, he had some issues versus bigger forwards that were able to win one-on-one battles against him deep in his zone.

SNB #26 LD Bell, Jason (2015): Another great skater on the Sea Dogs' blueline, Bell was quick to take advantage and rush the puck in the offensive zone when he saw an opportunity. He played on the power play with Luke Green, and has a big shot from the point. Bell played a feisty 2nd period, getting involved in different scrums and battles. He needs work defensively; he needs to be more active with his stick and play the man instead of the puck more, as he was beaten easily in one-on-one sequences.

SNB #16 C Dove-McFalls, Samuel (2015): Wears an 'A' in his second season in the league, a vocal player on the ice and on the bench. Didn't do much offensively today but was a key player on the PK unit when he was not in the penalty box himself. One of his penalties was when he ran over the Armada goaltender in his crease. Played a feisty game.

SNB #21 LW Joseph, Mathieu (2015): Joseph played in different situations, as his coaches are trying to find a way to give him ice time. Joseph showed some good anticipation on the PK, being very smart and using a quick stick to create turnovers. Showed flashes of how good his stickhandling could be on the power play, showing good puck control and I saw that he loves to challenge opposing defensemen one-on-one.

BLB #33 G Montembeault, Samuel (2015): An easy shutout for Montembeault, who made the saves he had to make and stayed calm in his crease, even after being run over multiple times. Didn't play the puck often out of his net; he had struggled in that area in my last viewing.

BLB #21 LW Mongo, Yvan (2015): Not a large player but still has good puck protection skills, using his back to shield opponents away. Scored a goal during the game, showing good patience with the puck on that two-on-one and got a lucky break after the puck deflected on Thomas Chabot in front of the net after he tried to make a pass at the other side of the net.

Feb. 4, 2015 – U.S.A. at Sweden (U-18 Five Nations Cup, Round Robin)

USA #2 LD Masonius, Joseph (2015) – A key contributor to the American effort tonight, as he was an offensive fixture on the point. Released a seemingly harmless wristshot from the high slot on the power play was potted in on the rebound by Jack Roslovic for the Americans' first goal of the game. Earlier, before that goal, he showed off a tremendously hard slapshot that just grazed the side of the net. Showed offensive promise, and wasn't a defensive liability.

USA #3 Jones, Caleb (2015) – Had a really strong game in all areas, but I especially enjoyed his contributions on the penalty kill. A very agile skater who will only improved with added strength. I loved his retrieval ability, as he spins off checks beautifully in his own end to outlet the puck. Made a couple masterful one-on-one moves to shut down opposition forwards coming down the wing on the rush.

USA #4 RD Fitzgerald, Casey (2015) – He made a couple nice pinches in deep that almost fooled the Swedish netminder, usually getting set up by Luke Kunin who would replace him up high at the blueline. Because the United States played so often on the penalty kill, I wasn't afforded the opportunity to watch Casey Fitzgerald too many times.

USA #7 LW Tkachuk, Matthew (2016) – Had yet another dazzling performance in what has been a long string of impressive viewings in my scouting book. Simply looks like a "pro's kids," as his level of hockey sense is far beyond his peers, and at a much younger age than should be realistically expected. Isn't a playmaker so much as he's a 'play follower'—one who recognizes opportunities off of a play and pounces on them like a tiger with unparalleled jump, skill, and pizazz. Holsters a great shot.

USA #9 LC Kunin, Luke (2016) – A downright pesky F-1 forechecker and a shrewd playmaker who can hem you into your own zone with his dangerous physical package of size, speed, and natural skills. He's become an incredibly faster skater since the last time I saw him, as his full-speed acceleration is now thrashing and explosive. Has good ability to stop and protect the puck with his head up, as he read plays and then possesses the requisite skills to re-write them in his own vision.

USA #10 RD Boka, Nicholas (2015) – Some really ugly turnovers came off of his stick in the first period, but I didn't think it was entirely Boka's fault, as Christian Evers defaulted to him in a couple hopeless situations. Skating wasn't bad by any means, but it will have to improve if he wants to continue taking chances like the ones he did in this game—his pinches were routinely poorly-timed and it almost cost his team on a few occasions. His passing game was by no means terrible.

USA #11 LW Warren, Brendan (2015) – Possesses decent size and positional skill, but overall had a fairly average game tonight, playing on a top line as the only 2015-eligible forward (middled by Luke Kunin and winged on the other side by Tage Thompson). I thought his hockey sense looked pretty good, but his skating and hustle were just alright on the whole. I wished he were more competitive.

USA #12 LW Greenway, Jordan (2015) – Playing on a second line that included Colin White at centre and Jeremy Bracco on the right wing, I thought Greenway looked like a bit of a weak link. Moving much slower than his linemates tonight, I didn't notice him too much outside of him using his big body to shield the puck along the boards, which he does particularly well in the offensive zone in order to extend life on the forecheck cycle. In fact, he made a bit of a speciality of it.

USA #19 Matthews, Auston (2016) C – He's earning the nickname "Crazy Horse" in my scouting booklet, as he has a tendency to fight so hard for the puck when it's near him that it's a little crazy. Indeed, he battles really hard for the puck any time it's near his stick, which makes him a dangerous player at all times and in all zones. A big presence and important part of the power play convergence-on-net set-play that was employed multiple times by the Americans. Also extremely important on the penalty kill, where—on a turnover he created off of some careless puckhandling by Oliver Kylington—he had a breakaway and almost scored a goal.

USA #20 RW Thompson, Tage (2016) – Outside of a few streaks of magic that really impressed me, Tage Thompson had a game that mirrored Brendan Warren's to a certain degree. He's a really good skater, as I thought he had some of the best acceleration spurts on his line, which featured Brendan Warren and budding speedster Luke Kunin. But other than that, I thought his game was fairly quiet with only a few quality chances from in tight to speak of.

USA #25 D McAvoy, Charles (2015) – Had an incredible game tonight, in which he was most successful when converging on net with funnelling passes and/or shots through fellow 2016-eligible prospect Matthew Tkachuk—(this is a theme worth following in the next few game reports). Skating skills are very good, but don't stand out to you immediately because his phenomenal positioning masks his quality footwork. Well planted most of the time, he doesn't need to move around the ice too frenetically so he almost appears slow at times.

USA #27 C White, Colin (2015) – Was usually the first player placed out on the ice in a penalty killing situation, but was also a regular and important contributor on the power play. He had some really good chances on the man advantage, and continues to go good skills on the cycle, but I thought he suffered a bit from over handling the puck at times and also over-passed it at others.

USA #28 RW Roslovic, Jack (2015) – Skating and hockey sense immediately come to the forefront when watching quick and clever Jack Roslovic. Footspeed was above the rest. Had an incredible first period, highlighted by a goal and an assist; first he pots in a rebound off of a power play wristshot from Joseph Masonius; and then he sets up Matthew Tkachuk on a streaking pass from behind the net for a one-timer goal. Later scores on a rebound from the weeds around the crease.

SWE #4 Younan, Alexander (2015) LD – Decent if not one-dimensional and made some awful giveaways that were hard to ignore. Sends a hard and quickly delivered first pass and an even harder and even slapshot that he loves to release from the middle of the blueline. Was a liability too often in reverse and in that sense, he was a bit of a one trick pony.

SWE #5 Carlsson, Lucas (2015) LD – Lucas Carlsson had a strong night. Did an amazing job of checking Colin Wilson and angling him off of any potential passing or scoring opportunities. Was definitely physical when he had to be, but otherwise used his tremendous footwork to jump in and out of passing lanes, which proved highly annoying for the American forwards. A good shooting option on the power play.

SWE #6 LD Kylington, Oliver (2015) – A smooth-skating and quick-footed left-handed defenseman-highly comfortable playing on either side. Made a bad giveaway early on, but was saved by a good effort from Gabriel Carlsson. Game improved slightly thereafter, as I noticed his tremendous passing along the blue paint in the offensive zone. This is a great puck mover from the point—or anywhere else for that matter. When he has his wits about him, that is.

SWE #7 Larsson, Jacob (2015) D – Had a strong defensive game in which he did a good job of remaining disciplined whilst also containing his opponents to well outside the prime scoring area. I liked his smooth skating, and the way in which it brought him into the corners and behind his net through tight and efficient turns and pivots that alluded any potential incomers on the forecheck. Become more physical and hard working since the last time I saw him (at the Ivan Hlinka tournament). A really good passer on the power play.

SWE #10 Dahlstrom, John (2015) C – Continues to score goals in international play, making me wonder why he isn't receiving more attention from the world's scouting agencies. Decently sized and deceptively fast—he has breakaway straight-ahead speed that he'll utilize at the most unexpected times. It allowed him to pull free from the pack with the puck on his stick numerous times in this one. His defensive game is far from a liability, too. Best of all, he has really good hands and he can finish in tight.

SWE #11 LW Ahl, Filip (2015) – Had a wild game in which he seemed to control the pace every time he was on the ice. Every one keeps their head on a swivel around Ahl who comes crashing onto the ice like a ten-foot diameter bowling ball. Created a couple breakaway opportunities with his speed and did a good job of crashing the net hard despite not scoring. Later, his physicality set up an easy goal for Joel Ek Eriksson in the slot. Can be excused for a few penalties he incurred, as he was stapling guys to the boards all night long.

SWE #12 RC Asplund, Rasmus (2016) C – Had a hell of a game, especially in terms of his puck movement on the power play, in which he gave Caleb Jones all he could handle on the penalty kill. His footwork is very good, and he has the hands to keep up. I love his 'surround sound awareness' and that he always has a multitude of passing options because of his exceptional vision in the offensive end. A really good passer.

SWE #27 Jesper Lindgren (2015) D – A force on the man advantage for Team Sweden in this one. That's especially true in terms of how he gained space in the attacking zone. Skillfully crafted his way across the opposition blueline through multiple stickchecks on various occasions. The only facet of his game that might have exceeded his skating and stickhandling abilities was probably his vision and passing, as he was able to see plays on the ice that couldn't be seen from a blimp.

SWE #28 RW Eriksson Ek, Joel (2015) – Had a heck of a game tonight, showing tremendous chemistry alongside the similarly large and fast Filip Ahl. Size, skating, vision, toughness and scoring drive were all on display in the Swede's first goal of the game, in which he kept the play alive by taking a punishing hit and making a behind the back blind pass from the slot to keep the play alive, and then continued crashing the net before driving home a wayward puck with the end of his backhand. This goal was indicative of his performance as a whole as his game exudes competitiveness and skill.

SWE #29 D Carlsson, Gabriel (2015) – Looked fairly average and raw in this one, playing a decent amount of minutes alongside Jesper Lindgren. While Lindgren shined, with the puck often being on his stick, Carlsson instead played second fiddle and provided a reliable counterpart on the other side of the ice. His plays with the puck were extremely quick and stupidly simple—exactly what his coaches were probably looking for.

Kingston Frontenacs at Barrie Colts, February 5, 2015

Score: 3-2 Barrie (SO)

Kingston

LW Lawson Crouse (2015) – Crouse's positioning in the defensive zone was excellent – especially on the PK – and he was always back to support. He forced a couple turnovers in the neutral zone, though he also turned it over a couple times. Crouse had a couple good rushes up ice, and showed good acceleration and speed skating the puck up ice. He showed good power in a couple shot attempts, but struggled to create his own lane and didn't do much offensively. He drew a penalty on a net drive, but really wasn't much of a threat in the ozone.

D Jarkko Parikka (2015) – Parikka played a pretty physical game. He used his body a lot along the walls, and took a penalty for checking from behind. His outlet passes were on and off, as some were accurate but he missed some others he should have made. He was effective on the penalty kill and was good defensively once everyone was set up, but his transition defense wasn't great and he seemed to struggle against small shifty players like Andrew Mangiapane and Kevin Labanc.

Barrie

LW Roy Radke (2015) – Radke played a pretty quiet game. He had a couple powerful shots that missed the net, and cycled well on occasion, but wasn't a huge threat offensively. Radke's defensive zone his positioning was solid, but in general not much happened in either end when he was on the ice.

C Matthew Kreis (2015) – Kreis was also pretty quiet. He was able to create some chances coming off the half-wall, but for the most part he played a perimeter game and wasn't able to generate any chances in the danger area. His backside pressure through the neutral zone forced some turnovers/dump-ins, which allowed the Colts to recover the puck and head up ice again. Kreis also danced around a defender in open ice early, but nothing came of it.

D Rasmus Andersson (2015) – Andersson consistently made good outlets, and was able to jump-start several odd-man rushes with a quick first pass. On the powerplay he moved the puck quickly and accurately. He got several pucks through towards the net, and when the game was tied late he had a couple end-to-end rushes that led to scoring chances. Andersson's 1-vs-1 defense was good, as he was able to knock the puck away from the oncoming forward (McGlynn once, Crouse another time) both times he was put in those situations. On the penalty kill he was able to clear it several times, and did a nice job waiting to pull forwards in before dumping it down the ice and maximizing the amount of time killed. When attackers took away Andersson's strong side he was able to hit open teammates with firm, accurate backhand saucer passes, which made him very tough to defend. Andersson did turn the puck over in the neutral zone on one occasion, which led to a shot against. He also fanned on one outlet that led to another shot against, but Blackwood was able to handle both with ease.

G Mackenzie Blackwood (2015) – Blackwood's rebound control was excellent in this one as there was rarely a 2nd chance opportunity for Kingston to pounce on. He wasn't tested a ton, but he was good when called upon, and came up huge stopping five of six in the shootout. He did allow a weak goal that squeaked through his five-hole, but the first one he had little chance as it was sniped short-side over the shoulder and just under the bar.

February 5, 2015, Sault Ste. Marie Greyhounds at Kitchener Rangers

SSM #6 D White, Colton (2015) - Made some good, smart plays at the offensive line to keep the play going. Had a little trouble carrying the puck into the zone today.

SSM #37 D Bouramman, Gustav (2015) - Skated in front of the slot with the puck, losing it which resulted in a scoring chance against.

SSM #9 RW Senyshyn, Zachary (2015) - Good forecheck off bench to force turnover. Good speed for size. Good patience then took puck up ice and drove net with stick on the ice for scoring chance. Good pass 2 on 2 after beating D wide for chance

SSM #38 C Verbeek, Hayden (2016) - Great skater, good pressure on puck carrier.

KIT #18 D Blaisdell, Doug (2015) - Great play with stick one on one. Kept it pretty simple and effective.

KIT #15 C Franzen, Gustav (2015) - Multiple good hits 1st shift good pressure and finishes. Great quick position in on on turnover then quick react for 3-1 goal. Great move in alone to score 5-1 goal on give and go.

KIT #17 C Kohn, Mason (2015) - Great penalty killing pressure to clear chances; PK 1. Excellent speed. Nice play on rush to shake checker go wide on D then threw pass towards slot. Great shot on one timer going to net 2 on one to score 2-0 goal. Great hands to control puck under pressure.

KIT #71 RW Miller, David (2015) - Slippery in traffic. Gets in passing lanes on forecheck but doesn't make contact with opponent

Final Score: Kitchener Rangers: 5 - Sault Ste. Marie Greyhounds: 1

Barrie Colts at Mississauga Steelheads, Feb 6, 2015

Score: 5-4 Barrie

Mississauga

RW Nathan Bastian (2016) – Bastian's positioning on the penalty kill was good, as he did a nice job taking away shooting/passing lanes. He finished his checks, battled hard along the walls and wasn't afraid to go to the dirty areas of the ice. Bastian deflected a couple pucks in front for scoring chances, though he couldn't convert any.

C Michael McLeod (2016) – McLeod was one of the best players on the ice. He was relentless after loose pucks, and didn't let up on the forecheck. He back checked very hard, too. He used his explosive strides to gain separation from the defense, and he was very good skating the puck up ice through the neutral zone. McLeod showed good vision hitting teammates for a couple back door plays, and was effective distributing the puck as a whole. He didn't shy away from contact, and scored a nice goal in tight on a one-timer.

D Sean Day (2016) – Day was not good in this game. He turned it over several times, one of which led directly to a goal against. He completely gave up on a back check when he was only a stride or two behind Kevin Labanc, and didn't show much effort in the defensive zone. He also took a minor penalty, and didn't seem at all engaged. He made a couple nice outlet passes and had one good rush, but he played poorly overall.

Barrie

LW Roy Radke (2015) – Radke regularly went to the dirty areas, and drove the net for rebounds on several occasions. He created a couple chances off the cycle, and was strong on the wall.

C Matthew Kreis (2015) – Kreis was pretty good playing limited minutes. He used his speed to stretch Mississauga's defense, and created some nice chances in the danger area. He did a nice job rotating high to intercept outlet passes to keep plays alive, and he regularly went to the net to open up lanes for outside shooters while going for rebounds in the process.

D Rasmus Andersson (2015) – As usual Andersson regularly got pucks through, and it led to a lot of offense for Barrie. Two goals were scored directly off point shots from Andersson. His ability to open lanes for himself and get pucks on net is exceptional. Andersson's outlet passes were regularly on target. Defensively he used his strong frame to seal opposing players off, and his active stick proved difficult for Mississauga players to get around.

G Mackenzie Blackwood (2015) – Blackwood didn't face a lot of rubber in the first 25-30 minutes, but he was peppered in the final frame and a bit. He flashed his glove for a few big saves, and showed good side-to-side and lateral movement. Barrie took a ton of penalties late, and Blackwood continually made big saves to bail them out and ensure Barrie didn't blow what was once a 4-0 lead.

Feb. 6, 2015 – Russia at U.S.A. (Five Nations Cup, Round Robin)

RUS #11 LD Volkov, Artyom (2015) – Had a good showing that saw him score a goal on the power play in the first period, when he scored on a dangerous wristshot from the point, utilizing a double screen set up his Russian forwards. Cleverly used his lateral mobility and puckhandling ability to wait the puck before finding an open shooting lane.

RUS #13 LW Yurtaikin, Danil (2015) – One of Russia's strongest players in a victory over the United States, especially in terms of his positioning and playmaking vision in the offensive zone and especially when on the power play. The continuity in his offensive game, the desire to keep his feet moving and get into new open space, led largely to the first period power play goal by Artyom Volkov, as it drew countless bodies below the goal-line or in front of Michael Lackey.

RUS #15 LD Sergachyov, Mikhail (2015) – Had a good game in which he contributed in all situations—although he probably looked most dangerous on the power play. Quarterbacked a tremendous power-play for Russia, showing really good one-touch passing ability and a clever slap-pass move that he used often and with a high degree of success. Moved the puck very quickly playing on his off-side on the offensive blueline. Almost looked like a power play specialist of sorts.

RUS #21 RW Kaprizov, Kirill (2015) – Had a strong showing in terms of displaying his dazzling array of stickhandling tricks. Undersized but fast. Showed some good work-ethic on the penalty kill, drawing a penalty on Charles McAvoy after beating him one-on-one off an individual rush. A flashy Russian with an appropriately flashy and alliterative name—see: Kirill Kabanov—he will inevitably find some fans in the armchair GM world.

RUS #25 RW Guryanov, Denis (2015) – Scored a goal, but probably would have had more had it not been for a major penalty incurred after a boarding call in the first period. Before being ejected, he showed off his breakaway speed on more than one occasion and was able to tap the puck home during a net drive to provide Russia with its first go-ahead goal in the first period. Later, he threw an absolutely vicious hit on Colin White that drew a raucous crowd in front of Team Russia's bench.

RUS #27 RC Zhukenov, Dmitry (2015) – Speciality appears to be his quarterbacking ability on the power play. Showed off a good one-timer slapshot as he finished off a tremendous one-time passing play, set up largely by Mikhail Sergachyov, during a five-on-three situation to put his team into a tied position in the middle of the first period. A really good stickhandler, passer, and shooter, he seemed able to create a lot of chances on his off-side from that small area just above the left faceoff circle.

USA #3 D Jones, Caleb (2015) – Not as dangerous as his defensive partner, Charles McAvoy, I thought Caleb Jones was nonetheless a stalwart on the back-end for U.S.A.'s power-play, largely because of his tremendous positioning, maneuverability, and hockey sense. Blessed with great hockey sense, good pokechecking skills, and a deep gas tank, he logged a ton of important minutes for his team, and looked highly dependable in all situations.

USA #7 LW Tkachuk, Matthew (2016) – Continues to buzz for the Americans, as he showed good net presence and speed in another good performance. Both players being 2016-eligile, the forward and defence duo of Matthew Tkachuk and Charles McAvoy seem to have made an art out of the deflection play from the point, as they connected again in this one for U.S.A.'s first goal of the game. His line, featuring Luke Kunin at centre and Jack Roslovic at right wing, was dangerous for the Americans on nearly every shift.

USA #9 C Kunin, Luke (2016) – Exhibited good speed and physicality, even though he seems to lose his temper a bit too often. He centred the team's five-on-three penalty killing unit, a testament to the coaching staff's level of trust in him. However, Kunin came unhinged during penalty killing duty and took a needless slashing call to put his team down on an extended five-on-three.

USA #10 RD Boka, Nicholas (2015) – A spirited fighter in his own end to start this game, as he saw a ton of ice-time killing a stretch of penalties incurred by the Americans. Also played on the power play, where he scored a goal set up by Jack Roslovic. I didn't see Boka a ton on even strength, and when I did, he didn't stand out too prominently. There was a bit too much "stand around and wait" to his game, as he didn't do enough to open up passing lanes for himself in the offensive zone.

USA #11 RW Warren, Brendan (2015) – Played a really good power game in this one, as he uses his big body and strength really well to muscle guys off the puck. I like that he has the agility and wherewithal to really track guys down in the offensive zone, not to mention the physicality and grunt to finish them off. You have to like the raw package of speed, size and a modicum of skill, as displayed in this game.

USA #17 LW Bracco, Jeremy (2015) – Undersized and not as consistent as I was hoping for, it's easy for Jeremy Bracco to go unnoticed for long stretches. But watch him long enough, and he's sure to do something spectacular. Looked like he was 6-foot-5 when he absolutely undressed Alexander Yakovenko en route to the goal, as he's surprisingly rangy for a player of his height and is capable of shifting the puck back-and-forth in complex motions with a remarkable level of control. Forced the play a bit too often for my liking.

USA #19 LC Matthews, Auston (2016) – Had just an okay showing early in this one, getting a couple nice chances towards the net. Has unnaturally long limbs and an uncommonly powerful skating stride, allowing him to dominate in terms of the north-south game. He's additionally good at getting his big frame in place to create screens and has the necessary hand-eye coordination to deflect shots past opposition goalies or finish off a play in tight quarters. Took a silly retaliatory penalty following the Guryanov hit on Colin White.

USA #21 LW Fischer, Christian (2015) – He has jersey-flapping speed through the neutral zone, and has the awareness and mentality to make a good entry into the offensive zone. I thought he was a bit stationary when completing his power play duties. Nonetheless, he's got really good awareness in all three zones and is a dependable F-3 forechecker thanks to a better than average shot from the high slot and because of his defensive mindedness.

USA #22 RD Gabriele, Grant (2015) – Has the requisite straight-ahead skating skills to rove down low and then back into position, but his overall positioning and decision-making in the offensive zone had me shaking my head at times. Needs to improve his set positioning, as he's a bit plodding in terms of his turns and pivots. Showed off a booming shot on the power play. And then, late in the third period, he made a crazy set-up to Charles McAvoy out of his peripheral vision off the rush to put Team U.S.A. into a 5-5 tie. You have to love that type of vision and poise from an otherwise big and rugged defenceman.

USA #23 C Terry, Troy (2015) – Had a good game, excelling in all areas including the faceoff circle. I loved his forechecking and physcality, as he drew several penalties through hard work and being tough to contain. Defensively reliable and showed good support work in the battles along the boards. Only downside was that he failed more than once trying to go one-on-one on Russian defenders in open space.

USA #25 RD McAvoy, Charles (2016) – Easily one of the U.S.A.'s better defenders in a losing contest with Russia. Showing off his tremendous skating ability, he drew a slashing penalty early in the first by cleverly using his speed and hockey sense to cleverly pinch on a dump-and-chase play. Later, he manned the right side on the ensuing power play and looked dangerous because of his patience, vision and shot. He and Matthew Tkachuk connected on yet another deflection in front of the net early in the first period.

USA #27 C White, Colin (2015) – I love the hyper-focused way in which he reads the game. Additionally, I love the way his superior skating abilities allow him to play the game exactly as he reads it. Unfortunately, he was the recipient of a crushing hit from Denis Guryanov, which resulted in the latter player being ejected from the game. Before that, he looked strong—putting a tremendously hard and accurate hashmark slapshot into the outstretched glovehand of Ilya Samsonov.

USA #28 RW Roslovic, Jack (2015) – Had an unspectacular start to the game, taking a couple ungraceful hooking penalties after falling behind the play. Later used his passing prowess to show good chemistry playing alongside 2016-eligibles Luke Kunin and Matthew Tkachuk. Sometimes he's a bit selfish. Other time, however, he's a playmaker. A charged offensive player who is depended on a lot in terms of power play duty, eventually setting up Nicholas Boka for a goal in the second.

Feb. 6, 2015 – Finland at Sweden (U-18 Five Nations Cup, Round Robin)

FIN #7 LD Juolevi, Olli (2016) – Sixteen-year-old Olli Juolevi had a memorable game, scoring a goal and recoding an assist as one of his team's key power play quarterbacks along with Veeti Vainio. Displays good skating ability, poise, and passing from the back end, particularly when his team is on the man advantage. Defensive game is simple but effective, as he likes to take the puck into the boards and to kill plays dead as a common tactic.

FIN #10 F Aho, Sebastian (2015) – A typical Finnish forward who works hard in the offensive zone and is a decent skater. Had a quiet first period before scoring a goal in the second. It was nice to see him score a goal as he stands out more as a playmaker than a finisher. For instance, prior to scoring his goal, he showed good vision on a nice behind the back pass to a teammate on the rush. Guarded the left point on the power play alongside Veeti Vainio, looking fairly dangerous from that position, again, because of his passing skills.

FIN #24 D Vainio, Veeti (2015) – An almost robotically smooth-skating defensemanwith particularly good backwards and side-to-side manoeuvrability. By "robotic," I mean that he is very cool and collected when he turns and pivots to face an oncoming player with the puck. Plays a head's-up game and is very difficult to get around on the forecheck. Superior hand-eye-foot coordination allow him to see the ice, the puck, and his man very well in one-on-one situations.

FIN #25 F Nattinen, Julius (2015) – An above-average skater and an aggressive forward who skates into his areas of play and into his hits with a lot of gusto. Has an intimidating North American-style presence on the ice in terms of hitting and intimidation tacticts—but he was a little too aggressive on the forecheck and was called for elbowing early in the first period. While defending the power play, he almost scored on a penalty kill breakaway that he created himself on a smartly timed neutral zone pokecheck. An all situations player with good size, great speed and world-class work-ethic.

SWE #5 LD Carlsson, Lucas (2015) – Continues to have a strong tournament, playing on a pairing that also includes Jacob Larsson. A talented skater which allows him to create offense in unique ways from the back end. Makes some really nice pinches, doing a good job of using his skating ability and offensive toolbox to extend life in the offensive zone. Showed good work on the penalty kill, as he generally looked calm under pressure and dropped down fearlessly to block shots. Made a couple bad givewaways.

SWE #6 LD Kylington, Oliver (2015) – Backwards skating is effortless and phenomenal, as he floats up and down his lane miraculously, keeping a watchful eye on anything entering his line of vision. A classical smooth-skating north-south defenceman. Unfortunately, that watchful eye worked against him a few times in this one as he had a tendency to get caught watching the game rather than being "involved," as they would say. Needs to show more compete and become more involved.

SWE #7 LD Larsson, Jacob (2015) – Not too dazzling, but not too daring, Larsson is a very dependable cog on the Swedish back end. A good skater with additional intangibles on the back end, I particularly liked Larsson's workmanship, hitting abilities, and pokechecking abilities as exhibited on a long 5-on-3 penalty kill in the second period.

SWE #10 Dahlstrom, John (2015) – You don't notice him until he scores, like he did in this in the first period on a simple wrister taken from in tight after being left alone. I've previously called him the "Master of the Wraparound" and he did little to dispel that myth in this one. A bit like Anthony Mantha two draft years ago, it's hard to fault a guy for doing nothing but score.

SWE #11 LW Ahl, Filip (2015) – An interesting player in that he doesn't fit the Swedish mould at all: an average skater with immense size and physicality and a hotheaded temperament. He had a really strong first period in terms of his determined and inspired efforts on the penalty kill playing alongside Joel Eriksson Ek. Folks came away from this tournament raving about the work-ethic of Joel Eriksso Ek, but I think that would underplay the performance of Ahl, who had just about as many chances but just had a little difficulty putting the necessary amount of finish on his plays.

SWE #19 LW Olund, Linus (2015) – It's hard not to notice his hard work in the offensive zone, his hockey IQ and clever playmaking ability. Continues to fit into that mould of "hard working Swedish forward" that I seem to have an affinity for. Had some nice shifts where hard work in the slot earned him a few chances on net. Additionally did a good job of tracking down loose pucks or in supporting his teammates engaged in board battles.

SWE #27 RD Lingdren, Jesper (2015) – His own end work was a frenetic product of Swedish strategy, as his pairing with Gabriel Carlsson was one with a clear design. You see, Lingdren's superior skating ability and light-footed agility allow him to rove from point A to point B to point C and back with tremendous ease, allowing a bigger and rangier defender like Gabriel Carlsson free to simply stand stationary and protect the front of the net.

SWE #28 RW Eriksson, Joel Ek (2015) – He and Filip Ahl were a two-man force on the penalty kill for Team Sweden in terms of positioning, physicality, and altogether toughness. Later, he showed his offensive skills by deflecting in a goal off of a beautiful one-time passing play set up first by Lucas Carlsson and then by Jesper Asplund. I like that he has the size and the speed to be dangerous in all situations, and that he was the work-ethic, fearlessness, and net-front presence to match.

SWE #29 LD Carlsson, Gabriel (2015) – Another fantastic skating defensemanwho plays an important part on Sweden's penalty kill where he uses his rangy arms and long stick to disrupt passing lanes. Cn be a real warrior at times when defending his net, not afraid to mix it up after the whistles. Had a few sloppy turnovers that were inconsequential. Other then that, I thought his game exhibited tremendous poise and good decision-making.

Feb. 6, 2015 – Red Deer Rebels at Vancouver Giants

RED #2 RD Strand, Austin (2015) – A smooth-skating defensemanwho calmly made good reads and kept plays alive in the offensive zone with smartly timed pinches. Blessed with good feet and awareness, it felt like the puck came to him whenever he roved down low in the offensive zone. Looked as dangerous in the offensive zone as he looked dependable in the defensive end. Unfortunately, a knee-on-knee penalty incurred in the last minutes of the game would prove very costly for his team.

RED #11 RC de Witt, Jeff (2016) – Had a fairly good game in which he centred the Rebels top line. He's a big kid but remains a bit slow-footed. His work in front of the net was noticeable, as he did a decent job of ploughing into the slot and getting in front of Cody Porter to create screens. Playing a fairly simple north-south game, I didn't notice him too much outside of being a starter for his club.

RED #16 LW Pawlenchuk, Grayson (2015) – A very good skater who showed breakaway speed on at least one occasion, he threw some enormous hits along the wall, whilst also making some nice shot blocks, defending on the penalty kill alongside Musil. On the whole, I really liked his shot blocking ability and team-oriented nature.

RED #25 LC Musil, Adam (2015) – Had a powerful and robust game tonight in which he recorded an assist. Showed good vision on that assist—dishing the puck from below the goal-line to an open defensemanat the point, who slapped one home. Otherwise, his game spoke most loudly in the defensive end. Was a workhorse much of the night. Did a good job of throwing his weight around in the corners and at collapsing down low to limit space around his goaltender.

RED #30 G Burman, Taz (2015) – Mental toughness seemed like a weakness, as he looked a bit deflated after letting in a weak goal. Thereafter Burman seemed a bit discombobulated, especially in terms of his rebound control. He also had difficulty covering the lower corners of the net, which proved costly as the boards are particularly stiff and active at the Pacific Coliseum. I liked his speed and awareness, though.

VAN #7 LW Ronning, Ty (2016) – Had a fantastic game, scoring the game winner with less than a minute remaining in game time. Quick-footed and agile, he is a fearless, some might even say 'reckless,' forechecker who excels on the dump and chase and at using his speed to create scoring opportunities off of the rush. That fearlessness sent him directly into Strand during what looked like a cataclysmic knee-on-knee collision. Shortly thereafter, Ronning returned to the game to score the game winner while dashing admirably into the slot.

VAN #8 LW Baer, Alec (2015) – Generally a streaky scorer, so the Giants head coach Claude Noel rode him pretty hard in this game after noticing he was hot. And indeed, Baer looked like he ate his spinach in this one, as he created turnovers and scoring opportunities through all three periods, utilizing his skating ability and making several smart reads. He continues to play on the perimiter a bit, where he tees up a heck of a slapshot from the high-slot.

VAN #21 RD Menell, Brennan (2015) – Responsibilities continue to accumulate with the Giants. Becoming known for his puck rushing ability and offensive prowess, he's now a regular fixture on the Giants power play. His lateral manoeuvrability makes him dangerous from the blueline as he puts a decent amount of deception on his shots. His wristshot from the point is particularly dangerous, as Vancouver has been looking for a formidable shooter from the point going back to the pre-season.

VAN #22 RD Osipov, Dmitry (2015) – Had the type of game I've come to expect from him—he was quiet in the offensive zone, while racking up several loud bodychecks in his own end. His one-on-one work in the corners, lane control, and pokechecking ability all continue to be strengths on home-ice. His passing game is also developing nicely, as he made nice straightforward outlets to get his team onto the offense in this one.

VAN #32 LC Bobylev, Vladimir (2015) – Vladimir Bobylev continues to prove himself as a serviceable fourth line centre for his Giants club, regularly exhibiting decent faceoff circles, good physicality, and a spatter of offensive punch. I really like his work ethic, even if he hasn't scored a ton of points this year. He seems to be slowing down a lot as the season drags on, however, and is making less and less of an impact on a game by game basis.

Sudbury Wolves at Barrie Colts, February 7, 2015

Score: 7-1 Barrie

Sudbury

D Kyle Capobianco (2015) – I thought Capobianco played a solid game considering his team lost 7-1. He displayed good hands in space, and was able to elude oncoming defenders several times throughout the game. He was confident skating the puck up ice, and was able to carry it into Barrie's zone with possession regularly. Capobianco got pucks through traffic, and made a good first pass coming out of his zone. He showed good anticipation intercepting passes in the neutral zone and taking them the other way. On the penalty kill he wasn't afraid to get in the shooting lanes, and blocked a couple shots while down a man. He took a couple penalties and at times he tried to do too much with the puck, but his teammates struggled to get open and really didn't give him anything to work with.

D Cole Mayo (2015) – Mayo's minutes were limited in this one; particularly in the first half of the game. Defensively he was calm defending on the rush, and disrupted Barrie's attack with an active stick. He laid the body when he could, but didn't play enough to make a big impact.

G Troy Timpano (2016) – The scoresheet would suggest Timpano was very bad, but that certainly wasn't the case. The Wolves left him hung out to dry. He stopped at least four or five clear cut breakaways, and made several sprawling saves. Timpano showed good athleticism, and was very quick in his crease. He played the puck regularly, though at one point he turned it over and it led to three great chances for Barrie in tight.

Barrie

LW Roy Radke (2015) – Radke was very smart with the puck in his zone, as he always made the safe play and would use the glass if nobody was open. He was dangerous coming from the corner on the cycle, and had a few net drives that led to scoring chances. He did take a penalty crashing the net on one play, but it's a penalty Dale Hawerchuk is probably fine with him taking.

C Matthew Kreis (2015) – Kreis was quick to read and react in this one. He pickpocketed Sudbury players several times, and had a couple nice give-and-go's off the rush. He was effective skating the puck through the neutral zone, and seemed more anxious to get to the net than usually, where he'd be OK taking the puck outside.

D Rasmus Andersson (2015) – Andersson made a nice play on his 2nd shift intercepting a centering pass on the PK, and leading a rush up ice for a scoring chance. His puck movement in the offensive zone – both at even-strength and on the PP – was exceptional. He consistently put it on the tape, and setup several one-timers. Whenever there was traffic he'd always take some power off his shots to make sure they get through, and Barrie had a few nice deflections in front as a result. Andersson made an excellent fake-slap pass to Stephen Nosad early in the game, and he added another three assists after that one. Defensively he was physical in the corners, and he used his stick to break up Sudbury rushes numerous times. Andersson had no problem making people miss in space, and pinched along the wall to keep plays alive. For my money he was the best player on the ice, and on one occasion he carried the puck from behind his net into Sudbury's zone, danced around a defender, passed the puck off the wall to himself, and then centered it for a Grade A chance. From start to finish he was excellent.

Feb 7th, 2015. Czech Republic vs Russia (U18 Five Nations)

CZE #3 LD Hajek, Libor (2016) – Just turned 17 but with legit size already, Hajek was able to skate the puck out of troubles eluding forecheckers most of the times. Showed a dynamic ability to take the puck away from the opponents' range. He looked less inclined to make plays with the puck, there was an occurrence where he clearly failed to recognize quickly enough the opponents' positioning and released a dangerous pass through the neutral zone. Still a promising performance.

CZE #12 RD Hronek, Filip (2016) – Struggled in the first period where he made some mistakes. A puck moving defenseman, on a rush into the offensive zone Hronek showed good ability to carry the puck and saw regular powerplay time. Probably saved a goal with a snap dive to block a shot in front of his net. Overall looked like another Czech defenseman worth monitoring next season. Needs to get bigger and become stronger on his skates.

CZE #15 C Spacek, Michael (2015) – The right handed center provided good defensive play, but had a few turnovers that wasted some of his efforts. Two of them were particularly bad and in those circumstances he gave the impression of not being 100% into it despite playing in front of a good home crowd; his puck poise can be an asset only as long as he maintains a maximum level of attention. Without the puck, Spacek appeared to be always very well positioned on both sides of the rink. He had a couple of good scoring chances, on the first one he misfired a one-timer from the slot, on the second one he made no mistake: was quick finding an opening on the short side after getting a bounce off the end boards to tie the game. Also of note for him, in this game the nifty puckhandler delivered a rare, legit hit.

CZE #19 LD Budik, Vojtech (2016) – The '98 born was solid under pressure and was used in all situations. One puck mishandled along his end boards was his only noticeable mistake. He looked comfortable on the powerplay, in his own end he was able to carry pucks out of troubles with his good skating ability, and went beyond that proving to be a deft puck carrier, consistently getting to the offensive blueline. Adding fearless work along the boards, accurate passes and very good use of his stick defensively, Vojtech put together an impressive performance and was certainly the most noticeable Czech among a corp of very young defensemen.

CZE #21 RW Jasek, Lukas (2015) – Jasek showcased good skating stride and will to work along the boards, getting there first to get puck possession. He completed some good passes on the PP and was consistently sharp in combining with his linemates at even strength. Took a little too much time to get his shot away on a 2 on 1 rush, failed to receive a couple of imperfect passes that could have given him good opportunities and was less active in the 3rd period, but was maybe the best player on the ice in the 1st and certainly was the best Czech forward over the first two periods. Made an ingenious pass early in the 2nd that out of nothing created a 2 on 1 for his linemates.

CZE #22 C Kase, David (2015) – The younger of the Kase brothers was the Czechs' #1 center, but despite his efforts he struggled to get things going in this game. His best chance came on the PP when he was quick getting open but his wrister only led to Krasotkin's best save of the game. His missed coverage on Yakovenko in overtime led to the Russian game winning goal.

CZE #27 LW Dufek, Jan (2015) – Dufek didn't show top six potential, but effectively used his speed backchecking and on the forecheck. He initiated some physical contact and was a helpful contributor, especially effective at creating turnovers in the offensive zone. Could have done a better job when entering the offensive zone with the puck on his stick.

CZE #30 G Vladar, Daniel (2015) – Vladar could move well in the net in spite of his height and also looked comfortable leaving the cage to play the puck when needed, without panicking under pressure. He was not fast enough to stop Sokolov's one-timer on a side to side powerplay pass by Zhukenov and was beaten cleanly by Kvartalnov's wrister coming in all alone. He probably over committed to Kaprizov approaching the slot in OT and couldn't recover on Yakovenko's one-timer GWG goal, but his only real mistake came when he mishandled a Guryanov's high shot which led to a big scoring chance on the rebound. Overall left a good impression and was voted player of the game for his team.

RUS #1 G Krasotkin, Anton (2015) – His size is far from ideal for a goaltender and Krasotkin tries to make up for it by staying very active in net. As apparent when he was able to stop Kase on the PP with a great recovery glove save, Anton can move quickly and was consistently good at challenging shooters. Was unable to completely shut down the short side on the first goal, but had no chances on the second goal when he was beaten on a 3 on 2 (basically an open net goal). His good performance was rewarded by being voted as the best player for Russia.

RUS #3 LD Sidorov, Mikhail (2015) – A right shooting defenseman playing the left side, despite being the only Russian defender to play more than 17 minutes Sidorov didn't have a good game. His play with the puck was average at best and his skating lacked jump. When he got starts in the offensive zone he was not quick enough in getting to pucks off faceoffs wins, in one occasion that led to a 2 on 1 for his opponents. He was also not quick enough in covering his guy on a sudden 3 on 2 that led to the Czechs' second goal.

RUS #7 RD Rykov, Yegor (2015) – Playing his off side, Rykov was consistently alert and kept his quick feet moving in order to be right on top of plays, quietly putting together a solid performance.

RUS #8 RW Chebykin, Nikolai (2015) – Chebykin showed good possession skills in the first period when he was able to use his good size and stickhandling to keep the play in the offensive zone. At this stage he seemed to lack some power and explosiveness to be able to generate offense playing that type of game. He was less and less visible as the game progressed.

RUS #14 RD Yakovenko, Alexander (2016) – Albeit small and light Yakovenko didn't seem to evade the physical play. In spite of a short choppy stride he showed pretty good straight forward acceleration and speed. For the most, the left shooting defenseman was able to conceal his current limitations; he was not too noticeable despite taking regular shifts but took full advantage of the right opportunity and of his nice shot to score the game winning goal with a quick one-timer in overtime.

RUS #15 RD Sergachyov, Mikhail (2016) – Born in June '98, this very young left shooting defenseman was used in all situations and played an almost error-free game; his only difficult moment came when he got beaten wide in the 3rd period and was rightly called for holding. Showed notable poise with the puck and a crisp passing game, making quick reads in recognizing where to dish the puck and when to jump in to keep the puck in the offensive zone or to pressure the opponent in the neutral zone. Often played as the only blueliner on the powerplay, was able to get his shots through a couple of times.

RUS #17 C Kvartalnov, Danila (2015) – A scrawny center that played a slowed down and savvy game, Kvartalnov didn't receive much help from linemates Yemets and Ivanyuzhenkov in this game aside from a Yemets' feed through the neutral zone which he took full advantage of, releasing a well placed wrister to beat the Czech goalie. He was constantly well involved in the play in his own end, his defensive efforts paid off and he was effective especially in the first half of the game. In the 3rd period he was assessed a 10 minutes misconduct for openly complaining about an offside call.

RUS #18 RW Sokolov, Dmitry (2016) – The elected shooter for Russia top PP unit, Sokolov was a constant feature on the right half boards, always looking for opportunities to exercise both his dangerous wrister and one-timer. That's how he opened the score. Despite being a shoot first type of player, Sokolov showed more than once that he can recognize when a linemate is open and passing is a better option than taking the shot. At even strength he benefited from the work of his linemates Kaprizov and Zhukenov, but on a couple of circumstances should have tried to use his powerful frame to park in front of the net instead of circling wide.

RUS #21 LW Kaprizov, Kirill (2015) – Showed very good puck control and agility, carrying the puck through the neutral zone and bringing possession to the offensive zone seemingly all game long. Quick recognizing opportunities for decisive passes, Kaprizov can deliver crafty ones. Worked hard and didn't mind boards play despite his short size. Easily the best Russian player in this game.

RUS #25 RW Guryanov, Denis (2015) – The offensive minded winger more than once didn't make the best decision with the puck in this game: a useless and unsuccessful one on one try along the boards instead of dishing the puck to his linemate and a similar turnover in the neutral zone being the main evidences of that. It is probably not a coincidence his best scoring opportunity came after circling back with the puck and looking for a combination with Kaprizov (who was momentarily on the ice with him instead of V.Barabanov); that give and go made his talent level obvious, showing his puckhandling skills and great skating ability. Unfortunately Guryanov's shot lacked accuracy in this contest and he missed the net from a very good scoring position. Denis was able to attack wide with great speed and get shots on net to generate a couple of rebounds, but had troubles against Czech defensemen's good stick work all game long. He still managed to draw a couple of penalties with his reach and mobility. Delivered a strong hit on the end boards in the 2nd period but was on the receiving end of a hard borderline hip-check in the third period.

RUS #27 C Zhukenov, Dmitri (2015) – Showed his good hands taming a difficult puck and feeding Sokolov back for his powerplay goal. Centering what was Russia best line, Zhukenov helped Kaprizov getting possession by winning faceoffs, bringing consistent effort and controlled play. He needs to add power to be able to do more on his own.

FINAL SCORE: 3-2 (OT) RUS

Feb 8th, 2015. Russia vs Sweden (U18 Five Nations)

RUS #5 LD Voronkov, Yegor (2015) – His size may not be ideal for a defenseman, but Voronkov certainly wasn't missing any inches in this game. With solid plays along the boards, good mobility and puck control he was probably the most effective Russian defenseman in the first half and his alertness only decreased when the game was already in his team's hands.

RUS #7 RD Rykov, Yegor (2015) – Another reliable performance by Rykov who moves quickly with and without the puck, often taking away from forwards time to make plays in his own end. Not very visible on the other side of the rink, he seems to struggle when he needs to recover from the offensive zone as his skating looks much better when it comes to agile moves rather than to straight forward speed.

RUS #10 C Vorobyov, Mikhail (2015) – Always involved defensively, Vorobyov worked deep in his own zone and made good use of any puck he could retrieve, showing good understanding of the game with and without the puck. His game is not flashy and he could use lighter feet, but good balance helps him in puck battles and along the boards. Wasted a great opportunity with a weak shot all alone in the slot, but made no mistake later on capitalizing on a bad rebound by Swedish goaltender Marmelind.

RUS #14 RD Yakovenko, Alexander (2016) – His current limitations were exposed on a Ahl's rush as he was basically passed over by the powerful Swede and he was not noticeable in the rest of a game, hanging in without making much of an impact.

RUS #15 RD Sergachyov, Mikhail (2016) – Never struggled against the Swedes' forecheck, played with confidence throughout the entire game, carrying the puck out of his zone more than once. Sergachyov appeared always in control and made it look easy.

RUS #17 C Kvartalnov, Danila (2015) – Kvartalnov was reliable defensively and showed good playmaking ability. His game makes you wonder whether he will still be able to effectively slow down the play at the next level or will inevitably need to learn executing faster after growing into his body.

RUS #18 RW Sokolov, Dmitry (2016) – His goal scoring prowess was again on display on the powerplay, as he roofed a rebound for his 1st goal and released a bomb of a one-timer from the half side boards on a 4 on 3 for his 2nd of the game. When attacking down the right side he made obvious he is not your ordinary 16 years old by the way he could protect the puck. Sokolov was able to stickhandle in tight spaces and make himself available around the slot. He could have scored more goals late in the game, but he missed the net at least a couple of times from good scoring positions.

RUS #21 LW Kaprizov, Kirill (2015) – Always alert, Kaprizov intercepted a pass on the penalty kill and at the end of that play was the player assisting on the shorthanded goal that opened the scoring. With his all around play and terrific passing game he makes players around him better, at least at this level.

RUS #25 RW Guryanov, Denis (2015) – Guryanov was sharing the puck more regularly in this game, had a couple of early rushes where he was not able to get his shot through but finished a strong first period displaying great speed to backcheck hard through the neutral zone, something he should do on a regular basis given his skating and athleticism. He promptly recognized openings in the slot delivering two passes from the right side that created good scoring chances. Generated other scoring chances coming down the wing with speed by creating rebounds with low percentages shots from sharp angles.

RUS #30 G Samsonov, Ilya (2015) – Samsonov was solid all game long and never let his level of attention to decrease when the game outcome had become obvious and the defense in front of him became porous, making save after save without losing his composure. He tends to slide out of position when forced to move fast from side to side, but especially for a big kid he shows good athleticism and was reactive on second and third shots.

SWE #6 RD Kylington, Oliver (2015) – More determined to complete his plays and try to impact the game with his puck carrying abilities, he backchecked effectively from his offensive rushes with his great speed. Kylington got hit pretty hard along the boards by Chebykin cause he didn't feel like turning to avoid the opponent, but his amazing agility was on full display on several plays. Definitely one of the best players in this game.

SWE #7 LD Larsson, Jacob (2015) – Larsson played a more dynamic game than against Finland, carrying the puck forward with better resolve. He moves very well laterally, his feet are first rate and he can move the puck with ease. Despite the overall lack of power Jacob can already hit legit one-timers.

SWE #11 LW Ahl, Filip (2015) – Some lack of agility led to a tripping penalty early on, but Ahl put together a strong first period. At this level he is hard to stop once he gets going with the puck and he managed to bully his way to the net more than once, setting up a scoring chance in the slot with a one hand pass. Ahl also delivered a strong open ice hit on his defensive blue line. He was less effective in the second period and with his team down 4-1 he didn't play in the third.

SWE #17 LW Grundstrom, Carl (2016) – Even if he was clearly missing Asplund's help (Rasmus didn't play in this one), Grundstrom was still Sweden's most dangerous forward. He delivered nice forehand and backhand passes to the slot, attacked the net mainly from the right side and was able to work his way into scoring areas. He makes plays that work at any level.

SWE #20 RW Looke, Jens (2015) – Was buzzing in this one, particularly in the first period but never let himself down despite the game slipping out of reach and despite his line not being able to produce much offensively.

SWE #27 RD Lindgren, Jesper (2015) – Paired with G.Carlsson, he was more visible than in the previous game, showed some smooth skating and stickhandling, but Lindgren still didn't show the confidence and the strength needed to try to make more of an impact.

SWE #28 C Eriksson Ek, Joel (2015) – He didn't have much going for him offensively in this game, but with some very good work defensively and in the faceoff circle Eriksson Ek was still an important contributor for his team in the first two periods. With Sweden down 4-1 after two, he only took one shift in the third period.

SWE #29 LD Carlsson, Gabriel (2015) – Consistently good at keeping the puck on his stick away from opponents, released several inaccurate passes but made good decisions regularly. Carlsson could have been more active in front of his net, his long limbs probably don't help him being very reactive on rebounds.

FINAL SCORE: 5-1 RUS

Feb. 10, 2015 – Seattle Thunderbirds at Vancouver Giants

SEA #4 RD Ottenbreit, Turner (2015) – Had a very good game that was unfortunately marred by a couple questionable calls. Skated well, logged top four minutes, kept his lane, and made a couple nice sweeps to escape with the puck. A decent skater of good size and physical ilk, his aggressiveness hurt him tonight on a few occasions, when he got called for interference.

SEA #9 C Pederson, Lane (2015) – He showed off some tremendous skills during the pre-skate warm-up, as he does an impressive passing exhibition with Matt Barzal that is bound to raise eyebrows. A good passer, he was a key contributor on at least two of Seattle's goals. I like the way he intercepts pucks at the offensive blueline, as he keeps his head on a swivel.

SEA #13 C Barzal, Matthew (2015) – Unfortunately, I can't say that I saw too much out of Barzal in this one outside of the pre-game warmup and the last five minutes of the contest, where—in all fairness—he looked electric. Before that he looked reasonably fast but fairly ineffective. At the very end of this one, his cycling game came to the forefront, as he showed good edgework, escapability, and passing skills in the corners, playing keepaway with his linemates during the last two minutes of game time.

SEA #25 LD Bear, Ethan (2015) – Had another solid if unspectacular game. Not tall or speedy, but he is stocky and difficult to knock off of his feet. Physicality behind the net and in the corners stood out as a strength, as he was able to rub larger opponents off of the puck with good hitting skills. Passing was also good, as he made some really clever outlets to the spring the Thunderbirds onto the offense.

VAN #17 LW Benson, Tyler (2016) – Had a great game tonight in which he was, once again, both a physical force and a scoring opportunity factory. His hitting is by far the most improved aspect to his game, while his shooting skills are also coming along nicely. He does suffer from a bit of tunnel vision at times, while he shows really good playmaking skills at others.

VAN #22 RD Osipov, Dmitry (2015) – While he's had some issues with discipline all season, Osipov has acclimatized nicely to his placement on the top defensive pairing alongside Colorado draft pick Mason Geertsen. There's a lot to like about this bruising defenceman—his small area skating, his crushing hits in the corners and along the wall, his simple outlets, and his ability to log big minutes being chief areas of skill for this Russian defender. Offensive upside remains limited.

Feb. 13, 2015 – Victoria Royals at Vancouver Giants

VIC #17 RC Soy, Tyler (2015) – Continues to exhibit the positive qualities that I've observed since the Delta pre-season tournament. A really good skater with better hands and a continuously growing frame, not only does he get himself to the high-traffic areas but he also connects on deflection opportunities with a startling accuracy. Defensive game is highly underrated as well, I think he's one of the better seventeen-year-old penalty killers in the league at this point.

VIC #29 LD Reddekopp, Chaz (2015) – A good showing, looking particularly impressive in terms of his puck movement—he springs the puck up ice quickly and conscientiously. A lot has been made of his skating deficiencies, but he's really good at positioning himself in front of the net despite being fairly slow-footed. It's hard to fault any of the Royals defensemanafter posting a shutout in a 'do-or-die' game for the Giants. One criticism I can see being levelled at Reddekopp, however, is that he isn't "mean" enough for a stay-at-home defensemanof his physical dimensions.

VAN #35 G Porter, Cody (2016) – He's had issues mishandling the puck this season—he made an insane giveaway in his own zone to Brandon Magee but then had the wherewithal to get back into position and make a quick glove save. Other than a few blunders with regards to giving away the puck, I continue to really like Porter's positioning and combination of upper-body reflexes and lower-body athleticism.

February 14, 2015 – Charlottetown Islanders vs. Shawinigan Cataracts (QMJHL)

CHA # 2 D – Deschesne, Luc (2015) - Deschesne is a smart defenceman, who showed some positives and negative aspects of his game against Shawinigan. Defensively he clogs up shooting lanes; forcing opposing forwards to the outside. He showed good gap control taking away time and space, although he was not very physical. Offensively he gets his slap shot off very quickly before the oncoming Shawinigan forward could set up for a block. He did however have a few mistakes in his own zone, turning over the puck when he was pressured in the corners.

CHA # 10 C – Kielly, Kameron (2015) – Kielly had a fairly quiet offensive game, but did show an impressive work ethic on the back check. On turnovers he would make smart plays to pick up a trailing forward or take away passing lanes on the back check.

CHA # 11 RW – Sprong, Daniel (2015) – Sprong is an explosive skater who possesses an electric offensive game. He accelerates very quickly and changes directions at high speed which creates space. He showed off good hands as he protects the puck by pulling the puck in close to his body or pushing out to his side making it tough for opposing defenders to take poke the puck away. He is constantly moving his feet and stickhandling at high speeds, off the rush he will push the puck out to his side to create a shooting lane. Sprong was very dangerous offensively whether it be off the rush, or setting up on the half wall in the offensive zone and feeding backdoor passes to his line mates. He also did not shy away physically; as he threw a couple hits on the fore check.

CHA # 14 C - Chlapik, Filip (2015) – Chlapik has an incredible game for Charlottetown, his compete level was top notch; one play in particular he battled down low in the corner, stick lifted the Shawinigan defensemanto steal the puck, then walked out towards the net and got a good shot off. In the neutral zone he was showing off good hands by weaving through opposing defenders and gaining offensive zone possession where he will set up plays from the half wall or wait for a trailer for a drop pass. He is a very smooth skater that protects the puck very well by spinning away from pressure. He makes smart decisions with the puck; one play in particular he scanned the zone finding space to cut towards for a shot on net.

CHA # 28 LW – Guilbeault, Olivier (2016) – Guilbeault Skates very low to the ice and generates a lot of power on his strides. He showed off good speed and was patient with the puck as he would spin away from pressure and make a pass.

CHA # 13 C – Getson, Keith (2016) – Getson battles hard in the corners, he keeps his feet moving; which allows him to power through checks. One play he spun off an opposing defender in the corner and cut out to the net for a shot then whacked at the rebound three times until a scrum started.

CHA # 44 LW – Balmas, Mitchell (2016) – Balmas showed good play making abilities, especially on the power play where he passed back door to Kielly who ended up getting robbed by the goalie. Another play he showed smart hockey sense when he passed down low on the power play; then cut to the net and opened up for a shot.

SHA # 91 C – Beauvillier, Anthony (2015) – Beauvillier showed off his quick decision making skills and explosive play making abilities vs Charlottetown. He is a smart player who is dangerous in the offensive zone. He made a quick play to steal the puck from a Charlottetown defensemanand got off a quick shot on net. He anticipates the play very well and follows the puck to the net and will go hard after rebounds; showing a willingness to go to the dirty areas to score.

SHA # 94 LD – Girard, Samuel (2016) – Girard is a smaller defensemanwith a beautiful fluid skating style. He is calm with the puck and makes crisp accurate outlet passes. He has a high hockey IQ, and great body positioning both help make up for his smaller size. Defensively he angles off opposing forwards well and broke up a 2 on 1.

SHA #11 RW – Yan, Dennis (2015) – Yan was relatively quiet in this game; however he did score a beautiful goal short side top corner; showing off a very quick release. He is patient with the puck and will not force a bad pass, instead will turn away from pressure and skate back to neutral zone with the puck looking to gain better entry into the offensive zone. Defensively he has an active stick and would try to break up passes or clog up passing lanes.

SHA # 37 LW – D'Aoust, Alexis (2015) – D'Aoust is a 96' birth year who plays an extremely physical style; he battles hard in the corners and looks to finish every hit. He is very strong on the puck, and is constantly moving his feet. This allows him to fend off back checkers and still get a shot off on net. He was particularly strong in the offensive zone when cycling the puck; as opposing defenders struggled to knock him off the puck. He was also strong defensively as he reads the play well, knowing when to stay high as the F3 position and not over commit down low.

February 14, 2015, Niagara Ice Dogs at Sarnia Sting

NIA #4 D Dunn, Vince (2015) - Protected puck in NZ to shake checker and move up ice. Quick to activate on pinch allowed him to win race to puck but caught deep in off zone too long. Jumped up on rush and finished on pass with good move 2-1. Made a few solid defensive plays on pp breaking up 2 on 1 and forcing opponents outside one on one. Played final minute of 4-3 game.

NIA #13 RW Knott, Graham (2015) - Good pass in low shot area for chance. Played all game situations. Great defensive position consistently pk and even strength

SAR #5 D Chychrun, Jakob (2016) - Great read to pinch and quickly bury rebound on high stick

SAR #6 RW Bushnell, Noah (2015) - Likes to hit every chance possible. Gets power in his hits. Skating hasn't improved. Mishandled pick own zone for turnover then took undisciplined trip penalty. Good position in slot then picked up puck to finish for 2-2 goal.

SAR #25 RW Kyrou, Jordan (2016) - Good shot off wing picked blocker side corner 1-0. Great chance on rebound but over handled puck causing tirnover. Mishandled puck on PL rushing to do too much resulted in icing. Good shot to score for 4-2 goal.

SAR #35 RW Korostelev, Nikita (2015) - Mishandled puck multiple times on rush and in offensive zone period 1. Good hit defensive zone. Passed up hit in offensive zone. Good play to help set up 2-2 goal. Then nice move to create scoring chance later on. Jammed him rebound/scramble in shot 5-2 goal.

Final Score: Sarnia Sting: 4 - Niagara Ice Dogs: 3

February 16, 2015, Sault Ste. Marie Greyhounds at Sarnia Sting

SSM #6 D White, Colton (2015) - Made some smart defensive plays on the penalty kill. Made some solid, simple and effective one on one plays. Competes hard down low and gets good power in his hits.

SSM #9 RW Senyshyn, Zachary (2015) - Good pass in neutral zone, then went to the net getting open.

SSM #37 D Bouramman, Gustav (2015) - Smooth skater, moves his feet to open up options, likes to rush. Jumps up too early sometimes and gets caught deep. Put puck on net which was deflected for 4-0 goal. Shows hands and quickness with puck but bad turnover for breakaway. PP2

SAR #5 D Chychrun, Jakob (2015) - Great calm under pressure with puck. Smart passes on powerplay. Unloaded several shots on powerplay with his cannon. It's NHL level already.

SAR #8 D Sproviero, Franco (2016) - Moved puck very well consistently making smart/accurate plays. Uses skating when options not there to move up ice. Good evasiveness down low to get away from checkers. Drew PP going to corner knowing there would be a big forward looking to hit him. He evaded the checker and was tripped up. Great pass set up chance when most would force low % shot.

SAR #10 LW Salinitri, Anthony (2016) - Really upped his compete level tonight against his former team and it resulted in multiple scoring chances.

Final Score: Sault Ste. Marie Greyhounds: 6 - Sarnia Sting: 0

Feb. 18, 2015 – Moose Jaw Warriors at Vancouver Giants

MJW #13 LW Smejkal, Jiri (2015) – Had a decent outing in which he showed slightly above-average skating ability and really good attention to detail in the neutral zone. Played hard in all situations, showing good stamina and durability. Shows good physicality in the corners and positioning in the slot as he has a good sense of when to converge on net and provide a nice screen. His shot blocking was a strength and his work on the cycle was additionally good.

MJW #19 C Point, Brayden (Colorado, 2014) – Was clearly an MVP for his Moose Jaw Warriors club in this one as he is clearly carrying the load for his club. There is a tremendous continuity to his game that makes him extremely difficult to contain. Frenetic in terms of foot and hand movement, you never know if Point is going to zig or zag. Net drives were fantastically difficult to predict and stick-handling skills were too much for the Giants defencemen, as he made a couple nice dangles that ultimately went without reward.

VAN #17 LW Benson, Tyler (2016) – Almost always an MVP for his Vancouver Giants club and tonight was no different. Sems to excel in these home games against beleaguered road warriors, as he plays an up-tempo and physical style that wears you down over three periods. After laying into you with a big check, Benson will dangle the puck around you and head straight towards the net with a quick-release wristshot.

VAN #22 RD Osipov, Dmitry (2015) – A fixture on the Giants top pairing alongside Colorado draft pick Mason Geertsen, I continue to like what Osipov brings to his club as a top pairing defender—especially in terms of physicality and consistency of effort. His aggressiveness is constantly increasing along with his confidence. Crease clearing skills are improving on a game-by-game basis. Still having some issues with discipline, however.

Owen Sound Attack at Barrie Colts, Feb 19, 2015

Score: 4-3 Attack

RW Ethan Szypula (2015) – Szypula was very responsible in this one, as he was always in position defensively. He did a good job tracking his man, and he regularly took away the shooting/passing lanes. Syzpula had a couple controlled zone entries, and showed good vision off the rush. He made smart decisions with the puck, and drew a powerplay, too. He was very quiet in the 2nd half of the game, though, and did also take a minor of his own.

D Thomas Schemitsch (2015) - Schemitsch definitely wasn't at his best in this game. He struggled to defend against speed off the rush, lost his man in the defensive zone several times, and lost several battles along the wall. For the most part his outlets were accurate, but he missed a few of those, too, and bobbled a couple pucks at the point that led to turnovers and chances against. He used his long reach to knock away the puck on a couple occasions, and didn't shy away from getting into the shooting lanes to block shots.

D Tyler MacArthur (2015) – He played a pretty defensively sound game. Offensively he didn't create much, but he was very physical in his own zone and did a nice job boxing out in front of the net. MacArthur had a good stick in the defensive zone, and was rarely caught out of position.

Barrie

LW Roy Radke (2015) – Radke did a better job of creating his own shots in this one. Most times he needs someone else to get him the puck in a shooting position, but that wasn't entirely the case vs Owen Sound. Radke won a lot of battles along the wall, and was very strong on the puck in the cycle game. He had a couple chances playing on the 2nd PP unit, but he was unable to convert on those opportunities.

C Matthew Kreis (2015) – Kreis started the game on the 4th line, but moved up several times throughout the game. He picked up the puck and safely skated it into the offensive zone numerous times, and was effective in the cycle; especially when he carried the puck out off the wall. Kreis did have a few offensive zone turnovers trying to force passes that weren't there, though he did forceda couple turnovers with good forecheck pressure.

D Rasmus Andersson (2015) – Andersson regularly made accurate outlets on both his backhand and forehand. He took a couple hits to make plays with the puck, and rushed the puck up ice if there was ever a lane for him to take. He had several controlled zone entries, and was able to get shots through traffic consistently. Andersson had a few nice pinches to keep plays alive, and stopped several pucks from clearing the zone. He also scored a powerplay goal on a blast from the point to get the Colts within one in the 3rd. Andersson played a pretty solid defensive game as well, though he did close his hand on a puck when Barrie was already shorthanded, which led to a long 5-on-3.

G Mackenzie Blackwood (2015) – Blackwood wasn't tested much in the 1st, but he did make a couple nice stops, and showed good athleticism stretching out to make a sprawling save. He allowed a few weak goals, including one on the ice with no traffic, in the 2nd before being pulled. He stopped just 17 of 21.

February 20, 2015, Owen Sound Attack at Sarnia Sting

OS #3 D Walters, Connor (2015) - Took huge hit to head resulted in leaving the game. Returned approximately six minutes later. Got shot through for chance. Trouble clearing zone.

OS #4 D Schemitsch, Thomas (2015) - Skating has improved. Bench tells him "go, go" and he fires it down the ice for icing. Gets caught flat footed down low. Played second power play unit.

OS #9 C Szypula, Ethan (2015) - Put pressure on in defensive zone but lacks strength which hurt him during puck protection. Competes but not physically mature enough. Slipped into slot and fired home Owen Sound's fifth goal. Struggled in face-off's tonight.

OS #11 LW Dunda, Liam (2015) - Great move for big guy beating defender then drove net hard with puck for chance. Ran over goalie but wasn't penalized.

OS #40 G McNiven, Michael (2015) - First goal good angle came out to make first save but too far off post and rebound slipped back door. Goes out a little too far on power play shots and beat five hole on second goal. Knows how to direct rebounds well but does sometimes leave them in the slot. Good save on first shot but lacked recovery one second shot for third goal. Then gave up rebound for 4th goal which was quickly banged in. Fifth goal beat him through traffic. Recovery needs to be quicker. Pulled after the fifth goal.

SAR #5 D Chychrun, Jakob (2016) - Hard shot from point on powerplay created rebound for Sarnia's first goal of the game. Sees plays others don't and vocalizes to teammates to involve everyone and create plays. Pinches very intelligently, knows when to inch in slowly and when to drop in quickly. Excellent shot on PP for Sarnia's second goal. Excellent play at line with pro strength to keep the play going.

SAR #14 C Zacha, Pavel (2015) - First game back from injury. Moved puck well early and landed big hit. Skated right to bench at a whistle with his head down in pain but kept going. Handled puck at top speed very well.

SAR #35 RW Korostelev, Nikita (2015) - Nice hands in close below goal line to score opening goal picking up rebound.

Final Score: Owen Sound Attack: 8 - Sarnia Sting: 5

February 21, 2015 - Sherbrooke Phoenix vs. Baie-Comeau Drakkar (QMJHL)

SHE # 2 RD – Gregoire, Thomas (2016) – Gregoire displayed patience with the puck on the break-out. He was very aggressive at keeping pucks in at the blue-line by pinching in and getting the puck back in down low. On Baie-Comeau's second goal Gregoire lost track of his man out front and caused a goal against.

SHE # 97 RD – Roy, Jeremy (2015) – Roy's skating was on display in this game as he was rushing the puck up the ice gaining weaving through the neutral zone then passing off once he was pressured. He has a soft passing touch, hitting his teammates in stride. Roy see's the ice very well as evident by sneaking back door for a pass or anticipating and breaking up opposing passes. His strength in skating allows him to keep a very tight gap control on opposing forwards as he is able to pivot and angle off to the boards. Roy was hit hard from behind in this game and retailiated with a massive two handed slash to the Baie-Comeau forward's ankle. He was kicked out and suspended.

SHE # 81 C – Fontaine, Gabriel (2015) – Fontaine played a 200 foot game, impacting on both the offensive end and especially defensively. In the offensive zone he set up plays through the cycle and on the half wall and would cut out to the net for a shot. Defensively he was always in the right position, making sure he was on the defensive side of the puck. Fontaine showed a tireless work ethic on the back check by staying with his man as he cut to the net and broke up a rebound opportunity.

SHE # 21 W – Thierus, Lucas (2016) – Thierus was very quiet in this game and made no noticeable impact.

SHE # 89 W – Shweri, Kay (2015) – Schweri similarly was quiet as his line was going up against a tough match up in Baie-Comeau's first line consisting of three overage players in Gamelin, St. Cry, and Ciampini.

BAI # 21 RD – Meloche, Nicolas (2015) – Meloche played a steady game for Baie-Comeau; he battled hard and did a good job defensively in his own end. He was fairly quiet offensively.

February 21st 2015, Fargo Force at Omaha Lancers

FGO #7 Stevens, Brody RW (2015) - Scored Fargo's lone goal right in front of the net off a goal-mouth scrum. Buzzes around, plays physical, chips in offensively. Doesn't do anything at an elite level, but plays a pretty solid overall game. Probably doesn't get the attention he deserves.

OMA #10 Henderson, Jake LW (2015) - Not a standout performance but not bad by any means. Didn't get involved too much offensively but threw a couple big hits in his own zone. Got a couple shots on net in transition which is encouraging to see. Confidence is growing with each game.

OMA #18 Angello, Anthony RW (2014, 5th Round Pittsburgh Penguins) - Scored a really nice goal at the end of the first period taking the puck from the corner to the front of the net out muscling the Fargo defender all the way there. Continues a streak of good play in a kind of inconsistent season to this point.

OMA #25 Spinner, Steven RW (2014, 6th Round Washington Capitals) - Two goal game. One on the power-play in the first and one in the third period. Was Omaha's first star tonight, realy impressive performance.

OMA #26 Forsbacka-Karlsson, Jakob (2015) - Came away really impressed with his game. Dominated in the face-off circle, don't believe he lost a draw all night. Didn't get on the score sheet in the 5-1 victory but showcased his elite playmaking skills. Like him that much more with each game I see him.

February 21, 2015 - Victoriaville Tigers vs. Cape-Breton Screaming Eagles

CBS # 27 RD – Leveille, Loik (2015) – Leveille displayed a high offensive skill set; he walked the line on the power play and can get off a quick half slap shot on net. He made a highly skilled play in the 3rd period to toe drag and pull the puck toward his body which changed the shot angle on net for a high percentage scoring chance. Leveille was tough to play against because of his puck possession skills rarely forcing turnovers. He has a lot of creativity and makes calculated passes back door. He is a good skater with his head up anticipating the play and jumped up to break up passes.

CBS # 37 W – Svechnikov, Evgeny (2015) – Svechnikov was flat out dominant against Victoriaville; he showed extremely high skill level and was the best player on the ice. He is dangerous on the power play because he reads the play so well and can find small seams to pass through. For example he made a gorgeous no look pass behind the net to the back door for an easy goal for his linemate. Svechnikov displayed incredible hands in the neutral zone where he had the puck on a string; somehow keeping the puck on his stick weaving through the opposition. He has his head up and is a good playmaker which stems from his zone entries where he opens up and looks for trailing teammates. Svechnikov competed hard in the corners and set up the winning goal for Cabe Breton.

VIC # 27 W – Gabriel, Gagne (2015) – Gagne is a big physical winger that plays a north/south style of game. In his own zone he made a big hit to take the puck away from the opposition; then carried the puck up ice and gained puck possession in the offensive zone. He has average hands but was effective on the cycle game.

VIC # 48 C – Lauzon, Felix (2016) – Lauzon is a speedy center that had a strong game for Victoriaville. He is smart with the puck and creates space for himself by cutting to the middle of the ice in order to get a shot off. Lauzon showed he reads the play well when he gained offensive zone possession and passed to a trailing forward. He also showed a variety to his game when on another rush up the ice he cut to the middle and used the opposing defensemanas a screen for a shot.

Niagara IceDogs at Barrie Colts, Feb 21, 2015

Score: 6-4 Barrie

Niagara

LW Graham Knott (2015) – Knott played a 200-foot game in this one. He was always one of the first back in his zone defensively, and did a nice job of getting in the shooting/passing lanes, especially on the PK. He had several clears, a couple blocks, and won several battles along the wall throughout. With the puck he made a couple nice passes, one of which led to a goal. Knott went to the dirty areas, and landed a couple heavy hits as well.

D Vince Dunn (2015) – Dunn was very good in this one. He made a good first pass with regularity, and had several end-to-end rushes that led to scoring chances. He made good D-to-D passes and was an excellent puck distributor on the PP. Dunn walked the line with poise, and did a good job stepping around opposing forwards, and changing angles to create his own lane, and get pucks through. Dunn had a few shots on goal, scored, and also recorded an assist. He wasn't as good without the puck and was caught pinching a couple times, however, he had good closing speed, was physical when he could be, and used an active stick to disrupt a couple rushes. He will need to do a better job defending around the net, though.

Barrie

LW Roy Radke (2015) – Radke played a solid pro-style game in this one. He finished his checks, was strong on the puck, and generated quite a bit in the cycle game. He also backchecked hard, and was a regular on the PK. With the puck he made some nice plays on the cycle. One play Radke skated the puck into the offensive zone with possession, and went wide before cutting towards the net and tucking a beautiful goal past Hope.

C Matthew Kreis (2015) - Kreis didn't see much ice in this one, and made a minimal impact. As usual he had a couple rushes up ice, but nothing came of them, and he lost a couple puck battles in the offensive zone that led to clears.

D Rasmus Andersson (2015) – Andersson didn't register a point, but he played a very effective two-way game. Defensively he used his strong frame to seal players off, and rub them out of the play along the walls. He was aggressive in the corners and around the net, and was involved in post-whistle scrums with several Niagara players regularly throughout the night. Andersson wasn't fazed by any of that, as he continued to make firm, accurate passes, and drive play up ice. He set up a few good one-time opportunities, picked his spots with pinches, and played a real sound game. Andersson also blocked shots on the PK, and had a couple clears. He wasn't on for any of Niagara's goals (they scored two on the PP, two at even-strength).

G Mackenzie Blackwood (2015) – Blackwood wasn't at his best, but he was good enough for Barrie to win. Blackwood did a nice job making the first save, and did have some nice flurries of saves, but he was coughing up rebounds pretty regularly throughout this one. He was also beat by an unscreened shot from a distance. Blackwood did make some excellent glove saves. Luckily for Barrie he didn't get rattled, and seemed to get better as the game went on despite a mediocre performance by his standards.

USA U18 vs MADISON CAPITOLS (2-21-15)

USA - #19 C - Auston Matthews (2016) – Managed 1 assist tonight after an impressive 2-2-4pts the night before. Auston dominated the play down low with the puck all night tonight. Used his frame well to shield defenders from the puck and seemed to be able to move the puck toward the front of the net at will. Had some incredible scoring chances in close where the goalie made some fantastic saves. Was able to stickhandle and get his shot off quickly in traffic. Matthews also was sound defensively coming back into his own zone and used good stick position to pick off passes and get the play going in the other directions. Has a long powerful skating stride that catches defenders off guard because it doesn't look like he is moving that fast and before you know it he is around the defender and driver the net.

USA - #7 LW - Matthew Tkachuk (2016) – Scored 3 goals tonight and all three were in different ways. Played a power forward style of game with plenty of skill. First goal was due to having a good net front presence on the power play which allowed him to tip a point shot home. Second goal was due to winning a battle in front of the net and banging home a rebound and the third goal was on a quick release snap shot from the slot that beat the goalie over the blocker. Tkachuk was physical in the corners tonight, won battles, got the puck to an open guy then went straight to the front of the net. Tkachuk was dominate all night I the offensive zone, charting 10 shots on goal.

USA - #17 C - Colin White (2015) – Colin didn't have a lot of impact in the game tonight. Made some good plays with the puck in the neutral zone and used his quick stick to win some battles along the boards. Moved the puck quickly on the power play and did have an assist on the game's opening goal.

USA - #3 D - Caleb Jones (2015) – Showed good skating ability both with and without the puck which allowed him to have good gap control at his own blue line when defending line rushes. Wasn't overly physical in the corners or in front of his own net but often managed to come away with the puck regardless. Jones made the simple passes well tonight but didn't try to do too much with the puck offensively.

USA - #17 RW - Jeremy Bracco (2015) – Showed good speed through the neutral zone all night. Liked to pull up with the puck in the offensive zone and feed the open man. Had good patients with the puck and was able to create time and space for himself until something opened up. Scored on a great cross ice feed by #44 Chad Krys (2016) D, that he got a quick shot off for the games opening goal.

USA - #11 LW - Brendan Warren (2015) – Warren and Tkachuk were easily USA's most physical forwards tonight. Warren separated players from the puck all night long, got in on the fore-check with speed and finished his hits on the opposition Defenseman. Warren's line along with Luke Kunin (2016) and Tage Thompson (2016) didn't create a lot offensively but played a solid checking role that created energy and pressured the puck.

USA - #44 D - Chad Krys (2016) – Showed slick puck moving ability in all zones. Got the puck out of his own end well, both by skating up the ice or finding the open guy in the neutral zone. I really liked his mobility with the puck at the offensive blue line, did a good job buying time and creating space for himself to make a play. Krys made several good plays to hold pucks in the offensive zone. Ended the evening with 2 assists a +3 rating and was on the ice for 4 of USA's 6 goals.

USA - #29 G - Luke Opilka (2015) – Opilka didn't see a lot of action in the first period with Madison only registering 2 shots on goal, so his rust early in the 2nd and letting in 2 goals in a 3 min span is somewhat understandable however Opilka did eventually settle into the game and made some solid saves late in the 2nd and 3rd periods, especially on the Penalty Kill. Has quick lateral movement and moves from post to post with ease. Rebound control was just ok tonight but managed to make the 2nd save a lot of the times.

MAD - #17 RW - Sam McCormick (2015) – Scored on a great release on a partial breakaway on a shot from the faceoff dot. Found himself in good scoring position with the puck numerous times tonight. Registered 5 shots on goal and had a few chances that just missed the net. McCormick's skating ability as well as his ability to think and react quickly gets him his chances each night and tonight was no exception. Still needs to add bulk going forward to win those 50/50 puck battles but his compete level in the hard areas was unmatched tonight.

North Bay Battalion at Barrie Colts, Feb 26, 2015

Score: 4-2 Battalion

North Bay

LW Brett McKenzie (2015) – He played a solid two-way game. Playing on the top line with Nick Paul, he did a nice job on the cycle and did create some offense. McKenzie had a good stick in the defensive zone, and was always one of the first guys back defensively. He finished his checks when he could, and also scored on a nice shot from outside the circle. McKenzie did take a minor penalty when North Bay was already down a man, but that was his only real mistake.

D Zach Shankar (2015) – Shankar got off to a rough start, as he was caught chasing several times early on. He settled down after a few rough shifts, and did a nice job of playing the body when he could. He also chipped in with an assist on the powerplay. He wasn't really noticeable, which was good news for North Bay.

Barrie

LW Roy Radke (2015) – Radke was very quiet in this one. He took a couple hits to make plays/get the puck out, but struggled to generate much offensively. Radke also had a terrible defensive zone turnover where he went up the middle and it was intercepted for a chance against.

C Matthew Kreis (2015) – Kreis had a few controlled zone entries, and used his speed effectively through the neutral zone. Like the rest of the Colts, he didn't create much in the offensive zone, though. He threw a couple pucks at net but otherwise wasn't much of a threat.

D Rasmus Andersson (2015) – Andersson has a quiet game by his standards, but was still pretty good. Barrie struggled to generate much of anything offensively, so he didn't contribute a ton in that regard. Defensively his positioning was good, and he was pretty physical in the corners. He was mixing it up after the whistle on several occasions, and did a nice job making a good first pass after coming out of the corners with the puck. Andersson didn't record a point, but he did make one pass from the circle in the defensive zone to the opposing blue line that sprung a Barrie forward on a breakaway.

G Mackenzie Blackwood (2015) – Blackwood wasn't tested much early, but he certainly made up for that as the game went on. Barrie didn't generate much offense, so a good portion of the game was spent in their zone. Blackwood's rebound control was good for the most part, and he made some impressive post-to-post stops. Blackwood also made a couple breakaway stops late while Barrie was on the PP, but Barrie never took advantage of the extra chances Blackwood gave them. He stopped 32-35 (.914SV%).

February 26, 2015, Ottawa 67's at Windsor Spitfires

OTT #6 D Orban, Ryan (2015) - Mishandled simple puck play, directly resulted in 0-1 goal. Made a few pick mistakes early. Slow first few steps. Uses long reach pretty well. Mobility struggles.

OTT #10 RW Addison, Jeremiah (2015) - Good hands going to the net beating defender for scoring chance. Penalized for good clean hit.

OTT #17 RW Konecny, Travis (2015) - Used as a D on 5 on 3 PK and cleared zone. Scored outstanding goal to beat defender then slip the puck between the pad and post for 1-2 goal. Good cross ice pass on PP set up 3-2 goal. Excellent pass on rush showing a higher percentage pass then executing perfectly on a more difficult pass that directly lead to a scoring chance. PP1. Moved puck extremely well on the powerplay, kept opening himself up for passes

OTT #96 C Salituro, Dante (2015) - Shot from bad angles. Handled contact well for small forward. Good compete level for pucks and isn't afraid to get involved physically. Lacks separation speed to escape forechecker

OTT #1 G Herbst, Liam (2015*) - Challenges shooter extremely well, uses size well in crease and generally was tough to beat on the first shot. Spent too much time on his knees when he needed to be getting back on his feet. Still has trouble going side to side quickly enough.

Final Score: Windsor Spitfires: 4 - Ottawa 67's: 3 OT

Feb. 27, 2015 – Kelowna Rockets at Vancouver Giants

KEL #12 LC Merkley, Nick (2015) – Though he's by no means an elite straight-ahead skater, his edge-work is truly remarkable, as he created a string of turnovers tonight with his deceptive stop-and-start ability. Took on the role of playmaker tonight. Creating his own turnovers in the offensive end, he then has the foresight to stop and weigh his options before dishing the puck off to a teammate who is open. Continued to show good physicality, with a couple of nice open-ice hits.

KEL #21 RD Stephens, Devante (2015) – Had a great game in which he looked fast and physical on almost every shift he played. His feet are moving at a much faster clip than they were earlier in the year, and his added size and strength have lent him a scarier presence in the neutral zone as he's beginning to hit more in open-ice and tends to do so at high velocity. Lowered the boom with a big open-ice hit on more than one occasion. His passing and shooting were both good, as well. He is adjusting to his increased ice-time very smoothly, playing in a protege role alongside Madison Bowey.

KEL #28 RD Gatenby, Joe (2015) – Had a decent game in which he logged significant minutes and provided a calming presence on the Rockets back end. Made several nice passes to spring the offense and did a good job of keeping the opposition outside of the prime scoring area in his end. His shooting prowess came to the surface once or twice, as he has a knack for getting a soft wristshot onto the net and creating a chaotic situation out front.

VAN #8 LW Baer, Alec (2015) – Alec Baer is showing an upward trend towards the end of a lacklustre season for the Giants as a whole. Developing greater strength, presence-of-mind and awareness and is becoming more difficult to hit and/or knock off of the puck. His skating, however, has taken a bit of a hit as he's playing a more 'head's-up' style now.

VAN #11 RW Stukel, Jakub (2015) – One of the most positive developments for the Giants this season has been the return of playmaking winger Jakub Stukel to full-time duty. He's known for making some spectacular net drives, as he did tonight on a few occasions. He's been a bit snakebitten all year, but I wouldn't be shocked if he put up a 50 point season next year.

VAN #21 LD Mennell, Brennan (2015) – You have to love his skating, puck rushing, passing and shooting abilities. He's a bit one-dimensional in terms of being too much of a defensive liability at this point, but I wouldn't be surprised if he were in serious consideration for top pairing duties next season.

February 27, 2015, Plymouth Whalers at Sarnia Sting

PLY #19 C Mercer, Cullen (2015) - Good compete down low on PP. Big hit at the end of the second period. Very physical on the forecheck. Used as only forward on OT Pk 4 on 3

PLY #41 RW Bitten, Will (2016) - Used what he has to protect the puck extremely well against a defender and drove the net with puck for chances. Used separation speed to get breakaway on the over but was robbed. Showed willingness to get involved physically

PLY #39 G Nedeljkovic, Alex (Carolina) - Made several outstanding saves early on. In the second he made a bad play with the puck giving an empty net but made a diving save to keep the luck out. Outstanding reflexes.

SAR #5 D Chychrun, Jakob (2016) - Made a few puck mistakes early. Mishandled puck on offensive line taking penalty. Early first put puck over glass own zone for penalty. Got out of bod for odd man chance but fell.

SAR #14 C Zacha, Pavel (2015) - Great scoring chance due to offensive positioning early but hit post. Not aggressive enough without puck. Great power move through two defenders for scoring chance. Good passes in transition in neutral zone. Went off the ice a few times in pain but still made it back out and made some good one on one moves to beat defender then great shot to score a beautiful goal. Struggled in face-off circle tonight, slightly uncharacteristic for him, however he is just returning from injury.

Final Score: Sarnia Sting: 3 - Plymouth Whalers: 2 - OT

March 1, 2015, Sudbury Wolves at Mississauga Steelheads

SBY #7 D O'Grady, Reagan (2017) - Got some ice on the second powerplay unit. Forced shot on powerplay resulted in blocked shot and play going the other way. Risky outlet pass was turned over by opposition and brought back into the offensive zone.

SBY #23 D Capobianco, Kyle (2015) - Smooth skating defenseman, played an effective two way game for Sudbury today. Got open on multiple rushes, but teammates couldn't get him the puck. One missed pass actually resulted in Sudbury's third goal. Made some smart plays at the line to keep the play going. Made some smart simple first passes up ice. Good gap control and did well in one on one match-up's. Likes to get his whacks in whenever he can and is a pain to play against. Fights through checkers well with the pick on his stick. Good puck rush, calmly changes directions well. Protects pick well in neutral zone.

SBY #27 RW Schmalz, Matt (2015*) - Outstanding size, great reach on the forecheck, his speed has improved but he greatly struggles with his turns taking slow wide turns which really affected him in transition. His first few steps also need a lot of work but a few steps in his skating speed has shown clear improvements. Cross-checked opponent in the face and turned down multiple requests to fight by the opponent. When the official came in and called a penalty on Schmalz he quickly dropped the gloves and landed the first punch. Considering the size and strength difference, the fight was a draw at best for Schmalz.

MIS #4 D Day, Sean (2016) - Effortless skater, showed calm and evasiveness pinching in from the point with the puck to generate a couple scoring chances in this game. He plays with a little more of an edge than previous viewings taking the body a few times but not a powerful checker. Lacked compete in the defensive zone a few times. Landed a huge hit on the backcheck after attempting to hold the line and failing. Made good play to pick off outlet pass but then went offside.

MIS #6 D Gibson, Stephen (2015) - Gibson has good size and is a very good skater for his size. Always keeps his feet moving. Made a smart pinch on the line keeping it simple winning the race to the puck then getting back in position. He got a little overconfident and chased the same pinch seconds later losing the race leading to a 3 on 1 which directly resulted in Sudbury's second goal. He tried to pinch everytime, losing more than half the time putting him out of position. In a 2 on 1 he backed into his goaltender resulting in Sudbury's third goal.

MIS #9 C McLeod, Michael (2016) - Good pass to set up scoring chance using his speed to get deep in the offensive zone. Has a good, hard shot but shoots from low percentage areas. Drew powerplay protecting the puck and driving the net.

MIS #12 C Dickerson, Marcus (2016) - Scored Mississauga's first goal of the game going to the net and banging home rebound.

Final Score: Mississauga Steelheads: 4 - Sudbury Wolves: 3

March 6, 2015, Sault Ste. Marie Greyhounds at Sarnia Sting

SSM #9 RW Senyshyn, Zachary (2015) - Flies up and down the wing, good quickness and reaction time to loose pucks offensively, but also has great hustle on the backcheck. Likes to drive the wing and try to take the puck to the net for scoring chances. Tenacious in battle and won more than his share. Protects the puck well around forecheckers to keep puck control.

SSM #26 LW Gettinger, Timmy (2016) - Great play offensively to drive the net and quickly finish for Greyhounds' first goal.

SSM #37 D Bouramman, Gustav (2015) - Nice drop pass at line to set up play. Misplayed pass resulted in breakaway chance.

SAR #5 D Chychrun, Jakob (2016) - Good shot on powerplay for goal. Shot from point got through and Zacha banged home on the rebound.

SAR #14 C Zacha, Pavel (2015) - Great speed and escapability to take puck up ice quickly then make smart accurate pass. Handled puck well in netural zone. Excellent pass on power play. Always gets open and blasted a few good shots just missing then nice pass to set up Sarnia's second goal. Outstanding passes in transition. Quickly banged home 3-4 goal on doorstep. Great in face-off's tonight.

SAR #35 RW Korostelev, Nikita (2015) - Hit or miss with passing. Showed some good physicality. Tried to get fancy and turned puck over for partial break.

Final Score: Sault Ste. Marie Greyhounds: 5 - Sarnia Sting: 4

Erie Otters at Barrie Colts, March 7, 2015

Score: 5-3 Erie

Erie

C Connor McDavid (2015) – McDavid was electric from start to finish. His dynamic skating ability was on full display, as he accelerated to top speed in just a few strides, and was able to blow past everyone on the ice. McDavid lost defenders with stops/starts on several occasions, and was very creative with the puck. He was able to pull defenders wide opening up the middle of the ice for his teammates before giving them tape-to-tape passes in the scoring area. McDavid made defenders miss in space, and eluded several big check attempts. Defensively his positioning was good, and he was able to pick pocket Colts forwards on a couple occasions. McDavid showed some grit in his game, as he had a couple firm checks, and got into it with Rasmus Andersson almost every shift in the 3rd. He was dangerous off the rush, showed consistent ability to create his own shot, and was a threat every time he was on the ice. That he was the best player in this game even though all he did was tally an empty-net goal speaks to just how good he is.

C Dylan Strome (2015) – Strome played a very good two-way game. Offensively he was creative with the puck, and he showed great vision finding teammates all over the ice. He made smart decisions with the puck, and was very patient allowing plays to develop rather than forcing them. Strome wasn't very physical, but he used his size effectively to protect the puck, and he was very strong on it. Strome forced several turnovers in the defensive zone, and was very good carrying the puck up ice for controlled entries into the offensive zone. He finished the game with a goal and an assist, and was one of the best players on the ice.

RW Alex DeBrincat (2016) – DeBrincat was a puck hound throughout the entirety of this game. He was relentless on the forecheck, backchecked hard, and forced several turnovers as a result. He was very shifty with the puck, and was tough to defend in tight spaces. DeBrincat didn't hesitate at all to go to the dirty areas of the ice, and had no problem getting involved in scrums to stick up for McDavid and other teammates. DeBrincat was dangerous off the rush, and made several nice passes to setup scoring chances for teammates. He had two assists in the win.

D Travis Dermott (2015) – Dermott played a sound game on the backend for Erie. He made a good first pass exiting his zone, and was calm under pressure from oncoming players. He was positionally sound, and did good work on the penalty kill getting in the shooting lanes, and letting the game come to him. Dermott distributed the puck well on the powerplay, and scored on a laser of a shot through traffic at even-strength. He regularly held the line in the offensive zone. Dermott was physical along the boards, and landed a couple big hits in this game. He did take an interference penalty in the neutral zone, though, as he tried to step up for a big hit before the puck arrived.

LW Matthew Kreis (2015) – With Brendan Lemieux out of the lineup, Kreis was moved back into the top-9. Kreis showed good vision coming off the halfwall, as he hit teammates across the ice for a couple good chances. He played with good pace, and forced Erie defenders to back off when rushing the puck up ice through the neutral zone. He was effective cycling the puck, too, and drew a penalty while doing so.

RW Roy Radke (2015) - Radke did a nice job carrying the puck up ice and safely into Erie's zone. He skated through contact on a couple occasions, and was very strong on the forecheck. Radke had some firm hits, and his pressure forced some bad passes. He didn't get on the scoresheet, but he was good.

D Rasmus Andersson (2015) – This was one of Andersson's most physical games. He finished guys off regularly, and was very aggressive in the corners. Andersson went at McDavid for much of the night, too, and at one point tried to get McDavid to fight. Andersson's gap control was good, and he did a nice job of getting his stick in the shooting lanes to deflect a couple pucks out of play, as well as to force turnovers. Andersson made a good first pass and, though he was physically engaged throughout the night, he didn't force any plays despite some strong forecheck pressure. In the offensive zone Andersson was able to get pucks to the net, and used the slap pass effectively to draw attention before feeding it to an open teammate.

G Mackenzie Blackwood (2015) – Blackwood made some very nice saves, and showed good athleticism stretching out for a few post-to-post stops, but he wasn't at his best in this one. He coughed out several big rebounds, and was beat by a couple shots without any traffic. After Barrie battled back from 3-1 down in the 3rd he needed to make some stops, and he allowed a five-hole goal to Nick Baptiste that he probably should have had.

March 7, 2015, Saginaw Spirit at Owen Sound Attack

SAG #3 D Stewart, Chase (2015) - Great play to get the puck up and out, playing on a 5 on 3 penalty kill and did a good job. Makes plays positionally and also solid in front of the slot. Good plays in one on one match-up's. Opponent tried to hit him and Stewart still got the best of it. Misplayed puck on the offensive line resulting in turnover. Got walked by speed getting caught flat footed. Skating is a little sluggish.

SAG #27 C Stephens, Mitchell (2015) - Plays with persistence and goes for hits. Impressive power in hits for his size. Good play after Owen Sound's second goal to drive net for scoring chance.

SAG #55 D Middleton, Keaton (2016) - Low panic level deensively resulting in several turnovers. Has trouble standing up at times; lacks balance. Made good play at line to keep play going in zone; lead to goal.

SAG #77 LW Barwell, Jesse (2015) - Good speed, good energy, made a few good puck handling plays.

SAG #35 G Cormier, Evan (2016) - Making a lot of saves but fighting the puck. Lots of rebounds. Struggled on potential break. Came well out to play penalty shot and stopped it five hole. Took too long to get across.

OS #4 D Schemitsch, Thomas (2015) - Doesn't get much on first few steps. Good wrister top corner blocker for goal. Struglled one on one vs speed when going wide or changing directions. Even without much speed when going wide he has trouble.

OS #11 LW Dunda, Liam (2015) - Landed several good hits. Missed on great scoring chance in slot.

Final Score: Owen Sound Attack: 5 - Saginaw Spirit: 2

Mar. 10, 2015 – Spokane Chiefs at Vancouver Giants

SPO #17 Yamamoto, Kailer (2017) – Had a tremendous game. Quick feet and good hands in tight are his bread and butter. His fancy handy work around the net created several opportunities for his team, before he eventually dished the puck to a teammate for his team's first goal of the game. Skating ability, quick hands, and the ability to finish all come together here in a dangerous offensive threat. Matched up against Mason Geertsen during most of the game, it's not often you see a sixteen-year-old give a player of Geertsen's calibre that much trouble.

VAN #7 LW Ronning, Ty (2016) – Used speedy first-step explosiveness to take off with the puck through centre ice and draw a hooking call. Like teammate Jakob Stukel, he's looked a bit snakebitten since returning from injury (outside of his fantastic goal against Red Deer a few weeks earlier). Still appearing a bit undersized, and looking like he lost a bit of development time following a broken collarbone in the preseason.

VAN #8 LW Baer, Alec (2015) – Alec Baer had a really good game tonight in which he moved far away from the perimiter game he's been employing over the last several months. He finally showed that net drive we've been looking for all year, taking the puck on a direct route to the front of the net to set up an easy goal for Jackson Houck. Getting involved in the "rough stuff," both between and after the whistles, his game showed a lot more gumption than I've seen previously.

VAN #11 RW Stukel, Jakob (2015) – Like teammate and often linemate Alec Baer, Jakob Stukel definitely showed a ton of offensive gusto early in this one, getting below the hashmarks with the puck and setting up a teammate for the Giants first goal of the game. A quick pivot and soft hands created a couple other opportunities from behind the net, this time coming off of Stukel's stick. At other times, his effort could wane or he would make over-ambitious plays with the puck.

Rouyn-Noranda Huskies vs Blainville-Boisbriand, March 12th 2015

RN #5 Lauzon, Jeremy LD (2015): Very good game from Lauzon who might have been the best player on the ice tonight, had a tough first shift of the game when he tried to be too fancy with the puck and caused a turnover. The rest of the game he was rock solid, very good job defending one on one with a good active stick and strong body positioning. He scored the 3rd goal for his team with a simple point shot with traffic that found his way in the back of the net. Strong kid, showed ability to take a hit to move the puck to a teammate. Lauzon played on both PP and PK unit.

RN #3 Neveu, Jacob RD (2016): Good game overall from Neveu, showed good strength while battling for the puck along the wall during the game. Nothing flashy about his puck movement but made simple outlet to get the puck out of his zone. Defensively had some trouble versus quick forwards from the Armada, had some tough shift versus Yvan Mongo. He's a regular on the Huskies PK unit. His reaction time is a bit slow and will need some improvement.

RN #6 Myers, Philippe RD (2015): Good job playing a physical game in his own zone today, not shy of finishing hits and had a strong compete level. Doesn't have the quickest of feet but did a good job one on one including one time versus the very quick Danick Martel. When he had opportunity he jumped into the play, does need to make quicker decision with the puck when trying to move it or getting his shot through.

RN #16 Beaudin, Jean-Christophe RW (2015): Beaudin scored the 5th goal for the Huskies today after a bad turnover by a BLB defenseman right in the slot, took a quick shot blocker side to beat Montembeault. He made some smart plays defensively in the neutral zone, good effort without the puck. On the power play he was used at time on the point, didn't get a ton of ice there but has been used there regulary this season. He showed off his playmaking abilities in the 2nd period where he made a nice pass to Ryan Penny to send him on a breakaway.

RN #24 Fortin, Alexandre LW (2015): Fortin did some good work down low using his size and strength to win puck battles. On the power play he was used in front of the net to screen the opposing goaltender. Fortin made some good passes in the offensive zone, including one to Zach Sill on the Huskies 2nd goal of the game. He was a bit slow at getting his shot through in the offensive zone.

RN #35 Jeremy Belzile G (2015): Belzile was good today for the Huskies, first half of the game had to really good as the Huskies had a tough time staying out of the penalty box. Belzile is not a big goaltender and had to fight to track the puck with traffic in front of him on the Armada PP, liked his compete level tonight and made the saves he had to made. His defense did a good job keeping things on the outside and clearing rebounds in front of the net. Only goal he allowed was in the first period when Marc-Antoine Bouillon was left all alone in front of him.

BLB #33 Montembeault, Samuel G (2015): Not the best game from Montembeault today, didn't get a lot of shot in the first half of the game as Rouyn-Noranda was on the PK most of the time. On most goal he allowed it was right after a turnover by a BLB players. Even in a average game, he showed good composure in his crease and late in the 2nd period he made two real good saves to keep his team in the game. He was slow to react on some of the goals he gave up including the first one where he could have poke check the puck instead of letting go back to Antoine Waked.

BLB #7 Schingh-Gomez, Olivier LD (2016): With the puck Schingh-Gomez kept his game simple, made short outlet or ice the puck, didn't turn over the puck. Big body in his own zone but could have play with a bit more physicality. Had some issues with his mobility and keeping in check RN speedy forwards.

BLB #18 Hylland, Tyler C/RW (2016): Played on a kid line with Miguel Picard and Brendan Hamelin today, did some good work on the forecheck; putting pressure on RN defense and did create a scoring chance out of it. Good active stick. Missed a pass which lead to RN 2nd goal of the game.

BLB #21 Mongo, Yvan LW (2015): Good game from the diminutive rookie forward, did a solid job on the forecheck using his speed to create some confusion in the RN defensive zone. Altough he's not tall Mongo has a strong lower body and is able to win puck battles like he did versus a much bigger Jacob Neveu on one sequence. He saw some power play time in the 2nd half of the game thanks to his effort in the 1st half of the game.

BLB #57 Picard, Miguel C (2016): Picard showed some flashes in the game in limited ice time, had a nice rush with the puck where he was able to beat him wide and center the pass in front of the net for a scoring chance. He was able to bring the puck to the net from the corner using his strength. Good effort on the backcheck, made a real nice block shot in front of Montembeault.

Owen Sound Attack at Barrie Colts, March 12, 2015

Score: 3-2 Barrie

LW Petrus Palmu (2015) – Palmu accelerated quickly through the neutral zone, and was effective in carrying the puck into the offensive zone with possession. He was dangerous off the rush, showing good vision hitting teammates with passes all over the ice. Palmu was aggressive on the forecheck, and was feisty in the corners despite his size. Palmu was very slippery in the offensive zone, and did a nice job finding soft spots in the defense and setting up shop. He had a couple good scoring chances just outside the paint, and had several shots on goal in the game. He finished with one assist.

C Ethan Syzpula (2015) – Syzpula didn't get a lot of ice time, but he made the most of his opportunities. He won several races to loose pucks, and was relentless on the forecheck. He back checked hard, too, and showed commitment to a 200-foot game. He accelerated quickly with the puck, and did a nice job generating speed through the neutral zone. Syzpula was creative in space, and didn't shy away from contact or battles along the wall.

D Tyler MacArthur (2015) – MacArthur was positionally sound in the defensive zone - especially on the penalty kill – and used his long reach effectively to break plays up and get pucks out of the zone. He did a nice job playing the body on the rush, and for the most part kept everything to the outside. MacArthur had a couple defensive breakdowns but generally was solid.

D Thomas Schemitsch (2015) – Schemitsch struggled defending speed off the rush at times, but was good defensively overall. He used an active stick to break up a couple rushes, and also did a nice job preventing a back door pass attempts; particularly when Barrie was on the powerplay. He broke down several zone entry attempts, too. With the puck, he made a good first pass, didn't force anything and looked confident during several rushes with the puck. One pinch led to a 2-on-1 against, but for the most part he picked his spot with pinches very well.

LW Matthew Kreis (2015) – Kreis protected the puck very well in the cycle game, and was shifty coming off the half-wall. He didn't shy away from the dirty areas, and had several scoring chances throughout despite not recording a point. Kreis was able to make accurate passes on both his forehand and backhand.

RW Roy Radke (2015) – Radke played a solid two-way game. He was strong on the puck, finished his checks and was very strong on his skates. Radke went to the dirty areas regularly, and stayed disciplined by not retaliating to some abuse he took in front. Radke did a nice job driving play up ice, and was effective carrying the puck from the defensive zone into the offensive zone. His forecheck pressure caused several bad passes and/or turnovers, and his line was excellent eating clock late while defending the lead.

D Rasmus Andersson (2015) – Andersson showed off some good hand-eye coordination early on picking a puck out of the air and holding the line in the offensive zone. Offensively Andersson did a nice job moving the puck on the powerplay, and picked up an assist on the man advantage. Defensively his gap control was good, and he was effective on the PK, blocking several shots while killing off penalties. Andersson played the first shift on a 3 vs 5, and was on the ice for the final 30 seconds defending the lead late, so clearly he has earned the trust of head coach Dale Hawerchuk.

G Mackenzie Blackwood (2015) – Blackwood had a real strong game. He didn't face many flurries of shots, but he was very good when called upon. Blackwood did a nice job squaring up to shooters, and didn't allow many rebounds. Whenever there was a rebound, Blackwood effectively steered them into the corners or towards his teammates. He helped out by playing the puck up ice a few times, and looked very confident.

March 12, 2015, Kitchener Rangers at London Knights

KIT #11 LW Kilgour, Jack (2016) - Big hit. Good speed for size.

KIT #15 C Franzen, Gustav (2015) - Had a great shift showing persists cd competing for puck, then went to the net with opponent all over him and scored the opening goal.

KIT #17 C Kohn, Mason (2015) - Gets knocked around a lot in board battles due to size and strength. Jammed home rebound in the slot for 7th goal.

KIT #27 LW Llewellyn, Darby (2015*) - Good pass to set up 4-1 goal.

KIT #74 C Bunnaman, Connor (2016) - Played big penalty kill minutes.

LON #6 D Gleason, Ben (2016) - Made good play two on one rush to break up play but gave the puck back to opponent for 6th goal against.

LON #14 D Crawley, Brandon (2015) - Ran around a bit in defensive zone. Good hit down low. Great in battles along the wall. Beat one on one in the slot, play created rebound resulting in Kitchener's 7th goal.

LON #86 D Martenet, Chris (2015) - Moved puck decent a few times. Let his man walk in and scored 7th goal for Kitchener. Let man into slot resulting in penalty, cross check.

LON #93 RW Marner, Mitch (2015) - Played point on powerplay. Didn't get much done tonight.

LON #1 G Parsons, Tyler (2016) - First goal quick pads to make first save, rebound quickly buried.

Final Score: Kitchener Rangers: 8 - London Knights: 1

March 13, 2015, Saginaw Spirit at Sarnia Sting

SAG #3 D Stewart, Chase (2015) - Great play down low to pick off pass then smart pass up ice; composed. Great first pass options chosen.

SAG #12 D Holmes, Michael (2015) - Great long distance pass. Great skater for size.

SAG #27 C Stephens, Mitchell (2015) - Scored nice 2-0 goal with defender all over him going forehand/backhand. Laser shot top shelf off the wing scoring Saginaw's third goal.

SAG #35 G Cormier, Evan (2016) - Looking much more poised than last viewing. Directing rebounds away well. First goal a little soft, slipped through. Great cross crease score 2 on 1.

SAR #14 C Zacha, Pavel (2015) - Good move to net first shift for chance. Good hit to open second period. Gets shot off quickly. Displayed excellent puck skills down low in offensive zone. Brilliant shot-pass set up big scoring chance. Good compete in defensive zone.

SAR #35 RW Korostelev, Nikita (2015) - Delivered several hard hits early in this game.

SAR #32 G Fazio, Justin (2015) - With 7:00 left in the first period, Fazio entered the game with the score of 3-0 for Saginaw. Made some good saves right off the bat. Made outstanding save 2 on 1 playing shot then rebound to second guy and dove to make the second save. Left hanging out to dry by his teammates in this one but made some highlight reel saves to keep them in it. Bad puck play late second nearly resulted in a goal.

Final Score: Saginaw Spirit: 4 - Sarnia Sting: 3

Barrie Colts at Mississauga Steelheads, March 13, 2015

Score: 5-2 Barrie

LW Matthew Kreis (2015) – Kreis regularly gained Mississauga's line with possession, allowing Barrie to setup in the offensive zone. He battled hard in the corners, however he was muscled off the puck at times. He back checked regularly and was back to support in the defensive zone. With the puck he didn't create a ton, and also had a couple neutral zone turnovers trying cross-ice passes.

RW Roy Radke (2015) – Radke's physical game continues to improve. He didn't take any needless runs or take himself out of position in the process, but he did have a few powerful hits on the forecheck. Radke recovered several loose pucks, which allowed Barrie to maintain possession and generate offense. Radke's positioning was good on the penalty kill, as he covered his points and had no problem sprawling to block shots. He took some hits to get pucks out and/or in deep while defending the lead, and played a solid 200-foot game.

D Rasmus Andersson (2015) – Andersson set the tone for his game early on when he blocked and/or intercepted consecutive centering passes. His positioning was good all night long, and he had no problems defending rotations in the cycle game. Once again Andersson was out for the first shift on a 3 vs 5, and was relied upon in all situations.

G Mackenzie Blackwood (2015) – Blackwood didn't face a lot of rubber – Barrie allowed just seven shots in the final 40 – but he was very good early, and was a big reason the Colts were tied after 20. Mississauga came out firing putting 15 pucks on net in the 1st, and they had plenty of chances in the slot area. Blackwood did a nice job controlling rebounds, and whenever they popped out he was there to make 2nd and 3rd stops.

C Michael McLeod (2016) – McLeod was Mississauga's most dangerous forward in this one. His quick decision making with the puck coupled with his high-end speed and overall pace gave Barrie a lot of problems; especially in the 1st period. McLeod was relentless after the puck, forced a couple turnovers and won several battles throughout. He finished his checks whenever he could, too. McLeod was elusive with the puck in space, stickhandling around oncoming checkers numerous times. He played a very good game, however, he showed a lack of discipline taking three minors in the final 22 minutes of the game.

RW Nathan Bastian (2016) – Bastian won puck battles all over the ice. He was strong on the puck, aggressive, and assertive while showing no fear going to dirty areas of the ice. Bastian finished his checks every shift, and had a couple big hits in this game. His puck pursuit paid off as he had a few pickpockets that led to scoring chances for Mississauga.

D Sean Day (2016) – Day played with an edge from start to finish in this one. He rubbed guys off the puck, took some healthy runs, and was very physical in the corners. Offensively Day showed good poise rushing the puck up ice, and carrying it into the offensive zone. His passes were accurate, and he moved the puck well on the PP picking up an assist on Brandon Devlin's goal.

March 14, 2015, North Bay Battalion at Kingston Frontenacs

NBY #8 D Bruce, Riley (2015) - Keeps it very simple from the back end playing a shutdown role. Skating is a bit uncomfortable.

NBY #12 LW McKenzie, Brett (2015) - Good burst of speed driving the net with the puck.

KGN #67 LW Crouse, Lawson (2015) - Tried to do too much early on. Made initial pass that lead to a great play by Sam Bennett for Kingston's first goal. He then made a nice move in the slot area where Bennett finished on the rebound created. On the powerplay he did a good job of covering for defenders. Quietly slips into good scoring area and quickly finished on Kingston's fifth goal. Protects puck extremely well. His direction changes need improvement.

Final Score: Kingston Frontenacs: 6 - North Bay Battalion: 0

Peterborough Petes at Barrie Colts, March 14, 2015

Score: 3-0 Barrie

Peterborough

C Jonathan Ang (2016) – Ang played a very effective two-way game. He was positionally sound defensively, made smart decisions with the puck, and was always on his man. Ang used an active stick to pick pocket a couple players, and didn't shy away from blocking shots. With the puck he set up a few chances, and had a couple of his own.

D Cam Lizotte (2015) – Lizotte was very physical from start to finish. He was aggressive in front of the net, and made it very uncomfortable for anyone trying to set up shop in front of Mancina. Lizotte blocked several shots on the PK, and he laid the body whenever he could. He was able to intercept a couple cross-ice passes while Barrie tried to enter Peterborough's zone, and he did a nice job of taking those pucks the other way to jump start the rush. He also made some good outlets, and skated the puck out of trouble when necessary.

D Matt Spencer (2015) – Spencer defended Peterborough's blue line well, as he broke up several entry attempts throughout. His positioning and gap control were good, and Spencer effectively kept a lot of Barrie's shots to the outside. With the puck he made a good first pass, and used a slap pass several times in the offensive zone to set up teammates in the danger area. A failed clear led to a couple Barrie shots, but he didn't really make any glaring mistakes.

LW Matthew Kreis (2015) – Kreis generated a fair amount of offense in this game. He did a good job skating the puck up ice and into Peterborough's zone with possession, and when he did so he regularly drew Petes defenders in before feeding it to open points. Kreis went to the net without hesitation, and was rewarded by registering an assist after whacking away in front.

RW Roy Radke (2015) – Radke did an excellent job of disrupting on the forecheck. He forced several turnovers over the course of the game, and pushed players off the puck numerous times. He showed good power in his shot, which generally weren't controlled and led to big rebounds in front. He was effective cycling down low, and a good cycle alongside Kreis and Cordell James led to Barrie's 3rd goal.

D Rasmus Andersson (2015) – Andersson pinched in on occasion to keep plays alive, but really picked his spots in that regard. He got a few pucks on net as well. Without the puck, Andersson used his stick to break up an odd man rush, and deflected several shot attempts out of play. He was pick pocketed once and that led to a quality Peterborough chance, but Blackwood managed to bail him out. Besides that, he played a pretty sound game.

G Mackenzie Blackwood (2015) – Blackwood played one of his best games this season. His side-to-side movement was excellent, and he would never over commit. Blackwood was squaring up to shooters, and eating up a lot of pucks. The Petes had the first 10 or 11 shots of the game, but Blackwood made several quality stops and gave Barrie some time to get their legs underneath them. He was tested early and often by a desperate Petes team, and he blanked them. Can't ask for much more than that.

March 15, 2015 - Rouyn-Noranda Huskies at Sherbrooke Phoenix

RNH #5 D Lauzon, Jeremy (2015) - Good patience with the puck. Doesn't rush plays, takes his time and make sure he's choosing the right options. Accurate puck decisions consistently throughout game.

RNH #24 LW Fortin, Alexandre (2015) - Goes to front of net and creates great screen despite size. Helped create Huskies' first goal.

RNH #1 G Harvey, Samuel (2016) - Made some quick reflex saves but gave up a ton of rebounds. Rebounds cost him a few goals tonight.

SHE #26 LW Poulin, Nicolas (2015) - Scored their goal in slot. Stopped on first attempt but rebound right back to him and finished on a somewhat soft goal.

SHE #89 RW Schweri, Kay (2015) - Excellent pass circling then entering pass to set up 2-1 goal.

Final Score: Sherbrooke Phoenix: 5 - Rouyn-Noranda Huskies: 1

March 20, 2015, Saginaw Spirit at London Knights

SAG #3 D Stewart, Chase (2015) - Walked bad on London's third goal by Max Domi.

SAG #7 D Henley, Troy (2015) - Pushed opponent into own net resulting in London's fifth goal. Will play opponents tough down low for someone his size. Lacks mobility.

SAG #12 D Holmes, Michael (2015) - Shot from the point slipped through pads and trickled in for Saginaw's first goal. Good physical play down low. and his man well one on one or two on two. Did get beat on one occasion by size and skill but was able to stick with play to prevent big chance. Good defensive zone positioning. Made smart/safe chip out of his own zone without icing it when under pressure.

SAG #27 C Stephens, Mitchell (2015) - Very quick release to get his chance on net. Provided good physical play all night. Played big minutes in all game situations. Persistent on the forecheck.

SAG #55 D Middleton, Keaton (2016) - Landed a huge hit on a big opponent. Was willing to block shots. Received secondary ice in all game situations. Stripped in the neutral zone for a breakaway opportunity.

SAG #62 C Felhaber, Tye (2016) - Great breakaway move for Saginaw's sixth goal.

SAG #88 RW Artemov, Artem (2015) - Has very quick hands, good pass into the slot to quickly score Saginaw's second goal. Skating is average despite quick feet. Lost battles down low in the offensive zone.

LON #6 D Gleason, Ben (2016) - Good on the puck rush, accelerates well through lanes. Generally chooses the right path when rushing with the puck.

LON #14 D Crawley, Brandon (2015) - Good cross ice pass created London's second goal. Moved puck very well on a few occasions in the neutral zone. Good long distance pass from own zone created a good odd man chance for London. Pinches at the right time in the offensive zone. Was a little too soft on a one on one match up. He was able to keep up with the opponent but still threaded a pass through resulting in a goal against. Showed good aggression in the slot and the corners after this occurrence. Made a good rush deep in the offensive zone and a good pass but a subsequent turnover had him caught deep and couldn't recover on Saginaw's sixth goal. Fired puck down the ice with an open net hitting the crossbar, but was rewarded with an assist.

LON #86 D Martenet, Chris (2015) - Pinched in to jump on rebound to score London's seventh goal. Uses long reach one on one to fend forwards off. Fell in a one on one match-up tripping over his own feet for a scoring chance against.

LON #93 RW Marner, Mitch (2015) - Great pass created the sequence that resulted in London's opening goal. Great shiftiness with puck, resulted in a powerplay that quickly became a power play goal for his team. Outstanding passing ability on display multiple times to create a wealth of scoring chances. Playing chippy and liked to get his whacks in.

LON #98 D Mete, Victor (2016) - Effortless skating, excellent speed, kept feet moving. Good stops and starts one on one making him very tough to get past.

LON #1 G Parsons, Tyler (2016) - Entered the game with nine minutes left in the second period. Excellent skating, so quick. Made some highlight reel saves in relief.

Final Score: London Knights: 8 - Saginaw Spirit: 6

Kingston Frontenacs at Barrie Colts, March 21, 2015

Score: 4-2 Kingston

LW Lawson Crouse (2015) – Playing on a line with Sam Bennett and Spencer Watson, Crouse was one of the best players on the ice. He skated through contact on several occasions, and regularly gained Barrie's line with possession of the puck. He was very aggressive on the forecheck, and used his body whenever he could. Crouse used his big frame effectively to protect the puck while driving the net. Crouse struggled to create his own shooting lane, but he was found open a couple times, and certainly made the most of it by ripping a powerful shot bar down for Kingston's 1st goal of the game. Crouse also showed good playmaking skills, making several touch passes and finding teammates all over the ice. Defensively he was always back to support, and his defensive positioning – especially on the penalty kill – was excellent.

D Jarkko Parikka (2015) – Parikka was part of a defensive breakdown on Justin Scott's goal that opened the scoring, but beyond that he played a sound game. Often times Parikka was almost unnoticeable, which is always a good thing for a defensive defenseman. He kept things smart and simple with the puck, and without it his positioning was good.

LW Matthew Kreis (2015) – Kreis played one of his better games this season. He was very shifty with the puck, and was able to make people miss in space a couple different times. One play Kreis danced around a Kingston defender gunning for a big hit, and completely took him out of the play before going in and getting a chance on a 2-on-1. Kreis was very good through the neutral zone in terms of carrying the puck up ice, but also by using his stick to break up some rushes, and pickpocket Frontenacs attackers. He went to the net to crash for rebounds, and showed no hesitation in his game.

RW Roy Radke (2015) – Radke caused havoc in Kingston's zone for much of the net. He finished guys off on the forecheck, and won several puck battles that led directly to scoring chances. He gained Kingston's line with possession easily at times, and showed good power protecting the puck while driving the net. Radke took several hits along the wall in the defensive zone to get pucks out or make plays, and showed a willingness to do whatever it takes to help his team.

D Rasmus Andersson (2015) – Andersson was playing with a burr under his saddle in this one. He was aggressive in front of the net, and wasn't shy with his stick work throughout the game. Andersson landed a couple solid hits, and did a nice job forcing attackers wide and finishing them off along the wall. He was involved in several scrums throughout, but didn't let that affect his play during the whistles. Kingston did a nice job clogging up the neutral zone and taking away outlets, so Andersson took it upon himself to rush the puck up ice, and into the offensive zone. Andersson showed good confidence skating with the puck, and stepped around a handful of Kingston players in the process. He played one of his better defensive games all year, however, after a Kevin Labanc turnover at the blue line, Andersson was eventually beat to a rebound by Juho Lammikko for a short handed goal.

Mar. 22, 2015 – Portland Winterhawks at Tri-City Americans

POR #7 LW Bittner, Paul (2015) – Had the type of game that I've become very accustomed to. Continues to get to the front of the net where he's practically irremovable. Doesn't absorb a ton of punishment there though, preferring to hang behind the net before popping out at opportune moments. It eventually earned him a goal, as he scored standing in front of the opposition goaltender with a patented rebound goal off a power play slapshot that came on and off of his stick in a heartbeat.

POR #23 RW Weingar, Evan (2016) – A total pest tonight, doing his best Brad Marchand impression. Despite being small, he doesn't back down from anyone, which makes him an annoying player to be placed up against. Levelled some absolutely huge bodychecks that were completely clean and drew the ire of the Americans, resulting in several earned power plays for his club. Offensive game also looked pretty good as he stickhandled his way into the slot to get a couple good chances on the net. The MVP for Portland tonight, in my opinion.

POR #44 RD Texeira, Keoni (2015) – Had a great game in which he made major contributions in his own end. While I've always liked his backwards skating ability, his straight-ahead skating continues to improve. On one play, he fearlessly blocked a shot one what would have been a sure-thing goal in the first period during a two-on-one. He plays a gritty game full of cheap shots and trash-talk. The opposition really seems to hate this guy.

TRI #31 G Sarthou, Evan (2016) – A tall and swivel-headed goaltender who likes to scan the offensive zone as much as possible. His butterfly technique is just okay, as it could be a little tighter. Otherwise he keeps his upper-body upright and tracks shots really well when transitioning to the standing position and back again. Both his glove-hand and his blocker looked excellent, and he has the natural reflexes to make a save with either in extraordinarily quick timing.

TRI #36 RD Carlo, Brandon (2015) – Brandon Carlo played his game to a tee tonight: kept things simple, cleaned out the front of his net with ease, and provided an intimidating presence on the back-end. He made some really nice keeps in the offensive zone and was an impenetrable wall when defending his team's prime scoring area. Once again, however, I thought he kept it a bit "too simple," as I would like to see him be a tiny bit more ambitious with puck-movement.

TRI #37 LD Wotherspoon, Parker (2015) – A great skater in all directions, but his hockey sense and positioning isn't always the best and he sometimes relies too heavily on his speed getting sucked out of position. Loves to weave-and-wind his way to centre ice, but doesn't have the anticipatory skills to make a successful entry or just the simple dump the vast majority of the time. On the positive end, he threw some nice hits and had several good takeaways along the boards.

March 27, 2015, Owen Sound Attack at Guelph Storm

Game #1 - OHL Western Conference Quarter-Finals

OS #3 D Walters, Connor (2015) - Connor played a pretty steady game. He was reliable defensively and consistently made a smart first pass. He took the hit to make the play down low. Made smart pinch at the offensive line. Scored Owen Sound's fourth goal of the game on a decent wrister, but a soft goal.

OS #4 D Schemitsch, Thomas (2015) - Schemitsch played a ton of minutes in all game situations for the Attack tonight. He struggled a little on the defensive side of the puck. He was a little hit or miss one on one, making a few good plays with his stick but made a bad play on Dickinson giving too much space and his stick in the wrong place, directly lead to Guelph's only goal. He struggled down low to contain opposing players of all sizes. Good puck movement in neutral zone. Smart fake shot to pass fooled goaltender and helped create Owen Sound's third goal. Mishandled the puck on the point a few times leading to a loss of offensive zone pressure.

OS #11 LW Dunda, Liam (2015) - Right off the start Dunda provided a very physical presence for the Attack. Smart play from behind the net to set up Owen Sound's first goal of the game.

OS #17 D Meyer, Jarret (2015) - Struggled a little tonight, got walked one on one falling when attempting to pivot. Iced the puck without hesitation when he got the puck in the defensive zone.

OS #25 LW Palmu, Petrus (2015) - Extremely small and shifty, played in all game situations tonight for Owen Sound. Struggled to create much offensively however.

GUE #4 D Carroll, Noah (2016) - Great composure down low with the puck under pressure to carry it out of trouble then make a smart pass in the neutral zone. Consistently strong on the puck rush, excellent timing on when to pass off and skates well. Maintains good positioning in one on one situations. Played top power play minutes for Guelph.

GUE #10 D Hall, Austin (2015) - Hall struggled a bit tonight. He got beat one on one which directly resulted in Owen Sound's second goal. In the second period he put the puck over the glass for a delay of game penalty, the power play resulted in Owen Sound's third goal. He is a decent skater but needs to read situations to better utilize his skating.

GUE #24 RW Smith, Givani (2016) - Right from his first shift, Smith provided an excellent physical presence for the Storm. He finished his check every opportunity. Givani protected the puck well down low and maintained possession for long periods of time using his size. He also assisted on Guelph's only goal of the game.

GUE #27 D McFadden, Garrett (2015) - McFadden did a good job in the slot tying up his man, usually bigger than him. Hard point shot. Very strong for his size, winning battles on the wall. Showed some pretty good moves when walking in from the point to get his shot off. Mishandled the puck on the offensive line a few times. Very aggressive when trying to hold the offensive line which had mixed results.

Final Score: Owen Sound Attack: 6 - Guelph Storm: 1

Mar. 29, 2015 – Kootenay Ice at Calgary Hitmen (Quarter Final, Game 2)

KTN #2 LD Murray, Troy (2015) – Good skating ability, calmness, poise, high hockey IQ—these are all qualities are that are clearly evident. Once again he made some good reads in the offensive zone without being too aggressive. His shooting accuracy could probably use some work. Despite good vision and timing, his outlet passes were strangely a bit off the mark and went astray far too often.

KTN #12 C Philp, Luke (2014) – A really good skater with a deep gas tank. Has many tools: a good skater, an equally good passer and shooter, and can hit very hard. Speciality appears to be tremendous hockey sense in the offensive zone's prime socring area—has a good sense for when to attack the net and when to play from the perimeter. Played on the point on the power play for a second game in a row—able to pinch in deep and converge onto the net with impunity as he's able to get back in good timing. Scores most of his goals from in tight, but doesn't hang out there forever and is capable of making the stretch pass from afar as well if necessary. Won the majority of his draws.

KTN #22 RW Zborosky, Zak (2015) – Another good skater who plays an admirable north-south energy game. Possesses above-average speed and hockey sense and utilizes those skills to retrieve pucks on smart dump-and-chase plays. He had a couple nice wristers on net. Works hard on the backcheck, too, although we wish he were more of a physical presence on a consistent basis.

CGY #4 LD Zipp, Michael (2015) – Not a great skater, but you have to appreciate the hard working nature of his game. He doesn't win the majority of his footraces, but has an active stick and finds ways to disposses guys of the puck along the boards after they beat him one-on-one. His passes were simple and effective.

CGY #9 C Karnaukhov, Pavel (2015) – Looked faster and more dangerous in Game 2 than he did in Game 1. Most effective when skating in direct lines towards the net: has the sandpaper to fight for position in the slot; has the agility to get himself in good position; and has the hands to finish in tight. Scored on a goal in-close on the power play off of a sloppy but smartly timed backhand. Discipline was a bit of an issue as he took an ugly elbowing penalty.

March 29, 2015, Erie Otters at Sarnia Sting

Game #3 - OHL Western Conference Quarter-Finals

ERI #17 RW Raddysh, Taylor (2016) - Excellent skating, explodes through neutral zone to get involved on the rush. Also played a good two-way game using his speed on the backcheck. Excellent offensive zone positioning. Gets his shot off quickly but was robbed. Played on the second power play unit.

ERI #19 C Strome, Dylan (2015) - Showing great poise when entering the offensive zone with the puck utilizing vision and distributing the puck well. Scored in the first period deflecting a shot from the point then was credited with his second in the second when an attempted pass was picked off by a defender and knocked into the net. Excellent on the penalty kill getting his stick in lanes and intercepting passes, took one down for short handed chance.

ERI #44 D Dermott, Travis (2015) - Good skating on puck rush, showed ability to keep opponents guessing on the rush. Good shoot/pass decisions on the powerplay point. Played top unit powerplay. Played opponents tough down low for his size and was tough to play against tonight.

ERI #97 C McDavid, Connor (2015) - Connor showed flashes of his speed and skill in the first period but was neutralized well by Sarnia. At the end of the period he got into a scrum which resulted in a power play. He then created two more powerplay when typical hockey contact was made with him. He was then penalized for protecting himself going into a corner resulting in an opponent getting stood up. Became very vocal with opposition and officials after this sequence in the first half of the game. Outstanding positionally and exceptional reaction time to play around him. Quick release off crossbar. Lightning quick hands. Made opposition nervous on second penalty kill unit and forced some turnovers clearing the zone and creating a few short handed rushes. In the third period, McDavid played with a lot more pushback and intensity in the third period getting after opponents and made some solid defensive plays. Does too much talking to officials after whistles. Nice play off the draw to cut across the slot with patience and roof the game winner 6-5 goal.

SAR #10 LW Salinitri, Anthony (2016) - Showed great puck control down low but made some blind passes to no one.

SAR #14 C Zacha, Pavel (2015) - Great one timer, goalie got a piece with his glove but went in for 2-0 goal. Excellent through traffic sign the puck on his stick. Great vision making tough passes look casual. Exceptional vision and ability to read the play around him.

SAR #25 LW Kyrou, Jordan (2016) - Does a great job of using his hands and speed to carry the puck end to end and control it in the offensive zone and create offense. However he tried to do way too much by himself with the puck playing with very good linemates and looked off some great passing options, eventually negating plays.

SAR #35 RW Korostelev, Nikita (2015) - Made the smart pass when he easily could have shot to setup 2-0 goal. Used his size very well protecting down low and delivered some solid hits in this game.

Final Score: Erie Otters: 6 - Sarnia Sting: 5

Game 2: Belleville Bulls at Barrie Colts, March 30, 2015

Final score: 8-2 Barrie

C Adam Laishram (2015) – Laishram started the game at center, but was shifted to wing to try and generate offense after the Bulls fell behind a few goals. Laishram used his quick acceleration to close gaps quickly, and pressure puck carriers. His positioning was good defensively, and he always played his man very tight. He was feisty in the corners, and had a non-stop motor while pursuing the puck. Offensively he created a few chances by pulling defenders to him before dishing it off to an open teammate. Laishram was able to lose his man with quick stops/starts, which gave him space to get off a couple good shots.

LW Trent Fox (2015) – Fox had a rather ineffective game. He struggled to generate anything offensively, and took a bad penalty in the offensive zone taking some extra shots in a scrum when Garret Hooey was already lying on the ice. Fox had a couple net drives, and finished his checks but otherwise was very quiet.

RW Matt Luff (2015) – Luff finished his checks, went to the dirty areas of the ice, and showed a good net-front presence throughout. He scored a goal on the man advantage with a nice deflection in front. Carrying the puck he had some problems, though, as he had several turnovers, one of which led directly to him taking a tripping penalty.

D Justin Lemcke (2015) – Belleville took seven penalties, and Lemcke played a ton on the PK. He made several clears, and blocked some shots in that span. Lemcke was out muscled in front of the net by Hooey on Barrie's 1st goal, and was walked a few times by Joseph Blandisi, Kevin Labanc and some of Barrie's faster players. He seemed to struggle against players going wide with speed. Lemcke did make some good defensive plays in this game, but he spent most of his time chasing play in his own zone, and he didn't create much offense, either.

LW Matthew Kreis (2015) – Kreis showed good awareness, positioning himself to intercept several cross-ice passes in this game. Offensively he did setup a couple good one-time opportunities, but none were converted on. Kreis was pushed off the puck too easily at times, and he was sealed off easily while skating wide.

RW Roy Radke (2015) – Radke was one of the best players on the ice in this game, and played the best game I've seen from him. He was very strong on the puck, and regularly skated through contact while driving the net. Radke had several good shots in tight, scored, and was causing havoc all game. Radke forced a few turnovers that led to scoring chances, and seemingly recovered every loose puck. He finished his checks, and didn't retaliate to any push back. Despite Barrie holding a big lead for much of the game, Radke continued to block shots and forecheck hard even with the game being well out of reach.

D Rasmus Andersson (2015) – Andersson made an impact in this game early, getting some pucks towards the net, setting up scoring chances, and hitting a post. When no outlets were available he served as a one-man breakout. Andersson was a regular on Barrie's penalty kill that killed off four of five opportunities, and he didn't hesitate to block shots. Andersson did a nice job using his stick to steer opponents wide, before sealing them off along the wall. He wasn't very aggressive in front of the net, however, he broke up a couple chances by tying up Belleville sticks.

G Mackenzie Blackwood (2015) – Blackwood had a poor start in this game allowing two goals on four shots in the 1st period. He didn't let that get to him, as he blanked the Bulls the rest of the way en route to a 25-save performance. Blackwood coughed out a big rebound on Belleville's 2nd goal, but otherwise his control was good. He showed good lateral movement gliding across the crease to stop pucks that were behind/beside him, and he never gave up on a play. Blackwood probably played the puck 10+ times in this one, and was helpful in breaking up Belleville's forecheck before it started.

March 31, 2015, Erie Otters at Sarnia Sting

Game #4 - OHL Western Conference Quarter-Finals

ERI #9 LW Maksimovich, Kyle (2016) - Fearless going into corners and battles despite size. Good positioning and a well placed shot for Erie's first goal of the game. Nice pass on the rush to initiate the overtime winning goal.

ERI #17 RW Raddysh, Taylor (2016) - Played on the Otters second power play unit. Smart positionally in the offensive zone. Displayed good vision and passing ability on the powerplay.

ERI #19 C Strome, Dylan (2015) - Getting involved in the offense making some smart passed but overall very limited through the second period. His play picked up in the third and overtime where he made smart plays then scored the overtime winner getting his initial shot blocked it went right back to him and was able to slip it past a recovering goaltender to win the game.

ERI #44 D Dermott, Travis (2015) - Multiple great rushes up ice. Very poised in traffic and went end to end a few times. This included Erie's second goal where he rushed end to end then fired a quick snapshot into the back of the net. Made several great plays one on one utilizing his stick but also knew when to take the body in these situations and did so very well.

ERI #97 C McDavid, Connor (2015) - Shadowed Zacha on the penalty kill. Received limited chances through the second period, every time he gets the puck, a Sarnia player is quick to knock him off. Connor created an assist on Erie's tying goal with great speed and hands on the rush the dropping it back for the goal.

SAR #14 C Zacha, Pavel (2015) - Pavel showed some aggression in his own zone protecting his goaltender. Great physical play at multiple points throughout the game. Made a great play at the offensive line to keep zone pressure and created a scoring chance. Made an excellent play on the backcheck with a defenseman caught up in the play to break up a 3 on 1 rush. Reads situations well and instantly knows where everyone else is. Great positional awareness. Zacha struggled in the face-off circle today losing most of his draws.

SAR #25 RW Kyrou, Jordan (2016) - Overhandles the puck a little too much sometimes. Has good puck skills and made a nice play using his hands to enter the zone then fired a wrister for Sarnia's third goal. Good speed and tenacity to win race to puck through a crowd and maintain zone control.

SAR #35 RW Korostelev, Nikita (2015) - Good puck protection going around the net not forcing his pass allowing him to create chances. Not nearly as physical tonight as he was in Game #3. Passing well early but as the pressure got heavier later in the game he stuck with shooting the puck every time. Rang one off the post and got a few other good shots on net.

Final Score: Erie Otters: 4 - Sarnia Sting: 3 - OT1

April 3, 2015, Kitchener Rangers at London Knights

Game #5 - OHL Western Conference Quarter-Finals

KIT #15 C Franzen, Gustav (2015) - Lacks speed but protected puck very well with pressure on rush. Quick hands save him allow him to possess puck for long periods of time without losing it. Made good defensive play on powerplay to prevent a direct scoring chance.

KIT #17 RW Kohn, Mason (2015) - Multiple excellent open ice hits, one of which was on Domi created huge scrum and a powerplay for his team. Great speed and consistently tenacious. Constantly mixing it up with opponents and frustrating them, getting the focus on him and away from his teammates. Mason was relentless with his intense style of play which won him many battles tonight. Good hands down low with the puck, cycles well.

KIT #44 D Hora, Frank (2015*) - Mishandled puck multiple times in his own zone, one sequence directly lead to London's first goal. Good powerful, accurate wrist shot from the point to score Kitchener's first goal. Played pretty rough down low own zone. Too slow on races to corner on the dump and chase.

KIT #74 C Bunnaman, Connor (2016) - Great backcheck to save a goal. Skating needs some work but does a good job protecting the puck and driving the net. Very intelligent player. Gets ice in all game situations. Protects puck very well down low.

LON #14 D Crawley, Brandon (2015) - Very passive in neutral zone early on. Good pinch with pressure to keep the play going in the offensive zone and got back into position well. Puck misplay resulted in a 2 on 1, then misplayed the 2 on 1 resulting in a scoring chance.

LON #86 D Martenet, Chris (2015) - Skating stride looks very slow on backcheck but was able to get to the wall pretty fast for his size to keep the puck in the offensive zone. Got caught deep in the offensive zone a few times with either skilled forwards covering point or no one at all. Glass and out under pressure.

LON #93 C Marner, Mitch (2015) - Great positioning in the offensive zone leads to defense drawing to him setting things up for linemates. Fell while down low in own zone, turnover directly lead to Kitchener's first goal of the game. Fired the puck over the glass with three seconds left in the first period for penalty. Forced turnover out of the box resulting in scoring chance. Excellent hands and vision always seeming to find the small passing lanes and threading it without hesitation. Nice diving play defensively to break up play.

LON #98 D Mete, Victor (2016) - Great rush, quick direction changes. Good hands when deep in offensive zone. Can get caught too deep at times but does have the speed to recover on some occasions. Multiple good zone clears on the second penalty killing unit. Good stick on 2 on 1 mismatch down low with man in slot to break up chance. Drew powerplay rushing into seam entering the offensive zone on a bit of a soft call.

LON #1 G Parsons, Tyler (2016) - Excellent quickness shown on recovery saves. Lightning fast glove. Third goal was a little soft.

Final Score: Kitchener Rangers: 6 - London Knights: 3

April 4, 2015, London Knights at Kitchener Rangers

Game #6 - OHL Western Conference Quarter-Finals

LON #14 D Crawley, Brandon (2015) - Doing an excellent job down low playing tough and frustrating opponents. Winning a ton of battles below the goal line. Battles hard not letting his man get a shot off.

LON #93 C Marner, Mitch (2015) - Played alright game by his standards. Good pass on the rush set up London's fourth goal.

LON #98 D Mete, Victor (2016) - Very smooth skating, uses it to open things up. Scored opening goal carrying the puck around the net and wrap around off defender and in.

LON #1 G Parsons, Tyler (2016) - Multiple great reflex saves. Doesn't give shooters very much time to set up due to quickness. Comes out and takes away angles on one on one plays.

KIT #18 D Blaisdell, Doug (2015) - Opened himself up well on point as passing option. Decent shot. Reliable positionally in his own zone.

KIT #74 C Bunnaman, Connor (2016) - Very persistent and tough forecheck punishing opponents and being very difficult to play against.

Final Score: London Knights: 5 - Kitchener Rangers: 0

April 4th 2015, Cedar Rapids RoughRiders at Tri-City Storm

CR #1 Larkin, Ryan G (2015) - Not a big guy, but plays out at the top of the crease and takes away a lot of the net. Got beat three times by Tri-City on the night but had no chance on two of the goals. Still not totally sold on him but his aggressive play and the way he cuts down angles makes me think the ceiling could be pretty high for Larkin.

CR #15 Fronk, Jiri RW (2015) - Not overly impressive tonight. He plays a good north-south game that can be tough for some defensemen to handle but was pretty much contained by Tri-City's good corps of defensemen. Looked a little lost without his regular linemate Erik Foley who was scratched.

CR #18 Gaudette, Adam RC (2015) - Another guy from Cedar Rapids that didn't play up to his potential. Just a bad game more than likely, but didn't do a whole lot well tonight. Plays well for the most part in his own zone and could develop into a really nice two-way center.

TRI #20 Wahlin, Jake LW (2015) - Pretty quiet game from Wahlin. Like his game with the puck on his stick, makes really quick decisions and not many mistakes. Fast thinker, fast skater. Doesn't do any one thing really well but plays a solid overall game.

TRI #44 Wilkie, Chris LW (2014 Undrafted) - Didn't get on the scoreboard but not for lack of effort. Really just dominates physically when he has the puck on his stick. Very hard to knock him off the puck.

April 4, 2015, Owen Sound Attack at Guelph Storm

Game #5 - OHL Western Conference Quarter-Finals

OS #3 D Walters, Connor (2015) - Made the smart simple play with the puck for the vast majority of this game.

OS #4 D Schemitsch, Thomas (2015) - Skates well for his size. Good outlet pass lead to scoring chance. Moves puck very well on powerplay, consistently on target. Held the line very well on multiple occasions. Pinches in from the point at the right times making him a scoring threat. Mishandled the puck down low own zone resulting in turnovers. Did better in the second period with the puck in his own end. Fumbled the puck at the offensive line getting stripped, directly resulted in Guelph's second goal.

OS #9 C Szypula, Ethan (2015) - Stole puck in the neutral zone then walked in and fired a laser for Owen Sound's first goal.

OS #11 LW Dunda, Liam (2015) - Intimidates opponents at this level when along the wall or going into the corner.

OS #20 D MacArthur, Tyler (2015) - Low panic threshold down low despite having the size to absorb contact. Fired puck over glass for penalty.

OS #25 LW Palmu, Petrus (2015) - Good puck movement in neutral zone and entering the offensive zone.

GUE #3 D Rhodes, Kyle (2016) - Dropped the gloves against the older Jaden Lindo and got beat pretty bad.

GUE #4 D Carroll, Noah (2016) - Midhandled puck on the rush when the pass was too far up to begin with, directly resulted in Owen Sound's first goal. Midhandled the puck later on in the neutral zone which also lead to an odd man scoring chance.

GUE #10 D Hall, Austin (2015) - Late first he had a shooting lane with a high percentage scoring chance and tried to force a pass down low that missed. Made bad decisions on a few first passes for turnovers. Takes the hit to make the play. Good stick a few times to break up developing play. Skating is above average in all directions which helped him keep up with the play. Engages physically but needs to add strength. Not a prospect.

GUE #22 LW Suter, Puis (2015*) - Good speed and persistence on the forecheck to steal pucks. Quick hands not forcing the play. Good work on cycle lead to Guelph's first goal recording an assist. Forced turnover on the point while penalty killing, used speed to turn it into a breakaway and scored Guelph's second goal, the eventual winning goal. Fired the puck over the glass with 1:40 left giving Owen Sound a powerplay to finish the game trailing a goal.

GUE #24 RW Smith, Givani (2016) - Skates well for size. Controlled puck well down low. Finishes his checks. Made great pass late in the third to create a big scoring chance late.

GUE #27 D McFadden, Garrett (2015) - Bad pass to defensive partner, direct lead to Owen Sound's first goal. Mishandled puck on the point a few times resulting in loss of zone pressure. Shot selection needs improvement as he tried to force some through, howevef has good power in his shot. Keeps up with his man well down low stopping/starting quickly. Unnecessarily fired the puck down the ice close to the red line with under two minutes left up a goal to allow Owen Sound to set up in the offensive zone and call a time out.

Final Score: Guelph Storm: 2 - Owen Sound Attack: 1

April 5, 2015, Ottawa 67's at Niagara Ice Dogs
Game #6 - OHL Western Conference Quarter-Finals

OTT #8 C Fanjoy, Ben (2015) - Good cycle down low, competes hard. Circles too much in offensive zone, not enough attacking the puck carrier. Blocked shot. Good skater. Rushed puck decisions.

OTT #10 LW Addison, Jeremiah (2015) - Finishes his checks. Quickly picks up his man on the backcheck very well. Puck skills have improved a fair amount since last season, also has a decent shot. Does a decent job getting open without the puck in the offensive zone. Played on the penalty kill.

OTT #74 RW Craievich, Adam (2015) - Hard shot but releases from low percentage areas a lot. Used sparingly in energy line role.

OTT #96 RW Salituro, Dante (2015) - Has a great shot but when matched up with a good defender he'll shoot from the perimeter a lot. Average forecheck, gets in lanes and pursues the puck carrier but lacks the speed, size, strength or persistence to make life difficult for the puck carrier. Good positioning to get open on a 2 on 1 rush and fired a laser that went glove and in for Ottawa's first goal. Good pass on a 3 on 2 to set up Ottawa's third goal.

OTT #1 G Herbst, Liam (2015*) - First goal of the night was a little soft through the five hole. Takes away initial shooting angle very well. Rebound control needs improvement and sometimes slow to jump on pucks around his crease, which would have prevented the third Niagara goal. He still struggled with side to side movement, which played a part in Niagara's fourth goal.

NIA #4 D Dunn, Vince (2015) - Quick reaction to pinch, saving zone pressure. Has the skating ability to recover. Has the skating and composure to rush the puck out of trouble in his own end. Tried to be too aggressive one on one to get beat in neutral zone. Too passive on 2 on 1 gave easy lane, resulted in Ottawa's first goal. Great pinch on Niagara's third goal to pick up the loose puck and quickly finish

NIA #13 LW Knott, Graham (2015) - Good offensive zone positioning, consistently goes where he needs to. Good skating for size. Played on the second penalty killing unit. Finished his checks. Great play in the slot with defender tying up his stick he kicked the puck out to a pinching defenseman creating Ice Dogs' third goal. Was hit or miss with his passing sometimes trying to force passes that weren't there.

NIA #23 LW Corneil, Johnny (2015) - Great compete down low to win battles; relentless in the corner. Smart pass under pressure created chance. Decent release on shot. Good skater.

Final Score: Niagara Ice Dogs: 4 - Ottawa 67's: 3

Game 1: North Bay Battalion at Barrie Colts, April 10, 2015

Score: 3-2 Barrie

LW Zach Bratina (2015*) – Bratina had a decent game while skating on a line with Nick Paul and Mike Amadio. Bratina showed good speed through the neutral zone, and was effective carrying the puck into the offensive zone with possession. He had some good shifts cycling down low, and made several nice passes into the scoring area throughout. He did take a bad cross checking penalty late in the 2nd, however, a dive was also called on the play against Joseph Blandisi.

C Brett McKenzie (2015) – McKenzie made some nice defensive plays in this one, and was always back deep in the defensive zone to help out. He back checked hard, and blocked shots whenever he could. Offensively he was a straight-line player; finished his checks, went to the net, etc. but was unable to create much in the offensive zone.

RW Roy Radke (2015) – Radke did some good and some bad in this one. He took hits to make plays in the defensive zone, finished his checks, drove the net, and caused some havoc in North Bay's end. That said, he forced a pass when he had a clear shooting lane from the danger area, and forced some shots on net when other players were available for passes.

D Rasmus Andersson (2015) – Andersson was tested early in this one, as he had to defend a couple different one-on-ones in the first period. Andersson did a nice job getting in the shooting lanes, and using his stick to steer players wide when they tried to create their own shot. Andersson didn't force anything that wasn't there, and used the boards to get the puck out when necessary. He made a good first pass, and had was able to get pucks through traffic numerous times; one of which led to a goal for Barrie. Though he played pretty well overall, he was late getting to Ryan Kujawinski at one point and it wound up in the back of Barrie's net.

G Mackenzie Blackwood (2015) – Blackwood was very good in this game. He didn't face many shots early on, but was good when called upon, and continued to get better as the game went on. For the most part he didn't give up many rebounds, and when he did he was there to make the stop on second chance opportunities. He tracked pucks well through traffic as well. Blackwood was particularly good in the 3rd, as he blanked North Bay despite an 11-2 shot advantage for the road team.

MUSKEGON LUMBERJACKS vs MADISON CAPITOLS (4-10-15)

MUS - #3 RD - Joseph Cecconi (2015) – Was Muskegon's best Defenseman tonight. Scored on a shot from the right faceoff circle beating the Madison goalie over the bad and under the glove. Has an effortless skating stride both with and without the puck. Had good body positioning along the boards and did a good job pinning players along the wall until support arrived. Ended the night with 1G and 1A.

MUS - #17 LW - David Keefer (2016) – Smaller stature forward, played a physical 200 foot game, wasn't afraid of the hard areas was physical on the fore-check.

MUS - #29 G - Eric Schierhorn (2015+) – Eric made a number of fantastic saves, stays calm and finds rebounds in traffic. Let in a couple of goals in the 3rd to let Madison back in the game. But played on top of his crease and was aggressive and confident all night.

MUS - #2 RD - Mitch Eliot (2016) – Physical game liked to step up on forwards coming into the zone but got burned on a couple occasions. Moved the puck well in his own end and in the neutral zone.

MUS - #6 LD - Christian Wolanin (FA) – Scored on a big slap shot off the rush on the left side. Played physical in front of his own net. Moved the puck well on the Power Play.

MAD - #37 LW - Haralds Egle (2015) – Madison leading point producer this season was impressive again tonight. Finished the night with 1G and 1A. Showed the ability to stick handle and get his shot off quickly in traffic. Got Madison's comeback started in the 3rd by banging home a rebound on the doorstep. Had good speed through the neutral zone all night.

MAD - #17 RW - Sam McCormick (2015) – Tied with Egle with 7SOG tonight. Ended up pointless despite getting a lot of chances. Was sprung on a breakaway on a great stretch pass from his own end as well as hit the cross bar on a quick release snap shot from the slot. Reads the play in his own end well, doesn't miss a chance to get out of his own end and try to get behind the opposing Defenseman but picks his spots well. Hockey IQ remains McCormick's greatest attribute, but his game has come along well as the year has progressed.

MAD - #29 RD - Tony Stillwell (2016) – The undersized D-man is only playing his 15th USHL game tonight after playing WI-HS in 14/15 and coming off winning the Wisconsin Mr. Hockey Award. Stillwell was a quick puck mover tonight. He did get caught out of position and taking unnecessary risks defensively.

Game 2: North Bay Battalion at Barrie Colts, April 12, 2015

Score: 3-2 North Bay

LW Zach Bratina (2015*) – Bratina played a real good two-way game for the Battalion. He was relentless on the forecheck, and forced several turnovers as a result. He regularly started in the defensive zone, and was able to drive play up ice and carry the puck safely into the offensive zone. Bratina was positionally sound on the PK, which made it tough for Colts blue liners to get pucks to the net. Bratina was elusive in space, and showed good vision waiting for plays to develop before finding open teammates.

LW Brett McKenzie (2015) – McKenzie played his typical north-south pro-style game in this one. He finished his checks, cycled well down low, and was tough to knock off the puck. He back checked hard, and was able to break up a couple odd man rushes by getting back. McKenzie also had a good net front presence on the man advantage. He did force some passes that weren't there, and struggled to gain separation from the defense to create his own shooting lanes.

LW Roy Radke (2015) – Radke regularly won battles along the wall, one of which led to a great scoring chance. He put pucks on net whenever he can, went to the dirty areas and scored a goal in front on a back door play. Radke had a couple punishing hits, and was able to pickpocket a Battalion forward while back checking in the neutral zone.

LW Matthew Kreis (2015) – After being scratched in Game 1, Kreis was very good in Game 2. He started on the 4th line, but was moved up and also saw some powerplay time as a result of his strong play. He played with great pace, and was able to carry the puck into the offensive zone with regularity. He didn't shy from contact, went to the dirty areas, and was creative below the paint in the offensive zone while setting up several chances. Kreis also picked up an assist on a gorgeous back-door pass to Radke.

RW Andrew Mangiapane (2015*) – Mangiapane was shifty with the puck, and very tough to contain in space. He was elusive, creative, and dangerous coming off the wall. He displayed excellent vision throughout, and consistently made accurate passes all over the ice. Mangiapane had several controlled zone entries that led to shots. Mangiapane started off a 5 vs 3 PK as the lone forward, and was able to pressure the points effectively to make them rush passes/shots. He finished his checks when he could, too, and didn't back down from anyone who tried to rough him up.

D Rasmus Andersson (2015) – Andersson did a nice job of pinching along the wall to keep plays alive. He didn't force anything, and moved the puck effectively at even-strength and on the powerplay. Defensively his positioning was good. On a couple occasions while defending 1 vs 1's he would steer the forward wide before extending his stick and deflecting shot attempts wide or into the stands. Andersson won some battles and, while he wasn't very physical, he did a nice job of stick checking opponents and tying their sticks up around the net. He didn't hesitate to block shots and did some good work while killing a 5 on 3. Andersson failed to block a centering pass from behind the net that resulted in a goal, but it was an excellent pass and he was only an inch or two away from intercepting it.

G Mackenzie Blackwood (2015) – Blackwood was exceptional in this one. After Barrie fell behind 2-0 in the 1st, he locked it down until the 3rd, and gave Barrie a chance to get back in it. He also made several great saves while North Bay was on a two-minute 5 vs 3. His rebound control was good, as there were very few for North Bay to try and pounce on. Blackwood did a nice job coming out to play the puck on a couple occasions, which forced North Bay to really pick their spots for dump-ins. If Blackwood wasn't on his game this probably wouldn't have been close.

April 12, 2015, North Bay Battalion at Barrie Colts
Game #2 - OHL Eastern Conference Semi-Finals

NBY #8 D Bruce, Riley (2015) - Great size. Leads with his stick a little too much when he should use his size. Good pinch but bad stick positioning on the pinch caused him to lose the battle and get caught up ice.

BAR #15 LW Kreis, Matthew (2015) - Small, good speed, persistent on the forecheck, keeps it simple, good compete level. Plays on second power play unit. Great cross ice pass set up 2-2 goal.

BAR #19 D Andersson, Rasmus (2015) - Top power play defenseman, consistent puck movement from the point. Good defensive positioning, picked up his man pretty quick. First pass is a bit risky sometimes. Had a few good puck rushes up ice as the game progressed. Good play to open himself up with skating relieving the pressure.

BAR #15 LW Kreis, Matthew (2015) - After being scratched in Game 1, Kreis was very good in Game 2. He started on the 4th line, but was moved up and also saw some powerplay time as a result of his strong play. He played with great pace, and was able to carry the puck into the offensive zone with regularity. He didn't shy from contact, went to the dirty areas, and was creative below the paint in the offensive zone while setting up several chances. Great cross ice pass to Radke set up Barrie's second goal.

BAR #22 LW Radke, Roy (2015) - Bad turnover down low early when he could have protected pick to keep play going. Finished his check well a few times in the first. Generates good speed for size. Got behind defender for breakaway chance. Made a good move but stopped. Got right back into the play and slipped into perfect positioning to one-time Barrie's second goal in. Good drop pass on rush set up scoring chance. Good hit on backcheck to break up scoring chance.

BAR #26 RW Mangiapne, Andrew (2015*) - Good compete and speed on the forecheck caused several turnovers. Excellent hand/eye coordination. Top power play unit on the point. Made quick and accurate decisions with the puck. Utilized as lone forward on a 5 on 3 penalty kill and did a great job blocking shot and quickly applying pressure to the point to frustrate the opposition. Great creativity with puck. Shoots into screen on power play at times. Good open ice hit.

BAR #29 G Blackwood, Mackenzie (2015) - Very fluid side to side for a big goalie. 1st goal completely screened, no chance. Quickly kicks leg out to make save. Excellent glove hand, always catches the puck. Followed play very well on a very fast paced 5 on 3 penalty kill.

Final Score: North Bay Battalion: 3 - Barrie Colts: 2

Apr 13th, 2015. Finland vs USA (Luzern – exhibition pre U18 WorldChampionships)

FIN #6 D Valimaki, Juuso (2017) – He made some good reads for a 16yrs old kid and didn't look out of place. However, he had some struggles defending against the most agile American forwards and had a bad play on the offensive blue line when he mishandled the puck and his feet couldn't react fast enough, generating an odd men rush for the US.

FIN #9 D Saarijarvi, Vili (2015) – This undersized defenseman was able to adjust to American forwards pace right from the start and displayed great mobility with the puck, always looking in control while escaping their forecheck. His stick work was good when defending, and terrific with the puck. He hit a couple of perfect passes through the neutral zone and made a great play at the red line where he showed poise and intelligence, initiating a rush by Puljujarvi with a backhand pass. Was regularly on the 1st PP unit, showing he also possesses a good shot already.

FIN #14 RW Niemela, Joonas (2015) – Consistently battling throughout the game, was able to win some puck battles along the boards despite his not ideal size. Offensively he was not able to get much going, aside from a nice backhand pass in the slot. His skating didn't look bad overall, but seemed to lack a top gear.

FIN #18 C Saarela, Aleksi (2015) – Centering Laine and Puljujarvi, Saarela was more effective on special teams than at even strength, where his line struggled defensively all game long, even if not for lack of trying. Aleksi was close scoring a shorthanded goal when his nice wrister hit the pipe, on the powerplay he was better at distributing the puck than at finalizing the play. His size seemed to limit him in battles, but he did have a good hit along the boards.

FIN #19 RW Tammela, Jonne (2015) – Played on both special teams, had a couple of take-aways early on and showed his speed through the neutral zone. Even if he wasn't very effective offensively he appeared 100% recovered from the concussion he recently suffered while playing for KalPa in the Liiga.

FIN #21 RW Puljujarvi, Jesse (2016) – A blocked shot and a rush on the right wing with a nice little toe-drag were his only noticeable plays along a disappointing first half of the game. More than once he had troubles keeping full control of the puck when carrying it up, and chasing it exposed him to the risk of a dangerous collision where he managed to avoid any injury. Puljujarvi turned it on in the 3rd period, he was much more active and the crossbar-in wrister that seemed to bring Finland back into the game was something special; calling it a NHL snipe wouldn't do it justice.

FIN #24 D Vainio, Veeti (2015) – A couple of times he managed to enter the offensive zone with the puck on his stick sneaking through opponents waiting for him with apparent ease, but overall his offensive impact was limited. Trying to spark his team comeback, had a costly turnover in the neutral zone when attempting a difficult pass in the 3rd period. Vainio was on the receiving hand of a couple of dirty plays and slashed two Americans in retaliation; he was not caught by the referee in either case, but he will certainly need to clean that up when the games will matter.

FIN #25 C Nattinen, Julius (2015) – Wasted his only two scoring chances wristing it just wide on a 2 on 1 and misfiring a one-timer. Perhaps more importantly, he was slow getting his shot off and getting to loose pucks on the powerplay. Nattinen was however very good at making himself available in the neutral zone, showing good speed and reading well the US defense. He was also very effective in the faceoff circle.

FIN #27 LW Laine, Patrik (2016) – Played an unselfish game trying to combine with his linemates rather than forcing his shots like in some previous viewings, however his passing game was not always accurate and his line struggled at even strength, even if the effort was there. Patrik was often backchecking pretty hard, showing decent speed. Battling for pucks, he tried to compensate for his lack of agility with strong stick work, but more than once it was not enough. Scored Finland 1st goal going top-shelf from the right faceoff circle with an impressive and perfectly placed one-timer like it was routine for him.

USA #4 D Fitzgerald, Casey (2015) – Made several good defensive reads in the neutral zone, even though in one circumstance he was caught trusting too much his anticipation and had to take an obvious penalty as a result. Among the US defensemen eligible for this year draft he was probably the most effective one in this game.

USA #7 LW Tkachuk, Matthew (2016) – Less visible than in other games during the first half, created more troubles for Finland defense as the game progressed and complemented Matthews' game very well. A quick one-touch pass and a nice top shelf backhand finish were his best moments.

USA #17 RW Bracco, Jeremy (2015) – Playing on a line with Matthews, Bracco enjoyed a 4 points game and was +5 by the end of it. While it's hard to argue with those numbers, it needs to be pointed out he was for the most capitalizing on the work of his linemates (one in particular). The most effective part of his game was making himself available in the right place at the right time. He could have used his good feet to get faster on loose pucks and wasted a great chance in the 2nd when he felt like out-waiting the goalie instead of shooting from an ideal position.

USA #19 C Matthews, Auston (2016) – Credited with 4 points, Matthews actually got 5 and dominated the game. Consistently buzzing around and creating danger in the Finnish zone, Auston seemed to remain equally effective even in the last part of longer shifts. He thinks fast and executes even faster, apparently too fast for the Finns today. When Pujujarvi brought Finland back into the game, it took him less than 40 seconds to re-establish the distance deking out the goalie with impressive ease at the end of a perfectly executed counter attack by his line.

USA #21 C Fischer, Christian (2015) – Fischer didn't really look into this exhibition game early on and he was not skating as hard as he usually does throughout the game, but to his credit he got better as it progressed and he ended up scoring a beautiful goal in the 3rd when on a counter attack he fooled both the D and G with a deke that allowed him to backhand the puck into the gaping net.

USA #25 D McAvoy, Charles (2016) – Had a couple of rough plays and missed wide a great chance on the powerplay, but overall had an impressive game, logging big minutes and consistently leading the play. He was able to complete accurate passes both off the rush and on the PP or to hold onto the puck and carry it deep instead. By far the best US defenseman.

FINAL SCORE: 7-2 USA

April 14, 2015, Erie Otters at London Knights

Game #4 - OHL Western Conference Semi-Finals

ERI #17 RW Raddysh, Taylor (2016) - Strong skater, goes hard into corners, tough down low winning battles. Finishes checks hard. Good puck mover on the rush. Excellent deflection in the slot to score the winning go with three minutes left in the third period.

ERI #19 C Strome, Dylan (2015) - Top powerplay minutes. Good at finishing great passing lanes and exploits them quickly. He doesn't have the speed to attack the opposition quickly but shows the smarts to be a threat in a hurry. Scored Erie's first goal.

ERI #44 D Dermott, Travis (2015) - Top power play unit. Good puck movement on point. Great compete to beat an opponent into the corner and get the puck. Smooth skater, good moves with quick hands to keep opponent guessing. Got walked a few times one on one by speed and skill. Early in 3rd period on penalty kill, took out man without puck, resulted in 5 on 3 kill.

ERI #97 C McDavid, Connor (2015) - Excellent creativity to set up a few chances. Even when it looks like a quiet period for him he finds a way to subtly make things happen. Took offsetting penalty engaging physically with Domi. Great play in the second driving wide beating defender and made a nice move. He was stopped but rebound resulted in easy empty netter for Strome on Erie's first goal. Outstanding long distance pass set up partial break. Exceptionally quick decision making.

LON #14 D Crawley, Brandon (2015) - Competes hard down low. Reaction time was a little off on a few occasions that he could have otherwise taken advantage of. Good shot late in tying game to find a way to get it through which created a scoring chance. Played man well one on one. Quick to get down low and battle for pucks, winning several battles on the wall. Was rewarded once again with extra ice in the third period tonight.

LON #86 D Martenet, Chris (2015) - Second penalty killing unit. A little panic to him with pressure when handling the puck. Consistently goes deep in offensive zone but lacks puck skills to sustain pressure or skating to recover. Carries puck up ice on rush by protecting it with size. Decent speed for big guy. Won physical battle vs big strong opponents.

Final Score: Erie Otters: 5 - London Knights: 2

Game 5: North Bay Battalion at Barrie Colts

Score: 7-5 North Bay

NB #12 LW Brett McKenzie (2015) – Offensively McKenzie was very quiet in this one. He struggled to create any offense on his own, and bobbled several passes. He also misplayed an odd-man rush, skating out of a good shooting lane prior to forcing a pass. Defensively he had one bad turnover in his own zone, but other than that was pretty sound.

NB #19 LW Zach Bratina (2015*) – Bratina was very good through the neutral zone. He used his acceleration to reach top speed quickly, which forced Colts defenders to back off and give him the line. He was creative with the puck, and showed good vision while distributing the puck all over the ice in the offensive zone. Bratina didn't shy away from contact, went to the dirty areas, and showed good hands deflecting a couple pucks in tight. He had a couple turnovers throughout, but definitely created more than he caused against North Bay.

BAR #15 Matthew Kreis (2015) – Kreis was one of Barrie's best players in this game. He regularly carried the puck into the offensive zone with possession, which led to several shots and chances for Barrie. He never gave up on a play, and was relentless after the puck. Kreis created offense almost every shift, and showed a commitment to defense by back checking hard as well.

BAR #22 LW Roy Radke (2015) – Radke didn't find the score sheet but he played well. He finished his checks, was effective in the cycle game, and did a nice job controlling the puck down low. Radke put pucks on net whenever he had the chance, and some big rebounds popped out as a result. He used his speed effectively while carrying the puck up ice, and drove the net whenever he had the chance. Radke also won his fair share of puck battles, and played a strong game as a whole.

BAR #26 LW Andrew Mangiapane (2015*) – Mangiapane may have been the best player on the ice. Despite his size he won a ton of puck battles, finished his checks, and didn't shy away from the dirty areas of the ice. He was creative with the puck, and very elusive in space. Mangiapane took hits to make plays, too. He scored a powerplay goal on a blast of a one-timer, and also picked up a beautiful assist on a backdoor pass to Kevin Labanc late in the game.

BAR #19 Rasmus Andersson (2015) – Andersson regularly had his stick in the shooting lane, which made it tough for North Bay to get shots through. With the puck Andersson made a good first pass, confidently rushed the puck up ice when given space, and distributed the puck well on the powerplay while recording an assist in the process.

BAR #29 Mackenzie Blackwood (2015) – Blackwood was not at his best in this one. He made some impressive saves throughout the game, but coughed out some big rebounds, and allowed a couple goals he'd certainly want back. On one occasion he knocked the puck into his own net. A few goals were scored through traffic, or on back-door plays, but it's hard to win a game when your goaltender allows seven goals on 36 shots.

CREDITS

I want to thank all the people who helped put this book together. Thank you to all our NHL Draft Scouts: Ryan Yessie, Jérôme Bérubé, Scott McDougall, Ron Berman, Russ Bitely, Justin Schreiber, Dusten Braaksma, Michele Portoni, Toni Rajamäki, Todd Cordell, Alex Stewart, Jeff Cox, Tyler Bilton and Ryan Minicola. I appreciate the huge number of hours in the rinks and the effort writing reports.

Once again for the 2015 NHL Draft, we travelled to rinks across Canada, USA and Europe. Our goal is to mirror what NHL scouting staffs do, albeit with a much smaller travel budget. In essence we try to act as though we are a 31st NHL team. With scouts based in numerous locations, we are able to scout hundreds of prospects. I travelled to Switzerland to attend the World under 18 Championship again this year. It's always one of my favorite events of the season. We also made our regular trips to all the other large events that take place during the scouting season.

As I write this, I just completed attending the 2015 NHL Combine which was relocated from Toronto to Buffalo this year. I always enjoy spending a day there and it allows us to include some information we gain from the combine and put it into this book.

I also want acknowledge the contributions of Kathy Kocur. Kathy assists with editing and also serves as our staff photographer. Her photos are used on our website.

Thanks to Paul Krotz and all the other media staff from around the NHL, CHL, the USHL and to Hockey Canada who help us out and are a pleasure to deal with.

Mark Edwards
Founder & Director of Scouting

www.ingramcontent.com/pod-product-compliance
Lightning Source LLC
Chambersburg PA
CBHW062124160426
43191CB00013B/2189